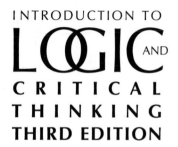

INTRODUCTION TO

LOGIC AND

CRITICAL
THINKING
THIRD EDITION

INTRODUCTION TO
LOGIC AND
CRITICAL
THINKING
THIRD EDITION

MERRILEE H. SALMON

UNIVERSITY OF PITTSBURGH

Harcourt Brace College Publishers

Fort Worth Philadelphia San Diego New York Orlando Austin San Antonio
Toronto Montreal London Sydney Tokyo

Publisher • Ted Buchholz
Senior Acquisitions Editor • David Tatom
Developmental Editor • Claire Brantley
Senior Project Editor • Steve Welch
Production Manager • Cynthia Young
Senior Art Director • Don Fujimoto

Cover Image: Photo © Bert Adler/Superstock

ISBN: 0-15-543064-5

Library of Congress Catalog Card Number: 94-72861

Copyright © 1995, 1989, 1984 by Harcourt Brace & Company

Address for Editorial Correspondence: Harcourt Brace College Publishers, 301 Commerce Street, Suite 3700, Fort Worth, TX 76102.

Address for Orders: Harcourt Brace & Company, 6277 Sea Harbor Drive, Orlando, FL 32887-6777. 1-800-782-4479, or 1-800-433-0001 (in Florida).

Printed in the United States of America

9   0   1   2   3   016   9   8   7   6   5   4

For
WBH
and
AHH

Preface to the First Edition

This book is designed to help students who are beginning college to acquire a deeper understanding of the relationships between logic and language and to increase their skills in critical thinking. Students must be equipped with these skills if they are to be able to recognize situations in which unsupported assertions require justification, to analyze and assess the arguments on their own.

Motivation for achieving these goals is provided by means of a variety of examples and exercises that show the usefulness of critical-thinking skills in everyday life. Students are asked to analyze exactly what claims are being made in various contexts and to determine whether reasons are given or should be given to support the claims they are asked to accept. Once assertions that require support have been distinguished from arguments (in which reasons are given for claims), three categories of argument types are distinguished: deductive arguments, inductive arguments, and fallacies. Standards for evaluating various types of arguments are presented. Many examples and exercises focus on the reconstruction of arguments in ordinary language.

A special feature of this text is the careful analysis of inductive reasoning prior to the treatment of deductive arguments. Several reasons can be given for this reversal of what has become the standard order in introductory texts.

- Inductive reasoning based on samples, arguments from analogy, statistical syllogisms, and arguments that attempt to establish casual connections have already been encountered frequently by students in their roles as consumers, citizens, and problem-solvers. Interesting real-life examples can be used to illustrate and explain the standards for evaluating these pervasive forms of argument.

- In their examination of familiar types of inductive reasoning, students gradually gain sensitivity to the structural features of arguments and to such important logical distinctions as the difference between universal and statistical generalizations. They are thus better able to appreciate the value of the more formal treatment of deductive reasoning that follows the analysis of inductive arguments.

- When inductive arguments are presented in this way, students are less likely to be left with the impression that only deductive arguments are really effective and that inductive reasoning is an inferior alternative to be relied on when nothing better is available.

After 16 years of teaching introductory logic courses to small groups of students and to large lecture groups with the assistance of teaching fellows, I am convinced of the value of treating induction before deduction. However, the text is designed so that it can be used by instructors who prefer the more usual order. Chapters 1, 2, 6, 8 (followed by Appendix 1), 9, and 10 may be followed by Chapters 3, 4, 5, 7, and 11.

Another unusual feature of this text is its treatment of fallacies. After a brief general account of fallacies is presented in Chapter 2, particular types of fallacies are addressed throughout the text within the context of analyzing the correct forms of inductive and deductive arguments that various fallacies resemble. In addition, some theoretical backround is supplied to show that fallacious reasoning frequently involves systematic types of error. One example is the belief that causes must somehow *resemble* their effects; another is the common tendency to overlook solid statistical data when presented with some particular vivid information that conflicts with the data. Such errors are not the result of carelessness, individual psychological quirks, or an intent to deceive. This approach to fallacies fosters a deeper understanding of correct as well as incorrect forms of reasoning.

The language used in the text is as simple and direct as possible. Technical vocabulary is introduced only when it is required and is redefined in Review sections at the end of each chapter. Formal methods are employed when they are useful for clarification, and even those students who begin the course with an aversion to formalization ("math anxiety") can usually master these methods with little difficulty. Instructors who wish to minimize attention to formal methods can omit the material on probabilities (Chapter 5 and Section VI of Chapter 7), the formal proof method in Appendix I, and Section VII on logic and computers in Chapter 8 without loss of continuity.

All the material in the text can be covered comfortably in a semester course that meets four times a week. If the course is fast-paced, most of the material can be covered in a semester course that meets three times a week. Fewer hours of class time may require more selective coverage, but the chapters and sections are designed so that this can be done easily. For example, Chapter 5, Section VI of Chapter 7, Section VII of Chapter 8, and the Appendix may be omitted. If time is short, Section IV on Venn diagrams in Chapter 9 may also be omitted, inasmuch as an alternative set of rules is presented for evaluating syllogistic arguments.

Over the years of teaching logic and thinking about how it should be taught, I have received much help from those who were my teachers, teaching assistants, and students. Although they cannot all be named, it is a pleasure to acknowledge their contributions. Special thanks go to Robert Fogelin at Dartmouth College, and to the reviewers, who offered valuable criticisms of a draft of this text: Donald Anderson, Los Angeles Pierce College; Paul Bassen, California State University, Hayward; Leslie Burkholder, Carnegie-Mellon University; Charles Chastain, University of Illinois at Chicago Circle; Allan S. Gnagy, University of Kansas; Russell Kahl, San Francisco State University; Walter H. O'Briant, University of Georgia; Ric Otte, University of California at Santa Cruz; Elliott R. Sober, University of Wisconsin; Eric Stiffler, Western Illinois University; and Robert Wengert, University of Illinois at Champaign-Urbana. Bill McLane of Harcourt Brace provided expert advice and editorial assistance for which I am most grateful.

Finally my deepest thanks go to my husband, Wesley C. Salmon, for his logical expertise, generous advice, and staunch support.

Merrilee H. Salmon

Preface to the Third Edition

While responses to earlier editions of *Introduction to Logic and Critical Thinking* have been gratifying, many who use it have suggested improvements. This third edition tries to respond to those suggestions. Because no textbook can have too many exercises, this edition contains about twenty percent more than the previous edition, at various levels of difficulty. Solutions to all of the odd-numbered exercises can be found at the end of the book. This edition discusses additional fallacies as well, in connection with the correct forms of argument that they resemble. As in the previous edition, the Index of Fallacies (Appendix 2) contains a list of all fallacies treated in the book, along with brief definitions and references to the discussions in the text.

A revised version of "Paying Special Attention to the Language of Arguments: Definitions" (Chapter 11 in earlier editions) is Chapter 2 in the third edition. This structural change responds to the belief of many teachers that the material covered in this chapter prepares students for later discussions of ordinary-language arguments by raising their sensitivity to linguistic issues.

One distinguishing feature of earlier editions—the treatment of inductive reasoning before deductive reasoning—remains the same. Many examples of inductive arguments (arguments from analogy, statistical syllogisms, inductive generalizations, reasoning to the truth of hypotheses, and so on) occur in everyday life. For this reason, students are likely to be familiar with these forms of argument and to have grappled already with some of the problems that inductive reasoning poses. As a result, they are prepared to pay serious attention to methods for analyzing such arguments.

Learning about matters of form in real-life contexts prepares them, in turn, to take seriously the more abstract features of deductive arguments. With a better understanding of the structure of inductive reasoning, many students who have experienced "math anxiety" in their earlier dealings with formalizations gain a new appreciation of the simplicity that formal treatments of deductive logic provide.

After the first three chapters present critical thinking and logic in a general way, a more detailed account of inductive reasoning follows in Chapters 4, 5, and 6. Chapter 7 provides a brief treatment of conditional (deductive) arguments in preparation for the discussion of inductive arguments of confirmation in Chapter 8.

Instructors who have their own reasons for preferring the more traditional approach, however, can proceed without loss of continuity from Chapter 3 to Chapters 7, 9, 10, and 11 before addressing Chapters 4, 5, 6, and 8.

As in the earlier editions, Appendix 1 presents a version of the popular "tree-method" for testing the validity of deductive arguments. This natural-deduction system for propositional logic is a variant of the proof method developed by Gerhard Gentzen. Although not to everyone's taste, this method interests students with a flair for formal reasoning, and some have set up machine programs to emulate the system.

A primary aim of this textbook is to present the study of logic and critical thinking in a way that makes it relevant to students' lives while at the same time providing a clear and rigorous treatment of technical matters that are a part of the enterprise. Reviewers of this and previous editions have helped immensely in this project by sharing their insights and expertise. It is a great pleasure to acknowledge the help of R. Boyd (Texas Christian University), J. Cargile (University of Virginia), D. Gilboa (University of Wisconsin, Oshkosh), D. Hillman (University of Pittsburgh), F. McGuinness (California State University, Northridge), H. Phillips (Whitman College), W. Salmon (University of Pittsburgh), E. Sherline (University of Wyoming), D. Stalker (University of Delaware), J. Tilley (Indiana University), R. Wahl (Idaho State University), and S. Wertz (Texas Christian University). Special thanks to Charlotte Broome for preparing the index.

During the years between the appearance of the second and third editions, the Andrew W. Mellon Foundation has generously supported my empirical research on reasoning in conversation. This work, done under the auspices of the Learning and Research Development Center at the University of Pittsburgh, and in collaboration with colleagues there, has informed the book in ways too numerous to mention. I am very grateful to R. Glaser and L. Resnick, Directors of the Center, to all of the members of Dr. Resnick's Pragmatics group, and most especially to C. Zeitz, for stimulating new ways of thinking about how to use what students already know to help them learn to reason well.

Merrilee H. Salmon

CONTENTS

CHAPTER ONE

CHAPTER TWO

CHAPTER FIVE

CHAPTER SIX

CHAPTER SEVEN

CHAPTER EIGHT

CHAPTER NINE

ARGUMENTS IN WHICH VALIDITY DEPENDS ON CONNECTIONS AMONG SENTENCES   285

CHAPTER TEN

CHAPTER ELEVEN

APPENDIX ONE

PROOF METHOD FOR TRUTH-FUNCTIONAL LOGIC   386

APPENDIX TWO

INDEX OF FALLACIES   398

Chapter One

INTRODUCTION TO ARGUMENTS

I. INTRODUCTION

"**D**on't believe everything you hear!"

This is familiar advice, and it's not merely a warning against liars. Even when a person's honesty is not in question, sometimes checking up on what that person says simply makes sense. Suppose, for example, you want to buy a new computer game for your niece's birthday. A store on the other side of town is the only place that sells this particular game. Your friend says that the store always stocks that game, but you don't want to make an unnecessary trip. So you call to check. After the salesclerk looks over the stock, he tells you that they have it.

When you make that phone call, you are seeking support, or *evidence*, for your friend's *assertion* that not only does the store's buyer make an effort to keep that game in stock but also that the game is available now—today, when you get there. When the clerk says that they have the game in stock, he supports your friend's assertion with *verbal evidence*.

Verbal evidence consists of sentences that state reasons for believing some other sentence. The clerk's assertion that the store has the game is supported by *physical evidence*—he has seen one on the shelf. In this case, though not always, verbal evidence is a description of some physical evidence.

Suppose, to take another example, that you want to go to a rock concert on the Fourth of July and plan to take a bus to the arena. Your father, who works near the arena, rides a bus to work regularly, and tells you that the buses run every ten minutes. Because you would hate to miss any of the concert, you find a bus schedule with the exact times the bus stops near your house. You learn the buses run only once an hour on holidays. You have obtained verbal evidence from the bus schedule (written, in this case, rather than spoken), but this time the evidence fails to support the assertion made by your father. He wasn't lying—he did not intend to deceive you—he merely forgot that the holiday bus schedule is different from the daily schedule.

Gathering evidence and determining whether it supports or undermines assertions are two aspects of *critical thinking*. Critical thinking also involves paying careful attention to what we hear and read so that we can understand and respond appropriately. We use language primarily to communicate with one another, and communication takes many forms. We engage in small talk just to "stay in touch" with others. We express our feelings of joy, sorrow, sympathy, anger, hope, and fear in language. We ask questions ("How old are you?"), make requests ("Please give me your phone number."), issue warnings ("Watch out for that car!") and commands ("Do not write in this book."). We also use language to convey information, often by asserting declarative sentences, such as "Thirty students are enrolled in the critical thinking class," or "The college volleyball team has nine scheduled games this year, but only three are home games."

We should seek evidence when it is important to know whether information is correct. In general, we prefer to be well informed and avoid error. But sometimes more is at stake than a desire for knowledge. We *act* on the basis of our beliefs, and our actions can have important consequences.

Knowing when to seek evidence requires sensitivity to the circumstances or context in which words are spoken or written. In some contexts, asking for evidence is silly. In casual conversation, for example, comments about unpleasant weather often serve to open a conversation or keep it alive. Asking for evidence when someone says "Rotten weather" after a week of rain could be done jokingly, but not seriously. In contrast, however, if you are planning to fly a in a small plane, atmospheric conditions are a serious concern and seeking evidence about the weather is not only appropriate but prudent.

When your close friend tells you that her head hurts or that chocolate ice cream is wonderful, she is expressing how she feels, and a request for evidence is not appropriate. In a different context, such as a survey conducted by a company selling pain killers or ice cream, seeking evidence to support what people say about their pains and preferences makes sense.

Requests for evidence are appropriate when we want to be sure that our information is reliable. Questions, requests, directives, and commands usually do not require evidence. When someone at the dinner table asks for the salt, information could be conveyed (perhaps the food needs salt), but the person who requests salt does not *assert* that the food needs salt, and it would be odd to ask for evidence.

Even though information is conveyed in songs and poetry, responding to these forms by seeking evidence is usually inappropriate. When we read an epic poem, such as Homer's *Iliad,* we normally do so to savor the poem's language and its portrayal of the human condition. That is to say, we are concerned with the expressive content of the poem rather than the information it presents about what might have happened in the eastern reaches of the Mediterranean some 3,300 years ago. We can respond aesthetically to the poem without raising the question of whether Helen of Troy existed and whether her kidnapping by a Trojan prince caused a war between the Greeks and Trojans. The *Iliad* is a work of art, and as such, can be enjoyed and appraised in aesthetic terms without raising questions of factual accuracy.

When we *do* ask whether the events described in Homer's *Iliad* actually occurred, we are reading the *Iliad* as a (possible) historical document, rather than—or in addition to—responding to it as epic poetry. In fact, many expeditions *have* been mounted to try to find evidence for the Trojan War, using Homer's work as a guide. Some physical evidence has been found, and a form of writing, Linear B, that may eventually yield verbal evidence for the Trojan War, has been deciphered. In the meantime, scholars continue to debate whether and to what extent the *Iliad* was based on actual historical events, and they use the poem as a set of clues to guide their research. These scholars are focusing on the information contained in the poem, rather than on its expressive features. In this sense, they are reading the *Iliad* as history rather than poetry. When the *Iliad* is treated as a historical document, analyzing it for evidence of the events it describes is not only reasonable but required.

As these examples show, context is all-important in determining whether to seek evidence. Context also influences the amount and type of evidence that is required. If a stranger tells me there is a fire in the office building where I'm working, I won't bother to acquire much evidence; I will get out as soon as possible. If that same stranger tells me a building where I used to work burned today, I might check it out before accepting what I have been told.

Examining evidence usually carries a price. While being misinformed can result in costly mistakes, gathering evidence also can be costly. Costs can be measured in time, money, and even good will. We risk offending people, for example, by questioning their accuracy or invading their privacy. Before we decide whether to collect evidence, we must balance the cost of doing so against the cost of being wrong.

Besides the abilities already mentioned (namely, figuring out what language means in various contexts, determining when evidence is required to support assertions, then marshaling that evidence), critical thinking also involves other abilities: being able to think coherently, to comprehend instructions and advice, to formulate problems and solve them, to judge whether bits of information are relevant to an issue, to survey possible outcomes of decisions and plans, and to decide how to make the best choices from those available. In this text, we are especially concerned with understanding the relationship between assertions and verbal evidence for those assertions, but we also are concerned with improving the other critical thinking skills mentioned here.

Although you probably have not studied critical thinking in a class before, you surely have engaged in critical thinking. At one time or another, for example, you have probably thought critically about advertising claims that promise quick and easy weight loss or those that guarantee to teach techniques that will make you irresistible to members of the opposite sex. If you are like most people, you distrust politicians' assertions about what they can accomplish if they are elected. You probably wouldn't take the word of a used-car salesman, without additional evidence, that the car you are interested in buying was owned by a little old lady who drove it only on Sundays.

A critical attitude towards claims people make comes easily in these cases, but we are less careful about seeking evidence when information comes from friends and various "authorities," such as teachers, television newscasters, and newspaper reporters. Trustworthiness of the source inclines us to accept what it says. Trust in a source, however, does not always override the need for further evidence, as the examples earlier about the bus schedule and the search for a computer game showed. We should insist on evidence when we plan to act on the basis of the information and when our actions have important consequences, especially if the consequences are potentially harmful. If a trusted friend tells you that a powdered substance produces a feeling of euphoria and well-being when inhaled, with no unpleasant side effects, you—knowing the risks—will be wise to seek further evidence before trying the substance yourself. The amount of evidence you require before you act depends in part on the type of consequences for you, or others, if the assertion turns out to be false.

To be critical thinkers, we must also understand the difference between *evidence* and other devices that people sometimes use to make us believe what they say. Advertisers are notorious for their ability to persuade people that what they say about their products is true. Some present physical evidence, such as washing dirty sweatsocks in different detergents and showing the results on television. Other advertisers describe tests performed by independent laboratories. These descriptions offer verbal evidence for the value of the product. Or, advertisers may present another type of verbal evidence in the form of testimonials from satisfied customers.

Many advertisements, however, do not present evidence. Instead, an ad may show smiling, beautiful, athletic, fashionably dressed people smoking the advertised cigarettes, or drinking the advertised brand of gin. These ads employ psychological pressure in place of evidence to persuade us to use their product. The ads are designed to suggest that if we use their products we will share the glamorous life portrayed in the ad.

Threats, which can be either subtle or blunt, are another nonevidential way to mold people's beliefs. Political campaigns often play on the fears of voters by showing scenes of violence and proclaiming that the candidate will reduce crime in the streets. This tactic exhibits the candidate's concern with crime. Pictures or descriptions of violent crime, however, obviously are not *evidence* that the candidate can do anything to reduce crime. Nevertheless, people are often convinced by such techniques that the candidate will stamp out crime.

Using means other than evidence to persuade people is not always wrong. It may be appropriate, for example, to appeal to people's sense of compassion to persuade them to aid victims of poverty or oppression. But it is not appropriate to believe, on the basis of such compassion alone, that a particular group is responsible for the oppression, that a particular type of aid is more appropriate than some other type, or that the democratic government of the impoverished people will collapse if the aid is withheld. Failure to distinguish between nonevidential persuasion and evidence that supports an assertion is a serious intellectual mistake. Such a mistake is called a *fallacy*. Avoiding fallacies is another aspect of critical thinking.

Defining the expression *critical thinking* is difficult because it refers to many different abilities and activities. Nevertheless, we can begin to understand what it means when we realize that thinking critically involves analyzing what is said, assessing it carefully, seeking evidence when appropriate, putting various pieces of information together in a coherent way, attempting to avoid mistakes in thinking, questioning things that do not make sense, and making decisions and plans in the light of the best available information.

Sometimes, just being aware of the pitfalls of not thinking critically is enough to spur us to more careful thought. As in many other areas of life, however, practice and exercise are the best way to improve critical thinking skills.

Exercise Set 1.1

These exercises are designed to raise your awareness of the distinction between unsupported assertions and those for which evidence is provided, as well as the need for evidence to support various sorts of claims.

1. Suppose a friend tells you about a special unadvertised sale of cassette tapes and compact disks at a nearby store. She says that you can pick up some

incredible bargains if you go quickly. You are not busy, you have a few dollars, and you share your friend's taste in music. Should you try to get evidence in support of your friend's assertion before shopping? Why or why not?

2. Some professors at your university have a reputation for being great teachers; others are regarded as so-so (or worse). On what sort of evidence are such reputations based?

3. Suppose you tell your professor that you missed an examination because of illness. What sort of evidence is the professor likely to ask for in support of your claim?

4. Earning a high score on the SAT test is supposed to be evidence for what sorts of abilities? Discuss some of the costs of gathering this evidence. Who pays those costs?

5. You read the following in a nonfiction travel book, *Prospero's Cell*, about the Greek island Corcyra (Corfu):

> Climb to Vigla in the time of cherries and look down. You will see that the island lies against the mainland roughly in the form of a sickle. On the landward side you have a great bay, noble and serene, and almost completely landlocked. Northward the tip of the sickle almost touches Albania and here the troubled blue of the Ionian is sucked harshly between ribs of limestone and spits of sand. Kalamai fronts the Albanian foothills, and into it the water races as into a swimming pool; a milky ferocious green when the north wind curdles it.
>
> —L. Durrell

Durrell says that from a given vantage point (Vigla) in summer (the time of cherries), you can see the sickle shape of the island. He describes (makes further assertions about) Corcyra's location with respect to surrounding geographical features, states, and towns. His language is expressive (for example, "the troubled blue . . . is sucked harshly between ribs of limestone") and is designed to convey the feelings of both serenity and untamed beauty that the island has inspired.

(1) Does the author offer any evidence for the assertions he makes?

(2) Suppose you are reading this book to acquire some information about the island because you hope to visit it someday. Should you gather evidence to support the accuracy of Durrell's descriptions?

(3) Suppose you are a military commander who plans an invasion of the island. Should you seek evidence for the truth of Durrell's descriptions?

6. You read the following account of *Amanita verna,* a type of wild mushroom, in *The Mushroom Hunter's Field Guide,* by Professor A. H. Smith, a recognized expert on mushrooms. He describes its appearance, which is similar to mushrooms you buy at the grocery; it is pure white (when fresh) and very beautiful. Then he says:

Edibility: Deadly poisonous. The symptoms are delayed, making applications of first aid almost useless. Never eat a white *Amanita*.

(1) What assertions does Dr. Smith make in the quoted passage?

(2) Is "Never eat a white *Amanita*" an assertion?

(3) Would you seek further evidence before following Dr. Smith's advice?

7. In "Make Your Soil Smile," *Organic Gardening,* March 1987, the method of shallow cultivation is offered as an alternative to the use of poisonous herbicides to control weeds:

Shallow cultivation is an effective way to control weeds. Experiments have shown that hoeing or tilling only the top 2–4 inches of soil *before seed sprouts can set* eventually exhausts most of the vast supply of weed seeds that lie dormant in the soil.

—P. H. Johnson

(1) What assertions does the author make?

(2) Is any evidence (physical or verbal) presented?

(3) If you are a backyard gardener who is trying to save money and avoid poisons, would you seek further evidence before trying shallow cultivation instead of herbicides to control weeds?

(4) If you are a truck farmer whose only income depends on the success of your crops, would you seek further evidence that shallow cultivation is an effective means of weed control?

8. Taken from an ad for a management consultant firm:

Whatever your problem, I'll solve it. Over two thousand men and women, doctors, lawyers, executives, have invested the time, money and effort to create a breakthrough in business, career, social life.

(1) What assertions are made here?

(2) Is any evidence offered? Should you seek any before you invest your time, money, and effort in a consultation with this firm? Can you suggest how to acquire evidence?

9. Taken from a story in a college newspaper, the *Arizona Daily Wildcat:*

A comparison of annual rates of four major insurance companies reveals that the costs of identical automobile insurance policies for college students vary by as much as $200.

[The comparison, described later in the same story, consists of telephone interviews with insurance agents from the four companies. The reporter inquired about rates for a 20-year-old male college student, who had no history of automobile accidents; she specified the automobile make, model, and year in each case.] So it pays to shop around and research the various types of coverage in order to get the best deal.

—Beverly Medlyn

What evidence supports the author's assertion that it pays to shop for the best deal in auto insurance?

10. Taken from a newspaper report:

Proponents of legalizing [marijuana] are apparently growing in number. They argue that it is less dangerous than alcohol, which kills thousands of Americans each year. No one becomes physically addicted to pot, they say, and it doesn't kill anyone under its influence. Marijuana, they assert, is safer than smoking regular cigarettes.

—Alton Blakeslee, Associated Press Science Writer

(1) Describe what evidence, if any, is offered for the assertion that marijuana is less dangerous than alcohol.

(2) Describe what evidence, if any, is offered for the assertion that marijuana is safer than smoking regular cigarettes.

(3) If marijuana really is no more dangerous than alcohol or cigarettes, is that a good enough reason to believe that marijuana should be legalized? Why or why not?

11. Taken from *"Don't* teach your children to read," *Carnegie Magazine,* May–June 1987:

The Commission on Reading recently reviewed decades of reading research and concluded that: "The single most important activity for build-ing the knowledge required for eventual success in reading is reading aloud to children." The experts also noted that this simple activity works as well or better than formal teaching of letters, sound, and words. Parents who want to do right by their children will be glad to know that they can throw away those baby flashcards and preschool workbooks in favor of engaging storybooks, books which quickly endear themselves to both child and adult.

—E. Segal and J. B. Friedberg

(1) Do you think that the title *"Don't* teach your children to read" accurately reflects the message in the article? (Isn't reading aloud a form of teach-ing?)

(2) What evidence is cited for the assertion that reading aloud to children is most important for eventual success in reading?

12. Taken from a *Chicago Daily News* story about the alleged decline of the institution of marriage:

> It is false to say that the institution of marriage is falling apart; it is true, I think, that people are demanding more of their marriage partners than they used to—which, in the long run, is a step forward despite the chaos it creates for our age. If marriage were *really* falling apart, divorced persons wouldn't be as eager as they are to find another partner as speedily as possible.

Here, the author says that divorced persons are eager to marry again as soon as possible, and regards this as evidence against the assertion that the institution of marriage is falling apart. Could someone admit that divorced persons are eager to remarry but still believe that a high divorce rate is evidence that the institution of marriage is falling apart? (Hint: Are there several different possible meanings for the sentence: "The institution of marriage is falling apart"?)

13. In a television commercial for a particular brand of travelers' checks, a young American couple is on vacation in the Orient. The woman, who looks worried, tells the man that she has lost her purse, which holds all their money, checks, and identification. Together they hurry to the tour director. After the tour director learns that their checks are the advertised brand, he assures them their worry is unfounded because they can get help at a nearby office.

(1) What method is used to persuade the viewer that this brand of travelers' checks should be purchased?

(2) Is any evidence presented here that this brand of travelers' checks is superior to any other?

14. Taken from a newspaper column, "Let's Explore Your Mind":

> *Why does it cost Dad more these days to send Daughter to college?* Changes in styles are responsible. When Matthew Vassar founded Vassar College in 1861, three nails were provided for each girl's clothing—one each for nightgown, day dress and Sunday frock. Nowadays, when a girl unpacks her trunks at college, she has far more feminine contraptions than a family of 10 daughters had 100 years ago. Poor Dad!
>
> —A. E. Wiggam

(1) Suppose it's true that women today go to college with far more clothes than women took to school 100 years ago. Is this a good reason to believe that changes in style are responsible for the great increase in the cost of a college education for women?

(2) Can you think of any evidence against Wiggam's assertion that changes in style are responsible?

15. In the final scene of Shakespeare's *King Lear,* the lifeless body of Lear's daughter Cordelia is placed in his arms. He says:

> She's gone for ever!
> I know when one is dead and when one lives;
> She's dead as earth. Lend me a looking glass,
> If that her breath will mist or stain the stone,
> Why then she lives.

The grief-stricken Lear first admits Cordelia is dead, and then hopes in vain that she is still alive. What evidence does he call for to settle the matter?

16. Taken from a newspaper letter to the editor, regarding the Supreme Court decision disallowing school prayer:

> Communism has won its greatest victory. Communists do not pray in school. Americans will not pray in school. . . . Without the sincere planting of the seeds of prayer in all of our children, Catholic, Protestant, and Jewish, we are finished. Communism has won. It's just a matter of time.

What does the author regard as evidence that the decision prohibiting school prayer is a victory for communism?

17. Consider Paul Ehrlich's position on lead poisoning, a serious illness that causes mental and physical decay and often leads to death.

> It is a sobering thought that overexposure to lead was probably a factor in the decline of the Roman Empire. . . . Romans lined their bronze cooking, eating, and wine storage vessels with lead. They thus avoided the obvious and unpleasant taste and symptoms of copper poisoning. They traded them for the pleasant flavor and more subtle poisoning associated with lead. Lead was also common in Roman life in the form of paints, and lead pipes were often used to carry water. Examination of the bones of upper-class Romans of the classical period shows high concentrations of lead—possibly one cause of the famous decadence of Roman leadership. The lower classes lived more simply, drank less wine from lead-lined containers, and thus may have picked up far less lead.
>
> —Dr. Paul R. Ehrlich, *The Population Bomb:*

Ehrlich portrays a decadent upper class, suffering from lead poisoning, leading Rome to ruin. However, he does not say whether any bodies of lower-class Romans have been examined for levels of lead.

(1) Assume it is true that the lower classes lived more simply and drank less wine from lead-lined containers. Does this persuade you that they picked up far less lead than the upper classes? Why or why not?

(2) What evidence might support the assertion that the lower classes were exposed to just as much lead? (Hint: Who was mining the lead, working with lead paints and lead pipes, and manufacturing lead-lined containers for wine?)

18. Taken from a United Press International newspaper story quoting Dr. L. Nelson Bell, a moderator of the Presbyterian Church:

> To deny the existence of Satan and the reality of evil spirits is to be more foolish than a soldier reconnoitering enemy territory without admitting that there is an enemy out there to do him harm.

Acknowledging that the "unseen power" of evil spirits is a difficult concept for the modern mind, Dr. Bell added:

> Electricity is also mysterious, but we do not question its existence or its power. We can be sure electricity is real, because we can see and feel the things it accomplishes, such as lighting and cooling homes. But if pain, hatred, war, suspicion, racism and other evils are manifestations of the devil's work, who is to say there is any lack of evidence in the modern world for his reality?

Dr. Bell compares the devil with electricity in the following way: both are "unseen powers" that are detected by their observed effects.

(1) Do we have any evidence that lighting or the cooling of houses are effects of electricity? (Could you demonstrate this to someone who doubts it?)

(2) Do we have any evidence that pain, hatred, war, and racism are the effects of the devil's work? (Could you give a similar sort of demonstration, or provide other evidence?)

19. On a recent sports news show on television, a football player comments on whether college football players should be paid for playing ball:

> Football players should be paid because they work five or six hours a day, and have to play—work again—on Saturdays. It is just like a real job.

(1) The player asserts that playing college football is just like a real job. Does he give any evidence for this?

(2) Can you think of any important differences between playing college football and working at a real job? (To answer this you may have to clarify the meaning of "real job.")

(3) Is it obvious that anyone who works five or six hours a day and again on Saturdays should be paid for that work?

II. ARGUMENTS

Evidence, as noted earlier, can be either verbal or physical. When you return damaged goods to a store to prove their condition before you collect a refund, you are presenting physical evidence to support your claim that the goods are damaged. Some situations—like requests for refunds—customarily require physical evidence. Remember all those detective stories which say that without a body no evidence exists to prove a murder was committed?

In this text, we are more concerned with verbal evidence than with physical evidence. Although in some situations physical evidence is absolutely necessary, in many others a description of the physical evidence will suffice and is more convenient to present. Verbal evidence may be oral or written and can include descriptions of physical evidence. A set of sentences consisting of an assertion to be supported and the verbal evidence for that assertion is called an *argument*. When we support sentences by offering verbal evidence for them, we are *arguing* for those sentences.

The terms *argument* and *arguing* are frequently used in another way: *argument* to refer to a dispute or disagreement and *arguing* to refer to the activity of engaging in verbal disagreement. The two ways of using these terms, while different, are not entirely unrelated. For when we are involved in a disagreement or dispute, we often try to show that our position is correct by stating evidence to support it.

In dealing with problems of critical thinking, however, the word *argument* most commonly refers to a set of sentences related in such a way that some of the sentences purport to provide evidence for one of the sentences, without any suggestion of dispute or disagreement.

Logic is the field of study concerned with analyzing arguments and appraising their correctness or incorrectness. The logician is interested in discovering and stating general principles by which to decide whether the alleged evidence in an argument would, if it were true, support some assertion. Thus, logic is an important part of critical thinking.

In the study of arguments, it is helpful to use special terms to refer to the separate parts of an argument. The sentences that assert the evidence are called *premisses;* and the sentence that is being argued for is called the *conclusion*. An argument can have any number of premisses, but (by definition) it can have only one conclusion.

The following argument, has only one premiss:

Mary has a twin sister.
_____
Therefore, Mary is not an only child.

The next argument has two premisses:

Abortion is the same as murder.
Murder is wrong.
_____
Therefore, abortion is wrong.

Many arguments have more than two premisses. Darwin once said that his entire book, *The Origin of Species,* is merely one long argument for a single conclusion: the truth of evolution.

A sentence acquires status as a premiss or a conclusion according to the role it plays in a given argument. The sentence "Abortion is the same as murder," which is a premiss in the preceding argument, might be the conclusion of a different argument in which someone tried to establish *its* truth, as in, for example:

Abortion is the deliberate killing of a human fetus.
Human fetuses are persons.
Any deliberate killing of a person is murder.

Therefore, abortion is murder.

Of course, we might want to develop other arguments with new premisses to support any of the premisses of any given argument, particularly if their truth is challenged.

Although it is always possible to question the premisses of an argument—and to ask for other arguments to support those premisses—this process normally ends when premisses that can be agreed on as a starting point are reached. Sometimes this happens quickly, especially when premisses state what easily can be observed as true. But when the arguments concern important issues, such as the morality of abortion or the legalization of marijuana, agreeing on premisses any less controversial than the proposed conclusions may be difficult. Sometimes, disagreements are so deep that opponents can not find any acceptable premisses they can share.

Usually, the point of an argument is to support the truth of its conclusion. Demonstrating the truth of a conclusion requires not only that the premisses are true* but also that the premisses provide the right type of support for the conclusion. *Logic* is concerned chiefly with the second point, that is, the relationship between the premisses and the conclusion. When we examine an argument in order to determine its *logical* strength, the question of whether the premisses are actually true may be set aside in favor of answering whether the premisses *would* support the conclusion *if* they were true.

Critical thinking is broader in scope than logic, for as critical thinkers we always must be concerned with whether the premisses are true, and perhaps with the possibility of finding further arguments to support any questionable premisses. However, even though we are concerned with the truth of premisses, it is important to treat that question of truth separately from that of whether the premisses, *if* true, *would* support the conclusion of a given argument.

Premisses and conclusions of arguments are usually stated in *declarative sentences*. These sentences are most commonly used in English for presenting information and making assertions and—in contrast to questions and com-

---

*An exception to this requirement for true premisses occurs in a form of reasoning called indirect proof, which is discussed in Chapter 3.

mands—asking whether declarative sentences are true or false is entirely appropriate.

Consider the following argument given by opponents of the legalization of marijuana:

Marijuana should not be legalized because it is potentially dangerous and not enough is known about its long-term effects and because use of marijuana leads to use of hard drugs.

Even though this argument is stated in a single sentence, we can divide that sentence into parts that are themselves sentences, and that stand in the relationship of premises and conclusion. The conclusion of this argument is the declarative sentence: "Marijuana should not be legalized." The three assertions, conjoined in a compound declarative sentence, that serve as premises are: "it is potentially dangerous," "not enough is known about its long-term effects," and "use of marijuana leads to use of hard drugs." Each of these component sentences is an assertion, the truth of which can be questioned. For this argument to establish the truth of its conclusion, all of these premises must be true *and* together they must provide reasons for accepting the conclusion.

Although premises and conclusions of arguments are usually declarative sentences, occasionally other forms are used. The following argument, taken from *Our Mutual Friend,* by Charles Dickens, is offered by Gaffer, a river boatman, to a friend who has just helped him empty the pockets in clothing taken from a body they found floating in the Thames. Gaffer tries to convince his friend that this is not robbery.

> And what if I had been accused of robbing a dead man, Gaffer?
> You COULDN'T do it.
> Couldn't you, Gaffer?
> No. Has a dead man any use for money? Is it possible for a dead man to have money? What world does a dead man belong to? T'other world. What world does money belong to? This world. How can money be a corpse's? Can a corpse own it, want it, spend it, claim it, miss it? Don't try to go confounding the rights and wrongs of things in that way.

The premises that support the claim that dead men cannot be robbed are stated here in a series of questions. But these are not ordinary questions. They are called *rhetorical questions* because they are based on the assumption that only one answer can be given to them. Thus, these questions are similar to sentences that say that something is so (they "state the facts") and are unlike ordinary questions. Sometimes rhetorical questions are used to dramatize the premises or the conclusion of an argument If Gaffer had flatly said, "Money cannot be owned, wanted, spent, claimed, or missed by a corpse," the information conveyed would have been the same, but the interest and color displayed in his speech would have been different, and his argument may have seemed less persuasive.

III. RECOGNIZING ARGUMENTS

Before beginning our detailed study of different types of arguments and their evaluation, we want to be able to recognize arguments as they occur in ordinary speech and writing. That is to say, we want to distinguish cases in which a sentence is merely being asserted from those in which the sentence is supported by other sentences. It makes no sense to accuse someone of presenting a poor argument for a case if no argument is being offered. The most we can reasonably do in such circumstances is to say that an argument *should* be given to support the assertion.

When we are trying to decide whether an argument is being presented, the first question to ask ourselves is what point the author or speaker is trying to make. When we have identified the sentence that makes the point (the conclusion, if it is an argument), then we can ask what assertions, if any, are intended as support or evidence for that point (the premises), for example:

> Cigarette smoking is a serious health hazard. Statistical studies show that cigarette smokers are not only at much greater risk for contracting lung cancer, but also have higher incidence of emphysema and heart disease.

In this example, the claim that cigarette smoking is a serious health hazard is the conclusion, and it is supported by referring to the statistical studies that show that smokers have higher rates of certain types of serious illness than nonsmokers.

Recognizing arguments is sometimes aided by the presence of certain words, called *indicator words*, frequently used to signal the presence of either premises or conclusions of arguments. In several of the arguments presented already, the word *therefore* served to introduce conclusions. This is such a common use of the term in English that whenever *therefore* occurs, we should look for an argument. Other terms that often introduce conclusions of arguments are *thus, and so, consequently, necessarily, hence, it follows that,* and *for that reason.* Words that frequently indicate premises are *because, since, for,* and *for the reason that.*

In the following arguments, the *indicator words* are italicized:

1. Taken from an ad paid for by the Mobil Corporation:

> *Since* private business is the most effective instrument of economic change, the government should utilize the resources of private business in its economic planning and decision making.

The main point here is stated in the sentence that follows the comma: "the government should utilize the resources of private business in its economic planning and decision making." The premiss offered in support of this conclusion is signaled by the indicator word "*Since* business is the most effective instrument of economic change, . . ."

2. Taken from a newspaper story:

> Women office workers work just as hard as men office workers, and are just as productive. *Therefore* women office workers should receive the same pay as men in comparable positions.

In this argument for equalizing pay between men and women office workers, the indicator word *therefore* introduces the conclusion of the argument. The premises are stated before the conclusion.

3. From a book, *The Vietnam War and the Right of Resistance:*

> Those who opposed the war by resistance to Selective Service may not fairly be charged with violating their moral obligation to obey the law of the land. *For* a condition of that obligation has been violated by government, and in so doing, government has forfeited its moral right to call upon citizens for obedience in this area.
>
> —J. G. Murphy

Murphy states the conclusion first and follows it with two supporting premises, introduced by *for.*

Although these indicator words often signal the premises or conclusions of arguments, they have other uses as well. Therefore, when we see these words, we cannot take it for granted that we have identified an argument. *Since,* for example, is often used to indicate passage of time, as in "Since Harry has been away at college he has been receiving his hometown paper in the mail."

Because is frequently used to express a causal connection between two events, rather than to offer evidence that one of those events occurred. An example of this use of *because* occurs in the sentence "Richard Nixon resigned the presidency because a scandal resulted from the Watergate break-in and subsequent investigations." Here, no attempt is made to prove that Nixon resigned. Presumably, that is so widely known that it needs no support. The sentence asserts, but does not argue, that a specific set of events caused him to resign.

If we want to *argue* that Watergate was the cause of Nixon's resignation, we would present evidence that the Watergate events were *causally related* to the resignation. For example, in our premises we might say that it was not merely coincidental that the burglary occurred before the resignation, that the motive of the burglary was political, not economic, that Nixon knew that such clandestine activities were authorized by his staff, that he believed the investigation ensuing from the burglary might result in his impeachment, and so on. Or the argument might try to show that other possible causes for resigning the presidency, such as a severe illness or Nixon's stated concern for national harmony, were not causally related to the resignation. Although sentences that merely assert a causal connection between two events are not themselves arguments, they can be premises or conclusions of arguments.

When the subject matter is unfamiliar, deciding whether a causal assertion or an argument is being presented may be difficult. If, for example, someone were to tell me that the National Collegiate Athletic Association will soon rule that football players can be paid by colleges for playing ball *because* so much pressure has been applied in favor of this move, I would not know whether that person was presenting evidence for the assertion that the rule would be changed or presenting an assertion about *why* the rule would be changed. I don't keep up with football news so I don't know what rulings have been made or are being contemplated.

If I am being told that pressure for paying players is a *reason to believe* that the ruling will change, the passage is intended as an argument. If I am being told that the new rule that is going into effect is a result of pressure that was exerted, the passage is a causal explanation. In many cases, we must ask questions, examine the context for clues, or make "educated guesses" about the intent of the person before we can decide whether a cause is asserted or an argument is presented.

The terms *for, since, thus,* and *therefore* are also used in causal explanations of why something happened: "He was invited to the wedding, since he's my mother's favorite cousin." "My dog ran away; therefore, I am putting up this sign to ask for help in finding him." "She sets high goals for herself; thus, she was disappointed to place third in the marathon."

Another use of *thus* and *therefore* is to introduce an example of some important point, as in "Not all mammals give birth to live young. *Thus* the platypus is an egg-laying mammal." Closely related to this meaning of *thus* is its use as a synonym for "in this way." "Every day during the last school term, I read over what I had written the previous day, crossed out the rough parts and rewrote bits of it. Thus I learned to write a decent essay."

Because *therefore, since* and the other indicator words have several uses, they are not absolutely reliable argument indicators. Another problem in recognizing arguments is that some arguments lack any indicator words. In these cases, we depend on the context as well as the meanings of the sentences to determine whether someone is presenting an argument or merely a series of assertions, none of which supports any of the others.

Here is an argument that has no indicator words. It is taken from a decision by the United States District Court of Appeals (District of Columbia; Bazelon, *Washington v. United States*):

> A judgment of acquittal by reason of insanity is appropriate only when a
> jury verdict of guilty would violate the law or the facts. We cannot say that
> this was the situation in Washington's case. The district court did not err
> in its refusal to enter a judgment of acquittal by reason of insanity.

The context (a decision by a court of appeals) is helpful in determining that this is an argument, because court rulings are supposed to be supported by reasons. The last sentence of the passage asserts that the district court's judgment was not in error, and the reasons for this (the premises) are given in the first two sentences. To decide whether an argument is present, we should ask ourselves (1) "What point is being made?" and (2) "What evidence is offered to support it?" In this case, we can spot the conclusion if we know that it is the business of district courts of appeals to decide whether lower court rulings are correct. Without background knowledge, however, deciding whether a given sentence is intended to be a premiss or conclusion can be difficult.

When no indicator words are present, one helpful technique is to insert them where appropriate—that is, premiss indicators before suspected premisses, and conclusion indicators before conclusions—to see whether the passage makes sense when it is reconstructed in this way. This method will not always work, because if we are unclear about the context, we may be unable to judge whether one way of constructing the passage makes more sense than another way. Assuming that the district court of appeals was ruling on whether the lower court was correct, if we insert indicator words in the previous example, it reads like this:

> *Because* a judgment of acquittal by reason of insanity is appropriate only
> when a jury verdict of guilty would violate the law or the facts and
> *because* we cannot say that this was the situation in Washington's case,
> *therefore* the district court did not err in its refusal to enter a judgment of
> acquittal by reason of insanity.

The meaning of the original passage is not changed when the indicator words are inserted; this supports our view that an argument is presented, and that we have identified its premisses and conclusion correctly.

When we insert indicator words to mark the premisses and conclusion of an argument, we must be sensitive to stylistic variations in the way arguments are presented in ordinary language. Frequently, for emphasis, the conclusion of an argument is stated before the premisses, but beginning an argument with *therefore*. is stylistically awkward. If we want to insert indicator words while ensuring that the passage retains correct English style, we sometimes must reorder the sentences, putting the conclusion sentence last.

In summary then, when trying to decide whether an argument is present a helpful technique is to consider the context carefully and to ask these questions:

1. What point is the speaker or writer trying to make?
2. Is the speaker or writer presenting evidence to support the truth of some assertion?
3. Is the speaker or writer trying to explain why something happened when the fact that it did happen is not in question?
4. Is an illustrative example—rather than an argument—being presented?

Exercise Set 1.2

> Part One. In each of the following arguments, use the indicator words to help identify the premisses and the conclusion. Rewrite the argument in *standard form*. That is to say, write each premiss on a line by itself, and underneath them, separated by a drawn line, write the con-

clusion. Although in standard form premisses are written above the conclusion, it is advisable to identify the conclusion first. Consider the following example. The *conclusion* is enclosed in parentheses, and each *premiss* is underlined:

(The earth is spherical in shape.) <u>For the night sky looks different in the</u> <u>northern and southern parts of the earth, and this would be so if the earth</u> <u>were spherical in shape.</u>

—Aristotle

In standard form, the argument, which has two premisses, looks like this:

The night sky looks different in the northern and southern parts of the earth. This would be so if the earth were spherical in shape.
_____

The earth is spherical in shape.

1. Since identical twins, who have the same genes, are more likely to have the same blood pressure than fraternal twins, who share half the same genes, we can conclude that high blood pressure is inherited.

2. Nuclear power plants violate principles of fairness because people who live close to them would suffer more in the case of an accident and they do not receive extra benefits to compensate for the increased risk.

3. In England under the blasphemy laws it is illegal to express disbelief in the Christian religion. It is also illegal to teach what Christ taught on the subject of non-resistance. Therefore, whoever wishes to avoid being a criminal must profess to agree with Christ's teachings but must avoid saying what that teaching was.

—B. Russell, *Skeptical Essays*

4. A coin has been tossed twelve times and has shown a "head" each time. Thus it is very likely that the next time this coin is tossed it will also show a "head."

5. A coin has been tossed twelve times and has shown a "head" each time, so the coin is probably unfair.

6. All 70 students who ate dinner at the fraternity house on Friday became ill during the night. None of the students who live at the house but who didn't dine there that night became ill, so the illness must have been food poisoning caused by something served for dinner at the house on Friday.

7. Since the exercise, training and development of our powers of discriminating among works of art are plainly aesthetic activities, the aesthetic properties of a picture plainly include not only those found by looking at it but also those that determine how it is to be looked at.

—N. Goodman, "Art and Authenticity"

8. We can suspect that the inventor [of eyeglasses] was not an academic, for professors delight in boasting of their inventions, and before the thirteenth century we have no record by any such self-styled inventor.

—D. J. Boorstin, *The Discoverers*

9. Over a period of two years now, I have tested my instrument [the newly invented telescope] (or rather dozens of my instruments) by hundreds and thousands of experiments involving thousands and thousands of objects, near and far, large and small, bright and dark; hence I do not see how it can enter the mind of anyone that I have simplemindedly remained deceived in my observation.

—Galileo, quoted by Boorstin in *The Discoverers*

10. Since creationism can be discussed effectively as a scientific model, and since evolutionism is fundamentally a religious philosophy rather than a science, it is clearly unsound educational practice and even unconstitutional for evolution to be taught and promoted in the public schools to the exclusion or detriment of special creation.

—H. Morris, *Introducing Creationism in the Public Schools*

11. Evolutionary theory merits a place among the sciences for . . . [i]t offers a unified set of problem-solving strategies that can be applied, by means of independently testable assumptions, to answer a myriad of questions about the characteristics of organisms, their interrelationships, and their distributions.

—P. Kitcher, *Abusing Science*

12. The integrated effect [of the Chernobyl nuclear power-plant accident] on the health of the world's population can be described by adding up all the calculated cancers, leading to a prediction of many thousand cancer deaths. But the effect is probably less than that caused by burning fossil fuels for 1 year in the Soviet Union. If, therefore, the average public health is the sole objective, and a Chernobyl accident happens less than once a year, the RBMK reactors in the Soviet Union can be considered less hazardous than coal-fired plants of similar size.

—R. Wilson, "A visit to Chernobyl," *Science* 236 (1987):1636

13. The [Great Fire of London (1666)] and rebuilding made little improvement in the sanitary and moral conditions of the slum populations. For the seat and origin of the plague had always been in the 'Liberties' outside the City, where the poorest dwelt. Now as these districts were not burnt down they were not rebuilt and in 1722 . . . 'they were still in the same condition as they were before'. It is therefore evident that the 'rebuilding of London' due to the Fire was not the main reason why the plague disappeared from London after its last great effort [of 1666].

—G.M. Trevelyan, *English Social History*

14. I say [Mr. Glass is] 'old' with intention, though not with certainty . . . my reason for it might seem a little far-fetched. The hair of human beings falls out in very varying degrees, but almost always falls out slightly, and with the [magnifying] lens I should see the tiny hairs in a hat recently worn. It has none, which leads me to guess that Mr. Glass is bald. Now when this is taken with the high-pitched and querulous voice which Miss MacNab described so vividly, when we take the hairless head together with the tone common in senile anger, I should think we may deduce some advance in years.

—G. K. Chesterton, "The Absence of Mr. Glass"

Part Two. In each of the following arguments, the conclusion is enclosed in parentheses. Try to insert appropriate indicator words before sentences that are premises or conclusions, then decide whether the passage makes sense. With some choices of indicator words, the sentences need to be rearranged.

1. Women tend to do better on essay tests than on timed, multiple-choice tests. Men tend to do better on timed, multiple-choice tests than on essay tests. SAT tests are timed, multiple-choice tests. (SAT tests are biased in favor of men.)

2. (The human mind is not the same thing as the human brain.) The human body, including the brain, is a material thing. The human mind is a spiritual thing. Nothing is both a material thing and a spiritual thing.

—K. Campbell, *Body and Mind*

3. (The year 1859 is perhaps the most important one in the history of biology to date.) In that year Charles Darwin published his theory of evolution by natural selection, which has deeply affected not only biology, but other branches of human thought as well.

—L. C. Dunn and T. H. Dobshansky, *Heredity, Race and Society*

4. (In spite of the general's years, he evidently is a little vain of his person, and ambitious of conquests.) I have observed him on Sunday in church eyeing the country girls most suspiciously; and have seen him leer upon them with a downright amorous look, even when he has been gallanting Lady Lilycraft with great ceremony through the churchyard.

—W. Irving, *Bracebridge Hall*

5. With no legal, regulated disposal facilities available, illegal dumping becomes more attractive. Far more damage will be done to the environment from illegal dumping than from regulated, legal disposal. (Hazardous-waste disposal facilities are essential to the protection of Pennsylvania's environment.)

—F. Kury, *Pittsburgh Post-Gazette*

6. After so much lying, even for purposes [Lt. Col. Oliver] North considered patriotic, (his protestations that now he only wants to tell the truth aren't worth much.) Why should he be considered believable, even under oath, when he testified under oath that he had so often considered other values more important than truth?

—T. Wicker, *The New York Times*

Part Three. In each of the following, the "indicator words" are italicized. Try to determine whether an argument is offered or whether the "indicator words" have some other meaning.

1. In some parts of the country parents have objected to students in high school reading *Romeo and Juliet because* it portrays teen lust, drug use, and suicide.

2. It is not fair of course to judge a book by whether its title is apt or not. All the more so, *because* often it is the publisher who decides the matter.

—A. Margalit, "The Birth of a Tragedy," *New York Review of Books* 33:16

3. *Since* the 1967 war the right wing in Israel has been speaking of the "Greater Israel," and the Labor party of the "demographic problem," the former in the name of the pleasure principle, the latter in the name of the reality principle.

—A. Margalit, "The Birth of a Tragedy," *New York Review of Books* 33:16

4. You're perfect, Raleigh. You're so perfect, you're going to lend me this money *because* rotten as I am, I'm still your brother and you've got to come through for me. That's what it's going to cost you to keep on being good old perfect old Raleigh.

—M. Malone, *Handling Sin*

5. This promotion of colleges to universities is consistent with the long-honored American custom of "raising" a thing by adding to the number of syllables used to describe it. For example, rain is raised to precipitation. College has only two syllables, and even seminary only four. But university, with five syllables, adds distinction. *Thus*: University of Montevallo, Alabama . . . Upper Iowa University . . . Midwestern University, Texas.

—P. Fussell, *Class*

6. Rock [music], Bloom says, "ruins the imagination," *so* it is difficult for students to have a relationship with the art and thought that are the substance of liberal education.

—"Insight," *The Washington Times*

7. Tipperary, made large by its fame and my imagination, is but one main street with a few stores and houses. This eerie scene repeated itself again and again during my visit to this most beautiful of European lands. *For* Ireland, contrary to the trend of most other countries, is a depopulated nation.

—S. Gould, *The Flamingo's Smile*

8. Most professors are specialists, concerned only with their own fields, interested in the advancement of those fields in their own terms, or in their own personal advancement in a world where all the rewards are on the side of professional distinction. They have been entirely emancipated from the old structure of the university, which at least helped to indicate that they are incomplete, only parts of an unexamined and undiscovered whole. *So* the student must navigate among a collection of carnival barkers, each trying to lure him into a particular sideshow.

—A. Bloom, *The Closing of the American Mind*

9. Describing how a process works is valuable *for two reasons*. First it forces you to make sure that you know how it works. Then it forces you to make sure that the reader will understand it as clearly as you do.

—W. Zinsser, *On Writing Well*

10. Taken from an interview with Benazir Bhutto, Pakistani political leader, in which she talked about her agreement to marry a man chosen by her family:

I did meet him, and *because* I felt he's nice and had a sense of humor and he seemed to be a tolerant person in that he could handle having a wife who had an independent career of her own, I thought it was wise to accept the proposal.

—H. Raines, *The New York Times*

IV. EXTENDED ARGUMENTS

Thus far, we have looked at arguments that offer one or more premisses in support of a single conclusion. Frequently, however, in real life, we meet not only arguments like this but also series of interrelated arguments—sometimes in a single paragraph or even a single sentence. We call these extended arguments. Some extended arguments attempt to establish a conclusion by stating premisses and, in addition, by producing evidence for those premisses. Thus the premisses of the main argument are conclusions of the subsidiary arguments. Some arguments display both the pros and cons of a position, and they present arguments for each side before selecting one conclusion. Other extended arguments present several different arguments in support of the same conclusion. Still others argue for several closely related conclusions. The techniques for analyzing these more complicated extended arguments, that is, for identifying premisses and conclusions, are just the same as for simpler arguments, with slight "bookkeeping" modifications.

First of all, as before, it is helpful to try to discover the main point the speaker or writer is trying to make, then to identify the reasons offered in support of that point. Once that is accomplished, we can begin to investigate whether any of the premisses of that argument are supported by reasons. If they are, we can say that the main argument contains *subarguments*, which can be investigated as well. This procedure can be messy. But our goal is to understand complicated arguments by reducing them to simpler parts.

Example

> Since there can be no talk of an independent ideology formulated by the working masses themselves in the process of their movement, (the only choice is either bourgeois or socialist ideology). There is no middle course. Hence {to belittle the socialist ideology *in any way, to turn aside from it in the slightest degree* means to strengthen the bourgeois ideology}.
>
> —V. I. Lenin, *What Is to Be Done?*

In this extended argument, brackets and parentheses have been added to clarify the structure of the argument. The main conclusion is stated last, in brackets, following the conclusion indicator word *hence*. The premiss that supports this conclusion is enclosed in parentheses, and is itself supported by the sentence following the premiss indicator word *since*. In this example, as in many extended arguments, after a conclusion of a preliminary argument has been stated, it is restated in simpler terms ("There is no middle course.") when used as the premiss of the next argument.

Exercise Set 1.3

Isolate the component arguments in each of the following passages, and identify their premises and conclusions. Write each component argument in standard form.

1. Nuclear fuel is cleaner than fossil fuels since its normal waste products do not cause significant atmospheric or water pollution. But the waste nuclear fuels does produce is very dangerous and lasts for centuries. This fact, combined with the possibility of dramatic pollution from escaped radiation, such as occurred at Chernobyl, leads to the conclusion that fossil fuels are cleaner than nuclear fuel.

2. Because publishers are aiming at a national market, the number-one criterion for any textbook is avoidance of controversy. Since they must respond to a variety of specific criteria from their buyers, this has resulted in what has been called the "dumbing down" of textbooks.

—C. Holden, "Textbook controversy intensifies nationwide"
Science 235 (1987):19

3. Cycads can, therefore, justifiably claim our interest if only because of their rarity and uncertain future. A further and possibly more important consideration is their value to students of plant evolution, for they appear but little changed from ancestors that flourished along with dinosaurs and our own insectivorous antecedents. They are, in a true sense, living fossils.

—K. Norstog, "Cycads and the Origin of Insect Pollination"
American Scientist (May–June 1987):75

4. Through analytic techniques of diverse kinds, through group therapies and encounter groups, by means of hypnosis, drug therapy, and brain stimulation, self-disclosure [the revealing of personal secrets] is aided and interpreted. But the therapeutic value of any one of these techniques is far from established; and the need for caution in choosing persons best qualified to listen to personal revelation is increasingly clear.

The caution is well founded. One cannot trust all who listen to confessions to be either discreet or especially capable of bringing solace or help. In addition, the act of confessing can in itself increase the vulnerability of persons who expose their secrets, especially in institutionalized practices. Studies have shown that when self-revelation flows in one direction only, it increases the authority of the listener while decreasing that of the speaker. In ordinary practices of confiding, the flow of personal information is reciprocal, as the revelations of one person call forth those of another; but in institutionalized practices, there is no such reciprocity. On the contrary, therapists and others who receive personal confidences are often taught to restrain their natural impulse to respond in kind.

—S. Bok, *Secrets*

5. The grouping of these drugs [LSD, DOM, DMT, psilocybin, mescaline, and their congeners as hallucinogenic] is not arbitrary or simply for the sake of convenience. They can be considered members of the same drug class for two important reasons. First, they elicit a common set of effects: sensory perceptual (distorted time sense; altered sensations of colors, sounds, and shapes, ultimately developing into complex, often

multimodal hallucinations; and synesthesia, or mixing of the senses); psychic (dream-like feelings; depersonalization; and rapid and often profound alternations of affect such as depression or elation); and somatic (dizziness, tingling skin, weakness, tremor, nausea, and increased reflexes). Second, and perhaps more important, these drugs display cross-tolerance—that is, a decreased efficacy of one drug taken shortly after another drug. Thus, if a person has a full-blown hallucinatory experience following ingestion of LSD, the normal hallucinatory response to mescaline or DOM taken the next day will be dramatically blunted or abolished. Therefore, even though it may be argued, and perhaps correctly so, that drugs such as marijuana and PCP should also be classified as hallucinogenic, they do not belong to the class of LSD-like drugs since they show no evidence of cross-tolerance with them.

—B. L. Jacobs, "How hallucinogenic drugs work,"
American Scientist 75 (July–August 1987):386

6. Background information: Victims of Guam disease (Guam ALS/P-D) exhibit symptoms of ALS (Lou Gehrig's disease), Parkinson's disease, and dementia. The study discussed here provides new evidence that all of these diseases could be triggered by some environmental factor.

> Scientists fed monkeys moderate amounts of amino acid, [beta-methylamino-L-alanine] and found that the animals developed severe nerve disorders similar to those in ALS. The severity of the disease and the time it took for symptoms to develop depended on the amount the animals ate.
>
> The chemical is found in the seeds of a cycad, the "false sago palm." During the wartime occupation of Guam by the Japanese, the seeds were used as nourishment and even medicine.
>
> After the war an unusual number of cases involving nerve degeneration began to appear among Guam's native inhabitants. . . . At the height of the outbreak in the early 1950s, it accounted for one death in five among natives over the age of 25.
>
> In more recent years, the Guam ALS has become much less common, indicating that the source of nerve damage is no longer present and suggesting to scientists that a slow-acting environmental cause was previously at work. Furthermore, the age at which patients developed symptoms has risen steadily, another strong indication of a causative factor that was present years ago but has since disappeared. After World War II, use of the cycad seed dwindled as other sources of food and medicine were made available.

—H. M. Schmeck, *The New York Times*

V. RECONSTRUCTING ARGUMENTS

1. Incompletely Stated Arguments

We have already considered the problem of identifying premises and conclusions when no indicator words are present. In addition to this problem, many arguments in English are incompletely stated, which is to say some premises, or even the conclusion, of an argument may be omitted. Once we recognize the presence of an argument, we frequently have to reconstruct it by supplying missing parts before we can evaluate its strength.

In ordinary language, arguments may be stated incompletely to avoid boring the listener or reader with information that is presumably obvious to all concerned.

Suppose you are wondering whether Jeb, your lab partner in a chemistry class who was worried about paying a tuition bill, has settled his account. Another friend who works in the registrar's office says, "Jeb must have come up with the money, since his application to graduate on Sunday has been approved." The approval of Jeb's application to graduate convinces you that his bill has been paid, because, as every student knows, degrees are not granted to those with unpaid tuition bills. The unstated premiss "No student with an unpaid bill can be graduated," is nevertheless a part of the argument that supports the conclusion that Jeb paid his tuition bill, for otherwise it would not be at all clear what the fact that Jeb is graduating has to do with his having paid his bills. Because you and your friend are both aware of the relevance and the truth of this premiss, however, mentioning the premiss is unnecessary.

Many but not all unstated premisses are *generalizations*. Sentences that say that *all* or *no* members of one class are members of another class are called *universal generalizations.* "No student with an unpaid bill can be graduated" is an example of a (negative) universal generalization. "All students know that tuition bills must be paid before graduation" is an example of an affirmative universal generalization.

"The Washingtons are probably wealthy, since they drive a new Cadillac" is another example of an argument with a missing—but presumably obvious—premiss: "Most families who drive new Cadillacs are wealthy." Generalizations, like this premiss, which state that some proportion of members of one class are members of another class, are called *statistical generalizations.* The universal generalization "*All* families who drive new Cadillacs are wealthy," would not be a good choice for the missing premiss in this argument because driving an expensive automobile is not an infallible mark of wealth. "Most families who drive new Cadillacs are wealthy" is more likely to be regarded as true than "All families who drive new Cadillacs are wealthy." An indication—not always present—that a statistical generalization is implied in the above argument is the word *probably*, which modifies the conclusion.

Statistical generalizations are sometimes stated numerically, as in "43 percent of American voters voted for Clinton in the '92 presidential election," or "14 infants out of 100 born to mothers with H.I.V. are also infected with H.I.V." Universal generalizations can be thought of as limiting cases of statistical generalizations. That is to say, a generalization is statistical if the percentage is greater than 0 percent and less than 100 percent; otherwise the generalization is universal. As we have seen, not all statistical generalizations are stated numerically; *most, usually, seldom, frequently,* and *rarely* are sometimes used to indicate a statistical generalization. Statistical generalizations, like universal generalizations, provide a link between the particular facts mentioned in the stated premises of an argument ("the Washingtons drive a new Cadillac") and the conclusion ("the Washingtons are wealthy").

In the context of an ordinary conversation or informal presentation of an argument, it is inappropriate to mention premisses that are obviously true. However, if we are concerned with checking the correctness of an argument, we may want to see that the argument is stated as completely as possible. This means that we must occasionally spell out even that which seems obvious to everyone.

Another reason for searching out the intended or assumed, but unstated, premisses in an argument is that when some hidden premisses are exposed, they turn out not to be obvious after all. Consider the following extended argument offered by a student who is trying to persuade a classmate of the benefits of nuclear power:

> Well, I'm for it because, first of all, we're eventually going to use up all our fossil fuels. And, if we don't do that soon, we're going to have really bad problems with acid rain, which we already have. The Canadians definitely feel the effects of acid rain. But, we don't think about that because we [in the United States] don't feel the effects right now. And, eventually we're not going to have an ozone layer left. Even though there are definite costs to nuclear power—I mean a disaster like there was at Chernobyl would be a nightmare—but if the plants were safely managed and operated, then a disaster like that would be less likely . . .

At this point, the other student in the discussion interrupted to point out that fossil fuels are not the only alternative to nuclear power. Other sources of fuel, power as wind, hydroelectric, and solar are available, she said. In this discussion (which was tape-recorded in a study of how students reason in ordinary conversation), the first student had not said "The only choice is between fossil fuels and nuclear power," but the second student correctly understood that this was a hidden premiss in her argument. The first student's argument for the use of nuclear power focused on problems with fossil fuels, but this line of reasoning would support nuclear power only if other alternatives were not available or were not adequate to meet our energy needs.

After the hidden premiss (which in this case was not a generalization) was pointed out and challenged, the first student revised her argument. She conceded the point that solar, wind, and hydroelectric power may eventually be feasible alternatives to nuclear power and fossil fuels, but said that at the present stage of technological development, the alternatives could not supply the nation's energy needs.

In the give and take of conversation, which is how most of us learn to develop our skills at critical thinking, premisses that are implicit (unstated) are most easily recognized when they are are not shared by all participants in the conversation. The first student in the recorded conversation knew about wind, solar, and hydroelectric power, but she didn't consider them real alternatives to nuclear and fossil fuels. The second student was more optimistic about the development and use of the alternate power sources, and so she was unwilling to accept the unstated premiss of the first student that one has to choose between the dangers of nuclear power and the depletion of fossil fuels and the pollution caused by their use.

The mistake of basing arguments on a premiss (either stated or unstated) that only two choices are available when a wider range of alternatives exist is common enough to be labeled a *fallacy*. This fallacy has several names (black-and-white thinking, false choice, false dilemma, and false dichotomy) and is especially insidious when the premiss that only two alternatives are possible is left unstated.

Unstated premisses that are shared by participants in a conversation can sometimes be recognized by noticing that the unstated premiss is referred to later in the conversation *as if it had been stated*. For example, in another recorded discussion of nuclear power, one student argued for nuclear power by using the stated premiss that it costs less than fossil fuels. Although another student challenged this premiss, the unstated assumption (which they both shared) went unchallenged, namely, that *the least costly alternative should be chosen*. At a later point in the conversation, however, when the second student had pointed out the higher cost of nuclear power when the costs of nuclear waste disposal (currently borne by the U.S. government) were calculated, he remarked that since the first student thought the least costly alternative should be adopted, the first student should not support nuclear power. Although the first student had not actually said that the least costly alternative should be adopted, he accepted the second student's remark as if he *had* said it, indicating that this was, indeed, an unstated premiss in his argument for the use of nuclear power.

The following two arguments depend on unstated generalizations that are somewhat more difficult to detect than the unstated premisses in the preceding examples.

The first argument is taken from *Crime and the Criminal Law,* by Barbara Wootton, one of the first women members of the British Parliament.

> To punish people merely for what they have done would be unjust, for the forbidden act might have been an accident for which the person who did it cannot be held to blame.

The conclusion of Wootton's argument is that punishing people merely for what they have done would be unjust (that is to say, without taking into account their intentions as well as their actions). The reason she offers for this conclusion is that the forbidden act may have been a blameless accident. The unstated premiss, required to connect actions for which persons are not to blame with actions for which they should not be punished, is a generalization: No one should be punished for acts for which they do not deserve to be blamed.

Is this general principle correct? In the British system of law, and in our own, actions committed with an evil intent or a "guilty mind" (*mens rea*) are distinguished from accidental actions. Most of us would agree that people should be *blamed* only for acts they intended to do, or at least were negligent in preventing. But both the American and British legal systems sometimes do punish people for "accidental" acts, even when no blame is warranted.

For example, if you are caught in an elevator between floors in an office building for an hour, and as a result find an expired parking meter (and a ticket) when you return to your car, you are not to blame for overparking. Nevertheless, you will still have to pay the fine because the law treats this as a case of "strict liability," or, in other words, the law recognizes no excuses. Many considerations can be offered to justify strict liability laws. In the case of parking fines, strict liability is justified by appealing to the good use the city makes of the money collected from this source, the minor nuisance of paying a small fine even when the violator is not to blame, and the excessive court costs of allowing defenses for simple parking violations.

If we accept the principle of strict liability for some kinds of action, we cannot accept the general principle that connects punishment with blame in an unqualified way. The apparent conflict between strict liability and the principle that conduct should be punished only if it is blameworthy can be resolved by restricting the application of strict liability to *noncriminal* cases. Wootton's book, *Crime and the Criminal Law,* clearly is concerned with criminal justice, and her remarks can be taken to apply to this context. The principle connecting punishment with blameworthiness is well established in Anglo-American criminal law.

The second example is taken from *A Treatise of Human Nature* by David Hume:

> Since reason alone can never *produce* any action or give rise to volition
> [desire], I infer that the same faculty [reason] is incapable of *preventing*
> volition or of disputing the preference with any passion or emotion.

Hume, writing in the eighteenth century, was concerned with the nonrational aspect of human life—the area of feelings and emotion. One of his famous sayings is "Reason is and ought only to be the slave of the passions." Hume's words are less startling when we realize that "passions" in those days referred in a general way to human feelings, not specifically to sexual passion. Hume believed that human morality must be founded on the sort of goodness that human beings—with all their biological limitations, natural feelings, and sympathies—are able to achieve, rather than on some intellectual view of an ideal form of goodness.

In this argument for "natural morality," Hume's conclusion is "reason is incapable of preventing volition or of disputing the preference with any passion or emotion." The words "I infer that" indicate a conclusion is being drawn. Hume offers as evidence the claim that "reason" (the human intellect) cannot by itself produce or cause our desires and wishes. The hidden premiss in this argument seems to be the claim that a general connection exists between the lack of power to cause something and the lack of power to prevent that same thing:

> Nothing that is powerless to cause an activity or event of a certain sort is powerful enough to prevent that activity or event.

Does this premiss seem obviously true to you? A wall can stop a rolling ball, but it cannot set the ball in motion. Sometimes it seems to me that I can just look the wrong way at machines and *prevent* them from operating properly, but I certainly have no power to cause those same machines to work the way they should. I can prevent my watch from operating by dropping it into dishwater, but I am powerless to build a new watch or to repair a damaged one.

Perhaps we could restate or qualify Hume's missing premiss so that it appears more plausible. If, for example, Hume was referring not to individual human capacities but to what humans in general can do, the example concerning my watch is no longer applicable, because human beings can both produce and destroy watches. Can you think of a case in which humans in general have no power to cause or produce something but do have the power to prevent its operation?

When we are reconstructing arguments, as when we are determining whether an argument is being offered, careful attention to context—written, spoken, or implied—is crucial. If we intend to deal seriously with Hume's or Wootton's arguments, we must consider them in the larger context of these authors' works, and use whatever information we can gather to supply missing premisses. When we are engaged in a discussion with another person who presents an argument, we should ask questions to clarify any unstated premisses. When we are presenting arguments of our own, we should be aware of any hidden premisses that, if stated explicitly, would undermine our conclusions.

When we are reconstructing arguments in situations that provide inadequate contextual information, we should supply the missing premisses that are the most plausible under the circumstances. This means that the missing premisses should have "the ring of truth." They should be premisses that, although they may not actually *be* true, at least are not known to be false or are not wildly unbelievable. The missing premisses should also be sentences we could reasonably expect the proponent of the argument to accept.

Identifying and exposing the missing premisses of arguments is a fussy business, complicated by the need to understand the context in which an argument is presented, the information available to the person who presents the argument, the intentions of that person, the purpose of the argument, and so on. As we learn more about the structure of different types of arguments, our task of finding missing premisses will be aided by a knowledge of some typical forms of argument.

Exercise Set 1.4

Part One. Identify each of the following sentences as a universal generalization or a statistical generalization. In some of the exercises you must depend on common sense or general background knowledge to determine the correct interpretation.

1. Few college baseball players make it to the major leagues.

2. College graduates earn more than those who have never been to college.

3. Fifty-five percent of students on the Dean's List are women.

4. Most hockey players are missing at least one tooth.

5. Soldiers are brave.

6. Zero percent of the ingredients of Brand X breakfast cereal are toxic.

7. Whales are mammals.

8. Politicians are honest.

9. No babies are Olympic swimmers.

10. Few computer programs are free of all bugs.

> Part Two. In each of the following examples, an unstated generalization is required to complete the premises of the argument. Write the argument as stated in standard form. Try to supply a plausible generalization to complete each argument. If no plausible generalization will make the argument succeed, try to explain why.

1. Women office workers work equally as hard as men office workers and are equally productive. Therefore, women office workers should receive the same pay as men in comparable positions.

2. Nuclear power should not be used because its use is unfair to those who live close to nuclear plants.

3. Nuclear power should be used because it is less damaging to the environment than fossil fuels.

4. Marijuana should not be legalized because it has potentially dangerous long-term effects.

5. Marijuana should be legalized because it is no more dangerous than alcohol, which is already legal.

6. Marijuana should be legalized because the laws against it are not respected, and this breeds contempt for law in general.

7. Marijuana should not be legalized because it leads to the use of harder drugs, such as heroin.

8. Tomatoes will be expensive in late winter because growers in Florida were hit by a hard freeze in December.

9. Since they have been rising for a long time now, prices are bound to drop soon.

10. Your tires should hold out for the coast-to-coast drive because they have made it six times before without any trouble.

11. A head will show on the next toss of the coin, for the past six tosses have been heads.

2. Contextual Clues for Reconstructing Arguments

We return to the problem of missing premises in later chapters, after we have had more to say about evaluating different types of arguments. For now, we turn to the question of identifying the premises and conclusions of arguments in contexts that contain additional material.

Sometimes an argument is framed in a context of background information that tells us something about the quality of the evidence, how it was gathered, or why it is relevant to the conclusion. Consider the following passage, taken from *Sexual Politics* by Kate Millett:

> A witty experiment by Philip Goldberg proves what everyone knows, that having internalized the disesteem in which they are held, women despise both themselves and each other. This simple test consisted of asking women undergraduates to respond to the scholarship in an essay signed alternately by one John McKay and one Joan McKay. In making their assessments, the students generally agreed that John was a remarkable thinker, Joan an unimpressive mind. Yet the articles were identical; the reaction was dependent on the sex of the supposed author.

Our first clue that this passage contains an argument is the assertion in the opening sentence that something is being proved. To *prove* something is to produce evidence that shows it is true. The conclusion of the argument (the sentence that is proved) is "having internalized the disesteem in which they are held, women despise both themselves and each other." The evidence for this conclusion is contained in the premise: "the reaction [to the identical essays] was dependent on the sex of the supposed author." Millett's premise is in turn supported by (is a conclusion drawn from) the outcome of Goldberg's experiment:

> Women undergraduates evaluated identical essays, which differed only in the sexually distinctive names of the supposed authors, as being the work of a remarkable thinker when the supposed author was male, and an ordinary thinker when the supposed author was female.

Additional background information provided in Millett's passage assures us that the conclusion was something already widely known and that the experiment was witty. We are also told that the experiment was a simple test. None of this information is evidence to support the truth of the conclusion, but it does tell us something about the *quality* of the evidence presented and helps us to understand the author's point of view.

Here is another argument stated in a context that contains additional information. This example is taken from a newspaper column entitled "How to Spot Rich People" by social commentator Andy Rooney:

> Another way to tell a rich person from a poor person is one I learned years ago when I worked for a morning news broadcast. We often had important people on it as guests and I began to notice one thing that the rich men had in common. They never wore overcoats.

> Nelson Rockefeller must have been on the show five times on different winter days and he never wore an overcoat or carried one. It was a long while before I realized he was so rich he didn't need one. He was never out in the cold because all he did was walk the 10 feet from his chauffeur-driven limousine to the building and anyone can stand that much cold. For all I know Rockefeller didn't even own a raincoat or an umbrella. Most of the restaurants a rich person like him would eat in have canopies extended to the street.

The conclusion of Rooney's argument is "They [rich men] never wear overcoats." His premises state that the sample of rich men he observed never wore overcoats. This evidence is strengthened by his suggestion concerning why rich men don't need overcoats. The rest of the passage contains information about how Rooney gathered his sample and humorous speculation about rich men's ability to dispense with raingear as well as overcoats.

Sometimes the context of an argument provides information that indicates something is true, while the argument itself attempts to establish that the situation is either good or bad. In the following argument, philosopher Bertrand Russell, after telling us that rats behave a certain way toward food, argues that rats are sensible to do so.

> Rats will eat food that contains rat poison. But if, before eating, they were to subject their food to scientific analysis, they would die of hunger meanwhile, and so they are well advised to take the risk.

Examples that illustrate a point often occur in the context of arguments. Such *illustrations* serve as neither premises nor the conclusion, but as clarifications of points that aid understanding by making general ideas concrete. Patrick Lord Devlin does this in the following passage from *The Enforcement of Morals:*

> No society can do without intolerance, indignation, and disgust; they are the forces behind the moral law, and indeed it can be argued that if they or something like them are not present, the feelings of society cannot be weighty enough to deprive the individual of freedom of choice. I suppose that there is hardly anyone nowadays who would not be disgusted by the thought of cruelty to animals.

Devlin supports his conclusion, which is stated at the beginning of the argument before the semicolon, with the premises that follow it in the complex sentence. (His argument also depends on a generalization that Devlin does not state here, but tries to establish elsewhere in his book: No society can live without morals.) Devlin's concrete example of disgust is provided in the last sentence of the quoted passage.

In addition to background information and examples that serve to illustrate and clarify points, arguments often contain remarks that are intended to put the reader or listener in a *properly receptive frame of mind* to accept their conclusions. Such additional material might convey an atmosphere of humor, fear, seriousness, or any number of other moods. Millett does this, in the argument quoted earlier, when she tells us that Goldberg's experiment proves "what everyone knows." Such a remark may intimidate a reader who feels inclined to disagree with Millett, because it suggests that anyone who does not agree with her conclusion is disputing common wisdom. This sort of claim can distract the reader from a critical examination of the argument.

When we examine the support that the evidence provides for a conclusion, we should separate carefully any additional material from the actual evidence. The extra material may appeal to our emotions and discourage us from taking a close critical look at the central issue: Does the alleged evidence support the conclusion?

Sometimes arguments repeat, in slightly different words, points that already have been made in a premiss or in the conclusion of the argument. When a conclusion is stated at the beginning of a passage, and is followed by reasons for accepting that conclusion, the conclusion may be restated for emphasis at the end of the argument. Restating points when arguments are long and complicated can clarify a presentation by keeping track of where the argument has been and where it is leading. Repetition can help ensure that the reader or listener does not fail to get the point.

Less savory motives, however, also inspire repetition. As advertisers have taught us, repeated exposure to an assertion can convince people that it is true, even when only flimsy evidence—or no evidence at all—has been offered. Thus an advertising campaign for Brand X soap might call for billboard signs, newspaper and magazine ads, television and radio spots, all flooding the market with the message "Brand X is the best soap."

A different use of repetition is found where the conclusion of an argument is repeated, but modified slightly to make it stronger or weaker.

Consider the following passage, taken from *The Odd Woman,* a novel by George Gissing, and try to decide what use is served by repeating the conclusion at the end of the argument after stating it initially:

> It is the duty of every man, who has sufficient means, to maintain a wife. The life of an unmarried woman is a wretched one; every man who is able ought to save one of them from that fate.

Exercise Set 1.5

Note: These exercises are demanding. Teachers may wish to defer assigning them until later in the term when various types of arguments, including categorical syllogisms, have been analyzed.

Each of the following passages contains at least one argument. Rewrite each argument in standard form. Discuss the role of any additional material in the passages.

1. Dear Readers: Here is the second part of Dr. George Ryan's testimony at a Senate Judiciary Subcommittee hearing on the human-life bill. [The bill, which was not passed, would have made abortion, the birth control pill, and the intrauterine contraceptive device illegal.]

Question: What economic effect would this bill have on those women?

Answer: Paradoxical. The president has promised to get government off our backs. This bill would not only LEAVE government on our backs, it would put government in our bedrooms. If this bill is passed and abortions are made illegal, it means at least another 700,000 babies will be born next year. A substantial percentage will be born to the poor and the very young—about two-thirds of whom will collect welfare.

Instead of a single cost of $125 for an abortion, we will pay $1,000 to $1,500 for a delivery, and at least $100,000 to support these welfare children until they reach maturity. This is a commitment of about 40 billion dollars each year.

Question: How did you come up with those figures?

Answer: Simple mathematics. I took the 1.4 million abortions [now being performed] a year—let's be conservative and say only half those women actually have babies. The other half would probably get illegal abortions or go out of the country to get one. But the remaining half are stuck—and probably poor. If two-thirds are on welfare, we are talking about 400,000 babies a year.

—Ann Landers' column

2. In the past there has been much argument whether, in the strategy of inflation control, one should seek to come to grips with the level of demand or whether one should seek to deal with the wage-price spiral. . . . The proper answer is that both are important. Inflation could be controlled by a sufficiently heavy reduction in the level of demand. It could also be controlled with a less drastic reduction if something could be done to arrest the interreactions of wages and prices, or, to speak more precisely, of wages, profits, and prices.

—John Kenneth Galbraith, *The Affluent Society*

3. Discrimination—refusing to admit someone to a public place or business on grounds of race, sex, or religion—is against federal law. However, the law also respects the rights of people to associate privately with whomever they wish.

Last year [the national organization of Jaycees] voted to kick out the women members they had previously recruited. They even voted to kick out the chapters who wouldn't kick out the women they had previously invited. (Who says that chauvinists are chivalrous?)

But in Minnesota, the courts ruled that the Jaycees were actually operating as a public business. They were soliciting memberships, and open to anyone so long as that anyone was a male. So, this duly designated public business was forbidden to discriminate.

—Ellen Goodman's column

4. "I could tell you things about Renaissance Popes that would make your hair stand on end," [said Leonie].

"I'm beginning to think there's something to be said for being a Protestant after all," said Clare.

"Oh, no, Clare," Nanda assured her, horrified at seeing the prospective convert wavering. "Don't you see it's just another proof that the Church really is divine and inspired: Any other institution would have been done for centuries ago with so much corruption in individual members. There really is something that keeps it going in spite of all that, and the gates of hell don't prevail in spite of all the horrors."

—A. White, *Frost in May*

5. "Most people wear some sign and don't know what it's saying. Choose your sign according to your audience," Malloy said. "A good dark suit, white shirt and conservative tie are a young man's best wardrobe friends, if he's applying for a white collar job in a big range of business and professional categories. They're authority symbols. It's that simple," he said.

—"Fashion," *Chicago Daily News*

6. An apparently progressive [evolutionary] advance may turn out ultimately to be a limitation. For instance, the insects successfully conquered the land by developing a method for breathing with the aid of fine air-tubes penetrating every tissue of the body. This constitutes an admirable mechanism so long as the creature remains small, but makes large size impossible. An insect as big as a rat just won't work properly; actually no insect is bigger than a mouse. This limitation of total size naturally sets a limit to the size of the brain, and so to the number of cells in the brain, which in turn sets a low limit to the degree of intelligence and the flexibility of behavior. That is why insects are never very intelligent, but have to depend mainly on the marvelous but always rigid and limited behavior-mechanisms we call instincts. This limitation of insect size is very lucky for us, because without it, man assuredly could never have evolved.

—J. Huxley, *New Bottles for Old Wine*

7. "A woman knows very well that all the talk about elevated subjects is just talk, but that what a man wants is her body and all that presents it in the most deceptive but alluring light; and she acts accordingly. If we only throw aside our familiarity with this indecency, which has become second nature to us, and look at the life of our upper classes as it is, in all its shamelessness—why it is simply a brothel. . . . You don't agree? Allow me, I'll prove it," he said, interrupting me. "You say that the women of our society have other interests in life than prostitutes have, but I say no, and will prove it. If people differ in the aims of their lives, by the inner context of their lives, this difference will necessarily be reflected in externals and their externals will be different. But look at those unfortunate despised women and the highest society ladies: the same costumes, the same fashions, the same perfumes, the same exposure of arms, shoulders, and breasts, the same tight skirts over prominent bustles, the same passion for little stones, for costly glittering objects, the same amusements, dances, music, and singing. As the former employ all means to allure, so do these others."

—L. Tolstoy, "The Kreutzer Sonata"

8. Other physicists, notably Arthur Holly Compton at the University of Chicago, contended that the cosmic rays were particles. There was a way to investigate the question. If they were charged particles, they should be deflected by the earth's magnetic field as they approached the earth from outer space. Compton studied the measurements of cosmic radiation at various latitudes and found that it did indeed curve with

the magnetic field; it was weakest near the magnetic equator and strongest near the poles, where the magnetic lines of force dipped down to the earth.

—I. Asimov, *The Intelligent Man's Guide to the Physical Sciences*

9. Theories, such as those of Peter Tompkins in his book *Mysteries of the Mexican Pyramids,* that link the pyramids of Egypt and Mexico also find little support in the available archaeological data. In fact, the last of the great pyramids at Giza on the Nile were built nearly 3,000 years before the great pyramids of the Sun and Moon at Teoti-huacan [Mexico], or the well-known pyramids in the Maya Lowlands. As Kurt Mendelssohn has pointed out, it is difficult to imagine a boatload of ancient Egyptians arriving in Mexico and introducing a monumental activity that had not been practiced in their homeland for millennia. Moreover, as many writers have argued, it is much more likely that a boatload of foreigners with no nearby support and no clear military or technological advantage would be killed before they got far from the beach rather than that they would be able to introduce a new architectural style all over ancient Mexico. In addition, the structures have major functional differences: the Egyptian pyramids come to a point and serve as tombs, while the Mexican ones are truncated and serve as foundations for temples, although they sometimes housed tombs as well.

—J. Sabloff, *The Cities of Ancient Mexico: Reconstructing a Lost World*

10. Inevitably historians are involved in selecting from the available sources the mater-ial they deem significant in the light of the problems under scrutiny. They never have access to all the facts anyway, and even those to which they do have access are selected to suit their own purposes. There is no history on a mortuary table. The 'facts' therefore do not simply 'speak for themselves'; the historian stage-manages their per-formance on the contemporary scene.

Selection, then, is inescapable.

—D. Livingstone, *The Geographical Tradition*

VI. REVIEW

This chapter introduces the subject of logic and critical thinking. In the remaining chapters, more detailed attention is given to various aspects of rea-soning and critical thinking that have been introduced here so that students can gain skill in assessing the thinking of others and improving their own rea-soning abilities. Skills that contribute to critical thinking include:

1. Sensitivity to different uses of language.

2. The ability to recognize when evidence is required to support an assertion.

3. Awareness of the distinction between the truth of sentences and the sup-port they would provide for some other sentence if they were true.

4. The ability to recognize arguments, to identify their parts, to supply missing premises that are unstated, and to sort the premises and conclusion of an argument from the context in which it is stated.

5. The logical skill of evaluating an argument in terms of how well the pre-mises support the conclusion.

All of these critical-thinking skills are useful and important in our everyday lives. Our language reflects what is important in human culture, and, as with other vitally interesting aspects of human life, a special vocabulary has been developed for discussing issues in logic and critical thinking. Because some of this vocabulary may be new to you, reviewing the following definitions of the most important terms will be helpful:

Argument: A set of sentences related in such a way that some of the sentences are presented as evidence for another sentence in the set.

Conclusion: The sentence in an argument that is supported by the evidence.

Declarative Sentence: Declarative sentences—as opposed to questions, commands, requests, and exclamations—assert or declare something: whether it it be that some thing exists; that some situation exists, perhaps to a specified degree; or some relationship exists, often qualified or quantified in some manner.

Evidence: Evidence is support that is offered for some assertion. It may be physical evidence, as when damaged goods are presented to support the claim that they are defective; or it may be verbal, in which case some sentences are offered to support the truth of another sentence.

Fallacy: A mistake in reasoning, in particular, of supposing evidence has been presented in support of an assertion—or pretending that it has been—when some form of nonevidential persuasion has been used instead.

Fallacy of Black-and-White Thinking: A mistake in reasoning that occurs when only two alternatives are considered available when in fact other alternatives are possible. For example, "It cannot be white; therefore it must be black" ignores the whole range of shades of gray. The fallacy is also called false choice, false dilemma, and false dichotomy.

Indicator Words: Words commonly used to signal premisses or conclusions of arguments. Examples of premiss indicator words are: *for, since, because,* and *for the reason that.* Examples of conclusion indicator words are: *hence, thus, therefore, and so, it follows that,* and *for that reason.*

Logic: The study devoted to analyzing and evaluating arguments and to developing general principles for these tasks.

Premiss: A sentence that is offered as evidence in an argument.

Statistical Generalization: A sentence that states that some proportion of the members of one class are members of another class. Common forms of these sentences are: *Most . . . are . . .* and *Most . . . are not . . . .* Statistical generalizations may also be expressed numerically, as in *x* percent of . . . are . . .

Universal Generalization: A sentence that states that all—or none—of the members of one class are members of another class. Common forms of these sentences are: *All . . . are . . .* and *No . . . are . . . ,* where the blanks are filled in by terms that denote classes of individuals.

The preceding terms in boldface are the most important terms introduced in Chapter 1 and are used throughout this text. Two other terms that are a part of the standard vocabulary of logic and critical thinking are so often misused that they should be mentioned here.

Infer: To infer is to conclude from something known or assumed. This is a mental activity that may be—but need not be—expressed in language.

For example, on the basis of the dark circles under my eyes, you may infer that I didn't get enough sleep last night, but you may be too considerate to mention that to me or to anyone else. However, if you argue that I didn't get enough sleep, you state the evidence (cite the dark circles) and the conclusion. Arguing, unlike inferring, is an activity that requires the use of language. When you state your reasons for drawing an inference—when you express in language the premisses and the conclusion—you transform the inference into an argument.

Imply: To imply is to provide a basis from which an inference may be drawn. Words, actions, looks, appearances may all "have implications"—that is, they may provide a basis for someone to infer something from them. It is also appropriate to speak of a person's implying something, through words, silence, looks, or some other feature, as in "Her smile implies approval." "Imply" also has another special meaning, in the context of deductive logic, which is explained later. Infer is sometimes confused with imply, as in "Your scowls infer that you disapprove of Mary Ann." As Fowler, in his *Dictionary of Modern English Usage,* says of imply and infer: "Each word has its own job to do, one at the giving end and one at the receiving."

The best way to review this type of subject matter is to work more exercises. If you can complete the exercises in the following section successfully, you will know that you have mastered the material covered in Chapter 1. Some of these exercises are difficult, so do not be discouraged if they require a lot of effort. Moreover, because these arguments are stated in ordinary language—which is not always as precise as we would like—and because the selected passages are all taken out of broader contexts, different interpretations of a given passage are possible. In a given case, for example, it may not be entirely clear whether the author is providing an argument or a causal explanation or whether the author is providing just one argument or several. If a premiss seems to be missing, the most plausible missing premiss to supply may not be clearly identifiable. Whenever you think that more than one interpretation is plausible, mention this and give your reasons for each interpretation. If the skills of logic and critical thinking you are developing in this course are to be useful to you in the ordinary situations you encounter in everyday life, you must practice with examples taken from such contexts.

Exercise Set 1.6

For each of the following passages:

1. Indicate whether the passage contains an argument (or several arguments).

2. Write the argument in standard form.

3. If the argument depends on a missing generalization as an implicit premiss, supply the generalization.

4. Discuss any cases in which nonevidence, such as a threat, might be mistaken for evidential support.

5. Indicate what role any additional material that is not part of the premisses or the conclusion plays in the passage.

1. At best, though, there is very little chance of a longtime future in smokejumping. To start with, you are through jumping at forty, and for those who think of lasting that long there are only a few openings ahead, administrative or maintenance.

—N. Maclean, *Young Men and Fire*

2. Throughout recorded history, most women have had little choice about becoming mothers. Married young, with no effective means of contraception or abortion, they had babies whether they wished to or not.

—Mary Anne Warren, "Is IVF Research a Threat to Women's Autonomy?"

3. Scientifically, it [Captain James Cook's first voyage to the South Pacific] was a hugely successful venture. The transit of Venus was accurately observed and recorded, kangaroos were discovered, ethnographic studies of indigenous peoples carried out, the New Zealand coastline was charted, and a vast amount of material collected and shipped back to the Royal Society—thousands of plants, five hundred fish preserved in alcohol, five hundred bird skins and hundreds of mineral specimens.

—D. Livingstone, *The Geographical Tradition*

4. "Your conversation looks more interesting than the others . . . Can I join you? . . . Or is this a private argument?"

"Not private, not even an argument, but trying to be . . . Would you say our train robbers were professionals or amateurs?"

"Never entered my head to doubt it—professionals. They've been very thorough. Amateurs never are."

—A. Cornelisen, *Any Four Women Could Rob the Bank of Italy*

5. Poetry, indeed, cannot be translated, and therefore it is the poets who preserve languages; for we would not be at the trouble to learn a language when we can have all that is written in it just as well in translation. But, as we cannot have the beauties of poetry but in its original language, we learn it.

—S. Johnson

6. Adam was led to sin by Eve and not Eve by Adam. Therefore it is just and right that woman accept as lord and master him whom she led to sin.

—St Ambrose

7. Men were thinking, writing, and creating, because women were pouring their energy into those men; women are not creating culture because they are preoccupied with love.

—S. Firestone, *The Dialectic of Sex*

8. [Pennsylvania] could lose about $91 million in federal highway construction aid because lawmakers have blocked the start of an emission-inspection program for autos in Pittsburgh and Philadelphia.

Senator Eugene Scanlon, D-Allegheny, a leading emission-program critic, said . . . he thought "the $91 million was worth it as a matter of principle."

He and his colleagues have maintained the federal government has no right to force a State Legislature to spend money for anything.

—Pittsburgh Post-Gazette

9. Pennsylvania may still have an out, if proposed clean-air-law revisions are enacted. [However, the Environmental Protection Agency] "feels the Clean Air Act as now written must be enforced because it is the rule of the land," Wassersug [EPA regional director] said.

—Pittsburgh Post-Gazette; same story as in #8

10. Hair analysis has been found to be a good test in screening large groups of people for exposure to toxic trace metals. It is not as widely used as blood analysis, but studies have shown that concentrations of lead, cadmium, arsenic, and mercury in hair provide a good record of exposure.

Also, since the metal grows out with the hair, lengthwise sections of hair can show the approximate time when a short, intense exposure occurred. Chromium is essential for the hormone insulin to work properly. Thus, in time, it may be that measurements of chromium in hair will be useful in identifying people with diabetes and in monitoring the course of the disease.

—Dr. J. Mayer and J. Goldberg, R.D., "Food for Thought"

11. My suggestion for a wine to accompany chocolate desserts is different [from wines made from the muscat grape]. I prefer a rich, slightly sweet red wine. Indeed, it was a chocolate dessert that led me to change my mind about late-harvest zinfandels.

The proper use for those alcoholic, full-fruited wines with considerable residual sugar is with chocolate. The very strength of the wine cuts through the rich heaviness of the chocolate.

—P. Machamer, Pittsburgh Post-Gazette

12. Dear Ann: I am boiling over with the statement that the Air Force spends $12.6 million per year for private pet service by veterinarians.

What nonsense!

Having put in 23 years in the armed forces, I happen to know that every base with a mess hall, in all branches of the Department of Defense, requires that all meat be inspected by veterinarians at the supply points. The meat is then distributed to the various units of the military. This is where the taxpayers' dollars go, and I'm sure you will agree it is a legitimate expenditure.

All services performed on privately owned animals must be paid for by the owners.

—Ann Landers' column

13. The thought tends to wrap itself in a joke because in this way it recommends itself to our attention and can seem more significant and more valuable, but above all because this wrapping bribes our powers of criticism and confuses them. We are inclined to give the thought the benefit of what has pleased us in the form of the joke; and we are no longer inclined to find anything wrong that has given us enjoyment and so spoil the source of the pleasure.

—S. Freud, Jokes and Their Relation to the Unconscious

14. It is incontestable that sense perception plays a crucial role in the natural sciences. It serves as the sole means through which we can gather information about the world around us. Knowledge of general laws is posterior, in the empirical sciences, to knowledge of particular instances, and for the latter the evidence of the sense is required.

> —R. Swartz, *Perceiving, Sensing and Knowing*

15. If a person is known to lie occasionally, it is not reasonable to accept something simply on the ground that he testifies to it. Similarly, once the senses have been discovered to be capable of deception, it is not reasonable to regard a belief as solid or permanent merely because it is based on sensory evidence. For it may turn out that the occasion on which the senses provided the evidence for the belief was one on which the senses were deceptive; and then, of course, the belief would have to be abandoned. Despite this, however, it may still be reasonable to regard some sensory beliefs as permanent and indubitable, if occasions on which the senses are absolutely reliable can be distinguished from those on which they are likely to deceive.

> —H. Frankfurt, *Demons, Dreamers, and Madmen*

16. Noting the diversity of Paraguayan languages, Dobrizhoffer comments: "Truly admirable is their varied structure, of which no rational person can suppose these stupid savages to have been the architects and inventors. Led by this consideration I have often affirmed that the variety and artful construction of languages should be reckoned among the other arguments to prove the existence of an eternal and omniscient God."

> —M. Harris, *The Rise of Anthropological Theory*

17. If great art is a product of a great soul only a critic of spiritual stature can hope to recognize and appreciate artistic greatness when he sees it. To the trivial all things are trivial. A critic with limited powers of observation, a weak imagination, and a restricted scale of values must remain blind to artistic greatness and incapable of distinguishing artistic profundity from artistic triviality.

> —T. M. Greene, *The Arts and the Art of Criticism*

18. Rules and regulations of the Securities and Exchange Commission compel the prospectus to dwell on all the problems and all the shortcomings the company faces in its competitive battle for survival and success. This is true, and since this is undoubtedly the first and last public occasion on which a company will stress the negative aspects of its situation, and since this is the point of entry for many new stockholders, the value (for investors) of reading the prospectus is enormous.

> —J. Diamond, *The Fine Art of Making Money in the Stock Market*

19. Despite abundant literature on the subject, the occurrence of human cannibalism in Old World prehistory remains an open question. We are concerned here with dietary cannibalism—the use of humans by humans as food—evidence for which is found in patterns of bone modification and discard. The key features of dietary cannibalism involve close, detailed similarities in the treatment of animal and human remains. If it is accepted that the animal remains in question were processed as food items, then it can be suggested by analogy that the human remains, subjected to identical processing were also eaten.

> —P. Villa et al., "Cannibalism in the Neolithic" *Science* 233

20. Encouragement of contempt for laws is more dangerous to society than occasional use of marijuana. Severe laws against marijuana do not discourage use of marijuana, but rather breed this contempt not only for drug laws, but for laws in general. Therefore severe laws against marijuana are more dangerous to society than the activity which they are designed to prevent.

> —A. Blakeslee, "Should Marijuana Be Legalized?" Associated Press

21. At this moment the King, who had been for some time busily writing in his note-book, called out "Silence!" and read out from his book, "Rule forty-two. All persons over one mile high to leave the courtroom."

". . . that's not a regular rule; you inserted it just now."

"It's the oldest rule in the book," said the King.

"Then it ought to be number one," said Alice.

> —L. Carroll, *Alice in Wonderland*

[Here, what is Alice's argument?]

22. In this passage referring to the island of Corsica, note the rhetorical questions:

> What can be found so bare, what so rugged all around as this rock? What more barren of provisions? What more rude as to its inhabitants? What in the very situation of the place more horrible? What in climate more intemperate? Yet there are more foreigners than natives here. So far then, is a change of place from being disagreeable, that even this place hath brought some people away from their country.
>
> —Seneca, *Ad Helviam de Consolatione,* quoted in J. Boswell, *Boswell on the Grand Tour*

23. Referring to a debate about whether humans have free will:

> We were eating cold fruit-soup. The soup was served in a huge tureen. It was a beautiful piece of china, and Maria was particularly fond of it. She hated things being broken, even a Woolworth tumbler. The veranda was surrounded by large polished panels of glass. I got up, by now trembling with anger, and lifted the tureen up from the table. I said:
>
> "Look, Maria, let us settle this problem in an empirical way, once and for all. If you continue to assert that I have a Free Will, you will thereby enrage me to the point when I cannot help smashing this tureen against the windowpane, for my actions are determined by your words. If you recognize that there is no such thing as a Free Will, the tureen will automatically be safe. But what is a tureen compared to the problem we are trying to settle?"
>
> "It is *my* tureen," Maria said, watching my hands with anguish.
>
> "I give you ten seconds to decide." I started counting—one-two-three, in a cold rage . . . At the count of nine, Maria said:

"All right, you win, put it down."

"You admit that I have no Free Will?" I asked, to make quite sure.

"*You* certainly haven't."

—A. Koestler, *The Invisible Writing*

24. [B]ecause the . . . rules are designed to benefit all and because the punishments prescribed for their violation are publicized and the defenses respected, there is some plausibility in the exaggerated claim that in choosing to do an act violative of the rules an individual has chosen to be punished.

—H. Morris, "Persons and Punishment"

25. And although it is utterly true that God's existence is to be believed in because it is taught in the Holy Scriptures and, on the other hand, that the Holy Scriptures are to be believed because they have God as their source (because, since faith is a gift from God, the very same one who gives the grace that is necessary for believing the rest can also give us the grace to believe that he exists); nonetheless, this cannot be proposed to unbelievers because they would judge it to be a circle.

—R. Descartes, "Letter to the Dean and Doctors of the Faculty of Sacred
Theology of Paris"

Chapter Two

PAYING SPECIAL ATTENTION TO THE LANGUAGE OF ARGUMENTS

I. INTRODUCTION

Understanding arguments requires paying special attention to the language in which the arguments are cast. Before we can decide whether a conclusion of an argument is supported by its premisses, we must understand the meanings of the premiss sentences and the conclusion.

The problem of linguistic meaning has received lavish attention from scholars of language and literature, from linguists to poets, from historians to philosophers. A sense of marvel at the power and effectiveness of language as an instrument of communication goes hand in hand with attempts to understand how languages originated and developed and how meanings are captured, transmitted, preserved, and lost in language. Experts disagree about even such basic matters as which elements of language are the primary bearers of meaning—words, phrases, sentences, or longer texts. This chapter considers only a small sample of problems concerning this vast subject matter of meaning. The selection of problems treated here is motivated by considering those that are most likely to arise in understanding and evaluating arguments.

II. AMBIGUITY

Because, considering its vast expressive power, language is a relatively compact instrument, ambiguity—the quality of having two or more meanings—is a necessary feature of its components. Ambiguity can occur at any meaningful level of language: words, phrases, sentences, paragraphs, and longer works, such as poems and plays. In literature, particularly poetry and drama, ambiguity allows for the richness of multiple interpretations and readings.

Consider, for example, Shakespeare's popular *Twelfth Night,* which is performed frequently and has been adapted to other media, such as musical comedy. Ambiguities begin once the principal characters, the twins Viola and Sebastian, are separated during a shipwreck. Viola, disguised as a male, enters the local duke's service, falls in love with him, but is set to the task of wooing the fair Olivia for the duke. Olivia is not interested in the duke, but is attracted to Viola, whom she takes to be a young man. The language that the two women use with one another is loaded with amusing ambiguities reflective of their situation. In the end, Viola weds the duke, and Olivia ends up with Sebastian, a more suitable suitor than his sister. Less fortunate is Olivia's steward Malvolio, who can be interpreted as either a self-deceiving fool or a tragic character. He is tricked by the ambiguous language in a forged letter to think Olivia is in love with him, and he is persuaded to wear strange clothes and engage in odd behavior as encouraged by the letter. Olivia, unaware of the letter, thinking he is ill with madness, asks "Wilt thou go to bed, Malvolio?"

Malvolio interprets that as a lover's invitation, and so it goes until he finds himself in prison. Because of the subtlety and rich texture of Shakespeare's language, the play as a whole, the speeches and all of the characters in it can be given various readings, allowing for continued enjoyment of the work of art.

Despite the enormous value of ambiguity for works of art, the same feature of language can be detrimental to communicating information. We do not appreciate ambiguity in directions for finding places, cooking food, or operating machinery. Yet we understand when we ourselves try to give directions that avoiding—or even recognizing— ambiguity is sometimes difficult.

This task of understanding the language of arguments can be complicated by the ambiguity of many English expressions. An expression is **ambiguous** if it has more than one distinct meaning. In English, the word *pen* is ambiguous; it can be used to refer to an instrument for writing, an enclosure for animals, or, as slang, to a penitentiary. Frequently, the sentence in which a word occurs clarifies its meaning. Sometimes, a broader context—several sentences, or an account of the circumstances in which the sentence is uttered or written—is needed to resolve an ambiguity. For example, in the sentence "Mark's pen won't write," the meaning of *pen* is clear. However, to understand the sentence "Mark couldn't get out of the pen" we may require more information to know whether Mark was trapped in an animal pen or in a penitentiary.

When we try to understand an argument, we should notice whether expressions are used in the same sense each time they occur. If an ambiguous expression is used in more than one way in the context of a single argument, the ability of the premisses to support the conclusion may be compromised. Consider the following argument, which for convenience is written in standard form:

Mad men should not be permitted to make important decisions concerning the lives of others.
My father is mad.

My father should not be permitted to make important decisions concerning the lives of others.

Suppose that this argument is offered in the following context: My father, whose mental competence is not in question, is mad at (angry with) me because I took a curve at a reckless speed and rolled his car. He has refused to let me drive his car in the future.

The first premiss is plausible only if the term *mad* is understood in the sense of *not mentally competent.* But if the second premiss is to be taken as true, the meaning of *mad* must be different. In the second premiss, *mad* means the same as *angry.* In this argument, the term *mad* is supposed to be the crucial link between the two premisses (its technical name is "the middle term"—see Chapter 10), but it cannot perform as a link because it refers to one property in the first premiss and to a different property in the second premiss.

When the persuasive force of an argument depends on shifts of meaning in ambiguous terms—called **equivocations**—the argument is said to commit the **fallacy of equivocation.** In the preceding example, the equivocation involves the single ambiguous word, *mad.* In other cases, the equivocation may result from the ambiguity of a whole sentence or larger unit of language. Consider the following extract from the *Journal* of John Wesley, the founder of the Methodist religion.

> 1751. London. I was carried to the Foundery and preached, kneeling (as I could not stand) on part of the Twenty-third Psalm.

Wesley had sprained his ankle and had preached in a kneeling position. His text was the Twenty-third Psalm. However, the sentence could be understood to mean that he knelt on a copy of the Psalm as he preached.

The type of ambiguity in Wesley's sentence is called **amphiboly,** and is the result of ambiguous sentence structure instead of a single ambiguous term. Such ambiguities can occur when commas are omitted or improperly placed or when grammatical rules for the placement of modifiers are ignored. For example, "He has two grown sons and a daughter in the nunnery" is a puzzling sentence for it suggests that the sons as well as the daughter are in the nunnery. The ambiguity is resolved when a comma is placed after *sons.* Another example is "The guards and prisoners who refused to join in the prison break were tied and left behind," which sounds as if some of the guards refused to break out of prison! Commas surrounding the phrase "and prisoners who refused to join in the prison break" would help to clarify the meaning of the sentence. Another ambiguous sentence is "They have brown and green eyes." This could mean that the persons referred to have multicolored eyes, but it is probably an attempt to express "Some of them have brown eyes and some have green eyes."

Other ambiguities arise through the use of adjectives and adverbs that are **relative terms.** The words *small* and *large* are examples of such terms. Although the terms themselves do not have more than one meaning, the context in which they occur determines how they are understood. A large mouse is not a large animal. A small skyscraper is probably not a small building.

Ambiguity can also result from shifting the **accent** or emphasis on certain words when a passage is read or spoken. Boswell, in his *Journal,* criticized a fellow lawyer for inferring that it was all right to lie *for* his client on the grounds that the Ninth Commandment, which is usually interpreted as a prohibition of lying, actually says "Thou shalt not bear false witness *against* thy neighbor."

No recipes exist for detecting and avoiding fallacies of equivocation; but awareness that many words have more than one meaning, that grammatical constructions can be misleading, and that shifts in emphasis can change the meaning of a passage provides some defense against the most serious mistakes. In some situations, asking for—or providing—a definition of an ambiguous term may be necessary to prevent misunderstanding. (Techniques for definition are discussed later in this chapter.)

When our primary purpose is to present or to evaluate evidence, we should resolve ambiguities to make all claims as explicit and precise as the context demands. Avoiding ambiguity is important in other situations, too, such as when giving instructions for operating a computer or receiving directions for taking medication. In general, we want to reduce ambiguity in the transfer of information.

Nevertheless, conveying information is not the only purpose of language. In other areas of language use, ambiguities play an important and valuable role.

We have already looked at some ambiguities in one of Shakespeare's plays. In the expressive language of poetry, the skillful use of ambiguous words and expressions to evoke a number of different images and to convey several meanings is highly valued. Puns and other forms of humor also depend on ambiguity. Our language would be greatly impoverished without such ambiguities.

Exercise Set 2.1

Discuss the ambiguities on which the following arguments depend.

1. Mary is a person who is a good dancer. Therefore, Mary is a good person.

2. Jumbo is a small elephant. Therefore, Jumbo is a small animal.

3. All women are not feminists. Betty Friedan is a woman. Therefore, she is not a feminist.

4. Camels are the ships of the desert. Ships, in order to move, must be propelled by motors, sails, or oars. Therefore, camels must be propelled by motors, sails, or oars.

5. In antiquity, the oracle at Delphi was consulted for advice about important undertakings. Croesus the Rich, king of Lydia, asked the oracle if he would succeed in a war against Persia.

> The only answer the Greek holy of holies gave him was that by going to war he would destroy a great empire. It happened to be his own, but, as the priestess pointed out, she was not responsible for his lack of wit.
>
> —Edith Hamilton, *The Greek Way*

(Discuss the ambiguity on which Croesus's inference depended.)

6. An ambiguity in the term *normal,* which can mean both "average or usual" or "healthy, correct, without fault," is sometimes the basis for fallacies of equivocation. Consider the following argument for the safety of nuclear power, and decide whether it depends on this ambiguity.

> All of us are exposed to a certain amount of background radiation from natural causes. Such background radiation forms part of normal atmospheric conditions which humans have lived with for ages. Thus, since nuclear power plants are responsible for increasing atmospheric radiation only by a factor of two, this is within the range of the normal and should not be condemned.

7. How does ambiguity figure in the following conversation?

Algernon: I don't think there is much likelihood, Jack, of you and Miss Fairfax being united.

Jack: Well, that is no business of yours.

Algernon: If it was my business, I wouldn't talk about it. It is very vulgar to talk about one's business. Only people like stock-brokers do that, and then merely at dinner parties.

—Oscar Wilde, *The Importance of Being Earnest*

III. VAGUENESS

An expression is **vague** if borderline cases for its application occur. For example, while the term *middle-aged* definitely applies to someone who is fifty years old, whether the expression is applicable to someone who is forty is less clear—most thirty-nine-year-olds would say "no." Vagueness differs from ambiguity in that an ambiguous term has at least two distinct, *nonoverlapping* meanings. Many English words, such as *kid,* are both ambiguous and vague. *Kid* is ambiguous because it can refer to a young goat or a young child. In the first sense, *kid* is not vague, for goats are no longer kids when they reach their first birthday. However, no clear cutoff point determines when a person is no longer a kid. In this section, we ignore possible ambiguities of the terms discussed so that we can concentrate on vagueness.

A standard example of a term that is vague in the sense that it has borderline cases of application is *bald*. A person with no hair at all is bald; a person with a full head of hair is not bald. But in some cases it is unclear whether the term "bald" is applicable. Other examples of terms that are vague in this sense are *old, happy, rich,* and *thin.* Many color terms (e.g., *mauve*) are also vague.

Vagueness also arises when several criteria exist for application of a term, with no specification of how many of the criteria have to be fulfilled, or to what degree. Consider the expression "Terry is a good friend." What are the criteria for being a good friend? Can a good friend let you down sometimes? How often or in what ways can someone do this and still be a friend? Can a good friend take something from you without permission? Some would say yes, but others would not agree, and most would say "It depends . . ."

Vague terms, like ambiguous terms, can cause difficulties in arguments. For example, the argument that concludes a person is not religious on the grounds of that person's failing to attend church regularly is defective because it does not recognize that *religious* is a vague term. A number of distinct criteria for being religious, include—but are not limited to—belief in a supernatural being; membership in an organized religion; adoption of an ethical code or set of altruistic values; performance of acts of devotion or piety; and a sense of reverence toward fellow humans, other living things, or even the entire universe. It is appropriate to call a person "religious" when all, or only some, of these criteria are applicable. Since "religious" is a vague term, it is unclear just how many of these criteria must be met in order to apply the term "religious" to someone. If all of them are applicable to some person, that person is religious. If none of these criteria applies, the person is not religious. Evidence that someone does not attend church appeals to only one of the criteria and is not enough to support the conclusion that the person is not religious.

Vagueness is a pervasive, important, and useful feature of language, and it would be foolish—if not impossible—to try to eliminate all vague terms. Ordinary social conversation would be severely hampered without such comfortable but vague expressions as "See you soon," or "I'll call you sometime," or "How have you been?—Just fine." International diplomacy depends heavily on vague language. Threats can be communicated by using such expressions as "The government has warned that it will take strong measures if its territorial waters are violated" without giving away any secrets or risking loss of face.

In some circumstances, however, vagueness should be reduced. For example, although the vagueness of the term *religion* poses few problems in most ordinary contexts, some historical situations demand a precise definition. For a long time in the United States, conscientious objectors to military service who were members of some religion were treated differently from conscientious objectors who were not. Religious objectors were assigned to alternate non-military service. Nonreligious objectors went to jail.

Leaving aside the question of whether any religious test should be applied to conscientious objectors, when something as serious as a prison sentence is at stake, stating precisely the conditions under which someone will be assigned to prison is very important. What is needed in this particular situation is a definition of *religion* that will reduce its vagueness. In the next section, various techniques for defining terms, as well as several types and purposes of definition, including definitions to reduce vagueness, are discussed.

Exercise Set 2.2

1. Have you ever argued with anyone about whether a tomato is a fruit or a vegetable? What are the criteria that determine whether something is a vegetable or a fruit? Can you think of a situation in which it would be important to clarify these vague terms?

2. Discuss any elements of vagueness (not ambiguity) in each of the following terms:

(1) girl

(2) bachelor

(3) house

(4) tree

(5) student

3. Can you think of any common nouns in English that are not at all vague?

4. What role does vagueness play in the following argument?

Lord Caversham: Good evening, Lady Chiltern! Has my good-for-nothing young son been here?
Mabel Chiltern: (coming up to Lord Caversham): Why do you call Lord Goring good-for-nothing?
Lord Caversham: Because he leads such an idle life.
Mabel Chiltern: How can you say such a thing? Why he rides in the Row at ten o'clock in the morning, goes to the Opera three times a week,

changes his clothes at least five times a day, and dines out every
night of the season. You don't call that leading an idle life, do you?

—Oscar Wilde, *An Ideal Husband*

IV. DEFINITIONS

In this section, we touch briefly on only a small part of this fascinating subject
of how to define words. Here, we are concerned primarily with the meanings
of words insofar as their meanings affect the understanding and evaluation of
arguments. Various ways of defining words (giving their meanings) are available, and are suited for different purposes.

1. Ostensive Definition

Often the best way to define a term is to point to or display the objects to
which the term applies, or to use some other nonverbal method of drawing
attention to the objects being defined. Parents use this technique to introduce
many words to their infants. They point to baby's eyes, nose, and ears, to dogs,
cats, and birds, and to other things in the world, while uttering the words that
refer to those things. This technique is called **ostensive definition** and is fundamentally important because it establishes a link between words and objects
in the world that are referred to by words.

Useful as it is, ostensive definition does not always work. Sometimes attention is directed to the wrong object. A baby may notice the pointing finger
rather than the nose when the word *nose* is uttered. Or the baby may suppose
that the whole face or the whole person is meant by *nose*. A general term,
such as *eye*, can be defined ostensively only by pointing to particular eyes,
thus allowing the possibility that some special feature of the particular eyes,
such as their color, will be mistakenly attached to the general term *eye*.

Definition by ostension is further limited because no objects of the right
type for a definition may be at hand. A New Yorker can offer ostensive definitions of skyscrapers in midtown Manhattan—but not in the New Guinea high-
lands—unless some appropriate pictures are available or can be drawn. Moreover, the technique of ostensive definition is not suitable for abstract objects,
such as numbers, the gross national product, or the average worker. Abstract
objects cannot be pointed to or displayed. Nevertheless, despite these limitations, ostensive definition is useful in many circumstances, and because it provides a crucial connection between language and nonlinguistic aspects of the
world, its importance should not be underrated.

2. Verbal Extensional Definition

Ostensive definition is sometimes called **nonverbal extensional definition.**
The *extension* of a term is the set of individuals, objects, or events to which
the term can be correctly applied. The extension of *boat* is the set of all boats;

the extension of *dog* is the set of all dogs; the extension of *prizefighter* is the set of all prizefighters. In ostensive definition, as we have seen, some member or members of the set to which the term applies are pointed to, pictured, or displayed in some way.

Verbal extensional definitions also select members of the set to which the term applies, but the selection is accomplished verbally by naming members of the set. For example, *prizefighter,* might be defined by naming some prizefighters, such as Muhammad Ali, Joe Louis, and Sonny Liston; *president of the United States* might be defined by naming Washington, Adams, Jefferson, Lincoln, Roosevelt, Bush, and Clinton.

Verbal extensional definitions, like ostensive definitions, have limitations. Common nouns, such as *prizefighter,* refer not only to all present and past prizefighters but also to future prizefighters. In such cases, providing a complete verbal extensional definition that lists all members of the class is impossible. When only a partial listing is given, misunderstanding can occur as a result of focusing on some property shared by all members of the list that is not the same as the term being defined. For example, Ali, Louis, and Liston are not only all prizefighters, each is also a heavyweight, a world champion, an American, and black.

Another limitation of the technique of verbal extensional definition is the difficulty of listing members of sets when the members have no names. Sometimes *subsets* (instead of *members*) of the set that is the extension of a term can be listed, and this may suffice to convey the meaning of the term. For example, we could define *marsupial* extensionally by naming various kinds of marsupials, such as opossums, kangaroos, and wallabies. But it would be very difficult to formulate a verbal extensional definition of *kangaroo*. Individual kangaroos do not ordinarily have names, and various types of kangaroos are not known by terms sufficiently familiar to convey their meaning to someone who does not know already what a kangaroo is.

3. Intensional Definition

The **intension** of a term is the set of *all and only* those properties that a thing must possess for that term to apply to it. For example, a person must possess the property of being a professional boxer for the term *prizefighter* to be correctly applicable. When a term is given an **explicit intensional definition**, a phrase equivalent in meaning to the term is stated, as in "Prizefighter" means "a professional boxer." All intensional definitions are verbal. We can distinguish several types of explicit intensional definitions by recognizing that definitions have various purposes.

i. Definitions that Show How a Word Is Commonly Used

Most dictionary definitions, such as the preceding intensional definition of *prizefighter,* are of this type. They are sometimes called **lexical definitions.** To work properly, a lexical definition should be neither too narrow nor too broad. The definition should state the set of properties possessed by all things to which the term applies, and only to those things. For example:

> "Knife" means "an instrument for cutting"

is too broad; some instruments for cutting, namely scissors, are not knives.

> "Table" means "a piece of furniture consisting of a flat top set horizontally on four legs"

is too narrow; some tables have fewer and some tables have more than four legs.

A definition can be both too broad and too narrow. For example:

> "Cat" means "domestic animal"

is too *broad*, because "domestic animal" applies to livestock, dogs, and various other pets as well. The definition is also too *narrow*, because many wild animals belong to the cat family.

In addition to being neither too broad nor too narrow, lexical definitions should not be circular. A **circular definition** incorporates the term being defined, or some variant of that term, in the definition. For example:

> "Full-time student" means "a person who is enrolled full time in school"

is a circular definition. Such definitions are not helpful in conveying the meaning of a word. Sometimes, circularity is not as apparent as it is in this example, because the circle is large enough to include several definitions. Consider the following set of definitions, taken from a recently published dictionary:

> "Grazing" means "feeding on growing grass."
>
> "Grass" means "any of various green plants that are eaten by grazing animals."

What we learn from these definitions is little more than that grazing animals feed on growing grass and grass is what is eaten by grazing animals. This pair of definitions comes close to being circular.

Exercise Set 2.3

What is wrong with each of the following lexical definitions?

1. "Politically" means "in a politic manner."
2. "Hamster" means "a small animal."
3. "Fork" means "a utensil for eating foods."
4. "Whale" means "an aquatic mammal."
5. "Overture" means "the orchestral opening to a symphony."

ii. Definitions that Introduce a New Word into the Language

Occasionally, as new situations arise, society changes, or our interests shift, new words enter the language. The definitions that introduce these new words are called **stipulative definitions.** For example, the term *astronaut* is a recent introduction to the language. At the time it was introduced, its meaning was stipulated:

> "Astronaut" means "a person trained to make rocket flights to outer space."

Before the middle of this century, no rockets flew to outer space and no persons were trained to make these flights. Thus, the language did not require a special term to refer to such persons. New words can always be introduced into a language when salient features of the world make them applicable. Sometimes the words are taken over from another language, as when the Europeans adopted the Nahuatl word for chocolate, a food that was unknown in Europe before the sixteenth-century Spanish invasion of Mexico. Sometimes new words are made by combining parts of old words (*astro* from the Latin word for star, and *naut* from the Latin word for sailor). Sometimes, especially in connection with a new technology, they are newly minted (*byte*).

The **conventional** nature of language is most apparent in stipulative definitions. Expressions in a language do not acquire their meanings as a result of some natural connection between the words and the things in the world that the words denote. The connection between the word *thunder* and the meteorological phenomenon of thunder is conventional—unlike the natural connection between thunder and lightning. Words have the meanings they do as a result of the widespread acceptance of proposals to use them in a certain way. This is not to say that the first humans who used language stipulated the meanings of all of the original expressions in a manner similar to the stipulation of the meaning of *astronaut*. Such a scenario seems highly unlikely, even though the origins of language remain shrouded in mystery. Nevertheless, given what we do know about the development of languages—the ways in which new words are added and words that are no longer useful are discarded—the conventional nature of language is indisputable. Different human languages use different words to refer to many of the same features of the world (the development of different languages involved the adoption of different conventions), but no language is more correct or "true to the world" than another language.

Although new words can be introduced into language and their meanings can be stipulated by whoever introduces them, stipulative definitions must meet at least the following two requirements if they are to be acceptable:

1. *A term that is stipulatively defined should not already have a widely accepted standard meaning.*

When Humpty Dumpty claims that he is the master of words—words mean what he wants them to mean—Alice protests that he is stipulating new and different meanings for words that already have established senses. Alice is justified in her complaint. Confusion obviously results from Humpty Dumpty's attitude toward words with established usage.

2. *A term that is stipulatively defined should be a useful addition to the language.*

Making up new words and offering stipulative definitions for them may be an amusing pastime, but unless the new words serve some useful purpose, it is unlikely that the proposed definitions will be incorporated into the language. Special interests or studies often require the stipulation of a new vocabulary; space technology, which has prompted the introduction of many new terms besides *astronaut,* is a case in point. The danger looms, however, that mere **jargon**—terminology that is incomprehensible to those outside a special-interest group—may be substituted for ordinary language, even though the special interest requires no new concepts and could be expressed in terms with accepted standard meanings. Stipulative definitions of this type are unfortunate because while they may satisfy the members of the special-interest group, they tend to result in the failure rather than the improvement of communication with those outside the group.

iii. Definitions that Reduce Vagueness

Sometimes, the meaning of a vague term must be clarified and made more precise. Definitions that do this are called **precising definitions.** *Full-time university student* is a vague term. In ordinary usage, it means roughly "a person who devotes a major part of his or her energies to acquiring some type of knowledge or skill through university courses." However, the vagueness of the term poses a problem for universities that assign fees and benefits on the basis of whether students are full time or part time. Universities typically solve this problem by offering a precising definition in their catalogs. One university lists the following definition:

> "Full-time student" means a "student who is carrying a course load of at least twelve units a semester."

Notice that this precising definition is not the same as a stipulative definition. No new term is being introduced, and a term already in use is not given a completely new meaning. In this precising definition, all borderline cases of the vague expression *full-time student* are simply eliminated by making a course load of at least twelve hours per semester the criterion for being a full-time student (at that university). This definition can be used to sort students at the university into two categories: those who are full time and those who are not full time.

Sometimes a word is given a special or technical meaning to be used in a particular context. We can classify this as a form of precising definition. In this text, we use many examples of such definitions. *Argument* and *fallacy* have already been defined in this way. For musicians, *beat* and *tempo* are technical terms; their technical meanings are different from the senses they carry in ordinary contexts. All disciplines employ some technical vocabulary that those who want to understand the field must acquire.

Not all cases of reducing vagueness are as simple as the precising definitions mentioned so far. When a term, such as *religion*, is vague because of a number of different criteria for applying the term, it can be very difficult to specify in a reasonable way exactly which criteria are most important or how many criteria must be met in order to apply the term. Recent debates concerning the definition of the *death of a person,* and the *beginning of life of a person* make us aware of the complexity of the problem. Even when such definitions are proposed in judicial rulings that take into account public debates and studies by experts, they do not go unchallenged, for the definitions have grave and far-reaching social consequences. The definitions that are offered in these cases not only reduce vagueness but also involve a theoretical account of what it means to be a person. In such cases, definitions are appropriately classed as theoretical. **Theoretical definitions** differ from **technical definitions,** for whereas a technical definition specifies the meaning of a term as it is used in some area of study, a technical definition does not necessarily carry any commitment to the truth of some theory.

Exercise Set 2.4

1. Discuss some of the problems that arise in formulating a precising definition of the term *adult.*

2. At most state universities, residents and nonresidents of the state are charged different tuition fees for the same educational programs. Suppose you are a state legislator assigned to a committee to define *resident* for the purpose of charging tuition fees. What considerations would guide your attempt? What definition would you propose?

3. What are some important technical terms in your major field of study (or a major you are thinking of choosing, if you have not yet done so)? Can you give an acceptable definition of one of these?

iv. Definitions for Theoretical Purposes

The term *theory* has several meanings, two of which concern us here. In one sense, *theory* refers to a general approach to, or belief about, some subject matter that is expressed in a set of interrelated statements concerning the nature of the subject. In this sense, we might speak of a theory of justice involving such statements as "Justice requires that all persons be treated similarly under similar circumstances," "Justice requires that individuals in a society be given equal opportunities and access to the good things in that society," "Justice demands that punishments should be tailored to the nature of the offense," and other such claims. Defining "death of a person" to mean "cessation of that person's brain functions" involves a theory in this sense, that is, a set of interrelated claims concerning the special character of human life. This theory is committed to the view that a human body that has totally and irreversibly lost the use of its brain but that may have its circulatory, respiratory, and other systems maintained by machine, is no longer a person. The term *veg-*

etable is sometimes applied as a slang term in such situations to mark the transformation of the body from the time that it was the body of a person, capable of thought and feeling, to its passive state after loss of brain function. One who holds this theory of what it means for a person to die would, for example, probably agree that removing a body that has lost all brain function from life-support machines is not immoral. In addition, the theory supports the view that no harm is done to the *person* if vital organs from that body are removed for transplanting. (Of course, while still conscious the person may direct how his or her body is to be used after death, just as the person directs the use of his or her personal property.)

A second sense of *theory* refers to a set of general but precise claims about the nature of society or the physical world. Such theories often involve appeals to unobservable entities that form the basis for many other statements that can be confirmed or disconfirmed by observing the behavior of relevant features of the world. Theories in the physical sciences often assume this form. Examples from physics are: the general theory of relativity, the theory of atomic physics, and the theory of classical mechanics.

Frequently, physicists take a term from ordinary language and redefine it for some theoretical purpose. For example, in classical mechanics, *work* is defined as "the product of force and distance" and *momentum* is defined as "the product of mass times velocity." In classical mechanics, as in other physical theories, many of the terms are defined explicitly by means of other terms in the theory.

Some terms, such as *force,* however, are not explicitly defined. Although the theory tells us how to calculate force (mass times acceleration), no expression synonymous with *force* is presented in the theory of classical mechanics. The meanings of such terms are given implicitly in the fundamental generalizations (or *laws*) of the theory. Newton's three laws of motion and his law of universal gravitation all say something about how forces behave (the effects of forces on bodies with respect to such other theoretical features as mass, acceleration, momentum, and distance). In a sense, we can say that the theory tells us what force is insofar as it tells us how forces operate under various circumstances.

Theoretical definitions are similar to precising definitions in that both reduce vagueness. However, in addition to reducing vagueness, theoretical definitions connect the term being defined with other terms in the theory. A complete understanding of the theoretical meanings of both explicitly defined terms such as *work* and implicitly defined terms, such as *force,* is gained only through an understanding of the theory.

v. Definitions Designed to Transfer Emotive Force

Definitions designed to transfer emotive force, such as feelings of approval or disapproval, are called **persuasive definitions**. Like other explicit intensional definitions, a persuasive definition should state the properties a thing must possess for the term to apply. However, persuasive definitions also convey an *attitude* toward what is being defined. For example, the definition

"Homosexual" means "one who has an unnatural desire for those of the
same sex"

is designed, through use of the term *unnatural,* to convey a negative or disapproving attitude toward homosexuals. An attitude of approval—although more
subtle than the disapproving attitude in the definition of *homosexual*—is conveyed by the following definition:

"Democracy" means "the acceptance and practice of the principle of
equality of rights, opportunities, and treatment; lack of snobbery."

An attitude of approval is present in this definition because most people place
a positive value on equality of rights and lack of snobbery. Perhaps, the emotive force of this definition of *democracy* can be seen more clearly if we contrast it with the definition

"Democracy" means "rule by majority."

Most people would not regard this definition as persuasive. Its emotive force is
probably neutral. "Rule by majority" does not engender the same degree of
approval as appeals to equality of rights and lack of snobbery do. If, however,
some people associate "rule by majority" with "mob rule," then the definition
of "democracy" that equates it with "rule by majority" may convey negative
emotive force to them.

As often happens, when more than one definition of the same term is
offered, these two definitions of *democracy* differ in their statement of intension as well as in their emotive force. "Rule by majority" and "the acceptance
and practice of the principle of equality of rights, opportunities, and treatment; lack of snobbery" do not refer to the same properties of a democracy.

Whether persuasive definitions are appropriate depends on the context in
which a definition is offered. Nothing is intrinsically wrong with trying to persuade others to share our attitudes. Insofar as as the attitudes themselves are
immoral or inappropriate in some way, however, trying to persuade others to
share them may incur punishment, blame or milder forms of criticism.

Persuasive definitions are often intended to be humorous. For example, *philosophy* has been defined as "a doubt which lives in one like a hookworm,
causing pallor and lack of appetite." In this persuasive definition, as in many
definitions proposed for humorous purposes, the intension of the term—the
properties a thing must have if the term is to apply—is partially or completely
ignored. When the purpose of a definition is entertainment, this can be perfectly acceptable. But if we are seeking the definition of a term for the purpose
of making its standard use known, then a persuasive definition is probably
inappropriate and can be deceptive or misleading.

Familiarity with the technique of persuasive definitions increases our awareness that words that refer to the same objects may differ sharply in emotive force.
It doesn't require much sensitivity to recognize the difference in attitudes carried
or conveyed by the terms *woman* and *babe,* or *black* and *nigger,* or *white* and

honky. Objectionable slang terms that are disrespectful to various ethnic, racial, and religious segments of the population are regrettably all too common.

Other expressions, however, can carry a similar negative emotive force in less obvious ways. Calling an airplane race in which the pilots are women a "Powder-Puff Derby" conveys the attitude that such races are to be taken less seriously than races in which men are the pilots. Calling a woman who writes poetry a *poetess* suggests that she is not quite up to the standards of a poet.

We should be especially sensitive to the emotive force of any expressions used in arguments, for emotively charged terms may lead us to accept or reject conclusions when this is not warranted by the evidence.

Exercise Set 2.5

Discuss the different **emotive force** (if a difference exists) for each of the following pairs of terms. If you ignore emotive force, do both members of each pair have the same intensional meaning (does each member of the pair refer to the same things)?

1. Fragile—weak
2. Public servant—bureaucrat
3. Mexican-American—Chicano
4. Sweat—perspire
5. Chairman—chairperson
6. Cop—police officer
7. Usher—usherette
8. Waiter—waitress
9. House—home
10. Footwear—shoes
11. College—university
12. Psychiatrist—shrink
13. Man—gentleman
14. Woman—lady

4. Syntactic Definitions and Implicit Definitions

Thus far, with the exception of implicit theoretical definitions, we have focused on defining terms by giving their intensions or extensions in an *explicit* manner. For the most part, the terms we have defined in this way have been common nouns and adjectives. Some words, however, such as prepositions, articles, and conjunctions, do *not* have an intension or an extension: they do not refer to things, events, persons, or activities, although they do have meanings and play an essential role in language.

These terms have primarily grammatical or **syntactic** meanings. Examples of such words are *and, or,* and *if . . . then.* Sometimes, these terms are defined explicitly, by presenting synonyms that have the same grammatical function ("and" means "also; in addition to; moreover; as well as"). More often, however, these terms are defined by stating their grammatical functions, and then giving examples (contexts) in which the term occurs. For example, a recent dictionary says that *or* is a *coordinating conjunction* that introduces an alternative, as in "I'll offer him beer or wine."

Or may also be implicitly defined as a word that connects sentences in such a way that the compound sentence that is formed is true whenever either of the sentences it connects is true—and which is false otherwise. Truth-table definitions of the logical connectives (see Chapter 7) are implicit definitions of this type.

Another kind of implicit definition presents an expression (context) equivalent in meaning to an expression in which the term to be defined occurs. For example, *unless* is contextually defined in the following:

> "We'll have a picnic unless it rains" means the same as "If it doesn't rain, then we'll have a picnic."

In this definition, no single expression synonymous with *unless* is explicitly presented. Instead, the defining expression is synonymous with the whole expression in which *unless* occurs, and it does not contain *unless.*

Exercise Set 2.6

1. Give a syntactic definition of *and* and give an example that shows how it is used.

2. Give a syntactic definition of *but* and give an example that shows how it is used.

3. Give an implicit definition of *Neither . . . nor . . .* by providing an expression in which it occurs and another equivalent expression in which it does not occur.

5. Operational Definitions

In addition to ostensive definition, another type of nonverbal definition has been of special importance to scientific studies. The technique of **operational definition** was first proposed by Nobel physicist P. W. Bridgman (*The Logic of Modern Physics,* 1927). Bridgman was aware of the different emotive and referential aspects of meaning. As a scientist, he was concerned about scientific terms meaning different things to different persons as a result of varying associations and contexts of use. He wanted to establish the meanings of scientifically important terms in a way that guaranteed that any scientist who used these terms would employ them in exactly the same way. Bridgman proposed specifying public and repeatable *operations,* such as measurement, to serve as criteria for application of scientifically important terms.

Consider the following example of an operational definition:

> "Each side of my table is three feet long" means that when a standard yard-stick is lined up with a side of my table, the ends of the yardstick coincide with the ends of my table.

The technique of operational definition is not intended to offer verbal definitions of abstract terms, such as *length*. Instead, a public and repeatable physical operation (such as measurement with a standard yardstick) is specified for determining whether a sentence containing specific expressions such as "is three feet long" can be applied correctly to a situation. Nothing is lost, Bridgman believed, by refusing to consider *length* in the abstract, because scientists use the concept of length only in specific contexts of measurement. Once we understand how to use sentences in which expressions such as "three feet long" occur, then we understand what such expressions mean. Because the operation of measuring with a standard yardstick is public and repeatable, this operational definition guarantees that scientists will all use the expression "three feet long" in exactly the same way.

With suitable instruments, many of the terms used by scientists can be defined operationally. For example, "This flame is blue" can be defined operationally as meaning that when subjected to analysis by a spectrometer, the flame registers between 4240 angstrom units and 4912 angstrom units. Operations other than measurement can also be used. For example, "The liquid in this jar is acid" means that when a piece of litmus paper is placed in this liquid, the litmus paper turns (or remains) pink. All that is required is a high degree of agreement among various observers as to the outcome of the operation and that the operation be repeatable.

The technique of operational definition has problematic features. For example, several different types of instruments and operations may be available for measuring a phenomenon such as temperature with no operation for coordinating the various results. In such cases, we cannot, strictly speaking, refer to "the temperature" of a particular object, but only, for example, to "the mercury thermometer reading" or "the alcohol thermometer reading." This introduces some awkwardness into scientific discourse. However, many scientists are willing to pay this price in order to specify the meanings of terms by tying them to observations and measurements.

Additional, more serious problems arise in trying to define operationally some of the more highly theoretical terms used by scientists. *Electron*, for example, unlike *temperature,* does not refer to anything that can be *directly* observed, though electron activity is inferred on the basis of detection devices, such as cloud chambers. Electrons are unobservable entities that are introduced to explain the behavior of what is observed. The existence and behavior of electrons is inferred on the basis of highly sophisticated ideas about the causes of reactions in various physical experiments. Electrons play a fundamental role in high-level physical theories about the nature of matter. Attempts to *reduce* these terms to terms that can be operationally defined have not been successful.

In light of the various difficulties surrounding operational definition, as things stand now, the program offers little hope for providing such definitions for *all* of the important terms used by physical scientists. Nevertheless, this form of definition is regarded as important in standardizing meanings of some words by establishing operational criteria for their application.

Even though operational definitions were first proposed for the physical sciences and have encountered serious difficulties there, many social scientists have become enthusiastic about the possibility of constructing operational definitions for the terms that occur in their own disciplines. Behavioral psychologists, for example, believe that operational definitions are the best way to handle so-called mental terms, such as *intelligence, belief, anxiety,* and *fear.* They have tried to specify publicly observable features of behavior or physiology in order to define particular concrete uses of such terms. Some examples are:

"John Jones is afraid of the dark" means that whenever Jones is in a dark place, he breaks out in a cold sweat and begins to tremble.

"Maria Garcia is very intelligent" means that she scored above 135 on the Stanford-Binet (IQ) test.

Although Bridgman admitted the importance of *symbolic* operations (such as test scores) as well as physical measurements with instruments such as rulers and balances, operationalist attempts to define mental terms are highly controversial and have been dismissed by some as completely inadequate. Two types of objections prevail. One has to do with the obvious difficulty of trying to handle multifaceted concepts such as *intelligence* in a quantitative manner. Measuring someone's intelligence is much less straightforward than measuring that person's height, just as monitoring the movement of electrons is less closely tied to direct observation than measuring a substance's temperature. The tests that have been proposed as measurements of intelligence have been criticized for being tied to specific cultural backgrounds and for measuring only some of the broad group of features that we believe make up intelligence in a human being. Similarly, physiological manifestations of fear, anxiety, and other mental states vary from person to person and culture to culture, making the specification of publicly observable criteria for determining the presence of such states problematic.

The second objection cuts deeper across the program of operational definition. An operational definition of a mental property is intended to equate that property with the outcome of some operation. Many people claim, however, that even if we devised satisfactory tests for measuring intelligence, what we would measure could not be the same thing as the score on the test. The test score, these objectors say, might be a good *indicator* of the degree of intelligence possessed by a person, but it would not be the *same thing* as intelligence. In other words, they hold that the meaning of someone's being in a particular mental state cannot be equated with the outcome of any measurement.

Despite these difficulties, some strong supporters of operational definition claim that a term is scientifically meaningful only if it is susceptible to operational definition. They hold that terms that cannot be defined operationally are of no use to science, or that only insofar as the terms are amenable to operational definition are the things they refer to suitable objects for scientific study.

Others take the more moderate view that although operational definitions play an important role in any science, their usefulness is limited, and trying to define *every* term used in a discipline in this way is inappropriate.

Exercise Set 2.7

1. Try to formulate *operational definitions* for each of the following:

(1) This lemon *tastes sour.*

(2) Joan *weighs 120 pounds.*

(3) Frank *believes that he (Frank) will win a scholarship next year.*

2. Social scientists often use questionnaires to formulate operational definitions. For example, they might be interested in arriving at an operational definition for uses of the term *alcoholic* if they wanted to correlate alcoholism with some other social phenomenon, such as working in a particular profession or being subjected to the stresses of student life. Try to formulate a questionnaire (using about ten questions) that would operationally define whether a person who answers the questionnaire is an alcoholic. Mention any difficulties involved in devising such a questionnaire.

V. REVIEW

If we want to be able to state our beliefs, opinions, and judgments clearly, so that others can understand us, and if we want to be able to assess ordinary-language arguments, we must recognize the many aspects of meaning—*extensional, intensional, grammatical (*also called *syntactical), emotive,* and *operational.* Various types of definitions are designed to capture these aspects of meaning, and it is important to know how to use definitions to achieve the type of clarity that is required in a given context. Definitions can be used to resolve ambiguities and to reduce vagueness, but they have many other uses as well. Most definitions are verbal, but two important types of definition (ostensive, and operational) are nonverbal. These are especially important for providing a link between language and the world. A review of the terminology introduced in this chapter follows.

Ambiguous: An expression is *ambiguous* when it has several distinct, *non-overlapping* meanings. Words with more than one distinct meaning are ambiguous, and ambiguities can also arise in larger units of language as a result of their grammatical structure or of the possible changes in meaning due to changes in emphasis.

Equivocation: The use of an ambiguous expression in more than one of its senses in a single context. When an argument depends on equivocation to establish a conclusion, the **fallacy of equivocation** is committed.

Extension: The set of objects to which a term refers.

Implicit Definition: A form of definition in which terms are defined by showing how they are used in a given situation or situations. Examples include implicit definitions of theoretical terms and definitions that present an expression in which the defined term occurs, along with a synonymous expression in which it does not.

Intension: The set of *all and only* those properties a thing must possess for the term to apply to it.

Intensional Definition: Defining a term by stating the properties a thing must possess for the term to apply to it. All intensional definitions are verbal. Further distinctions can be made among intensional definitions by considering the purposes of definition:

Lexical Definition: To present the accepted standard use of a term.

Stipulative Definition: To introduce a new term into the language.

Precising Definition: To reduce the vagueness of a term.

Persuasive Definition: To express or evoke an attitude, such as approval or disapproval, toward things referred to by the term.

Theoretical Definition: To construct a theory. Theoretical definitions may be *explicit*, in which case terms are defined by giving *synonymous expressions* formulated in the vocabulary of the theory or *implicit*, in which case terms are defined according to their use in the laws or generalizations of the theory.

Operational Definition: Specifies a publicly observable and repeatable operation with a specified outcome that determines whether a sentence containing the expression is correctly applicable to a given situation.

Ostensive Definition (*nonverbal extensional definition*): A nonverbal form of definition in which pointing or some other way of indicating the extension of a term is used to give the meaning of the term.

Syntactic Definition (*grammatical definition*): Terms that have no intension or extension are sometimes defined by indicating their *syntactic* or *grammatical* role in a language. These definitions are often supplemented by presenting a context in which the term occurs. (Example: *A* is an indefinite article, used in such expressions as "A dog ran out in the road.")

Vague: A term is *vague* if there are borderline areas in which it is unclear whether the term applies. *Vagueness* is a useful feature of language, but definitions that reduce vagueness are required in some circumstances.

Verbal Extensional Definition: Defining a term by listing or naming members of its extension.

Exercise Set 2.8

Part One. Classify each of the following definitions as to type:

1. "Communism" means "an economic theory or system of ownership of all property by the community as a whole."

2. "Communism" means "a form of government characterized by rigid state planning and control of the economy, ruthless suppression of all opposing

political parties, suppression of individual liberties under a dictatorship, and expansion by military action and subversion."

3. "Nucleus" means "the central part of an atom, the fundamental parts of which are the proton and the neutron. It carries a positive charge and constitutes all the mass of the atom. It is what remains after the orbital electrons have been stripped away."

4. "The Big Ten" means "Indiana University, Ohio State, Michigan, Michigan State, Northwestern, Illinois, Wisconsin, Purdue, Minnesota, and Iowa.

5. "Monotreme" means "platypuses and echidnas."

6. "Monotreme" means "egg-laying mammal."

7. "Naturalistic" means "glorifying all the meanness of human nature and the sordidness of human existence, emphasizing the disgusting, crude, animal part of human nature."

8. "Overweight" means "exceeds the United States government's standard chart's recommended weight per height by at least 10 percent."

9. In order to save space in the written reports of the curriculum committee, we will let "FLC" mean "first-year logic course."

10. It's just as "I believe in God" often means "I prefer not to think," so does "I love you" often mean "I want to own you."

—John Fowles, *Daniel Martin*

11. "Water freezes *only if* it has a temperature of 32° F or lower" means "*If* water freezes *then* it has a temperature of 32° F or lower."

12. "Living ex-president of the United States of America" means "Gerald Ford, Jimmy Carter, Ronald Reagan, George Bush."

13. "Superfluous" means "unnecessary."

14. "The" is a definite article that is used to refer to a particular person, place, or thing.

15. "Lecturing" means "a boring way of teaching in which the teacher drones on for nearly an hour while the students try to stay awake."

16. "Properly dressed for dining at local restaurants" means "wearing shoes and a shirt."

17. "The best age of a person" means "the age at which the person is old enough to know what's what and not old enough to show it."

18. Some anthropologists define "culture" as "a set of attributes and products of human societies, and therewith of mankind, that are extrasomatic and transmissible by mechanisms other than biological heredity."

19. "State university" means "an institution of higher learning that grants advanced degrees and is supported by taxes."

20. "Abortion" means "the deliberate murder of a human fetus."

Part Two. What sort of definition is needed to settle the following question?

Should a travel trailer or camper be assessed as a mobile home?

If the camper and travel trailers are considered to be mobile homes, the property tax must be paid in the same year that they are assessed. If the assessor considers the camper to be a recreational device and actually a part of the owner's personal property, the camper is considered in the same category as a boat or an automobile, and the tax is not paid until the year after it is assessed.

There is widespread inconsistency in assessing campers. Lawrence County is assessing them as mobile homes. Several other southern Indiana counties, including Monroe, are considering them personal property.

It seems to us that this amounts to discrimination, and there should be a uniform rule regarding the assessing of campers. It also seems to us that when a camper is owned by a permanent resident, who lives in a house and parks the camper or travel trailer on the premises, the trailer is truly no more than a recreational device and should be considered as personal property.

—Editorial, *The Indianapolis Star*

Chapter Three

DEDUCTIVE ARGUMENTS, INDUCTIVE ARGUMENTS, FALLACIES

I. INTRODUCTION

The premisses of an argument are put forth as reasons for accepting its conclusion. When confronting an argument, a natural first question is whether its premisses are true, because we are not required to accept a conclusion based on false premisses. To decide whether premisses are true, we need information about the world, often of a specialized sort. For example, if a stock analyst argues that the market will go up because the government is going to reduce interest rates, we want to know whether interest rates really will be reduced. To find out about the interest rates, we may have to investigate the source of the claim. Is the analyst depending on an insider's tip or an official announcement?

The analyst's argument relies also on an unstated premiss about the connection between falling interest rates and a rising market. Students of the market know that this correlation often holds, but they are aware of important exceptions. In some circumstances, lowering rates will not stir a sluggish market.

A reconstruction of the analyst's argument in standard form looks like this :

The government will reduce interest rates.
Very often, when interest rates fall, the market rises.

The market will rise.

Besides asking whether the premisses of an argument are true, we can ask whether the argument is "logical," that is to say, whether the premisses offer any support for the conclusion. One way of expressing this concern is to say that we want to know whether the premisses *if true* would either guarantee or make it probable that the conclusion is true as well. For example, with respect to the preceding argument, suppose you cannot find out whether the analyst is right about rates falling, and, further, that you have not heard of the historical connection between falling rates and a rising market. Even though you do not know whether the premisses are true, you could still say that *if* the analyst has the facts straight (i.e., both premisses are true), and if other relevant information is not being ignored, the market probably will rise.

The logical correctness of an argument depends on meaningful connections between expressions that occur in the argument and on its various structural features. To investigate the logic of arguments we need to know about the contexts in which they occur (discussed in Chapter 1), about the meanings of the terms in the argument (a topic briefly covered in Chapter 2), and about the structure of arguments. Structures can be studied in a general way, without reference to specialized factual knowledge. In the preceding sample argument, for example, an important structural feature is that the claim made in the first premiss is linked with the claim made in the conclusion by a generalization that says that these two types of things (falling rates and rising markets) regularly go together. This structural feature of the above argument is shared by other arguments with different content, and can be discussed without reference to particular facts. We can thus discuss in a general way the structures that various arguments share, as well as how structural features strengthen or weaken arguments.

In this chapter, we focus on a way of organizing arguments to address such structural questions. We classify arguments into three important groups. Our classification is based on whether the premises of an argument, if true, (1) guarantee that the conclusion cannot be false, (2) make it probable that the conclusion is true, or (3) fail to provide support for the conclusion. We can study arguments in this way without knowing whether premises and conclusions of arguments are actually true.

When the premises and conclusion of an argument are related in such a way that the truth of the premises guarantees the truth of the conclusion, the argument is said to be a **valid deductive** argument. The relationship of **deductive support** holds between premises and conclusions of deductive arguments. In these arguments, *if* the premises of the argument are all true, then the conclusion *must* be true.

The type of support provided by the premises for the conclusion of an inductive argument is different. In these, *if* the premises are all true, then *probably* the conclusion is true, but might be false.

Into the third category fall the **fallacies.** In a fallacy, or fallacious argument, the alleged evidence offers only very weak support or is irrelevant to the conclusion. Many fallacies superficially resemble correct deductive or inductive arguments, but violate some standard that is appropriate to deductive or inductive reasoning. For this reason, some are called *deductive fallacies* or *invalid deductive arguments* and others are called *inductive fallacies* or *incorrect inductive* arguments. The premises of fallacious arguments, even if true, neither guarantee nor even make it probable that the conclusion is true. The conclusion of a fallacious argument *might* be true, but the premises of the argument are not good reasons to believe that this is so.

Arguments (either deductive or inductive) that provide the proper kind of support for their conclusions and in addition also have *all true premises* are called **sound arguments.** (Some writers prefer to apply the term *sound* only to deductive arguments, reserving another term such as *good* or *cogent* to refer to an inductive argument with all true premises.)

In this chapter, we examine both deductive and inductive arguments and learn more about the differences between them. Recognizing each type is important because we apply different standards for evaluating inductive and deductive arguments. We also discuss some general characteristics of fallacious arguments, and consider some examples of fallacies.

II. DEDUCTIVE ARGUMENTS

In a valid deductive argument, if all the premises are true, the conclusion cannot be false. This guarantee—that true premises will yield true conclusions—is the outstanding characteristic of deductive arguments, and it is obviously a valuable feature. How is the truth preserved? The conclusion of a deductive argument puts together or restates information that is contained in the premises without adding new information about the world. For example, the conclusion of the argument might depend on the definition of some term or expression in the premisses:

Jack is a bachelor.

He has no wife.

In this argument, the conclusion makes explicit something about the meaning of *bachelor*. Because the truth of the conclusion depends solely on the truth of the premiss and conventional linguistic meanings, we say that the conclusion contains no new information about the world.

The conclusion of a deductive argument might be an instance of a general principle stated in the premiss, for example:

Addition is commutative.

$3 + 4 = 4 + 3$.

Again, to see that the conclusion cannot be false if the premiss is true, we need only to understand the meaning of the premiss sentence (i.e., in the mathematical operation called *addition*, reordering the terms to be added does not change the value of the sum) and to understand that the conclusion states that the value of the sum of 3 and 4 is the same as the value when the terms are reordered with 4 placed before 3.

Alternately, the conclusion of a deductive argument might follow as a result of connections drawn among the premisses by important logical terms, such as *and, or, not, all,* and *some:*

(1) Either Jeb is not graduating or he has paid his tuition bill.
    But he is graduating.

    He has paid his tuition bill.

(2) All whales are mammals.
    All mammals are warm blooded.

    All whales are warm blooded.

The next argument is as old as the first text in logic—about 2,300 years old! It is so commonly used in logic classes that you can hardly escape it, so you might as well be exposed to it now.

All men are mortal.
Socrates is a man.

Socrates is mortal.

The first premiss is a universal generalization. It contains the information that *all* members of one class, or type of thing (the class of men) are also members of another class (the class of mortals). The second premiss provides the information that the individual whose name is Socrates is a member of the class of men. The conclusion of the argument combines the information contained separately in the two premisses but does not introduce any additional information. It is fairly obvious in this example that, strictly speaking, the conclusion contains no "new" information that is not already present in the premisses. Neither premiss says explicitly (in exactly those words) what is said in the conclusion, but the information in the conclusion is there in the premisses *implicitly.* Moreover, this is true not only for the simple arguments in our examples but also for every argument in which the conclusion follows deductively from its premisses.

When we say that deductive arguments preserve truth because they recombine and restate information contained at least implicitly in the premisses, we point to a limitation on the powers of deductive reasoning. For although the conclusion of a deductive argument can restate or recombine information, put it together in novel ways, and thus can make explicit what was formerly only implicit, the conclusion of a deductive argument cannot go beyond what was already present, at least implicitly, in the premisses to advance our knowledge of what the world is like. Deductive arguments are *truth-preserving,* but they cannot extend factual knowledge.

If deductive arguments cannot give us any new information that was not already present in the premisses, what purpose do they serve? Why should we bother to state a conclusion if all of the necessary information is already provided in the premisses? If all arguments were as simple as the example about Socrates, stating conclusions would be unnecessary. The mere mention of both premisses together would be sufficient for most people to "get the point" or "to put two and two together." Sometimes such simple arguments are presented without their conclusions. For the same reason that premisses can be omitted, conclusions can also be unstated. It is boring and can be condescending to dwell on the obvious.

Not all deductive arguments are simple, however. Sometimes the chain of reasoning that connects the premisses to the conclusion is long and complex. When this is so, even though the conclusion contains no new information (in the sense that it only selectively *recombines* information stated in the premisses), the conclusion will be new to us because we had not put together the information in the premisses in precisely that way. Even the person constructing the argument might be surprised to see where the premisses lead, because although the conclusion is contained implicitly within the premisses jointly, the conclusion is not merely a restatement or a specific instance of one of the premisses. We can say that although the conclusion of a correct deductive argument can contain no new information, it can put information together in ways that might not have occurred to anyone before. We can—and do—reach conclusions that are new from a psychological standpoint. Even when the conclusions of deductive arguments are novel, surprising, or startling in this sense, however, they can only draw out what was already there in the premisses.

The following deductive argument reaches a conclusion that is apt to be psychologically new and surprising, even though its conclusion contains no new information. Smith presents the argument to her neighbor, Jones, who commutes from his suburban home to a job in the city, to convince Jones that he is spending three weeks of every year riding a commuter train.

Jones: Three weeks a year—that's ridiculous!
Smith: No, it's a simple matter of logic. You ride the train to and from work, one hour each way, five days a week, for a total of forty-nine weeks a year, allowing for your vacation and holidays. Using simple arithmetic, that comes to a total of 490 hours per year on the train. There are 24 hours in a day, and if you divide 490 by 24, you get 20 and 10/24 days. That's almost 21 days, or three weeks a year you spend on the train.
Jones: Ouch.

The reasoning in this argument depends on the use of mathematics. Mathematical arguments are almost exclusively deductive in character. Although mathematicians may believe on inductive grounds that, for example, a theorem holds in every case because it has held in every case tested so far, mathematicians are not satisfied that the theorem has been *proved* until it has been established as the conclusion of a deductive argument with acceptable premises. Especially in our use of mathematics (including simple arithmetic calculations), deductive arguments pervade our everyday lives. Balancing checkbooks, counting change, and setting up a budget all require deductive reasoning. Although you might not use geometry much in your everyday life, if you studied it in high school you were intensely involved in constructing and evaluating deductive arguments. You began the course in geometry with a set of first principles— axioms, postulates, and definitions—and then proceeded to derive theorems (conclusions!) on the basis of those first principles. This was an exercise in deductive reasoning, and, as you no doubt remember, some parts of it were subtle. Even though you had all of the necessary premises in hand, it was not at all obvious in many cases how these premises could be combined to deduce the theorem you were supposed to prove.

All other areas of mathematics, including those that, unlike geometry, are not formulated as axiomatic systems, essentially depend on deductive arguments. All mathematical *proofs*, including proofs in the areas of statistics and mathematical probability, are deductive arguments. Furthermore, we can regard mathematical proofs as the purest form of deductive reasoning, because even the premises contain no information about what the real world is like. The mathematical principles that form the basis for mathematical proofs are themselves usually considered to contain no factual information but rather to be true by definitions of the terms involved or to be true claims about abstract constructions of the human mind, such as numbers or geometric figures. This is what Bertrand Russell was referring to when he said "I fear that, to a mind of sufficient intellectual power, the whole of mathematics would appear trivial, as trivial as the statement that a four-footed animal is an animal" *(My Philosophical Development).*

Russell does not mean to say that all mathematics is trivial to *our* minds, for our intellectual powers are limited. When we *apply* mathematical reasoning to factual claims, as we did in the preceding example (in which the premises included the information that Jones spent two hours on the train each working day), the results may seem surprising—just as the results of a complicated mathematical proof may seem surprising. The point is that the use of mathematical calculations in an argument does not introduce any new *information about the world* that goes beyond what is already stated in the premisses.

Many arguments concerning ethics—in which the proponent attempts to show that an action is right or wrong or that a moral principle is acceptable or unacceptable—are deductive arguments. A standard way to establish that some kind of action is right (or wrong) is to show that all actions of that type are right (or wrong) because they fall into a broader class of right (or wrong) actions. The following argument provides an example:

All deliberate killing of helpless persons is wrong.
Euthanasia (mercy killing) is a deliberate killing of a helpless person.

Euthanasia is wrong.

In this argument, as in all correct, or valid, deductive arguments, *if* the premisses are true, then the conclusion cannot be false. The question of whether the premisses *are* true (or acceptable, if one objects to regarding moral claims as true) is an important and interesting question, but the deductive character of the argument is independent of the answer to that question.

Other arguments commonly employed in ethics attempt to show that a particular moral principle is not acceptable because it would condone or permit actions that we consider to be immoral. This pattern of argument is somewhat more complicated than the preceding, for it contains subarguments within a larger argument. The following example is an argument of this type:

First Subargument:

Whatever is done as an expression of love is morally acceptable.
Mrs. X, who believed her baby's soul was possessed by demons that could be
  driven out only by beating, beat her baby severely because she loved him.

Mrs. X did something morally acceptable when she beat her baby.

Second Subargument:

The conclusion of the argument in the first part is obviously false.
But that argument is deductive (if all its premisses are true, then so is its
  conclusion).

At least one of the premisses of the first argument is false.

Third Subargument:

At least one of the premisses of the first argument is false.
The second premiss states a fact about Mrs. X's behavior, and its truth is
  not in question.

The first premiss is false. (It is not true that whatever is done as an
  expression of love is morally acceptable.)

This method of proving that a sentence is false—taking it as a premiss, and showing that it, either alone or in combination with other premises whose truth is not in doubt, leads deductively to an obviously false conclusion—is common, not only in ethical arguments, but in mathematics and many other fields as well. Beginning an argument with a premiss that is believed to be false may seem odd. Nevertheless, this often happens in dialogues, when one person makes a statement and the other person tries to show that it is false, as in the following example:

He: You don't love me anymore.

She: Don't be silly. Suppose that I don't love you. If a woman doesn't love a man, she doesn't care what happens to him, she doesn't want to spend time with him, and she doesn't give him presents. But I do care what happens to you, I do want to spend time with you, and I do give you presents. So you see, I do love you.

This way of arguing is called *indirect proof.* (Mathematicians sometimes call it *proof by contradiction.*) We examine the logical structure of this useful form of deductive argument more carefully in later chapters.

An important feature of some ethical arguments is that they apparently acknowledge exceptions to general principles of morality, such as the general prohibition against killing other humans. Because exceptions to general principles of morality do exist, it might seem that these principles are statistical generalizations rather than universal generalizations. An examination of how exceptions are treated, however, clarifies those cases in which moral principles are regarded as universal generalizations, and reveals that ethical arguments employing them are intended to be deductive.

For example, although the deliberate taking of human life is morally unacceptable, exceptions are recognized. If Jones deliberately kills Smith in self-defense, the killing is not necessarily considered wrong. Such actions are permissible according to a different general principle that allows killing in self-defense. The important point about such exceptions is that they too are governed by universally general principles, which may be somewhat more limited in their application. Therefore, to show that a particular killing was not a wrongful act even though it was deliberate, we might show that the circumstances surrounding the act make it a case of "killing in self-defense" rather than another sort of killing. Then according to the principle that killing in self-defense is morally justifiable, the act would not be considered morally wrong. When an apparent exception to some accepted moral principle is encountered, another deductive argument, based on a different acceptable general principle, may be invoked to handle the exception.

Remember, in a valid deductive argument, if the premises are true the conclusion *cannot* be false; accordingly, certain words and phrases are often used in ordinary language to mark the strong support provided in these arguments. Expressions such as *must, it must be the case that, necessarily, inevitably, certainly,* and *it can be deduced that,* are frequently used to indicate that an argument is deductive. The terms *entail* and *imply* are also used to indicate a deductive connection between premises and conclusion.

Sometimes the same terms that indicate that an argument is deductive are used in strong inductive arguments. That is to say, they are used when a conclusion is very strongly supported by evidence, but when the truth of all the premisses is nevertheless compatible with the falsity of the conclusion. For example, "Mary must have gone to the party because she accepted the invitation" is not a deductive argument. To test whether an argument is deductively correct, ask the question: *Is it impossible for the conclusion to be false if the premisses are true?* To answer this question for any except the simplest arguments, however, we need to know how to judge the nature of the relationship between premisses and their conclusion, and we need to understand the meaning of *impossible* in this context. We concentrate on these points in later chapters, but in the meantime, the clues provided here regarding the contexts in which deductive arguments are normally used and the special words used to indicate the presence of a deductive argument provide some guidance. If the proponent of an argument intends it to be deductive (here again we may need to grasp the context to see this), we can judge the argument by the standards for correct or valid deductive arguments.

Our task can be complicated when arguments in ordinary language are stated incompletely. Then it is especially difficult to determine whether, for example, the missing premisses are universal or statistical generalizations. Contextual clues for judging whether arguments are deductive are particularly useful at this stage, because they help us to supply the appropriate type of missing premiss. If a missing premiss is to provide nontrivial support for the conclusion, however, it should be more plausible than the conclusion itself. If we ignore this caution about plausibility, we could transform *any* argument into a deductive argument with the addition of some premiss. (For example, adding the conclusion itself as an additional premiss would make the argument deductive!)

Occasionally, terms such as *necessarily* are used to bolster an argument or to make it look stronger than it is. Consider the following argument, taken from an advertisement paid for by a large oil corporation:

> Because it is keyed so closely to the marketplace and so responsive to it, private business is *necessarily* the most effective instrument of economic change.

Private business is indeed closely tied to what people buy and sell, and this might provide a *good* reason to believe that private business is the most effective instrument of economic change. Nevertheless, the linkage to the marketplace is hardly a compelling reason to believe that private business is the most effective instrument of econmic change. The government, for example, with its power to control the money supply, interest rates, taxes, import duties, and other aspects of the economy might be a far more effective instrument of economic change than private business, even though private business is more closely tied to the marketplace. It is true that many large, private corporations, like the one that paid for this ad, would prefer that government refrain from using those powers and let a free market determine the state of the economy.

The preferences of the corporation, however, are irrelevant to whether the premisses of the argument support its conclusion.

In Arthur Conan Doyle's stories about master detective Sherlock Holmes, arguments are characterized as deductive although the truth of their premisses does not guarantee the truth of the conclusions. We can recognize and admire the impressive logical powers of Holmes in these stories, but we should realize that most of what he calls "deductions" are really strong inductive arguments, according to logicians' definitions of the terms. That is to say, if Holmes's premisses are true, then very probably his conclusion is true as well. Consider the following passage from "A Scandal in Bohemia," in which Dr. Watson visits Holmes after a long absence. Although Watson hasn't told him so, Holmes figures out that Watson has returned to the practice of medicine.

"And in practice again, I observe. You did not tell me that you intended to go into harness."

"Then, how do you know?"

"I see it, I deduce it. How do I know that you have been getting yourself very wet lately, and that you have a most clumsy and careless servant girl?"

"My dear Holmes," said I, "this is too much. You would certainly have been burned [as a witch] had you lived a few centuries ago. It is true that I had a country walk on Thursday and came home in a dreadful mess; but, as I have changed my clothes, I can't imagine how you deduce it. As to Mary Jane, she is incorrigible, and my wife has given her notice; but there again I fail to see how you work it out."

He chuckled to himself and rubbed his long nervous hands together.

"It is simplicity itself," said he; "my eyes tell me that on the inside of your left shoe, just where the firelight strikes it, the leather is scored by six almost parallel cuts. Obviously they have been caused by someone who has very carelessly scraped round the edges of the sole in order to remove crusted mud from it. Hence, you see, my double deduction that you had been out in vile weather, and that you had a particularly malignant boot-slitting specimen of the London slavery. As to your practice, if a gentleman walks into my rooms smelling of iodoform, with a black mark of nitrate of silver upon his right forefinger, and a bulge in the side of his top hat to show where he has secreted his stethoscope, I must be dull indeed if I do not pronounce him to be an active member of the medical profession."

The fiendishly clever Holmes is right on all counts, as usual, and his "deductions" would no doubt stand as proof in a court of law. It is *possible*, however, that Watson cleaned his own boots and that the signs of medical practice were the result of Watson helping out in an emergency rather than setting up his own practice. In some cases we may want to analyze arguments such as those Holmes gives here as if they are *intended* to be deductive arguments in which a universally general premiss has been left unstated. Here, however, such an approach is unlikely to work, because the required premisses, such as "Every pair of boots scored by cuts was cleaned by a clumsy servant," are no more plausible—in fact, less plausible—than the conclusion. Holmes's conclusion goes beyond a clever recombination of the information he states in his premises, and so his argument, although ingenious and persuasive, is not a truth-preserving deductive argument.

As we all know, linguistic usage is variable, and Holmes is not to be criticized for calling his inferences "deductive." In studies of logic, however, the term has a more restricted use, as explained before. Even among logic texts, the term *deductive argument* is used in slightly differing ways. The term *deductive argument* in this text is normally used in the sense of a *correct* or valid deductive argument—that is, to refer to arguments that contain premisses, which if true, lead to a conclusion that cannot be false. Sometimes, an argument's proponent intends it to be deductive, but the premisses are not related to the conclusion in the correct way. An argument may also seem to be deductive, for example, when it uses expressions that indicate that necessarily the conclusion follows from the premisses, even though this is not the case. Some texts define *deductive arguments* as arguments in which the premisses *purport* to provide complete support for the conclusion, or in which the proponent *intends* the argument to be deductive. Others, such as this text, define deductive arguments as those in which the premisses (including implicit premisses) actually provide the appropriate level of support. Each way of defining the term *deductive argument* has advantages and disadvantages. The disadvantage of defining the term as "an argument in which if all the premisses are true, the conclusion cannot be false" is that all deductive arguments are then valid by definition, and the usual way of referring to fallacies that mimic deductive arguments as "invalid deductive arguments" is awkward. An advantage of this definition is that it does not suggest that inductive arguments are defective because they are deductively invalid. The structure and perspective of this textbook reflects the belief that it is better to recognize inductive arguments as a separate type of argument with a special role and value instead of viewing them as failed or weak versions of deductive arguments. Students, nevertheless, should be aware of the two ways of defining deductive arguments. In this text, we specify *correct* or *valid* deductive argument if the context does not make this clear. When we talk about fallacies that superficially resemble correct (valid) deductive arguments, we adopt the usual practice and call them *deductive fallacies* or *invalid deductive arguments*.

Exercise Set 3.1.

Part One. If we define a deductive argument as one in which it is impossible for the conclusion to be false if all the premisses are true, which of the following sentences are true?

1. A deductive argument can have a false premiss.

2. A deductive argument can have a false conclusion.

3. A deductive argument can have all false premisses and a false conclusion.

4. A deductive argument can have all false premisses and a true conclusion.

5. A deductive argument can have all true premisses and a false conclusion.

Part Two. For each of the following arguments, indicate in a general way the definitional or structural features that make it deductive. If the argument requires the addition of an obviously true, but unstated premiss, say what it is.

1. John is Mary's brother. Therefore, Mary has a brother.

2. Mary is Michael's sister. Therefore, Michael is Mary's brother.

3. Black swans live in Australia. Therefore, not all swans are white.

4. Every senior can register for this class. Carlos cannot register for this class. Therefore, Carlos is not a senior.

5. The Student Council meeting began at 11 a.m. and ended at 2 p.m. Thus, the Council meeting lasted three hours.

6. If the Americans pursue their present policies in the Persian Gulf, they will antagonize the leaders of Iran. If the leaders of Iran are antagonized, they will start a war. So, if the Americans pursue their present policies in the Persian Gulf, the leaders of Iran will start a war.

7. Four tickets to graduation ceremonies are reserved for each graduating senior. There are 150 graduating seniors. So 600 graduation tickets are reserved for seniors.

8. A person should not be judged guilty of murder if he was certified as insane at the time of the act of killing another person. But the court has accepted the doctors' certification of Smith's insanity at the time. Therefore, Smith should not be judged guilty of murder.

9. JLH paid $3000 to have 500 copies of his drawing printed for sale at the art festival and $200 to rent space for his work. Since he is charging $50 for each print, he will need to sell at least 64 of them to recover his costs.

10. The letter *k* does not occur in the Italian alphabet. Therefore, any word in Italian speech or writing that contains a *k* is a borrowed or foreign word.

Part Three. Describe a situation in which the conclusion of each of the following arguments could turn out to be false even though the premisses are all true.

1. Every political survey has indicated that the next governor of the state will be a Republican. Therefore, the Republican candidate will win the governor's seat in the next election.

2. Every senior can register for this class. Sally is not a senior. Sally cannot register for this class.

3. Greer was rushed to the hospital yesterday, apparently suffering from heat exhaustion. Therefore, Greer will not win the marathon today.

4. Students admitted to this college have the ability to perform well in college classes. You have been admitted to this college. Thus, you will perform well in this logic class.

5. [To reduce unreimbursed overhead costs in hospitals,] all hospital rooms should be converted to single occupancy. Although it may seem that single rooms are an inefficient luxury, they are actually more cost-effective than multi-bed rooms for several reasons. For one, gender and illness restrictions in the latter force hospitals to provide about 15 percent or 20 percent more such beds than the market may need. Single beds avoid that over-capacity.

—M. Bobrow and J. Thomas, *The New York Times,*
Viewpoints, July 25, 1993.

III. INDUCTIVE ARGUMENTS

In an *inductive argument*, all of the premises can be true, and can support the conclusion in the sense of contributing to or upholding its probability, but the conclusion could be false. Inductive arguments lack the definitive and the most valuable feature of deductive arguments—the ability to preserve truth. However, this apparent shortcoming is more than offset by a feature of inductive arguments that is lacking in deductive arguments. Inductive arguments can extend our factual knowledge. Their conclusions contain new information that is not present, even implicitly, in the premises of the arguments. Although the field of mathematics is well suited to the almost exclusive use of deductive reasoning, in all other fields of human endeavor—natural science, the social sciences, history, literary criticism, ethical judgments, and the practical knowledge of everyday affairs—inductive inferences and arguments are indispensable.

Inductive arguments figure strongly in reasoning about causes. Holmes's arguments that so impressed Dr. Watson frequently were used to support a claim about causes. Thus Holmes inferred that the cause of the bulge in Dr. Watson's top hat was a hidden stethoscope, and that the cause of Watson's carrying a stethoscope was a return to medical practice. The following argument, which is the opening passage in Charles Darwin's *The Origin of Species,* is also causal:

> When we compare the individuals of the same variety or sub-variety of our older cultivated plants and animals, one of the first points which strikes us is, that they generally differ more from each other than do the individuals of any one species or variety in a state of nature. And if we reflect on the vast diversity of the plants and animals which have been cultivated, and which have varied during all ages under the most different climates and treatment, we are driven to conclude that this great variability is due to our domestic productions having been raised under conditions of life not so uniform as, and somewhat different from, those to which the parent species had been exposed under nature.

Darwin noted the impressive differences among individuals of the same species of domestic plants or animals, such as dogs. The range of types from miniature poodles to Great Danes is far more varied than that found in wild species such as elephants, which come only in two varieties. Darwin concluded that this is so because humans breed these plants and animals under a much greater variety of conditions than the conditions to which wild species are exposed. Humans have bred dogs for centuries in almost every part of the world—for sport, show, work, and a variety of other purposes. Elephants flourish in highly specialized environments in only two or three specific places.

Causal arguments are among the most frequently presented inductive arguments. Other common types of inductive arguments are:

1. Arguments in which we conclude something about the future on the basis of what has happened in the past.

> That a stone will fall, that fire will burn, that the earth has solidity, we have observed a thousand and a thousand times; and when any new instance of this nature is presented, we draw without hesitation the accustomed inference.
>
> —D. Hume, *Dialogues Concerning Natural Religion*

Philo, the speaker in this passage of the dialogue, does not actually state the obvious conclusion—that in the future stones will continue to fall; fire to burn; the earth to be solid—but his meaning is clear.

2. Arguments in which we conclude something about the past on the basis of present evidence.

> Pollen grains, though microscopic, are preserved in peat bogs in a remarkable manner for hundreds and even thousands of years. Since the pollen of every plant has its own special form, it is possible with the microscope to establish what plants were growing at different points in time. The distinct layers in peat-bogs thus become, as it were, the pages of a great picture book illustrating the changing flora of the land through the ages.
>
> —P. V. Glob, *The Bog People*

Here, the pollen, which is observed in the present, provides the basis for reconstructing the types of vegetation that grew in prehistoric times. Historians, geologists, archaeologists—all who are concerned with knowledge of the past—use inductive reasoning in this way.

3. Arguments in which we generalize on the basis of a sample of observations or experiments.

This is the type of inductive reasoning that is used by persons who conduct public opinion polls to determine who is a favorite political candidate or to learn about the public's attitude toward a particular piece of legislation. You have seen or heard such arguments, particularly in election years. Here is an example of this form of reasoning, taken from a newspaper report about some recent research:

> Los Angeles—Equal property splits in divorces make men richer and women substantially poorer, a California study has found, buttressing nationwide efforts to include a husband's earning potential in settlements.

> The study of 3,000 divorces by a Stanford University researcher shows men improved their standard of living an average 42 percent in the first year after a divorce, while the living standard for women and children dropped 73 percent when income was compared to need.
>
> —J. Matthews, *The Washington Post*

In this passage, the reporter not only provides the conclusion and the evidence on which it is based but also includes additional information about the effect the conclusion may have on future financial calculations for divorce settlements. Generalizing on the basis of samples is one of the most useful ways in which we extend our knowledge through inductive reasoning.

4. Arguments that conclude something about a particular case on the basis of what happens usually, or frequently, but not always.

The following passage, taken from Mark Twain's *Notebook,* is an amusing example of this common form of inductive argument:

> At bottom I did not believe I had touched that man. The law of probabilities decreed me guiltless of his blood, for in all my small experience with guns I had never hit anything I had tried to hit. And I knew I had done my best to hit him.

5. Arguments that conclude that a particular kind of similarity holds on the basis of other known similarities between two types of things.

This form of reasoning is often used in making a decision to buy a particular brand of merchandise on the basis of good performance by other items of the same brand. Similarities in materials, methods of manufacturing, and other product qualities provide evidence to support some further, as yet unobserved, similarity (such as durability). This kind of reasoning also provides the focus for much of our medical research. Investigators observe the effects of various substances on experimental animals, which are similar to humans in certain respects, and conclude that those substances will affect humans in similar ways. Here is an example:

> Marian C. Diamond, professor of anatomy at the University of California at Berkeley, warned recently that birth control pills may inhibit development of the brain.
>
> Dr. Diamond said that research reveals that female sex hormones contained in birth control pills limit growth of the cerebral cortex, a part of the brain which regulates intelligence.
>
> Dr. Diamond has been working with female rats into which she has injected a hormone equivalent to a birth control pill. Such rats showed less growth of the cerebral cortex than rats not injected with the hormone.
>
> —*Parade Magazine*

Recognizing contexts in which inductive arguments are appropriate help us to determine whether a given argument is inductive or deductive, although, of course, the real test of a deductive argument is to ask: Would the premisses, if true, make it impossible for the conclusion to be false? In an inductive argument, the falsity of the conclusion is compatible with the truth of the premisses, but the premisses should make it *probable* or *likely* that the conclusion is true as well. As in deductive arguments, special terms draw attention to the inductive nature of the link between the premisses and the conclusion. These terms include *probably, usually, tends to support, likely, very likely,* and *almost always.* When Mark Twain said "The law of *probabilities* decreed me guiltless," he indicated that his argument was inductive. The terms *may* or *might* are sometimes used to point to the tentative nature of an inductively drawn conclusion, as in Dr. Diamond's claim that "birth-control pills *may* inhibit development of the brain."

An important difference between deductive and inductive arguments is that whereas deductive support is an all-or-nothing affair (either the truth of the premisses is incompatible with the falsity of the conclusion or not), inductive support may vary in strength. The terms that indicate an argument is inductive might also provide information about the degree of strength of the argument. For example, *may, might,* and *possibly* indicate weak or moderate support; whereas *almost always, highly probable,* and *highly likely* indicate strong support. The expressions *with practical certainty* or *with moral certainty* indicate a very high degree of inductive support. They are used when the evidence is overwhelmingly strong. Nevertheless, strong inductive support differs from that demanded in deductive arguments. The phrase *beyond all reasonable doubt* is often used to indicate a strong inductive argument, but it is sometimes used to signal a deductive argument as well.

Still another difference between inductive and deductive arguments concerns the effect of additional information on the strength of the argument. Suppose you have received $1,000 from the estate of a distant relative. You want to invest it in a mutual fund, and your main objective is preservation of capital with reasonable income from your investment. You select a fund that has paid a dividend every quarter for forty years while showing moderate growth. Your decision was based on the following argument:

Fund X has a forty-year record of paying regular dividends while maintaining
  a slow growth of capital.
My investment objectives are regular income and preservation of capital.

Fund X is a suitable investment for me.

Suppose you later learn that Fund X has just been reorganized, and that the new managers have a reputation for picking speculative stocks with aggressive growth potential. With the addition of this new information to your original argument, the support for the conclusion is considerably weaker.

Alternatively, additional information can strengthen an inductive argument. Consider some recent research conducted to study the role of heredity in alcoholism. On the basis of a ten-year study of 202 alcoholic men, Dr. T. Reich, at the Alcohol Research Center at Washington University, learned that 38 percent had alcoholic fathers, 21 percent had alcoholic mothers, 57 percent had alcoholic brothers, 15 percent had alcoholic sisters, 32 percent had alcoholic sons, and 19 percent had alcoholic daughters. When we realize that in the general population, alcoholism will eventually develop in only 3 percent of women and 8 to 10 percent of men, this information supports the conclusion that hereditary factors are important in the development of alcoholism. Additional information from Swedish studies of adopted children, which clearly showed that the children of alcoholics are four times more likely than other children to become alcoholics even if the children are adopted early in life by people who do not abuse alcohol, makes the argument in support of the hereditary character of alcoholism even stronger.

Thus, as these examples show, additional information can either strengthen or weaken an inductive argument. In contrast, if a deductive argument is valid, then the addition of premises cannot either strengthen the argument (the truth of its premises is already incompatible with the falsity of its conclusion) or weaken it in the sense of making it invalid. Since *if* the premises in the original argument were true, then the conclusion would be true as well, adding anything (even a false premiss) to the premises cannot change that relationship. As we have said before, an argument that purports to be deductive is either valid or invalid—validity cannot be expressed in degrees. Premisses of inductive arguments, however, can offer a range of support—from very strong to moderate to weak—for their conclusions. So additional premisses can make an inductive argument either stronger or weaker. When the support in an inductive argument is extremely weak, but the argument superficially resembles a correct inductive argument, the argument is called an inductive fallacy.

Some arguments, particularly those used in science, combine inductive and deductive elements. An argument used by Louis Pasteur is an example. Pasteur is well known for his method of pasteurization, a gentle heating process used to destroy harmful organisms in fresh milk. Before he tried pasteurizing milk, he suggested the process as a solution to the problem of wine turning sour during the aging process. Yeast cells, which are living organisms, are responsible for the fermentation necessary to make wine. Using a microscope, Pasteur discovered that there were several types of yeast in wine. He hypothesized that after the fermentation yeasts had done their work, some of the other yeasts caused the wine to sour during the aging process. He reasoned that if all yeast cells in the wine were destroyed by gentle heating *after* fermentation was completed, the wine could age without souring. His method worked and earned him the enthusiastic thanks of the wine industry in France. The deductive part of Pasteur's argument is

Yeast cells are the cause of souring in wine.
Gentle heating destroys yeast cells.
_____
Gently heated wine does not sour.

After experiments showed that heated wine did not sour, Pasteur *inductively* concluded that his belief about yeast *causing* the wine to sour was correct.

This conclusion follows inductively, rather than deductively; although the yeast cells were killed by heating, it is *possible* that some other agent that was destroyed by heating caused the wine to spoil. Even with a deductive component, arguments of this type have an overall inductive structure, because the conclusion about the *cause* does not follow with certainty from the success of the experiment. Arguments of this type, which are fundamental to scientific reasoning, are examined more closely in Chapter 8.

Exercise Set 3.2

Part One. Find an example of an inductive argument in a newspaper, magazine, or other contemporary source. Reconstruct the argument in standard form, and tell whether it falls into any of the six categories described in this section.

Part Two. Identify the premises and the conclusion of each of the following inductive arguments. If the argument belongs to one of the six common types of inductive argument discussed in this section, tell which one.

1. The introduction of cooperative marketing into Europe greatly increased the prosperity of the farmers, so we may be confident that a similar system in the United States will greatly increase the prosperity of our farmers.

2. The *Farmers' Almanac,* which has an excellent record on such matters, predicts that we are in for a hard winter this year. So there is going to be a tough winter ahead.

3. A team led by J.H. Dwyer studied 6,634 men and women. They discovered that people who consumed at least one gram of calcium per day lowered their risk of high blood pressure by about 12 percent. They concluded that calcium guards against hypertension (high blood pressure).

—*Science News,* vol. 142, p. 340

4. Although the bay upon whose shores Cerros (Mexico) now sits is a fairly choppy body of water, the archaeological discovery of certain plant and fish remains at the site indicates that, in the late Preclassic, Cerros lay on the shores of a calm lagoon.

—J. Sabloff, *The Cities of Ancient Mexico*

5. There are events which are foreknown by persons who have applied their observation to that end. Of this kind are tempests and gales of wind, produced by certain aspects of the Moon, or the fixed stars, towards the Sun, according to their several courses, and the approach of which is usually foreseen by mariners. . . .

Since it is thus clearly practicable, by an accurate knowledge of the points above enumerated, to make predictions concerning the proper quality of the seasons, there also seems no impediment to the formation of similar prognostication concerning the destiny and disposition of every human being. For by the constitution of the Heavens, at the time of any individual's primary conformation, the general quality of that individual's temperament may be perceived . . . [and] an event dependent on one disposition of the Heavens will be advantageous to a particular temperament, and that resulting from another unfavorable and injurious. From these circumstances, and others of similar import, the possibility of foreknowledge is certainly evident.

—Ptolemy's *Tetrabiblos,* quoted in P. Suppes,
A Probabilistic Theory of Causality

6. When the elaborate methods of preparation of some of the plants used to break down the monotony of life are studied, it becomes quite evident that primitive man must have possessed something other than chance to reveal to him the properties of food and drug plants. He must have been a keen observer of accidents to discover fermentation, the effects and localization of alkaloids and toxin resins, and the arts of roasting and burning a product to gain from it the desired narcotization or pleasing aromas (coffee).

—O. Aimes, quoted in *Technics and Human Development,* by L. Mumford

7. It is clear that our *Iliad, Odyssey, Erga,* and *Theogony* are not the first [hexameter poems]. These ostensibly primitive poems show a length and complexity of composition which can only be the result of many generations of artistic effort. They speak a language out of all relation to common speech, full of forgotten meanings and echoes of past states of society; a poet's language, demonstrably built up and conditioned at every turn by the needs of the hexameter metre. There must therefore have been hexameter poems before our *Iliad.*

—G. Murray, *The Literature of Ancient Greece*

8. *Note:* The long-lost bowerbird was found in the Foja Mountains of west New Guinea, and its bower and display were discovered. The bower is a stick tower on a rimmed moss platform, adorned with separate piles of fruit of three different colors. The displaying male extends toward the female a blue fruit set against his golden crest.

> In many other kinds of birds, males court females and stimulate them to ovulate by constructing real or mock nests and by ritualized offering of food (courtship feeding). If bower building developed as an exaggerated form of such courtship behavior the bower may represent a gigantic courtship nest. The decoration of bowers by colored objects has been viewed as derived from courtship feeding, since males of all species for which the display is known pick up a decoration and hold it in the bill toward the female, and since these objects are sometimes edible (fruit).

—J. M. Diamond, "Rediscovery of the Yellow-Fronted Gardener Bowerbird," *Science* 216 (1982):431

9. The economy will soon be in good shape. A pair of government reports pointed yesterday to an improving economy. The Commerce Department reported that construction spending rose 1.4 percent in December, the second straight monthly gain, and orders to U.S. factories for new manufactured goods rose a strong 4.8 percent.

—Newspaper report

10. [The Assistant Secretary for Health of the Department of Health and Human Services] released the results of the National Household Survey on Drug Abuse, which

examined a national sample of Americans over age 12, and the High School Senior Survey.

The surveys showed that one out of three Americans over age 12 has tried some kind of illicit substance.

—Newspaper report

IV. FALLACIES

Fallacies or fallacious arguments might appear to provide support for their conclusions. As we know, however, appearances can deceive. Committing a *fallacy* is different from simply making a *factual error.* Although in ordinary language, the term *fallacy* is sometimes used to refer to false beliefs (particularly those that are believable because they are attractive to us), we reserve the term to refer to mistakes in reasoning. From this standpoint, merely being in error about something should not be regarded as committing a fallacy. To believe, for example, that Thomas Jefferson did not own slaves is erroneous but not fallacious. The person who does not believe that Jefferson owned slaves is ignorant of certain facts, but that person's logical ability to draw conclusions on the basis of evidence might not be at fault. To commit a fallacy, we must offer or accept nonevidence as evidence for a claim.

Chapter 1 contains an example of the fallacy of black-and-white thinking, in which a range of energy alternatives was overlooked while just two (fossil fuels and nuclear power) were considered in the premiss of an argument. Chapter 2 shows that mistakes in reasoning can result from equivocation, or shifting the meaning of an ambiguous expression, during the course of an argument. In the following chapters of this book, we examine standards that have been developed to characterize valid deductive and strong inductive arguments. Fallacies occur when these standards are not met.

Fallacies can mislead for many reasons. Sometimes a conclusion is so attractive that we are ready to accept almost anything that is offered as evidence in support. Swindlers and confidence men present preposterous "evidence" for the reliability of their money-making schemes, but they count on the desire for money to cloud the judgment of their victims. Alternatively, an assertion may be so repugnant that we will accept almost any statement as evidence against it. Critical thinking requires us to separate the psychological desire to believe or deny a claim from considerations of how well supported that claim is.

In other cases, we may be moved by a strong like or dislike, or respect or disapproval, for the *person* making a claim, which so prejudices us that we fail to consider the nature of the evidence. Fond parents are notorious for their willingness to accept a child's word as sufficient evidence for fantastic claims. Critical thinking requires us to be on guard in this respect as well.

When a fallacy is presented in the context of a threat or an enticement, we may not notice that no evidence is being offered. An "argument" that substitutes a threat of force for evidence has, like many fallacies, a special name. It is called "appeal to force," or (in Latin) *"ad baculum."* This fallacy appeals to an emotion (fear) rather than our reasoning ability. Although a threat may be a "good reason" (in the sense of serving your best interests) to do something, a threat should not be confused with evidence for the truth of a claim. In a totalitarian regime, for example, threats against one's life are good reasons not to openly disagree with the party line—but are not evidence for the truth of the line.

Another fallacy that plays on emotions is called "appeal to pity" or *"ad misericordium."* This occurs when we confuse feeling sorry for someone with evidence for the truth of an assertion that is made by or about the person. A well-known scientist, a victim of cancer, made an appeal to pity when he said in response to challenges to a theory he was trying to defend: "I can say these things . . . because this is my last hurrah, and I have to tell the truth." Appeals to pity are often presented by lawyers who defend their clients against criminal charges by saying that the client was ill, was mistreated, has suffered enough, and other such considerations. Any of these claims may be relevant to the type of punishment inflicted on the criminal, if convicted. Such claims are probably not, however, relevant to the issue of whether the defendant committed the crime. To suppose that they were would be fallacious.

Aside from exerting emotional pressure, a fallacy can deceive us by its resemblance to a correct form of argument. One of the reasons for studying the formal structure of arguments, as we do in the following chapters, is to be able to recognize such fallacies. A few examples suffice here:

(1) Since things that are causally connected regularly occur together, the premises of causal arguments often include statements to the effect that such regularities have been observed. But to argue for a causal connection *merely* on the basis of the fact that things have occurred together occasionally in the past is to argue fallaciously. Further evidence is required to show that the observed co-occurrences are not coincidental. All sorts of things happen together without any causal connection existing between them. For example, in 1993, Hanna Gray ended her tenure as president of the University of Chicago and Mike Ditka ended his tenure as coach of the Chicago Bears. Neither announced any definite plans for the following year. Yet, it is unlikely that these matters are causally linked, and even more unlikely that, as a Chicago alumnus suggested, "Hanna Gray is Coach Mike Ditka in disguise."

(2) In Woody Allen's *Love and Death*, the hero offers this argument to demonstrate his skill in logic:

> All men are mortal. Socrates is mortal. Therefore, all men are Socrates.

The way in which this fallacious argument parodies the classic example of deduction is transparent enough to make it amusing rather than deceptive. Life would be simpler if all fallacies were so easy to detect.

Sometimes fallacies are committed because relevant evidence is ignored. This can happen as a result of thinking in terms of *stereotypes*—fixed, rigid, or conventional mental patterns that leave little room for noticing individual variations in information received or for classifying new information appropriately. A blatant example of this kind of fallacy would be to argue that a person is intelligent because that person is a member of some racial or ethnic group. This argument ignores the well-known fact that individual members of every ethnic or racial group vary considerably in intelligence. Prejudicial judgments of this type are a particularly insidious form of thinking in terms of stereotypes.

Stereotypic thinking is not always this obvious (or obnoxious). Psychologists have demonstrated that fallacious reasoning involving stereotypic thinking is common even in the absence of any racial or ethnic prejudice. Two psychologists presented the following problem to several groups of students and professional colleagues (A. Tversky and D. Kahneman, "Judgments Under Uncertainty," *Science* 185 [1974]:1124).

Persons to whom the problem was presented were told that the following description had been drawn at random from a collection of 100 descriptions (30 of lawyers and 70 of engineers):

> John is a 39-year-old man. He is married and has two children. He is active in local politics. His favorite hobby is the collecting of rare books. He is competitive, argumentative, and articulate.

The problem is to tell whether John is an engineer or a lawyer.

A large majority answered "lawyer," even though no specific information about John's profession occurs in the description and descriptions of engineers outnumbered descriptions of lawyers by more than two to one, making it much more likely that a description drawn at random would be a description of an engineer. Yet, almost all participants ignored these factors, and concentrated instead on the description itself.

On the basis of the results of this and similar experiments, the psychologists who conducted the study concluded that people are the captives of stereotypes pertaining to lawyers and engineers. Presumably, the general stereotype of a lawyer is formed by the media's representation of high-powered trial lawyers, who are competitive, argumentative, and articulate. Collecting rare books can be an expensive hobby, and many lawyers earn large incomes. In addition, many high-level political offices are held by men and women trained in the law. None of the information presented in the description is incompatible with the engineering profession, however, and a large number of lawyers lead less glamorous lives than those lawyers who exemplify the stereotype. If the solid information that the descriptions of engineers in the sample far outnumber those of lawyers is ignored, then the judgment that a lawyer (not an engineer) is being described could be accounted for by stereotypic judgments.

Exercise Set 3.3

Point out the fallacious reasoning in each of the following:

1. Lizzie Borden, who is being tried for killing her mother and father, pleads innocent on the grounds that she is an orphan.

2. In college, you can either be a serious student or establish beneficial social contacts. In later life, however, whom you know is more important than what you know, so you would be well-advised to let your studies slide in favor of an active social life.

3. Crime in the streets, especially crime committed by gangs of teens, is increasing at an alarming rate. Senator Ess shares your concern about this issue. Therefore, to reduce crime in the streets, vote for Ess.

4. Remark of a congresswoman who agreed to jog with (large, heavy) President Clinton:

> I thought he'd chug along like a caboose.
> —*The New York Times*, July 26, 1993

5. Eating fish causes migraine headaches. I know that because the last time my brother ate fish for dinner, he had a sick headache the next day.

V. REVIEW

In this chapter, we have learned to distinguish deductive arguments from inductive arguments and to understand the general nature of fallacies. Once it becomes apparent that an argument is being presented, the pertinent questions to ask and to answer are:

1. What is the conclusion?

2. What evidence is offered in support of the conclusion?

3. Is it possible for the premises to all be true while the conclusion is false?

4. If the answer to the third question is unclear, look at the context in which the argument is offered.

   a. Is the context mathematical?

   b. Does the reasoning in the argument depend on mathematical calculations?

   c. Is the context one of ethical reasoning in which a particular kind of action is shown to be an instance of a general principle?

   d. Does the reasoning depend largely on drawing out the meanings of terms in the argument?

Such arguments are likely to be deductive.

If the argument is not deductive, is it an argument that tries to establish something about the future or the past on the basis of present evidence? Is it an argument designed to show that something is the cause of something else (a causal argument)? Is the argument based on a sample study, or on something that "happens most of the time"? Does the argument conclude that two things are similar in some respect on the basis of other similarities? Such arguments are probably inductive.

Remember, too, to look for words such as *probably* and *necessarily*, because they can indicate the type of argument.

If the argument bears some resemblance to a correct deductive or inductive argument, but has premisses that only appear to support the conclusion, the argument is fallacious. Being aware of different types of fallacies helps to avoid committing them and being deceived by them.

The most important new terms introduced in this chapter are defined in the following list.

Appeal to Force: A fallacious form of reasoning in which the threat of force is inappropriately put forth as evidence for a conclusion.

Appeal to Pity: A fallacious form of reasoning in which sympathy or pity for the circumstances of somebody is inappropriately put forth as evidence for a conclusion.

Deductive Argument: An argument constructed such that if all of the premisses are true, the conclusion cannot be false.

Factual Information: Information about what the world is like, in contrast to what is true merely by definition of the terms involved or true by the principles of mathematics.

Fallacy (*Fallacious argument*): An argument in which the premisses provide only very weak support, or no real support, for the conclusion.

Indirect Proof: A way of arguing in which one shows that a contradiction or an obviously false sentence follows deductively from the assumption that the claim to be proved is false. Because a deductive argument with a false conclusion must have at least one false premiss, we use this method to show that the assumption that the claim is false is itself false, or, in other words, that the claim is true.

Inductive Argument: An argument that is not deductive, and one in which if the premisses are all true, then *probably* the conclusion is true as well.

Sound Argument: A correct inductive or valid deductive argument in which all the premisses are true.

Valid Argument: A correct deductive argument, that is, an argument in which the premisses, if true, guarantee the truth of the conclusion.

Exercise Set 3.4

Reconstruct all of the arguments in the following passages. Write them in standard form, and then categorize them as inductive or deductive. Try to identify and supply any missing premisses. If you use any clues from the context of the argument to identify either the type of argument, or any missing premisses, or both, describe them.

1. Fluorescent light is good for houseplants. In an experiment in a commercial nursery, a group of houseplants was exposed to four hours of fluorescent light in addition to

normal daylight. These plants grew much more quickly than others that were not exposed to the additional lighting. They were also generally greener and healthier looking.

—Newspaper article, *Arizona Daily Star*

2. Of course, the human brain [which weighs about 1,500 grams] is not the largest in the animal kingdom. The elephant's brain weighs 2,500 grams (some five and a half pounds), and the brains of the biggest whales are twice that size.

—I. Asimov, *The Intelligent Man's Guide to the Biological Sciences*

3. If we ask precisely wherein consists the greatest good of all, which ought to be the aim of every system of legislation, we shall find that it is summed up in two principal objects, *liberty* and *equality*. Liberty, because any individual dependence is so much force denied to the body of the State; equality because liberty cannot subsist without it.

—J.J. Rousseau, *The Social Contract*

4. We are bound in duty to pay due respect, not only to what is truly the right of another, but to what, through ignorance or mistake, we believe to be his right. Thus, if my neighbor is possessed of a horse which he stole and to which he has no right, while I believe the horse to be really his and am ignorant of the theft, it is my duty to pay the same respect to this conceived right as if it were real.

—T. Reid, *Essays on the Active Power of Man*

5. From an account of Joseph Lister's search for an antiseptic chemical to prevent deaths that followed surgery:

At the end of 18 months, Lister had used the carbolic acid treatment on 13 cases of compound fracture, with results that could be tabulated as follows:

Death	2
Hospital gangrene	2
(amputation and recovery 1)	
(recovery without amputation 1)	
Recovery without complications	9

These were not enough cases to prove conclusively that carbolic acid was the weapon which Lister sought to fight hospital diseases, but they represented a mortality of only 15 percent as against the usual record of more than twice that figure.

—A. Young, *The Men Who Made Surgery*

6. The vandals mutilated five sacred statues, destroyed a sacred book, smeared black paint around, and scribbled obscenities and racial remarks on walls.

Temple leaders said the attack seemed to be planned. They noted that the vandals had to bring the paint with them.

—Report about the desecration of a Hindu temple in suburban Pennsylvania, from the *Pittsburgh Post-Gazette*

7. An *association* between two or more elements within a geological deposit in no way implies a systematic, behavioral, or dynamic relationship between the components. All that is implied is a roughly coincidental contextual relationship for the events of which the elements were derivatives. For instance, the finding of a whale bone and a tuna vertebrate in a geological deposit in no way implies that whales ate tuna or for that matter that tuna ate whales! Nevertheless, the depositional context of an aquatic environment may be indicated.

—L. Binford, *Bones*

8. I recommend that you close the sales tax loopholes which currently exempt cigarettes, alcoholic beverages sold in bars and restaurants, arcade games, cable television, confection products, paper and cleaning products, and non-prescription drugs—most of which are taxed, in fact, in a majority of our states today.

Surely we must question a system that taxes furniture while exempting cigarettes, or taxes the radio while exempting the arcade game, or taxes the prime rib in a restaurant while exempting the martini from the bar of that same restaurant.

—Pennsylvania Governor Richard Thornburgh's Budget Address,
Pittsburgh Post-Gazette

9. From a report of an excavation of a Mesolithic site in Ireland, inhabited approximately 9,000 years ago:

> At what times of year were the Mount Sandel huts occupied? Could the site have served as a year-round settlement? Our excavations have uncovered much evidence with seasonal connotations. For example, the salmon bones are evidence of summer occupation. Today the main salmon run up the Bann is in mid-summer: June, July, and August. In Mesolithic times there may also have been an earlier run, say in April or May. Although the lower water temperatures [at that time] make it unlikely that the salmon run would continue beyond the fall, eels do run downstream in the fall: September, October and November are the best months of the eel run. Hence the eel bones at the site are evidence of fall residence. So is the presence of hazelnuts, which are ready for picking by mid-fall, and of water-lily seeds, which are best collected in September.

—P. C. Woodman, "A Mesolithic Camp in Ireland,"
Scientific American 2 (1981):126

10. [Approximately 10 million people are living or will live in western Russia outside the 30-kilometer zone around Chernobyl during the next 70 years.] Outside the 30-kilometer zone, radiation exposure [from the nuclear accident at Chernobyl] was of course much lower, but because millions of people were affected, the anticipated number of excess cancers could be very large. As a rough estimate, the report calculates that exposure to relatively short-lived radionuclides from the Chernobyl accident will increase cancer mortality by about 0.05% in western Russia. [Thus there would be] some 5000 additional deaths over 70 years.

—*Science* 233 (1986):1031

11. "Is it possible that he was conscious all that time?" asked Peter Ivanovich. "Yes," she whispered. "To the last moment. He took leave of us a quarter of an hour before he

died, and asked us to take Voloyda away." The thought of the sufferings of this man he had known so intimately, first as a merry little boy, then as a school-mate, and later as a grown-up colleague, suddenly struck Peter Ivanovich with horror, despite an unpleasant consciousness of his own and this woman's dissimulation. He again saw that brow and that nose pressing down on the lip, and felt afraid for himself. "Three days of frightful suffering and then death! Why that might suddenly, at any time, happen to me," he thought, and for a moment felt terrified.

—L. Tolstoy, *The Death of Ivan Ilych*

12. Doctors in Texas have reported finding a virus in patients with multiple sclerosis, a discovery that could help explain the origin of the disease and possibly lead to a way to prevent it.

> "What's exciting is that the virus has been found at the time people have the disease," Dr. Melnick said. Melnick and his colleague, Edward Seidel, analyzed spinal fluid taken from 12 patients with nerve diseases and 27 others without such illnesses.
>
> The virus was found in four of the 12 patients with the diseases; it was not found in any of the patients without nerve ailments. The scientists bolstered their case by also finding antibodies to the virus in the blood serum of the four patients with the virus. That provides additional evidence that the virus was not a contaminant picked up accidentally in the laboratory.
>
> —Associated Press newspaper story

13. [E]verything would seem to be heading up for the beer business. Per capita consumption of the golden brew in the United States last year reached an all-time high, currently equaling about a six-pack a week for every American 18 and over. Beer sales for the past several years have been going up 4 percent to 5 percent annually; so far the rise this year is running around 2 percent—not bad for a recession year.

—*Time Magazine*

14. An attorney offers the following argument in a burglary case to prove the defendant's innocence:

> Assume that the defendant was burglarizing the store at 7:30 p.m., on Friday the 13th of October. This is the time that the burglar alarm sounded. No fewer than six of his co-workers can testify that he was at his job from 4 p.m. until midnight on that day. In order to break into the store, he would have had to have been in two places at the same time.

15. The question of nutrition is closely related to that of locality and climate. None of us can live [just] anywhere; and he who has great tasks to perform, which demand all his energy, has, in this respect, a very limited choice. The influence of climate upon the bodily functions, affecting their retardation or acceleration, is so great, that a blunder in the choice of locality or climate may not merely alienate a man from his duty, but may withhold it from him altogether, so that he never comes face to face with it. . . . Enumerate the places in which men of great intellect have been and are still found; where wit, subtlety, and malice are a part of happiness; where genius is almost necessarily at home: all of them have an unusually dry atmosphere. Paris, Provence, Florence, Jerusalem, Athens—these names prove this: that genius is dependent on dry

air, on clear skies—in other words, on rapid organic functions, on the possibility of continuously securing for one's self great and even enormous quantities of energy.

—F. Nietzsche, *Ecce Homo*

16. A layman seldom sets out the premises from which he is arguing, so it is generally impossible to tell whether some false conclusion is the result of thinking illogically about true premises, or the result of thinking logically about false premises. Or both!

—G. A. Miller, citing John Stuart Mill, "Is Scientific Thinking Different?" *Bulletin of The American Academy of Arts and Sciences,* February 1983.

17. An important element in the analyses used to justify the counterforce [nuclear weapons designed to destroy the nuclear weapons of the adversary] race is the idea that it might be possible to fight a nuclear counterforce war in a carefully controlled manner. However, because the means of command and control are inevitably vulnerable to nuclear destruction, it is extremely doubtful that a nuclear war could be limited and prevented from escalating into an all-out civilization-shattering exchange. Moreover, even if a nuclear exchange could be strictly limited to military targets, a strategically significant counterforce attack would probably cause tens of millions of civilian deaths.

—H. Feiveson and F. von Hippel, "The Nuclear Freeze—Pro and Con," *Physics Today* (1983):40

18. Paleolithic inhabitants who decorated the [Lascaux] cave were predominantly right-handed. Not only do the majority of the animals face right (an orientation generally preferred by right-hand draftsmen) but also the "fossilized" rope depicted . . . was obviously the work of a right-handed individual. Since the natural twisting motion involves the overhand rotation of the thumb away from the body, the twist in this case must have been imparted by the right hand.

—Letter from T. A. Reisner, *Scientific American* 4(1982):7

19. Although incest taboos do possess social functions, these cannot account for their origins, because it is impossible to believe that early men who instituted these rules could have known their possible social advantages.

—A. de W. Maalfjit, *Images of Man*

20. Yes, and if oxen and horses and lions had hands, and could paint with their hands, and provide works of art, as men do, horses would paint the forms of gods like horses, and oxen like oxen, and make their bodies in the image of their several kinds.

The Ethiopians make their gods black and mule-nosed; the Thracians say theirs have blue eyes and red hair.

—Xenophanes, *Fragments*

21. To be able to read the classics you have to know "from where" you are reading them, otherwise both the book and the reader will be lost in a timeless cloud. This, then, is the reason why the greatest "yield" from reading the classics will be obtained by someone who knows how to alternate them with the proper dose of current affairs.

—I. Calvino, trans. by P. Creagh, "Why Read the Classics?"

22. Workers should vote for a program that will see that they get their fair share of the products of industry. Whenever taxes go up, prices go up; whenever prices go up, profits go up; and whenever profits go up, the workers get less than their fair share of the products of industry. So workers should vote for lower taxes.

23. The last four presidents of the United States have supported equality of races and civil liberties. But we do not have equality of races, and the erosion of our civil liberties continues. Therefore, Congress or some other force must be preventing our presidents from bringing about the reforms they want.

24. If a man's destiny is caused by the star under which he is born, then all men born under that star should have the same fortune. But masters and slaves and kings and beggars [whose fortunes differ greatly] are born under the same star at the same time. Thus, astrology—which claims that a man's destiny is caused by the star under which he is born—is surely false.

—Pliny the Elder, *Natural History*

25. Skin hue is neither a necessary nor a sufficient condition for being classified as black in our culture. That looking black is not in our culture a necessary condition for being black can be seen from the phenomenon of passing. That it is not a sufficient condition can be seen from the book *Black Like Me,* by John Howard Griffin, where "looking black" is easily understood by the reader to be different from being black.

—R. A. Wasserstrom, "Racism, Sexism, and Preferential Treatment," in *UCLA Law Journal* 3(1977):581

26. The real justification (perhaps a cynical one) for progressive taxation is that the wealthier receive more benefits from government and, therefore ought to pay more. This may not be true in a strict accounting sense; the middle and upper classes don't use food stamps. But in this country, the essence of government is to preserve the social order. The well-off benefit from this far more than do the poor.

—R. Samuelson, "Economic Focus," *Pittsburgh Post-Gazette*

Chapter Four

A CLOSER LOOK AT INDUCTIVE ARGUMENTS

I. INTRODUCTION

In this chapter, we take a closer look at specific types of inductive arguments. Generally, the aim of any argument is to establish its conclusion. By definition, however, the conclusions of inductive arguments may be false even when all the premises are true. The premises of an inductive argument, however, should make it *probable* that the conclusion will be true. The very least we can expect is that an inductive argument will give us some measure of how likely we are to be correct if we draw a conclusion on the basis of the evidence presented.

Our study of inductive arguments is eased by classifying them according to *form*. The **form of an argument** refers to its structural features, without regard to its subject matter or content. Although you may not have thought about forms of argument before, the term *form* in the sense used here is not new to you. You have undoubtedly been concerned with structures in many real-life situations.

For example, most secondary schools require a civics course in which various forms of government are discussed. The United States has a democratic constitutional form of federal government composed of three main branches—executive, judiciary, and legislative. The powers and responsibilities of each of these branches are outlined in the Constitution.

The British form of government, in contrast, is a constitutional monarchy composed of a legislative branch (Parliament), a judiciary branch, and a crowned king or queen, who—except in cases of abdication—holds office for life. The head of government is the prime minister, but unlike the president of the United States, the prime minister is not the head of state. The powers and responsibilities of the various branches of the British government are also outlined in a constitution.

Forms of government other than constitutional democracies and constitutional monarchies exist. Libya, for example, has a dictator. Forms of government can be studied *abstractly*, without notice of the individuals who fill the positions that are determined by the form of government. When we study forms of government in this way, we learn something about their parts and how these parts are related to one another. Similarly, when we study forms of arguments, we learn something about their parts and how they relate to one another.

In the sections that follow, we identify several forms of inductive argument and consider standards for determining how well the premises in the various argument forms support the conclusions. The correctness of an inductive argument is not determined, however, only by its form. Inductive arguments are presented against a background of information that provides a source for unstated premises and other considerations that affect the ability of the premises to support the conclusion. Inductive arguments are open-ended in the sense that additional information can weaken or strengthen an existing argument. Thus, considerations of context are particularly important in the evaluation of inductive arguments, a point that is emphasized in the examples presented in this chapter.

II. STATISTICAL SYLLOGISMS

The word syllogism is derived from the Greek and literally means "a putting together of ideas." The use of the term in logic is related to this meaning. *Syllogisms* are arguments with two premisses, and a conclusion that "puts together" information presented in the premisses. The following argument is an example of a deductive form of syllogism.

All men are mortal.
Socrates is a man.

Socrates is mortal.

In an inductive form that closely resembles the deductive form of this syllogism, the general premiss is a statistical generalization, rather than a universal generalization. The form is therefore called a **statistical syllogism.** The following argument is an example of a statistical syllogism.

90 percent of freshmen at State University are residents of the state.
Elena is a freshman at State University.

Elena is a resident of the state.

We use arguments with the form of statistical syllogism when we argue that what is generally, but not universally, true (or false) is also true (or false) for a particular case. The statistical generalization in the premisses is not always stated numerically. *Almost all, most, very often, almost never,* and other terms can be used, as in the following example:

Hardly any freshmen had a philosophy course in high school.
Oscar is a freshman.

Oscar did not have a philosophy course in high school.

Inductive arguments are sometimes contrasted with deductive arguments as follows: In deduction, one goes from general premisses to a particular conclusion, whereas in induction, one goes from the particular to the general. Statistical syllogisms are exceptions to this often-offered (but incorrect) characterization of inductive arguments. As you can see, this form of inductive argument proceeds from a generalization in the premiss to a claim about a particular individual in the conclusion. Because arguments of this form may have false conclusions even though their premisses are all true, they cannot be deductive. However, as with other inductive forms of argument, statistical syllogisms vary in strength.

Reasoning in the form of a statistical syllogism is common in everyday life and guides many of our decisions and beliefs. We do not plan outdoor picnics in Chicago in January because the weather usually won't be favorable. If we are fortunate enough to travel in southern France, we expect to find good food at country inns because that's usually the case. A summons for an audit of our tax return is dreaded because audits of tax returns are normally costly and unpleasant.

1. Form of Statistical Syllogisms

With the preceding examples in mind, we are ready to look at the abstract form of statistical syllogisms:

X percent of all F's are G's.
a is an F.
_____

a is a G.

In this form of argument, F and G represent classes of individuals or properties that determine those classes. The lower-case letter a represents an individual person, place, or thing. The class denoted by F is called the **reference class,** that is, the class that the individual mentioned in the second premiss belongs to, or is *referred to.* The class denoted by G is called the **attribute class,** that is, the class that has the property *attributed to* the individual in the conclusion. In the preceding argument about the individual Oscar, the reference class is *freshman* and the attribute class is *persons who have had a philosophy class in high school.*

2. Standards for the Strength of Statistical Syllogisms

The most obvious standard for judging the strength of a statistical syllogism is the closeness to 100 percent (or 0 percent in the negative case) of the statistical premiss. If the premiss in the preceding sample argument had stated that 99 percent, instead of 90 percent, of the freshmen at State University were state residents, a stronger case would be made for the conclusion that "Elena is a state resident." Similarly, the argument would have been weaker if only 85 percent, rather than 90 percent, of all the freshmen were state residents. If only 51 percent of all freshmen were state residents, the argument would be so weak that we would call it fallacious. Even when the statistical premiss is not expressed numerically, this criterion applies. For example, "Almost all F's are G's" supports the conclusion that a, who is an F, is also a G more strongly than "A sizable majority of F's are G's."

A second criterion of strength of statistical syllogisms is whether all available relevant evidence has been considered in selecting the *reference class.* This requirement, which is called the **rule of total evidence,** is designed to address problems that arise as a result of individuals belonging to an indefinite number of classes. Elena, for example, belongs not only to the class of freshmen, but also to the class of women students, and many other classes as well. Assume that we have the following information about Elena:

Besides being a freshman at State, she has brown hair, she is 18 years old, a supporter of equal rights for women, a part-time office worker, and a member of the Foreign Students' Club.

Each of these properties of Elena marks a class to which she belongs. In constructing an argument with the conclusion "Elena is a state resident," we must take into account *every* class that Elena belongs to that might affect the probability that she is a state resident. Suppose, for example, we already know that only 2 percent of the members of the Foreign Students' Club are state residents. If we assign Elena to this reference class, ignoring all the other information, we can construct the following argument with true premisses:

2 percent of all members of the Foreign Students' Club are state residents.
Elena is a member of the Foreign Students' Club.

Elena is *NOT* a state resident

Both this argument and the original argument have true premisses, and their statistical premisses are very close to 100 percent and 0 percent. So, if we were to use only the standard that requires a strong statistical generalization, both arguments would appear to be strong. Yet their conclusions cannot both be true because they contradict one another. The conclusion of the first argument says that she is a state resident; the conclusion of the second that she is not. Following the rule of total evidence can help us avoid this unfortunate situation. The rule requires us to assign Elena to a reference class of freshmen at State who are members of the Foreign Student Club and who are also members of *any other classes relevant to state residency* to which she belongs (and for which information is available).

Background knowledge plays an all-important role in helping us to decide which classes are relevant. On the basis of common background information, for example, we know that her hair color and age are irrelevant. (Her age would be relevant, however, if she were much older than the average college freshman.) Working in an office *might* be relevant, because some residence restrictions apply to student eligibility for such jobs. If we do not know or cannot find out about that, however, the information is not available and cannot figure into our construction of the proper reference class. Suppose that the only classes for which information relevant to state residency is available are the class of freshmen and the class of Foreign Students' Club members. A check of school records for past years shows us that generally only 5 percent of freshmen who are state residents join the Foreign Students' Club. We are now in a position to construct the appropriate statistical syllogism that embodies all available relevant evidence:

5 percent of all freshmen at State University who are members of the Foreign Students' Club are state residents.
Elena is a freshman member of the Foreign Students' Club.

Elena is *NOT* a state resident.

In many statistical syllogisms, the statistical premiss is not stated when it is assumed to be part of our common background knowledge. For example, the argument

> The student who sits next to me in logic class doesn't have a home telephone, for he isn't listed in the telephone directory.

could be reconstructed as a statistical syllogism with the implicit premiss, "Almost all phone owners are listed in the telephone directory." When we are concerned with evaluating such arguments, however, we should try to state any implicit premisses. Sometimes when implicit premisses are exposed, we find that they are questionable or fail to represent all available relevant evidence. When the implicit premiss in this argument is exposed, we realize that the student could belong to a class of persons who usually do not have their home phone numbers listed under their own names (for example, the class of persons who have changed residences recently or who live with a group of others). If so, then the argument is weak because the reference class in the implicit premiss violates the requirement of total evidence.

Exercise Set 4.1

Part One. Each of the following arguments is or can be reconstructed as a statistical syllogism. (i) Identify the reference class and the attribute class and (ii) assess the strength of the argument, using the criteria discussed in this section.

1. About 95 percent of all professional hair dyes and a considerable portion of home dyes now contain paraphenylenediamine or related chemicals (also called peroxide dyes). My hair was dyed at the hairdresser's. Therefore, peroxide dye was used on my hair.

2. That cat will probably never learn to use a litter box because she was separated from her mother at only two weeks of age and was not "mothered" by another cat.

3. Of all the students who registered this term, 75 percent favor the university's requiring students to pay an activity fee to support the projects of the student government association. Since Ellen is registered this term, she undoubtedly is in favor of the fee.

4. Very few people dislike chocolate, so Jill will be pleased with the chocolate dessert you made.

5. Since most German shepherds are easy to train, your German shepherd puppy should do well in dog-training school.

6. Stocks typically outperform bonds in the first recovery year after a recession. Since this is such a year, stocks should outperform bonds.

7. Only about 3 percent of cigarette smokers actually die from lung cancer, so my smoking won't result in death from lung cancer.

Part Two. Each of the following passages gives advice that is based on a statistical syllogism. In each case, reconstruct the argument in standard form and explicitly state the statistical premiss, the premiss that refers to a particular individual, and the conclusion.

1. Always remember that the odds in this hobby are heavily against the collector. He is gambling the price of a mess of mushrooms against the doctor and hospital bills. With such odds in mind it is up to the collector to be critical of what he collects.

—A. H. Smith, *The Mushroom Hunter's Field Guide*

2. Dear Dr. Molnar: I am 56 and considering an operation. Would you advise against it? I've had a loss of hearing since about age 12. On a recent checkup my doctor said two bones have grown together in the middle ear. He thinks there is an 85 percent chance of improvement to "very good"; 10 percent chance of no improvement; 5 percent chance of further damage.

Answer: Why should I advise against the operation? Only one chance in 20 of being worse off; 17 chances in 20 of being better off. There are few if any operations in which 100 percent success can be guaranteed. If I were the patient in such a case, I'd take the 17 to 1 odds.

—"Doctor Molnar," syndicated newspaper column

3. At a Democratic committee meeting the incumbent prosecuting attorney loses his party's endorsement. He considers running as an Independent, but his advisers tell him not to because hardly any Independents could receive enough votes to win an election in that city.

4. Take your umbrella when you go out today because there is a 70 percent chance of rain in your area.

5. More than two-thirds of the students who enter this college earn their degrees. So don't bother studying for your finals tonight; come to the party with us.

3. The Fallacy of Incomplete Evidence

When the reference class (the class denoted by F in "X percent of F's are G's") in a statistical syllogisms is not based on all available relevant evidence, the argument is fallacious. What we mean by relevant evidence is any evidence that might influence the probability that the individual (a) has the property attributed to it in the conclusion (G). Although we can define *relevant* in this context, we need background knowledge to determine what evidence is relevant.

It is also difficult to say in a general way what *available* means in this context. How much research is required to be sure that we have accounted for all available relevant evidence? We are seldom in a position to spend years of our lives—or even hours—acquiring evidence that is "available" in the sense that it is part of the storehouse of human knowledge. Often, we must make judgments and take actions (such as agreeing to an operation) in the absence of evidence that may be "available" but that we cannot afford to obtain. The rule of total evidence is not intended to place unrealistic restrictions on reasoning. It only demands a reasonable effort to find appropriate reference classes. The rule of total evidence says that we must not ignore—through carelessness, prejudice, or laziness—evidence that is within our reach, and we must not suppress evidence that is known to be relevant. Consider the following example of a fallacy in the form of a statistical syllogism

90 percent of Harvard's medical-school faculty are men.
Dr. Shirley Jones is a Harvard medical-school faculty member.

Dr. Shirley Jones is a man.

This argument appears to be a strong one only if we ignore the well-known fact that *Shirley* is a name that is rarely given to males in the northern part of the United States. If we accept the argument as it stands, we will be more likely to accept a false conclusion than a true one, for the probability that a faculty member named Shirley is male is very low. Even though we do not have exact figures to assign a probability to the reference class of Harvard medical-school faculty members named Shirley, we can see that this additional evidence is relevant and that it undermines the original argument.

The argument that some celebrity has no phone because she is not listed in the phone directory ignores the information that many celebrities have unlisted numbers. Similarly, it would be a violation of the requirement of total evidence to infer that your bus for work, which is normally on time, will be on time when the city streets are covered with ice.

In statistical syllogisms, the rule of total evidence is designed to ensure that we select an appropriate reference class. The rule of total evidence more broadly understood applies to all other forms of inductive argument as well. To construct good inductive arguments, we must take account of any available relevant information that could affect the truth of the conclusion of the argument. The rules of critical thinking do not permit us to construct arguments in which we selectively choose evidence that supports our conclusions while we ignore available evidence that would undermine them.

Exercise Set 4.2

Each of the following arguments commits the fallacy of incomplete evidence. In each case, discuss the relevant information that is ignored.

1. Most Russians don't speak English, so the newly appointed Russian ambassador to the United Nations probably doesn't speak any English.

2. Most movie actors aren't politicians, so Ronald Reagan, a former movie actor, is not a politician.

3. Most Americans earn less than $100,000 a year, so the president of General Motors earns less than $100,000 a year.

4. Only about 2 percent of college football players ever play professional ball after college, so the Heisman trophy winner probably won't play pro ball after he is out of college.

5. Most American women in their fifties do not exercise. Since Jane Fonda, who has produced a number of exercise videos and books, is now in her fifties, she probably does not exercise.

4. Special Types of Statistical Syllogism

A number of special uses of statistical syllogism are so common that they, and the fallacies that resemble them, have standard names.

i. Arguments from Authority

We all rely on the advice and counsel of those who know more than we do. Sometimes when we present arguments, we appeal to what experts have said on the matter instead of presenting direct evidence to support the claims that we make. Critical thinking allows this, for it would be difficult and wasteful to always reiterate what others have established. Although in some circumstances appeals to authority are fallacious, in others an argument from authority can be construed as a strong statistical syllogism. The principle that guides the difference between correct and incorrect uses of authority is based both on the nature of the authority's expertise and on the nature of subject matter.

It is reasonable to take the word of an authority if:

(i) the authority is an expert on the matter under consideration, and

(ii) there is agreement among experts in the area of knowledge under consideration.

Authorities achieve their status through training, talent, and experience. These qualities enable them to understand and evaluate evidence in areas that are not easily accessible to others. Condition (i) is designed to rule out taking the word of an expert in one field about matters outside the authority's area of expertise. This happens more frequently than one might think. Expertise in physics, chemistry, or another one of the physical sciences does not make a person an authority on social matters or ethics. Expertise in sports or the arts does not make a person an authority on world peace, urban renewal, or the various commercial products athletes and actors are often called upon to endorse.

Condition (ii) recognizes that some areas of knowledge are sufficiently controversial that persons with comparable training, experience, and all other credentials of a genuine authority disagree with one another. Appeals to authority in such a circumstance are feeble because different "authorities" give conflicting opinions on the matter. Although economists, for example, agree in some areas of their discipline, expert economists may hold conflicting views about ways to stimulate the economy, defeat inflation, increase employment, and other such matters. In psychiatry, also, qualified doctors disagree. Thus in criminal trials, when both prosecutor and defense attorney call expert witnesses to support their opposing positions, the prosecutor's expert psychiatrist might pronounce the defendant sane at the time of the crime, while the defendant's expert psychiatrist will testify to the defendant's insanity.

When the two conditions for being an authority on a given subject are fulfilled, however, we can say that most of what the authority has to say about the subject matter in which she or he is an authority is correct. In such a case, the argument from authority is a statistical syllogism of the following form:

Most of what authority *a* has to say on subject matter *S* is correct.
a says *p* about *S*.

p is correct.

The first premiss is a statistical generalization; the second premiss is a statement about a particular assertion (a member of the reference class of assertions in the authority's field of expertise); and the conclusion attributes the property of being correct to that assertion.

Arguments from authority are rarely presented in this strict form. Usually the authority is merely cited or quoted in support of some conclusion. For example, a point in the theory of relativity might be argued by quoting Einstein's view on the matter; a claim concerning the best way to bake a soufflé might cite Julia Child. Sometimes, a group of authorities is cited: "All leading physical scientists agree that the earth is more than a million years old." Regardless of the way arguments from authority are stated, they are acceptable only when the conditions (i) and (ii) are fulfilled.

Because arguments from authority are inductive, the conclusion of an argument from authority can be false even when the premisses are true and the conditions for authority are satisfied. In a correct argument from authority with true premisses, however, probably the conclusion will be true. Nevertheless, in using arguments from authority, it is wise to remember that history, including the history of science, offers many examples of expert authorities who were mistaken in their beliefs and were proved wrong in the light of new evidence. New evidence must be assimilated (often a slow process) before experts in the field recognize its significance and change their opinions. Despite these cautions, arguments from authority have an important place in both scientific and everyday reasoning.

Arguments that resemble correct arguments from authority but that cite an alleged authority who lacks expertise in the area of concern or that ignore disagreements among experts are fallacious. Such arguments can deceive us in several ways.

First, when someone is a genuine expert in a particular field of knowledge or has achieved success in a difficult and highly competitive enterprise, that person is properly entitled to prestige and recognition for those accomplishments. Such people are often asked to express their views on a wide variety of issues, many of which are completely outside their field of expertise. Famous physicists are asked their opinions on moral questions; a football hero testifies to the virtues of one brand of panty hose. Their statements cannot carry the weight of a legitimate appeal to authority, for they are speaking about subjects beyond their area of expertise. We must be careful not to accept arguments that rely on the glamour or prestige of an authority in one field to support the truth of claims in another, unrelated area of knowledge.

Second, some persons set themselves up as authorities—or their followers set them up—even though they lack the expertise of a genuine authority. Authoritative knowledge of modern science, for example, requires years of training and study under the supervision of experts. Yet, some people claim to have achieved such knowledge through self-study of obscure texts, visions, inspirations, revelations, or other questionable means. They claim to have found cures for diseases that have eluded standard medical research or they claim to be able to explain major cosmic events in ways that defy the truth of well-accepted scientific theories. These people, called "cranks" by all but their followers, are not reliable authorities in the subject areas in which they profess expertise. We should not accept arguments that appeal to such "authorities," and must be especially careful to scrutinize them carefully when their conclusions—such as a new cure for a hitherto incurable disease—are ones we wish were true.

Finally, in many branches of knowledge, widespread disagreement obtains among those who have all the right academic and professional credentials. Economics and psychiatry, already mentioned, are merely two examples. It is probably no exaggeration to say that in every discipline in which scholars are actively engaged, there are some areas in which the experts disagree. The U.S. Civil War, for example, has been extensively studied and analyzed by historians, most of whom hold similar beliefs about many aspects of this conflict. To settle a noncontroversial point, an appeal to a distinguished historian of that period would suffice. Nevertheless, different schools of U.S. history dispute the precise role of slavery as a causal factor in the War between the States, and so appeals to authority on that topic are weak. Scientists avidly debate whether birds are descendants of dinosaurs, as many paleontologists believe, or whether, as some ornithologists hold, the two developed in parallel evolutionary paths. The *evidence* presented by the experts can be considered and evaluated on its own merits, by those qualified to judge. When such evidence is considered and evaluated, however, the form of argument is not that of an argument from authority but some other type.

In determining whether an argument from authority is fallacious, background knowledge must be called upon to judge both whether an alleged authority is genuine and whether the area of knowledge is one in which experts disagree.

Exercise Set 4.3

1. Creation scientists, who claim that scientific evidence supports the biblical account of creation more strongly than it supports evolutionary biology argue for their view by listing the many supporters of creationism who hold Ph. D. degrees in various branches of science, from earth science, to chemistry, to

nutrition—but almost none in biology. Critics of creation science say that the creationists are using a fallacious argument from authority. On what grounds do they make this claim?

2. Many nuclear scientists argue that we in the United States should be willing to live near nuclear power plants because U.S. plants are constructed on different principles from the one that exploded at Chernobyl, and that many safety features of U.S. plants make the probability of such a nuclear disaster very small. Critics of nuclear power do not dispute the nuclear scientists' estimates of the probability of nuclear accidents, but say that the people who must live with the risk are the ones to say what risk they will tolerate. Thus we can say while that the critics are willing to accept the argument from authority for the amount of nuclear risk, they not willing to accept the argument from authority for the *acceptance of nuclear power risk.* Which of our two conditions does the second argument violate?

ii. Arguments against the Person (*Argumentum Ad Hominem*)

Arguments against the person (also known by the Latin name *argumentum ad hominem*) are the inverse of arguments from authority. These arguments conclude that a statement is *false* because it is made by a particular person or group. Such arguments are legitimate only with reason to believe that most of the claims made by the individual or group concerning a particular aspect of that subject matter are false. Arguments against the person are often made when lawyers want to attack the credibility of witnesses for the opposition. If a lawyer can show that a witness has committed perjury when questioned about the subject at issue, and can also show that a lie would benefit the witness, the argument may be strong. Like arguments from authority, correct arguments against the person can be construed as statistical syllogisms:

Most of what individual *a* says about a particular subject matter *S* is false.
a says *p* about *S*.

p is false.

Although the forms of argument from authority and argument against the person are similar, we are not often in a position to claim that most of what an individual says about a subject is false. Whereas many genuine authorities exist, few individuals almost always speak falsely about a subject. Truth-telling, rather than lying, is the normal mode of communication. Indeed, communication would soon break down if it were not so. Moreover, most people do not make pronouncements about subjects on which they are more often wrong than right. For these reasons, special care should be exercised when arguments against the person are encountered.

With this warning, we can mention some circumstances (other than the perjury example) in which legitimate arguments against the person can occur. One concerns the pronouncements of scientific cranks whose views conflict with the collected wisdom of scientists. In the area of their weird theories, cranks are more apt to be wrong than right. Similarly, the exaggerated claims made by high-pressure salespersons for their products are probably more often false than true, especially when the products are made by companies that have bad records with the local chamber of commerce. The performance records of some stockbrokers are so poor that their clients would be advised to hold off when those brokers say "Buy."

Arguments that a claim is false on the grounds that it was made by a particular individual or group are fallacious *unless* most claims made by the individual or group on that subject are false. This statistical premiss, as we have seen, is rarely true. Nevertheless the fallacy is fairly common. We may commit this fallacy, or be taken in by it, for several reasons. We may dislike the person who is making the claim, or we may disapprove of the person's looks, clothing, views, habits, religion, ethnic origin, or some other personal characteristic or association. Obviously, such prejudices should not be allowed to intrude on our critical judgments of the evidence for truth or falsity of claims.

A second reason why we are sometimes misled by fallacious arguments against the person is our desire to deny the claim made by the person. When we disagree with a claim someone makes, we may, in the absence of any counterevidence, try to discredit it by attacking the person's character or qualifications, however irrelevant they may be to the issue. An old joke advises lawyers who have no case to "abuse the person." In a similarly sophistical (intentionally misleading, but clever) bit of reasoning, Samuel Johnson defends the fallacious use of argument against the person in such cases:

> "When there is a controversy concerning a passage in a classic, or concerning a question in antiquities, or some such subject, one may treat an antagonist with politeness and respect. But where the controversy is concerning the government or religion of my country, it is of such vast importance to have the better, that the *person* of the opponent is not to be spared. If a man firmly believes that religion is a great treasure, he will consider a writer who endeavors to deprive mankind of it as a robber; he will look on him as odious even though the infidel may think himself in the right. . . ."
>
> Dr. Johnson said that when a man voluntarily engages in an important controversy, he is to do all he can to lessen his antagonist, because authority from personal respect has much weight and often more than reasonings.
>
> "If," said he, "my antagonist writes bad language, though that may not be essential to the question, I will attack him for his bad language."
>
> —J. Boswell, *The Ominous Years*

Johnson is probably correct in saying that people are more often moved by their respect (or lack of respect) for a person than by the strength of argument. It is an unfortunate fact that people usually pay less attention to reasons than to the person who provides them. Nevertheless, as critical thinkers, we do not want to be deceived by such ploys.

When an argument against the person (or *ad hominem* argument) attacks the character of an individual, the argument is called an "abusive *ad hominem*." When argument attacks not the person *per se*, but some circumstances of the person, such as religion, nationality, or membership in a political party, the argument is called a "circumstantial *ad hominem*."

Another variant of *ad hominem* arguments is called "*tu quoque*," which can be translated "you, too." This occurs when someone counters an attack on a position by accusing the person who offers it of being in a position similar to that being criticized. Example: "You can't call me slow or lazy since you haven't finished any of the work you were assigned to do either." These arguments are almost always fallacious.

Regrettably, fallacies of all these types occurred in a recent interchange among distinguished scientists. The focus of the discussion was the contention by Dr. Luis W. Alvarez, a Nobel Prize winner in physics for work on nuclear particles, and his son, Dr. Walter Alvarez, a geologist, that the impact of a large comet 65 million years ago was responsible for the extinction of the dinosaurs. The main evidence for the comet's impact is a layer of metallic iridium found in sedimentary rock all over the world. The evidence that this impact caused the extinction of dinosaurs is far from conclusive, and most paleontologists (scientists who specialize in fossil evidence of extinct life forms) reject the Alvarezes' theory that a single catastrophe caused the extinction. The paleontologists say that the fossils show that the extinction took place over a very long period. This controversial situation has all of the features that promote the use of fallacious arguments from authority and fallacious arguments against the person: a distinguished expert in one field (L. Alvarez, a nuclear physicist) speaking in an area (paleontology) outside his field of expertise and disagreement even among expert paleontologists about the nature of fossil evidence.

In the quoted portions of this report from *The New York Times* fallacies are identified in square brackets:

> Dr. Luis Alvarez also criticizes three earth-sciences professors at Dartmouth College, Charles B. Officer, and his colleague Charles L. Drake as well as Robert Jastrow, who all reject the cometary impact hypothesis. "It is now clear," Dr. Jastrow said in an interview," that a catastrophe of extraterrestrial origin had no discernible impact on the history of life as measured over a period of millions of years."
>
> Dr. Alvarez responded: "There isn't any debate. There's not a single member of the National Academy of Sciences who shares Jastrow's point of view." (Dr. Alvarez is himself a member of the Academy.) [Fallacious appeal to authority: members of the academy are scientists distinguished in many different fields, but do not constitute a legitimate authority in paleontology.]
>
> He added: "Jastrow, of course, has gotten into the defense of Star Wars, which for me personally indicates he's not a very good scientist. In my opinion, Star Wars doesn't stand a chance." [Circumstantial *ad hominem*; Jastrow's conclusion about extinction is rejected because Jastrow has aligned himself with supporters of the government's Strategic Defense Initiative.]
>
> In rejoinder, Dr. Jastrow noted that Dr. Alvarez had personally flown on the nuclear raid that destroyed Hiroshima, and that in 1954, Dr. Alvarez had been one of only five physicists willing to appear before the Atomic

Energy Commission to denounce J. Robert Oppenheimer as a security risk. . . . [*Tu quoque*; in response to Alvarez's accusation that Jastrow is aligned with questionable government science policy, Jastrow points out Alvarez's own connection with other questionable government science-related activities.]

In his public barbs at Dr. Officer, Dr. Alvarez asserted that the Dartmouth geologist was laughed to scorn at a 1985 meeting of the American Geophysical Union and that the incident had shorn Dr. Officer of scientific credibility [Abusive *ad hominem*]. . . . Dr. Officer responded: "This is a misstatement. There was no outburst of laughter following Walter's brief comment, and no direct or implied derision of me as a scientist by the audience. . . ."

Closer to home, Dr. Alvarez has harsh words for some of his colleagues at Berkeley. Among them is Dr. William A. Clemens, a paleontologist who recently reported in *Science* that he had found abundant dinosaur fossils along Alaska's North Slope. The dinosaurs would not have faced the danger of freezing since temperatures were much milder then, but at such high latitudes, total darkness must have persisted for several months each winter, thereby halting the growth of plants and curtailing food supplies.

That the dinosaurs nevertheless survived such conditions, Dr. Clemens contends, undermines the comet theory because a cometary impact would not have blocked sunlight for nearly as long as the polar winter.

Dr. Alvarez responds by saying that he considers Dr. Clemens inept at interpreting sedimentary rock strata and that his criticisms can be dismissed on grounds of general incompetence [abusive *ad hominem*], a charge Dr. Clemens rejects.

—*The New York Times*

iii. Arguments from Consensus

In an **argument from consensus** (in Latin, *ad populem*) some assertion is held to be correct, or incorrect, on the grounds that most people believe, or reject, the assertion. An automobile advertisement argues that one brand of car is best by stating "50 million Americans can't be wrong!" Advertisers, politicians, and others try to persuade people to act by stating that "everyone" does it. Such arguments, when they are correct, can be cast in the form of a statistical syllogism:

When most people agree on a claim about a subject matter S, the claim is true.
p is a claim about S that most people agree on.

p is true.

The similarity between this argument form and that of the argument from authority is easy to see. On which subject matters, we need to ask, is consensus (which means "agreement, especially in opinion") or general opinion an authority? Background knowledge is essential to know whether the subject matter is understood by enough people in the group being polled for an argument from consensus to work. For example, most residents of New York who have been to high school there know that Albany is the state capital. If a large group of New York high school graduates were asked about the state capital, the consensus would probably be the correct answer. Consensus of the same group on the capital of New Mexico or of Slovenia (assuming that some consensus would emerge—"no opinion" rather than a systematic error in naming the capital city would probably be the result of attempting to find a consensus) would not be so reliable. Moreover, even in the cases in which consensus is a reliable authority, running an opinion poll may not be the most efficient way to argue for a claim. Such factual matters as the location of capitals are relatively easy to settle by checking reference books or asking a single reliable authority.

When—for whatever reason—consensus of a group is an unreliable authority on the subject matter, an appeal to consensus is fallacious. Fallacious appeals to consensus often depend on prejudice as the source of the second premiss: "Everybody knows those people are cannibals [or witches, thieves, infidels, and so forth]."

Claims about the most popular brand of beer or the current favorite sport of young people are commonly supported by appeals to consensus. In these cases, however, the arguments are deductive, because they are grounded in a definition (*popular* means "what is liked by the people or by most people"), rather than inductive. Such an argument could fail to have a true conclusion only if it had a false premiss—such as a claim for consensus that did not hold. In contrast, to argue on the basis of popular appeal that a given product is most nutritious, most healthful, or best in some other feature is fallacious if the consensus is merely a popularity contest. Majority opinion can deductively support a claim about what is most popular, but may not even provide weak inductive support for many other claims.

Majority opinion *by definition* validates the truth of some claims. One example is the recent judicial ruling that a movie is pornographic if it violates local standards of decency (that is, if most people in that community would consider it pornographic). Under these circumstances, the following argument would be correct:

A movie is legally pornographic if most people consider it pornographic.
Most people consider movie *M* pornographic.

Movie *M* is legally pornographic.

Careful examination of this argument reveals that it does not have the same form as the argument from consensus. The first premiss is not a statistical premiss; instead the first premiss states something that is true as a result of a definition (in this case, the legal definition of *pornographic*). The second premiss, although a statistical generalization, states that the circumstances for the application of the definition have been fulfilled for the movie in question; the conclusion states that the movie belongs to the class of pornography thus defined. If the premisses of this argument are true, then, necessarily, the conclusion is true. The argument is not inductive, but deductive. The argument is correct, but is not an argument from consensus.

If we turn our attention to the statistical *premiss* in such an argument and ask how it is supported, then we may appeal to another sort of inductive argument, called **inductive generalization**, discussed in Section IV.

5. Missing Premisses in Statistical Syllogisms

Once the form of an argument is identified, it is easier to identify any missing premisses that are required to complete the argument. We have already noted that the statistical premiss in a statistical syllogism is frequently suppressed, particularly when it represents a claim that is widely known. In such cases we appeal to general background information as well as to what is stated in the argument to construct a plausible and relevant statistical generalization. As critical thinkers, we construct and evaluate arguments because we want to arrive at new true beliefs on the basis of those we already have. Thus, we are trying to minimize ignorance and maximize knowledge. In arguments from authority, arguments against the person, and arguments from consensus, the statistical premiss is almost always suppressed. However, we need to supply this premiss to evaluate those arguments because their correctness depends on whether most of what an authority says is right, or whether most of what a person says about a subject is false, or whether majority opinion on a subject is reliable. Once the suppressed premiss is stated, we can call upon background knowledge to assess its truth. The acceptance of fallacious arguments can often be prevented merely by exposing their suppressed premisses.

6. An Incorrect Form of Inductive Argument

As shown at the beginning of this chapter, the statistical syllogism resembles a correct form of deductive argument. The inductive form differs from the deductive in substituting "X percent" or some nonquantitative expression such as *most* for *all*.

Deductive Form:	**Inductive Form:**
All *F*'s are *G*'s	*X* percent of *F*'s are *G*'s
a is an *F*	*a* is an *F*
a is a *G*	*a* is a *G*

The (valid) deductive form that the statistical syllogism resembles is called the **quasi-syllogism.** To say a deductive form is valid means that if an argument has this form it cannot have all true premisses and a false conclusion. The structural features alone guarantee that any argument with that structure (form) is valid.

Unlike a valid deductive form, a correct inductive form is never sufficient to guarantee—or even make probable—that the conclusion of arguments in this form will be true if their premisses are true. Arguments in the inductive form of statistical syllogism may have true premisses and a false conclusion. However, if background knowledge assures us that the reference class is correctly chosen and that the percentage in the statistical premiss is appropriately high (or low in the negative case), we can say that in arguments with the form of statistical syllogism, *probably* the conclusion is true if the premisses are true. Given these qualifications, the statistical syllogism is a correct inductive form of argument.

The following argument is an example of another correct deductive form called a **categorical syllogism**:

All humans are mammals.
All mammals are animals.

All humans are animals.

Letting upper-case letters represent class terms, we can exhibit the form of this argument as follows:

All F's are G's
All G's are H's

All F's are H's

When we replace *all* with *most* in the syllogistic form just shown, the following form results:

Most F's are G's
Most G's are H's

Most F's are H's

This form is not, however, inductively correct. Even when we are careful about taking account of all available relevant evidence, this form of argument is not likely in general to lead us from true premisses to true conclusions. Consider the following argument:

Most physicists are men.
Most men are non-physicists.

Most physicists are non-physicists.

Despite its true premisses, the conclusion of this argument is a self-contradiction. This incorrect form exemplifies the danger of supposing that all correct inductive argument forms are just slightly weakened versions of deductive forms.

Exercise Set 4.4

Part One. Reconstruct each of the following arguments. Identify those that are instances of a correct inductive form and those that are fallacious. If the background knowledge required to evaluate the argument is missing, discuss what would be needed.

1. Charles Colson, a former White House aide and a convicted perjurer, charged that the CIA knew about the Watergate break-in in advance. Referring to Colson's charge, William Colby, former CIA director, said, "His lack of credibility should cause the charge to fall of its own weight. (Reconstruct Colby's argument.)

2. My favorite fashion model says that Cover Girl cosmetics are safest for delicate skins. Therefore Cover Girl is the safest brand for sensitive skin.

3. Many prisoners have complained that conditions in the county jail are unsanitary. However, these persons are all criminals, so we do not need to believe what they say about the jail.

4. Both the American Medical Association and the American Dental Association have formally endorsed fluoridation of drinking water. Therefore, fluoridation promotes dental welfare and is not generally harmful to people's health.

5. Most people believe that smoking marijuana is dangerous to one's health. Therefore, smoking marijuana is dangerous to one's health.

6. In recent years, all economic advisers to both Democratic and Republican presidents have agreed that the best way to encourage U. S. residents to conserve oil would be to impose a tariff of at least three dollars a barrel on imported oil. Therefore, such a tariff would be the best conservation measure.

7. Congresswoman Sanders, a former professor of political science, has argued that failure to restructure our foreign policy in the Mideast will result in an outbreak of war. She is a woman, however, and we all know that feminine logic is not reliable when it comes to affairs of state.

8. You are in no position to challenge my argument that my school's team will defeat yours in the big match, for you are just as biased in favor of your school as I am in favor of mine.

9. The following argument supports the use of folk medicines:

> I know they have been well reported of and many wise persons have tried remedies providentially discovered by those who are not regular physicians, and have found a blessing in the use of them. I may mention the eminent Mr. Wesley [the founder of Methodism], who, though I hold not altogether with his Arminian doctrine, nor with the usages of his institution, was nevertheless a man of God.
>
> —George Eliot, *Felix Holt*

10. Now you are better equipped to analyze this argument that appeared in Chapter 1:

After so much lying, even for purposes North considers patriotic, his protestations that he now only wants to tell the truth aren't worth much. Why should he be considered believable, even under oath, when he testified under oath that he had so often considered other values more important than truth?

—Tom Wicker, *The New York Times*

Part Two. In this passage the author attempts to defend Creationism against the charge that it is unscientific. Identify the type of *Argumentum ad Hominem* committed here.

Thus, for a theory to qualify as a scientific theory, it must be supported by events, processes or properties which can be observed, and the theory must be useful in predicting the outcome of future natural phenomena or laboratory experiments. An additional limitation usually imposed is that the theory must be capable of falsification. That is, it must be possible to conceive some experiment, the failure of which would disprove the theory.

It is on the basis of such criteria that most evolutionists insist that creation be refused consideration as a possible explanation for origins. Creation has not been witnessed by human observers, it cannot be tested experimentally, and as a theory it is nonfalsifiable.

The general theory of evolution also fails to meet all three of these criteria, however.

—D. Gish, *Evolution? The Fossils Say No!*

Part Three. Although we normally go to a dictionary to check the standard pronunciation of some unfamiliar or disputed word, linguists who construct dictionaries formulate the dictionary entry after listening to determine how most people pronounce the word. Thus, the way most people pronounce the word constitutes the standard for how it should be pronounced. Shifts in the standard pronunciation of many words account in part for the need to revise dictionaries from time to time.

With the preceding as background information, consider whether the argument with the premiss that most English speakers pronounce the word *otiose* as ó-shi-oś, inductively supports the claim that this is the correct pronunciation. (In other words, is this an argument from consensus?) Is the premiss itself supported by inductive or deductive reasoning?

Part Four. In Section 6, an example was given of an argument in the following form with true premises and a false conclusion.

Construct another example of an argument in this form with true premises and a false conclusion:

Most *F*'s are *G*'s
Most *G*'s are *H*'s

Most *F*'s are *H*'s

Hint: Choose classes such that *F* is a much smaller class than *G*, so that it is possible for most *F*'s to be *G*'s and most *G*'s to be *H*'s, while most or even no *F*'s are *H*'s, because the *H*'s could be merely all the things that are not *F*'s.

Part Five. Identify the fallacy being attacked in the following:

> One of the hardest things to remember is that a man's merit in one sphere is no guarantee of his merit in another. Newton's mathematics don't prove his theology. Faraday was right about electricity, but not about Sandemanism. Plato wrote marvelously well, and that's why people still go on believing his pernicious philosophy. Tolstoy was an excellent novelist; but that's no reason for regarding his ideas about morality as anything but detestable, or for feeling anything but contempt for his aesthetics, his sociology, and his religion. In the case of scientists and philosophers this ineptitude outside their own line of business isn't surprising. Indeed, it's almost inevitable. For it's obvious that excessive development of the purely mental functions leads to atrophy of all the rest. Hence, the notorious infantility of professors and the ludicrous simplicity of the solutions they offer for the problems of life.
>
> —A. Huxley, *Point Counter Point*

III. ARGUMENTS FROM ANALOGY

When we point out an observed similarity between two things or two types of things, we draw an **analogy** between them. In everyday life, we often notice and comment on similarities. Analogies that are unusual and surprising are the stuff of which literature, especially poetry, is made. Thus Boswell *(In Search of a Wife)* draws an analogy between his character and a kind of fabric: "I am a weaker man than can well be imagined. My brilliant qualities are like embroidery on gauze." Lawrence Durrell *(Reflections on a Marine Venus)* compares the close of days in Rhodes to falling fruit: "In Rhodes the days drop softly as fruit from trees." Open almost any page of Shakespeare and you will find beautiful analogies, which in literature are called *similes* and *metaphors:*

> How far that little candle throws his beams! So shines a good deed in a naughty world.
>
> —*The Merchant of Venice*

When, on the basis of analogies, we conclude that items that are similar in observed ways are also similar in some further, as yet unobserved, respect, we employ an **argument from analogy.** In an example in Chapter 3, analogical reasoning from the observed effects of the birth-control hormone on rats (which are physiologically similar to humans) was used to conclude that birth-control pills may affect human brain development.

Not every use of analogy is an argument from analogy. For an argument to be present, a conclusion must be drawn on the basis of an analogy. The examples from Boswell, Durrell, and Shakespeare are not arguments from analogy; for the analogies stated there are not used to support some further unobserved similarity. Instead these analogies enhance our ability to see the world in a new way by directing our attention to an interesting similarity.

1. Form of Arguments from Analogy

Although arguments from analogy are stated in various ways, they can be reconstructed to exhibit the following basic form:

Objects of type X have properties F, G, H, and so on.
Objects of type Y have properties F, G, H, and so on, and also an additional
 property Z.

Objects of type X have property Z as well.

Both premisses of these arguments mention the respects (F, G, H, and so on) in which the two types of objects have been observed to be similar. The second premiss also mentions a property (Z) that has been observed in one type of object. The conclusion states that the other type of object has that property as well.

In the argument that concludes that birth-control pills may affect human brain development, the properties F, G, H, and so on—although unspecified in the premisses—are the physiological properties that humans (objects of type X) and rats (objects of type Y) have been observed to share. It is because rats possess these properties that they are used in medical experiments. The further property Z, of brain development being affected by the birth-control hormone, has been observed for rats and is inferred to hold for humans as well.

In the absence of sufficient information about the effects on humans of potentially harmful substances, tests are performed on experimental animals. Such tests are used to conclude (inductively) that humans will be similarly affected. This form of reasoning is understood not only by scientists but also by the general public. In view of widespread familiarity with the role of experimental animals, the similarities between these animals and humans are not always stated explicitly. When the conclusions of such arguments are challenged, however, mention is often made of relevant dissimilarities between the animals used in the experiment and human beings. The results of tests on laboratory rats, for example, are often challenged on the basis of the disparity in size between rats and humans.

When we reconstruct analogical arguments to judge their strength, we should try to state explicitly any *implicit* points of analogy contained in the premisses. Specialized knowledge might be needed to state the implicit similarities. For example, most of us do not know enough physiology to be able to state precisely how various experimental animals resemble humans. We must then rely on experts' claims that the similarities are present, but we should at least be aware that the nature of these similarities is crucial to the argument.

2. Standards for the Strength of Analogical Arguments

The strength of an argument from analogy, or an **analogical argument,** depends heavily on the *relevance* of the similarities mentioned in the premisses to the similarity stated in the conclusion. One feature is relevant to another if the presence of the first increases (is positively relevant to) or decreases (is negatively relevant to) the probability that the second feature will also be present.

In the argument about birth-control pills that we have been discussing, the conclusion states that the birth-control hormone produces a physiological effect in humans similar to the physiological effect it produces in rats. The implicit premiss asserts the existence of physiological similarities between rats and humans. The similarities employed in the implicit premiss are relevant to the similarity drawn in the conclusion, because similar physiological features are relevant to whether the same substance will produce a similar physiological effect.

As noted, however, the physiological features of rats are not exactly similar to those of human. Rats are smaller, their brains are less complex, and rats and humans undoubtedly differ in other important (relevant) ways. Such dissimilarities between rats and humans account in part for the tentative nature of the conclusion of this argument, which is indicated by the use of the term *may.*

The *number* of relevant similarities in the premisses and the number of relevant dissimilarities between the two types of objects are also important in judging the strength of analogical arguments. Obviously, the more relevant similarities the two types of objects share, the stronger the argument that the feature mentioned in the conclusion will also be shared. For this reason, the results of experiments on our closest mammalian relatives, the large primates, are considered more likely to apply to humans. By the same token, the greater the number of relevant dissimilarities, the weaker the argument.

Consumer decision making frequently employs arguments from analogy. You may, for example, decide to buy another car made by the U.S. manufacturer of your old car because it has been so reliable. If your conclusion that the new car will be reliable is based on a suitable number of relevant analogies between the old car and the new one, and if few relevant dissimilarities exist, your argument will be strong.

Some features that we believe to be relevant to automotive reliability are incorporated in the type of engine, the braking system, the transmission, and the suspension systems. If these features are similar in the new car and the old, the conclusion that the new car will be reliable may be strongly supported. If, however, the new car has many innovations (perhaps a different type of fuel-injection system and a redesigned starter) or if your old car is a sedan and the new car is a sports model with radically new design features, your argument from analogy is weakened by these relevant dissimilarities. Not every feature of a car is relevant to reliable performance. The color of the car and the style of upholstery probably make little difference.

Other criteria for determining the strength of analogical arguments are the number and the variety of instances mentioned in the premisses, or in other words, the size and diversity of the sample, which forms the basis for the analogy. The special value of a larger and more varied set of instances is that this facilitates recognition of exactly which similarities *are* relevant. If the similar properties mentioned in the premises and the similarity stated in the conclusion go together in a variety of otherwise dissimilar circumstances, we have reason to believe that their connection with one another is not accidental—that a causal connection or some other real connection exists between the properties mentioned in the premises and the property mentioned in the conclusion.

Suppose, for instance, that you had owned not only one reliable car made by the same manufacturer but had owned and driven six of this manufacturer's cars, in various models and styles. Your argument that another car made by this manufacturer will be reliable will be strengthened, because the additional evidence would tend to show that the manufacturer produces a variety of reliable cars and that yours was not just a fortunate exception.

Similarly, if experiments had shown that birth-control hormones had an adverse effect on brain development not only in rats but also in rabbits, pigs, and other experimental animals, then the conclusion that birth-control hormones have an adverse effect on humans would have been strengthened. The additional evidence would tend to show that nothing is special about the reaction of rats that makes them relevantly dissimilar to other mammals (and possibly to humans) in their response to the hormone.

The principle that a variety of cases strengthens an analogical argument may seem to conflict with the principle that says relevant dissimilarities between instances in the premises and the instance in the conclusion weaken an analogical argument. However, these two principles do not really conflict. The instances mentioned in the premises can have properties that differ in *irrelevant* ways, and also be similar in ways that are relevant to the property inferred in the conclusion.

3. Fallacies Associated with Analogical Arguments

An argument in the form of analogical reasoning, might yet fail to meet the standards for strong analogical arguments. These fallacious arguments may attempt to establish a conclusion on the basis of irrelevant analogies. In *A System of Logic* (first published in 1843), John Stuart Mill named this fallacy the **fallacy of false analogy.** For example, to argue that Joan is probably lazy because her brother John is lazy is fallacious, for the similarities between Joan and John that are implicit in the premiss (whatever similarities siblings typically share) are not particularly relevant to the property of laziness. Many families have both lazy and industrious children.

One of Mill's own examples of this fallacy is the argument that a paternalistic form of government is superior to other forms of government, because paternalistic governance works well in families, and families and states resemble one another in many ways. Mill points out that the *relevant* qualities for the successful paternalistic governance of a family—affection of the parents for the children and parental superiority in wisdom and experience—are conspicuously absent in most paternalistic forms of state government. States and families are therefore relevantly dissimilar to one another with respect to how they should best be governed.

Many examples of false analogy are found in early anthropological studies of tribal cultures. Because scholars falsely assumed that certain aspects of these cultures were similar to our own, they viewed the behavior of individuals in tribal societies as perverse or bizarre. For example, early observers noted that in some aboriginal societies the words for *mother* and *father* refer not only to the biological parent, but also to the parent's sisters and brothers. In our own society this would be attributed to confusion about the identity of the biological parents, so they concluded that the same was true in these societies. Because, however, the people they were observing seemed to suffer no such confusion, the researchers further inferred that at some time in the past there had been a system of group marriage in which the terms that mean *mother* and *father* were applied to a variety of persons—because the child could not know which members of the group were actually the biological parents. Later, and more detailed, anthropological studies—notably those of A. R. Radcliffe-Brown—showed that the kinship terminologies used in our society and in tribal societies are relevantly dissimilar but equally systematic ("logical") and useful in their own contexts. It is no more mysterious for a child in a society with a different kinship terminology to call his or her mother's sister *mother* than it is for a child in our own society to use *aunt* to address his or her mother's sisters, father's sisters, father's brother's wife, mother's brother's wife, elderly female cousins, and even mother's friends.

4. Analogy in Archaeology and in Legal and Moral Reasoning

We have already discussed the use of analogy in medical research. Archaeology is another science that depends heavily on arguments from analogy. Archaeologists study humans by examining the material remains of their implements, artifacts, and buildings. Because the people who made these objects are no longer alive, archaeologists cannot directly observe how these things were used by their makers. Written records are of little help in the study of prehistoric peoples, because, as the term *prehistoric* indicates, these people had no writing system, left only fragmentary records, or wrote in languages that we do not yet understand.

Archaeologists note, however, that other people, who are living now or whose lives are historically documented, use or once used items *similar in form* to those found in archaeological excavations. On the basis of these observed similarities, archaeologists infer by analogy that the prehistoric items were *used for similar purposes.* Archaeologists working in caves in Oaxaca, Mexico, for example, found awl-like objects made from sharpened deer bones that were analogous in virtually every relevant respect (including patterns of wear) to bone tools used by contemporary Oaxacan farmers. Because the farmers were using these tools to scrape kernels from corn, the archaeologists, who found remains of corn in the caves as well, unhesitatingly attributed the same function to the prehistoric objects.

Judges rule on the legality of actions and cases brought before them in hearings and trials. In a civil court, for example, a trial might be held to determine whether a proposed merger between two companies involves a violation of the antitrust laws. To rule on such actions, judges must be aware of any laws that are applicable to the particular case being tried before them. In addition to being guided by laws—which are usually broadly stated and difficult to apply to complex cases—judges are guided in their rulings by *precedent.* Legal precedents are previous judicial rulings (interpretations of the law for particular cases).

Analogical reasoning plays an important role in the legal process with regard to the use of precedents. For example, lawyers who are arguing that a corporate merger should be declared illegal examine previous rulings on mergers. In particular, they look for a decision important enough to constitute a precedent. If such a "controlling case" rules against the merger, the lawyers try to present relevant similarities between the case they are arguing and the controlling case in which the merger was denied. Lawyers who are arguing in favor of a merger try to point out the lack of analogy (or relevant dissimilarities) between the controlling case and the case in question.

In the absence of a controlling case, lawyers on both sides search through reports of court decisions on mergers and cite relevant similarities between their case and those decisions that are favorable to their position as well as point out relevant dissimilarities between their case and those decisions that are unfavorable to their position. The judge, after hearing the arguments, decides whether the case in question should be regarded as relevantly similar to the mergers that were denied or permitted in the past.

Analogy plays an important role in moral as well as legal reasoning. When we claim that a given act deserves blame, for example, we may try to show that the act is relevantly similar to other actions that are classified as blameworthy. If we can conclude that the act is relevantly similar to other blameworthy acts, then we can use the ethical principle that like acts should be treated similarly to argue *deductively* that the act in question deserves blame. Or someone might argue analogically, for example, that a particular case of promise-breaking is relevantly similar to other cases in which ignorance was an important excusing factor. Then a further deductive argument (not an argument from analogy) would conclude that this case of promise breaking should be excused, because it occurred under conditions of ignorance that generally excuse failing to keep promises.

We use analogical reasoning also to attribute characteristics, motives, desires, and feelings to other people. For example, we might judge a politician to be too weak to be able to handle the stresses of high office because he behaved irresponsibly in situations of similar, but less severe, stress on other occasions. I might excuse a friend who behaves crossly if she had all four wisdom teeth pulled yesterday, for I could not help my bad temper the day after my own teeth were pulled. We infer that other persons, who are similar to us in many observable respects, share similar hopes, fears, and feelings when confronted with situations that would inspire those hopes, fears, or feelings in ourselves.

Exercise Set 4.5

Reconstruct the analogical arguments contained in each of the following passages. Identify the points of analogy in the premises—including any unstated premises—and the analogies argued for in the conclusions. Assess the strength of the arguments on the basis of the criteria presented in this section. Discuss any cases in which further background knowledge is required to determine relevance.

1. Tar (extracted from cigarette smoke) when smeared on the skin of mice in laboratories causes skin cancers. Therefore, cigarette smoking causes lung cancer in humans.

2. My last pair of Brand X running shoes were comfortable, gave excellent support to my feet and ankles, and lasted a long time. I expect my new pair of Brand X running shoes, which have the same design, to give the same kind of service as my old pair.

3. A perfect thought can only come from someone who is perfect. After all, you can't get heat from something cold.

4. In field trials where the soil was a moderately heavy clay and natural rainfall the only source of water, the roses offered in this catalogue bloomed heavily and were untroubled by disease. Therefore, they will perform well in your own garden.

5. Technology was once thought to be a uniquely human attribute, but the discovery of tool use in apes, otters, birds, and even wasps has scotched that. Nevertheless, the extent and nature of tool use among apes remains a subject of considerable importance in relation to the development of technology among the earliest members of the human family, the hominids. William McGrew of Stirling University, Scotland, therefore decided to survey what has been observed among our simian cousins. . . . "For most of my career I've worked with chimpanzees," he said, "and I have tended to generalize from chimps to the other apes. Great apes [gorillas, orangutans, gibbons] have usually been considered to be of similar intelligence, and I expected similarities in tool use to what I had known about chimps."

—*Science* 236 (1987):776

6. Wives, be subject to your husbands as to the Lord, for the husband is head of the wife as Christ also is the head of the church; as the church is subject to Christ, so wives are to be subject to their husbands in every respect.

—St. Paul, Ephesians, 5,22

7. The force that binds planets to the sun (gravity) obeys the same general form of law as the electrical force that binds electrons to the nucleus of an atom. (Both gravity and electricity decrease in strength with the square of the distance between the bodies or particles.) Therefore the electron particles, which

have negative charges, when attracted by the positive electricity of the nucleus, should move around it in the same way that the planets move around the sun.

Note: This was British physicist Ernest Rutherford's argument for the planetary model of the atom. He rejected a "plum pudding" model that arranged the electrons randomly throughout the atom like raisins in a pudding.

8. From an editorial written in response to a rejection by voters of a measure that would have provided money for additional officers of the court:

> Anyone who has bought a cheap used car knows that paying less for repairs now may prove to be more expensive later. This basic truth is often forgotten by people who call for reduced federal spending. The tendency to let tomorrow take care of itself is exemplified in America's approach to the administration and enhancement of justice. . . .
>
> The path to justice is never easy. Those truly committed to the promotion of justice must be willing to pay the price—a price that must take into account future costs of present inaction. We must not forget principles of preventive medicine when undertaking to remedy social ills. If the public truly desires to ensure the nation's long-term health, it must be willing to pay the doctor's bill for the cures.
>
> —Judge I. Kaufman, *The New York Times*

9. In the case of *Langridge v. Levy* (1837), the court allowed recovery to the plaintiff, who said that the defendant sold his father a defective gun. The gun had blown up in the plaintiff's hand, and the court ruled that the seller had falsely declared the gun safe when he knew it was defective.

> In *George v. Skivington* (1869), a chemist who compounded a secret hair wash was liable to the wife of the purchaser for injuries caused by the wash. . . . [The court] thought that the imperfect hair wash was like the imperfect gun in the *Langridge* case. It chose to ignore the emphasis in the *Langridge* case on the purported fact that the seller knew the gun was defective and lied. It said, "substitute the word "negligence" for "fraud," and the analogy between *Langridge v. Levy* and this case is complete.
>
> —E. H. Levi, *An Introduction to Legal Reasoning*

10. Remains of *Homo erectus* were found at Choukoutien, China. The skulls there had been carefully opened through the base, presumably to extract the brain. Some archaeologists interpreted the skulls as the remains of a cannibalistic meal.

> We tend to think of cannibalism as a bestial and inhuman practice, but in fact nothing better demonstrates the humanity of the Choukoutien people. Among living peoples, cannibalism is never a matter of nutrition; no animal, human or nonhuman, eats its dead for food. Rather, it is a solemn ritual act, sometimes to express family piety toward the deceased or magically to impart the deceased's spirit and qualities to the living. We may be

confident that the atmosphere of Choukoutien during the cannibal meal was closer to Mass than to McDonald's.

—C. Jolly and F. Plog, *Physical Anthropology and Archaeology*

11. Johnson told me that he went up thither without mentioning it to his servant when he wanted to study, secure from interruption; for he would not allow his servant to say he was not at home when he really was. "A servant's strict regard for the truth (said he) would be weakened by such a practice. A philosopher may know that it is merely a *form* of denial [that is, a "little white lie"], but few servants are such nice distinguishers. If I accustom a servant to tell a lie for *me*, have I not reason to apprehend that he will tell many lies for *himself*?"

—J. Boswell, *Life of Johnson*

Reconstruct the argument that Johnson believes his servants would use if he allowed them to lie for him.

12. In the following passage, an analogy is drawn between shade trees and knowledge, or the habit of intellectual activity. The analogy is used to argue for the importance of educating persons during their youth. Discuss the relevance of the similarities.

Knowledge is a comfortable and necessary retreat and shelter for us in an advanced age; and if we do not plant it while young, it will give us no shade when we grow old.

—Lord Chesterfield, *Letters*

13. 'Tis education forms the common mind; Just as the twig is bent, the tree's inclined.

—A. Pope

14. It seems that the Latin races are far more deeply attached to their Catholicism than we Northerners are to Christianity generally, and that consequently unbelief in Catholic countries means something quite different from what it does among Protestants.

—F. Nietzsche, *Beyond Good and Evil*

15. Now, pro-life folk need to understand that just as it can be said that some highly civilized folk believed that slavery was a normal human institution (St. Paul, John C. Calhoun) so some people feel that way about abortion. And as long as people feel that way, they are perplexed, indignant and outraged at condemnations of their behavior, let alone efforts to restrict it.
It is for this reason that one should be no more tempted to scorn a woman who terminates a pregnancy by abortion than one would have been to associate with Thomas Jefferson, a slaveowner.

—W. F. Buckley, Jr., syndicated newspaper column

16. The anti-climatic fact is that, as a matter of general opinion, scientists concluded years ago that sexual orientation is not chosen. How? The answer seems startlingly low tech: basically the same way they concluded that left-handedness is not chosen,

through common sense. Left-handers tell us they don't choose to be left-handed. Aspects of left-handedness, like homosexuality, almost universally appear in early childhood.

—C. Burr, *The New York Times,* Op-Ed, 8/2/93

17. The following argument is offered against D. Gish's antievolutionary claim that no transitional forms exist between reptiles and mammals.

> Imagine that we have a sequence of color patches, forming a continuous gradation from yellow through orange into red. For purposes of convenience, we divide them into two classes, the red ones and the yellow ones, by choosing some criterion of demarcation. (We might pick, for example, some wavelength in the middle of the orange range.) It would be absurd to object that we do not have a continuous sequence of colors on the grounds that all of the patches in the yellow class fail to satisfy the criterion for being in the red class.
>
> This analogy is easily applied to the reptile–mammal transition. The fossil record supplies a sequence of organisms showing gradual changes into a number of characteristics. For taxonomic purposes, zoologists want to split these organisms into two classes, the reptiles and the mammals. Paleontologists are aware that they are imposing a division on a continuum. . . . The series is divided by using the criteria of jaw mechanics, ear structure, and features of the teeth.
>
> —P. Kitcher, *Abusing Science: The Case against Creationism*

18. Wyman (1874) listed four reasons underlying his conclusions [that human remains from aboriginal Floridan middens indicated prehistoric cannibalism]:

> 1. The bones . . . were not deposited there at an ordinary burial of a dead body.
>
> 2. The bones were broken as in the case of those of edible animals, as the deer, alligator, etc.
>
> 3. The breaking up of the bones had a certain amount of method.
>
> 4. There is no evidence that the bones were broken up by wild animals.
>
> — T. White, *Prehistoric Cannibalism at Mancos 5MTUMR-2346*

19. State the implicit analogies required for the following arguments to succeed.

> Three arguments, however, can be used to support the conclusion that the gold [from a late Neolithic (*c.* 4000 BC) cemetery in Bulgaria] was indeed of great worth:
>
> 1. Its use for artifacts with evidently symbolic status: e.g., to decorate the haft of a perforated stone axe which, evidently through its fine work and friability, was not intended for use.

2. Its use for ornaments at particularly significant parts of the body: e.g., for face decorations, for a penis sheath.

3. Its use in simulation: sheet gold was used to cover a stone axe to give the impression of solid gold; such a procedure normally indicates that the material hidden is less valuable than the covering material.

—C. Renfrew and P. Bahn, *Archaeology: Theories, Methods, and Practice*

20. What use of analogy is made in the following legal decision (*Paton v. British Pregnancy Advisory Service Trustees,* 1979)?

> In the discussion of human affairs and especially of abortion, controversy can rage over the moral rights, duties, interests, standards and religious views of the parties. Moral values are in issue. I am, in fact, concerned with none of these matters. I am concerned and concerned only with the law of England as it applies to this claim. My task is to apply the law free of emotion or predilection. . . .
>
> The foetus cannot, in English Law, in my view, have a right of its own at least until it is born and has a separate existence from its mother. That permeates the whole of the civil law of this country . . . and is, indeed, the basis of the decisions in those countries where law is founded on the common law, that is to say, in America, Canada, Australia. . . .
>
> —Sir George Baker P, as quoted in *Embryo Experimentation*, edited by Singer et al.

5. Analogy and the Slippery Slope

Three of the exercises in Exercise Set 4.5 (#11, #17, and #20) are concerned with making distinctions—or failing to make distinctions—among analogous things. Johnson believes, for example, that his servants will not be able to mark the distinction between social lies told for his convenience and lies they want to tell for their convenience. Kitcher criticizes creationists for thinking that an evolutionary continuum does not exist because scientists have divided it into taxonomic classes to simplfy their studies. Sir George Baker interprets English law to say that before birth a fetus has no rights of its own and after birth it acquires those rights.

Many persons involved with the moral issues surrounding abortion, *in vitro* fertilization, and experiments on human embryos are trying to identify a developmental stage in the life of the embryo that marks the point at which the embryo should be treated as a person with the full complement of human rights. Sir George Baker represents one extreme view on when this status is achieved—birth is the marker event. The Roman Catholic Church represents the other extreme—the moment of conception is the marker event. Other markers that have been proposed are segmentation (the point at which twinning can no longer occur), the end of the first trimester of pregnancy, the end of the second trimester, the development of the fetal nervous system, "quickening," that is, the mother's awareness of movement in the womb, and viability, that is, the capacity to live outside the womb. Although each of the proposals has something to be said for it, none is entirely satisfactory, for fetal development is a process without sharply divided stages. Even conception and birth are not instantaneous events but are themselves processes that extend over some time. Nevertheless, despite the difficulty of drawing nonarbitrary distinctions at any point along the continuum of fetal development, it would be fallacious to conclude that no meaningful distinctions could be drawn between the beginning of the process and the end, or between early, middle, and late stages in fetal development. To argue in that manner is to commit the **fallacy of the slippery slope.** Those who would allow abortions and those who would outlaw them can both recognize that a nine-month fetus is far more similar in morally relevant ways to a newborn than to a newly fertilized human egg. Arguments can be formulated against destroying early-stage embryos that do not rely on the continuity of the process of fetal development, and these may avoid the slippery slope.

Johnson, in saying "few servants are such nice distinguishers" sees them as sliding down the slippery slope—telling white lies for him will lead to telling other sorts of lies for themselves. Kitcher accuses the creationists of the opposite mistake—they suppose that because a distinction has been drawn a natural gap exists.

During the time of the Vietnam War, the U.S. government propounded what was then called "the domino theory." According to that view, if a single Southeast Asian country "fell" to the communists, then its neighbor would fall as well, and so on until the whole area—or the whole world—was under communist rule. Critics called the domino theory a slippery slope argument, objecting that the conditions that allowed a takeover in one country were not always relevantly similar to those in neighboring countries.

The slippery slope is an ancient form of reasoning. According to van Fraassen (*The Scientific Image*), the argument is found in Sextus Empiricus that incest is not immoral, on the grounds that "touching your mother's big toe with your little finger is not immoral, and all the rest differs only by degree." Van Fraassen himself is concerned with the slippery slope character of arguments that challenge the distinction between observable and nonobservable objects. This topic and the closely related distinction between observable and theoretical entities in science are subjects of intense debate in contemporary philosophy of science. In an argument that van Fraassen criticizes, G. Maxwell says:

> . . . there is, in principle, a continuous series beginning with looking through a vacuum and containing these as members: looking through a windowpane, looking through glasses, looking through binoculars, looking through a low-power microscope, looking through a high-power microscope, etc., in the order given. The important consequence is that, so far, we are left without criteria which would enable us to draw a non-arbitrary line between "observation" and "theory".
>
> —G. Maxwell, quoted in van Fraassen 1980, p. 16.

In trying to determine the import such arguments have, it is useful to examine the notion of an "arbitrary" distinction. The term *arbitrary* in this context can mean that no justification at all can be given for drawing the distinction, or it can mean that different justifications can be given for various ways of drawing the distinction, and that the choice of where to draw the distinction is to be justified by the purpose of the distinction. For example, although having achieved the age of 18 years is no clear marker of having reached the level of maturity required to vote, serve in the armed forces, and take on other adult responsibilities, by that age a great many people have matured sufficiently to qualify as adults. For all kinds of practical reasons, some age must be chosen to mark the age of majority. Thus, the choice of 18 is arbitrary in the second sense—19 years might serve the purposes mentioned as well as 18, but not in the first sense of the term.

Slippery slope arguments often occur in moral and legal reasoning, for contexts in which decisions can have lasting impact on people's lives and well-being. For this reason, the arguments need to be examined carefully to determine the sense in which considerations of analogy, or similarity, support drawing distinctions, the purposes those distinctions are intended to serve, and the effects of any actions to be taken on the basis of such distinctions.

Exercise Set 4.6

The following argument against abortion at any stage of fetal development has been called a slippery slope argument:

Since it is clearly wrong to kill a human being the day it is born, and since the fetus is the same person the day before it is born as the day it is born, it is also wrong to kill it on that day, and on the day before, and the day before that, and so on back to the first moment of that being's life.

Some opponents of euthanasia ("mercy-killing") support their position by a slippery slope argument. Try to construct such an argument, and then criticize it.

IV. ARGUMENTS BASED ON SAMPLES

Arguments based on samples share a common form called **inductive generalization.** Other names for the same form are **simple induction, induction by enumeration,** and **statistical generalization.** Inductive generalizations are arguments from the particular to the general. They do have the characteristic that has been inaccurately attributed to all inductive reasoning. As we have seen, statistical syllogisms and some analogies draw particular conclusions from general premises. The premises of inductive generalizations, however, are about particular cases (the cases that make up the sample), while their conclusions are generalizations about a population. Moreover, inductive generalization is such a common form of inductive argument that those who define induction as arguing from the particular to the general may be excused for focusing on this one important type.

Inductive generalization is the argument form that political pollsters use to forecast election results. Before an election, polltakers interview a sample of the population of registered voters and, on the basis of what members of the sample say about how they will vote, the pollsters predict how the population will vote. The information contained in the premises (called *the statistics*) is extended in the conclusion to apply to the entire population. Such an argument might look like this:

1,200 (60 percent) of the 2,000 voters polled plan to vote for the incumbent.

60 percent of all voters plan to vote for the incumbent.

Although the predictions based on such polls are often incorrect, their overall record of success is impressive. Such success motivates us to understand how this powerful type of argument works.

Inductive generalization is also used in quality-control studies. Suppose that a manufacturer wants to know what proportion of its products are defective. The company can employ an inspector to examine a portion of the items as they come off the assembly line. If, for example, during a one-year period, the plant produces approximately 5,000 stereo receivers (the population) and 100 receivers are inspected (the sample), with only two showing defects, the following argument can be constructed:

98 out of 100 receivers that were examined were without defects.

98 percent of the receivers produced at the plant are without defects.

Inductive generalizations are used in many scientific studies. New drugs are tested by giving them to selected individuals; if the members of the sample suffer no ill effects, the drugs are deemed safe for the general public. The functions of various features of animals, such as distinctive patterns of coloration, are studied by performing experiments on a sample group, and noting effects. The findings are then generalized to apply to all animals of that type. Investigators recently used this form of reasoning when they used black paint to mask high-contrast wing stripes on tropical butterflies and noted that neither survival nor wing damage was affected.

You have probably noticed that inductive generalizations are similar in some ways to arguments from analogy. Indeed, in strong inductive generalizations a high degree of relevant analogy holds between the sample and the population it represents. We can distinguish between the *form* of inductive generalizations, in which a general claim is based on what happens in a sample, and the *form* of analogical arguments, in which a conclusion about an unobserved similarity is based on similarities that have been observed. In ordinary language, however, because arguments are often incompletely stated, many could be reconstructed in either form. Relevant similarities are crucial to the evaluation of both types of arguments.

Generalizations that are the conclusions of arguments from samples can be either universal or statistical. **Universal generalizations** state that *all* (100 percent) or *none* (0 percent) of the members of a class have a certain property. **Statistical generalizations** state that some percentage less than 100 percent, but more than 0 percent, of members of a class have the property. Recall also that statistical generalizations can be stated nonnumerically, using such terms as *most, almost all,* and *very few.* Whether the conclusion of an inductive generalization should be statistical or universal depends on the information contained in the premises. If *all* members of the sample exhibit the property in question, then the conclusion that all members of the population exhibit that property *may* be appropriate—provided certain other conditions are satisfied.

1. Preliminary Account of the Form of Inductive Generalization

We are now ready to present a preliminary version of the abstract form of arguments based on samples:

X percent of observed F's are G's.
_____
X percent of all F's are G's.

The letters F and G in this form represent expressions such as *voters, voters for the incumbent, receivers,* and *items without any defects,* which refer to classes of individuals or to properties possessed by all members of a class. The conclusion of an inductive generalization states that the percentage in the *population* of F's that are G's is the same as the percentage in the *observed sample.*

2. Standards for the Strength of Inductive Generalizations

When are arguments in this form that have true premises likely to lead to true conclusions? The answer depends largely on whether the sample mentioned in the premiss is *representative* of the population referred to in the conclusion. When a sample is representative of the population from which it is taken, the conclusion based on the sample is strongly supported. To say that a sample is *representative* is to say that the features of the population that concern us in an argument (for example, features that determine how people will vote) are reflected in the sample. When this is the case, what is true of the sample will probably be true of the population as well. Traditionally, the following criteria are offered for representative samples:

1. The sample must be large enough.
2. The sample must contain sufficient variety.

Background information about the subject matter of the argument is used to determine whether a sample has sufficient size and variety. If we have reason to believe that a population is highly uniform with respect to the properties that interest us, information about a small sample can support a strong generalization; in larger, more diverse populations, a larger sample is required to capture that diversity. A sample of only five voters, all of whom say they will vote for the incumbent, will not support the conclusion of a landslide victory in a national election. Such a sample is so small that it is almost worthless. A sample of five voters, all family members, however, might well support the conclusion that Smith will be elected chairman of a small family-owned company. A cook in a kitchen on top of a mountain who wants to determine the boiling point of water at that altitude can use a sample of only one—or perhaps two (to check the reading)—pans of water, because that population is highly uniform with respect to the property of boiling point.

Noticing that a small sample may be adequate to represent a large population *provided* the population is highly uniform suggests the importance of having varied samples when a population is not uniform. Indeed, even very large samples may lack suitable variety. In a national election, a sample of 100,000 voters would not be representative if all members of the sample were wealthy business executives. Nevertheless, in some circumstances, sufficient size may be viewed as an important (and in some conditions the most important) aid to achieving appropriate variety in samples. A sample that is too small automatically fails to provide the requisite variety.

We now turn to the problem of generating representative samples. A sample taken haphazardly from a population may, through luck, closely resemble the population with respect to the properties that interest us in an argument. However, arguments based on samples that are gathered without attention to sufficient size and variety do not form a basis for strong arguments. Several methods are used to obtain representative samples. These methods do not *guarantee* that a sample will be representative, but their use increases the probability that it will be so.

A sampling method called **random sampling** is often used. In random sampling, each member of the population has an equal chance of being chosen as a member of the sample. A random sample of students at a university can be generated, for example, by printing the student identification number of each student on a different ticket, mixing the tickets in a rotating drum, and performing a blind drawing of tickets to select a sample of the appropriate size.

The value of larger samples can be shown by taking random samples from an ordinary deck of playing cards, in which one half of the population is red, and the other half is black, and considering how much information samples of various size give us about this population. Keeping the cards face down, shuffle the deck so that each card has an equal chance of being selected for the sample. Then select a sample of two cards, replacing the card drawn and shuffling after each draw. There are four possible outcomes of such a selection (or trial): The first card is red and the second is black; the first card is black and the second is red; both cards are red; or both cards are black (RB, or BR, or RR or BB). In only two of the four possible outcomes (half the time) do we get a sample that is truly representative of the population.

Now suppose that we start again, only this time our sample consists of four trials. The sixteen possibilities are: RRRR; RRRB; RRBR; RRBB; RBRR; RBRB; RBBR; RBBB; BRRR; BRRB; BRBR; BRBB; BBRR; BBRB; BBBR; or BBBB. In only six of the sixteen possible outcomes (three-eighths of the time) are exactly half of the cards red and half black. However, and this is critical, in all but two outcomes (seven-eighths of the time), a mix of between one-fourth and three-fourths' red cards occurs, and in only one-eighth of the outcomes (as opposed to one-half in the smaller sample) could we be misled into thinking the deck contained cards of only one color. So when our sample size is four instead of two, we are more likely to get an answer that is *close to* half red cards, and less likely to get an answer that the deck is all red or all black. In general, as our sample size increases, a proportion of red and black cards occurs that is *closer* to the true proportion in the deck. This is so, even though as the sample size increases, our chances of getting exactly the true proportion (1/2) gets smaller. (When the sample size is two, half the possible outcomes were exactly half red; when the sample size is four, three-eighths of the possible outcomes are half red; in a sample size of ten, one-fourth of the possible outcomes are exactly half red—but in about two-thirds of the possible outcomes of sample size ten, between 40 percent and 60 percent are red cards.) Therefore, as sample sizes increase, we can be more and more confident that a randomly selected sample will resemble the population from which it is drawn.

Stratified random sampling is a form of random sampling that is useful when information is available about the nature of variation in a population. When we know something about how segments of the population would be apt to differ with respect to the property that interests us in the conclusion (such as voter preference) and when we also know the proportion of each segment in the population, we can "stratify" the different layers in the population, and then select randomly within each layer. We know, for example, that voting preferences are often shared by persons of similar social class, occupation, and religious or ethnic background. If we also know the proportion of each of these groups in the population of voters, we can sample randomly *within* the groups to construct a sample that "matches" those proportions. Stratified random sampling has been refined by professional polltakers to permit the construction of relatively small representative samples for huge populations. The Gallup Poll and the Harris Poll, for example, are reliable indicators of voter preference in national elections and other matters of public opinion even though their samples, which must represent hundreds of millions of eligible voters, usually consist of fewer than 2,000 persons.

Random sampling and stratified random sampling are very good ways to generate representative samples, and constitute an ideal standard for premises of strong inductive generalizations. Unfortunately, however, theoretical and practical barriers prevent using these techniques in many cases. Gathering statistics is expensive in terms of time and money. Decisions must sometimes be made and actions taken before the best information can be gathered and processed.

From the discussion thus far, we can see the importance of background knowledge when trying to assess the strength of an inductive generalization. We not only must examine the premises of the argument but also we must consider whether the sample is representative—and this requires information that is not contained in the premises. When we cannot tell whether a sample is large enough or varied enough, we cannot determine whether an inductive generalization is strong. This dependence on background knowledge—on information that is not a part of the premises—is a feature of all inductive arguments. Success at critical thinking does not demand that we acquire the background knowledge to judge every case. It demands instead that we be aware that certain questions must be raised and know how the answers to these questions affect the arguments that we construct or evaluate.

In thinking critically about arguments, keeping the *truth* of a conclusion separate from the *strength* of an argument is of utmost importance: Bad or weak arguments may turn out to have true conclusions, and good or strong arguments may turn out to have false conclusions. In inductive logic, the standards for correctness are designed to make it *probable* that if the premises of the argument are true, the conclusion will be true as well. If we adhere to these standards, conclusions that are based on true premises will usually, but not always, be true.

3. Fallacies Associated with Inductive Generalizations

We are now ready to consider some fallacies that are associated with inductive generalizations. One fallacy arises from failing to meet the requirement of obtaining a large enough sample. This fallacy has a number of common names: the **fallacy of insufficient statistics, hasty generalization,** and **leaping to a conclusion.**

If a friend snaps at you when you ask a question, you commit the fallacy of hasty generalization if you conclude that this one instance of unfriendly behavior showed that he is no longer your friend. If you conclude that no one likes artichokes because none of your friends do, this too would be a hasty generalization. The psychological reasons for leaping to a conclusion are fairly obvious in these cases. In the first, hurt feelings may color your judgment; in the second, personal interest in opinions of friends may obscure the fact that they are only a small part of the population. To avoid making hasty generalizations, we should dispassionately consider the size of the sample before we draw any conclusion from it. If feelings are not clouding our judgment, but we lack the appropriate background information on which to decide whether a sample is large enough, we should try to acquire the information. If this is not possible, suspending judgment is better than jumping to a conclusion.

The second fallacy associated with inductive generalizations is the **fallacy of biased statistics.** To say that statistics are biased means that the sample lacks proper variety. Biased samples are not representative; they fail to capture, or represent, the variety present in the population from which the sample is taken. Again, background information is required to judge whether a sample is sufficiently varied. Knowing, as we do, that business executives are apt to think alike on political matters, the set of statistics generated by a sample of voters that comprises only business executives (no matter how many executives), would be considered biased if these statistics were being used to infer the outcome of a national election.

A recent example of biased statistics, taken from a newspaper, reported a study in which the investigator tried to show that usually when a person is falling in love with someone, the other person is likely to reciprocate the affection. But the investigator's sample was biased, for the group he questioned consisted entirely of couples who had recently become engaged!

In another newspaper story, the reporter surveyed residents of a large city to see whether they would object to having a streetcar line out of service for several months while a new subway was being built. Every person questioned objected to the plan, but all the persons surveyed were riding that streetcar line during the hours when most riders are going to work or returning from their jobs. Riders who depend on the streetcar for getting to and from work do not constitute a representative sample of city residents.

Still another fallacy associated with inductive generalization consists of rejecting a generalization that is strongly supported by premises that cite sufficient and unbiased statistics. This sometimes happens when we acquire new information that apparently conflicts with the statistics. The following situation provides an example.

Someone is planning to buy a new car, and carefully collects all the appropriate statistical information. The statistics include comparisons of thousands of automobiles, in terms of performance, safety, repair bills, and other important features. On the basis of these statistics, the person concludes that a certain brand of automobile is the best buy. Before the purchase is made, however, the person announces the decision to a friend at a party and is informed that the friend's cousin bought the same model of car, which turned out to be a real lemon. The friend describes all the things that went wrong with the car in vivid detail. If the person then rejects the conclusion that the chosen brand is the best buy, a fallacy is committed. Can you see why?

It is not that new information should be ignored. Additional information—either in the premises themselves or in the form of new background information—can strengthen or weaken inductive arguments. But this new information concerns only one case, and one new case cannot outweigh all the statistical information that has been carefully collected. The statistics already take account of defective automobiles. The information that some cars of the chosen brand are lemons is recognized, but presumably this brand comprises relatively fewer lemons than other brands. This is what the statistics say, and no reason has been given to doubt their reliability.

Contemporary psychologists R. Nisbett and L. Ross (*Human Inference*) have studied instances of this fallacy, which David Hume had already noticed and commented on in the eighteenth century. The psychologists agree with Hume's explanation of why the fallacy occurs. The problem, they say, is that new information received about a car from a friend at a party is more vivid than an impersonal collection of statistics. When you actually know someone (or someone who knows someone) to whom the lemon belongs, the information seems more startling and impressive than a "mere statistic." The vividness of the new information about a single car psychologically cancels out the far more complete, but less vivid, information about thousands of cars. The expense and inconvenience of owning a lemon is brought home to the prospective buyer in an alarming way that tends to override the better information. It is a fallacy nevertheless to allow a single vivid case to outweigh strong statistical data. This mistake in reasoning can be called the **fallacy of misleading vividness.**

4. The Revised Form of Inductive Generalization

Thus far, we have discussed two criteria for evaluating inductive generalizations (size of sample and variety in the sample), the fallacies resulting from the failure to meet these criteria, as well as the fallacy of rejecting a strongly supported conclusion when faced with a small amount of vivid information. A further criterion for evaluating the strength of inductive generalizations applies to all other forms of inductive reasoning as well. This criterion is concerned with the strength of the conclusion relative to the strength of the premises in the argument. Remember that an argument is a whole that is composed of parts (the premises and the conclusion). The strength of the whole is determined by considering how much support the premises provide for the conclusion. Thus, an argument can be strengthened by providing better premises (a larger or less biased sample) to support the original conclusion. An argument can also be strengthened, however, by weakening the conclusion, while leaving the premises unchanged. A statement is said to be weaker when it is qualified or guarded in such a way that it presents less information, or less specific information, than the original statement.

Suppose, for example, a poll is taken by the student newspaper to determine the outcome of a student-body election. The reporter lacks the resources to construct a truly random sample, but tries to avoid bias by talking to beginning and advanced students, and members of fraternities and sororities, as well as unaffiliated students and students in other special-interest organizations. The reporter interviews 100 of the approximately 2,000 students who are expected to vote in the election. Of those interviewed, 40 (40 percent) say they will vote for the Student Conservative Party, and 60 (60 percent) say they will vote for the Student Liberals. The following argument could be constructed:

60 percent of those interviewed said they would vote for the Liberals.

60 percent of the students plan to vote for the Liberals.

Based on our discussion of random samples from a deck of cards, we know that it is unlikely that the percentage of Liberal voters in the population of students will be *exactly* the same as the percentage in the sample. Thus, it is common to build into the conclusion of inductive generalizations a "margin of error." This deviation in the conclusion from the percentage in the sample by a little less or a little more is an example of "weakening" the conclusion relative to the premises. The altered argument might look like this:

60 percent of those interviewed plan to vote for the Liberals.

60 percent (plus or minus 10 percent) of the students will vote Liberal.

In this example, the margin of error is 10 percent on either side of 60 percent. Because the sample size was 100 students (and because we can make certain reasonable assumptions about the nature of voting behavior) this margin of error would make it very probable (about 95 percent probable) that reasoning in this way will lead to a true conclusion.

If 500 students are sampled, then we could choose a smaller margin of error, about plus or minus 5 percent, and be just as confident (with 95 percent probability) that our method leads to a true conclusion. Alternatively, if our sample is small, say, only about 30 students, then to achieve the same confidence level, we would have to increase the margin of error to roughly plus or minus 20 percent.

Statisticians have calculated the margins of error associated with various sample sizes for estimating percentages in populations with various probabilities of reaching true conclusions (confidence levels). Their calculations are based on random sampling and some reasonable assumptions about how properties are distributed in a population. Although some of the arithmetic can be complicated, the basic idea is the same as that discussed in our example with the playing cards. Assuming that the property we are interested in is distributed normally in the population and that the sample is chosen randomly, the larger the sample size, the more likely that what is true of the sample will also be more or less true of the population. The confidence level is a measure of the likelihood that use of the method leads to a true conclusion. The margin of error is a measure of the degree to which (more or less) the sample resembles the population.

Margin of error, confidence level, and sample size are intimately related. How much **sampling error** to take account of in an inductive generalization is connected with the desired confidence level for reaching true conclusions. If you want to be almost certain of being correct, you are better off with a wider margin of error. You pay for the extra certainty, however, with a loss of precision. If you are willing to accept a lower confidence level (that is, a greater chance of being wrong), then you can adopt a smaller margin of error for a comparable sample size. So, to use the sample of 100 students from the preceding example, we might have concluded that between 55 percent and 65 percent of the students would vote Liberal—but then our confidence level in the method would only be about 70 percent rather than 95 percent. If we want to retain the higher confidence level (95 percent) *and* reduce our margin of error to a plus or minus 5 percent, then we must increase our sample size to about 500.

Confidence levels and margins of error are sometimes stated informally rather than numerically. For example, if all members of a large sample have some property, the conclusion might be *almost* all the members of the population will have this property, and the confidence level might be expressed by some other phrase such as "It is very likely that. . . ." Or, if half the members of the small sample have the property, the conclusion might state that *roughly* half the members of the population have the property, and the confidence level could be "It is probable that. . . ."

Because samples, no matter how carefully constructed, infrequently present an *exact* picture of the population, the conclusion of any inductive generalization should include some allowance for a margin of error. In light of this ever-present possibility of *sampling error,* we represent the form of inductive generalization in the following way:

X percent of observed F's are G's.

X plus or minus z percent of all F's are G's.

In this form, z represents the degree of departure in either direction from the observed percentage in the sample. It is possible to measure precisely the margin of error in some carefully conducted statistical studies, and margins of error are sometimes stated in reports of political surveys and other polls. You should be aware, however, that these quantities need not be expressed numerically in every inductive generalization.

Exercise Set 4.7

Decide whether each of the following arguments is an acceptable inductive generalization or a fallacy. Identify the premises and the conclusion of each argument. In the case of a fallacy, explain what is wrong. Discuss what sort of additional background information, if any, is needed.

1. A chemistry student is told to determine the boiling point of copper. The student tests two very pure samples of copper and finds that each sample has a boiling point of 2,567° Celsius. The student concludes that this is the boiling point for copper.

2. A nationwide poll of a random sample of thousands of homeowners revealed that 70 percent of them are opposed to increases in welfare payments. Therefore, roughly 70 percent of the adult population opposes such increases.

3. An investigator studied several thousand heroin users and learned that 70 percent of them had used marijuana before they tried heroin. He concludes that roughly 70 percent of all marijuana users will go on to try heroin.

4. It has rained during the past two home football games at our school. Therefore, it will probably rain at all the home games this year.

5. Pueblo sites (prehistoric Native American "apartment villages") are located in many places in Arizona, New Mexico, and Colorado. To determine the number of rooms in pueblo sites that were located by surface surveys but were not excavated, archaeologists examined the relationship between the size of the surface rubble mound prior to excavation and the number of rooms that were ultimately uncovered in each of six sites excavated in the Upper Little Colorado River region. The number of rooms in each excavated site was equal to (.10 $\times$ area of rubble mound in square meters) + 4.

6. [A]t the University of Pennsylvania, psychiatrists conducted a study to determine the social factors that affect the well-being of coronary patients. There were 93 patients in the study; slightly more than 50 percent of them had pets of some kind (dogs, cats, fish, and one iguana). At the end of a year, one-third of the patients who did not own pets had died but only three animal owners had succumbed. The psychiatrists concluded that pet ownership may have a positive effect on the health of humans.

7. There is no overestimating the importance of pets to people, it seems. Katcher [the psychiatrist in charge of the study mentioned in Exercise 6] reported that in one questionnaire, on which people were given the opportunity to indicate whether they thought their pet was an animal or a human member of the family, 48 percent responded that the animal was a human family member.

> —"Human-Animal Relationship under Scrutiny," *Science* 214 (1981):418

8. Jonathan must travel to a distant city. He wants to take the safest mode of transport, so he compares statistics from the past ten years on accidents involving buses, trains, automobiles, and planes on routes between his city and the one he will visit. Jonathan determines that a bus is safer in terms of lives lost than any of the other forms of travel. As he is about to purchase his ticket, however, he sees a newspaper story about a bus accident in which six people died. Jonathan decides not to buy the bus ticket and to drive instead.

9. When all his sophisticated electronic equipment fails to help him move his boat as fast as he would like, Conny van Rietschoten resorts to more primitive methods. He tosses coins into the sea, "for luck, to bring wind." Who's to say if such tribute influences the gods? But it can be reported from personal observation that during last June's Annapolis-Newport tuneup race, when van Rietschoten tossed several Dutch guilders into a flat sea on two different occasions, the wind subsequently picked up.

> —*The New York Times*

10. The English national authors are in all hands and read by all people. . . . My landlady, who is only a taylor's widow, reads her Milton; and tells me that her late husband fell in love with her on this very account; because she read Milton with proper emphasis. This single instance would prove but little; but I have conversed with several people of the lower class, who all knew their national authors, and who all have read many, if not all of them.

> —Moritz (1782), quoted in G. M. Trevelyan, *English Social History*

11. Women are believed to talk too much. Yet study after study finds that it is men who talk more—at meetings, in mixed group discussions, and in classrooms where girls or young women sit next to boys or young men. For example, communications researchers Barbara and Gene Eakins tape-recorded and studied seven university faculty meetings. They found that, with one exception, men spoke more often, and without exception, spoke for a longer time. . . .

When a public lecture is followed by questions from the floor, or a talk show host opens the phones, the first voice to be heard asking a question is almost always a man's. And when they ask questions or offer comments from the audience, men tend to talk longer. . . [A study by M. Swicker is cited. The mean was 23.1 seconds for women, 52.7 for men]

—D. Tannen, *You Just Don't Understand*

12. Most labs test [for rabies] only bats that are submitted because they are rabies-suspect. Results are often reported in a manner that implies that these bats are representative of bats in general. An extreme case involved a claim that 50% of a state's bats were rabid because one of only two bats examined tested positive.

—M. Tuttle, *America's Neighborhood Bats*

V. EXTENDED INDUCTIVE ARGUMENTS

Our discussion has treated separately the various forms of inductive arguments. In real life, they frequently occur in combination with one another. Different forms of argument can be presented together to support the same conclusion. No inductive argument provides conclusive support, and no combination of inductive arguments can provide conclusive support either. A conclusion can be more strongly supported, however, when several types of favorable arguments can be mustered for it. Arguments against the person, arguments from authority, and arguments from consensus are often presented in combination with other arguments.

The conclusion of an inductive generalization is sometimes used as the premiss of a statistical syllogism. For example, a person might read a report citing statistics about the dangers of off-the-road bikes, and conclude that most off-the-road bikes are unsafe. Then, using that generalization as a premiss, the person might conclude that the off-the-road bike that he or she owns is unsafe, even though it has not given any trouble so far. No new techniques are needed for evaluating these extended arguments, beyond sorting out the different components and applying the appropriate standards to each.

VI. PRO AND CON ARGUMENTS

Frequently we are confronted with not merely one argument, or an extended argument, to support a single conclusion, but rather with a situation in which some "pro" arguments are presented *for* a conclusion along with "con" arguments *against* the same conclusion. This can happen when participants in a debate disagree about the truth of premisses. Not surprisingly, different sets of premisses can lead to different conclusions. In still other cases, different (and conflicting) conclusions can be drawn because of different views about how evidence should be interpreted.

Consider, for example, the pro and con arguments centering on the career of Casanova. He was an eighteenth-century libertine whose twelve volumes of *Memoirs* present detailed accounts of his seduction of hundreds of women from all walks of life—noblewomen to servants and nuns to prostitutes. From the first publication of *Memoirs* (nearly a quarter of a century after Casanova's death), historians have questioned the veracity of the work, citing inconsistencies as well as the use of many pseudonyms. Recently, however, a former U.S. diplomat, J. R. Childs, published a book in which he argues that Casanova was telling the truth. He tries to show that the pseudonyms can be matched to real people, that the apparent inconsistencies in time and place can all be explained, and that the *Memoirs* provide a valuable piece of social history. He also says that if Casanova were not telling the truth that he never would have presented himself in such an unflattering light.

In a review of Childs's book, however, Angeline Goreau (*The New York Times*) contends that in order for Childs to identify real persons with the pseudonyms, we must assume that Casanova was telling the truth in the first place—but this is exactly what is denied by his critics. Goreau points out that in the *Memoirs,* the author himself repeatedly proclaims his powers of deceit and his ability to deceive "without the slightest qualm of conscience." Goreau also says that even if Casanova is not trying to dupe us in his autobiography, we must place his *Memoirs* in the context of the times in which works of this sort were written. She says that such documents are dubious as social history because they were designed rather to make some religious or philosophical point (Casanova was preaching the philosophy of moral relativism), or to justify the author in the eyes of posterity.

Neither side in this dispute denies the basic premisses: inconsistencies and pseudonyms abound in the *Memoirs,* and Casanova presents himself as a deceiver. However, these premisses are used in different ways. On both sides, the arguments employed are inductive. Childs uses inductive generalization when he tries to go from individual instances of Casanova's truth telling (supported by identifications of pseudonymous characters) to a general claim that Casanova was telling the truth. Statistical syllogism is used when Childs argues that most persons who lie, unlike Casanova, do not present themselves in an unflattering light, so Casanova is not a liar. Goreau uses analogical reasoning when she argues that Casanova's *Memoirs* are similar to other autobiographies of his time in their propensity to promote some religious, philosophical, or justificatory theme; these other autobiographical works are not reliable guides to social history, so Casanova's work is not a reliable guide either. She also accuses Childs of committing the **fallacy of circular reasoning**, because he assumes as a premiss precisely what his book is supposed to prove as a conclusion, namely, that Casanova was telling the truth.

Circular arguments are deductively valid, in the sense that their conclusions cannot be false if all their premisses are true. Accusations of circular reasoning are usually directed at arguments based on premises no more plausible than the conclusions they support. Such circular arguments fail to convince those who doubt their conclusions, for the truth of the premises is contested.

In deciding which conclusion about Casanova to accept, readers try to assess the evidence for both sides according to the information available to them. They should keep an open mind when doubts can be raised about the correctness of either the evidence or the conclusion. Additional evidence can sometimes resolve the issue, as can new arguments about how the evidence should be interpreted, but some disputes remain insoluble.

VII. REVIEW

In Chapter 4, we have examined three important and commonly used forms of inductive argument:

1. Statistical syllogisms

2. Arguments from analogy

3. Inductive generalizations (arguments based on samples).

In evaluating arguments in these forms, a number of criteria have been suggested. Some of these criteria apply only to particular forms; others apply to all forms of inductive reasoning.

The strength of *inductive generalizations* depends on whether the sample described in the premiss is representative of the population. Two factors are important here: the size of the sample, and the degree of variety in the sample. *Random sampling,* in which each member of the population is equally likely to be a member of the sample, and *stratified random sampling,* in which relevant variety in the population is proportionately matched in the sample, are two good methods to obtain representative samples.

The strength of *arguments from analogy,* or *analogical arguments,* depends crucially on whether the similarities mentioned in the premises are *positively relevant* to the similarity inferred in the conclusion. A similarity mentioned in the premises is *positively relevant* to the similarity in the conclusion if the similarity mentioned in the premiss increases the probability that the similarity in the conclusion will obtain. Whether analogies are relevant depends on background information that is not usually contained in the premises of the argument. The *number* of relevant similarities and relevant dissimilarities, as well as the *variety* in the instances cited in the premises, are also important determinants of the strength of these arguments.

Statistical syllogisms are judged on the basis of the strength of their statistical premises and also on whether they meet the requirement of *total evidence.* In statistical syllogisms, the requirement of total evidence demands that we choose the appropriate *reference class* in the premises of the argument. Background knowledge is required to select the reference class.

A number of special cases of statistical syllogism—*argument from author-*

ity, argument against the person (argumentum ad hominem), and *argument from consensus*—have also been discussed. In their correct form, these arguments depend on a statistical premiss to the effect that, in most cases dealing with the subject matter under consideration, the person who makes the claim speaks truthfully (authority), or the person who makes the claim speaks falsely (against the person), or the majority opinion is correct (consensus).

In evaluating any inductive argument, we must consider the strength of the premisses relative to the strength of the conclusion. Arguments can sometimes be strengthened by additional supporting evidence, such as a larger or more varied sample for an inductive generalization, additional relevant analogies in an argument from analogy, a stronger statistical premiss, or a more appropriate reference class in a statistical syllogism. Arguments can also be strengthened by *weakening their conclusions.* Because the strength of an argument is determined by how well the premisses support the conclusion, a conclusion that is qualified by allowing a margin of error—or is weakened in some other way, relative to the same evidence—results in a stronger argument.

All inductive arguments, not merely statistical syllogisms, are subject to the requirement of total evidence. In statistical syllogisms, the requirement of total evidence obliges us to choose the reference class that embodies all available relevant evidence about the individual mentioned in the conclusion. When we construct inductive generalizations, the requirement of total evidence forbids us to ignore or disregard any relevant evidence in selecting a sample. In an argument from analogy, relevant dissimiliarities cannot be ignored.

A number of fallacies are associated with these correct forms of argument. In each case, a fallacy occurs when some standard is violated. Not every fallacy has a special name, but many do. A list of common inductive fallacies follows:

Fallacious Argument Against the Person: Occurs in the absence of good grounds for believing that a claim is false simply because a particular individual says that it is false. (The appropriate statistical premiss—most of what the individual says about a particular subject matter *S* is false—cannot be accepted.) The fallacious forms of *ad hominem* are frequently identified by the special names: abusive *ad hominem,* circumstantial *ad hominem,* and *tu quoque.*

Fallacious Argument from Authority: Occurs when the authority cited is not a genuine expert in the field of concern, or when the authority is speaking outside his or her field of expertise, or when experts in the area of concern disagree among themselves.

Fallacious Argument from Consensus: Occurs when majority opinion does not constitute a good reason to believe the truth or falsity of a claim.

Fallacy of Biased Statistics: Occurs when the sample is not sufficiently varied to represent the population, usually through failure to approximate a random sample.

Fallacy of Circular Reasoning: Occurs when the truth of the conclusion is already assumed in the premisses that are supposed to support the conclusion, especially when the premisses are themselves questionable.

Fallacy of False Analogy: Occurs when the types of objects in the premisses of an analogical argument are relevantly dissimilar.

Fallacy of Hasty Generalization (also called *insufficient statistics,* or *leaping to a conclusion*): Occurs when the sample in an inductive generalization is too small.

Fallacy of Incomplete Evidence: Occurs when the requirement of taking account of all relevant available evidence is violated.

Fallacy of Misleading Vividness: Occurs when a small amount of particularly vivid information is allowed to outweigh a substantial amount of statistical support for a conclusion.

Slippery Slope: Occurs when one denies that any distinction can be made on the grounds that any distinction would be an arbitrary break in continuum of similar things.

In addition to the names of the forms of arguments and fallacies discussed, you should be familiar with the meanings of the following terms:

Attribute Class: The class represented by *G* in the statistical premiss of the form "*X* percent of all *F*'s are *G*'s" in a statistical syllogism. The conclusion claims that the individual mentioned in the argument is (or is not, in negative cases) a member of this class.

Reference Class: The class represented by *F* in the statistical premiss of the form "*X* percent of all *F*'s are *G*'s" in a statistical syllogism. The other (particular) premiss claims that the individual mentioned is a member of this class.

Syllogism: An argument with two premisses.

Exercise Set 4.8

1. The following report contains a statistical syllogism, in which the statistical premiss is supported by an inductive generalization. Reconstruct both arguments, and try to evaluate them in light of the criteria developed in this chapter. Are any other argument forms used to bolster either conclusion?

> For a dozen years, Dr. Joseph Stolkowski has researched a theory that a potential mother can dictate the sex of her baby by regulating her diet.
>
> Dr. Stolkowski is no quack. He is the distinguished chairman of the physiology department of the Pierre and Marie Curie University in Paris. His papers on the preconception selection of sex in humans have been published in the respected medical journals.
>
> He contends that a woman who wants to give birth to a boy should eat foods rich in potassium and sodium—such as meat, fish, vegetables, chocolate, and salt—beginning at least six weeks before she wishes to become pregnant. A woman who wants to have a girl should eat foods rich in calcium and magnesium, such as milk, cheese, nuts, beans, and cereals. . . .
>
> In a study of 47 French couples from 1970 to 1980, he says, 39 of them produced a child of the sex they wanted after the wives had followed special diets. In Canada, a study of 224 couples on special diets reveals an 80 percent success rate with this method.
>
> Asked recently how his research was going, Stolkowski told us: "Better than ever. We now have five health centers in Paris and five outside the city where couples are taking their special diets and producing the boy or girl babies they want. Our success rate is approximately 90 percent."
>
> —Lloyd Shearer, *Parade Magazine*

2. Consider the following inductive generalization and tell whether, as well as *why*, the argument would be strengthened, weakened, or unaffected in strength if it were modified in each way suggested. Where applicable, discuss the importance of background information.

> All of the 5,000 swans observed in North America and Europe have been white, and no nonwhite swans have been observed. All swans are white.

(1) Suppose only female swans had been observed.

(2) Suppose only 500 swans had been observed.

(3) Suppose all observations were made during winters.

(4) Suppose swans had been observed in Africa and Australia as well as in Europe and North America.

(5) Suppose the conclusion were "All European and North American swans are white."

(6) Suppose only adult swans had been observed.

(7) Suppose all observations were made on weekends.

(8) Suppose all observations were made in areas within 300 miles of a city.

(9) Suppose reports from world travelers about black swans had been recorded in seventeenth-century journals—but that no living person had seen a black swan.

3. Samuel Johnson presents the following case supporting the right of a schoolmaster to beat his pupils. What kind of arguments does Johnson employ? Does he commit any fallacies?

> The government of a schoolmaster is somewhat of the nature of a military government; that is to say that it must be arbitrary according to particular circumstances. A schoolmaster has the right to beat, and an action of assault and battery cannot be admitted against him unless there is some great excess, some barbarity. Pufendorf [an outstanding legal scholar in Johnson's day] maintains the right of a schoolmaster to beat his scholars.
>
> —J. Boswell, *Boswell for the Defense*

4. In the following passage, taken from "Joint Custody as a Fundamental Right," what form of argument is the author using? Identify the premisses and the conclusion of the argument.

> The fundamental right of parental autonomy [the right of parents to share in the companionship, care, custody, and management of their minor children] arguably is identical both within the traditionally recognized nuclear family unit and outside that traditional family unit so long as the relationships maintained outside the unit are "family-like" in the previously specified sense [both parents have an active interest in making parental decisions, and neither is prevented from doing so by reasons of distance, disability, or any other incapacitating factor]. Since the state's right to

interfere with these rights within the family is limited by a principle far more restrictive than "the best interest of the child," it is hard to see why state interference should become any less restricted after divorce. Normally, the state may interfere with parental rights only to prevent harm or abuse to the child. . . . Why should a comparable limitation on state judicial power not be present after divorce as well?

—E. Canacakos, *Arizona Law Review*, 1982

5. The following passage is taken from a newspaper report concerning the efforts of a consumer group to have the government ban Bendectin, a prescription drug used to treat morning sickness associated with pregnancy. The consumer group claims that the drug has been linked to birth defects in humans. On what type of argument supporting the drug's harmful effects does the group base its petition? Discuss any implicit premises.

The consumer group's petition cited an unpublished study from the Max Von Pettenkofer Institute in Germany, which found that 16 of 861 rats exposed to high doses of Bendectin developed a condition in which intestines protrude into the chest through a hole in the muscle separating the lung from abdominal muscles. The group also cited another study conducted in California that used monkeys. That research raised the possibility of an association between the drug and heart defects, the group said.

—*Pittsburgh Press*

In each of the following examples, identify the form of argument used and evaluate each argument according to standards for that form.

6. The pope, the spiritual leader of millions of Roman Catholics, who believe that he speaks infallibly on matters of faith and morals, has—as have previous popes—proclaimed abortion to be a form of murder. Therefore, abortion is murder.

7. In dozens of trials conducted by an independent laboratory, generic brands of laundry detergent performed just as effectively as more expensive name-brand detergents. Therefore, generic brands are just as effective as name-brand detergents for all laundry purposes.

8. In a recent Harris Poll, 47 percent of a sample (carefully matched to the population) of 2,500 American adults said that they approved of the president's economic policies. Therefore, approximately 47 percent of all American adults approve of the president's economic policies.

9. The movie star whose recently divorced young wife receives alimony of $150,000 per year probably won't have to pay it for very long, because most young women who are divorced remarry within a year of the divorce. (Alimony payments cease upon remarriage.)

10. *Background:* Lead is sometimes added to molten bronze to increase its fluidity. The amounts normally added range from 5 percent to 25 percent of the volume of bronze.

The analyses of Bronze Age Greek artifacts made by Craddock, supplemented by those of Renfrew and the Stuttgart group for the Early Bronze Age, show that most copper, arsenical bronze, and tin bronze objects contain less than 1 percent lead. Indeed, out of a total of 185 analyses of Early and Late Bronze Age axes, chisels, swords, daggers, knives, spearheads, arrowheads, and figurines, 161 show lead contents of less than 1 percent, and only nine show more than 3 percent. Catling and Jones found that of 141 Late Minoan II copper and bronze objects from the unexplored Mansion, Knossos, Crete, only three objects had as much as 1 percent lead. . . . The evidence that lead was rarely deliberately added to copper or bronze objects in the Greek Bronze Age seems compelling and indicates that the lead in ancient copper or bronze objects below about 1.5 percent (and certainly below 0.5 percent) is present as an accidental impurity from the copper ore.

—N. H. Gale and Z. A. Stos-Gale, "Bronze Age Copper Sources in the Mediterranean," *Science* 216 (1982):12

11. In the outbreaks of human poisoning from methylmercury in Japan and later in Iraq, one of the most consistent signs in adults was deficits in visual function. . . . The visual system of macaque monkeys resembles that of humans and exhibits the same signs and pathological lesions as that of humans when exposed to methylmercury. Macaques are therefore excellent models for testing the effects of methylmercury on the visual system.

—D. C. Rice and S. G. Gilbert, "Early Chronic Low-Level Methylmercury Poisoning in Monkeys Impairs Spatial Vision," *Science* 216 (1982):759

12. What steps would you take to find an unbiased sample if you wanted to conduct a poll to determine student opinion at your college or university about the legalization of marijuana?

13. What kind of argument supports the conclusion that is stated in the first sentence of the passage below?

Over wide areas of Australia the tame dingo was by no means an effective hunting dog and it contributed relatively little to the Aborigine's larder.

At Warburton, the Aborigines denied ever having used dingoes in hunting, especially when pursuing large animals, and this view was echoed by Jankuntjara [in South Australia, at the southeastern end of the Western Desert] informants interviewed by Hamilton. Nor were dingoes ever used for hunting by the desert-dwelling Aborigines we observed in the Clutterbuck Hills-Tikatika region in 1966—1967 or at Pulykara, near Mt. Madley, in 1970.

—R. A. Gould, *Living Archaeology*

14. Can you think of any plausible example in which the opinions of most Americans would constitute the basis for a nonfallacious argument from consensus?

15. Recently, the city of Pittsburgh decided to enforce collection of a personal property tax on stocks and bonds held by city residents. All residents who

own such property are supposed to file statements listing their property. The city's resources for detecting ownership of these properties are practically nonexistent, since the city does not have access to federal income-tax returns filed by residents. Despite this, a letter claiming that the recipient owns stocks, bonds, or both was sent by the city to each head of household whose earned income exceeded $40,000 per year. (A city income tax is deducted from wages, so these persons were identifiable.) On what type of argument do you think the city based its claim to know that persons earning more than $40,000 owned stocks or bonds?

16. The following passage is taken from a letter to the editor of *Science News* 6/12/93 concerning land use in the Americas prior to 1500. Name the mistake in reasoning that the author is worried about. Tell what form of argument the author uses against the argument he criticizes.

> Data from one lake in central Mexico are extrapolated to Native Americans in general. Given the diversity and complexity of Native Americans, this is astonishing.
>
> Could a parallel assertion be made, for instance, after researching long-term erosion patterns into Lake Como in Italy and then issuing a blanket statement about the land use practices of Eurasion peoples? Most researchers would not be so foolish as to make such a pronouncement.
>
> —Philip Snyder

17. In the following, name the mistake in reasoning that the author of the letter accuses Gajdusek of making. Also tell what form of argument Schryer employs against Gajdusek.

> I must question the relevance of Gajdusek's argument that "the whole of Australia knows these people are cannibals". . . [This] may well be true, but proves nothing. At one time virtually the whole population of Europe and much of Britain and America "knew" that witches existed and countless persons were not only arrested but put to death for allegedly practicing witchcraft. Nevertheless, it is now generally acknowledged that witches, defined as persons with supernatural powers of diabolical origin, do not exist and never did. Gajdusek may or may not have other proof for the existence of cannibalism in New Guinea, but he does his case no good by arguing, in effect, that if a lot of people, including civil authorities, believe in the occurrence of some questionable practice then it must be so.
>
> —Letter from D. R. Schryer in *Science* 233 (1986):926

18. The following is taken from a letter to the editor of *Science News* 8/7/93. Identify the fallacy that the author of the letter suggests that the person who wrote the article commits.

> You make statements about alcoholics in general on the basis of a study using entirely male samples. My experience as a member of Alcoholics Anonymous, however, has suggested that there are significant differences

between female and male alcoholics. This is particularly noticeable with regard to the incidence and severity of depression.

—Anita A.

19. Current debates flourish about the wisdom of raising the automobile speed limit in certain areas from 55 to 65 miles per hour. Both sides agree that preventing traffic accidents and saving lives are worthwhile goals. Proponents of the measure argue that the increase in the speed limit helps to save lives because it promotes smoother traffic flow and reduces the time in which motorists are on the road and exposed to accidents. Opponents of the measure can agree that higher speed limits promote smoother traffic flow and reduce accident exposure time, while insisting that statistics have shown that the years in which the 55 mph limit was strictly enforced were years in which deaths from traffic accidents were greatly reduced. On the basis of these statistics, they argue that the lower speed limit saves lives. Proponents do not deny the statistics, but say that the figures have been misinterpreted and even manipulated and that this has resulted in a falsification of the true picture.

Can you construct (or reconstruct) some pro and con inductive arguments on the basis of the preceding information or from other sources? In your opinion, which side has the stronger support? Why?

20. Discuss the forms of argument used in the following discussion of banning tobacco advertising and products:

> Advertising bans can be particularly helpful in reducing cigarette consumption among adolescents, with whom we should be especially concerned on grounds of "informed consent." There is good evidence that cigarette advertising in general, and sport sponsorship in particular, appeals to children [several statistical studies are cited]. Conversely, banning advertising of cigarettes in Norway in 1975 led to a sharp decline in the percentage of teenagers who subsequently have become daily smokers [again, statistical studies are cited]. . . .

> Against bans on the use or sale of tobacco, the Prohibition analogy is standardly urged. Already we have evidence of substantial "bootlegging" (or "buttlegging") of cigarettes between states with low cigarette taxes and those with high ones. Any more serious ban on sale or use of tobacco would no doubt lead to even more illicit activity of this sort. Even accepting such slippage, however, this strategy is still bound to reduce smoking substantially. Whether more would be lost in terms of respect for the law than would be gained in terms of public health remains an open question.

—R.E. Goodin, *No Smoking*

CAUSAL ARGUMENTS

I. INTRODUCTION

Many of the inductive arguments discussed thus far are causal arguments. The conclusions of such arguments state that a causal relationship holds (or fails to hold) between two types of things or events. For example, one argument in Chapter 4 concludes that birth-control hormones may affect brain development. Another concludes that obliterating the high-contrast wing stripes on tropical butterflies does not affect wing damage or survival.

Statements about causes (causal claims) occur as the conclusions of different forms of argument. Some causal arguments have the form of inductive generalizations; others are arguments from analogy. Arguments from authority, which, when correct, are statistical syllogisms, are also used to support causal conclusions. In this chapter, we pay special attention to a variety of ways of establishing causal claims. We call any argument in which the conclusion is a causal claim a **causal argument,** but, remember, the term *causal argument* does not refer to any single *form* of argument.

Causal connections are a focus of concern in everyday life. For example, when cars break down, when buses are late, when classes are canceled, when we do poorly in an examination, or when personal relationships take a turn for the worse, we look for causes.

Research by psychologists R. Nisbett and L. Ross (*Human Inference*) shows that people readily generate causal accounts of events on the basis of little evidence. Nisbett and Ross also found that spontaneous causal analysis occurs frequently in ordinary conversation. In one experiment, the investigators "bugged" thirteen haphazardly selected conversations at singles' bars, at a picnic for economically underprivileged senior citizens, and at student bull sessions. Using a set of categories that included "Gives Information," "Gives Evaluation," "Gives Advice or Suggestion," "Makes Prediction," and "Gives Causal Analysis," they classified each utterance of the speakers. Statements expressing or requesting causal analysis accounted for roughly 15 percent of all utterances recorded. Even though, as the investigators admit, their sample was not random, the proportion of ordinary speech devoted to causes was impressive. The search for causes is not confined to scientific investigations; it is also important in our daily lives.

In this chapter, we look closely at some methods that have been proposed as aids to discovering causes and to supporting claims about causes. Although the *discovery* of causes is an important part of everyday life, critical thinking is more particularly concerned with the *justification* of causal claims than with how causes can be discovered. Inadequate evidence for causal claims should be challenged or supplemented. Thus we need to know how to evaluate arguments with causal conclusions. We should also be aware of common mistakes in causal reasoning (causal fallacies) and learn to avoid them.

II. MILL'S METHODS FOR ESTABLISHING CAUSAL CLAIMS

The justification of causal claims is primarily a problem in *inductive* logic. The reasons offered for the existence of a causal connection are usually less than conclusive, although some causal arguments are better than others. Inductive logic is a much newer branch of knowledge than deductive logic. The latter has been studied continuously since it was developed—almost single-hand-edly—by the Greek philosopher Aristotle 2,300 years ago. (This is not to say that no one reasoned logically before Aristotle, but he was the first to formulate *principles* of logical reasoning.) In the nineteenth century, John Stuart Mill—the author of *Utilitarianism; On Liberty;* and *On the Subjection of Women*—tried to spell out the rules of inductive logic, as Aristotle had done for deductive logic.

Mill recognized that knowledge of scientific laws is based on inductive reasoning and that reasoning about causes is central to acquiring such knowledge. He was distressed with the flimsy basis for many causal claims put forward by scientists of his own day. To correct the problem, he formulated standards that he believed to represent sound scientific practice that would serve as guidelines in reasoning about causes. Mill believed that causal claims should be based on careful observation and experiment; he thought that if he could formulate some rules about how to use observation and experiment to gain knowledge of causes, then people could become more skilled at causal reasoning. The methods that Mill outlined, although they do not always measure up to his exaggerated claims for their success, still provide an important basis for scientific reasoning.

Mill's methods are also useful in ordinary causal reasoning. He outlined and discussed the five methods that we examine in this chapter. Mill presented his methods both as aids to discover causes and instruments to justify causal claims. Scientists use them both ways.

1. The Method of Agreement

Shortly after a recent flight from Japan landed in Copenhagen, 144 passengers were hospitalized. Another 51 were treated but did not require hospitalization. All of the affected passengers exhibited symptoms of a gastrointestinal disorder. Doctors immediately suspected food poisoning. The passengers had eaten food taken aboard during a refueling stop in Anchorage. All those who later became ill had eaten omelets prepared by a cook who worked for the airline's catering service in Anchorage. During a two-week investigation, it was learned that this cook had an infected sore on his finger. Officials concluded that bacteria from this infection had been the source of contamination and the cause of the food poisoning suffered by the passengers.

The investigators' pattern of causal reasoning exemplifies *Mill's Method of Agreement*. When we use the Method of Agreement to identify the cause of some event or condition, we look at antecedent circumstances (the events or conditions that occurred earlier) to see whether some antecedent circumstance is common to each occurence of the event for which a cause is sought. If only one common antecedent circumstance can be identified, then it is likely to be the cause—or, at least, a part of the cause—of the event or condition under investigation.

Finding a common antecedent circumstance is not sufficient to justify a causal claim, for many antecedent circumstances are causally irrelevant. In this case, for example, all the passengers who became ill also boarded the plane in Tokyo, but we have no reason to believe that boarding a plane in a particular city causes gastrointestinal illness. Causal reasoning is guided by general background knowledge about the types of causes that bring about the condition or event in question. In the airline incident, the illness was diagnosed as *food poisoning*. This diagnosis structured the search for a cause. It is well known that food poisoning is caused by bacterial contamination of food. Something is also known about how contamination occurs. Harmful bacteria grow when susceptible foods are not stored at the proper temperature. Food can also become contaminated through contact with unclean utensils or unclean hands. The relevant antecedent circumstance common to the hospitalized passengers was that before becoming ill, all had eaten omelets prepared by the cook with an infected finger.

Schematically, the Method of Agreement can be presented in the following form, where E represents the event or condition for which the cause is sought, and S-Z represent a selection, guided by general background information, of antecedent conditions. The left-hand column numbers each separate case in which E occurs.

Case	Antecedent Circumstances	Event for Which Cause Is Sought
1	X, Y, Z	E
2	X, U, V, Y	E
3	X, W, S	E
4	X, T, Z, W	E
etc.	$X, \ldots$	E

In this schematic representation, X is the only antecedent circumstance in which all occurrences of E agree. Thus, the use of Mill's Method of Agreement supports X as the cause—or a part of the cause—of E. Applying the scheme to our example, the number of cases is 195, the total number of cases of food poisoning (E). The antecedent circumstance X represents the circumstance of eating an omelet prepared by the cook with an infected finger. The other letters represent various other antecedent circumstances that were possible causes of the disease. In our example, these antecedent circumstances included foods and beverages, other than the cook's omelets, that were taken by passengers who became ill.

The use of the Method of Agreement does not guarantee that a cause will be discovered. Moreover, the method does not guarantee that the *suspected* cause is the *real* cause of the illness. (This is an inductive form of reasoning, not a deductive form.) The investigators could have overlooked the true source of contamination, and the cook with the sore finger might have been only coincidentally connected with the illnesses. However, this investigation was thorough, and other evidence supported the same cause of illness, so officials believed there was little room for doubt.

The use of Method of Agreement is not mechanical, because we are faced with an unlimited number of antecedent circumstances in most cases of causal inquiry. Using background knowledge, we need to confine our attention to those antecedent circumstances that are possible causal agents. Unless an investigator has some idea of the type of cause sought, the Method of Agreement is nearly useless.

Another limitation of the Method of Agreement is that ignorance or error might lead to overlooking a possible cause when constructing the list of antecedent circumstances. If the true cause is not on the list, the Method of Agreement will not disclose it, and the method may lead to a false conclusion. Another problem that can arise is that an antecedent circumstance and a particular effect might not be directly related, yet both could be effects of some common underlying cause. This is a general problem for causal reasoning, not just for the use of Mill's Method, and it is discussed in Section VI.

The method is most likely to lead to a true conclusion when we possess general information about the types of causes that bring about the condition or event in question. Then the method can be used to narrow the search for a cause within that general framework or *causal theory*. In our example, the causal theory that guides the search for a cause of the passengers' illness is the general information about the symptoms and causes of food poisoning. It is known that vomiting, stomach cramps, and diarrhea can occur several hours after eating contaminated food. Also, harmful bacteria multiply rapidly in foods typically cooked at low temperatures—such as omelets, custards, and cream sauces. Such foods receive special scrutiny during investigations of food poisoning. Furthermore, harmful bacteria can be introduced into foods from cuts, unwashed hands, and the like. All of this background information, not just the use of Mill's Method, helped to solve the problem of the passengers' illness.

Exercise Set 5.1

For each of the following situations, suggest some possible common antecedent circumstances that you might investigate to find the cause of the event described.

1. You have a flat tire on the way to work. When you finally get there, you find that three of your coworkers also had flat tires on the way to work.

2. When you arrive home in the early evening, you try to turn on some lights and find that none of them works.

3. Although it is early summer, all of the trees in the woods near your home are turning brown.

4. When you go to a concert downtown and try to park in the lot you normally use, you find that it is full. All of the other parking lots in the area are full as well.

5. When you turn on a faucet, the water has a rusty color. Your neighbors complain about the same condition in their water.

6. Three students in a class turn in identical term papers.

7. An unusually high number of students from your former high school earn scholarships at major universities year after year.

2. The Method of Difference

Although the newspaper report from which the food poisoning example was taken did not present all the details, it was clear that the investigation to find the cause of the illnesses used another of Mill's methods, the **Method of Difference,** to eliminate some possible causes of the disease. Once the illness was tentatively diagnosed as food poisoning, the search for a cause concentrated on foods eaten by the various passengers. According to the report, everyone in the first-class section of the plane was served an omelet prepared by that cook, but many of the tourist-class passengers were not. The cook prepared between 207 and 215 omelets, but only 195 passengers became ill. However, no one who had not eaten an omelet prepared by the cook with the infected finger became ill.

Mill's Method of Difference tells us that to find the cause of an event, or condition E, we should look at antecedent circumstances when E is present, and compare these to antecedent circumstances when E fails to occur in order to see how the antecedent circumstances in the two cases differ. Schematically, the Method of Difference can be represented:

Case	Antecedent Circumstances	Event for Which Cause Is Sought
1	X, S, R, U, V, W	E occurs
2	X, S, R, U, V	E does not occur

Suppose, for example, that a husband and wife were on that flight from Tokyo and were served identical meals. Suppose, further, that the wife is allergic to eggs, so she did not eat the omelet, although she ate all the other foods, and—except in that one respect—ate the same things as her husband. If she did not become ill but her husband did, the omelet would be judged to be the cause of the food poisoning according to Mill's Method of Difference. The only difference between E's occurring and failing to occur is the presence of W (eating an omelet) in the antecedent circumstances of E. Under these conditions—because unless W occurs, E fails to occur—Mill's Method of Difference states that W is the cause, or an indispensable part of the cause, of E.

The Method of Difference is subject to the same limitations as the Method of Agreement. If the real cause is not listed in the antecedent circumstances, the method cannot isolate it. Similarly, the method works best when the choice of antecedent circumstances is guided by a causal theory. In our example, a well-established causal theory suggests possible causes of food poisoning. In the presence of such causal theories, uses of Mill's methods constitute strong evidence for causal claims.

Exercise Set 5.2

For each of the following situations, suggest some antecedent circumstances that might account for the presence of the effect on the one hand and its absence on the other.

1. A friend gives you two tomato plants, which you set out in your garden. One plant produces two dozen tomatoes; the other plant fails to yield a single one.

2. You and a friend go on a hike together. The next day she breaks out with a case of poison ivy, but you don't have any signs of it.

3. You bake a birthday cake and it turns out just right. You make a second cake a week later, but this one fails.

4. You normally fall asleep within ten minutes of going to bed, but last night you lay awake for at least two hours before you fell asleep.

5. Your new cotton shirt fit perfectly the first time you wore it two weeks ago, but it is now too tight around the collar and its sleeves are an inch too short.

6. You and a friend submit identical solutions to a puzzle contest. He wins a prize, but you do not.

7. You have claimed the same deductions for five years on your federal income tax return and have not been challenged until this year.

8. Your dog refuses to eat the brand of food that he has been eating for four nights in a row.

3. The Joint Method of Agreement and Difference

In many causal investigations, like that of the food poisoning case, Mill's Method of Agreement and Method of Difference are combined. If both methods point to the same cause, support for a causal claim is strengthened. Whenever possible, in important investigations, the Method of Agreement is applied to all cases in which the condition occurs and again to all cases in which the condition does *not* occur; the Method of Difference is then used to compare the two *sets* of cases.

The two methods are combined so often as to merit a special name—**The Joint Method of Agreement and Difference.** Schematically, the joint method looks like this:

Cases	Antecedent Circumstances	Event for Which Cause Is Sought
1-*b*	*X, S, T, U*	*E* occurs
i-n	*S, T, U, V*	*E* does not occur

In the schematic representation, the cases (1-*h*) in which *E* occurs are grouped together. (In our example, the 195 cases of food poisoning.) The cases (*i-n*) in which *E* does not occur are also grouped together.

The newspaper report from which our example was taken did not specify the number of cases in which passengers did not become ill, but the plane was a jumbo jet and carried many such persons. The letters *S-U* represent foods eaten by each passenger. The letter *V* represents an alternative food to *X* (for example, an omelet prepared by another cook or a different type of main dish). Although *V* represents a difference between the two groups, it is not judged to be the cause of the illness, because persons who ate *V* did not become ill.

Because it is so powerful, the Joint Method of Agreement and Difference is widely used to study the causes of and cures for diseases. For example, if only two persons are given a flu vaccination and one escapes the flu but the other is stricken, we know little about the effectiveness of the flu vaccine. In some cases, apparent exposure to a cause does not produce the effect. The person who did not get the flu may have had a natural immunity or may not have been exposed. We know also that vaccination itself can, in some cases, cause a case, usually mild, of the disease it is designed to prevent. If everyone in a rather isolated community receives a flu vaccine and little or no flu occurs, use of the Method of Agreement would tell us the vaccine was effective. But we cannot be too confident about this result, for the community may simply not have been exposed to the flu virus. If, however, hundreds of students are vaccinated for the flu at the student health clinic and only a few of them get the flu, but a very large proportion of hundreds of unvaccinated students at the same school get the flu, the Joint Method of Agreement and Difference tells us that there is good reason to believe the vaccine is effective in preventing flu.

Although Mill's methods are most effective when they are applied within the structure of a specific causal theory to provide evidence for causal claims, they can also be used to guide and restrict the search for causes when no specific causal theory is available. In this way Mill's methods help investigators formulate causal theories that can be subjected to further testing. Early studies of cholera, discussed by B. MacMahon and T. Pugh (*Epidemiology*), illustrate this point. Even before the germ theory of disease was developed, observers noted that cholera spread when persons came into contact with infected persons and that the occurrence of cholera was associated with poverty, overcrowding, refuse, and filth. General causal theories of the time suggested that the common factor was exposure to the fecal matter from cholera patients.

In 1854, a perceptive observer, John Snow, noticed that during a cholera epidemic in London, the frequency of the disease was highly variable in one neighborhood. Five years earlier, in 1849, all groups in London had been uniform with respect to frequency of the disease. Using the Joint Method of Agreement and Difference, Snow looked for antecedent circumstances that would account for the different frequencies of cholera present in the two groups in 1854. He discovered that families in the area were served by two different water companies. Those supplied by the Southwark and Vauxhall Company, had a much higher incidence of cholera than those supplied by the Lambeth Company. Between 1849 and 1854, the Lambeth Company had changed its supply source—which had been near the area where the Southwark and Vauxhall Company obtained its water—to a place farther upstream on the Thames River. As a result of its move, the Lambeth Company no longer drew its water from an area where large amounts of sewage poured into the river. Snow believed this confirmed his suspicion that fecal contamination was the cause of cholera.

In the wake of Snow's investigations, efforts were made to provide the citizens of London with clean drinking water, and the incidence of cholera declined significantly, even though the exact cause of the disease (the specific germ) was not known until much later. This use of Mill's methods by Snow was an important step in the development of the germ theory of disease.

The search for causes and cures of disease often begins when investigators notice differences in the geographic distribution of a disease. When a disease is prevalent in one area and much less common in another area, it is natural to look for causes in such general features as differences in diet, soil (which affects food grown there), and water supplies.

Not all attempts to use Mill's methods as aids to discover causes have been as successful as Snow's work on cholera. An incident reported in the *Diary* of Samuel Pepys shows the perils of using Mill's methods in the absence of a causal theory.

During an epidemic of the bubonic plague in London in the 1660s, someone noticed that not a single London tobacco seller died of the plague. On these grounds, reasoning by what would now be called the Joint Method of Agreement and Difference, tobacco was believed to prevent plague. Accordingly, at Eton, outside London, all the schoolboys were ordered to smoke tobacco. Eton is one of the few boarding schools in history where boys were flogged for failing to smoke! Unfortunately, smoking did not prevent bubonic plague at Eton—the use of tobacco was apparently unrelated to avoidance of the disease. Whatever spared the London tobacconists remains unknown; their escape from plague may have been simply a coincidence. We now know that the bubonic plague virus is transmitted through the bite of fleas that are carried on rodents. After the rats die of the disease, the hungry fleas begin migrating to other hosts; when they bite people, the disease is transmitted into the human population. The great plague episodes in England during the seventeenth century resulted when rats escaped into the cities from ships that brought the rats—and the disease—from foreign ports. This causal connection between rats, fleas, and plague was not discovered, however, until a hundred years after the worst plague epidemics—and it was much later before the immediate cause, a specific virus, was isolated.

In our own time, medical research expends many resources to discover causes and cures for cancer, AIDS, and other scourges. Mill's methods are frequently applied at various levels of research. It has been observed, for example, that cervical cancer is almost nonexistent among nuns, although it is a rather common form of cancer among women in general. Use of the Joint Method of Agreement and Difference leads investigators to suspect that some aspect of sexual activity or the reproductive process is causally related to cancer of the cervix.

4. The Method of Concomitant Variation

The Method of Difference and the Joint Method of Agreement and Difference are applicable only when the suspected causal source can be observed to be present in some cases and absent in others. In the investigation of the cause of food poisoning, the suspected foods were eaten by some passengers but not by others. In the study of cholera, London households received water from two distinct sources. In these cases, as in all cases for which the Method of Difference and the Joint Method of Agreement and Difference are applicable, we can distinguish between exposure and nonexposure to the suspected cause.

As in the cholera example, the event or condition that results from the cause may be an increased or decreased *rate* or relative frequency of occurrence in a group of persons, rather than an occurrence of the condition corresponding to each exposure to the suspected cause. Cholera was not present in each case in which the suspected cause (contaminated water) was present. Nevertheless, the water supply was judged to be the cause (or part of the cause) of cholera because many more customers of Southwark and Vauxhall contracted the disease than did customers of the Lambeth Company. Background knowledge informs us that some people are more susceptible to disease than others and also that people drink water from sources other than the taps in their own dwellings.

Sometimes when we want to investigate a causal question, we are faced with circumstances in which the effect and the suspected cause are always present to some extent. This inhibits use of the Method of Difference and, consequently, the Joint Method. Of course, the Method of Agreement might prove useful, but if there are several common antecedent circumstances, this method might not distinguish among them. If, however, the condition or event under investigation *varies in degree or strength* from one case to another, the **Method of Concomitant Variation** could be the tool to use. Mill's idea behind this method was that a change in the strength of the effect is to be accounted for by a change in the strength of the cause. Therefore, to find the cause of an effect that varies, look for an antecedent condition that varies. The variation in the effect may be in direct or inverse proportion to variation in the suspected cause. Use of the method is demonstrated in the following example.

High blood pressure (hypertension)—a widespread condition among people in all parts of the United States—is regarded as a major contributor to fatal heart attacks. According to a newspaper report in the *Arizona Daily Star*, about 23 million Americans—10 percent of the population—suffer from high blood pressure. However, the frequency with which fatal hypertension attacks the population varies from place to place. Two scientists noted that the death rate from hypertension-related heart attacks in Tucson, Arizona, was 41 percent below the national average. They suggested that the lower death rate could be explained by the causal relationship between a relatively high content of selenium in Arizona soil and lower incidence of hypertension in the population of Arizona residents.

Selenium is a metal found in small quantities in almost all soils, and, like other "trace minerals", finds its way into the human body in minute amounts through incorporation into the food chain. Current physiological theory acknowledges the role of some trace minerals in preventing diseases. The scientists studied 45 cities. They used the selenium levels measured in grazing food or forage crops as a gauge for amounts of selenium present in state soils. Tucson was among nine cities in seven Western states with high selenium levels and relatively low hypertension-related death rates. The death rates attributed to high blood pressure in selenium-poor states (Connecticut, Illinois, Ohio, New York, Oregon, Massachusetts, Rhode Island, Pennsylvania, Indiana, and Delaware) are three times greater than these rates in selenium-rich areas.

In this example, the association between selenium levels in the soil (the antecedent circumstance) and death rates from high blood pressure (the condition for which a cause is sought) suggests that selenium might be a causal factor in the prevention of fatal high blood pressure. The method used to discover this connection—or to justify the claim that a causal connection exists between higher selenium levels in the soil and lower incidence of fatal high blood pressure—is Mill's Method of Concomitant Variation. Here is a schematic representation of this Method:

Cases or Groups	Antecedent Circumstances	Event or Condition for Which Cause Is Sought
1	$X+, Y, Z, \ldots$	$E+$ (or $E-$)
2	$X-, Y, Z, \ldots$	$E-$ (or $E+$)

The far left-hand column represents individuals, events, or circumstances—or groups of the same—classed according to the severity or degree of strength of the condition under investigation. There may be more than two such cases. For example, instead of dividing the individuals into two groups according to whether a condition is present in severe or mild degree, we might divide the individuals into three groups—severe, mild, and moderate. The letter X represents the antecedent circumstance that varies in strength—either in the same direction as the condition under investigation or in the opposite direction. In our example, the death rate from hypertension decreased ($E-$) as the selenium level increased ($X+$). The letters Y, Z, and so on, represent any other common antecedent circumstances suspected of being causally connected with the condition under investigation. In the newspaper report, no other antecedent circumstances—such as different trace minerals or average hours of sunshine per day—were mentioned. Presumably, the scientists decided to focus on the role of selenium in this study.

Another study of disease provides a classic example of the use of the Method of Concomitant Variation. Every day, in large cities, people die from respiratory problems. Although now smog alerts keep people inside in times of heavy air pollution, until recently people were unaware of the close connection between fatal respiratory events and air pollution. This changed with a dramatic discovery in the early 1950s. In counting the number of deaths in London that occurred during a time of severe atmospheric pollution (formerly called "London fog") from November 29 to December 16, 1952, it became

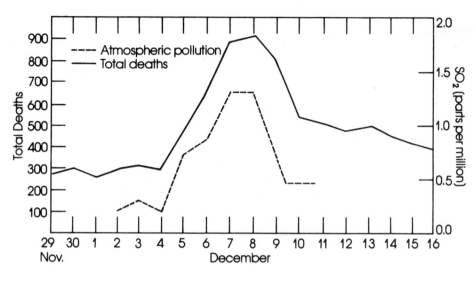

FIGURE 5–1

Atmospheric pollution (in parts per million of sulfur dioxide) and numbers of deaths per day in London, from Nov. 29 to Dec. 16, 1952. *Source*: B. MacMahon, T. Pugh, and J. Ipsen, *Epidemiologic Methods* (Boston: Little, Brown, 1960), page 6.

apparent, based on Mill's Method of Concomitant Variation, that the intense smog had caused approximately 4,000 deaths. Information concerning the antecedent circumstances (pollution measured in parts per million of sulphur dioxide, SO_2) and the event whose cause is sought (increase in number of deaths) is reproduced in Figure 5-1. This graph shows clearly that the increases and decreases in the number of deaths ($E+$) almost exactly match the increases and decreases in parts per million of sulfur dioxide in the atmosphere ($X+$).

The Method of Concomitant Variation, like Mill's other methods, is most useful within the framework of a specific causal theory. Such a causal theory provides guidance as to which antecedent circumstances among an indefinite number of available antecedents are plausible candidates for causes. If little is known about the specific causal nature of a widespread disease, such as cancer or hypertension, and different frequencies appear to be present in different geographic areas, investigators use the Method of Concomitant Variation to select broad environmental features, which vary with intensities that match the variation in frequency of the disease. This helps narrow the search for causes, and sometimes bringing a disease under control is possible even when the precise causal agents are unknown.

5. The Method of Residues

Mill's **Method of Residues** not only recognizes the complexity of situations in which multiple causal forces are operating, but also offers a way to separate those components in causal analysis. Suppose, for example, that you have planted a dogwood tree that is not growing well. You consult a knowledgeable neighbor who suggests a number of causal possibilities for slow or poor growth in these trees. She asks if the tree has been getting enough water, and explains that the tree requires at least an inch of water each week during the growing season. You have been giving the tree adequate water, however, so that is not the problem. Then she asks whether the proper amount of fertilizer has been used—too little or too much can harm the tree. But you have followed the recommended dosage of feeding once a year. She inspects the tree and notices that grass is growing right up to its trunk. This is known to inhibit dogwood growth. So you clear a circle two feet wide around the trunk of the tree, and keep the grass away from it. In the next growing season, the tree shows signs of more vigourous growth. In this example, a complex effect, abnormally slow growth of dogwood trees, is brought about by several causes: inadequate water, improper fertilization, and turf cover growing directly against the trunk. But the slow growth in your tree is not a result of the first two causes, and so, by the Method of Residues, the third cause is judged responsible.

A famous use of the Method of Residues occurs in the history of astronomy. From ancient times until late in the eighteenth century, astronomers thought that our solar system contained only six major planets. After the seventh planet, Uranus, was discovered by Herschel in 1781, its orbit was discovered to be irregular. For a while the irregularity was suspected to be the result of an error in calculation. But when the young astronomer H. Leverrier verified the calculations, he suggested that a different cause—the gravitational pull of a still more distant eighth planet—would account for the irregular orbit. At Leverrier's suggestion about where to focus their search, astronomers discovered Neptune in 1846, about one degree from where Leverrier had suggested.

Although discrepancies in the orbit of Neptune were used in the same way to predict the existence of the ninth solar planet, Pluto, the success of the Method of Residues in that case is questionable. Although Pluto was found in the region of the sky predicted by the calculations, that planet is much too small to exert the gravitational pull on Neptune indicated by Neptune's irregular orbit. Apparently, the discovery of Pluto, in 1930, can more reasonably be attributed to a careful search of the sky, using powerful new telescopes at the Lowell Observatory, than to the use of the Method of Residues.

The Method of Residues works by using known causes to account for as much of the complex effect as possible, and then invoking an additional cause to account for the remainder. The Method is verified by identifying the postulated new cause if possible. Schematically the Method of Residues can be characterized:

Components of causal complex	**Complex effect**
$X, Y, (Z?)$	$E_1 \cdot E_2 \cdot E_3$
X accounts for	E_1
Y accounts for	E_2
Z accounts for	E_3

Exercise Set 5.3

In each of the following exercises:

(1) Identify the condition or event for which a cause is sought. Be sure to tell whether specific occurrences or rates (relative frequencies) of occurrence are being investigated.

(2) Identify all antecedent circumstances mentioned in the example.

(3) State which of Mill's methods is being used.

(4) Identify the cause, according to the use of Mill's methods.

> Notice that some of the exercises are taken from newspaper reports and that less than complete information is available. If more background information is required to make a judgment, discuss why this is so. Being aware of what is needed to pass critical judgment on a problem is part of critical thinking! The evidence we receive in newspapers, magazines, and other sources is often incomplete with respect to the conclusions stated there.

1. From a report in *The New York Times* on the use of a new antiviral drug, called "ara-A," in the treatment of herpes simplex encephalitis:

> Of 28 cases of the disease, 18 received ara-A, and 10 were given an inert substance for 10 days. Five persons in the first group died, and seven in the second group. Thus the mortality rate of the untreated group was 70 percent; the rate of the treated group was 28 percent.

2. Alzheimer's disease is a serious form of senility that afflicts from 5 to 10 percent of all persons over age 65. Recently, researchers discovered that patients who die of Alzheimer's disease have much smaller amounts of a particular enzyme in the cortexes of their brains than persons the same age who do not suffer from the disease. The loss of this enzyme activity has been suspected as a cause of the lesions found on the brains of Alzheimer's patients. In postmortem examinations of five Alzheimer's patients and five people without the disease, all the diseased patients were found to have lost neurons from the nucleus basalis (a tiny area deep in the brain; its function is not understood by neurologists), while all the people without the disease had the normal number of cells in this area. Scientists who conducted this study believe that the loss of neurons from the nucleus basalis may be responsible for the decreased activity in the cortex.

3. An antismoking campaign aimed at junior high school students has shown significant results. . . . The study involved 750 Houston seventh graders. One group of students was asked about smoking habits—31 percent said they had smoked at least one cigarette in the previous month—and was asked the same question again ten weeks later. No antismoking instruction was given to them. [They are members of the control group.] Other groups of students were asked the same question [The report does not tell how they responded], and then participated in various kinds of anti-smoking instruction. By the end of ten weeks, 18.3 percent of the control group—those who were not shown antismoking propaganda—had taken up smoking. Among the other groups, fewer students had started smoking—ranging from 8.6 percent to 10.3 percent.

—Arizona Daily Star

4. *Background:* We now know that the disease beriberi is caused by a dietary deficiency in the B complex of vitamins, particularly vitamin B1. Whole grains provide a common source of this vitamin. The following episode occurred before anything was known about vitamins. The research was conducted in an insane asylum. Cured rice has been treated to preserve some of the outer hull. Uncured rice (now usually called "polished rice") is rice from which the outer hull—which contains most of the vitamins—is removed.

> The lunatics are housed in two exactly similar buildings on opposite sides of a quadrangle surrounded by a high wall. On December 5, 1905, all the lunatics at that time in the hospital were drawn up in the dining shed and numbered off from the left. The odd numbers were subsequently domiciled [housed] in the ward on the east side of the courtyard, and no alteration was made in their diet. They were still supplied with the same uncured rice as in 1905. The even numbers were quartered in the ward on the west of the quadrangle and received the same rations as the occupants of the other ward with the exception that they were supplied with cured rice. . . . On December 5, there were 59 lunatics in the asylum; of these, 29 were put on cured rice and 30 on uncured rice. The next patient admitted to the asylum was admitted to the cured rice ward, and the one admitted after him to the uncured rice ward, the next to cured, and so on alternately to the end of the year.
>
> In the middle of the year, the patients in the east ward were moved to the west ward and those in the west ward to the east, but they continued to receive the same diets. By the end of 1906, among 120 patients eating uncured rice, there had been 34 cases of beriberi and 18 deaths. Among the 123 patients assigned to cured rice, there had been only 2 cases and no deaths, and both cases had been manifested at the time the patients were admitted to the asylum.
>
> —B. MacMahon and T. Pugh, *Epidemiology*

5. In England, which imports most of its sucrose [sugar], records of the last 100 years show a steady increase in per capita consumption of sucrose, from about 20 pounds per year in 1820 to over 100 pounds per year today. Present consumption of sucrose in the United States is about the same. This represents 15 to 20 percent of an individual's caloric requirements. Concomitant with this increased consumption of sucrose has been an almost parallel rise in the prevalence of caries [cavities]. Conversely, surveys in Europe and Japan demonstrated that caries was dramatically reduced during periods of wartime restrictions of sugar, syrup, and all sugar products.

> —E. Newburn, "Sugar and Dental Caries: A Review of Human Studies,"
> *Science* 217 (1982):418

6. Several years ago, newspapers ran a story about a doctor in New Jersey who was suspected of—and later tried and acquitted for—murdering a number of patients in a private hospital. Empty vials that had contained curare ("arrow poison") were found in the doctor's locker. The doctor claimed that the curare was used for experiments on dogs, but the man who was supposed to have supplied the dogs denied that he had given or sold any dogs to the doctor. The bodies of the patients, all of whom had been in the hospital for

minor operations and who had been in good health otherwise, were exhumed. Sophisticated tests found traces of curare in each of the bodies. On the basis of this evidence, other doctors at the hospital and the authorities insisted that a warrant be issued for the arrest of the suspect.

7. An alarming number of malignant skin cancer cases have been discovered among members of the District of Columbia Police Dept. who were repeatedly exposed to tear gas during the riots and demonstrations of 1968-1971 here.
Dr. Robert F. Dyer, director of the D.C. Police and Firemen's Clinic, said Thursday that one chemical component of tear gas apparently causes cancer.
"Over the past five years I personally have collected a series of 12 patrolmen with malignant melanoma [a form of skin cancer], which in a group of 4,800 men is higher than I would expect," Dyer said. All 12 officers reported being present at one or more of the many riots and demonstrations quelled with tear gas between 1968 and 1971, he said.

—Washington Star

8. Aspirin, taken in large doses by sufferers of arthritis, is being looked at for its effect on the liver.
Gall [The physician conducting the research] said his interest in aspirin and the liver began when a 20-year arthritis sufferer, who had taken aspirin for many years, was found to have high levels of an enzyme in her blood, usually one indicator of hepatitis, a disease of the liver. When doctors took the woman off aspirin, the high enzyme levels dropped back to normal, Gall said. The test was conducted several times, and each time, the high enzyme levels corresponded to the times when aspirin was taken.

—Arizona Daily Star

9. A federal study of 46 cities has concluded that fluoridating water to prevent tooth decay has no adverse effect on public health.
The study by the Center for Disease Control in Atlanta was undertaken to investigate claims that fluoridation is linked to higher cancer rates.
"There is no evidence to suggest that fluoridation does any harm," Dr. J. David Erickson, who conducted the study, said in an interview.
Erickson studied the causes of death of 922,000 people over three years in 46 American cities—24 of them with fluoridated water and 22 without. After taking into account differences in race, age, sex, education, and population density between the people in the two groups of cities, Erickson found that there was virtually no difference in the death rates. There were 1,124 deaths per 100,000 persons per year in the cities with fluoridated water and 1,137 in those without.

—Associated Press

10. In a study at Vipeholm, a mental institution in southern Sweden, 436 adult patients on a nutritionally adequate diet were observed for several years. They were found to develop caries [cavities] at a slow rate. Subsequently, the patients were divided into nine groups to compare the effect of various changes in their carbohydrate intake. Sucrose was included in the diet as toffee, chocolate, or caramel, in bread, or in liquid form. Caries increased significantly when food containing sucrose was ingested

between meals. Not only the frequency but the form in which sucrose was ingested was important: sticky or adhesive forms were more cariogenic [cavity-producing] than forms which were rapidly cleared from the mouth. After two years on the test diets, the patients were again placed on the control diet, and the caries activity reverted to the pretest pattern.

—E. Newburn, *Science* 217 (1982):419

11. LUNG CANCER FROM "SMOKY COAL" IN CHINA
Women in China's Xuan Wei County heat their homes and cook their meals with "smoky" coal (coal which when burned releases enormous numbers of tiny organic carcinogenic particles that remain airborne for a long time and can eventually lodge in the residents' lungs). . . . Lung cancer incidence is higher among the women who spend their time indoors than among the men, most of whom are farmers and spend the day outside.

—*Science* 235 (1987):139

12. Pheromones are discrete chemicals produced by insects. Pheromones allow insects to communicate with other members of their own species by signaling the presence of food, enemies, or willing mates. The chemicals can be produced in laboratories and sprayed on crops to confuse the insects that produce the chemicals naturally. Scientists who are concerned about damage to the environment hope that the use of pheromones will provide a safer alternative to toxic pesticides.

> In the San Joaquin Valley of California, cherry tomato plots were treated with a pheromone that disrupts mating between tomato pinworm moths. Peak infestation during the long growing season was less than 3%. On the control fields sprayed with insecticides, infestation reached 33%.
>
> —*Science* 239 (1988):135

13. Hypertension specialist William Elliot, armed with results from an eight-year study of 108 set of ears, has proposed a new wrinkle on earlobe utility: a diagonal crease in an earlobe may foretell heart disease. . . .

Among patients with no diagnosed disease, those with a crease were nearly eight times as likely to experience a cardiac event as those without.

—*University of Chicago Magazine*, August 1991

14. An international scientific team suggests that elevated concentrations of Lp(a) [which carries cholesterol] in the bloodstream may cause smooth muscle cells within the artery wall to proliferate. . . .

Biochemist David J. Grainger and molecular biologist Richard M. Lawn grew smooth muscle cells taken from healthy human arteries in laboratory dishes. When the team exposed those cultured cells to Lp(a), the cells began to divide more rapidly than usual.

—*Science News,* June 12, 1993

15. Results of a study linking increased rate of suicide to smoking in a sample of 100,000 females:

Compared with those who had never smoked, women who smoked one to 24 cigarettes daily displayed twice the likelihood of committing suicide, and those smoking 25 or more cigarettes daily exhibited four times the likelihood of committing suicide, Hemenway's team contends.

—*Science News*, February 13, 1993

III. CONTROLLED EXPERIMENTS

Many of the preceding exercises present reports of **controlled experiments** that are used to establish causal claims. Controlled experiments often use Mill's Joint Method of Agreement and Difference or the Method of Concomitant Variation. In a controlled experiment the investigator studies two or more groups that are similar except for their exposure to the suspected cause.

For example, in a controlled experiment to study the effects of a birth-control hormone on brain development in rats, two groups of 100 laboratory rats are selected from the relatively uniform population of laboratory rats. The two groups are treated the same in all respects, except that the food of one group (the experimental group) is supplemented with doses of the birth-control hormone, and the food of the other group (the control group) is not supplemented. If retarded brain development (or a higher frequency of retardation) occurs in the experimental group, but fails to occur in the control group, the experiment supports the claim that the birth-control hormone is the cause of retardation in laboratory rats. If after this treatment, however, the two groups do not differ with respect to retardation, the experiment does not support the causal claim.

When controlled experiments are used to establish causal claims, the argument form of inductive generalization plays a role as well. The experimental group of rats in the study just described is randomly selected from the population of laboratory rats. The experimental group thus represents the population from which it is drawn. Because this is so, what happens to the experimental group in the experiment provides a basis for generalizing to what *would* happen to any population of laboratory rats, if all were exposed to the hormone. Similarly, the control group is another randomly selected, representative sample of rats, and the results obtained from the experiment can be generalized to what would happen to the population of laboratory rats if they were not exposed to the hormone. Being able to say what *would* happen under various circumstances is especially important in causal reasoning, for when we make a causal claim (for example, birth-control hormones cause brain damage in rats), we mean to say not merely that taking hormones was *correlated* with brain damage in the rats that were studied, but that *if* any population of rats were exposed to the hormone, then those rats would suffer a greater rate of brain damage than a population not so exposed. Correlations between events may be established by observation, and statistical studies may be used to prove that such correlations exist. But when we want to make the stronger claim about a causal relationship, we need to go beyond observation to what would happen in unobserved cases. Controlled experiments provide us with inductive support for such causal claims.

The type of controlled experiment performed on the rats in the preceding example is called a **randomized experimental study,** because the experimental group and the control group are randomly chosen from the population they represent prior to being manipulated for the purposes of the experiment.

In the physical sciences, it is possible to perform similar randomized experiments to study various properties of physical substances. For instance, any bit of pure sodium is a representative sample of that metal, so investigators can perform controlled experiments to discover the causal properties of sodium without difficulty. (Sometimes, however, scientists find it difficult to isolate the item on which they wish to perform a controlled experiment: Nobel Prize-winner Marie Curie had to handle tons of pitchblende to isolate enough radium to perform her experiments on radioactive materials.)

When humans rather than animals or inanimate materials are studied, randomized experiments are subject to severe moral and legal restraints. Although these restraints are not relevant to whether causal claims are supported by experimental studies, they are extremely important to the ethics of science. Perhaps you felt uneasy when you read about the treatment of "lunatics" in the beriberi experiment described in the preceding section. It seems cruel to compel a group of helpless people to eat a diet suspected of causing a serious disease like beriberi. In fairness to the researchers who first suspected that diet was the cause of beriberi, however, a diet of polished rice was not unusual for many people outside institutions during that time. Nevertheless, restrictions on scientific and medical research would not allow such an experiment today. The government—with some unfortunate lapses—enforces strict guidelines for experiments involving human subjects, with the result that experiments in which humans are forced to participate are less likely to occur. Federal regulations also require that subjects who volunteer for experiments be informed about any suspected dangers so that they can give informed consent. Some of the same protections against harming experimental subjects are extended to animals. Recently animal-rights activists have raised serious questions about the treatment of experimental animals, and have protested acts of apparent cruelty.

Not all controlled experiments involve manipulation of subjects. In some types of studies, no treatment at all is imposed. In **prospective studies,** for example, the experimental group may be drawn from individuals who have already been exposed to the suspected causal factor, often by "self-selection." The control group in a prospective study is then "matched" to the experimental group in all features thought to be relevant to occurrence of the effect (except the causal factor under consideration). Instead of manipulating the experimental group, as in a randomized experimental study, the experimenter merely observes and waits to see what happens. This type of controlled study has been used to investigate the harmful effects of smoking. A sample of persons who already smoke (the experimental group) is matched for such features as age, sex, occupation, place of residence, ethnic background, history of disease, and so on with a sample (control group) of nonsmokers, and both groups are observed over a period of time to see whether rates of various illnesses (or death rates from those illnesses) differ in the two groups. Such studies can be very costly, because of the time required for the effects to develop, but are an important way to gather necessary information about the course of disease and the adequacy of various forms of treatment. Ongoing studies, for example, compare the long-term cure rate of mastectomy (removal of the breast) and lumpectomy (removal only of diseased tissue) for similar forms of breast cancer. Prospective studies are also used to study the outcomes of various social and educational reforms, such as how educational programs in prisons affect recidivism, how preschool education for the children of impoverished families influences later academic performance, and whether distribution of free hypodermic needles to drug addicts reduces incidence of AIDS.

When prospective studies would be too costly or would take too long to gather urgently needed information, **retrospective studies** can sometimes be employed. In a retrospective study, the experimental group is chosen from a population that already exhibits the suspected *effect*. The experimental group is matched to a control group that lacks the effect, but is similar in all other respects that are presumed to be relevant. Then a backward-looking study of the histories of the two groups is conducted in an effort to justify a causal claim about some difference in antecedent circumstances between the two groups.

A retrospective study investigated the cause of a particular type of disturbed sleep in infants. The experimental group of 28 newborn infants all showed more rapid-eye-movement sleep and less quiet sleep than the 30 newborns in the control group. The infants in the experimental group had all been chronically exposed in the womb to low doses of methadone. (The mothers were former heroin addicts on a methadone maintenance program.) The control group of infants were children of mothers whose age, nutrition, care during pregnancy, and other properties believed to affect the welfare of newborns were similar to the mothers of infants in the experimental group, except that none of them was on methadone or similar drugs.

Although prospective studies and retrospective studies avoid some of the moral and legal objections to randomized experimental studies on humans (and animals), they do not avoid all objections. Sometimes intrusive questioning in retrospective studies forces patients to expose personal histories that they would prefer to leave undisturbed. The benefits to persons in the control groups in these studies are unclear. Prospective and, more especially, retrospective studies are flawed by possible bias, which compromises their scientific value. Because the samples in both types are *not* randomly selected, they are not likely to be representative. In prospective studies, for example, the apparent "self-selection" of the experimental group may mask some other underlying cause for the effect. As the tobacco companies remind us, smokers may not freely choose to smoke, but be drawn to smoke because of some underlying condition. That, in turn, may contribute to an illness that the study suggests is smoking-related. Retrospective studies are subject to the same bias as prospective studies, and they have the added problem of possible errors in the records and reports that are used to reconstruct antecedent circumstances.

Many prospective and retrospective studies of human disease draw on hospital patients as subjects, but this practice is almost sure to produce biased samples. Depending on their location, some hospitals attract patients from one economic group of the population; others, from different economic classes. People who enter a hospital for the treatment of one disease may be more susceptible than the general public to other diseases. In evaluating the effects of curative or preventive treatments, it is important to know about the medical history of a patient's family, but this information is often difficult to obtain. For these reasons, medical scientists are very cautious about projecting the results of controlled studies of hospital patients onto the general population.

Another problem and possible source of bias associated with controlled studies of humans is the difficulty of obtaining samples large enough to be statistically valid. In the study that concluded that the sleep of newborn infants was affected by drugs taken by their mothers when the infants were in the womb, experimenters made an effort to select two groups of babies who were as alike as possible except for their sleep patterns, but both the experimental group and the control group were small. It is often difficult to obtain samples that are large enough to be representative of even a special subgroup of the human population, such as the subgroup of newborns.

When we can study the difference between a control group that is a representative sample of a population, none of which is exposed to the suspected causal agent, and an experimental group that is a representative sample of a population, all of which are exposed to the suspected causal agent, then we are justified in concluding that the results of the study will yield reliable information about what *would* happen if the population were exposed to the suspected causal agent. Insofar as samples are not representative, conclusions are less strongly supported.

Studies performed on experimental animals often come close to the ideal conditions of a randomized experimental study. The animals are bred for uniform characteristics, so that almost any group of animals is a representative sample of the population. Such animals are not, however, a representative sample of the *human* population—because only the population of laboratory rats, guinea pigs, or other experimental animals is used. If we want to use the results of animal studies to draw conclusions about humans, we need to construct arguments from analogy as well. Any relevant differences between the experimental animals and humans weaken the conclusions of such studies.

One further problem that should be mentioned in connection with controlled studies of humans is the need to eliminate psychological influences that might affect the purity of the results. It is well known that human illnesses often improve when the patient *believes* in the treatment that is being administered, regardless of any specific physical influence of the drug or whatever physical means are employed to effect a cure. The technique of a **double-blind experiment** attempts to eliminate such psychological influences in judging the effectiveness of possible cures. In an experiment to test a new drug, for example, members of the control group are given some inert substance (called a *placebo*) such as a sugar pill, while members of the experimental group are given the drug. The people receiving these substances do not know whether they are members of the control group or the experimental group; they are "blind" to the type of substance they receive. In addition, the investigators dispense the drugs and placebos "blindly"; the substances are identified by codes, and those performing the study cannot tell the placebo from the drug at the time of the experiment. In this way, the experimenters are able to make judgments about success of treatment in each case and learn who received the drug and who received a placebo only after the experiment is completed.

Double-blind experiments are used in most drug tests, and in other tests as well. Recently, the U.S. government completed a three-year study of the effectiveness of cloud seeding in enhancing rainfall. The technique of seeding clouds involves flying over them and sprinkling them with fine particles of silver iodide. None of the experimenters in the study "knew at the time on which days they were actually seeding clouds with fine silver iodide particles, and on which they were merely sprinkling them with an inert sand 'placebo'" (R. A. Kerr, "Test Fails to Confirm Cloud Seeding Effect," *Science* 217 (1982):234). Neither those who decided which clouds to seed nor those who judged the amounts of rain that fell from seeded clouds knew whether the clouds had been seeded with silver iodide or sand. After three years, a locked vault that held the secret record of the silver iodide seedings was opened. The experimenters were disappointed to find that this particular double-blind experiment failed to confirm the effectiveness of cloud seeding, but they planned further, more refined experiments and were convinced that weather-modification researchers must continue to use such controlled experiments to test the effectiveness of various weather-modification procedures.

Despite all the problems with controlled experiments, these studies of both humans and animals play an extremely important role in causal investigations. We do not really have any better method for ferreting out causal relationships.

Exercise Set 5.4

1. Review the set of exercises at the end of the previous section on Mill's methods, and note any that exemplify controlled experiments. When you identify the controlled experiments, describe the experimental group and the control group and say whether the study is randomized experimental, prospective, or retrospective in design.

2. The following report suggests a causal connection between severe head injury early in life and violent behavior. What types of controlled experiments are suggested to substantiate this? What moral considerations constrain such experiments?

> A study of 13 men and 2 women convicted of murder and awaiting execution in American prisons has shown that all had experienced severe head injuries earlier in life.
>
> Asked to comment on these findings, Dr. J. Engel of UCLA, a specialist in seeking the roots of violence, noted the difficulty in assessing the relative roles of environmental factors and physical damage to the brain.

Individuals such as those examined in the studies, he pointed out, often grow up in a world in which they both witness violence and are subjected to it.

Animal studies have shown that damage to certain areas of the brain can lead to violent behavior, but, Dr. Engel said, "Humans are much more complex than a cat or rat." To identify whether a person's environment or physical damage is more important, he added, would require a series of studies. For such studies, those who suffered specific brain damage and became violent without having been subject to emotional abuse would be matched with a comparable population lacking brain injury. Likewise, those who became violent after a childhood of exposure to violence, but without physical injuries to the brain would be compared statistically with a nonviolent population of similar background.

—*The New York Times*

3. Tell how the following study, reported in *Parade Magazine*, might have been improved by the use of a controlled experiment:

A Chinese worker developed a toothpaste that was mixed with the Chinese herbs traditionally prescribed for colds. The toothpaste was tested clinically on 3,600 persons who had colds. The Chinese said that 63 percent of the subjects tested reported marked improvement.

4. Identify the type of experiment (randomized, prospective, retrospective) described in the following:

Starting in 1978, Klatsky's team collected information on 81,825 men and women who said they drank alcoholic beverages. Over the next 10 years, the researchers also recorded deaths in this group attributed to heart disease.

—*Science News,* November 28, 1992

5. In what ways does the study described in the following fall short of a randomized experimental design?

"There's a lore in Alcoholics Anonymous," [Harriet de Wit] continues, "that a single drink can lead to a drinking binge." But no one had ever shown— under controlled conditions—if this was true for the so-called average drinker. Earlier this year, de Wit and her coworkers decided to find out. In a double-blind study, the researchers gave a placebo drink or a little bit of alcohol to a small group of volunteers—mostly graduate students—who were "light to moderate drinkers." A short while later, the team asked the volunteers to choose between a second drink or a small amount of money—usually about $10. The people who had received the alcohol "preload" were twice as likely to choose alcohol.

—*University of Chicago Magazine,* August 1991

6. Find a description of a controlled experiment in an outside reading source. (Some good sources are the magazines *Science* and *Scientific American* and

the "Science" sections of weekly news magazines. Other possible sources are newspaper stories and Sunday supplements, such as *Parade*.) Characterize the important features of the experiment (whether it was double-blind, how the control group was matched to the experimental group, and so on).

7. Design a controlled experiment to test a causal claim that interests you.

IV. DIFFERENT USES OF "CAUSE"

For want of a nail, the shoe was lost,

For want of a shoe, the horse was lost,

For want of a horse, the battle was lost,

And all for the want of a horseshoe nail.

—Nursery rhyme

Our references to "the cause" of some event or condition conceal different meanings of the word *cause* and the complexity of most causal situations. How we use *cause* depends on how much we know about a situation and on our practical or theoretical interest in a causal relationship.

Consider a murder trial in which the defendant is accused of shooting the victim. The prosecuting attorney, who is interested in showing that the defendant is legally responsible for the gunshot wound that led to the victim's death, says that the defendant's action was the cause of death. But the medical examiner has a different interest. If the victim died immediately after being shot, for example, the cause cited might be "massive internal bleeding." If the victim did not die immediately, but was taken to surgery and suffocated after an allergic reaction to an anesthetic, the medical examiner's report would cite suffocation as the cause of death. The causal accounts given by the lawyer and the coroner, although different, do not conflict with one another; although suffocation was the *proximate* physical cause of death (the causal physical circumstance closest to the event), the action of the defendant was an important earlier part of the causal chain that led to the suffocation. The law is interested in one part of that chain (*who* is to blame), and the medical specialist is interested in another (which of the body's systems stopped working).

The causal chain leading to the victim's death undoubtedly contains more links. The ambulance that took the victim to the hospital may have been delayed by traffic. The anesthetist may have failed to check the victim for allergies. The shooting may have been provoked (caused) by a quarrel resulting from the victim's attentions to the defendant's spouse; the victim's attentions might have been encouraged by the spouse; and so on. All of these events and conditions were a part of the complex causal process leading to the death of the victim. Only a special interest in some part of the complex set of events and processes (such as who is legally responsible or what should be put on the death certificate) leads us to refer to one part of this complex process as "the cause."

Even this account of the *chain* of causal events that results in the death of the victim is oversimplified, for it fails to consider various other chains of events that might be interwoven with these events and that could reinforce or counteract them. Thus, the analogy of a "causal network" rather than a "causal chain" may characterize the process more appropriately.

Diverse interests of the lawyer and the medical examiner in the preceding example lead them to focus on different aspects of the causal network. The lawyer wants a conviction; the medical examiner must determine the physical events leading to the victim's death. In other circumstances, such as a scientific investigation, a feature is singled out as "the cause" because it is more susceptible to control than other aspects of the causal process. In the story of the defeat of yellow fever, for example, the anopheles mosquito is usually cited as "the cause." While the mosquito plays a causal role by transferring the disease from one human to another, the specific yellow fever virus must be present in the bloodstream for the mosquito bite to cause the disease. Nevertheless, the discovery of the insect vector of the disease, and the realization that the disease was not transmitted by physical contact with a victim of yellow fever or other common sources of contamination, was of crucial importance in the control of the disease. Even though a vaccine for yellow fever was developed in the 1930s, programs to control the disease, like those to control maleria, are still primarily aimed at eliminating the mosquito rather than controlling the specific virus.

The importance of naming that part of the causal process that is susceptible to our control with the term *the cause* is shown by an interesting contrast between identifying "the cause" of diseases in some plants and in humans. Many humans have natural immunities to various diseases. All of us have known some of those lucky few who never seem to catch the flu, even when they haven't had shots and almost everyone around them comes down with the disease. We do not, however, try to control the spread of human infectious diseases through selective breeding, and a lack of natural immunity is almost never cited as "the cause" of human disease. In contrast, when a disease-resistant strain of some plant is discovered, plant breeders immediately try to propagate the new strain and market it for this valuable property. Breeding resistant strains rather than attacking the specific organism responsible for the disease is an accepted and effective method of controlling diseases in plants. Because of this, we sometimes say that a plant succumbed to disease *because* it lacked the immune characteristic.

The mosquito carrier of yellow fever is a "necessary causal condition" of the disease. Without the mosquitoes the disease does not survive in nature. A condition is called "necessary" if the effect cannot occur without that condition. The presence of oxygen (or hydrogen gas), for example, is a necessary causal condition for the existence of fires. Our attention most often focuses on causally necessary conditions when we are interested in *eliminating* some undesirable effect. When medical scientists try to eliminate a disease, they look for some necessary causal condition, such as the mosquito carrier of yellow fever. No one, however, would think of trying to prevent forest fires by reducing the oxygen in the atmosphere near forests, even though this would be effective. Unlike the mosquito in the yellow-fever example, oxygen is never referred to as "the cause" of forest fires even though, like the mosquito, it is a causally necessary condition. The difference between the two cases is that the mosquito is something we can eliminate to prevent the problem; oxygen is not.

When we are interested in bringing about some effect, rather than eliminating an effect, we often look for a causally sufficient condition that we can control. A condition is "causally sufficient" for some effect if whenever the condition is present the effect must occur. Vaccination is sufficient for the prevention of smallpox. Decapitation of a person is a causally sufficient condition for that person's death. Scientists search for wonder drugs ("magic bullets") that will bring about causally sufficient conditions for curing human diseases.

It is unusual, however, to be able to isolate a single causally sufficient condition. Frequently, the term "sufficient condition" refers instead to some important causal factor that, against a background set of necessary conditions, is especially proximate, or interesting, or easy to control. For example, it is reasonable to claim that bringing water up to a temperature of 100° Celsius is sufficient to make that water boil. This is true, however, only when certain necessary background conditions, such as relative freedom of the water from impurities and normal atmospheric pressure, are operative. Turning a light switch to the "on" position suffices to produce light only when power is available, the lamp is in working order, the bulb is not burned out, and so forth. When the background conditions are fairly standard, or are not subject to great fluctuation, or are not usually under our direct control, we typically ignore them and use the term "sufficient causal condition" to refer somewhat loosely to an event or process that we can control directly and which, under standard background conditions, will produce the desired effect.

Sometimes we say that a set of causal conditions is "individually necessary and jointly sufficient" for some event to occur. The conditions individually necessary and jointly sufficient to cause germination in viable grass seed, for example, are (1) adequate water, (2) suitable temperature, (3) oxygen, and (4) light. When all of these conditions are present jointly in the appropriate degree (proportions vary for different types of grasses), germination occurs.

Frequently, however, even when we know a lot about the causes of some type of event, we are unable to specify individually necessary and jointly sufficient complete sets of conditions. An example follows.

Dental caries, the localized destruction of tooth tissue by microorganisms, is a process familiar to most of you, and this process is well understood by medical scientists. Three main causal factors are: (1) the hosts (saliva and teeth), (2) the microorganisms (particularly one called *Streptococcus mutans,* which is found in dental plaque), and (3) the diet.

Experiments have shown that rats fed through stomach tubes do not develop cavities even when the caries-producing *S. mutans* is present. Similarly, rats do not get cavities when they are fed orally if their mouths are kept sterile. It would seem then that the presence of teeth, microorganisms, and food are individually necessary and jointly sufficient for cavities in rats.

However, rats do not *always* develop cavities under these circumstances—although groups of them do develop cavities at "the normal rate." Some rats, like some humans, apparently are able to resist cavities better than others. For this reason, we cannot say that the presence of the three necessary conditions (teeth, microorganisms, and a food supply) jointly form a sufficient causal condition for the disease.

Further necessary conditions may be specifiable in this case (for example, lack of fluoride protection and genetic susceptibility to the disease), but frequently the causal situations are too complex to permit us to identify a complete set of conditions. The effort medical scientists are willing to expend in search of additional necessary conditions for a particular type of event depends largely on practical concerns, such as how much knowledge is necessary to *control* the causal process. Although diet receives emphasis in some studies of dental caries, other research focuses on host factors (fluoride treatment of teeth and drinking water) and on microorganisms (the possibility of immunization).

We have been looking at some of the different ways in which the term *cause* is used. The point of this discussion is that many correct uses of the term are available. Different uses of *cause* are suitable in different circumstances. We need to understand the various ways that *cause* is used so that we can identify and understand important causal relationships.

We especially want to be aware that causal connections are possible in which the cause is neither a sufficient nor a necessary causal condition for the effect. Cigarette smoking, for example, is neither necessary nor sufficient for contracting lung cancer. Even if you do not smoke, you may get lung cancer. Likewise, you may escape lung cancer even if you are a heavy smoker. Yet, it would be foolish, with all the evidence now available, to deny that smoking causes lung cancer. Smoking is a probabilistic cause of the disease. We call a causally antecedent condition a **probabilistic cause** when its presence makes the occurrence of the condition under investigation more probable than it would be in the absence of the antecedent condition. Strong evidence points to smoking as an antecedent condition that is related to lung cancer in this probabilistic way. Many of the controlled experiments examined in this chapter provide evidence for assigning probabilistic causes. Although Mill did not think of causes in a probabilistic way, he designed the methods to find and justify *partial* causes as well as complete sets of necessary or sufficent conditions. His methods, particularly the method of concomitant variation, are widely used in modern research to study the variations in frequencies that provide a basis for probabilistic causal claims.

The following example, taken from a syndicated newspaper medical advice column, shows the danger of confusing probabilistic causes with sufficient causal conditions:

> Dear Dr. Steincrohn: Thinking about premature death has caused a serious depression in my husband. Although only 38, and, according to our doctor, physically sound he lives in fear of dying early.

He blames it on his poor heredity. His father died of a coronary attack at the age of 59 and his mother had a stroke at about the same age. One uncle suffers from extremely high blood pressure.

With that kind of family history, he asks, "What chance have I got?" As a result he smokes too much. Drinks a lot. Has let himself get fat.

He figures how he lives won't make any difference. Have you run into similar problems?

In answering this letter, the doctor correctly notes that "there may be a hereditary disposition to stroke and heart attacks," but he points out that the man is not inevitably doomed to an early death. He cites records of patients who had good family histories and poor living habits who died earlier than their counterparts who had bad heredity traits. The husband, at least if his wife's description of the situation is accurate, seems to regard his poor heredity traits as causally sufficient for an early death rather than as factors that increase the probability of early death. As a result of this misunderstanding, he ignores other factors, such as not smoking, which could counteract a possible predisposition to cancer.

Exercise Set 5.5

For each of the following causal claims, discuss whether *cause* is used in one or more of the following ways:

(1) A proximate or nearest cause in a chain or network of causes

(2) An agent causally responsible for some action or event

(3) A necessary causal condition

(4) A sufficient causal condition

(5) A sufficient causal condition against a background of accepted, stable necessary conditions

(6) A probabilistic cause.

1. Martha failed the exam because there wasn't enough time to finish it.

2. Jason will graduate in June because he passed every course he took this year.

3. William went to the party because Jean invited him.

4. An arsonist caused the fire at the museum.

5. The house burned down because oily rags were stored in a closet.

6. The criminal confessed because he was promised a light sentence.

7. Nathan caught the measles because he played with the boy next door who had the measles.

8. The crops are poor this summer because there hasn't been enough rain.

9. Rice takes much longer to cook at the observatory because it is on top of

an 8,000-foot mountain. At that altitude, the boiling point of water is considerably less than it is at sea level.

10. The ice on the sidewalk is melting because salt was thrown on it.

11. The condemned murderer died by lethal injection at 6 A.M.

12. Rats that were injected with massive doses of saccharine developed tumors at a much greater rate than a control group of rats that did not receive saccharine, thereby demonstrating that saccharine causes tumors in rats.

13. The assassination of Archduke Ferdinand at Serajevo in August, 1914, was the cause of World War I.

14. The heavy penalties imposed by the Allies on the Germans after the First World War caused the Second World War.

15. Worry about the national deficit caused the crash of the stock market in October, 1987.

16. Atmospheric testing of nuclear bombs produces levels of radiation that are hazardous to humans and other animals in the areas near the test sites.

17. The pear crop was poor because no bees were around for pollination.

18. Harry's heart attack was a result of his shoveling heavy snow for two hours.

19. "T-cells, a type of immune cell that helps defend the body against disease, may play a villain's role in the drama of atherosclerosis, the buildup of plaque that clogs arteries and causes heart attacks. . . .Compared to the controls, the 11 people with the most severe heart disease had 35 percent fewer T4 lymphocytes, a particular type of T-cell in their blood."

—K. Fackelmann, *Science News,* Nov. 28, 1992

20. "Of the usual clinical tests for assessing the fertility of a male—sperm number, morphology (shape) and motility (movement)—only sperm motility is correlated with fertilizing ability. If a sperm sample contains less than 20% motile sperm, fertilization will not occur."

—K. Dawson, *Embryo Experimentation,* ed., Singer et al.

V. HUME'S ANALYSIS OF CAUSATION

Thus far in our discussion, we have not proposed a definition of *cause* that would cover the various uses of the term. Even though we all seem intuitively to grasp the meaning of the term, it turns out to be difficult to define *cause* precisely. In the eighteenth century, David Hume offered an analysis of the meaning of statements of the general form "*A* causes *B*." Hume was trying to solve the problem of how to justify causal inferences. To keep things simple, he analyzed the type of causal relationship that holds between two uncomplicated events, or types of events (the striking of two billiard balls and their movement after the collision). Hume said that he could find nothing in the *ideas* of striking and subsequent motion to connect the two events. That is to say, the concepts of striking and of motion are not related through their meanings in the way that synonyms (such as *bachelor* and *unmarried male*) or mathematical equalities (2 + 2 and 4) are to one another. It is certainly possible to conceive of a ball being struck without subsequent motion.

Failing to find a relation of ideas (such as a definitional connection), Hume turned to experience (matters of fact) for a better understanding of causal claims. The features he could *observe* in such relationships were:

1. *A* and *B* are joined with one another in space and time. ("No action at a distance.")

2. *B* follows *A*. (The "effect" does not precede the "cause.")

3. Whenever *A* occurs, *B* occurs. ("Constant conjunction.")

Hume realized that all three of these relationships might be observed between two events that were only coincidentally connected with one another. (Remember the London tobacconists' avoidance of bubonic plague.) Hume therefore believed that his analysis of the observable features of causal relationships failed to uncover any "real"—as distinguished from coincidental—connection between the two events. The only additonal feature he could find that accounts for our linking *A* to *B* in such cases was a habit of expecting *B* when presented with *A*. His analysis pushed the matter still further, for he showed that no logical reason—no correct noncircular deductive or inductive argument—supports the view that constant conjunctions that have been observed in the past will continue to hold in the future.

Hume was not entirely satisfied with his results, and he challenged others to find a "real connection," but his own conclusion was skeptical: The inference from cause to effect is based on a psychological habit of expectation, formed as a result of observing the connections in the past. The inference, Hume said, is apparently not grounded in *reasoned* knowledge of real connections but in habit or custom. Because we tend to think that our knowledge of causes, especially what we have learned from scientific investigations, is based on more than mere habit, Hume's well-argued and startling conclusion has troubled all who have thought seriously about this problem.

Hume's arguments have been the subject of many philosophical works as various authors have attempted to solve the problems he raised. Many of these reluctantly accept Hume's skeptical conclusion that no logical reason supports the view that constant conjunctions that have been observed in the past will continue to hold in the future. Nevertheless, most people also believe that genuine causal connections can be understood as something more than constant conjunction and the habit of expecting repetitions of these conjunctions.

We should understand that Hume was *NOT* recommending that we cease our causal investigations or that we give up causal reasoning altogether. He thought that this would be not only foolish but also psychologically impossible. A number of philosophers and scientists have adopted the following pragmatic stand in view of Hume's analysis:

Although we have no logical reason for believing that the future will resemble that past, *if* it does, then our causal judgments that are based on observations of continued regularities (using reasoning of the sort recommended by Mill) will be the ones that provide useful and important information about the world. If the world changes in such a way that the present regularities no longer hold, no other method now available can give us any better information about what regularities—if any—we can expect in the future.

You may have noticed that in this presentation of Hume's analysis of "*A* is the cause of *B*," a cause is understood to be a "causally sufficient condition." This is expressed in the third statement of his analysis: "Whenever *A* occurs, *B* occurs." Causally sufficient conditions are sometimes called "deterministic" causes. A **deterministic cause,** unlike a probabilistic cause, inevitably results in its effect.

Determinism is the philosophical principle that everything that happens is a result of causally sufficient conditions. Determinism does not claim that we know, or even that we will someday know, what these conditions are in each case. Determinism is a view about what the world is like, not a view about the knowledge we can obtain about that world. According to the principle of determinism, the fundamental causal structure of the world is deterministic, and references to probabilistic causes reflect our ignorance of some part of the causal complex—some "hidden factors" that, if understood, would complete the causal story.

Whether all fundamental causes are deterministic is another difficult—and, as yet, unanswered—philosophical question. If the causal structure of the universe is fundamentally deterministic, then our talk about probabilistic causes could simply reflect our ignorance of hidden, deterministic causal factors. In Hume's time, the most advanced science of the day was Newtonian physics. Newton's genius had unearthed an impressive set of deterministic causes, expressed in his Law of Universal Gravitation and in his three Laws of Motion. In view of Newton's successes, it was widely believed that future scientific advances would uncover more and more deterministic causes in cases in which previous knowledge had been probabilistic.

Consider our view that smoking is a probabilistic cause of lung cancer. Certainly, further scientific investigation might uncover a genetic property, present in some but absent in others, that predisposes humans to lung cancer when they smoke heavily. Medical scientists might someday be able to specify a set of individually necessary and jointly sufficient causal conditions for the disease.

Nevertheless, there are some areas of modern science, particularly quantum physics, in which—unlike the situation in Hume's time—the best theories available not only admit probabilistic causes at the most fundamental level but cannot even accommodate the discovery of "hidden factors." That is to say, quantum physics, unlike our incomplete causal theory about lung cancer, cannot absorb additional causal variables that would transform it into a deterministic theory. This point is difficult to understand without an appropriate background knowledge of quantum physics. Nevertheless, it is so important that some scientists have considered it the most revolutionary feature of modern science—comparable to Newton's great discoveries in the seventeenth century. Many scientists hope that eventually a different—and, to their minds a more satisfactory—deterministic theory of quantum physics will be discovered. But they recognize that the present theory cannot be expanded or modified to become a deterministic theory without giving up even more firmly held principles about causality, such as *an effect cannot occur earlier than its cause*. The finest experimental results currently available cannot be accounted for by a deterministic causal theory.

Thus, quantum physics differs from medical science. Medical scientists have discovered that specific microorganisms are causally responsible for such diseases as cholera, plague, tuberculosis, and Legionnaires' Disease and that deficiencies in specific substances (vitamins) are causally responsible for such diseases as beriberi, rickets, and scurvy. Medical theory is heavily committed to the discovery of such specific causal agents, which when present or absent—against a standard background of necessary causal conditions—are sufficient for the occurrence of specific diseases. In other words, the history of medical science can be viewed in terms of searches for deterministic causes and success in finding such causes. With the ever-growing importance of understanding the genetic component of disease, this deterministic approach may be modified, for some genetic changes (mutations) are not governed by any known deterministic principles. Seventeenth-century physics, which reached its peak in Newton's work, enjoyed great success in identifying deterministic causes. Until quite recently, Newton's (deterministic) physics represented the most advanced science. The most advanced theory of physics in the twentieth century, however, depends on probabilistic causes.

Probabilistic causation would remain important even if all fundamental causes were deterministic, for at any point in the investigation of a subject area, probabilistic knowledge may be the most accurate or the most accessible knowledge available. Furthermore, the search for deterministic causes is frequently guided and motivated by the observation of probabilistic (statistical) regularities. In the practice of science as well as in everyday life, we will continue to be concerned with probabilistic causes.

One final remark: Hume's worries about causation are not solved by replacing a deterministic notion of causality with a probabilistic explanation. Hume's arguments apply to conjunctions that hold only with probability as well as they apply to constant conjunctions.

VI. CAUSAL FALLACIES

Mistakes in causal reasoning, or causal fallacies, can arise when some important aspect of the causal relationship is ignored or distorted. Hume's analysis of the causal relationship suggests that causes are *repeatedly* connected with their effects. This feature of the causal relationship holds whether we are talking about causally necessary conditions, causally sufficient conditions, proximate causes, or probabilistic causes. We expect causes and their effects to occur together with some degree of regularity. Hume noticed also that no cause occurs later in time than its effect. The following three causal fallacies normally occur because of insufficient attention to or misunderstanding of these features.

1. Confusing Coincidental Relationships with Causes (*Post Hoc*)

Sometimes people focus on the second standard feature just mentioned, and infer that *A* is the cause of *B simply because* event *B* occurs later than event *A*. To reason this way is to commit a causal fallacy. The fallacy is common enough to be given the special name **post hoc,** which is derived from the first two words of the Latin expression that describes the fallacious pattern of reasoning: *"Post hoc, ergo propter hoc"* ("After this, therefore because of this").

Ordinarily, we would not claim that a causal connection exists between two events merely on the grounds that one event occurred later than the other. We constantly observe successions of events without drawing causal connections between them. But sometimes when the events are striking, unusual, or important to us, we mistake a coincidence for a true causal connection, particularly if such a connection fits roughly within some accepted causal framework. If, for example, an air-conditioning unit breaks down the day after it receives routine maintenance service, we might suspect that the tinkering of the person who worked on the unit was responsible. But to draw a causal conclusion on the basis of such evidence would be *post hoc.* Further investigation could show that, for example, a worn-out timing switch was the cause of the breakdown. Mechanical systems can go wrong in so many ways that are unrelated to the maintenance work that drawing a causal conclusion would be premature in this case. In our critical moments—when we are free from the annoyance of having to pay for a second service call—we realize that the such a succession of events may be coincidental. *Post hoc* fallacies arise under circumstances similar to those that promote hasty generalizations. When a conclusion is attractive to us, whether through laziness, prejudice, fear, hope, or another strong psychological motivation, we are tempted to accept insufficient evidence for it.

Conclusions of *post hoc* reasoning can be true even though not well supported by their premises. We might, for example, consider the astronomers' postulation of an additional planet as the cause of irregularities in Neptune's orbit an example of *post hoc* reasoning, because such an event had occurred only once before—when Uranus's orbital irregularity was explained by postulating Neptune's existence. As it turned out, another planet, Pluto, was out there, but it was too small to be the cause of the observed gravitational pull on Neptune. (Many astronomers would protest calling the reasoning that led to Pluto's discovery *post hoc* because it fit within a well-supported scientific theory of planetary motion, and thus could be said to be based on more than a single previous successful discovery.)

Post hoc reasoning underlies many superstitious beliefs. If, for example, I eat bacon and eggs for breakfast instead of the cereal I usually have and then perform brilliantly on a math examination, it would be a *post hoc* fallacy to conclude that the special breakfast was the cause of my unusual performance on the examination. If I receive bad news on three successive Wednesdays and conclude that Wednesday is my unlucky day (that this day of the week somehow causes me to receive bad news) I am committing a *post hoc* fallacy. A 1993 article in the *The New York Times Magazine,* citing numerous disturbing events that occurred during August, the traditional month for presidential vacations, asked "What is it about August?" Suggesting the fallacy was part of the humor of the piece. Not much effort is required to recall momentous events that have occurred in other months of the year.

Another source of *post hoc* fallacies is the belief that effects *resemble* their causes—or that the cause must somehow *contain* whatever is in its effect. Mill was especially scornful of this mistake, which he considered to be an undesirable holdover from crude medieval attempts to reason scientifically by reading the signs present in nature. Mill maintained that proponents of the resemblance theory of causation might as well argue that pepper had to be in the cook, because there was pepper in the soup! Belief in the efficacy of many folk medicines is based on this kind of reasoning, which is associated with the teachings of Paracelsus. Herbal cures were selected on the basis of resemblance between the form of plant and the afflicted part of the body. The leaves of the wildflower Hepatica (Liverwort) are shaped something like the human liver, so the plant was used as a cure for liver ailments. The leaves of Pulmonaria (Lungwort) resemble human lungs, and were therefore considered to be an effective lung medicine. The "medicine" seemed to work in some cases. Because many human illnesses clear up regardless of treatment—or lack of treatment—however, we should not believe that a cure has been found simply because improvement follows treatment in a few cases.

Controlled experiments are the best way to distinguish coincidental from causal relationships. When a controlled experiment is impossible or impractical, then we should try to make further observations to determine whether the observed connection, for example, between "medicine" and cure, persists. After smoking tobacco failed to prevent the plague at Eton in the seventeenth century, observers realized that the connection between using tobacco and avoiding the plague had been coincidental. Mill understood that it was important to use his methods repeatedly to test suspected causal connections. His views are reflected in the modern use of controlled experiments and observations. Besides checking for repetition of connection between suspected cause and effect, controlled experiments are designed to eliminate factors irrelevant to the causal process. In the absence of opportunities for checking the persistence of regularities, critical thinkers may want to suspend judgment about whether a connection is coincidental or causal.

2. Ignoring a Common Cause

Even when observation and experiment assure us that a regular connection exists between a suspected cause and some effect, we must be careful to distinguish among various direct and indirect causal connections. For example, when archaeologists excavate sites in Central and North America, they find that sites that contain pottery frequently have fragments of grinding stones (used for grinding corn) as well. But they do not conclude that the presence of pottery causes the presence of grinding stones or that the presence of grinding stones causes the presence of pottery. To do so simply because the two are found in conjunction with one another would be to commit the fallacy of **ignoring a common cause.** Pottery fragments and grinding-stone fragments are not directly causally related to one another. Their joint occurrence is a result of an underlying common cause, namely human habitation of those sites.

Examples of regular associations that depend on a common cause are frequently encountered; thus, if we fail to consider this possibility we are liable to commit a causal fallacy. The measles virus causes both red spots and fever in those people who are afflicted with the disease; although the spots and fever always occur together, neither directly causes the other. Measles is so familiar to us that distinguishing the symptoms from the underlying cause does not seem problematic. Medical researchers must, however, take great care to distinguish symptoms from causes in many less familar diseases.

A common cause, namely, a sharp drop in atmospheric pressure, accounts for the regular association between stormy weather and falling barometers. The tips of many pine trees in Los Angeles turned brown in the late 1980s. Investigation by the forestry department showed that this happened not because of infection spreading from one tree to others, but as the result of a common cause—an atmospheric inversion that allowed atmospheric fluorides to concentrate in the foliage of the pines.

When two or more events are causally related to one another through an underlying common cause, they are sometimes said to be indirectly causally related. The expression *indirect causal relationship* is also used, however, to refer to the relationship that holds between events that are part of the same linear causal chain, but which are separated from one another by one or more intervening links. In this latter sense, for example, we say that the "want of a horseshoe nail" indirectly caused the loss of the battle.

If an adequate causal theory is available, it can be used to identify common causes, and to distinguish them from their multiple and indirectly related effects. Given what we know about measles and about weather, for instance, we know that "treating the symptoms" will not cure the disease and that placing barometers in pressurized cabins will not prevent storms. But sorting out symptoms from common causes in many other situations requires the use of controlled experiments or other sophisticated forms of inductive reasoning.

3. Confusing Cause and Effect

A third causal fallacy, the fallacy of confusing cause and effect, arises when evidence supports a direct causal relationship between two types of events, but the *direction* of the relationship is not given adequate consideration. An example of confusion about the direction of causality occurs in one of Graham

Greene's spy novels, *The Human Factor*. Two secret agents discuss a method to "eliminate" a colleague suspected of leaking secrets. One of the agents suggests using peanuts as a weapon, and offers the following account to his baffled coworker:

> "Peanuts when they go bad produce a mold. Caused by *aspergillus flavus*—but you can forget the name. It's not that important, and I know you were never any good at Latin."
>
> "Go on, for heaven's sake."
>
> "To make it easy for you I'll concentrate on the mold. The mold produces a group of highly toxic substances known collectively as aflatoxin. And aflatoxin is the answer to our little problem."

The condescending spy has no reason to be smug about his knowledge of aflatoxin, because he mistakes a cause for its effect. The peanuts do not *produce* a mold when they go bad. The mold attacks the peanuts and is the *cause* of their going bad. The mold, in other words, is a cause—not an effect—of spoiled peanuts. Although the spy was mistaken about the direction of causality, it is not clear that he committed a fallacy. For a fallacy to occur, one must draw a conclusion that is not justified by the evidence. In this case, no indication is given in the novel of the basis for the agent's claim.

Because effects cannot precede their causes, a way to avoid the fallacy of confusing cause and effect is to pay careful attention to the *temporal order* of two events that have a direct causal relationship to one another. For example, it is well known that the rise in the incidence of lung cancer and the increase in cigarette smoking have been regularly connected during the past 50 years. Most people believe a direct causal relationship exists between these two events—that the increase in tobacco use is the cause, and the increase in cancer is the effect. However, some people have said that the rise in the incidence of lung cancer may have caused the increase in smoking, because having cancer may create a craving for tobacco. This seems to be a case of the fallacy of confusing cause and effect, for we know that most smokers who develop lung cancer have smoked heavily for years. Their smoking habits were fixed long before they contracted the disease. No evidence indicates that people who contracted lung cancer increased their smoking thereafter.

Although the question of which came first—smoking or lung cancer—seems clear, in many situations sorting earlier from later parts of a causal complex is not simple. For example, archaeological evidence shows that certain areas of the southwestern United States were occupied for a prolonged period by one group of people (Anasazi), whose abrupt disappearance was succeeded by the presence of a different ethnic group (Athabascans). The agreed-upon temporal order of this series of events is subject to various causal interpretations. The invasion of the newcomers might have caused the former residents to abandon these areas, or the influx of the newcomers might have been caused, or partially caused, by the decision of the former residents to depart, thus leaving an area open for occupation.

Another example of the difficulty of sorting out cause and effect occurs in studies of schizophrenia. A well-supported, regular association holds between schizophrenia in young adults and unstable or disturbed relationships in their families. But it is not known whether the unhappy family situation is a cause, or part of the cause, of schizophrenia or whether the hardship of living with a schizophrenic tends to cause disturbance in the family. Both schizophrenia (or at least some symptoms of the disease) and unhappy family situations usually develop over an extended period of time. In such situations, determining which event occurred first is almost impossible.

In some cases, further observation or controlled experimentation that attempts to interfere with some part of the causal process can enable us to determine the direction of a causal relationship. On the basis of many studies of the development of lung cancer and the smoking history of victims of this disease, we can reject the claim that cancer causes an increase in smoking.

In their studies of the abandonment of pueblos in the Southwest, archaeologists look for evidence of warfare and evidence of unfavorable conditions for agriculture, as well as for other evidence—such as the exact dates of leaving and arrival of the different groups—that would help them to decide whether invasion by new people was the cause of pueblo abandonment or an effect of the abandonment.

In some cases, such as with schizophrenia, experimental determination of causal direction is very difficult. One experiment that could be performed would be to remove the schizophrenic from the family situation and then to use Mill's Method of Difference to observe whether family relationships improved. The results of such an experiment might not be entirely convincing, however. The family situation may have deteriorated to the point that family patterns of uncooperative behavior are too fixed to be changed simply by the removal of the original source of the difficulty. Moreover, concerns can be raised about possible negative effects of removing the schizophrenic patient from the family.

Although no effect can precede its cause, the elaborate complexity of many causal relationships hampers a proper causal ordering of all their components. Multiple, interacting causes reinforce and counteract one another to such a degree that isolating the various parts in order to observe or control them separately may not be feasible. In such situations, awareness of the possibility of an underlying common cause, or of the possibility that cause and effect may be confused with one another, can prevent us from accepting inadequately supported causal claims.

4. Genetic Fallacy: Reasons and Causes

The term *genesis* is synonymous with *origin*. The **genetic fallacy** is a mistake in reasoning that occurs when some factor concerning the origin or causal source of a claim is offered as evidence for the truth of that claim or accepted as such evidence.

Unlike the three preceding fallacies, the genetic fallacy does *not* involve misunderstanding the sort of evidence required to support a causal claim. The genetic fallacy is treated in this section, however, because the discussion of the nature of causes puts us in a better position to understand the difference between the *cause* of holding a belief and the *evidence* for the truth of that belief.

When evidence is presented in a logically correct argument, the premisses that embody or describe the evidence are *reasons* for accepting the conclusion as true. That is to say, if the premisses are true, and the argument is a correct inductive argument, then probably the conclusion is true as well. In correct deductive arguments, the conclusion cannot be false if all the premisses are true. Sometimes, however, beliefs are not held on the basis of reasons but arise from (are caused by) various psychological factors. These factors may include devotion to the person from whom the belief was acquired, social pressures to conform, and the implantation of a belief at an early age. Any of these factors can be a causal source of a belief—and can be cited in an explanation of why someone holds the belief—although they do not constitute evidence for the truth of the belief.

An adult who is afraid of the dark may believe a physical harm, such as suffocation, will result from being in a dark room. This belief may be the result of being locked in a closet as a child. The frightening childhood experience is part of a (correct) causal explanation of that person's fear of the dark. We have good evidence that cruel treatment of children causes fears that persist into adulthood. However, none of this is evidence that being in the dark will suffocate the person. To confuse the causal explanation of the belief with reasons (in the sense of evidence) for its truth is to commit the genetic fallacy.

Fallacious appeals to authority, fallacious appeals to consensus, and fallacious *ad hominem* arguments can also be considered forms of the genetic fallacy, for they involve mistaking some feature of the genesis of a claim (the person who is the source of the claim) as evidence for (or against) the truth of that claim. If I argue that my senator's description of some proposed legislation is false because he is a pompous windbag, then my so-called argument is a fallacious abusive *ad hominem*, and I also commit the genetic fallacy. (This is so even if the windbag's account is in fact false.)

5. Confusing the Harm or Benefits that Result from Holding a Belief with Evidence for It

Closely related to accepting or rejecting a claim because of its source (rather than because of evidence) is accepting or rejecting a claim because of the harm or good that might be caused by holding the belief (its consequences). This fallacy has no special name (the **Consequential Fallacy** has been suggested) but it can occur whenever our desires intrude on our reasons for belief. Suppose, for example, that I am a heavy smoker, and that I want very much to continue smoking. If I can make myself believe, despite all the evidence, that cigarette smoking will not harm me, then why should I give up smoking? Here, holding the belief that smoking won't harm me has the apparent benefit of continuing my pleasure in smoking, and because of that result, I believe it. (Of course, smoking is harmful, regardless of whether I believe it, and cannot be counted overall as a benefit; confusing the apparent benefit of holding a belief with evidence for the belief can be dangerous.)

Swindlers and confidence men offer preposterous claims about easy money schemes and depend on the greed of their "marks" to override any evidence against the truth of those claims. If we very much want the prize that would result if a claim were true, we find it more difficult to pay attention to evidence.

Some fundamentalist religious groups have rejected Darwin's theory of evolution not because of evidence against it, but because they believe that if the biblical account of creation is not accepted as literal truth, the standards of morality will become drastically lowered. Darwin's own cousin held similar views and wrote to him that she hoped he was wrong about evolution, but that if he was not, she hoped at least that people would not learn about his ideas. Although we may be legitimately concerned about the consequences of a claim if it is true, that question should be kept distinct from the question of evidence for the claim. Moreover, we can reasonably demand some evidence for the claim that a belief will have the consequences that its detractors fear it will have. The supposed relationship between the truth of evolutionary theory and a lapse in moral standards is hardly self-evident, for example.

Holding beliefs is not always cost-free. If I believe that a friend is loyal, I enjoy a benefit. If someone presents me with evidence that the friend has betrayed me, I have a problem. If I admit that the friend has betrayed me, I pay the price of lost or diminished friendship. It is not hard to understand why I do not want to pay that price. But if I take avoiding that cost as a justification (in the sense of evidence) for denying the betrayal, I confuse the effect of holding a belief with a reason for the belief, and I engage in fallacious reasoning.

To avoid the genetic fallacy, we must distinguish the source of a belief from reasons for it. Similarly, we have to distinguish the resultant harm or benefit of holding a belief from reasons for it to avoid this other fallacy.

A different fallacy concerned with origins assumes that the originating cause of some event is also necessary to sustain that event once it has originated. Some theologians argue that just as the Creator was necessary for the original act of creating the world, so is that same being required to sustain the world at each moment of its existence. Other theologians reject this argument in favor of a Creator who does the job once and then leaves things to develop on their own. On a more down-to-earth level, we can think of many processes that once set in motion—nuclear chain reactions, for example—do not require further intervention to continue.

Before closing the subject of causal fallacies, we should note that the fallacies described in this section treat only some of the most common errors in causal reasoning. Because of the complexity of causal arguments and of the many forms they take, causal reasoning can go wrong in a wide variety of ways. Pointing out the most common fallacies should serve to raise our critical awareness of the hazards of causal reasoning.

VII. REVIEW

The aims of Chapter 5 have been to increase understanding of the complexity of causal reasoning, to offer standards for assessing causal arguments, and to point out some common types of fallacious causal reasoning. The new terminology introduced included the names of Mill's methods for discovering causes and justifying causal claims: the **Method of Agreement,** the **Method of Difference,** the **Joint Method of Agreement and Difference,** the **Method of Concomitant Variation** and the **Method of Residues.** Look again at Section II, in which these methods are discussed to be sure that you are able to recognize examples of the use of these methods.

In our discussion of the term *cause,* several types of causes were distinguished:

Necessary causal condition: *A* is causally necessary for *B* means that without *A*, *B* will not occur.

Sufficient causal condition: *A* is causally sufficient for *B* means that whenever *A* occurs, *B* will also occur.

Deterministic cause: sufficient causal condition.

Probabilistic cause: *A* is a probabilistic cause for *B* if the presence of *A* increases the probability that *B* will occur.

Proximate cause: the causal condition in a causal complex that is nearest in time or space to the event caused.

Another important concept discussed in this chapter is the controlled experiment, in which an experimental group is subjected to a suspected causal agent but the control group is not. The controlled experiment provides a context for the application of Mill's Joint Method of Agreement and Difference or the Method of Concomitant Variation. The technique is especially valuable when we can be reasonably confident that the control group and the experimental group differ only with respect to the suspected causal agent and are similar in all other relevant respects. In one type of controlled experiment, the **randomized experimental study,** the control group and the experimental group are selected in such a way that they form representative samples of the population. Thus, it is reasonable to infer by inductive generalization that what happens to these groups in the presence or absence of the suspected cause would also happen to the population they represent. To avoid subjecting humans to unpleasant and possibly harmful causal agents, these randomized experimental studies are often performed on experimental animals. If we want to make inferences about what would happen to humans on the basis of these animal studies, additional analogical arguments are required.

Another type of controlled study is the forward-looking **prospective study,** in which an experimental group that has already been exposed to the suspected cause is matched with a control group that has not been exposed. The experimenter then waits to see what happens in each group. These experiments are inferior to randomized experiments for demonstrating causal claims because of questions about the ability of the experimental and control groups to provide representative samples. Nevertheless, these studies provide valuable information. Because humans "self-select" themselves into the population from which the experimental group is drawn, these studies avoid some of the moral objections to performing randomized experiments on humans. They also circumvent the need for additional analogical arguments to draw conclusions about humans.

Retrospective (backward-looking) studies are another type of controlled study. In these, the experimental group is chosen from individuals that already exhibit the effect. A matched control group that lacks the effect is chosen, and the histories of the two groups are examined to see whether a difference in past exposure to the suspected causal factor can be found. These studies suffer from all the problems of prospective studies, and introduce additional bias into the samples. They are the weakest form of controlled study, but because they give quicker results than prospective studies, they can provide useful information, such as early warnings about the dangers of some medical treatment. They can also be used to gain information for conducting a more thorough prospective study.

Causal fallacies discussed in this chapter include:

1. **Post Hoc:** the fallacy of arguing that *A* is the cause of *B* simply because *B* comes later than *A*. A relationship that is coincidental is judged—on the basis of insufficient evidence of a regular connection—to be causal. Many superstitious beliefs involve this fallacy.

2. **The Fallacy of Ignoring a Common Cause:** When evidence supports the view that a regular connection holds between two events or types of events, the nature of the connection must be investigated before making a causal judgment. *A* and *B* might be regularly connected through some common underlying cause *C*. In such cases, neither *A* nor *B* directly causes the other. Both *A* and *B* are effects of a common cause.

3. **The Fallacy of Confusing Cause and Effect:** When two events or types of events are regularly connected and do not result from a common cause, care must be taken to define which is cause and which is effect. Effects cannot occur earlier than their causes. In complex causal relationships, however, the temporal order of the various parts of the complex may be difficult to investigate.

4. **Genetic Fallacy:** This fallacy occurs whenever something about the genesis (origin, source or cause) of a claim or a belief is taken as evidence for its truth.

5. **Fallacy of mistaking some consequence of a belief with evidence for it.** The long name describes the fallacy. The shorter name **Consequential Fallacy** has been suggested for it.

6. **Fallacy of confusing an orginating cause with a sustaining cause.** Here we assume that because a particular cause was required to bring something into existence it is necessary to maintain that thing's existence.

Exercise Set 5.6

Part One

1. Some people have argued that both smoking and lung cancer are caused by some unknown factor, perhaps an obscure hereditary condition. Which fallacy would these people say that those who claim smoking is the cause of lung cancer are committing?

2. Two students in a large class turn in identical term papers. The teacher accuses them of copying from one another, even though the students can prove that they did not know one another and had no access to one another's work. The teacher maintains that copying could be the only cause of the identical papers. What fallacy does the teacher commit?

Part Two. Identify any fallacies involved in the following arguments:

1. Mrs. Jones, who is 89 years old, died two days after receiving a flu shot. Therefore, the flu shot caused her death.

2. Psychologists who have tested thousands of people working in U.S. businesses have discovered that top executives generally have much larger vocabularies than lower-level employees do. Therefore, if you want to rise to the top in business, you can make this happen by developing a very large vocabulary.

3. Every time little Johnny approaches the supermarket door, he says "Abracadabra" and then the door swings open. Johnny concludes that saying this magic word causes the door to open.

4. The results of surveys conducted by a computer company indicate that college students who own computers are, on the average, better students than college students who do not own computers. So if you want to succeed in your college studies, you should get a computer.

5. It has been widely observed that when young children who are usually well-behaved become irritable and difficult, they exhibit the symptoms of a cold or viral infection the next day. It is clear that their misbehavior causes these illnesses.

6. During the looting and rioting in Detroit in the summer of 1967, the items most commonly stolen were color television sets. Some people argued that one way to prevent such riots would be to distribute free color television sets to those who want them.

7. Tom is being quite reasonable when he regards all his coworkers with suspicion and fear because he feels that they are trying to take over his responsibilities. After all, he grew up in a tough situation and had to fight for everything he has achieved. He became impressed at an early age that others were out to get him.

8. Some people argue that emotional distress is the cause of cancer. Their evidence is the well-known fact that many patients with terminal cancer are severely depressed and unusually irritable.

9. A number of legislators are opposed to legalized abortions on the grounds that women undergoing abortions may be damaged psychologically. We can dismiss the truth of their claims, however, for these legislators are Catholic, and everyone knows the Catholic Church is opposed to abortion.

10. A football coach who is trying to bring his team out of a slump studies the statistics of past games. His research on several teams over a number of years shows that many more passes and attempted passes are almost always made by the losing team than by the winning team. From this information, the coach infers that he can make his team win by restricting the number of passes they throw.

11. "Since modern civilization came into being through Christianity, it would not survive once its supernatural basis were removed."

—Evelyn Waugh.

12. Computers cannot really *think*, because if we were to admit that there are thinking machines, that would mean that we humans might be mere machines as well, a very degrading situation!

Part Three. The following examples are taken from Friedrich Nietzsche's *Twilight of the Idols*, in which he discusses errors in causal reasoning. Identify the fallacy in each example.

1. Everybody knows the book of the famous Cornaro in which he recommends his slender diet as a recipe for a long and happy life—a virtuous one too. . . . The worthy Italian thought his diet was the *cause* of his long life, whereas the precondition for a long life, the extraordinary slowness of his metabolism, the consumption of so little, was the cause of his slender diet.

2. The church and morality say: "A generation, a people, are destroyed by license and luxury." [I] say: when a people appproaches destruction, when it degenerates physiologically, then license and luxury *follow* from this (namely, the craving for ever stronger and more frequent stimulation, as every exhausted nature knows it).

3. This young man turns pale early and wilts; his friends say: that is due to this or that disease. I say: that he became diseased, that he did not resist the disease, was already the effect of an impoverished life or hereditary exhaustion.

4. The newspaper reader says: this [political] party destroys itself by making such a mistake. [I] say: a party which makes such mistakes has reached its end; it has lost its sureness of instinct.

Part Four. In each of the following, identify the mistake in causal reasoning that the reader is warned against.

1. Has sodium been getting a bum rap? For a decade, health organizations, government agencies, and physicians have urged everyone to cut back on the intake of all forms of sodium.

R. Curtis Morris, Jr., of the University of San Francisco's General Clinical Research Center, thinks such recommendations may be wrong. "It has never been demonstrated," he says, "that any form of sodium other than sodium chloride [table salt] can raise blood pressure." This means, for example, that the sodium ingested as sodium bicarbonate in baked goods or antacids probably does not affect blood pressure and should not be lumped together on food labels with the sodium of sodium chloride.

—Scientific American 258:2,32

2. Breast cancer patients are more likely to survive the disease if they have a happy, positive frame of mind than if they feel hopeless and depressed, according to a study by a team of scientists at Pittsburgh and Yale University. . . .

[Dr. Sandra] Levy emphasized that the findings do not necessarily mean that cancer can be cured by making patients happy. The scientists don't know whether happy feelings cause longer survival, perhaps through an enhancing effect on the body's own healing process, or whether the patient's positive feelings are simply an effect, possibly resulting from an inherent stamina.

—H. Pierce, *Pittsburgh Post-Gazette*

3. The following is taken from a letter to the editor of *Science News*, 8/7/93, concerning an article on the causes of alcoholism. One conclusion of the article was that depression does not cause alcoholism ("depressed people rarely resort to uncontrolled alcohol use").

> [The article] says that the city men "from some of the poorest parts of Boston . . . tended to descend into alcoholism between age 21 and 30," whereas the Harvard men succumbed two decades later.
>
> Doesn't this suggest that distinctions in economic class were significant? In spite of the conclusion that "depressed people rarely resort to uncontrolled alcohol use," might not a similar but more gradual wearing away have been in operation? Clearly, the city men faced a harder economic reality than the more buffered Harvard men, and some of them may have succumbed earlier to personal desperation.
>
> —Seth Zimmerman

4. The following is taken from a letter to the editor of *Science News*, 2/13/93. The article that the writer comments on ("Rest for the weary dialysis patient") maintains that dialysis causes sleep apnea (holding one's breath while asleep).

> I do not believe that dialysis causes sleep apnea; it is more likely that sleep apnea and other sleep disorders contribute to kidney failure by causing hypertension.
>
> I have suffered from sleep apnea since about 1969. Once I was correctly diagnosed and treated, my problem with slowly increasing blood pressure

went away completely, despite the fact that I am still overweight, over 40, and both of my parents were hypertensive. After about a week of using a nasal CPAP [to stimulate regular breathing], my blood pressure went down to its current 110/70, without medication or change in diet.

—Howard Harkness

Chapter Six

PROBABILITIES AND INDUCTIVE LOGIC

I. INTRODUCTION

In an inductive argument, true premisses and a correct form make it probable that the conclusion is true as well. We know that inductive arguments vary in strength. Evidence presented in some inductive arguments makes it highly probable that their conclusions are true; in others the support is weaker. The probabilities that we are talking about here refer to the degree of support offered by premisses for a conclusion, not to the conclusion itself, even though it is sometimes (loosely) said "given the evidence, the conclusion is probably true." So far, we have relied on a common-sense understanding of the words *probable and probability*. In this chapter, we take a closer look at the concept of probability and its relationship to inductive logic.

Chapter 4 explains that the statistical premiss of a statistical syllogism can be stated numerically, as in "90 percent of all first-year students are state residents." On the basis of such information, and assuming that the reference class embodies all relevant information, it is natural to say that with a probability of 90 percent a randomly selected first-year student (for example, Maria) is a state resident. When we want to take some action, such as investing money or placing a bet, we have a practical interest in knowing how to assess probabilistic support in a precise numerical way. Consider, for example, the sentence "A blind draw from a standard deck of cards will result in a nonheart," (that is, a spade, a diamond, or a club will be drawn). We can argue for that conclusion using the following statistical syllogism:

Most cards in a standard deck are nonheart cards.
a is a card drawn "blind" from a standard deck.

a is a nonheart card.

This argument is reasonably strong. If, however, we are going to bet that a nonheart will be drawn, we want to know how to assign a numerical probability to "a is a nonheart," so we can know what sort of bet is fair.

Background information about standard decks of cards tells us that a deck contains 39 nonhearts and 13 hearts. Therefore, the first premiss could be stated quantitatively: 39/52 (or 75 percent) of the cards are nonhearts. With this information—which encompasses all relevant available information, given blind drawing of the card—we can say that the probability of drawing a nonheart is 75 percent, or 3/4.

This probability can be used to determine proper betting odds that a nonheart will be drawn. In an even-money bet, the amount won or lost is equal to the "stake" (the amount that is put at risk). An even-money bet is proper when, as in the toss of a fair coin, two equally likely outcomes are possible. If you win such a bet, your stake is returned along with an equal amount, so that you double your money. When the probabilities of various outcomes are not equal, the betting odds must be altered in an appropriate way to assure fairness. For example, betting odds of "3 to 1," in which the return for a winning bet is three times the stake, are fair for an outcome with a probability of 1/4, or 0.25.

The "odds" refer to the difference in favor of one side and against the other. For an outcome with a probability of 1/4, such as blindly drawing a heart from a standard deck that contains 39 nonhearts and 13 hearts, there are three times as many ways of losing as there are of winning. In other words, the odds are 3 to 1 against winning. A payoff of 3 to 1 balances this disadvantage and makes the bet fair. For an outcome with a probability of 3/4 (drawing a nonheart), the odds against winning are only 1 to 3, so an accordingly smaller payoff balances this advantage.

Numerical probabilities are sometimes used to assess the strength of inductive generalizations. Chapter 4 also explains that by increasing the sample size, we can reduce the margin of error while retaining the same confidence level. Alternatively, by increasing the sample size, we can retain the same margin of error but increase the confidence level. The confidence level can be understood as the minimum probability that arguing in this way will lead to a true conclusion. As shown in that chapter, in certain circumstances, we can state these probabilities numerically. One example uses a sample of 100 students to determine voting behavior. Based on the information that 60 percent of the sample planned to vote for the Liberals, we concluded, with a confidence level of 0.95 that between 50 percent and 70 percent of the student population would vote for the Liberals. Assigning this confidence level is equivalent to saying that the use of this statistical method of reasoning will lead to a true conclusion at least 95 percent of the time.

Probabilities play an important role in judging the outcomes of controlled studies, for as we have seen, such experiments use information about what happens in the experimental and control groups to tell us what probably would happen in populations. Probabilities also enter into judgments of whether an outcome of a study is statistically significant.

We know that the properties of random samples rarely match exactly the properties of the populations from which they are selected. But, within a margin of error, samples should resemble the population most of the time. For example, assume a coin you hold is fair (that is, not weighted or altered), and begin a series of tosses. Stop after five tosses. This series is your sample. Suppose further that the sample contains no heads. Although this happens relatively infrequently, it is possible. The probability of getting no heads in five tosses of a fair coin is slightly more than 3 percent (1/32). In other words, you can expect at least one head in five tosses of a fair coin with a probability greater than 95 percent. Your sample in this case is statistically significant at the 0.05 level because it is the kind of sample you would expect less than 5 percent of the time if the coin is fair. Statistical significance is obviously dependent on sample size. In a series of two tosses of a fair coin, an outcome of no heads would not be significant at the 0.05 level—heads fail to turn up about 25 percent of the time.

Although traditionally a criterion of statistical significance at the 0.05 level (corresponding to a 95 percent confidence level) is adopted for most scientific studies, use of statistical significance at the 0.01 level is not uncommon. A result is statistically significant at the 0.01 level if the probability of obtaining such a result is less than 1 percent. A series of ten tosses of a fair coin that results in no heads has a probability of less than one in a thousand. A sample composed of such a series would be statistically significant at the 0.001 level and could even be used to challenge the assumption that the coin is fair.

A branch of mathematics, called the probability calculus, provides rules for determining unknown probabilities when some probabilities are known. If we know, for example, that the probability of obtaining a head on a single toss of a fair coin is 1/2, then we can use the mathematical theory of probability to calculate the probability of obtaining all heads on two, three, or more tosses of a fair coin. Because the method of calculating unknown probabilities on the basis of known probabilities is a part of mathematics, it belongs properly to deductive logic rather than to inductive logic. However, the probability calculus has such important applications for inductive reasoning that serious studies of inductive logic always include some treatment of probabilities.

The mathematical theory of probability was developed during the seventeenth century in two different places, to solve two different types of problems. On the European continent, where gambling with cards and dice was a major form of amusement for the nobility, an interest in setting fair betting odds for complicated gambling situations motivated probability studies. One game involved tossing a pair of ordinary dice, with the goal of tossing a "double six." Each die has six sides; the side turned up is called the *face,* and 36 different combinations of two faces are possible when a pair of dice is tossed. Only one of these possibilities shows six dots on the faces of both dice. Thus, the probability that one toss of a pair of fair dice will result in double sixes is 1/36. Parisian gambling houses were offering even money bets that at least one pair of double sixes would show in 24 tosses. The Chevalier de Méré, wondering whether these betting odds were fair, put the following question to his friend the mathematician Blaise Pascal:

How many tosses are required for the probability of getting a double six to be at least 1/2 ?

The concept of *probability* that is used to assign initial probabilities in most games of chance assumes a set of equally possible alternatives (for example, each card is equally likely to be drawn from a deck; each face on a die has an equal chance of showing), and identifies the probability of any of these alternatives as the ratio of favorable to possible outcomes. In coin tossing, if the coin is fair, two outcomes are equally possible: heads or tails. Whichever one of these two outcomes is chosen is favorable. The ratio of favorable to possible outcomes in a fair coin toss is therefore 1/2. In dice games, each die has six sides. Assuming the die is balanced, the outcome of a particular face showing in a roll of a single die is 1/6. In card games, a standard deck contains 52 cards, divided into 4 suits, each containing 13 cards in denominations from ace through 10, jack, queen, and king. The probability of blindly drawing a particular single card from a well-shuffled deck is 1/52; of drawing any card of a particular suit, 13/52 (1/4); of drawing a particular denomination, such as an ace, 4/52 (1/13).

Remember that the mathematical calculus of probability is used to calculate probabilities on the basis of some initially known probabilities. Considerable mathematical skill is required to use the known probability of obtaining a double six on a single toss of a pair of fair dice to determine how many times a pair of dice must be tossed to yield a probability of obtaining at least one double six equal to or greater than 1/2. In working out answers to complicated problems such as this, Pascal, Fermat, and other French mathematicians constructed the foundations of the mathematical theory of probability. The usefulness of their results goes far beyond helping gamblers to get fair payoffs for their risks. The techniques developed to solve de Méré's problem are also used, for example, to determine the relationship between size of sample, margin of error, and confidence level in experimental studies.

At about the same time that French gamblers were asking mathematicians to help solve their problems, a different interest motivated studies in mathematical probability in England. There, the problem was not how to figure fair betting odds for games of chance but rather to determine the fair cost of insurance to cover burial expenses. This was the beginning of actuarial science—the calculation of risks and associated insurance premiums.

The Great Plague struck London in 1664-1665. Previous epidemics of this disease (bubonic plague, sometimes called "black death") had wiped out from one-fourth to three-fourths of the population. When the plague arrived this time, people formed associations to share the burden of funeral and burial expenses. Even after the plague ended, participation in this type of insurance continued. To determine fair costs of membership in burial associations, it was necessary to know, for example, the probability that a prospective member would survive another 5, 10, 15, or 20 years. The gamblers' understanding of "probability" as a ratio of favorable to possible outcomes was not appropriate in these circumstances. Years of life are not dealt like cards from a deck, with any year being viewed as an equally possible year for death to occur. A different concept of probability from the one used in connection with games of chance was required.

Probability in this actuarial context is connected with the observed frequency with which events of a certain type occur. Information about the ages at which death had occurred for persons living in various areas and following assorted trades and occupations was gathered, mostly from church records, by the burial associations. The information was compiled in "mortality tables," which were used to determine the relative frequency with which persons in given situations survived to reach various ages. On the basis of the information in a mortality table, for example, it could be observed that 90 percent of the 25-year-old carpenters living in London during a specified period of time had survived their thirtieth birthdays. A burial association might then use this information to assign a probability of 0.9 (or 90 percent) that Hawkins, a 25-year-old carpenter from London, would be able to pay dues in the association for at least five years and to charge accordingly for his five-year membership.

Mortality tables are still used by insurance companies to figure the probabilities that determine the cost of life-insurance premiums. The information compiled in modern tables is far more extensive than the data contained in seventeenth-century tables. Similar tables, based on records of automobile ownership and accidents, are used to determine automobile-insurance premiums. These records show, for example, that males under twenty-five years of age have more accidents than females in the same age category. Before insurance companies were challenged on the basis of sex discrimination, they used this information to charge young male drivers correspondingly higher rates. Health-insurance costs also are based in part on actuarial tables that are compiled from meticulous records of the frequency of various illnesses and diseases and the costs associated with their treatment.

From these historical examples, we see that *probability* has at least two different meanings: the ratio of favorable to other equally possible outcomes, and the relative frequency of events of a particular type in some reference class of events. Both senses of probability lend themselves naturally to quantitative (numerical) expressions of probability values. When probabilities are expressed quantitatively, the probability of a sentence describing an event is stated as a single real number (integer, fraction, or irrational number) between 0 (the lowest possible value) and 1 (the highest possible value). A probability may be expressed as a ratio between two numbers (1/4), as a decimal fraction (0.25), or as a percentage (25 percent).

Probability is commonly used another way, too. When, for example, I assign an extremely low probability to the statement that my mother will attend a Grateful Dead concert in the city where she lives, *probability* does not mean "ratio of favorable to possible outcomes." Nor is my probability assignment based on the relative frequency of her attendance at Dead concerts, because the band has never played in her city. Instead, here *probability* is used as a measure of the degree to which it is rational to believe certain statements. My belief that my mother will not go to hear the Dead is based on my knowledge of her taste in music, her lack of interest in pop culture, her dislike of crowded places, and a lot of information about how she prefers to spend her leisure time. The "degree of rational belief" concept of probability can be expressed numerically, but it does not lend itself so naturally to quantification as the other meanings of *probability*. If numerical values are assigned to these degrees of rational belief, however, the mathematical rules for calculating unknown probabilities on the basis of known probabilities can be applied to them as well.*

II. THE RULES OF PROBABILITY

Before we look at the mathematical rules, we should note that any assignment of a probability value is based on general background information or on evidence regarding specific conditions. Probability assignments are always conditional on the assumed truth of some such information. Thus, the probability of "a single toss of a die shows six dots on the face" being equal to 1/6 is conditional on the die having the usual design and being balanced in the usual (fair)

---

* For further discussion at an elementary level of different meanings of "probability" and related matters, see W. Salmon's Foundations of Scientific Inference (1967).

way. Regarding the examples considered in the preceding section, the probability of the 25-year-old carpenter's surviving his 30th birthday, for instance, is conditional on the statistical data and no evidence of a fatal disease; the low probability of my mother's attending the Dead concert is conditional on background information and on no one's offering her a large sum of money to go.

Statements of probability values are standardly written as:

$$Pr(h|e) = n$$

which can be read, "The probability of a statement h, on evidence e, is equal to n." Sometimes, however, when it is clearly understood that a probability value is conditional on general background information and not on any special evidence, we write

$$Pr(h) = n$$

omitting any reference to evidence.

Rule 1.

The value n in a sentence of the form $Pr(h|e) = n$ must be a single real number between 0 and 1, inclusive.

In view of Rule 1, the following assignments of probabilities are improper:

Pr(Jones will win the Sweepstakes|Jones bought a Sweepstakes ticket) = −1.
(No probability values can be negative numbers.)

Pr(The Democrats will win the next presidential election) = 1.25.
(No probability value can be greater than 1.)

Rule 2.

If h follows deductively from e, then $Pr(h|e) = 1$.

To say that h follows deductively from e means that if e is true, then h must be true also. If this is so, then the probability of h, on evidence e, is 1.

Examples

(a) Pr(Mrs. Jones is married|Mrs. Jones has a spouse) = 1.
(b) Pr(A black or a red card is drawn|A card is drawn from a standard deck) = 1.

In (b), e is "A card is drawn from a standard deck" and h is "A black card or a red card is drawn." If a card is drawn from a standard deck, that card will be either black or red; no other possibilities exist. Thus, $n = 1$.

The probability value of 1 is not reserved exclusively for sentences that follow deductively from the available evidence. Sentences that are certainly true ("sure things") are assigned a probability equal to 1. The type of certainty that is involved here may be practical certainty, rather than certainty based on strict relationships of deductive logic.

Example

Pr(A six-year-old child, using materials found in an ordinary home workshop, cannot build a spaceship that will reach Mars) = 1.

Notice that no statement of evidence (*e*) is given in this example; here, the probability is conditional on general background information. This sentence is so likely to be true on the basis of everything we know (it has "practical certainty") that the assignment of 1 is appropriate.

The lowest probability value (0) is assigned to sentences that either are inconsistent with the evidence sentence or that are false as a matter of "practical certainty."

Examples

(a) Pr(5 aces are drawn | 5 cards are drawn, without replacement, from a standard deck) = 0.

Here, the sentence "5 aces are drawn" is inconsistent with the evidence that the deck is standard. (Standard decks contain only 4 aces, and the cards are drawn without replacement.)

(b) Pr(A human being, without any artificial aids, can leap tall buildings in a single bound) = 0.

Given our background knowledge of human physiology, we have "practical certainty" that this sentence is false.

Rule 3.

If two sentences h_1 and h_2 are mutually exclusive (if they cannot both be true), then, on the same evidence in both cases, the probability that their disjunction (h_1 or h_2) is true is equal to the sum of their individual probabilities.

A disjunction is a compound sentence with its major components connected by *or* (or an equivalent connective, such as *unless*), as in "The coin came up heads or the coin came up tails," or "The coin came up heads unless the coin came up tails." Symbolically, Rule 3 can be expressed

$$\text{Pr}(h_1 \text{ or } h_2 | e) = \text{Pr}(h_1 | e) + \text{Pr}(h_2 | e)$$

Although this rule is stated for any two mutually exclusive sentences, it can be generalized to any number of mutually exclusive sentences. This rule allows us to calculate the unknown probability of a disjunction when each disjunct is incompatible with all the others, and the probabilities of all the individual disjuncts are known.

Examples

(a) Using as evidence the claim that a fair die is tossed a single time, we know that the probability of throwing a six is equal to 1/6, and that the probability of throwing a two is 1/6. Because the sentences "A six is thrown" and "A two is thrown" are mutually exclusive for a single throw, Rule 3 tells us that the probability of "A six is thrown or a two is thrown," is 1/6 + 1/6, or after performing the addition [2/6] and reducing the fraction, 1/3.

(b) Conditional on the same evidence as in (a), the probability of "A six or a two or a three is thrown," is equal to (1/6 + 1/6 + 1/6), or 1/2.

(c) Conditional on the same evidence as in (a), what is the probability of "An even number of dots will show on the face of the die thrown"?

The sentence stating that an even number of dots will show means the same as "Either two dots or four dots or six dots will show," and this sentence is a disjunction composed of three mutually exclusive disjuncts, each with a probability of 1/6. To calculate the probability of the disjunction, use Rule 3, and add the individual probabilities: (1/6 + 1/6 + 1/6) = 1/2.

Rule 4.

The probability of the conjunction of two sentences is equal to the probability of the first sentence multiplied by the probability of the second sentence on the condition that the first sentence is true.

A conjunction is a compound sentence with its major components connected by *and,* or some other expression such as *moreover,* or a semicolon, which indicates that the sentence as a whole is true just in case all of its components are true. "A six showed on one of a pair of dice, and a five showed on the other" is an example of a conjunction. Rule 4 allows us to calculate the probability of a conjunction when the probabilities of the individual conjuncts are known. Symbolically, Rule 4 can be expressed

$$\Pr(h_1 \text{ and } h_2 | e) = \Pr(h_1 | e) \times \Pr(h_2 | e \text{ and } h_1)$$

Like Rule 3, Rule 4 can be generalized to any number of cases, but for simplicity here, it is stated to cover only two conjuncts. When more than two conjuncts are involved, calculations become more complicated because the probability of each successive conjunct is conditional on the truth of all the preceding conjuncts.

Examples

(a) Suppose that a fair coin is tossed twice (the evidence sentence). What is the probability that both tosses yield a head?

Rule 4 tells us to multiply the probability that the first toss will yield a head (1/2) by the probability that the second toss will be a head, on the condition that the first toss yields a head. This probability is also 1/2, because what happens on the first toss has no effect on the second toss (the probability of a head on the second toss is 1/2 regardless of whether the first toss is a head or a tail). Multiplying 1/2 by 1/2 yields 1/4, which is the probability of "two heads appear on two tosses of a fair coin."

(b) Suppose that two cards are drawn blindly from a standard deck and placed in a drawer together (the evidence). What is the probability that both cards are aces? We want to know the probability of the conjunction "The first card is an ace and the second card is an ace." The probability that the first card is an ace is 4/52. (There are four aces in a standard deck of 52 cards.) The probability that the second card drawn is also an ace, if the first card drawn is an ace, is 3/51. (At the time of the second draw, the deck contains 51 cards; if the first card drawn is an ace, only three aces remain in the deck.) The product of 4/52 and 3/51 is 12/2,652. This fraction can be reduced to 1/221, which is the probability of drawing two aces from a standard deck in two draws (without replacing the first card drawn).

In example (b), unlike example (a), the probabilities are not the same for the first and second conjuncts. When a fair coin is tossed, what happens on a second or a third toss is independent of what happens on any previous toss. When cards are drawn from a deck without replacement after each draw, the probabilities of drawing a particular card are not the same for successive draws. The deck is different after each draw. What happens on the second draw is not independent of what happens on the first draw. If, however, the cards are replaced and the deck is shuffled after every draw, the outcome of each draw is independent of previous draws from the deck.

(c) What is the probability of drawing three aces in three draws from a standard deck without replacement?

Here, we want to apply Rule 4 to more than two conjuncts. The probability that the first draw is an ace is 4/52. The probability that the second draw is an ace, given that the first card drawn is an ace is 3/51. The probability that the third card is also an ace, given that the first and second cards drawn are aces is 2/50. Multiplying these three probabilities (a calculator is helpful for such problems), we find that the probability of three aces being drawn from a standard deck in three draws without replacement is equal to 24/132,600. This fraction can be reduced to 1/5,525.

In these examples of the application of Rule 4, it is easy to tell whether the events being considered are independent. Tosses of coins and rolls of dice are independent events. Draws from a deck, when cards previously drawn are replaced and the deck is reshuffled, are also independent. When cards drawn from a deck are not replaced or, as in games such as 21 (Blackjack), when cards that are exposed are then placed on the bottom of the deck and the deck is not reshuffled, successive draws are *not* independent. In applying Rule 4 to real-life situations, we must pay attention to whether events are independent. For example, suppose that the probability of getting a busy signal when calling any one of your close friends is 0.05. The probability of getting a busy signal when you call one friend and then getting another busy signal when you call a second friend immediately afterwards is not equal to 0.05×0.05 *if* those two friends are also friends of one another, because the busy signals are then not independent events. If your first friend is on the phone, this raises the probability that you will also get a busy signal when you try to call the second friend. It may be difficult to assign probabilities for dependent events, but we should at least be aware of how a lack of independence can affect the calculation of probabilities.

Rules 1–4 (sometimes called axioms) form the entire basis of probability theory, just as the axioms of geometry form the basis for that area of mathematics. Without deriving any theorems here, we take note of one useful theorem that simplifies calculations:

Theorem

$$\text{If } \Pr(h \mid e) = n, \text{ then } \Pr(\text{not } h \mid e) = 1 - n.$$

Here, "not *h*" is the negation, or denial, of the sentence *h*.

Examples

(a) What is the probability of not drawing an ace from a standard deck when a card is drawn blindly?

Because the probability of drawing an ace is 4/52, the probability of not drawing an ace is $1 - 4/52 = 48/52 = 12/13$.

(b) What is the probability of obtaining at least one head in two tosses of a fair coin?

Rule 3 is not applicable in this problem because "a head occurs on the first toss" and "a head occurs on the second toss" are not mutually exclusive sentences. Heads could occur on both tosses. If we were (mistakenly) to add the probabilities of obtaining a head on the first toss and of obtaining a head on the second toss, the probability would be equal to 1. Obviously, this is incorrect, because it is by no means certain that a head will occur in two tosses. However, the sentence "At least one head occurs in two tosses of a fair coin," is equivalent to the sentence "Tails do not occur on both tosses of a fair coin." We can use Rule 4 to calculate the probability of obtaining tails on both tosses $(1/2 \times 1/2 = 1/4)$. Then, we can use the theorem to calculate the probability of not obtaining a tail on both tosses $(1 - 1/4 = 3/4)$.

The Rasmussen Report, issued in 1975, is the most complete study by the U.S. government on the safety of nuclear power. The report, which has been criticized by those opposed to nuclear power, offers an interesting and important application of this theorem. Critics say that the report misrepresents the probability of a serious accident at a nuclear-power plant (K. S. Shrader-Frechette, *Nuclear Power and Public Policy*).

According to federal government figures, the probability of a serious accident is 1/17,000 per year, per reactor. "Serious accident" in this context refers to a core melt, which, again, according to government estimates, would be equivalent to 1,000 Hiroshimas. The probability of 1/17,000 per year, per reactor may sound like a very low probability. However, critics point out that each reactor presently operating at 65 nuclear power plants has an estimated lifetime of 30 years. The critics believe we should be concerned with the probability that a serious accident will occur at any one plant during its 30-year lifetime.

We can apply the preceding theorem twice to calculate the probability that a core melt will occur in at least one of these 65 nuclear-power plants during their 30-year lifetimes. This probability is equal to 1 minus the probability of no serious accidents in any of these 65 plants during their 30-year lifetimes. The probability of no core melts—using the government probability of 1/17,000 per year, per reactor that a serious accident will occur, and assuming that the events (core melts per year, per reactor) are independent—is equal to

$$[1 - (1/17,000)]^{65 \times 30}$$
$$\text{or}$$
$$(16,999/17,000)^{1950}$$

which is equal to 0.8916.

We can then apply the theorem a second time to determine the probability of at least one serious accident. "There will be no serious accidents (core melts)" is the denial of "There will be at least one serious accident." To calculate the probability that at least one serious accident will occur, we subtract the probability of no serious accidents (0.8916) from 1:

$$1 - 0.8916 = 0.108$$

Therefore, according to government figures, the probability of a nuclear-power disaster equivalent to 1,000 Hiroshimas occurring in the United States is slightly more than 10 percent.

In considering the probability of a serious nuclear accident, difficulties in applying the probability calculus to life situations become apparent. First of all, we can ask whether it is reasonable to assume that the probability of a serious accident in a nuclear-power plant is the same throughout each of its 30 years of use. In addition, the assumption of independence for per-year, per-reactor core melts is probably false. Nuclear reactors are built along similar designs and have almost identical safety devices. Therefore if the threat of a serious accident is connected with the design of the reactor itself or the failure of its protective devices, such accidents could not be considered independent. Another possible source of serious accidents is sabotage. We might judge an isolated instance of a sabotage-caused accident as independent of other such acts, but the sabotage could be a part of a terrorist campaign against nuclear power reactors. Another factor that would undermine an assumption of independence is that publicity about the sabotage at one plant could be a causal factor in other instances.

An additional difficult question is whether the lack of independence would raise or lower the estimate of the probability that an accident will occur in at least one plant during its 30-year lifetime. Some critics of nuclear power have also objected that the figure of 1/17,000 is an unrealistically low estimate of the probability of a serious accident per year, per reactor.

Such questions cannot be answered by simply applying the rules to calculate probabilities. The assignment of initial probabilities and the determination of whether events are dependent or independent require us to assemble and evaluate evidence, using means far beyond the probability calculus. With suitable evidence in hand, many of the argument forms we considered in earlier chapters—inductive generalizations, statistical syllogisms, and analogies—may be useful in assigning appropriate initial probabilities.

Exercise Set 6.1

1. What is the probability of obtaining either an ace or a king in a single, blind draw from a standard deck of cards?

2. What is the probability of not obtaining either an ace or a king in a single, blind draw from a standard deck of cards?

3. What is the probability of obtaining three heads in three tosses of a fair coin?

4. What is the probability of obtaining at least one tail in three tosses of a fair coin?

5. What is the probability of obtaining either a head or a tail in a single toss of a fair coin?

6. What is the probability of drawing an ace and a king in two blind draws from a standard deck without replacement?

7. Suppose you are playing a card game in which 4 cards are dealt to each person. What is the probability that you will be dealt 4 aces? What is the probability that you will be dealt the four following cards: Jack of Hearts, 2 of Diamonds, 3 of Clubs, and 6 of Spades?

8. Consider a Health Club with 100 members (60 men and 40 women). Each member uses the club for only one favorite activity, and men and women are equally likely to engage in any of the activities. Twenty members of the club are swimmers; 30 play racquet ball; 24 take aerobics classes; 16 lift weights; and 10 play indoor tennis.

   a. Suppose a member of the club is randomly selected:

   (1) What is the probability that the member selected is a weight lifter?

   (2) What is the probability that the member is either a swimmer or takes aerobic exercise classes?

   (3) What is the probability that the member selected is either a tennis player or a racquet-ball player or a weight lifter?

   (4) What is the probability that the member selected is a woman weight lifter?

   (5) What is the probability that the member selected is a man who takes aerobic classes?

b. Suppose that two members of the club are randomly selected:

(1) What is the probability that both are tennis players?

(2) What is the probability that the first one selected is a tennis player and the second one selected is a racquet-ball player?

(3) What is the probability that a tennis player and a racquet-ball player are selected?

9. Suppose the probability that a 22-year-old male will survive his forty-seventh birthday is 0.840 and the probability that a 22-year-old female will survive her forty-seventh birthday is 0.910. A man and a woman, who have been close friends at college, are both graduating at the age of 22. They promise to meet each other at their twenty-fifth reunion.

(1) What is the probability that both friends will be alive to keep that promise?

(2) If these good friends fall in love and marry one another after college, would this affect the independence of each living another 25 years?

10. Assuming that you know what your birthday is but do not know what mine is, what is the probability that we share the same birthday (day only—not year)?

11. Suppose that you hold three aces and two different small cards in a game of draw poker. If you discard the two small cards, what are your chances of improving your hand on the draw? The hand will be improved either by drawing another ace and any other card or by drawing a pair. (Hint: Because this is a fair game and you do not know what cards are in the other players' hands, treat their cards as if they were part of the deck.)

12. If my chances of being apprehended for committing some crime are 0.7, my chances of being convicted if I am apprehended are 0.6, and my chances of serving time if I am apprehended and convicted are 0.5, what is the probability that I will serve time if I rob the local grocery store?

13. You are taking a True-False test that has ten questions, and you need a score of 60 percent to pass. You know the answers to only five of the questions. For the other five, you toss a coin and answer True if it comes up heads and False if it comes up tails. What is the probability that you will pass the exam? (Think about this as the probability of getting at least one right answer in five tries.)

III. DECISION THEORY: USING PROBABILITIES TO PLAN A COURSE OF ACTION

"Probability," as Bishop Butler remarked in the eighteenth century, "is the very guide of life." None of us can see what the future holds. We make most choices, decisions, and plans as best we can in the face of less than complete knowledge about what the state of the world will be and what others will do. Probabilities play an important role in many of these decisions, because we are often in a position to judge the probabilities of various states of affairs before we make decisions. We all depend on probabilities in our daily lives. For example, if we care about seeing a movie from the beginning, we try to arrive at the theater before the show is scheduled to begin because it will probably start on time. We pursue our college educations because we believe that what we learn in college will probably enhance the quality of our lives.

The probability that some event or condition will occur is not the only consideration on which we base a decision to act. We are concerned with costs and benefits as well. In problem number 12 in Exercise Set 6.1, the surprisingly low probabilities given for apprehension, conviction, and incarceration are not unrealistic, based on government crime statistics. Although the probability that someone would actually serve time for robbing a store is low, even an immoral or antisocial person who contemplates such an act should reflect not only on the probability of serving time but also on the unpleasantness of that prospect. It is prudent to avoid even a fairly small risk of falling into such an unhappy situation. Conversely, we think it is reasonable to expend great effort to achieve some goals, even though the probabilities of attaining them are small, if the potential benefits are very attractive.

The term *utility* is often used to refer to the desirability (positive utility) or undesirability (negative utility) of a situation. The term *value* (which can also be positive or negative) is sometimes used as well. Thus, we say that serving time in prison has such great negative utility that this should be considered along with the probability of serving time when contemplating an action that could result in a prison sentence.

Decision theory is the study of how to decide what to do in contexts that vary with respect to the knowledge available. (Here, a *decision* is a decision to take some action.) The goal of decision theory is to develop criteria for rational (reasonable) decision making. In our brief look at decision theory, we consider three general contexts in which decisions occur:

1. Decisions under risk: Contexts in which we can assign probabilities to the states of the world that we believe are relevant to our actions. Our knowledge in these contexts is said to be partial or incomplete.

2. Decisions under certainty: Contexts in which the relevant state of the world is assured. In these contexts, our knowledge of states relevant to our actions has "practical certainty."

3. Decisions under uncertainty: Contexts in which various relevant states of the world are possible, but of unknown probability.

1. Decisions Under Risk

In one example of a statistical syllogism in Chapter 4, a patient whose doctor had suggested an ear operation was trying to make a decision under risk. If the patient decides to have the operation, three different states of the world or conditions are relevant, each associated with a probability (the condition of improved hearing to "very good": 0.85; the condition of no improvement: 0.10; the condition of further damage to ear: 0.05). The probabilities in this case are based on statistics gathered from other similar operations. No utilities for the various outcomes are mentioned, though clearly the first outcome has the greatest utility as well as the highest probability; the second outcome has a lower utility (the hearing problem is unimproved and the patient must endure the pain and expense of an operation); and the third outcome has the lowest utility. If the patient decides against the operation, it is almost certain that the ear condition will neither improve nor worsen. The utility of this outcome ranks higher than utilities of having an unsuccessful operation (no improvement or no improvement and further damage) but ranks lower than the outcome of an operation that results in hearing improvement. Should the patient have the operation? The decision problem can be represented in the following array, which displays the states of the world and the probabilities associated with them in the light of the two actions:

States of the World

Actions	Improved hearing	No change	Worse off
1. Have operation	0.85	0.10	0.05
2. Refuse operation	(almost) 0	(almost) 1	(almost) 0

The patient could act as if the most probable result of the operation will occur. However, "Always act as if the most probable state will occur," is a poor decision-making rule because it ignores the utilities of various states and it will lead to apparently irrational decisions in some cases. Following this rule, for example, would lead an immoral robber to hold up the local grocery store on the grounds that no prison sentence was the most probable result of that action. The improbable sometimes happens, and in this case has highly negative utility. Following this rule would also lead a homeowner to refuse to purchase fire insurance, even at a very favorable price, because the probability (based on statistics) that a given house will catch fire is very low.

Another possible decision rule is "Always choose the action that could result in a state of affairs with a higher utility than any other possible state of affairs." If the patient follows this rule, the operation will be chosen, for a restoration of hearing is clearly the state with the highest utility, and this condition is possible only if the patient has the operation. But this rule ignores the known probabilities involved in making a decision under risk, and like the rule "Always act as if the most probable state of affairs will occur," it can lead to decisions that most of us would regard as foolish.

To illustrate that this rule is not effective, consider the following case. Suppose that Hilary has $10,000 to cover college costs. Hilary places a high utility on having money but also strongly desires a college education, and college would be out of the question if this $10,000 were lost. Someone offers Hilary a chance to invest that $10,000. The probability that the $10,000 investment will return a profit of $100,000 is 10 percent, but the the probability that the original $10,000 stake will be lost is 90 percent. What action should Hilary take? Given the high value placed on a college education, most people would consider it unreasonable to invest the $10,000 under these circumstances, even though one possible state of affairs associated with this action (money for education and a lot left over for other things) has the greatest utility.

To evaluate correctly these decisions under risk, a rule that accounts for both utilities and probabilities is required. "Choose an action that maximizes expected utility" is such a rule. This is not the only rule that takes probabilities and utilities into account, and in some cases it appears to give bad advice. Nevertheless, it is a good rule for many ordinary decision problems and is a good tool for beginning to think about decision problems. To understand the rule of maximizing expected utility, we need to know how to calculate expected utilities. To do so, we first need to quantify, or measure, utilities; only then can a calculation be performed.

The problem of measuring utilities is by no means simple. How can we assign a quantity to the value of hearing properly, or undergoing an unsuccessful operation, or losing one's hearing? Objectivity is not the issue here. The measurements of utilities need not be objective in the sense that the assigned quantities must be acceptable to any reasonable person. All that is required is that the person confronted with the decision measure his or her utilities, but even that is difficult in many cases.

Studies of decision theory usually begin with examples of decisions about spending money, such as decisions concerning bets or investments. An investment that will return $30,000 seems—all other things being equal—three times as desirable as (has three times the utility of) an investment that will return $10,000. If dollars are correlated in this manner with units of utility, it is not difficult to assign a measure of the utility of various amounts of money lost or won, for money already comes in measurable units. Consider a problem that involves only money to illustrate how expected utilities work before returning to the problem of the ear operation.

I am committed to attend a school fair and spend at least $2 there playing a game of chance. I have to decide whether to risk $2 on a punchboard or on a dice game. If I choose to play the punchboard, four states of the world are relevant to my action: the state in which I win $10, the state in which I win $5, the state in which I win $2, and the state in which I win nothing. Given the way the punchboard is designed, the respective probabilities associated with these states are 0.05, 0.10, 0.20, and 0.65. If I play the dice game, and roll any matched pair, I win $10; otherwise I win nothing. To assure that units of utility correspond to the amounts of money won or lost, I assume that the dice game is no more or no less amusing to me than the punchboard and that I desire to gain as much money as possible from my $2 play.

The expected utility of a $2 punch can be calculated by multiplying each payoff with its associated probability, summing the results, and subtracting the $2 cost:

$$[(10 \times 0.05) + (5 \times 0.10) + (2 \times 0.20) + (0 \times 0.65)] - 2 = (0.50 + 0.50 + 0.40) - 2 = -0.60.$$

In the dice game, the expected utility is similarly calculated by multiplying payoffs with their associated probabilities, summing the results, and subtracting the $2 cost. In general, the rule for calculating the expected utility of some decision is to multiply the probability of each relevant state of affairs by the number of units (the total amount) of utility associated with that state. The sum of these products, minus the initial cost (also measured in units of utility), if any, is the expected utility of that decision.

In the dice game, the probability of rolling a pair of ones, twos, threes, fours, fives, or sixes is 1/6. This probability can be calculated in several ways. The probability of rolling any one pair is 1/36. You can win by rolling any of six mutually exclusive pairs, and (1/36 + 1/36 + 1/36 + 1/36 + 1/36 + 1/36) = 1/6. Or the problem can be viewed another way. The first die shows some number on its face. The probability that the second die will show the same number is 1/6, and this is also the probability that you will roll a pair.

The utility associated with rolling a pair (the payoff) is $10. The probability of not rolling a pair is 5/6 (1 minus the probability of obtaining a pair). The payoff for not rolling a pair is $0. Because $10 × 1/6 = $1.67 and 0 × 5/6 = 0, we sum these amounts and subtract the $2 cost (1.67 + 0 − 2 = − 0.33). Therefore, the expected utility (measured in money) of a play on the punchboard is −$0.60 and the expected utility of the dice game is −$0.33. If I followed the rule of maximizing expected utilities, I would choose the dice game and thereby cut my losses.

Let us return to the problem of measuring the utilities associated with the ear operation. Remember that the measures I assign are my own in such a situation. You might assign values differently, and could not be criticized for doing so. The units I assign are simply "units of utility." The arithmetic operations of addition, subtraction, multiplication, and division can be performed on these units of utility, but the units need not—and perhaps can not—be translated into monetary amounts.

(i) Units of utility of three states associated with decision to undergo operation (probabilities are enclosed in parentheses):

> Hearing improvement to "very good": 10 (0.85)
> No improvement: −2 (0.10)
> Further damage: −10 (0.05)

(Notice that the three states are mutually exclusive and exhaust the possible relevant states; therefore the sum of their probabilities is equal to 1.)

(ii) Units of utility associated with the only state with nonzero probability relevant to the decision not to undergo the operation:

> No change: 0 (1)

Using these figures, the expected utility of the operation is [(10 × 0.85) + (−2 × 0.10) + (−10 × 0.05)] = 7.8. The expected utility of not having the operation is (0 × 1) = 0. The "cost" of the operation was not calculated separately here; it was "figured in" when the utilities were assigned to various states of the world. Following the rule of maximizing expected utility, if I were the patient, I would choose the operation.

The discussion about candidates for the best rule to follow when making decisions under risk shows that different rules can lead to the same decision in some cases. By far the most probable state of affairs after the operation was also the state with the greatest utility. But the rule "Choose the action that maximizes expected utility" is adequate when other proposed rules appear to offer unreasonable advice. This happens frequently when a state with a low probability has a very high utility, or when a state with a high probability has a very low utility. That is why the rule for maximizing expected utility is generally accepted as a good rule for rational decision making when the probabilities of the various states are known. This rule is applicable when other rules would lead to decisions that seem unreasonable.

2. Decisions Under Certainty

In some situations, we must choose among various actions when each action is associated with only one state of affairs. These decisions are called decisions under certainty, but this is something of a misnomer, because the future is never absolutely certain. The world around us might change in an unpredictable way between the time of the decision and the completion of the action. For example, you are deciding between studying for a test in your room and studying for a test in the library. Ordinarily, only one state is relevant to each choice in a decision under certainty—you study in your room if that is your decision, or you study in the library if that is your choice. It is, however, possible though unlikely that after you decide to study in the library, it closes because of an unexpected electrical power failure. In general, when we talk about decisions under certainty, we simply ignore such unusual possibilities.

Decisions under certainty do not require the calculation of any probabilities. The probability associated with the single state of affairs relevant to the action is always so close to 1 that it may be treated as 1. The rule to apply when making decisions under certainty is simple: "Choose an action with the highest utility." If no single action has the highest utility, it is reasonable to choose any of the actions that have the highest utility.

Even though calculating probabilities for decisions under certainty poses no problems, comparing utilities can be difficult. For example, some products (such as automobile tires and batteries) are sold at different prices that depend on the the length of the guarantee period. If I buy tires with a two-year guarantee at a specified price, I can calculate the cost per year and compare it to the cost per year of tires with a three-year guarantee. But other factors may enter into the decision. How long will I keep my car? How much trouble is it to replace worn tires? Are both sets of new tires equally safe throughout their guarantee period? Suppose the tires are identical; only the guarantee is different. Is it worthwhile to pay for the longer guarantee period as a kind of insurance against having to pay for new tires?

Comparing utilities almost always involves more than monetary considerations, and these additional factors should not be ignored just because they make the decision more difficult. In many cases (as in the tire-buying decision), the consideration of additional factors involves probabilities that can change a decision under certainty into a decision under risk. For example, it may be possible to assign a probability to your car lasting two years, and a different probability to its lasting three more years.

Utilities for decisions under certainty are more easily compared than for decisions under risk. To evaluate decisions under certainty, the utilities need only be ordered by rank (highest, second highest, and so on). Because the utilities are not multiplied by probabilities, units of utility are not required. In other words, in a decision under certainty, we do not need to ask whether the highest utility is ten times higher than the next highest utility, or six times higher, or exactly how much higher. Units of utility are required, however, to perform arithmetic operations involved in decision under risk, such as multiplication, for these operations make no sense otherwise.

3. Decisions Under Uncertainty

In decisions under uncertainty, as in decisions under risk, our knowledge is incomplete. In decisions under risk, however, we at least can make judgments about the probability of various states of the world. When we face decisions under conditions of uncertainty, we are aware that different states are relevant to our decisions, but we are unable to assess the probabilities of the various states. We cannot even say whether one relevant state is more likely, less likely, or equally as likely to occur as any other. Such situations may be unusual; in most cases, we have sufficient knowledge to make at least very rough assignments of probabilities on the basis of past experience or information gathered from other sources. If we can make even crude probability judgments, we should follow the rule for making decisions under risk (choose the action that maximizes expected utility). For the sake of completeness, however, and because of some interesting problems associated with decisions under uncertainty, most accounts of decision theory have something to say about these decisions. Because when we make decisions under uncertainty, (by definition) we have no information about probabilities, we base our choices entirely on our consideration of the utilities that are associated with various states of affairs. As in decisions under certainty, in most cases of decision under uncertainty, a rank ordering of utilities is sufficient. (One rule for decisions under uncertainty does require units of utility, but not all decisions require this rule.)

Sometimes decisions under uncertainty are simple, for any state of the world associated with one of the actions will be no worse than any state resulting from any other action. For a simple decision between two actions, each associated with two states, this situation can be represented thus:

States of the World, Ordered by Rank

(1 is highest)

Actions	I	II
I	4	3
II	2	1

In this table (or decision matrix), two possible states of affairs are associated with Action I. These are ranked lowest and second-lowest in utility. Action II also has two associated states, ranked highest and second-highest in utility. In this situation, Action I is said to be dominated by Action II. Assuming that our decision has no effect on the probabilities of the states of the world, it would be irrational to choose Action I because either state associated with Action II is better than either state associated with Action I.

In the following case of a decision under uncertainty, one action dominates. Mark, a football player is offered two nonathletic scholarships—one at State University and one at Out-of-State University. He is unable to assign probabilities to making the team at either university. He'd like to play ball, but he wants the best education possible, regardless of whether he plays ball, and he believes the academic program at State is better. His utilities are ranked (1) play ball at State, (2) be a nonplayer at State, (3) play ball at OSU, (4) be a nonplayer at OSU. Thus, he will be better off at State, regardless of whether he plays ball. Going to State is the rational decision for him.

States of the World, Ordered by Rank

(1 is highest)

Actions	Make the team	Do not make the team
Go to State	1	2
Go to OSU	3	4

Suppose, however, that Clark, another football player, assigns the highest priority to playing ball, and perceives State as the best place to play. If, however, he cannot play ball, he would prefer an easier academic program so he will be free to pursue other interests. Faced with the same scholarship offers as Mark, his ranking of utilities are (1) play ball at State, (2) play ball at OSU, (3) be a nonplayer at OSU, (4) be a nonplayer at State.

States of the World, Ordered by Rank

(1 is highest)

Actions	Play ball	Do not play ball
Go to State	1	4
Go to OSU	2	3

In this decision under uncertainty, neither action dominates. Going to State is associated with the most highly valued state, but also with that with the lowest value. Because no dominant action is available, the next question is whether only one satisfactory action is available—an action that is not associated with any unacceptable states of affairs. If the second player would be satisfied with a utility ranked three or higher but would not be satisfied with a utility ranked lower than 3, then choosing State would not be a satisfactory action for him to take. He should follow the rule: "Choose the action that is satisfactory," and go to OSU.

Suppose, however, that no utility is completely unacceptable to the football player. He could accept being a nonplayer at State, although for him that outcome has the lowest utility. The rule for choosing the satisfactory action does not apply if there is more than one satisfactory action. At this point, several strategies (rules for decision) are open to the player.

In cases in which no action dominates and no single "satisfactory action" exists, various other decision rules may be used. Which rule the football player follows will depend in part on the player's personality. Decision theorists categorize three different types:

1. The Gambler: In situations in which only one action is associated with the state of affairs with the highest utility, one decision strategy is to take that action. The gambler is willing to take a chance to get the best. If our player is a gambler, he'll go to State.

2. The Cautious Player: The cautious player determines the lowest, rather than the highest utility for each outcome. The choice is based on which action is associated with the highest of the low utilities. The cautious player wants to protect against losses, to "maximize the minimum." Using this strategy, our second football player will choose OSU, for the lowest utility associated with that action is 3, whereas the lowest utility associated with State is 4.

3. The Calculator: The calculator must assign units of utility in order to calculate the average utilities of the various actions. An average utility cannot be determined merely on the basis of a rank ordering. The strategy is to choose the action with the highest average utility.

If our football player is a calculator, he might assign the following units of utility: play at State (10); be a nonplayer at State (2); play at OSU (8); be a nonplayer at OSU (6). The average utility of an action is calculated by adding the utilities of each possible outcome for that action and dividing the total by the number of possible outcomes. The average utility of the decision to go to State is then $(10 + 2)/2 = 6$, and the average utility of the decision to go to OSU is $(8 + 6)/2 = 7$. Following the rule of choosing the action with the highest average utility, our player will go to OSU.

If we examine the calculator's decision-making rule, we can see that when average utilities are assigned, the decision under uncertainty is similar to a decision under risk in which each possible state of affairs is considered to be equally as probable as any other. This method would not be appropriate if available information indicated that one state, or condition, was much less or much more likely than another. In these situations, the problem should be treated as a decision under risk, and probabilities should be assigned in a suitable way. Even when no available information indicates that one state is more likely than another, the assumption that they can be treated as equally likely is dubious because in effect it transforms a lack of information into a statement that probabilities are equal. Nevertheless, the calculational strategy that allows this transformation is recognized by many decision theorists.

In thinking about the choices open to the football players, we can see the importance of assuming that one's decision should not affect the probabilities of relevant states of the world. Sometimes, this assumption is fair; our decisions have no effect on states of the world. My decision to schedule a picnic has no effect on whether it rains that day. The (perhaps unknown) probability of rain remains the same whatever I decide. For the football players' decision problem, the assumption may not hold. If Mark decides to go to State, and Clark learns this then Clark may go to OSU to avoid the competition. If Clark decides to do this, however, then Mark's chance of making the team at State is improved because Clark is no longer a competitor there, so the state of the world "Mark plays ball at State" has a higher probability as a result of Mark's decision to attend State. In such ways, decisions may affect probabilities of states and even result in canceling the dominance of an action.

4. The Prisoner's Dilemma

An interesting puzzle about decisions under uncertainty, entitled "The Prisoner's Dilemma," has been widely discussed by decision theorists. Here is one statement of the problem:

A man and a woman are arrested on suspicion of operating a ring of burglars. The police have sufficient evidence to make the arrests, but the District Attorney doubts that enough evidence is available to convict the pair. In an effort to obtain further evidence, the prisoners are prevented from consulting with one another, and the District Attorney makes each of them the following offer:

> Confess to the crime. If your partner does not confess, you will receive a light sentence of one year in prison, but your partner will receive the maximum sentence of five years.

Each prisoner wants to know what will happen if he or she does confess and the other partner also confesses. The District Attorney tells each prisoner that if both confess, each will receive a three-year-sentence. The District Attorney also reveals that if neither partner confesses, the case will collapse, but that sufficient evidence is available to convict both partners of a lesser crime, for which they will each receive the maximum sentence of two years.

In making such a bargain, the District Attorney is confident that both partners will confess, even though they would be better off if neither partner confessed. Can you see why this is so?

We have assumed that each partner is unable to assign a probability to whether or not the other partner will confess. Thus, each partner is faced with a decision under uncertainty. If units of (negative) utility are correlated with the length in years of the possible prison terms, each prisoner is faced with the following choice of actions and the utilities associated with the possible outcomes of those actions (utility rankings are shown in parentheses):

	Partner Confesses	Partner Does Not Confess
Confess	−3 (3)	−1 (1)
Do Not Confess	−5 (4)	−2 (2)

In this situation, no action dominates, for one outcome of confessing carries a lower utility than a possible outcome of not confessing, and vice versa. If a satisfactory action *does* exist, it is to confess, for the lowest utility attaches to a state of affairs associated with not confessing. If either partner follows the rule of choosing the satisfactory action, that partner will confess. However, if no satisfactory action is available, and either partner follows any other rule surveyed thus far for making decisions under uncertainty, the prisoner will also confess.

The gambler's strategy would be to take the action associated with the state with the highest utility (confess). The cautious strategy would be to maximize the minimum utility—in this case, also, to confess. (At worst, the prisoner would spend three years in prison, versus a possible five-year prison term for not confessing.) The calculator would determine that the average utility of confessing is

$$(-3 + -1)/2 = -2$$

whereas the average utility of not confessing is

$$(-5 + -2)/2 = -3.5$$

and would also confess.

The District Attorney believes that both partners will make a rational decision. Whatever reasonable rule they follow, both partners will confess.

The Prisoner's Dilemma raises interesting problems about decision rules. It is crucial to note that separating the partners, thereby preventing their communication and cooperation, affects their decisions. A condition of the problem as a decision under uncertainty prevents the partners from working out a solution between themselves that would benefit both. Even if they were able to communicate with one another, however, each partner would be faced with the problem of whether the other partner could be trusted. If each partner's decision about trusting the other partner is a decision under uncertainty, the dilemma arises again.

The Prisoner's Dilemma is an artificial problem, but decision problems that resemble the dilemma can arise in real life. Consider, for example, a group of prosperous manufacturers located along a river into which they dump manufacturing wastes. The river is in danger of becoming severely polluted as a result of their behavior, and if pollution levels rise significantly, the manufacturers will be charged stiff penalties. Each plant is also trying to decide whether to expand, a move that would add to pollution. The profits of each manufacturer would increase if its plant could expand without paying a penalty. If most of the manufacturers expand, however, the pollution levels will be high enough to result in penalties, which will reduce profits below present levels.

The Board of Directors of Plant X is considering expansion. The members of the board figure that if they expand but no other plant expands, the pollution levels will not rise noticeably and Plant X can count on a 10 percent increase in profit. If Plant X does not expand, but the other plants do, then Plant X not only will have to pay a share of the penalty but, unlike the other plants, will not accrue any additional revenue from an expanded facility to help offset this loss. In such a case the profits of Plant X would sink 10 percent below the present level, but the profits of the other plants would sink to only 5 percent below the present level. In the absence of any information about the other manufacturers' plans, the board members of Plant X are in a situation similar to "The Prisoner's Dilemma"; moreover, each manufacturer considering expansion is in the same state as Plant X.

	Others Expand	**Others Do Not Expand**
X Expands	P − 0.05 P	P + 0.10
X Does Not Expand	P − 0.10 P	P

Problems like this in the logic of decisions under uncertainty have challenged decision theorists to think carefully about such issues as free will, cooperation, individual utilities versus what is most valuable for a social group, and whether "rational choice" means the same thing in decisions under certainty and decisions under risk. (See B. Skyrms, *The Dynamics of Rational Deliberation*, especially Chapter 1, for a brief history and outline of a new proposal to resolve these issues.)

5. The Petersburg Paradox

Another famous problem in the history of probability and expected utilities, the Petersburg Paradox, raises questions about decision rules and about equating units of value with units of money. The problem arises in the context of a game of chance with clearly defined probabilities and payoffs. It was formulated in the seventeenth century by the Swiss mathematician Daniel Bernoulli. Bernoulli, one of the famous scholarly guests of Catherine the Great at her court at St. Petersburg, also offered a solution to the problem.

The game can be played this way. Begin by tossing a fair coin and continue to toss the coin until a tail appears. As soon as a tail shows, the game is over. If the first toss is a tail, the game is over without any payoff. If one head shows before a tail appears, the payoff is $4. If two heads show, the payoff is $8. If three heads show, the payoff is $16, and the payoff doubles for each successive head that occurs before a tail appears.

The paradoxical aspect of the game arises when we attempt to determine a fair price to charge for a play of the game. Normally, in games of chance, a price is considered fair if it is equal to, or reasonably close to, the expected value of a play of the game. If units of value are equated with dollars, the expected value of a play can be calculated in the usual way—by multiplying the probability of each relevant state of affairs by the associated payoff for that state and summing the results. The mutually exclusive states relevant to a play of the Petersburg game are "game ends after one toss," "game ends after two tosses," and so forth, for an indefinite number (n) of tosses. The probability that a game will end after one toss (that a tail will appear on the first toss) is 1/2, and the associated payoff is $0; the probability that a game will end after two tosses (H, T) is 1/4, and the payoff is $4; the probability that a game will end after three tosses (H, H, T) is 1/8, and the payoff is $8; and so on. In other words, the expected value in dollars is

$$(1/2 \times 0) + (1/4 \times 4) + (1/8 \times 8) + (1/16 \times 16) + \ldots + (1/n \times n) + \ldots$$

Each of the terms after the first term in this series is equal to 1, and because no mathematical limit restricts the number of tosses, the mathematical sum of the series is an infinite number of dollars! It would seem that the game is worth playing no matter how much a play costs, for any finite cost would be less than the infinite expected utility of the game.

An endless coin-tossing game is unrealistic, but the situation is hardly less puzzling if some reasonably large limit is placed on the length of a game. For example, let us say that the maximum number of tosses in a play is 1,001 tosses. The expected value of that game is $1,000; however, only the most reckless gambler would pay $1,000 to play such a game.

Many different solutions to the Petersburg Paradox have been proposed. You may be able to think of a few yourself. Bernoulli's solution is particularly interesting because in it he introduced a significant concept in economic theory—the diminishing marginal utility of money.

Bernoulli distinguished the "physical" value of money from its "moral" (or "practical") value to explain why the addition of a certain fixed amount of money to a large fortune has less value (except to a miser) than the addition of the same amount of money to a small fortune. The principle of the diminishing marginal utility of money can be stated:

> If a certain gain is added to an initial fortune f_0, the utility of this gain decreases as f_0 increases.

According to this principle, a person whose initial fortune is $100 will place a greater value on an additional $100 than a person whose initial fortune is $100,000. The "physical" value of the $100 is the same in both cases, but the "moral" value is much greater in the first case than in the second. In deciding what price to pay for a play of the Petersburg game, a reasonable person who is aware of the decreasing marginal utility of money will consider the moral value, as well as the physical value, of the expected winnings, and will also consider the moral value of the money that must be risked to play the game. In terms of moral value, the loss of even a small amount of one's stake could be hard on a poor person; the win of a large amount might not mean much to a rich one. (See John Maynard Keynes, "The Application of Probability to Conduct," in J. R. Newman's *The World of Mathematics,* for further discussion of solutions to the Petersburg Paradox.)

6. The Law of Averages and the Gamblers' Fallacy

If a fair coin is tossed repeatedly, then "on average" roughly half the tosses will result in heads, and as the series of tosses grows longer (that is, the sample grows larger), the proportion of heads continues to hover around one half. Suppose you toss a coin and get a head on the first toss and tails on the next eight tosses. Should you use the law of averages to argue that the next toss will be a head? Many people not only argue this way but bet money accordingly.

Another tail in the series would be the ninth in a row. A series of nine tails in nine tosses has a very low probability [$(1/2)^9 = 1/512$]. Nevertheless, such series do occur (about once in 500 times). If the coin is fair, the probability that the next toss will be a head is 0.50, the same as for any other toss. What happens on earlier tosses has no effect on the next toss, because the events are independent. The law of averages tells us that if the series of tosses is long enough, the eight tails in a row will eventually become insignificant. After a thousand tosses, for example, a slight excess might prevail in the proportion of tails to heads, but the proportion will be roughly half and half. The law of averages does not have anything to say about what happens in the tosses that immediately follow the improbable series of eight tails. To suppose otherwise is to commit the gamblers' fallacy.

The preceding account of how to understand the law of averages assumes that the coin is fair and that the tosses are independent. Suppose those assumptions are false. Then would it be reasonable to assign a high probability to the next toss being a head? If the coin is weighted (unfair) but the tosses are independent, then the evidence that eight tails have appeared in succession makes the probability that the next toss will be a head less than 0.50. The evidence suggests that the coin is weighted for tails. If the coin is cleverly designed so that a hidden magnet controls which side lands up, and is programmed so that after a certain number of tails, a head appears, then not only is the coin unfair, but also the tosses are not independent. Without information about how this magnet is adjusted, though, it is not reasonable to assign a probability of greater than 0.50 to heads on the next toss.

Another instance of the gamblers' fallacy occurs when statistical records are misused in the following way. Suppose your favorite baseball player has ended his past four seasons with batting averages that range from 0.330 to 0.340. This means that he gets hits "on average" about one of three times at bat. It is now about the middle of the season; his average so far this year is 0.330; but he's in a slump and hasn't had a hit in his past fifteen times at bat. Unlike the coin tosses, hits are not independent events. Psychological factors such as a burst of confidence after several hits or physiological factors such as an injury that becomes progressively more painful each time the batter takes the box can affect the probability of the next hit. If we are going to use past performance as our guide to the future, then we take account not only of the published statistics, but also the hot streak or the slump. We commit the gamblers' fallacy if we think that the batter has somehow used up his allotted number of failures, and will have proportionately more (or fewer) hits from now on to keep his average intact.

IV. REVIEW

In Chapter 6, we have considered applications of the mathematical calculus of probability to inductive logic. The term *probability* has been used to refer to the ratio of favorable to possible outcomes of some action or event, to the relative frequency with which events of a certain type occur in some series of events, and to the degree to which it is rational to believe certain statements. Whatever interpretation of *probability* is adopted, however, probabilities should behave in accord with the mathematical rules of probability. These rules allow us to calculate unknown probabilities when some probabilities are known.

Probabilities play an important role in everyday decision making. Decision theory offers an analysis of decisions and criteria for making rational decisions. Several rules or strategies for making decisions in the face of less than complete knowledge were proposed. The rule "Choose an action that maximizes expected utility" seems the most acceptable rule for choosing among actions when the probabilities of the states relevant to these actions are known. The rule for decisions under certainty, "Choose an action that maximizes utility," is reasonable when faced with several actions, each of which is associated with a single known state of affairs. In deciding among actions that are associated with more than one state when the probabilities of the states are unknown, the rule "Choose a dominant action" should be followed if one is available. If no action dominates, but one satisfactory action is available, it should be chosen. If neither of these rules applies, reasonable decisions can be made using either the gambler's strategy, the cautious strategy, or the calculating strategy.

Decision theory offers criteria for making reasonable decisions, depending on the type of information available, but it cannot provide the information required for making sound decisions. Many decisions would be inappropriate and even dangerous in the absence of accurate information. The following letter from the president of the Travelers Aid Association, published in Ann Landers's newspaper column, makes the point:

> Since January, vast numbers of job-seekers have gone to the Deep South in search of employment. Recently, it came to our attention that many of these people are victims of a heartless scam. Ads in newspapers and flyers are offering thousands of fabulous jobs in the offshore oil industry. Information for these jobs costs $10 to $12. For this, the advertiser sends a list of offshore oil companies in Texas and Louisiana.

Travelers Aid Societies in Houston, New Orleans and elsewhere are seeing an enormous increase in clients who have spent the last of their money on a bus ticket, only to be bitterly disappointed after weeks of fruitless searching for a job.

The unemployed persons who were desperate enough to risk their last savings on the search for a job thought they were making a reasonable decision, for it appeared, on the basis of deceptive advertising, that the probabilities of finding work were high. In terms of following the rule of maximizing expected utilities, they did not act unreasonably. However, when the stakes are so high (as they were in this case), it is imprudent—and a violation of the principles of critical thinking—to make judgments about the probabilities of various outcomes on the basis of such poor sources of information. Newspaper advertisements, paid for by profit-seeking organizations, cannot be considered authoritative sources of information. When available evidence allows us to frame strong inductive generalizations, statistical syllogisms (including legitimate appeals to authority) or arguments from analogy, probability judgments may be accurate and useful. Without reliable probabilities, high-utility decisions can be perilous.

A list of some important terms introduced in Chapter 6 follows:

Conjunction: A compound sentence that is true just in case all its major components (conjuncts) are true. *And* is commonly used to conjoin the elements of conjunctions. Other words in English, such as *moreover, in addition to,* and *but* are also used to form conjunctions. These words differ in rhetorical force from *and* (for example, *but* suggests a contrast between the elements it conjoins), nevertheless (another conjunction!), they all have the logical force of conjoining elements in such a way that the truth of the whole depends on each element's being true. (See Chapter 9 for more on conjunction.)

Decision Under Certainty: A decision in which a single known state of the world is associated with each action.

Decision Under Risk: A decision in which the probabilities of the various states associated with the actions are known.

Decision Under Uncertainty: A decision in which the probabilities of the various states associated with the actions are not known.

Disjunction: A compound sentence that is true if any of its major component sentences (disjuncts) is true, but is false if all disjuncts are false. *Or* is commonly used to join sentences to form a disjunction.

Dominating Action: In a decision, if no state associated with an action has a utility lower than those associated with any other action in the set, then that action dominates.

Expected Utility: The utility of some event is its value or desirability, which may be positive or negative. To make decisions that require calculations involving probabilities and utilities, we need to assign units of utility to relevant states associated with actions. The expected utility of an action is calculated by multiplying the probability of each state associated with the action by the utility associated with that state, and summing the results.

Gamblers' Fallacy: This fallacy occurs when one appeals to "the law of averages" to infer that an unusual series of events will be reversed in the short run. For example, if a series of five coin tosses have all been heads, the "law of averages" cannot be used to infer that the next toss will be a tail. If the coin is fair, the tosses are independent, and the probability of a tail is 1/2. If the coin is not fair, the tosses are still independent, but the series of five may support the claim that the coin is weighted to land heads.

Independent Events: Events are independent of one another when the occurrence of one event does not affect the probability of the occurrence of the other event. Tosses of a fair coin are independent of one another; draws from a deck of cards without replacement and reshuffling are not independent of one another.

Mutually Exclusive Events: Events are mutually exclusive if the occurrence of one precludes the possibility of the occurrence of the other. On a single roll of a pair of fair dice, rolling a total of six points and rolling a total of five points are mutually exclusive events. Sentences are mutually exclusive when the truth of one rules out the truth of the other. If the sentences that form a disjunction are mutually exclusive, only one of them can be true.

Satisfactory Action: In a choice among several actions, if no action dominates, but an action is associated with no states with unacceptable levels of utility, that action is a satisfactory action.

Exercise Set 6.2

1. The state in which you live operates a lottery. The proceeds of the lottery are used to supplement the state's unemployment insurance fund. You can play the lottery for $1. To play, you choose a three-digit number from 000 to 999, inclusive, and receive an official ticket with that number printed on it. Each evening, a ball is drawn blindly from a container that holds 1,000 balls, each marked with a different three-digit number. If the number on your ticket is selected in the daily drawing on the date you play, you receive $500 for your ticket. Otherwise you receive nothing.

(1) What is the probability that a chosen number will win?

(2) What is the utility (in dollars) of a single play?

(3) Suppose that you decide to play three times in one day, and that you choose the same number each time. (You hold three tickets at a cost of $3.) What is the expected utility (in dollars) of your triple play?

(4) Suppose that you decide to play three times in one day, and that you choose a different number each time. What is the expected utility (in dollars) of this triple play?

2. An investor has $1,000 to invest for a period of one year. She must decide whether to invest the money in a stock her broker recommends or in a money-market fund. If she invests in the fund, she will collect $1,200 (her original $1,000 + a profit of $200). If she invests in the stock and a merger occurs, she will realize $1,800 (her original $1,000 + a profit of $800). If she invests in the stock and no merger occurs, she will receive only $900 (a loss of $100). The probability of a merger is 0.40. Assume that units of utility can be correlated with dollars (no other utilities are involved in this decision).

(1) What is the probability that no merger will occur?

(2) What is the expected utility of investing in the money-market fund?

(3) What is the expected utility of investing in the stock?

(4) What decision rule should the investor use?

(5) What is the rational decision in this case?

3. You are in charge of organizing a dinner party that is held for the sole purpose of raising money for a worthy cause. You must decide whether to schedule an outdoor picnic or an indoor buffet supper. This event must be planned so far in advance that you have no way of assigning a probability of rain on the day of the party. On the basis of past events of this type, you have the following information:

> If it does not rain the outdoor picnic will yield a profit of $500, and the indoor buffet supper will yield a profit of $170.

> If it does rain, the outdoor picnic will yield a profit of $80, and the indoor buffet supper will yield a profit of $440.

(1) Is this a decision under risk, a decision under certainty, or a decision under uncertainty?

(2) Is it reasonable in this case to correlate units of utility with dollars gained for the worthy cause?

(3) What decision rule would you follow in this case?

(4) Apply the decision rule, and state what decision you would make. (Show your work.)

4. The same conditions stated in Exercise 3 exist, except that on the basis of weather records for the date of the party, you can reasonably assign a probability of 1/3 to rain on that date.

(1) What type of decision are you faced with now?

(2) What decision rule should you follow?

(3) On the basis of that rule, what is the decision? (Show your work.)

5. You are a restaurant manager who is responsible for planning the "daily specials." You are considering whether to introduce a new Thursday special. If the special is successful, the restaurant will show a profit of $250 for the night; if the special is not successful the restaurant will lose $50. If you serve the usual Thursday special, the restaurant will show a profit of $100. On the basis of past introductions, you assign a probability of 0.50 that the new dish will be a success. You've been doing a good job at the restaurant, so you are not afraid that you'll be fired if you make the wrong decision this time. However, you share in the profits, so the decision does affect your pay.

(1) What decision rule would you use in this situation?

(2) What would your decision be? (Show your work.)

6. You can enter one of two contests at no cost, but cannot enter both. In the

first, the prize is $5,000, and the probability of winning, if you enter, is 0.001. In the second, the prize is $100, but the chance of winning is 0.10. What decision would you make? Explain your reasoning and tell which rule you follow.

7. As an enthusiastic opera fan, you are considering a purchase of a season ticket. If you buy a $100 season ticket, you can see five operas for the price of four single tickets ($25). Your work schedule is erratic, however, and you figure that the probability that you can attend only three is 1/3, that you can attend only four is 1/3, and that you can attend all five is 1/3. Should you buy a season ticket? In your answer, describe the relevant states of the world, and the probability and utilities (in dollar cost of tickets) associated with each.

8. A famous problem in decision theory, called "Pascal's Wager," was formulated by the French mathematician and philosopher Blaise Pascal in the seventeenth century. Pascal, who was a devout Christian, offered several formulations of the problem. Here is one way of looking at "Pascal's Wager":

The two possible states of the world are: either God exists, or He does not. You are faced with two choices: Believe in God, or refuse to believe. If God does exist and you are a believer, you will be rewarded with infinite happiness in Heaven. If God does not exist and you believe He does, your life will be as usual, without any supernatural benefits or penalties. If, on the other hand, you refuse to believe and God exists, you can expect everlasting punishment in Hell. If you do not believe and God does not exist, your life will be the usual rewards of life with no Heaven or Hell to face.

(1) Is this version of "Pascal's Wager" a decision under certainty, uncertainty, or risk?

(2) If you accept this formulation, does any action dominate?

(3) Do you think that this way of presenting the problem is reasonable? To answer this, consider, for example, whether only two choices are available and two states are associated with each. Is "life as usual" the same for the believer and the nonbeliever? Does Pascal make any assumptions about what God is like? (See I. Hacking, *The Emergence of Probability,* for a fascinating discussion of various forms of Pascal's Wager.)

9. Flu shots can offer valuable protection against the flu, particularly in an epidemic year. The shots, however, are not entirely unproblematic. Some people experience an allergic reaction to flu shots—a kind of miniflu. This reaction is less severe than a real case of flu and lasts a much shorter time. Another problem is that in order to be effective, the flu shot must be administered before it is known whether an epidemic is on the way. Suppose that you are trying to decide whether to get a flu shot. Public health doctors assign a probability of 0.6 that this year will be an epidemic year in your city. You have never had flu in a nonepidemic year and believe the probability that you will get flu is 0 if no epidemic occurs. If an epidemic strikes your city and you are not vaccinated, your chances of getting the flu are 0.4, and you will be ill with the flu for nine days. If you are vaccinated, the probability is 0.1 that you will have a reaction and be ill for two days.

Flu vaccination is free at the student health clinic, and you do not particularly mind getting shots. Thus, it is reasonable to equate units of (negative) utility for this decision with days of illness.

(1) What is the probability that you will get the flu if you are not vaccinated?

(2) What is the expected utility of not being vaccinated?

(3) What is the expected utility of being vaccinated?

(4) If you follow the rule of maximizing expected utilities, will you get the flu shot or not?

10. Suppose that a person who needs $1,000 to stay in business (the business is the person's only means of support) is offered the choice between a $1,000 gift or a gamble on a prize of $100,000 if any number but a six is rolled on a single throw of a fair die (but nothing if the six shows). Also suppose that the person has no other way of obtaining the money needed to stay in business.

(1) Is it rational for the person to choose the gamble rather than the gift?

(2) Why or why not?

(3) What does this problem suggest about the practice of equating units of utility with units of money?

(4) What does this problem suggest to you about considering risks as well as possible gains when contemplating an action?

11. You need a jacket and are considering buying one you really like at an outlet store. The ticket price is $100 now (reduced from $200), but if the jacket is not sold in three days, the price will drop to $50. Suppose that the probability that the jacket will stay on the rack three more days is 0.50. If you do not get this jacket, you will be forced to buy one you like less at the nonsale price of $110. Construct a decision matrix for this problem, treating it as a decision under risk.

12. You have had some success selling your work at art fairs, and have a watercolor of sheep grazing in a field that many people have asked about. You want to have prints made to sell, and need to decide how many. The cost is $1,000 for 50 prints, and $1,500 for 100 prints. To simplify your decision problem, you consider only three mutually exclusive results of your attempt to sell the prints: On the basis of past experience, you assign a probability of 0.90 that you will sell 50 prints at $50 each, a probability of 0.07 that you will sell 60 prints at that price, and a probability of only 0.03 that you will sell 70 prints. (You think 70 is the total number of possible sales.)

Construct a decision matrix for this problem. On the basis of the information available would you have the larger number of prints made? On what rule do you base your decision?

Chapter Seven

DEDUCTIVE REASONING: CONDITIONAL ARGUMENTS

I. INTRODUCTION

This chapter examines conditional arguments, a common form of deductive reasoning. Arguments of this type, important in their own right, also play a central role in the overall *inductive* pattern of reasoning that is used to confirm and disconfirm hypotheses. The topic of confirmation is addressed in Chapter 8. The discussion of conditional arguments thus forms a necessary prelude to that chapter as well as to the final three chapters, which continue the discussion of deductive reasoning.

II. PROPERTIES OF DEDUCTIVE ARGUMENTS: VALIDITY AND THE IMPORTANCE OF LOGICAL FORM

The distinguishing feature of (correct) deductive arguments is their ability to preserve truth. That is to say, if the premises are all true, then the conclusion cannot be false. When an argument is truth-preserving it is said to be *valid.* Strictly speaking, because deductive arguments are characterized by this truth-preserving feature, all deductive arguments are valid. Terminology varies, however; some writers prefer to distinguish two types of deductive argument: those that are truth-preserving, or valid, and those that fail to preserve truth but which are put forth as valid by their proponents. The latter type, arguments that merely *purport* to be valid, these writers call *invalid deductive arguments;* whereas this text classifies as fallacies those arguments that purport to be valid but are not.

The term *valid* has other uses in ordinary English. People speak of valid beliefs, valid reasons, and valid claims. In various contexts *valid* applies to what cannot be objected to because it conforms to law, logic, or the facts. Thus, I might claim to have a valid case against my neighbor if a survey shows that her fence is built inside my property line. In this text, however, *valid* and *validity* are reserved for the truth-preserving feature of deductive arguments. Thus, inductive arguments are never valid, no matter how strongly their premisses support their conclusions.

Inductive arguments differ from deductive arguments in another important respect. The correctness of an inductive argument depends partly on its form, but also on other matters, such as background information and the inclusion of all relevant evidence. Earlier chapters discuss forms of several types of inductive arguments: analogy, inductive generalization, and statistical syllogism. As noted there, the **form** of an argument refers to logically important structural features that pertain to the argument regardless of its particular subject matter or content. Statistical syllogisms, for example, have two premises: one, a statistical generalization that relates an attribute class to a reference class, and the other, a sentence that says a given individual is a member of that reference class. The conclusion of a statistical syllogism places the individual mentioned in the premise in the attribute class. Symbolically, the form of statistical syllogisms can be represented as

X percent of F's are G's
~~a is an F~~
_____

a is a G

When an argument is an instance of this form *and* fulfills the other requirements, such as the selection of an appropriate reference class and the requirement of total evidence, we can say it is a strong inductive argument.

In deductive arguments, however, validity can be guaranteed on formal criteria alone. The famous example of a deductive argument:

All men are mortal.
Socrates is a man.
_____

Socrates is mortal.

exemplifies a general pattern or form of argument that can be represented

All F's are G's
a is an F
_____

a is a G

When we say that this pattern is a valid form of argument, we mean that any argument in which the first premiss says that all members of one class *(F)* are also members of a second class *(G)*, and the second premiss says a particular individual is a member of the first class validly yields the conclusion that the same individual is a member of the second class as well. It is impossible for an argument that exemplifies this pattern of reasoning (i.e., is an **instance** of this form) to have all true premisses and a false conclusion. Consider, for example, another argument in this form:

All horses are quadrupeds.
Shamu is a horse.
_____

Shamu is a quadruped.

Because Shamu is a whale, the second premiss of this argument is false. Obviously, the conclusion in this argument is false as well. Nevertheless, given the form of this argument, the conclusion could not be false if all its premisses were true.

Although *validity* refers to the truth-preserving character of deductive arguments, arguments can be valid even when their premisses or their conclusions are *not* true. Paradoxically, an argument can be truth-preserving even when it contains no truth to be preserved, that is, when all the premisses and the conclusion are false. To say that an argument is valid is to claim that in all possible circumstances in which the premisses are true, the conclusion is also. If an argument is an instance of a valid form, however, like the argument about

Shamu, it is valid, even though it may contain false premisses and a false conclusion. Examples (1) through (4) demonstrate this claim and serve to emphasize the difference between having true premisses and having the truth-preserving feature of deductive validity. In the presentation of arguments (1) through (4) below, nothing has been done to *prove* validity. At this point, as with the argument about Socrates, we are relying on intuitive ability to see that if the premisses of these arguments were true, then their conclusions would be true also. Later on, we show how to prove that these arguments are valid.

Example (1)

No mammals can fly.	(false premiss)
All dogs are mammals.	(true premiss)
No dogs can fly.	(true conclusion)

Example (2)

No mammals can fly.	(false premiss)
All bats are mammals.	(true premiss)
No bats can fly.	(false conclusion)

Example (3)

No mammals can fly.	(false premiss)
All birds are mammals.	(false premiss)
No birds can fly.	(false conclusion)

Example (4)

All birds can fly.	(false premiss)
All bats are birds.	(false premiss)
All bats can fly.	(true conclusion)

Valid arguments in which all of the premisses are true are called "sound arguments" (see Chapter 3). Soundness is obviously a desirable property of many arguments. If we present a deductive argument in order to persuade someone that the conclusion is *true*, the argument should not only be valid but also should have true premisses. As critical thinkers, however, we are also sometimes interested in the validity of arguments apart from the truth of their components. We may want to trace the consequences (the conclusions that follow deductively) of a variety of premisses, not all of which can be true. We might ask ourselves what would follow if *A* and *B* were true and, alternatively, what would follow if *A* were true and *B* were not true. Sometimes we want to identify the consequences of sentences but have no way of determining their truth or falsity at the time the argument is constructed. For example, suppose that you are considering whether to cut class on a Friday to drive to a friend's wedding. You might want to trace out the consequences for your final grade in the class if the teacher gives a quiz that day, and assigns an automatic F for unexcused absences, as well as the consequences for your friendship if you miss the wedding because of a possible quiz.

If we do not know whether some premisses are true, but we see that they lead deductively to some false conclusion, then we know that at least one of those premisses must be false. Suppose, for example, that before going on a vacation, you arrange to have a leaky roof repaired, and when you return you see no evidence that the work was done. You are annoyed that the roofer did not follow your instructions. On the first night home, however, very heavy rain falls, and the roof does not leak. You can then reason that your premiss was false; the repairs must have been made because otherwise the roof would certainly have leaked.

Deductive arguments (1), (2), and (3) above are all instances of the same form, which can be represented, using upper-case letters for class terms, as

No *F*'s are *G*'s
All *H*'s are *F*'s

No *H*'s are *G*'s

The dependence of validity on the *form* of arguments simplifies the evaluation of deductive arguments. When we evaluate inductive arguments, we must take into account all sorts of background information that could affect the strength of the argument. We need to be concerned, for example, with the size of samples, the lack of bias, the relevance of analogies, whether any evidence has been suppressed, and other matters. On the basis of all of these considerations—not only the form—we judge whether the premisses support the conclusion, and if so, how strongly.

In evaluating deductive arguments, we do not need to consider any background information beyond the information required to state implicit premisses. If an argument is an instance of a **valid argument form,** then that argument is valid. Moreover, validity is an all-or-nothing affair, unlike the degrees of strength in correct inductive arguments. An argument is either valid or not valid—validity does not exist in degrees.

With this reminder of the important general characteristics of deductive arguments we can turn to a closer look at conditional arguments. Following a discussion of the nature of conditional sentences, we introduce some common forms of valid conditional arguments and discuss some fallacies associated with conditional forms of argument.

III. CONDITIONAL SENTENCES

Conditional arguments are arguments that contain conditional sentences as premisses, as conclusions, or both. **Conditional sentences** have two main clauses, the **antecedent** and the **consequent.** The antecedent is frequently introduced by *if* and the consequent by *then.* Conditional sentences are used when we want to say that the truth of one clause depends on (is conditional on) the truth of the other.

Examples

1. If I study, then I will pass my math exam.
2. Maisie will recover from mono, provided that she takes care of herself.
3. John wouldn't have taken that position if he had not been forced.
4. You will break your leg climbing that way if you are not careful.

1. The Structure of Conditionals

Each of these conditional sentences (or, briefly, **conditionals**) is a *compound* sentence—a sentence that contains another sentence as one of its parts. A sentence that is not compound is a *simple* sentence. Conditionals are composed of (at least) two sentences—the antecedent that states the condition, and the consequent that depends on the stated condition. Antecedents and consequents can also be compound sentences. For example, the antecedent of "If I get enough rest and eat properly, I will soon recover from my illness" is a conjunction.

In example (1), the antecedent is "I study" and the consequent is "I will pass my math exam." In (2), the antecedent is "she takes care of herself" and the consequent is "Maisie will recover from mono." In (3), the antecedent is "he had not been forced" and the consequent is "John wouldn't have taken that position." In (4), the antecedent is "you are not careful" and the consequent is "you will break your leg climbing that way."

Even this small sample reveals some of the variety of ways in which conditionals are expressed in English. Different verb tenses (past, present, and future) and moods (indicative and subjunctive) are used. Various terms indicate the presence of a conditional: *if . . . then* and *provided that*. Sometimes the word that signals the presence of the conditional also functions in another way in the sentence. For example, a sentence equivalent to (4) is "You will break your leg climbing that way *unless* you are careful," where *unless* does the same work as *if not* in the original conditional. Sometimes, as in (1), the antecedent comes before the consequent; sometimes the antecedent follows the consequent, as in (2), (3), and (4). Subjunctive conditionals, such as (3), are most often used in English to express what would happen if something else were to occur (a possibility) or what would have occurred if something else had happened, when, in fact, it did not. These latter subjunctive conditionals are called **counterfactual conditionals.** They are used to talk about events that might once have been possible, but which never happened. For example, one can speculate about what the outcome of World War II would have been if the Allied invasion of Normandy had failed.

Conditional sentences are used to express the relationship that holds when the truth of one component depends on the truth of the other. If we distinguish honorary degrees from earned degrees, for example, we can say that being enrolled as a student is a *necessary* condition for receiving a degree from the university. In other words, if someone is not enrolled as a student, then he or she cannot earn a degree. Another way of expressing this same conditional is "A person can earn a degree from the university *only if* that person is enrolled as a student." Alternatively, we can say "A person cannot earn a degree from the university *unless* that person is enrolled as a student."

Conditional sentences are also used to express the relationship that holds between their components when the truth of one is *sufficient* for the truth of the other. As every student is aware, being enrolled as a student is not sufficient for earning a degree. Other matters, such as course credits, distribution requirements, grade-point average, and payment of fees and library fines are also necessary to earn a degree. The sufficient condition for earning a degree is so complex that several pages in the school's catalogue are devoted to it.

In other cases, it is not so difficult to state a sufficient condition. For example, being enrolled as a student is sufficient for being eligible to purchase basketball tickets at the student rate. Thus we can say that *if* someone is enrolled as a student, *then* that person is eligible to purchase basketball tickets at the student rate.

Because the validity of conditional arguments depends on form, and the form of the argument in turn depends to some extent on the forms of the sentences that are its premises and conclusion, we want to be able to represent the form of conditional sentences in a standard way. To do so, we ignore some differences in conditionals as well as some rhetorical features that characterize different ways of stating conditionals in English. Such refinements are suppressed for the sake of focusing on features of logical structure.

The relationship between antecedent and consequent clauses is the crucial logical relationship in conditional sentences, just as the relationship between classes is the crucial relationship in universal generalizations (see Chapter 4). Thus it is of primary importance to identify which sentence is antecedent and which is consequent. When conditionals are written in the standard way—"If (antecedent), then (consequent)"—their form is readily apparent. This practice makes it easier to recognize the structure of conditional arguments. Example (1) is in standard conditional form. We can rewrite examples (2), (3), and (4):

2. If Maisie takes care of herself, then she will recover from mono.
3. If he had not been forced, then John wouldn't have taken that position.
4. If you are not careful, then you will break your leg climbing that way.

English expressions in addition to those in the examples above are used to indicate conditionals. The following sentences contain some of them.

1. Whenever I see a kangaroo, I run. (If I see a kangaroo, then I run.)
2. I run only if I see a kangaroo. (If I do not see a kangaroo, then I do not run.)

Note that this is *not* the same as (1) but that it is the same as "If I run, then I see a kangaroo."

3. Given that I see a kangaroo, I run.

Note that this is the same as (1).

4. A sufficient condition of my running is my seeing a kangaroo.
   Same as (1).
5. A necessary condition of my running is my seeing a kangaroo.
   Same as (2).
6. I don't run unless I see a kangaroo.
   Same as (2).

Exercise Set 7.1

Rewrite each of the following sentences in standard conditional form: *If* (antecedent), *then* (consequent).

1. You can do well in math and logic classes only if you keep up with the assignments.
2. Unless you want a ticket, you won't park in the faculty parking lot next to the classroom building.
3. Whenever you want something very much you work hard to achieve it.
4. You will get the job provided that you complete your degree this term.
5. Without complications, life is uninteresting.
6. In case the teacher asks about her, Jane missed the test because she was ill.
7. You can pass this class if you really want to pass it.
8. Having a grade-point average of C or better is a necessary condition for a student's being graduated.
9. Passing one course in logic is a sufficient condition for a student's fulfilling the logic requirement.
10. Only if you care little for your safety will you ride a bicycle on Main Street during rush-hour traffic.

2. The Truth of Conditionals

In English, conditionals are used to express various kinds of conditional relationships between the antecedent and the consequent, including causal, logical, counterfactual, and material relationships. The conditional "If Maisie takes care of herself, then she will recover from mono," for example, expresses a *causal* connection between Maisie's caring for herself and her recovery. Subjunctive conditionals often express causal relationship: If Maisie were to take care of herself, she would recover more quickly. Conditionals can also express **logical,** or **definitional,** connections between sentences, as in "If two and two are added, then they equal four" and "If porpoises are aquatic, then they live in water."

The truth of a causal conditional depends on whether the situation described in the antecedent stands in the appropriate causal relationship to the situation described in the consequent. If Maisie's taking care of herself is causally irrelevant to her recovery from mono, (1) is not a true causal claim. Similarly, a conditional intended to express a logical or definitional relationship is not regarded as true unless that connection holds between the antecedent and the consequent.

Occasionally, we encounter conditional sentences in which the truth of the consequent does not really depend on the truth of the antecedent because the consequent is true regardless of whether the antecedent is true.

Examples

(1) If Jake continues to smoke, he will eventually die.

Jake will *eventually* die regardless of whether he continues to smoke—although "eventually" will probably be sooner if Jake smokes than if he doesn't smoke. Perhaps that is the intended interpretation of the sentence.

(2) If the forecaster predicts rain, then either it will rain or it won't.

In this conditional, the consequent must be true regardless of what the forecaster predicts.

A **material conditional** expresses another type of connection, neither causal nor logical, yet sharing with those types the feature that its truth depends on not having a false consequent with a true antecedent. An example of a material conditional is "If humans live on Jupiter, then my great-grandmother was an astronaut." Although no natural link connects the antecedent and consequent in this conditional, its meaning is clear. The point of this sentence, and others like it in English, is to emphasize the falsity of the antecedent. It is a way of expressing, forcefully and humorously, that no humans live on Jupiter.

Although material conditionals are often intended humorously, we can learn from examining them something logically important about the role of conditionals in valid arguments. In a material conditional, the *if . . . then . . .* that connects the component sentences is called a material or **truth-functional** connective. This means that the truth of the conditional sentence is determined by (is a function of) the truth of its component sentences. The only circumstance under which a material conditional is false is when it has a true antecedent and a false consequent. That is why the compound sentence "If there's human life on Jupiter, then my great-grandmother was an astronaut" can be used to state the falsity of "there is human life on Jupiter." The consequent of the conditional ("my great-grandmother was an astronaut") is obviously false. Yet the sentence as a whole is taken as true. But if the antecedent were true, then the conditional would be false, for it would have a true antecedent and a false consequent. Thus, a material conditional of the form *If (antecedent) then (consequent)* can be said to be true unless the antecedent is true and the consequent is false.

The form of a sentence can be studied without regard to its content (what it is about, what it says, or means). In studying the form, we may be interested in the logical relationships between the subject and the predicate of the sentence or between the various sentences that make up a compound sentence. For example, when we express the form of generalizations such as "All *F*'s are *G*'s," what "*F*" and "*G*" represent is suppressed to focus on the logical relation of inclusion, that is, every member of *F* is also a member of *G*. Similarly, when we use lower-case letters to represent sentences in the conditional form—"If *p*, then *q*"—we can ignore the content of *p* and *q*, and focus on the truth functional relationship.

However, this approach to form will not tell us whether a conditional is a causal conditional, a logical conditional, or a material conditional. This difference is important for some purposes. From the perspective of grasping the logical relationship between validity and the form of arguments, however, it is useful in introductory studies to focus on the relationship that is expressed in a material conditional. More complicated systems of logic have been developed to treat causal conditionals, but they depend on the basic understanding of the conditional relationship developed here.

Moreover, causal conditional sentences and definitional conditional sentences resemble material conditionals in the sense that if their antecedents are true and their consequents are false, then they are false conditionals. (For example, the causal conditional "If the match were struck, then it would light," is shown to be false if the match is struck and the match does not light.) Causal conditionals, however, unlike material conditionals, cannot be judged true merely because they have true antecedents and true consequents. As noted before, the appropriate causal relationship must hold between antecedent and consequent. But to know this requires knowledge of the world as well as knowledge of the meanings of the component sentences. Similarly, for a definitional conditional to be true, the appropriate relationship must hold between the meaning of the antecedent and the meaning of the consequent. Counterfactual conditionals pose special problems because their antecedents are always false. If their antecedents were true, they would not be *counterfactuals.* Thus we cannot say that, like simple causal conditionals and material conditionals, they are false *if* their antecedents are true and their consequents are false. Such an interpretation would place us in the difficult position of saying that no counterfactual is false. In using counterfactuals, we want, for example, to be able to recognize the difference between "If the Allied invasion of Normandy had failed, then the outcome of World War II would have been different," and "If the Allied invasion of Normandy had failed, then the outcome of World War II would not have been different." The logic of counterfactual statements requires more apparatus than can be developed in an introduction to logic. We avoid the special problems raised by counterfactuals by excluding them from our discussion of conditional arguments. Like the more advanced logical systems that attempt to handle the complexities of causal conditionals and the arguments that employ causal conditionals, these topics are beyond the scope of a beginning text.

To study the validity of conditional arguments by examining their *forms,* logicians ignore such "extralogical" considerations as the meanings of the component sentences and look only at what happens when various combinations of truth and falsity are assigned to the component sentences. The truth-functional relationship between the antecedent and the consequent in material conditionals thus serves as a minimal model for other types of conditionals, capturing at least the notion that a conditional cannot be true when it has a true antecedent and a false consequent. We can learn interesting things about validity and the structure of arguments in a simplified system that focuses on material conditionals. This does not mean that all conditionals *really* are material conditionals or that other types of conditionals are unimportant to logicians. The logic of truth-functional connectives, such as the *if . . . then* in a material conditional, does, however, provide a relatively simple introduction to deductive reasoning.

In summary, we can state the general circumstances under which a conditional statement is regarded as true by considering only the truth or falsity of its component parts. The four possibilities are listed in the following table:

Antecedent	Consequent	Conditional Sentence
True	True	True
True	False	False
False	True	True
False	False	True

Exercise Set 7.2

I. In the following exercises, the letters "*p*" and "*q*" represent component sentences in conditionals. Suppose that "*p*" is a true sentence, and "*q*" is a false sentence. Rewrite each conditional in standard form, and state whether the conditional is true or false. (You may wish to refer to the preceding table.)

1. *p* if *q*.
2. *q* if *p*.
3. *q* if *q*.
4. If *p*, *q*.
5. *p* provided that *q*.
6. *q* whenever *p*.
7. *p* is necessary for *q*.
8. *q* is sufficient for *p*.
9. *p* unless *q*.
10. *p* only if *q*.

II. The difficulty of treating counterfactual conditionals as truth-functional compound sentences has been mentioned. Also, other types of compound sentences exist that are not truth-functional compounds (that is, the truth of the compound does not depend only on the truth of the component parts).

Examples:

(1) Jack believes that Sally won the marathon.
(2) Frank has admired Gloria since he was sixteen years old.

(3) Rita phoned Larry before she went to his apartment.

(4) Frank hopes that Gloria feels the same way about him.

1. Identify the component sentences in the compound sentences (1), (2), and (3), and (4).

2. Formulate at least three other compound sentences that are not truth functional compounds.

IV. CONDITIONAL ARGUMENTS

In this section, we examine two common forms of conditional arguments. Each of these forms has two premisses, one of which is a conditional sentence. In one of the forms, the second premiss affirms (is the same as) the antecedent; in the other form, the second premiss denies (is the negation of) the consequent. The character of the second premiss provides the name for each of these argument forms.

1. Affirming the Antecedent

The following argument is an example of **affirming the antecedent:**

If we drive nonstop to the coast, we will need two days to recover.
We are driving nonstop to the coast.

We will need two days to recover.

Like many argument forms, it also is known by a Latin name, *modus ponens,* which means (roughly) "the way of affirming." Using the lower-case letters "p" and "q" to represent the component sentences of the conditional, and those letters to represent the same sentences when they occur elsewhere in the argument, we can exhibit the form of the argument as follows:

If p then q
p

---

q

The argument when stated in English is readily seen as valid. If its premisses are true, it is easy to see that the conclusion must be true as well. However, with the understanding that there is only one circumstance in which a material conditional can be false, we are in a position to prove that any argument that has this structure (form) must be valid. We need to show only that under no circumstances are the sentences represented by "If p then q" and "p" both true while "q" is false.

If the second premiss (p) is true, then the antecedent of the conditional premiss is true. But a conditional with a true antecedent is true only if its consequent (q) is true as well. However, q is not only the consequent of the conditional, it is also the conclusion of the argument. So, if "If p then *q*" and "*p*" (the premisses) are true, then "*q*" (the conclusion) must be true as well.

In showing that this argument form is valid, we did not take into account any meanings of the sentences that the letters "*p*" and "*q*" might represent. Thus, the validity of the form does not depend on the content of the sentences. All that is needed to demonstrate the validity of an argument form is to rule out the possibility that the premisses could all be true while the conclusion is false. Because one of the premisses is a conditional, and the other premiss "affirms the antecedent" (claims the antecedent is true), while the conclusion affirms the consequent of the same conditional, both premisses could not possibly be true while the conclusion is false.

By showing that this argument form is valid, we have also shown that any argument in English that "fits" this form, or is an instance of this form, is also valid. This means that any argument with two such premisses (one a conditional; the other, a sentence that affirms the antecedent) and a conclusion that is the consequent of the conditional is valid. Some examples of English-language arguments that are instances of affirming the antecedent follow.

Examples

1. Sally will go to the dance if Charlie will. But Charlie will certainly go, so Sally will be there.
2. Here comes Rover. Whenever Rover appears, Kitty-cat is not far behind. Therefore, Kitty-cat will be along soon.
3. With persistence, you'll be elected. So you will be elected, for persistence is your strong point.
4. A man cannot be robbed unless he can own, spend, claim, or want money. It is impossible for dead men to own, spend, claim, or want money. Therefore, dead men cannot be robbed.

   (This is a reconstruction of Gaffer's argument in *Our Mutual Friend* in Chapter 1.)

Exercise Set 7.3

Rewrite each of the four arguments above in standard form, listing the conditional premiss first.

2. Denying the Consequent

The second type of conditional argument, **denying the consequent,** is at least as common as affirming the antecedent, and is only slightly more complicated. The Latin name of this form is *modus tollens* ("the way of denying").

Example

If Japanese beetles are present in the garden, then leaves take on a lacy, skele- tonized appearance.
The leaves in the garden have not taken on a lacy, skeletonized appearance.

Japanese beetles are not present in the garden.

In this argument, as in affirming the antecedent, one premiss is a conditional. The other premiss denies the consequent, or says that the consequent of the conditional premiss is false. The conclusion of the argument says that the antecedent of the conditional is also false. Again, using the letters "p" and "q," we can represent the form of this argument in the following way:

If p then q

Not q
_____

Not p

As before, we appeal to the circumstances under which material conditionals are true or false to show that this argument form is valid. In addition, we must consider the logical force of *not*, which renders true sentences false, and vice versa. In English, this logical function of **negation** can be accomplished in a number of ways. Sentences can be negated by replacing the main verb of the sentence with the negation of that verb: "You can do this."—"You can't do this." A verb that means the same as the denial of the verb in the original sentence may be used: "They passed the test."—"They failed the test." The expression "it is not the case that" may precede the sentence to be negated: "You can do this."—"It is not the case that you can do this." Although "it is not the case that . . ." is an awkward phrase, it is favored by logicians because it can be placed at the beginning of any sentence to negate the original sentence without otherwise altering its structure. These features of negation are familiar to competent speakers of English, but here are a few more examples to remind us of the variety of ways in which negation can be accomplished:

1. Harry is happy. Harry is unhappy.
2. She will do it. She won't do it.
3. Jack loves Jill. It is false that Jack loves Jill.
4. Skeletonized leaves are present. Skeletonized leaves are absent.

As with conditionals, subtleties of English usage are ignored to concentrate on the logically important feature of negation. Negation is an operation that changes a true sentence into a false one, or changes a false sentence into a true one. This is the feature that is important to the validity of arguments. For this reason, just as conditionals are written in standard form, negations are also standardized: Write "not" in front of the letter that stands for the sentence that is negated ("Not p").

Now we are ready to consider the validity of the form of denying the consequent. One premiss of the argument says that the consequent of the conditional premiss is false. Thus, if the conditional premiss is true, it must have a false antecedent. But the conclusion of the argument simply states that the antecedent of the conditional premiss is false. So, if both premisses are true, the conclusion must be true as well.

Any English-language argument that fits the form of (is an instance of) *denying the consequent* is a valid argument, just as any that fits the form of *affirming the antecedent* is valid. Here are some examples of arguments in English that are instances of *denying the consequent.*

Examples

1. If you really wanted that car, you would get a job to pay for it. So you must not really want the car, since you won't get a job.

2. Stupid savages could not devise complex languages without God's help. The languages of these people are complex. Therefore, God helped to construct the languages.

Example (2) is a reconstruction of Dobrizhoffer's argument at the end of Chapter 1. To write the argument as a standard-form *denying the consequent,* requires double negation:

If God did not help to construct the languages of savages, then these languages could not be complex.
It is not the case that these languages are not complex.

It is not the case that God did not help to construct the languages of savages.

Exercise Set 7.4

Rewrite (1) above in standard form, showing it to be an instance of denying the consequent.

3. Unstated Premisses in Conditional Arguments

In written works and ordinary speech we find many incompletely stated conditional arguments of the forms *affirming the antecedent* and *denying the consequent.* Either the second (unconditional) premiss or the conclusion can be omitted. Occasionally, both the conclusion and the unconditional premiss are missing, and we must depend on the context to tell us that an argument, rather than merely the affirmation of a conditional sentence, is intended. This suppression of premisses and conclusions is acceptable in many situations because the forms of conditional argument are so well understood. For example, in the Bible, St. Paul is obviously arguing for the truth of Christ's resurrection from the dead when he says "If Christ has not risen, vain then is our preaching, vain too is your faith" (I. Cor. 15). Paul intends the argument to be interpreted in the form of denying the consequent.

Exercise: Supply the missing premiss for Paul's argument.

When premisses are not actually stated, the danger is that what is intended as a *modus tollens* may be interpreted as a *modus ponens.* For example, John Wesley (the founder of the Methodist Church), counting on his listeners' faith, is supposed to have said, "If you give up belief in witches, then you give up belief in the Bible."

Exercise: Complete Wesley's argument—first as a *modus ponens* (affirming the antecedent), and then as a *modus tollens* (denying the consequent). Which form do you think Wesley intended? With respect to Wesley's conditional, Bertrand Russell once said, "I agree." How did Russell interpret Wesley's argument? (Russell was not a Methodist!)

V. FALLACIES ASSOCIATED WITH CONDITIONAL ARGUMENTS

Arguments that are offered as deductive can fail to meet the truth-preserving standards for deductive validity. When these invalid arguments bear a superficial resemblance to valid arguments, they are called **deductive fallacies.** Whether a proponent of an argument intends it to be deductive may be difficult to determine but remains an important consideration. Inductive arguments, for example, are not meant to be deductive, and the standards for assessing their strength differ from the standards for evaluating deductive arguments. Although inductive arguments are not truth preserving, it would be inappropriate to regard all inductive arguments as fallacious.

1. Fallacious (Invalid) Forms of Arguments

Before addressing the question of fallacious arguments in English, we consider what it means to say that an argument form is "invalid." An argument form is **invalid** (not valid) if it is possible for an instance of that form to have all true premises and a false conclusion. Invalid argument forms that closely resemble valid argument forms are called **fallacious** forms of argument. The following form, which resembles affirming the antecedent, is an invalid form of argument:

If p then q

q
_____

p

To show that this form is invalid, we need to note only that if "q" were true and "p" were false, the conclusion would be false but both premises would be true. This is because a material conditional with a false antecedent is true whether its consequent is true or false. Not surprisingly, this fallacious form is called **affirming the consequent.** The following argument is an instance of this form:

If Cincinnati is the capital of Ohio, then Cincinnati is in Ohio.
Cincinnati is in Ohio.
_____

Cincinnati is the capital of Ohio.

The second fallacious form of argument, which superficially resembles denying the consequent, is called **denying the antecedent.**

If p then q
Not p
_____

Not q

The invalidity of this form is evident if we consider that the second premiss denies the antecedent of the conditional premiss (says it is false). But conditionals are true when their antecedents are false, regardless of whether they have false consequents (as the conclusion states) or true consequents. Because the truth of the premisses cannot guarantee the truth of the conclusion, the argument form is not valid. Again, we can supply an argument in English with true premisses and a false conclusion that is an instance of this form:

If bats are birds, then bats have wings.
Bats are not birds.

Bats do not have wings.

To show that an *argument form* is invalid, we need only to show that it is logically possible for an argument with all true premisses and a false conclusion be an instance of that form. As with *denying the antecedent,* we can do this abstractly by discussing the circumstances under which sentences of a certain form are true or false. Alternatively, we can exhibit an English-language argument that fits the form and obviously has true premisses and a false conclusion. This latter method is called "providing a counterexample."

2. Invalid and Fallacious Arguments

Incorrect arguments are normally called fallacious if they somehow resemble correct arguments. Arguments that resemble deductively correct arguments but are invalid are called deductive fallacies. Unless an argument has premisses that are all obviously true and an obviously false conclusion, it is more difficult to show that a given argument is invalid than it is to show that an argument form is invalid. An argument that is offered as deductive is invalid only if it is not an instance of any valid argument form. (No inductive argument, no matter how strong, is an instance of a valid form. In this discussion of fallacies, we consider only arguments that somehow resemble valid deductive arguments.)

The number of valid argument forms is infinite. Thus far, we have considered only two valid argument forms—affirming the antecedent and denying the consequent. We cannot prove an argument is fallacious merely by showing that it fails to fit either of these forms. For example, the classic example of a valid argument does not fit either form:

All men are mortal.
Socrates is a man.

Socrates is mortal.

One problem we encounter is that a single English-language argument can fit several different argument forms. Forms of argument reflect certain structural features of the components of the argument. Sometimes we are interested in structural (formal) relationships *among* various simple sentences in an argument, as when we analyze conditional arguments. In other arguments, such as the syllogism about Socrates, validity depends on structural relationships *within* the simple sentences that make up the argument, such as the relationships between the subject and the predicate in a sentence. If the validity of a given argument depends on *intra*-sentence structures, we will not prove that it is valid by representing its form in terms of *inter*-sentence structure.

If an English-language argument has obviously true premises and an obviously false conclusion, we know that it is invalid, for it could not be an instance of any valid form. For this reason, we can be confident that the examples we presented of English-language arguments that were instances of *affirming the consequent* and *denying the antecedent* are fallacious. In addition, because deductive validity is a matter of form, when we are more familiar with the various types of argument structure and when we can be reasonably certain we have not overlooked any hidden structure by virtue of which some arguments could be valid, we may say that it is highly probable that these arguments are fallacious. For the time being, however, we are on safer ground when we speak of fallacious *argument forms.* When we are presented with an English-language argument that is an instance of one of the known fallacious forms, we should suspect it of being fallacious, and it is reasonable to challenge whoever is presenting the argument to prove that it is not.

VI. REVIEW

Because the most important material in Chapter 7 can be described in the new vocabulary that was introduced here, the chapter can be reviewed by listing those new terms and their meanings:

Compound Sentence: A sentence that contains another sentence as one of its parts.

Conditional Argument: An argument that contains at least one conditional sentence as a premiss. In this chapter, we studied two valid forms of conditional argument: *affirming the antecedent* (or *modus ponens*), and *denying the consequent* (or *modus tollens*):

Modus Ponens	*Modus Tollens*
If p then q	If p then q
p	Not q
———	———
q	Not p

We also studied two fallacies associated with conditional arguments:

Affirming the Consequent	Denying the Antecedent
If p then q	If p then q
q	Not p
———	———
p	Not q

Conditional Sentence (Conditional): A compound sentence consisting of an *antecedent* (the sentence that states the condition) and a *consequent* (the sentence that depends on the stated condition). The standard form of a conditional is: "If (antecedent) then (consequent)" or "If p then q."

Deductive Fallacy: An invalid argument that bears some resemblance to a correct deductive argument.

Invalid Argument (or, loosely speaking, **Invalid Deductive Argument**): An argument is invalid if it is meant to be truth preserving, but fails to meet the standards for deductive validity. An invalid argument is not an instance of any valid form of argument.

Invalid Argument Form: An argument form is invalid if it is possible for an argument in that form to have all true premises and a false conclusion. Invalid argument forms that resemble correct forms are called *fallacious* forms.

Material Conditional: A conditional sentence in which the connection between the antecedent and the consequent is truth functional, rather than some "real" causal, definitional, or logical connection. A material conditional is false only when its antecedent is true and its consequent is false.

Truth-Functional Connective: When components of a compound sentence are joined by truth-functional connectives, the truth or falsity of the compound sentence depends entirely on the truth or falsity of its component parts. "If . . . then," *when interpreted in the sense of a material conditional,* is a truth-functional connective. "Not" is also a truth-functional connective. If a sentence "p" is true, then "Not p" is false. If a sentence "p" is false, then "Not p" is true. In contrast, "if . . . then" in subjunctive counterfactual conditionals (for example, "If Nixon had not resigned, then he would have been impeached") is not a truth-functional connective. The truth of a counterfactual conditional is not a function of the truth of its component parts.

Valid Argument: An argument is valid if no circumstances exist under which it is possible for all of its premises to be true and its conclusion to be false. *Valid* is the term applied to correct deductive arguments, those that actually preserve truth rather than merely purport to preserve truth. Any instance of a valid argument form is a valid argument.

Valid Argument Form: An argument form is valid if it is impossible for an argument in that form to have all true premises and a false conclusion.

Exercise Set 7.5

Each of the following exercises contains a conditional argument. Treat all the conditionals as material conditionals. Assume that all the arguments purport to be deductive, and rewrite each argument (in English) so that its premises and conclusion are on separate lines. If the conditional premiss is not in standard form, rewrite it. Supply missing premises or conclusions, if necessary. When doing so, adopt a principle of "charity" and give the proponent of the argument the benefit of the doubt. Then tell whether the rewritten argument is in the form of *affirming the antecedent, denying the consequent, affirming the consequent, or denying the antecedent.*

1. If our school's team wins all its football games this season, then they'll be invited to play in a postseason bowl game. They will be invited to play in a bowl game. Thus, they will win every game this season.

2. State will play in a bowl game only if State has a winning season. State will not have a winning season, so State won't play in a bowl game.

3. Headlines in sports pages on two successive days:

IF STEELERS BEAT OILERS, THEY GO TO PLAYOFFS

STEELERS BEAT OILERS; GO TO PLAYOFFS

4. You can do well in math and logic classes only if you keep up with the assignments. You keep up with the assignments, so you do well in math and logic classes.

5. The picnic will be held on Thursday, provided that it doesn't rain. But according to the weather reports, there will be no rain on Thursday, so we'll have the picnic.

6. Without complications, life is uninteresting. But life is interesting, so there are complications.

7. If primitive peoples did not cross the Pacific Ocean, there would not be a strong resemblance between Polynesian artifacts and South American artifacts. But there is a strong resemblance between these artifacts, so primitive peoples did cross the Pacific Ocean.

8. Since there are holes in the carpet, there must be moths in the house; for if there are moths in the house, then they make holes in the carpet.

9. Coyotes howl only when there's a moon, but there's a moon tonight, so they'll be howling.

10. All forms of pantheism [which involves the belief that man is a part of God] must be rejected, because if man is actually a part of God, the evil in man is also in God. But there is no evil in God.

> —Bishop of Birmingham, quoted in B. Russell, *Religion and Science*

11. If 2 is not a prime number, then there is a positive integer smaller than 2 and greater than 1 which evenly divides 2. But there are no positive integers smaller than 2 and greater than 1. Therefore, 2 is a prime number.

12. If morals could be taught simply on the basis that they are necessary to society, there would be no social need for religion. But morality cannot be taught in that way.

> —Patrick Lord Devlin, *The Enforcement of Morals*

13. We would not be at the trouble to learn a language when we can have all that is written in it just as well in translation. But as we cannot have the beauties of poetry but in its original language, we learn it.

> —S. Johnson

14. The earth is spherical in shape. For the night sky looks different in the northern and southern parts of the earth, and this would be so if the earth were spherical in shape.

> —Aristotle, *Physics*

15. A judgment of acquittal by reason of insanity is appropriate only when a jury verdict of guilty would violate the law or the facts. We cannot say that this was the situation in Washington's case. Therefore, the district court did not err in its refusal to enter a judgment of acquittal by reason of insanity.

> —Bazelon, *Washington vs. United States*

16. All history shows that the progress of humanity is accomplished not otherwise than under the guidance of religion. But if the race cannot progress without the guidance of religion—and progress is always going on, and also in our own times—then there must be a religion of our times.

> —L. Tolstoy, *What Is Art*

17. One could argue that given raw materials of more-or-less equally ideal qualities for axemaking, a simple utilitarian model would predict a wide but more-or-less even pattern of dispersal of axes in all directions from the quarry source. However, such uniformity of dispersal of greenstone [for making axes] from Mt. Williams is emphatically what one does not find in southeastern Australia.

> —R. A. Gould, *Living Archaeology*

18. Because the financial burden of radioactive waste storage is simply taken on by the government [and not by the operators and customers of nuclear power plants], the tax-paying public is the victim of an inequitable practice. . . . If the public as a whole bears the cost of waste storage, but only a subset of society receives the benefits of atomic power, then the costs and benefits of nuclear generation of electricity are not borne equitably.

> —K. S. Shrader-Frechette, *Nuclear Power and Public Policy*

19. "What I said was," said Cantrip, "that if it wasn't the Major, then it was the Bruce chap. And it wasn't the Major, so it is the Bruce chap."

> —S. Caudwell, *Thus Was Adonis Murdered*

20. A postal regulation requires that sealed letters carry first-class postage. Suppose you are given the task of verifying that the regulation has been followed. Obviously, if you see a letter without first-class postage, you must turn it over to see whether it is sealed. Three other possibilities exist: (1) letters stamp-side up with first-class postage; (2) letters back side up that are sealed; (3) letters back side up that are unsealed. Which of the three types, if any, do you have to turn over to see whether the regulation has been followed? Describe the form of reasoning that you use to answer the question.

Chapter Eight

CONFIRMATION
OF HYPOTHESES

I. HYPOTHESES

The first time I baked muffins, they tasted fine but looked funny. They were cracked, crooked, wobbly, and peaked. When I told an experienced cook about my muffins, she said they had been baked in an oven that was too hot. This surprised me, for I had followed cookbook directions carefully, but I decided to test her claim. If she is right, I thought, and if I make the muffins the same way but bake them at a lower temperature, they should turn out all right. I baked another batch, lowering the oven temperature 50 degrees. This time the muffins looked the way they were supposed to, and I believed the cook had been correct in saying that my first muffins had been baked in an oven that was too hot.

This experience illustrates the type of reasoning to be examined in Chapter 8. To check whether the cook's claim that the oven was too hot is true, we "test" the claim, by making a prediction based on the claim and seeing what happens. Claims that are tested in this way are called "hypotheses." Webster defines **hypothesis** as "a supposition used as a basis from which to draw conclusions." *Hypothesis* has other uses in ordinary language. Sometimes, it means a guess or suspicion that something is the case: "Our hypothesis is that it will rain on graduation day." Other times, "hypothesis" is used to refer to a belief that is not well established: "The existence of life on any other planet in our solar system is only a hypothesis." In this chapter, the term *hypothesis* refers to any sentence that we want to test by checking the truth of predictions that follow from it. Scientists test hypotheses by performing experiments or making observations to check the truth of predictions. The results of such tests, however, usually do not *conclusively* establish hypotheses. Results that inductively support hypotheses are said to **confirm** them; predictions that turn out to be false inductively **disconfirm** hypotheses. In this chapter we examine the logic of confirmation, which is an important part of inductive logic.

Hypotheses can be formulated about any subject matter. Many hypotheses are causal claims. (In Chapter 5, Mill's Methods were used to test causal claims. These methods are closely related to the form of reasoning discussed in this chapter.) Some hypotheses are universal generalizations: "All human languages have terms for kinship relations." Others are statistical generalizations: "49 percent of all Americans approve of the way the President is handling foreign affairs." Hypotheses that are not generalizations can also be tested: "A mouse is in the kitchen."

Conditional arguments, introduced in Chapter 7, play an important part in arguments to confirm or disconfirm hypotheses, for a conditional sentence expresses the relationship between the hypothesis and the prediction that follows from it, and a nonconditional sentence affirms or denies the truth of the prediction. As we will see, however, arguments of confirmation are not conditional deductive arguments, for they combine aspects of deductive and inductive reasoning.

II. THE HYPOTHETICO-DEDUCTIVE METHOD

Texts for science classes in high school and college typically present the following oversimplified version of the **hypothetico-deductive method** of testing scientific claims:

> To see whether a hypothesis is true, derive some prediction from it. If the prediction is true, then the hypothesis is confirmed. If the prediction is false, then the hypothesis is disconfirmed.

In this chapter we develop an account of hypothesis testing that more nearly reflects scientific practice.

The form of reasoning we want to examine can be illustrated with a famous example—Galileo's use of the telescope to check a prediction based on the *heliocentric* hypothesis that the earth and other planets revolve around the sun.

The prevailing sixteenth-century *geocentric* hypothesis had been proposed 1,400 years earlier by Ptolemy, a Greek astronomer. The Ptolemaic system regarded the earth as fixed, with the other planets and the sun revolving around it. Using such a model and making careful observations, Ptolemaic astronomers calculated and accurately predicted the positions of stars and planets. In other words, the geocentric hypothesis had resulted in many true predictions, and thus, seemed well confirmed.

In 1543, Copernicus, a Polish astronomer, proposed a new *heliocentric* system in which the earth and other planets revolve around the sun. Copernicus did not base his system on any new observations, nor did he make predictions that were different from those of the Ptolemaic system. The Copernican system did simplify the process of calculating orbits because with the sun at the center, planetary orbits are more regular and nearly circular. About 50 years after Copernicus's book was published, a Danish astronomer, Tycho Brahe, introduced still another planetary system in which the earth was motionless, the sun orbited the earth, and the other planets orbited the sun. The geocentric Tychonic system had the same mathematical advantages as the Copernican system—it offered simpler orbits with easier calculations than the Ptolemaic system—and it was in accord with all observational evidence. Moreover, in a time when scripture was considered by many scholars to be relevant to such matters, the Tychonic system agreed with biblical remarks about the earth's not moving, found in such passages as Psalm 104: "O Lord my God . . . who laid the foundations of the earth, that it should not be removed for ever." (See O. Gingerich, "The Galileo Affair," *Scientific American*, 247:2, 133.)

All three of these planetary systems were proposed before 1609, the year the telescope was invented. Galileo did not invent the telescope, but he built one that same year and was the first to use the instrument for astronomical observations. Soon after Galileo built his telescope, a student suggested that if

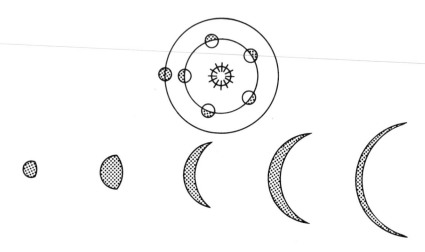

FIGURE 8-1
Phases of Venus

In the Copernican system, Venus can appear nearly full as it passes behind the sun, and its size varies greatly. *Source:* Richard S. Westfall, *The Construction of Modern Science: Mechanisms and Mechanics* (Cambridge, UK: Cambridge University Press, 1971). Used by permission of the publisher.

the Copernican system was correct, then Venus, as it moves in its orbit between earth and sun, should show a range of phases similar to the phases of the moon—from almost dark to crescent to nearly full. Galileo turned his telescope on Venus, and, over a period of several months, he was able to observe the phases. (You can observe this yourself with a good pair of binoculars.) Galileo interpreted these data as evidence that the Copernican (heliocentric) system was correct—that the apparently immobile earth actually revolved around the sun.

As a first approach to understanding the hypothetico-deductive method, we can reconstruct Galileo's reasoning in the form of a conditional argument. His hypothesis is "The Copernican system is correct." On the basis of this hypothesis, Galileo (with the help of his student) deduced a prediction that could be checked by observation and would be true if the hypothesis were true. The prediction in this case is "Venus will show phases." The conditional argument can be stated:

If the Copernican system is correct, then Venus will show phases.
Venus shows phases.

The Copernican system is correct.

Galileo's argument for his hypothesis, thus formulated, fits one of the patterns of conditional arguments discussed in Chapter 7. This way of reasoning to the truth of a hypothesis can be stated generally:

If the hypothesis is true, then the prediction is true.
The prediction is true.

The hypothesis is true.

As we have formulated it, this argument is an instance of *affirming the consequent:*

If p, then q
q

---

p

Affirming the consequent is, however, a fallacious argument form. An argument that is intended to be deductive and is in this form is suspected of being fallacious unless the argument is also an instance of some valid form of argument.

Remember, though, that arguments offered in support of hypotheses are intended to be inductive arguments, not deductive arguments. The truth of their premises only makes it probable that their conclusions are true. *Confirmation* refers to positive inductive support rather than to a guarantee of truth. At the same time, it would not be satisfactory to regard fallacious deductive forms of argument as satisfactory inductive forms. Fortunately, the form of reasoning used by scientists to confirm hypotheses is more complicated than *affirming the consequent* and depends on premises not represented in that invalid form.

III. COMPLEXITIES IN THE HYPOTHETICO-DEDUCTIVE METHOD

The *deductive* part of the hypothetico-deductive method refers not to the overall structure of the arguments, but rather to the *connection* between the hypothesis and an observable prediction that is deduced from it. To say the connection between the hypothesis and the observable prediction is deductive means that if the antecedent (hypothesis) is true, then the consequent (prediction) cannot be false. The conditional sentence that states this relationship is but one premiss in a confirmation argument.

1. Auxiliary Hypotheses

Galileo's test of the heliocentric hypothesis requires additional premisses to connect the hypothesis deductively with the observable prediction. These premisses, typically unstated but assumed to be true, are called auxiliary hypotheses. These premisses are usually not stated because they form part of a generally accepted theoretical background or standard conditions of the observation or experiment. Although they are assumed to be true in the context of testing the hypothesis for which they are auxiliaries, they can themselves be tested in other contexts. One of Galileo's assumptions (auxiliary hypotheses) was "Venus lies between the earth and the sun." Because this assumption was a part of the standard view of astronomy at that time (and still is), it was not in question. Another auxiliary hypothesis was "The telescope is a reliable instrument for observing celestial bodies." If both auxiliary hypotheses were stated rather than assumed, the conditional premiss in Galileo's argument would be:

> If the Copernican system is correct, and if the telescope is a reliable instrument of observation, and if Venus lies between the earth and the sun, then Venus will show a complete set of phases.

Of the two main types of auxiliary hypotheses, one has to do with **proper testing conditions.** In general, these auxiliary hypotheses are concerned with whether all of the equipment (such as the telescope) and materials used in a test are in proper working order and whether the observers are capable of correctly assessing the outcome of a test.

The second type of auxiliary hypothesis refers to **theoretical background knowledge.** Hypothesis testing is carried out against a background of presumed knowledge, such as the knowledge that Venus is between the earth and sun. Tests of hypotheses concerning the curative powers of drugs assume that certain theories of human physiology and microbiology are true. The physical theory of optics plays a background role in any tests that use microscopes or telescopes. When theoretical knowledge is not itself being tested but its truth is assumed in a test of some other hypothesis, that theoretical knowledge functions as an auxiliary hypothesis.

When we recall that Galileo was the first to use a telescope to record observations of the heavens, we can see how vulnerable hypotheses about the reliability of telescopes were at that time. In the tremendous controversy that followed Galileo's discovery (he was censored, then silenced, and finally tried by the Inquisition and placed under house arrest by the Catholic Church), he suggested that his critics look through the telecope to observe what he had seen. With his instrument he had observed not only the phases of Venus, but also the moons of Jupiter and the mountains on our own moon. Many critics refused to look, on the grounds that what was seen through a telescope did not count as *observation* because telescopes could not be relied on to show what was really there.

In Galileo's time, the questions raised about his telescope were chiefly theoretical. That is to say, the optical principles used to construct telescopes were considered dubious. Curved lenses and mirrors were used in those times, as they are now, for *distorting* images, as, for example, in "fun houses" in amusement parks. Intelligent critics thought it implausible that putting together two curved lenses—each of which would distort the appearance of objects—could enable an observer to see far away objects more clearly.

When an entrenched belief is challenged by new test results or new observations, auxiliary hypotheses receive special attention. When things go as expected, and widely held beliefs are confirmed by tests, we don't take the trouble to ask what assumptions are involved. But those assumptions—auxiliary hypotheses—always are important in hypothesis testing.

Awareness of the role of auxiliary hypotheses in the logic of confirmation requires us to revise the simplified form of hypothetico-deductive reasoning. The form of the revised argument, in which H denotes the hypothesis that is being tested, $A_1, \ldots, A_n$ represent auxiliary hypotheses , and P stands for the observable prediction, is:

If H and $A_1, \ldots, A_n$, then P.
P is true.

H and $A_1, \ldots, A_n$ are true.

This form of argument is not deductively valid. It is an improvement over the first version of an argument for confirmation, however, because it includes the auxiliary hypotheses in the premises, and makes the role of these hypotheses in the argument explicit. Further revisions are required.

2. Alternative Hypotheses

The form of argument to support the truth of the preceding hypotheses fails to represent the full complexity of the logic of hypothesis testing, in part because it does not account for the importance of **alternative hypotheses.** Alternative hypotheses, as their name suggests, are alternatives to the hypothesis that is being tested. That is to say, they are distinct (nonequivalent) hypotheses that have the same observational predictions as the hypothesis that is being tested.

In Galileo's time, three competing models of the planetary system were proposed by leading astronomers. Whereas Ptolemy's system did not predict the phases of Venus, Tycho's system, which was a different *geocentric* system from Ptolemy's system, predicted *the same phases of Venus that Galileo observed.* Thus the Tychonic hypothesis is an alternative to the Copernican. Tycho's system agreed with the Copernican system in *all* points of observation that could be obtained using the telescopes of that day. Our previous account of confirmation, even with the added complexity of auxiliary hypotheses, does not say anything about how to choose among incompatible alternative hypotheses with the same observable predictions. Because both Tycho's system and the Copernican system predict the phases of Venus, how do we choose one rather than the other? Before trying to answer that question, consider another example of alternative hypotheses that account for the same observational data. The context is the question of when the first humans arrived in America.

The first American immigrants are believed to have come from Asia, probably crossing the Bering Strait on an "ice bridge." From there, they (or their descendants) spread across the North and South American continents. The big question—When did this happen?—is especially puzzling because much evidence indicates that humans were widespread on both continents about 12,000 years ago. Presumably, this far-flung dispersion required a great deal of time. However, almost no evidence indicates that humans were anywhere in North America much before 12,000 years ago—and the little evidence available has been highly disputed.

Several years ago, two archaeologists (W. Irving and C. Harrington, "Upper Pleistocene Radiocarbon-Dated Artifacts from the Northern Yukon," *Science* 179 (1973):335) made an important discovery that they interpreted as confirmation of the hypothesis "Humans were in Beringia 27,000 years ago." In what is now Alaska, they found mammoth bones that showed traces of having being shaped by humans. Bones can be "worked" (shaped into tools) only when they are fresh. After a relatively short time, they become so brittle that they splinter. We know from finding projectile points in mammoth carcasses that human hunters coexisted for a time with now-extinct mammoths in the New World. The worked bones that Irving and Harrington found were subjected to radiocarbon dating, which showed that this mammoth had died approximately 27,000 years ago. (The correctness of radiocarbon dating is an important auxiliary hypothesis.)

Nevertheless, many archaeologists did not accept these bone tools as confirmation of the hypothesis that humans were in America 27,000 years ago. They preferred an alternative hypothesis that could accommodate the dates of the worked bones just as well. This hypothesis states that the bones were from an animal that died 27,000 years ago and subsequently remained frozen in the tundra for another 15,000 years. Then, during a thawing period around 12,000 years ago, the mammoth remains were found by newly arrived humans, who worked the bones. The long freeze had preserved the bones from brittleness, so that when they thawed they could be worked like fresh bones.

Though this alternative hypothesis may seem farfetched, in recent times, long-frozen mammoths were heaved from the earth in Siberia during thawing and freezing cycles. Their meat was eaten; their ivory tusks were sold on the market; their stomachs were examined to see what food they had eaten before they died—and their bones were worked to make tools. Moreover, at the time of the discovery of the worked bones, no other evidence supported the presence of humans in that region before 12,000 years ago. So some archaeologists regarded the hypothesis that the bones had been frozen for 15,000 years before being worked initially more plausible than the hypothesis of early occupation of the area by humans*.

Let us return to our question of how we choose among alternative hypotheses that have the same observable predictions. We could say, like the archaeologists who rejected the claim that humans were in Beringia 27,000 years ago, that when the same true prediction follows from different hypotheses, then the hypothesis that was more plausible (or had a higher *prior probability*) before the test occurred is the hypothesis confirmed by the test. Before the worked bone was found and dated, the hypothesis that humans were present 27,000 years ago was much less probable than the hypothesis that frozen bone

---

*This situation may change. Archaeologists continue to search for signs of early human occupation of the Americas. They are encouraged by recent discoveries that show that humans were in Australia—long thought to be the most recently populated continent—40,000 years ago.

can be salvaged and worked. But either hypothesis can account for the presence of worked bone that is from an animal that lived 27,000 years ago. If we think of tests as resulting in the increase or decrease of the probability of a hypothesis rather than as settling its truth or falsity, then a test that supports two alternative hypotheses equally well leaves their probabilities relative to one another unchanged. In other words, because either alternative could account for the result, the one that was more probable before the "test-observation" remained more probable after it.

On this view, the prior probability of a hypothesis—the probability that the hypothesis is true before taking account of a particular test of that hypothesis—is important in the logic of confirmation. Not only do these probabilities help us to decide which hypothesis among several alternatives is confirmed by a particular test, they also help us to decide which hypotheses are worth taking the trouble to test. If a hypothesis is very implausible (if its truth is almost impossible to imagine), scientists are reluctant to spend time, effort, or money on testing it. Furthermore, if a hypothesis has a very high prior probability—such as the geocentric hypothesis in Galileo's time—then, even when tests apparently disconfirm it, efforts are made to "save the hypothesis" by questioning auxiliary hypotheses. The debate between supporters of the heliocentric system and the geocentric system continued for nearly 100 years after the Copernican system was first published. For much of that time, prior probabilities favored the geocentric hypothesis. The Law of Universal Gravitation and the Laws of Motion, formulated by Newton, who was born the year Galileo died, severely undercut the geocentric hypothesis. These laws, which were accepted by almost all scientists, showed that Tycho's proposed geocentric system required motions that were impossible. Newton's work, along with observations (such as stellar parallax) made with better instruments in the nineteenth century, drastically reduced the probability of the geocentric hypothesis.

The prior probabilities of hypotheses depend on a number of factors. Previous studies or tests may have contributed to the probability of a hypothesis. The prior probability of a hypothesis that is compatible with well-established scientific theories is greater than the prior probability of a hypothesis that conflicts with accepted views. A hypothesis proposed by a legitimate "authority" has greater prior probability than a hypothesis proposed by a crank. In some cases, only rough estimates of prior probabilities can be made. In others, precise quantitative values can be assigned, as is shown in Section VI on Bayesian confirmation.

3. Form of Inductive Arguments of Confirmation

We can now present the structure of reasoning that is used to confirm hypotheses. It is considerably more complex than the first simple formulation of the hypothetico-deductive schema, which treated arguments of confirmation as simple conditional arguments. This new formulation shows how conditional arguments play a part in reasoning about hypotheses, but it also exhibits the overall inductive structure of these arguments.

The structure of arguments to confirm hypotheses can be summarized:

1. The hypothesis is initially plausible. (It has some degree of prior probability.)

2. If the hypothesis, and the auxiliary hypotheses, are true, then the observable prediction is true.

3. The observable prediction is true.

4. No alternative hypothesis has as high a prior probability as the hypothesis that is being tested.

5. Therefore, the hypothesis is true.

Arguments of confirmation thus have four premisses. The first premiss states the plausibility of the hypothesis to be tested. The second and third premisses are the same premisses found in the (invalid) conditional argument form of affirming the consequent. The fourth premiss again appeals to prior probabilities to compare the hypothesis being tested with alternatives that give rise to the same prediction. If a test confirms several alternative hypotheses, the hypothesis that is best confirmed *after* the test is the one that *started out* with the greatest degree of plausibility (prior probability). A positive prediction that follows deductively from several hypotheses confirms each of them; after the test, however, the hypothesis that was most probable before the test remains most probable. The only way to change this relative ranking is by negative (disconfirming) evidence, as explained in Section V.

Although the conclusion of the argument of confirmation is "the hypothesis is *true*," we must remember that because the argument is inductive, the strength of support that the premisses can give to the conclusion is variable. In a case, for example, with several alternative hypotheses that have prior probabilities only slightly lower than the hypothesis being tested, the argument for the truth of the hypothesis will not be very strong. The hypothesis will be supported only a little better after the test than it was before. In another case, with apparently no other plausible alternatives, the argument can be strong. In a case where the the prior probability is low, the succesful prediction may not raise the probability greatly.

Another factor to consider in judging the strength of arguments of confirmation is the nature of the hypothesis itself. On the one hand, a low-level empirical hypothesis, such as "There's a mouse in the kitchen," can be strongly supported by a small amount of the right kind of evidence; if we predict and then find mouse "tracks" on the countertop, and we can rule out someone's trying to trick or deceive us, little doubt remains that the hypothesis is correct. On the other hand, a theoretical hypothesis as high-level and wide-ranging as the Copernican hypothesis will not be strongly confirmed by a few observations with a brand-new scientific instrument. Although we will address quality of evidence briefly, a discussion of the amount and type of evidence it takes to support broad theoretical hypotheses is beyond the scope of our text. The general framework for confirmation arguments developed here, nevertheless, is intended to apply to both high-level and low-level hypotheses.

Finally, any conclusion about what the world is like is revisable in the light of further evidence. This should be clear from our insistence that inductive arguments can be strengthened or weakened by the inclusion of additional evidence. Ptolemy's theory was strongly supported for a very long time by all the available evidence. It was overturned gradually as new evidence accumulated and could be evaluated and absorbed by the scientific community. Some of our own best-supported theories will undoubtedly go the way of Ptolemy's, and new theories will emerge.

4. Confirming a Causal Hypothesis

Edward Jenner's confirmation of the hypothesis that an attack of cowpox confers immunity to smallpox is a classic in the history of medicine. In 1980, the World Health Organization announced that smallpox, long dreaded for its power to kill and disfigure, has at last been completely eliminated; not a single case of the disease remains in the world. Because smallpox spreads only by contact among humans (no other carriers of the disease are known), this is a significant step toward the achievement of worldwide health.

Smallpox is highly contagious. When Columbus's sailors first brought it to America, entire tribes of the Indians, who had never been exposed, were destroyed by the disease. Smallpox epidemics were common in Europe and the Middle East before the twentieth century, and until only a few years ago, the disease remained a serious problem in some parts of the world. In the 1960s, New York City was thrown into near panic when it became known that a foreign traveler with an active case of smallpox had spent several hours in Grand Central Station.

For centuries, doctors tried to discover a way to prevent smallpox. It was known that those who survived an attack of the disease were immune to further infection. It was also well known that some persons contracted a relatively mild form of the disease. Thus, one method of trying to protect against a severe case of smallpox was to be scratched with the infectious material from a sore of someone with a mild case of the disease. This method of "inoculation," widely practiced as early as the seventeenth century, was hazardous and frequently resulted in the very condition it was designed to prevent.

In England, persons who lived and worked near dairy farms were susceptible to a much milder disease, "cowpox," that attacked both cows and humans. The disease was never fatal, and left only a few faint scars. Jenner—a doctor who lived and worked in the dairy country of Gloucestershire—was aware of the belief, commonly held in that area, that an attack of cowpox conferred immunity not only to further attacks of that disease, but to smallpox as well.

Jenner decided to test the hypothesis "An attack of cowpox confers immunity to smallpox." A report of his test is given by Isaac Asimov in *The Intelligent Man's Guide to the Biological Sciences*:

> In 1796, Jenner decided to chance the supreme test. First, he inoculated an eight-year-old boy named James Phipps with cowpox, using fluid from a cowpox blister on a milkmaid's hand. Two months later came the crucial

and desperate part of the test. Jenner deliberately inoculated young James with smallpox itself.

The boy did not catch the disease. He was immune.

We can reconstruct Jenner's argument, using the model for confirmation provided in the preceding section.

1. *The hypothesis "An attack of cowpox confers immunity to smallpox" is initially plausible.*

It was widely believed in Gloucestershire that an attack of cowpox produced this benefit. Dairymaids and others who worked around cows, although susceptible to cowpox, never seemed to get smallpox, even during epidemics. The plausibility of the hypothesis was also enhanced by an analogy. Mild attacks of smallpox conferred immunity to further attacks, and cowpox produced symptoms similar to those of *extremely* mild cases of smallpox. All of this made the hypothesis worth testing.

2. *If an attack of cowpox confers immunity to smallpox, then Phipps, who has had cowpox and is inoculated, is immune.*

In the preceding conditional, the consequent follows deductively from the antecedent, with the aid of three three auxiliary hypotheses:

    (i) The smallpox matter with which Phipps was inoculated had not lost its potency.

    (ii) Jenner knew how to inoculate, and he was qualified to observe whether Phipps actually had cowpox and whether he had contracted smallpox.

    (iii) Persons who are inoculated and who do not contract even a mild case of smallpox are immune.

The first two auxiliary hypotheses refer to the conditions of the test; the third is a theoretical background assumption, based on past experience with the disease.

3. *The observable prediction is true.*

Phipps was immune.

4. *No alternative hypothesis has as high a prior probability as the hypothesis that is tested.*

Jenner's hypothesis is a causal hypothesis (having cowpox *causes* immunity to smallpox). Causal hypotheses are difficult to test because of alternative causes that could account for what is observed. For example, some persons have natural immunities to some diseases. Phipps could have been one of those fortunate few who are naturally immune to smallpox. The alternative causal hypothesis "Phipps has natural immunity to smallpox," supports exactly the same observable prediction: Phipps is immune.

The hypothesis of natural immunity, however, has a lower prior probability than the cowpox hypothesis. Although exact statistics were unavailable, epidemics of the disease showed that natural immunity to this highly contagious disease was relatively rare compared to the immunity apparently conferred on dairymaids by prior cases of cowpox.

5. *Therefore, an attack of cowpox causes immunity to smallpox.*

The hypothesis is confirmed.

Exercise Set 8.1

In each of the following:

(1) Identify the hypothesis.

(2) Try to state some observable predictions that follow from the hypothesis. Identify any auxiliary hypotheses that are required for your predictions.

(3) Try to formulate an alternative hypothesis to account for what has been observed.

(4) Compare (in a rough, non-numerical way) the prior probabilities of the original hypothesis and the alternatives you suggest. Indicate the sources on which your probability assignments are made. (For example, you might assign a very high prior probability to *H* because it fits well with established scientific theories; or you might assign a very low prior probability to *H* on the basis of your past experience with similar types of hypotheses.)

1. Medical scientists have noticed recently that the incidence of severe heart attacks in young and middle-aged men is far greater in a particular small area of Finland than in any other region of the world. Most of these men work as lumberjacks. Their diets consist of large amounts of meat, eggs, cream, and rich pastries—foods that are high in cholesterol. Medical scientists believe that diet is the cause of the high incidence of heart attacks.

2. A plastic surgeon who specializes in facelifts commented that his youngest patients are frequently actresses. He believes that actresses seek facelifts at an earlier age than other women because actresses' faces "fall" as a result of extensive massaging when they put on and take off their makeup.

3. In the chapter from S. J. Gould's *The Mismeasure of Man*, entitled "The Real Error of Cyril Burt," Gould discusses the views of one of the leading developers of "intelligence testing." Answer questions about Burt's hypothesis.

> [Burt] wonders about the intellectual achievements of Jews, and attributes it, in part, to the inherited myopia [nearsightedness] that keeps them off the playing fields and adapts them for poring over account books.

4. On the basis of annual data, Mr. Ehrenhalt [regional Commissioner for the Bureau of Labor Statistics] said, fewer teen-agers (16 to 19 years old) in proportion to the youth population are working in New York City than in other central cities. While New York

is at the bottom in the proportion of its young people actually holding jobs, he said, the city's rate of unemployment for that group has run below that in the major middle western cities hard hit by the recession.

The seeming contradiction, he explained, stems from the fact that a large element of youths here in the 16- to 19-year-old bracket have not been looking for jobs and, in many cases, have probably not even been thinking about working because jobs for young people are so hard to get here. Consequently, they are not counted as unemployed in population surveys, he said.

—D. Stetson, *The New York Times*

5. Counseling and home placement programs can substantially reduce the number of juveniles locked up for minor status offenses, according to a federally funded study.

The study, done by University of Southern California researchers, evaluates a program undertaken at eight sites where efforts were specifically made to help juveniles stay out of detention facilities.

The Southern California researchers reported there was a reduction of 43 percent from preprogram levels in the total number of juvenile status offenders placed in detention at the eight sites.

Their evaluation added "Although this does not constitute proof that the program caused the reduction, since such reductions were part of the larger national trend in any case, knowledge of particular program activities makes us confident that a substantial portion of the reductions can be attributed to the program."

—H. Benedict, Associated Press

6. [J. F. McLennan (1827-1881)] was a student of the early history of society, and charged that no one before him had attempted to reconstruct the social conditions of primitive peoples. . . .

His major item of reconstruction was bride capture, which is still carried out in mock battles in some contemporary societies. Thus, among the Kalmucks, a prospective groom would go to the village of his bride, pay the bride price, and then carry the girl away on his horse, while the people of her village pursued them or made mock resistance. Or again, among the Welsh, the groom and his friends engaged in a mock battle with the friends of the bride, until the latter inevitably lost. Postulating that these customs were survivals from former actual situations of bride capture, McLennan set out to explain why women should have been taken in this manner. He arrived at the logical conclusion that there must have been a shortage of women [due to the practice of female infanticide].

—A. de W. Malefijt, *Images of Man*

7. A rare Amazon "sea cow," one of only two manatees of its kind in the nation, died yesterday at the Pittsburgh Zoo.
The 200-pound, $5\frac{1}{2}$-foot creature was found dead in its tank at 8 A.M. It had been in apparent good health.

An autopsy by Robert Wagner, zoo veterinarian, failed to reveal the cause of death, but zoo officials speculated that a drop in water temperature during a heating failure Monday night might have been a contributing factor.

"It wasn't an old animal, as manatees go," Goodlett [director of the Aquazoo] said. "They're believed to live about 35 years." [The 15-year-old manatee had been in the zoo for 13 years.]

Goodlett said the building's furnace went off at about midnight Monday night. Tuesday morning, the water temperature stood at 64 degrees F., he said. The water is usually kept at 75-78 degrees F.

—H. Pierce, *Pittsburgh Post-Gazette*

8. In the following excerpt from *The Bog People*, P. V. Glob refers to studies of three Iron Age men, found in Danish peat bogs, where they had been buried for nearly 2,000 years. The circumstances of the burials, as well as their location, showed that the men had been deliberately killed, probably in conjunction with some ceremony. Bog water, which is saturated with soil-acids, prevented deterioration of the bodies, and the contents of the stomachs and intestines of the three men were examined and analyzed.

In each of these last meals no trace was found of summer or autumn fruits, such as strawberries, blackberries, raspberries, apples, or hips; nor was there any trace of greenstuffs. There are thus grounds for thinking that all three men met their deaths in winter or early spring, before everything had come into leaf. From this we may conjecture that the deaths took place at the time of the mid-winter celebrations whose purpose was to hasten the coming of spring. It was on just such occasions that bloody human sacrifices reached a peak in the Iron Age.

9. Catfish slime, a gel-like substance secreted by the fish, has remarkable properties that help heal wounds. . . . Richard S. Criddle, a professor of biochemistry and biophysics at the University of California at Davis, said that when a local Gulf species of catfish is caught, it secretes a slime over its entire body.
"I have used it myself on cuts," he said. "They heal entirely in 3 days, instead of the usual 10."

—S. Blakelee, *The New York Times*

10. EMOTIONAL PREPARATION AIDS SURGICAL RECOVERY
A study of 60 men undergoing coronary bypass grafts at the University of Iowa Medical Center was conducted recently. The men were divided into two groups. One group received the hospital's standard preparation for patients about to undergo surgery: a brochure on the procedures and a short visit from a nurse to answer questions. The other group watched a videotape called "Living Proof" that followed a patient through the operation and recovery. While 75 percent of those with the standard preparation suffered after the surgery from acute hypertension—a condition that can endanger coronary bypass patients in the first 12 hours after surgery—only 40 percent of those who viewed the tape had the problem.

—*The New York Times*

11. Salvesen's team [of Norweigian scientists] did find a weak association between ultrasound exposure in the womb and the chances of being a leftie [left-handed] by age 8 or 9. The link appeared independent of a family history of left-handedness.

However, those findings could be the result of chance, the team cautions in the July 17 BRITISH MEDICAL JOURNAL.

Alternatively, they say, the sound waves employed by ultrasound scanners may influence the migration of neurons in the developing fetus. Changes in fetal brain formation could cause a child to favor its left rather than its right hand.

—*Science News* 144, Sept. 18, 1993

IV. INCREMENTAL CONFIRMATION AND "ABSOLUTE" CONFIRMATION

Most tests, such as Jenner's test of the cowpox hypothesis and Galileo's test of the heliocentric hypothesis, confirm in a relative or *incremental* sense. This means that the probability of the hypothesis *after* such a test is greater than it was prior to the test. A hypothesis is said to be confirmed in the "absolute" sense only when it is so strongly supported by evidence that it is almost certainly true. (Its probability is close to 1.) Many tests may have to be performed before a hypothesis is "absolutely" confirmed.

Even when a hypothesis is "absolutely" confirmed, new evidence could overturn it. Before Europeans learned about platypuses, the hypothesis "All mammals bear live young" was considered absolutely confirmed. When Europeans first heard reports of Australian egg-laying mammals, they assumed that the aboriginal Australians who described these strange animals were either mistaken or dishonest. However, the aboriginals were correct; platypuses are mammals that lay eggs.

Newton's Laws of Motion, long regarded as universally applicable and absolutely confirmed, are now—in light of Einstein's work on relativity— either regarded as only approximately true, or they are restricted in application to particles that are not moving at speeds close to the speed of light or that are not located in strong gravitational fields. To say hypotheses are "absolutely" confirmed means they are very strongly supported, and that no evidence is known to count against them. It does not mean that no chance exists of ever rejecting them in light of future evidence.

Controlled experiments and Mill's methods can be used to test causal hypotheses. Observable predictions deduced from hypotheses are often predictions about the outcome of controlled experiments. The Method of Difference and the Joint Method of Agreement and Difference can sometimes eliminate alternative hypotheses. In controlled experiments, special attention is paid to auxiliary hypotheses that might affect the outcome of a test. The use of varied samples and the repeated use of Mill's methods contribute to the confirmation of hypotheses, for no important hypothesis is firmly accepted or rejected on the basis of a single test.

Any observable prediction that can be deduced from a hypothesis can be used to test it, but some predictions are more important than others. Consider, for example, the hypothesis that the mastodons and other large mammals (megafauna) that once roamed North America and Australia became extinct because humans "overhunted" them. One "prediction" that follows from the overhunting hypothesis is that these mammals coexisted with humans over a period of time. Archaeological investigation has proved this to be true. But this evidence does not confirm the overhunting hypothesis nearly so strongly as archaeological evidence of massive "kill sites" or "butchering sites" would, and such evidence has not been found. In fact, many archaeologists believe that the long period of coexistence between humans and these animals counts *against* the overhunting hypothesis, and indicates an ecological balance between hunters and hunted.

In general, we can say that the more unlikely it is for a prediction to be true *unless* the hypothesis is true, the better the truth of that prediction confirms the hypothesis. In some cases, it would be very surprising if a prediction turned out to be true unless the hypothesis that gave rise to it were also true. A long period of coexistence for humans and megafauna would not be particularly surprising or unlikely, even if the animals became extinct as a result of some cause other than overhunting by humans. While extinctions can be attributed to human predation, they can also result from the destruction of habitat—which may be a result of human activities, of some natural force, such as a severe drought, or a combination of both. Giant pandas in China are now threatened with extinction from loss of a suitable habitat, despite human efforts to prevent the loss. Thus, the evidence of coexistence does not weigh very heavily either for or against the overhunting hypothesis.

Proponents of pseudoscientific theories try to find acceptance for their theories by pointing to successful predictions based on these theories. An example of this is found in *dianetics*—a pseudopsychological theory that predicts the remission of neurotic symptoms for people who undergo the therapy prescribed by dianetic theory (see W. Salmon, *Foundations of Scientific Inference*, 1967, p. 119). Many persons who submitted to this treatment did improve, so proponents of dianetics can say truly that their predictions were true. The spontaneous remission of neurotic symptoms, however, is common. Because many people recover from neuroses with no treatment, the true predictions of dianetics do not constitute strong confirmation for the theory.

Astrology attracts many believers, who faithfully read their "horoscopes," follow the advice given, and observe that many astrological predictions turn out to be true. Consider some typical examples of forecasts, which are printed in many daily newspapers:

What appeared to be immovable will now prove to be flexible.
Apparent obstacle actually proves to be a stepping-stone toward goal.
Be ready for significant change which could ultimately result in journey.
Member of opposite sex does care, will plainly show it.
Many people miscalculate when judging your capabilities.

All of these "predictions" are phrased so vaguely that they can be applied to different situations that are not at all unusual or surprising in the lives of most people. The truth of such "predictions" does nothing to confirm the hypothesis that our lives are influenced by the positions of the stars and planets.

Exercise Set 8.2

1. For the following example, adapted from *Fads and Fallacies*, by Martin Gardner,

    (1) Identify the hypothesis at issue.

    (2) Identify any mistake in reasoning.

Mr. Smith is unable to get rid of an annoying cold. He decides to try a new doctor he has heard about. The doctor's methods are unorthodox, but he has been strongly recommended. The doctor assures Mr. Smith that his cold will be cured. The treatment requires Mr. Smith to take off his shoes and stockings and let the doctor shine infrared light on his feet for ten minutes. Mr. Smith returns for several more treatments at a cost of $15 each. After a week or so, Mr. Smith's cold has vanished, and he becomes one of the doctor's loyal boosters.

2. Find an example of a prediction made by some pseudoscientific theory, and explain why the prediction either does or does not support the theory.

V. DISCONFIRMATION

Science textbooks often say that scientific hypotheses cannot be *proved*; they can only be *disproved*, and that scientists should therefore try to falsify, or disconfirm, hypotheses rather than try to confirm them. Let us examine this suggestion in connection with the heliocentric-geocentric controversy.

    According to the Ptolemaic system, Venus will not show a full set of phases; it will always have a crescent appearance, although the crescent will vary somewhat in width (see Figure 8-2).

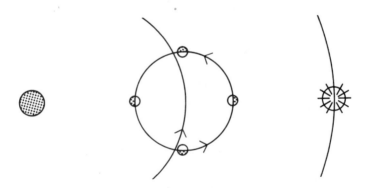

FIGURE 8-2

In the Ptolemaic system, Venus must always appear more or less crescent shaped. *Source*: Richard S. Westfall, *The Construction of Modern Science: Mechanisms and Mechanics* (Cambridge UK: Cambridge University Press, 1971). Used by permission of the publisher.

Galileo could have used the following argument to *disconfirm* the hypothesis "The Ptolemaic (geocentric) system is correct." The observable prediction that follows deductively from this hypothesis is "Venus will not show a full set of phases."

If the Ptolemaic (geocentric) system is correct, then Venus
 will not show a full set of phases.
Venus does show a full set of phases.
_____

The Ptolemaic system is not correct.

In the conditional premiss of this argument, the hypothesis is the antecedent, and an observable prediction—which must be true if the hypothesis is true—is the consequent. This time, however, the observable prediction turns out to be false. The argument fits the *valid* conditional form of *denying the consequent*:

If p, then q.
Not q.
_____

Not p.

Thus, an apparent difference emerges between the *confirmation* of hypotheses, which we have said depends on complex inductive reasoning rather than a simple conditional argument, and the *disconfirmation* of hypotheses, which can be deductively valid. This discrepancy accounts for the greater enthusiasm that many scientists express for the method of disconfirming hypotheses. The method looks particularly attractive when it seems that by the method of elimination the true hypothesis will emerge. For example, if the geocentric hypothesis is rejected deductively, then the heliocentric hypothesis wins by default. However, as we have seen in looking at the geocentric-heliocentric controversy in its historical context, proponents of a hypothesis can try to "save" it by rejecting one or more of the auxiliary hypotheses that are required to connect the hypothesis with the unfavorable prediction. Although the Ptolemaic system is now rejected by astronomers, in Galileo's time its prior probability was too great to be outweighed by observations with an instrument that was not guaranteed to be reliable. If the disconfirming argument were fully stated along with the important auxiliary hypotheses, it would read:

If the Ptolemaic system is correct, and if the telescope is a reliable instrument
 of observation, and if Venus lies between the earth and the sun, then Venus
 will not show a complete set of phases.
Venus does show phases.
_____

Either the Ptolemaic system is incorrect, or the telescope is unreliable, or
 Venus is not between the earth and the sun.

Faced with this disjunctive conclusion, many of Galileo's contemporaries were willing to reject the reliability of the telescope rather than the Ptolemaic system. (See Galileo's own argument for the reliability of his telescope, Exercise Set 1.2, #9.)

The general form of this argument for disconfirmation is:

If H and A_1 . . . An, then P.
P is false.
_____
Either H is false or A_1 or . . . or An is false.

In this argument form, the conclusion follows deductively from the premises, but the conclusion is not simply a rejection of the hypothesis. The conclusion says instead that either the hypothesis is false or one of the auxiliary hypotheses is false.

In scientific practice, it is not appropriate to reject or replace an auxiliary hypothesis merely to "save the hypothesis." The arbitrary rejection (or addition) of an auxiliary hypothesis to save a favored hypothesis is called "*ad hoc* reasoning" and is regarded as fallacious. Although everyone agrees that arbitrary rejection of auxiliary hypotheses is inappropriate, they do not always agree about whether a particular rejection is "arbitrary." Galileo thought his opponents were being arbitrary because they refused to look through the telescope. His opponents did not think they were being arbitrary because they knew that curved lenses distorted images, and so did not think that what they saw through a telescope could support Galileo's case.

When an auxiliary hypothesis is called into question and can be tested, it should be. It cannot be tested in isolation, any more than the original hypothesis could be. When an auxiliary hypothesis becomes the focus of attention, still other auxiliary hypotheses will have to be called in to connect it with its predictions. This sort of complexity makes the rejection of hypotheses no less complicated than their acceptance.

Even when auxiliary hypotheses are accepted, deriving the true hypothesis with deductive certainty by eliminating incorrect hypotheses will not work. No theoretical limit can be imposed on the number of possible false hypotheses that have to be eliminated. Although we are not often faced with an abundance of *plausible* hypotheses for testing, we may nevertheless overlook or be unaware of some that should be tested. A situation in which there are only two plausible competing hypotheses and in which the rejection of one "forces" us to accept the other hypothesis seldom occurs. Even if Galileo's arguments persuade his contemporaries to reject Ptolemy's geocentric hypothesis, for example, the Copernican hypothesis is not thereby established, for Tycho's geocentric hypothesis is also compatible with the full set of phases of Venus.

1. Crucial Tests

Occasionally, scientists do find themselves in the happy situation of agreeing about auxiliary hypotheses and being faced with an observable prediction that confirms one of only two competing hypotheses at the same time it disconfirms the other. These **crucial tests** have received much attention in the history of science. Jenner's test of the cowpox hypothesis on young Phipps comes close to exemplifying a crucial experiment. The small chance that Phipps was naturally immune to smallpox did not pose a threat to deciding between: "Cowpox confers immunity to smallpox," and "Cowpox does not prevent smallpox."

In this case, as in most examples of crucial testing, the test that seems to settle the question definitively in favor of one of the hypotheses emerges only after prolonged investigation and many noncrucial tests. It is unrealistic to call even this kind of scientific reasoning "purely deductive," for the deductive rejection of one hypothesis is embedded in a series of complex inductive arguments. These inductive arguments serve to support the truth of auxiliary hypotheses, to establish prior probabilities, and to eliminate some alternative hypotheses. Such work is usually necessary before reaching the stage of performing a crucial test. The following example illustrates what typically happens in attempts to disconfirm well-established hypotheses. Like arguments of confirmation, arguments for disconfirmation of a hypothesis involve considerations of prior probabilities and the availability of alternative hypotheses as well as the relation between the hypothesis, auxiliaries and the observable prediction.

2. Disconfirming a Causal Hypothesis

Different Indian groups, each with distinct languages and cultures, live in the region of the Amazon River. Some of these groups are constantly engaged in violent warfare with neighboring tribes. The Yanomamö are among the most warlike. Many anthropologists have long believed that the cause of their hostile behavior is the scarcity of protein in their diets. The warlike tactics, say those anthropologists, are ecologically advantageous. They enable the Yanomamö to compete for scarce resources in an environment that is inadequately supplied with enough protein for those who live there.

However, when the hypothesis "Warlike behavior among the Yanomamö is caused by a diet deficient in protein" was tested during the late 1970s, it was rejected by the two anthropologists who conducted the test (N. Chagnon and R. Hames, "Protein Deficiency and Tribal Warfare in Amazonia: New Data," *Science* 203 (1979):910). Chagnon and Hames spent 13 months living with the Yanomamö, carefully recording the foods they ate and calculating the amounts of protein in those foods. They found that the protein intake of the Yanomamö was greater than standard minimum daily requirements—that their diet was not deficient in protein. The argument for disconfirmation can be reconstructed as follows:

1. *The hypothesis has initial plausibility.*

This hypothesis was the prevailing view among the anthropologists who had studied Amazonian tribal societies. The hypothesis is consistent with one widely accepted theoretic approach to the study of human culture, which views the material conditions in which people live as the chief factors in determining their behavior. It is also known that protein deficiencies have various effects not only on human physiology but also on human behavior.

2. *If warlike behavior among the Yanomamö is caused by a diet deficient in protein, then the diet of the Yanomamö will exhibit protein deficiency.*

The observable prediction of protein deficiency in the Yanomamö diet follows deductively from the hypothesis and three auxiliary hypotheses:

(i) The methods used by the investigators to measure amounts of available protein in the diet of the Yanomamö were accurate.

(ii) The field study that lasted 13 months was long enough to provide a correct picture of the normal eating patterns of the Yanomamö.

(iii) The "minimum daily requirement of protein" is a good measure of the amount needed to avoid protein deficiency.

The first two auxiliary hypotheses refer to the conditions of the test. The third auxiliary hypothesis is part of generally accepted theoretical knowledge of human nutritional requirements —the theory that is the source of information you see printed on boxes of breakfast cereal.

3. *The diet of the Yanomamö is not deficient in protein.*

The observable prediction is false.

4. *Therefore, warlike behavior among the Yanomamö is not caused by protein deficiency in their diet.*

Although the observation that the diet is not deficient in protein disconfirms the hypothesis, it does not conclusively establish that this hypothesis is false. This argument, like the arguments that confirm hypotheses, is inductive—if we regard the falsity of the hypothesis as its conclusion. Deductively, all we can say is that either the hypothesis is false or some auxiliary hypothesis is false.

Some anthropologists have questioned the second auxiliary hypothesis, that is, whether the 13-month study was long enough. Those who study the diets of people like the Yanomamö, who live by hunting and gathering, have found significant variations in the the amounts of available protein from one year to another. Too much or too little rain or epidemic diseases in animals that are hunted (events that do not occur on a yearly basis) affect the availability of protein-rich food. Hunter-gatherers cannot count on steady supplies in stressed environments. The study that forms the basis for the argument of disconfirmation may have been conducted in an unusually good year for gathering and hunting.

No one denies that the results of this 13-month study are important. However, no single study will convince those who believe that the prior probability of the protein-deficiency hypothesis is very high. Additional tests, carried out over a period of years, could (if the results were similar to the results of the 13-

month study) eventually disconfirm "absolutely" the hypothesis. In this situation, it is difficult to see what sort of crucial test could be devised to help us choose between the hypothesis being tested and some other hypothesis. No other causal hypothesis (except the negative "Warlike behavior is not caused by protein deficiency") was even formulated in this study.

Exercise Set 8.3

> For each of the following, identify the hypothesis that is disconfirmed, and reconstruct (insofar as possible) the disconfirming argument, with reference to plausibility, disconfirming observations, and alternative hypotheses.

1. A student tells the teacher that a family crisis may require a trip out of town at the time of the next class period when a test is scheduled. The student fails to appear for the test, and the teacher surmises that the student left town to deal with the crisis. Then, immediately after the test ends, the teacher sees the student with a group having lunch at the Student Union.

2. You oversleep and are concerned about missing an appointment, so you dress hurriedly, skip breakfast, and leave the house as quickly as you can. When you return in the evening, you find the front door ajar and immediately suspect that a burglar is responsible. When you go inside, however, nothing is disturbed. The house looks exactly the way it did when you left in the morning, so you stop worrying about a burglar.

3. Cauterization was the only known treatment [for gangrene]; sometimes the patient was cured by it and sometimes the gray slough would reappear. Most surgeons regarded hospital gangrene and the other septic diseases as inescapable scourges, without troubling to do more than to speculate about their causes. Young Lister, [J. Lister, 1827-1912, who revolutionized surgery with the introduction of antiseptics] however, examined the results of the cautery treatment and reasoned that if some patients recovered and some did not, though all had been exposed to the oxygen in the air which most doctors vaguely assumed to be the cause of the trouble, then oxygen could not be responsible.

—A. Young, *The Men Who Made Surgery*

4. Researchers [at the national Centers for Disease Control] say they are convinced that, despite earlier worries, the [new hepatitis B] vaccine is not linked to the deadly acquired immune deficiency syndrome.

The vaccine, which became generally available last July, prevents one common type of hepatitis, a viral infection that causes inflammation of the liver.

Of more than 200,000 people who have been given the vaccine, only 118 became ill. Fifty-six of the illnesses were found to be unrelated to the vaccine. Only six of the people were seriously ill, the centers said.

The centers found no cases of immune deficiency in people who had received the vaccine since July, and just two cases, both in homosexual men, in the initial study and trial of the vaccine. . . .

Hepatitis B vaccine, first licensed in 1981, is made from the blood plasma of donors who have hepatitis B, most of whom are homosexual men. Because most of the donors are homosexual men, the centers said, there has been concern that the vaccine could be linked to acquired immune deficiency.

—*The New York Times*

5. In an attempt to make ecological sense out of a diversity of practices, including food choices and taboos, much attention has been given to protein as a necessity in potentially short supply. These various studies identify a particular potential for protein scarcity in a given situation and seek to demonstrate that the ecologically most important effect of certain aspects of behavior is the alleviation of this scarcity. Support for these interpretations has been offered in the form of the almost universal preference for meat over plant foods, a preference that, while not instinctual, is "biologically and culturally conditioned" and makes good nutritional sense as well.

Yet this general "Protein Hypothesis" faces a number of problems. Proteins per se are not recognized by most peoples of the world and thus are not considered in their evaluations. Furthermore, all meat is not preferred over all plants, and preference orders among animal foods do not correspond to protein contents. Certainly, high-quality protein is a requirement for survival, but since many people can give reasons for their food preferences, and since these reasons do not include the protein content of different foods, it becomes necessary to explore the link between stated preferences and nutritional consequences that include protein intake. One possible link between the two is the suggestion that, for lack of a better name, may be called the "Fat Hypothesis."

There are numerous examples of stated preferences for fat as a major attribute of food desirability. Animal foods are often clearly ranked according to fat content.

—M. A. Jochim, *Strategies for Survival*

6. Background: Some birds, such as Clark's nutcracker, hide seeds and recover them later.

Few people would want to wait several months near a nutcracker's cache, hoping to learn whether it was eventually dug up by the bird that buried it.
Diana Tomback of the University of Colorado at Denver reasoned, however, that much could be learned from the way Clark's nutcrackers search for caches. She took advantage of the fact that birds leave a record of their searches in the form of beak marks in the snow and the earth where they dig. Moreover, successful searches can be identified by the presence of piñon-seed coats next to the holes from which seeds were taken. If nutcrackers search at random, successful probe holes and clusters of unsuccessful holes should be more or less evenly distributed over landscapes where the birds have searched. Tomback found, on the contrary, that unsuccessful probes were clumped around successful ones. The pattern indicated that nutcrackers were not searching for caches by trial and error. Furthermore, in the early spring (before rodents had found many of the caches), about two-thirds of the probes were successful, far more than one would expect of a random search.

Tomback's observations do not prove unequivocally that the birds could remember where their caches were. They might have smelled them (although again it is an unlikely possibility). Alternatively, they could have searched mainly in places of the kind that are likely to contain caches. Recent laboratory studies done by Stephen B. Vander Wall at Utah State University seem to rule out these possibilities.

—S. J. Shettleworth, "Memory in Food-Hoarding Birds,"
Scientific American 248:3, 106

7. In 1678 the Dutch physicist Christian Huyghens suggested [contrary to the accepted theory that light was made up of tiny particles] that light consisted of tiny waves. If it was made up of waves, there was no difficulty about explaining the different amount of refraction of different kinds of light through a refracting medium, provided it was assumed that light traveled more slowly through the refracting medium than through air. The amount of refraction would vary with the length of the waves: the shorter the wavelength, the greater the refraction. This meant that violet light (the most refracted) had a shorter wavelength than blue light; blue, shorter than green; and so on. It was this difference in wavelength that distinguished colors to the eye. And of course, if light consisted of waves, two beams could cross without trouble. (After all, sound waves and water waves crossed without losing their identity.)

But Huyghens' wave theory was not very satisfactory either. It didn't explain why light rays traveled in straight lines and cast sharp shadows, nor why light waves could not go around obstacles, as water waves and sound waves could. Furthermore, if light consisted of waves, how could it travel through a vacuum, as it certainly did in coming to us through space from the sun and stars? What medium was it moving?

> —I. Asimov, *The Intelligent Man's Guide to the Physical Sciences*

8. Most any textbook [on the subject of pre-Neanderthal man] tells us that the men of Choukoutien cooked meat over hearths, predominantly ate venison, but also ate elephants, rhinoceroses, beavers, bison, and wild pigs, and on occasion one another.

Evidence for the use of fire was summarized by Teilhard de Chardin as so extensive as to need no further comment! In this judgment I must agree, but the evidence hardly justifies the picture one gets from textbooks of early man seated around his hearth roasting meat and carrying on a fireside chat.

"The thickest layer of ash, in the upper-middle part of the cave deposit is up to *six meters* [more than 19 feet] deep. Stone tools and fossilized small vertebrates—rats and bats—were numerous in this layer, *sometimes indeed forming their own layers*. The ash deposit here is not in piles, but spread out in even layers, apparently the result of water movement. In the lower-middle part of the cave deposit, the ash layer is thicker near the south wall. *At its maximum, it is four meters deep.* It was around the fringe of this ash layer that most of the human fossils and stone tools were unearthed."

> —Lan-Po, *The Cave Home of Peking Man*, quoted in L. Binford, *Bones*

Note: The emphasis in the quoted passage is Binford's. His alternative hypothesis to the claim that early humans were cave-dwelling hunters of large animals is that early humans were scavengers who used caves, but who did not live in them, and who feasted mainly on the marrow in bones left by animal predators.

9. Hot water bottles, electric heaters and warm blankets may be no help at all to people suffering the effects of extreme cold, according to six Canadian researchers who found out the hard way. . . . They sat in tubs of ice water for one to two hours, until their body temperatures dropped as much as 8 degrees Fahrenheit, from the normal of 98.6 degrees.

Then they tried three alternative methods of getting their temperatures back up from those dangerously low levels. They sat in front of heaters. They exercised. Or they just shivered.

Shivering warms the body from the inside by letting muscles produce waste heat. It worked surprisingly fast—about three times faster than previous researchers have found.

Surprisingly, external heat appeared to make no difference. "We surmise that the heat blunted the shivering response," said Gordon Giesbrecht [one of the researchers]. "Paradoxically, when we kept the skin cool, it maintained the shivering stimulus and let the body do what it does best."

Exercise, which hypothermia [extreme cold] victims cannot always manage, was best of all, warming the body three times faster than shivering alone.

—J. Gleick, *The New York Times*

10. Until 1967, when a measles vaccine was licensed, about 500,000 cases of the disease were reported each year in the United States.

The disease was believed to be headed for eradication in 1983, when only 1,497 cases were reported, but the case count surprised researchers by rising in 1984, 1985, and 1986 [6,255 cases].

Nearly half the cases reported in the first six months of 1987 were in patients who had been vaccinated against measles.

One-third of those people had been vaccinated at 12 to 14 months of age. Researchers now believe that at that age the vaccine may be less effective.

—Associated Press

VI. BAYESIAN CONFIRMATION

When arguments for confirmation and disconfirmation are supplemented with considerations of prior probabilities, as suggested in preceding sections of this chapter, and when the requisite probabilities can be expressed quantitatively, *Bayes's Theorem*—a theorem of the mathematical calculus of probability (discussed in Chapter 6)—provides a formal model for arguments of confirmation and disconfirmation. In this section, we look first at Bayes's Theorem, and then we see how arguments similar to those we have already examined can be analyzed along Bayesian lines.

1. Bayes's Theorem

The probability calculus is used to calculate unknown probabilities on the basis of known probabilities. Thus we can use the "multiplication rule" (Rule 4, Chapter 6, Section II) to calculate the probability of a conjunction, when the probabilities of individual conjuncts are known:

$$\Pr(h_1 \text{ and } h_2 | e) = \Pr(h_1 | e) \times \Pr(h_2 | e \text{ and } h_1)$$

Sometimes, when we have information about a "set-up," such as the composition of a deck of cards, we are interested in the probability of some outcome that has not yet occurred, such as drawing an ace. Such "pretrial" problems were discussed in Chapter 6. Other times, however, we may have already observed an outcome, such as four successive tosses of a coin resulting in a head, and we may be interested in what kind of set-up gave rise to that outcome. (For example, was the coin a fair coin?) Bayes's Theorem, which can be derived from the four rules of probability presented in Chapter 6, enables us to calculate these "inverse" or "post-trial" probabilities when certain other probabilities are known. To illustrate the theorem, we consider the question raised about whether a coin that lands heads four times in a row is a fair coin.

To use Bayes's Theorem, some prior probabilities must be known. In our example, we need to know the prior probability that the coin is fair as well as the prior probability that the coin is unfair. (Here, let us say that "unfair" means the coin is weighted to yield a head on every toss.) These prior probabilities are usually assigned on the basis of background knowledge. If the coin is received in change from the grocery store, then the prior probability that it is a fair coin is high. But if the coin is in the possession of a person who is known as a prankster or a gambler whose winnings are suspiciously heavy, we might assign a low prior probability to the fairness of the coin. For the sake of our example, we will assume the slick gambler holds the coin and that the prior probability that it is fair is only 0.1. Then, because the coin is either fair or not fair, the prior probability that it is *not* fair is $1 - 0.1 = 0.9$.

The next probabilities we need to know are the *likelihoods* that the observed outcome (four heads in a row) would have happened if the coin was fair and if the coin was not fair. If the coin is fair, the probability of obtaining four heads in a row is $(1/2)^4$, or 0.0625. If the coin is unfair (weighted to show only heads when it is tossed) the likelihood of getting four heads in a row is 1, because the *evidence statement* follows deductively from the hypothesis.

In addition, we need to know the probability that the observed evidence would occur without regard to whether the hypothesis is true. This is called the *total probability* for the evidence statement. It is based on the prior probabilities of each of the hypotheses that could give rise to the observed evidence as well as the probability that the evidence would occur, given the truth of each of the hypotheses. Suppose, for example, that we want to know the probability that a white ball will be drawn (e) when the ball may be drawn blindly from either of two jars (h_1) or (h_2). Suppose further that each jar has an equal probability of being selected (the prior probability for h_1 is equal to the prior probability for h_2 and both are 1/2). But suppose that the first jar contains 50 white balls and 50 black balls, while the second jar contains 75 white balls and 25 black balls. If the ball is drawn from the first jar, the probability that it will be white is 1/2; but if it is drawn from the second jar, the probability that it will be white is 3/4. The total probability of drawing a white ball, regardless of which jar is selected is:

$[Pr(h_1) \times (Pr(e|h_1)] + Pr(h_2) \times [Pr(e|h_2)]$ which, in this case, is $[1/2 \times 1/2] + [1/2 \times 3/4]$. This is equal to $1/4 + 3/8$, or $5/8$, which is the total probability of "A white ball will be drawn, given that it is drawn from one of the two jars, each with a probability of 1/2 of being selected, one of which contains 1/2 white balls and the other of which contains 3/4 white balls."

Finally, Bayes's Theorem is applicable only when the prior probability of the hypothesis that is tested is greater than zero. The reason for this becomes clear when we look at the mathematical formulation of the theorem. This limitation does not affect the usefulness of Bayes's Theorem as a model of hypothesis testing because we are not interested in testing totally implausible hypotheses.

We can now assess the fairness of the coin held by the slick gambler. In the following representation of Bayes's Theorem, h represents the hypothesis "The coin is fair," let $\sim h$ (not h) represent the other hypothesis "The coin is unfair," and let e represent the evidence "Four heads appeared in four tosses of the coin." Therefore, $\Pr(h)$ is the prior probability that h is true, and $\Pr(\sim h)$ is the prior probability that $\sim h$ is true. $\Pr(e|h)$ is the likelihood that four heads will appear if the coin is fair, and $\Pr(e|\sim h)$ is the other likelihood. Finally, $\Pr(h|e)$ is the *inverse probability* that we want to calculate—the probability that the coin is fair, given the evidence of four heads appearing in four tosses.

Bayes's Theorem. Assuming that $\Pr(h)$ is not equal to 0

$$\Pr(h|e) = \frac{\Pr(h) \times \Pr(e|h)}{[\Pr(h) \times \Pr(e|h)] + [\Pr(\sim h) \times \Pr(e|\sim h)]}$$

(The probability in the denominator is the total probability for e. This is the probability that four heads will occur, regardless of which hypothesis is true. Also, we can see that if $\Pr(h)$ were zero, then the value on the left would be zero as well.)

Inserting the values for likelihoods and prior probabilities just assigned into this equation gives us

$$\Pr(h|e) = \frac{0.1 \times 0.0625}{[0.1 \times 0.0625] + [0.9 \times 1]} = 0.0068$$

The quantity on the right, called the **posterior probability** of the hypothesis that the coin is fair, is lower than the prior probability of that hypothesis. In other words, after examining the evidence of four heads in a row, the probability that the coin is fair has been reduced from the prior probability of 0.1 to a posterior probability of 0.0068. The hypothesis that the coin is fair is thus disconfirmed.

Exercise Set 8.4

1. Among 300 freshmen attending a small college, 100 are from out of state and 200 are state residents. Cars are owned by 50 of the out-of-state students and by 50 of the state residents.

a. If a student is selected randomly (if each student has an equal probability of being selected), find:

(1) The probability of selecting an out-of-state student without a car.

(2) The probability of selecting a state resident without a car.

(3) The probability of selecting a student with a car.

b. If the student who is selected randomly has a car, find:

(1) The probability that the student is an out-of-state student.

(2) The probability that the student is a state resident.

2. A total of eight points on a pair of dice can be rolled the "hard way" (4-4), or the "easy way" (3-5, 5-3, 2-6, 6-2). Rolling an eight the hard way has a prior probability of 1/36, and rolling an eight the easy way has a prior probability of 4/36. (Can you see why this is so?)

Suppose you know that someone has rolled an eight (this is the evidence), but you did not see the way the dice came up. What is the probability that the eight was rolled the hard way?

3. The object of a game of chance is to draw a white ball blindly from one of two jars, each of which contains 100 balls. One of the jars contains 75 white balls and 25 black balls. The other jar contains 25 white balls and 75 black balls. The outcome of a toss of a fair die determines from which jar the ball is to be drawn. If the die shows a six, the ball is drawn from the jar with 75 white balls. If any other face shows, the ball is drawn from the jar that contains only 25 white balls. Suppose you agree to play the game.

(1) What is the prior probability that you will be able to draw from the jar with 75 white balls?

(2) What is the prior probability that you will have to draw from the jar that contains only 25 white balls?

(3) What is the likelihood that you will draw a white ball if you draw from the jar containing 75 white balls?

(4) What is the likelihood that you will draw a white ball if you must draw from the jar containing only 25 white balls?

(5) What is the total probability that you will draw a white ball (the probability of drawing a white ball no matter which jar is selected)?

(6) Suppose that an opponent plays the game and loses by drawing a black ball. What is the probability that your opponent's ball came from the jar containing 75 white balls and 25 black balls?

4. A candidate for state office has a breakfast meeting at one end of the state and is supposed to appear at an evening dinner in a city at the other end. Her campaign manager goes ahead of her to help with arrangements for the dinner. The candidate plans to fly over in time for the dinner, but her flight is canceled. She figures that if she drives, her chances of arriving on time for the dinner are fifty-fifty (Pr = 0.50). Someone offers to fly her in a small plane, but she loathes small aircraft and is reluctant to accept the offer even though it means that she would be practically certain of of making the dinner that way.

She calls her campaign manager, and he tries to persuade her to accept the small-plane ride. He figures that his arguments had only about a 40 percent chance of winning her over. He goes to the dinner not really expecting to see her and she walks in on time. What is the probability that she took the small plane?

2. Using Bayes's Theorem to Test Hypotheses

In this section, we see how Bayes's Theorem can be used to disconfirm a hypothesis concerning prehistoric agriculture in America: "The diet of people in Ecuador during the Valdivian Phase (sixth century) was based on intensive maize agriculture." The prehistoric beginnings of agriculture are of great interest to anthropologists, and the claim that maize agriculture was practiced at this early date in coastal Ecuador has been strongly defended by some investigators. This hypothesis was also initially plausible because the ecological setting in coastal Ecuador is similar to many other areas in which evidence of early agricultural activity is found. Although in this case—unlike the exercise in which the prior probability of selecting one of the jars depended on the outcome of a toss of a fair die—we have no precise way of assigning a prior probability to the practice of maize agriculture, we do know that the prior probability is rather high, so we will assign 0.7 to it. Then, the prior probability that the diet was not agriculturally based is $1 - 0.7 = 0.3$. Bayes's Theorem formally requires that $\Pr(h)$ be greater than zero, and this is reflected in our informal requirement that the hypothesis be plausible.

Anthropologists learn what prehistoric peoples ate by examining their skeletal teeth. Dental caries (cavities), for example, are most frequent and severe in people whose diets are agriculturally based, less severe in gathering-collecting-hunting peoples, and least severe among strictly meat-eating hunters. (This is an important auxiliary hypothesis.)

The agricultural hypothesis was tested by a physical anthropologist, C. Turner ("Dental Caries and Early Ecuadorian Agriculture," *American Antiquity* 43 (1978):694). His evidence consisted of a sample of 76 teeth recovered from six crania of individuals who had been buried in a Valdivian-period cemetery. These individuals were judged to have lived to an age at which they would be susceptible to caries (another auxiliary hypothesis). Two additional auxiliary hypotheses were stated by Turner:

(i) Maize, as it is usually prepared for eating, has strong cariogenic potential (it clings to the teeth and causes cavities).

(ii) T. D. Stewart's dental pathology review (*American Journal of Anthropology*, 1931) provides a good measure for incidence of dental caries among prehistoric Central American Indians whose diet was agriculturally based. (According to Stewart's review, 15.5 percent of all teeth of these individuals have one or more carious lesions.)

Using the agricultural hypothesis and these auxiliaries, the observable prediction was that in a sample of 76 teeth, approximately 12 (76×0.155) should have had at least one cavity. However, when the teeth were examined, not a single cavity was found on any of the teeth. (This is the evidence *e*.)

Using the expected average of 12 bad teeth in a sample of 76 to determine the likelihood of finding no cavities when our hypothesis is true and making certain assumptions about the randomness of the sample and the normal distribution of cavities in the population, there is only about one chance in 100 of finding no cavities in a sample of 76 teeth: $Pr(e|h) = 0.01$.

Because our auxiliary hypotheses assure us that the incidence of cavities is much lower when the diet is not agriculturally based, let us assign the likelihood of 0.1 to discovering no cavities if the diet is not agriculturally based:

$$Pr(e|\sim h) = 0.1$$

Now we are ready to apply Bayes's Theorem to determine the posterior probability of the hypothesis in light of the evidence:

$$Pr(h|e) \frac{0.7 \times 0.01}{[0.7 \times 0.01] + [0.3 \times 0.1]} = \frac{0.007}{0.037} = 0.19$$

The posterior probability that the diet was agriculturally based during the Valdivian period has been dramatically reduced by this test—from 0.7 to 0.19. The probability that the diet was not agriculturally based (because that is the only alternative) has been correspondingly enhanced—up from 0.3 (its prior probability) to 0.81.

The role of alternative hypotheses, which was not explicit in the first simple formulation of the hypothetico-deductive method, is apparent in Bayesian confirmation. The amount of support that evidence lends to a hypothesis depends on how probable the evidence would be if the hypothesis were false—that is, if some alternative hypothesis were true. To simplify the example, we considered only two alternatives, but we could have treated each alternate hypothesis about subsistence strategy (hunter-gatherer-collector, hunter, and agriculturalist) separately by assigning each one a prior probability and considering the likelihood that the evidence would occur for each case.

Bayes's Theorem helps us to understand why some tests are more valuable for confirming or disconfirming hypotheses than other tests. Finding no cavities is particularly damaging to the agricultural hypothesis because the absence of cavities would be so unlikely if the hypothesis were true. Furthermore, many hypotheses that we would like to test do not deductively imply any observable predictions even when we invoke auxiliary hypotheses. In these cases, it is reasonable to ask how *likely* (or probable) a certain prediction would be if the hypothesis were true or if some alternative hypothesis were true. Bayes's Theorem helps us to see how these *likelihoods* raise or lower posterior probabilities by various amounts. The posterior probability is changed less by an outcome that is likely to occur regardless of whether the hypothesis is true than by an outcome that would be surprising unless the hypothesis were true. Thus, this Bayesian pattern, or model, for arguments of confirmation and disconfirmation seems to capture our insights and intuitions about using the outcomes of predictions to judge whether a hypothesis is true or false.

Exercise Set 8.5

1. Approximately one out of every twenty women in the United States develops breast cancer by age 50. Early detection is important to prevent fatalities. Suppose that doctors develop a screening test that is inexpensive and "noninvasive" (it does not involve X rays or any surgical technique). Although the test apparently does not give false negative readings, studies indicate that it produces a false positive reading 20 percent of the time. When a test is positive, the patient is advised to undergo further testing with X rays. Mrs. Griffen, age 50, has no symptoms but she is considering having the screening test performed.

   (1) What is the prior probability that Mrs. Griffen has breast cancer?

   (2) Suppose that Mrs. Griffen has the test and that the result is positive. What is the posterior probability that she has breast cancer?

2. Suppose you see an announcement that all cars of your make and model are being recalled to correct a suspension problem. These models were produced at two plants: X and Y. You cannot determine which plant produced your model, but plant X produced about 80 percent of the make and model of your car, whereas plant Y produced only 20 percent. The automobile manufacturer estimates that about 90 percent of the models produced by plant Y have the suspension problem but that only 50 percent of the models produced by plant X have this problem.

   (1) What is the probability that the suspension in your car will be defective?

   (2) Suppose you take your car in to be tested and find out that the suspension is defective. What is the probability that your car was produced by plant X?

3. Based on recent statistics, the probability that a smoker who lives in a rural area will die from lung cancer is 0.00065. The probability that a smoker from an urban area will die from lung cancer is 0.00085. The probability that a nonsmoker from an urban area will die of lung cancer is 0.00015, while the probability that a rural nonsmoker will die of lung cancer is 0.00001. Approximately 70 percent of the population live in urban areas, and about 30 percent live in rural areas. Assume that 20 percent of urban dwellers are smokers and that 10 percent of rural dwellers are smokers.

   (1) What is the probability that an urban dweller will die of lung cancer?

   (2) What is the probability that a person from a rural area will die of lung cancer?

   (3) Given only the information that a person died of lung cancer, what is the probability that this person was an urban dweller?

   (4) Given only the information that an urban dweller died of lung cancer, what is the probability that this person was a smoker?

4. A murder has been committed, and the police have brought in two suspects on the basis of circumstantial evidence. The suspects are similar in physical appearance, but one has red hair and the other brown. The police believe that one of the two suspects almost certainly committed the crime, but they think the greater chance (80 percent) is that the redhead, who has a previous record, is guilty. A witness who saw someone running from the scene of the crime says that the person had brown hair, so the brunet is brought to trial. The defense attorney insists that the witness be tested for reliability, and a test is set up. In lighting and other circumstances similar to those in which the crime occurred, the witness is correct about 90 percent of the time in distinguishing redheads from brunets.

(1) Taking the performance of the witness into account and accepting the prior probabilities offered by the police, what is the probability that the brunet is guilty?

(2) If the witness had correctly distinguished the redhead from the brunet in only 50 percent of the test cases, what would be the posterior probability that the brunet is guilty?

5. In the 1980s, an advisory group of the National Cancer Institute turned down a proposal to study the possible link between breast cancer and fat consumption. The proposal was for a 10-year prospective study of women across the country, 10,000 of them on a low-fat diet to see whether their risk of breast cancer was lower than the additional 22,000 women who would form the control group. The reason the panel of experts gave for the turn-down, according to *Science,* was: "The hypothesis that dietary fat is a cause of breast cancer among women is plausible, but only weakly supported at present." Explain, in terms of the Bayesian model of confirmation, why the consideration raised by the expert critics is important.

VII. REVIEW

This chapter introduced the logic of confirmation. The methodology developed here allows statements that are not accessible to direct observation to be inductively supported or undermined by checking the truth or falsity of *observable predictions* based on those claims. In scientific reasoning and in everyday life, confirmation employs deductive arguments as well as inductive arguments, but its overall structure is inductive. Because these arguments offer conclusions that go beyond what is observed, future observations can lead us to reject claims that we currently consider to be highly confirmed.

Several simple formulations of the *hypothetico-deductive method of confirmation* were considered. These were then supplemented by considerations of prior probabilities and recognition of the role of alternative hypotheses to bring them into line with sound scientific practice. Thus supplemented, the hypothetico-deductive method can be viewed as a *Bayesian model of confirmation.* Brief definitions of the key concepts examined in this chapter follow.

Ad hoc reasoning: This fallacious form of reasoning occurs when auxiliary hypotheses are rejected (or brought in) arbitrarily, merely to save a favored hypothesis.

Alternative Hypotheses: Hypotheses that are distinct from the hypothesis being tested, but that could yield the same observable predictions.

Auxiliary Hypotheses: Auxiliary hypotheses are used in conjunction with the hypothesis being tested to derive observable predictions. These claims, not always explicitly stated, are assumed to be true in the context of a test of a hypothesis. Two chief categories of auxiliary hypotheses are: (1) those that claim that the conditions of the experiment or observation are "normal" (that reliable instruments are used by competent observers, and so on), and (2) theoretical auxiliary hypotheses that assume the truth of background theories.

Bayesian Confirmation: A method of confirmation that, like the simpler hypothetico-deductive method, considers the observable predictions derived from the hypothesis and the auxiliary hypotheses. In addition, Bayesian confirmation requires taking into account the prior probabilities not only of the hypothesis being tested but also of the alternative hypotheses. A true prediction confirms one hypothesis, relative to alternatives, if that hypothesis had a higher prior probability than any of the alternative hypotheses. The Bayesian model of confirmation also accommodates observable predictions that follow inductively rather than deductively from the hypothesis and the auxiliary hypotheses. When numerical values can be assigned to the requisite probabilities, *Bayes's Theorem* provides a quantitative model for Bayesian confirmation.

Confirmation: Positive inductive support for hypotheses. "Confirmation" is used in both an *incremental* and an "absolute" sense. Hypotheses are incrementally confirmed by tests that raise their probability. Hypotheses are considered to be "absolutely" confirmed only when they are strongly supported and when no available evidence counts against them. However, it is always possible for "absolutely" confirmed hypotheses to turn out to be false.

Crucial Test: A test that confirms one and disconfirms the other of two plausible but incompatible hypotheses that are the only candidates for acceptance.

Disconfirmation: Inductive support for rejection of a hypothesis. Like "confirmation," "disconfirmation" is used in both an incremental and an "absolute" sense.

Hypothesis: A sentence to be tested by finding a prediction that follows from it and checking the truth of that prediction.

Hypothetico-Deductive Method: A method of testing hypotheses by deriving an observable prediction from the hypothesis along with any auxiliary hypotheses. The simplest version of the method says that if the prediction is true, the hypothesis is confirmed; and if the prediction is false, the hypothesis is disconfirmed. To provide a realistic account of scientific method, the simple version must be supplemented by considerations of initial plausibility of the hypothesis and by how the tested hypothesis compares to alternative hypotheses with the same observable predictions.

Likelihood: The probability of a piece of evidence relative to the truth of some hypothesis. Likelihoods are one of the types of probabilities required for using Bayes's Theorem as a model of confirmation.

Posterior Probability: The probability that a hypothesis is true after taking into account the results of a particular test. When Bayes's Theorem is used as a model of confirmation, the hypothesis is said to be confirmed if the posterior probability is higher than the prior probability, and disconfirmed if the posterior probability is lower than the prior probability.

Prior Probability: The probability of a hypothesis *before* taking into account the results of a particular test or observation.

Exercise Set 8.6

1. Suppose some hypothesis *H* is similar to other well-supported scientific hypotheses and that it does not conflict with any well-confirmed hypotheses. How is this information relevant to the confirmation of *H*?

2. Can prior probabilities be based on objective evidence rather than on personal beliefs about how likely a hypothesis is to be true? Give an example to support your answer.

3. Give an example of a hypothesis that you believe to be false but which can be used as a basis for true predictions. Be sure to say what one of the predictions is.

4. When different alternative hypotheses have the same observable predictions, how can you choose among them?

5. Can true predictions establish conclusively a scientific hypothesis? Explain why or why not.

6. In the hypothetico-deductive method, is the argument from the truth of the observable prediction to the truth of the hypothesis deductive or inductive?

7. Is it usually possible to deduce an observable prediction directly from a scientific hypothesis without any additional assumptions as premisses? Explain why or why not.

8. "No matter how carefully a scientific hypothesis is tested, it may be rejected later in light of the discovery of new evidence." If this sentence is true, does it follow that hypotheses can never be confirmed but can only be disconfirmed or rejected?

9. Is it true that in most cases there is only one scientific hypothesis that is compatible with all the available evidence? Explain your answer.

10. If a hypothesis has a very strong degree of confirmation, do further successful predictions raise its probability very much? Explain why or why not.

11. Is it always possible to construct and carry out a crucial test to determine once and for all which of two competing hypotheses is correct?

12. Are good scientific hypotheses typically nothing more than a summary of the observable evidence on which they rest?

13. When testing a hypothesis, can we simply assume that all of the auxiliary hypotheses required to support the observable prediction are true?

14. Can auxiliary hypotheses ever be tested? Explain.

15. If the prior probability of a hypothesis is zero, then why is it not suitable for testing using the Bayesian method of confirmation?

16. Can a hypothesis have a very low prior probability initially but become strongly confirmed as a result of a single favorable test? Explain.

17. Under what circumstances can a series of favorable tests fail to raise the probability of a hypothesis very much?

18. Suppose that you are taking a course in which you have done well on the midterm exams and homework, and that you studied for the final and thought you did well in that too, but then you receive a "D" when your grade report arrives. Given the hypothesis—"There was an error in the grade report"— what can you say about the hypothesis's prior probability?

19. A Neanderthal skull, pierced at its base and surrounded by a "ring" of stones was found in a cave (Grotta Guattari) near Naples, Italy. This was interpreted as evidence for ritual cannibalism. Can you suggest an alternative hypothesis to account for the condition of the skull and the placement of the stones?

20. You receive a letter from a friend who tells you she won an award for a chemistry project immediately after she consulted a fortune teller who predicted that she would win. You do not believe in fortune telling, and have assigned the hypothesis "The fortune teller has a supernatural ability to predict future events" a very low probability. Discuss the degree to which this successful prediction raises the probability of the hypothesis.

Chapter Nine

ARGUMENTS IN WHICH VALIDITY DEPENDS ON CONNECTIONS AMONG SENTENCES

I. INTRODUCTION

This chapter continues the analysis, begun in Chapter 7, of deductive arguments in which validity depends on *truth-functional* connections among sentences. We have already discussed *affirming the antecedent* (*modus ponens*) and *denying the consequent* (*modus tollens*)—as well as the fallacious forms that mimic these valid forms of inference. Two sentential connectives— expressed by "if . . . then" and "not" in English—are discussed in Chapter 7. The truth-functional sense of "if . . . then" is given in the following table, where "*p*" and "*q*" represent any two sentences:

p	q	If p then q
True	True	True
True	False	False
False	True	True
False	False	True

The table can be summarized by noting that the conditional is true whenever the antecedent is false or the consequent is true.

The truth-functional meaning of negation is given in the following table:

p	Not p
True	False
False	True

The table can be summarized by noting that a negation is false whenever the original sentence is true, and vice versa.

Additional connectives (terms used to form compound sentences)— expressed in English by *or, and,* and *if and only if*—can be assigned truth-functional definitions, thereby allowing a large class of English-language arguments to be analyzed in truth-functional terms. This chapter examines some common forms of truth-functional arguments, as well as a general method for determining the validity or invalidity of *any* argument form in which validity depends on truth-functional connections among sentences.

The area of logic concerned with such intersentential connections is called *truth-functional logic, sentential logic,* or *propositional logic.* It is based on two important principles:

1. Every sentence is either true or false.

2. No sentence is both true and false.

The first principle is called the *principle of the excluded middle;* the second, *the principle of contradiction.* The first principle assures us that a sentence such as "It is raining" is either true or false; the second principle assures us that the sentence "It is raining" cannot be both true and false. These principles apply to sentences in a *specific context of utterance.* For example, the time and place to which the claim "It is raining" refers is either understood or expressed. If this were spelled out explicitly, the sentence would include a reference to the time and place: "Rain is falling on March 15, 1993, at Washington Square in New York City." The sentence "It is raining" is true when it applies to places and times when it is raining, and it is false when it applies to places and times without rain. When the sentence "It is raining" is understood as referring to a particular time or place, the principles of excluded middle and contradiction apply. Some sentences (generalizations) are understood as referring implicitly to all times and all places ("All men are mortal"). Properly understood, the principles of the excluded middle and contradiction seem obvious enough, and we accept them in our study of logic.

1. Hypothetical Syllogisms

Hypothetical syllogisms are made up of two conditional premisses and a conditional conclusion. The antecedent of the conclusion is identical to the antecedent of one of the premisses and the consequent of the conclusion is identical to the consequent of the other premiss. The following argument is an example of a hypothetical syllogism:

If inflation can be controlled, then businesses will expand.
If businesses expand, then unemployment will decrease.

If inflation can be controlled, then unemployment will decrease.

As in the conditional arguments discussed in Chapter 7, the conditional sentences in hypothetical syllogisms are treated as *material conditionals.* The connective "if . . . then" yields a false compound sentence only if the antecedent is true and the consequent is false. The form of this argument can be represented by letting "p," "q," and "r" stand for the antecedents and consequents in the premisses and conclusion, using the same letter for the same component sentence in each case:

If p, then q.
If q, then r.

If p, then r.

If this argument form were *invalid*, it would be possible for the conclusion to be false while both premisses were true. However, this is not possible, because the only way the conclusion could be false would be for p to be true while r is false. But if p is true, then q must also be true for the first premiss to be true. If the second premiss has a true antecedent (q), then its consequent (r) must also be true, or it will not be a true premiss.

In other words, if this form were invalid, and if *p* were true, the sentence represented by *"r"* would have to be categorized as false in the conclusion and as true in the second premise. But no sentence can be both true and false, so the argument form is valid. The hypothetical syllogism concerning inflation control is an instance of this valid form, so it is a valid argument.

In offering proofs of validity, we follow this general procedure: Show that one cannot consistently assign truth and falsity to component sentences in such a way that all the premises are true and the conclusion is false.

2. Dilemmas

In English, the term *dilemma* usually refers to a situation in which a choice between two disagreeable alternatives must be faced ("Tom is in a dilemma; he must either give up the big party weekend or fail some of his midterms next week"). Another meaning of *dilemma* refers to a form of argument in which one of the premises states the choice between the two alternatives. The two meanings are connected, for someone like Tom who is in a dilemma often faces the following sort of argument:

If I spend the weekend partying, then I will fail some midterms.
If I spend the weekend studying, then I will miss out on some good times.
I will party this weekend, or I will study.

I will fail some midterms, or I will miss out on some good times.

This argument is valid. (Remember, for an argument to be valid the premises do not have to be true. If it is impossible for the argument to have all true premises and a false conclusion, then the argument is valid.)

This argument is similar to, but slightly more complicated than, arguments that take the form of "affirming the antecedent." The form of this argument, called the **constructive dilemma,** has two conditional premises. The third premise states that one or the other of the antecedents is true, and the conclusion states that one or the other of the consequents is true. Using letters to represent simple sentences, this form of argument can be symbolized:

If *p*, then *q*.
If *r*, then *s*.
p or *r*.

q or *s*.

The validity of this argument form depends on the truth-functional meanings of the sentential connectives *or* and *if. . . then.* Compound sentences that are connected by *or* are called **disjunctions.** Some disjunctions are **exclusive,** in which case *or* is understood to mean *one or the other, but not both.* When a menu states "Soup or salad is included in the price of the meal," we understand that the disjunction is exclusive. If you want both soup and salad, you must pay extra.

Other disjunctions are **inclusive.** In these sentences, *or* means *one or the other, or possibly both.* When a road sign says "This bridge is open to automobile or truck traffic," we understand that the disjunction is inclusive. The English word *or* is thus ambiguous; it has two distinct meanings. Some languages, such as Latin, have two different words for the two senses of *or.*

For the purpose of analyzing forms of arguments, it is desirable to eliminate ambiguity in the important sentential connectives by agreeing on a single meaning. Logicians have selected the inclusive sense of *or.* The truth-functional meaning of the inclusive *or* is given in the following table, where "*p*" and "*q*" represent any two sentences:

p	*q*	*p* or *q*
True	True	True
True	False	True
False	True	True
False	False	False

The table can be summarized by noting that a disjunction is true whenever one or both of its components (**disjuncts**) is true, and false only when both disjuncts are false.

Now we can see that the constructive dilemma form of argument is valid, for when the truth-functional meanings of *if. . . then* and *or* are adopted, if all the premisses are true, the conclusion will be true as well. For the disjunctive premiss ("*p* or *r*") to be true, at least one of its disjuncts must be true. Then, the conditional premiss that has that disjunct as its antecedent must have a true consequent to be true. But this means that "either *q* or *s*" (the conclusion) is true if all of the premisses are true. The English argument representing Tom's dilemma is valid, because it is an instance of a valid argument form.

Another version of the dilemma, called the destructive dilemma, is closely related to *denying the consequent (modus tollens).*

Example:

If the reporter was doing his job, he was present at the political meeting.
If the reporter is intelligent, he knew what was happening there.
Either the reporter wasn't present at the meeting, or he didn't know what was happening there.

Either the reporter wasn't doing his job, or he isn't intelligent.

The form of this argument is represented:

If *p*, then *q*.
If *r*, then *s*.
Not *q* or not *s*.

Not *p* or not *r*.

This argument form is valid. (You can convince yourself that this is so by analyzing the form in the same way that the constructive dilemma was analyzed.)

In another variation of the dilemma, the antecedent of one of the conditionals (not *p*) is the denial of the antecedent of the other conditional (*p*), and the disjunctive premiss has the form "*p* or not *p*." In ordinary language, an obviously true disjunctive premiss is usually left implicit. In many dilemmas of this type, the conclusion is also unstated.

James Boswell, in his *Journal*, describes such an argument, offered by Pasquale de Paoli, the "George Washington of Corsica," when Paoli was trying to decide whether to marry:

> If he [the commander of a nation] is married, there is a risk that he may be distracted by private affairs and swayed too much by a concern for his family.
>
> If he is unmarried, there is a risk that not having the tender attachments of a wife and children, he may sacrifice all to his ambition.

Can you complete Paoli's dilemma with an appropriate premiss of the form "*p* or not *p*" and a conclusion?

In another variant of the constructive dilemma, both conditionals have the same consequent:

If I win a scholarship, I'll have enough money for tuition.
If I get a part-time job, I'll have enough money for tuition.
I'll win a scholarship, or I'll get a part-time job.

I'll have enough money for tuition.

This obviously valid argument illustrates another feature of dilemmas. Dilemmas can present *attractive* alternatives in the disjunctive premiss. "Happy dilemmas" as well as an unhappy ones can occur.

3. False Dilemmas

When presented with two choices, we often consider the consequences of each and reason about them using one or another of the dilemma forms. When we do so we must be careful not to be misled by this form of reasoning into thinking that the number of alternatives is always limited to two. Suppose, for example, that a young woman has received two proposals of marriage. Suitor A is charming, but lazy and poor; Suitor B is dull but rich. The young woman might construct the following argument:

If I marry A, then I'll be poor.
If I marry B, then I'll be bored.
I must marry A or B.

Therefore, I'll be poor or bored.

If she reasons this way, however, she constructs a false dilemma for herself. First, she can choose not to marry either suitor. Second, she does not have to assume that her own income is determined by her husband's. Alternatively, she could tell the lazy charmer that she'll consider his proposal when he settles down to work, or she could persuade the other suitor to expand his horizons.

4. Disjunctive Syllogisms

In **disjunctive syllogisms,** one of the premisses is a disjunction and the other premiss denies one of the disjuncts. The conclusion affirms the truth of the other disjunct.

Either the home team will win the pennant, or the fans will be unhappy.
The home team will not win the pennant.
_____

The fans will be unhappy.

This argument is an instance of the following valid form:

p or q.
Not p.
_____

q

If the first premiss is true, then at least one of the disjuncts (p, q) must be true. The second premiss says that one of those disjuncts (p) is false. The conclusion simply says that the other disjunct (q) is true, which must be so if both premisses are true.

A variation on the disjunctive syllogism is

p or q.
Not q.
_____

p

In this form, the second disjunct is denied in the second premiss, and the conclusion affirms the truth of the first disjunct.

Because *or* is understood in its inclusive sense, the following argument *form*, which resembles disjunctive syllogism, is *not* valid:

p or q.
p.
_____

Not q.

Because "p or q" is true not only when one of the disjuncts is true but also when both disjuncts are true, affirming the truth of one of the disjuncts in the second premiss does not rule out the truth of the other disjunct. However, the conclusion in this argument form states that the other disjunct is false.

Nevertheless, the following English-language argument is valid:

Joshua either failed the exam, or he passed it.
Joshua failed the exam.
_____

Joshua did not pass the exam.

In this argument, *or* is clearly understood as exclusive, because it is impossible for Joshua to both fail and pass the same exam. However, because we have agreed to use *or* only in its inclusive sense, we cannot represent the form that demonstrates the validity of this argument unless we find another way to express the meaning of the exclusive *or*. We could do this by introducing a *new* connective (we could call it "eor"):

p	*q*	*p* or *q*
True	True	False
True	False	True
False	True	True
False	False	False

This table can be summarized by noting that an exclusive disjunction is true only when one of its disjuncts is true and the other is false.

It is possible, however, to use *or, and,* and *not* in the following way to express *or* in its exclusive sense:

p or *q*, and not both *p* and *q*.

The valid form that the English argument instantiates is:

p or *q*, and not both *p* and *q*.
p.
_____

Not *q*.

(The meaning of *and,* another important truth-functional connective, is discussed in the next section.)

A fallacy similar to **false dilemma** arises when disjunctive premises in these syllogisms rule out legitimate alternatives. Suppose, for example, that you want to buy a car. The owner wants a thousand dollars in cash, and you have only $500. You could argue:

Either I come up with $1000 or I can't get the car.
I can't come up with $1000.
_____

Therefore I can't have the car.

Although this argument is formally valid, the first premiss probably does not represent all the available options. Perhaps you could persuade the owner to arrange terms that would allow you to pay $500 down and the rest later. Perhaps the owner is willing to lower the price for a quick sale. The mistake of looking only at the two extremes when intermediate alternatives are available is sometimes called **the fallacy of black-and-white thinking** (see Chapter 1).

Exercise Set 9.1

>Which of the valid argument forms or fallacies discussed in this section best characterizes each of the following English-language arguments?

1. If Roxanne knew that Cyrano spoke to her, she would have fallen in love with him. If she had fallen in love with Cyrano, Christian would have been disappointed. So, Christian would have been disappointed if Roxanne knew that Cyrano was speaking.

2. If stocks go up, bonds go down. If interest rates rise, bonds go down. Therefore, because stocks or interest rates will go up, bonds will go down.

3. Tina has volleyball scholarship offers at State University and at Smalltown College, one of which she'll accept. But she certainly won't take the offer at Smalltown, so she'll go to State University.

4. To pass a logic class, you must work exercises. To get a degree, you must pass a logic class. So if you intend to get a degree, you should do your logic exercises.

5. If the team wins next week, they'll go to the bowl game. If the team ties next week, they'll win the conference championship. But they will either win or tie next week, so they'll go to the bowl game or win the conference championship.

6. Either you buy a lottery ticket for the school library fund, or you care nothing about the library. But surely you care about the library, so you'll buy a lottery ticket.

7. If your lottery ticket wins you'll receive a good book for a prize; if your lottery ticket loses, you'll be supporting the school library fund. So either way, you'll get something good for your ticket.

8. If I stay up late to cram for the exam, I'll do poorly because I am so tired. If I don't stay up late to cram, I'll do poorly because I haven't read the material. So it looks like I'll do poorly on the exam.

9. If I keep up my studies during the term, I won't have to cram for the final exam. If I don't have to cram for the final, I'll do well on it. So if I keep up my studies during the term, I'll do well on the final.

10. Either extraterrestrial visitors have landed in the United States or the honest people who have reported seeing them are liars. But these people are not liars, so the extraterrestrial visitors must have landed in the United States.

11. If global warming continues during the next 50 years, glaciers and polar ice caps will begin to melt. If glaciers and polar ice caps begin to melt, sea levels will rise by several feet, pushing Florida's coast inland by 1,000 feet. So if global warming continues, Florida's coast will move inland.

12. Either people must forgo such amenities as personal automobiles, air conditioning, and consumption of large quantities of beef, or global warming will continue. But people are not willing to forgo their present lifestyles, so global warming will be a fact of life.

II. SYMBOLIZING CONNECTIVES

When validity is treated as a matter of logical form, symbols can be used to represent logical operations, such as negation, disjunction, and conjunction. This simplifies writing argument forms, and reminds us that the truth-functional meanings of such expressions as *if . . . then, or,* and the other connectives are considerably more restricted than the meanings of these terms in ordinary language. The following symbols are used to represent truth-functional connectives:

1. *Arrow* ($\rightarrow$): The connective *if . . . then* is represented by a $\rightarrow$ (called an "arrow") between two sentences. The arrow connects the antecedent and the consequent of a conditional sentence.

2. *Tilde* ($\sim$): The connective *not* is represented by a $\sim$ preceding the sentence that is negated. The tilde forms the negation of a sentence.

3. *Wedge* (v): The connective *or* is represented by a v between two sentences. The wedge connects two disjuncts in a disjunction.

4. Dot ($\cdot$): The connective *and* is represented by a $\cdot$ between two sentences. The dot connects two conjuncts in a conjunction.

In ordinary English, a conjunction with two conjuncts, such as "John went to the movies, and Mary played racquetball," is true just in case both conjuncts are true. Otherwise, it is false. This is the logically important feature of a conjunction, and it expresses the whole of the truth-functional meaning of *and*, as shown in the following table, in which "True" and "False" are represented by "T" and "F":

p	*q*	*p* $\cdot$ *q*
T	T	T
T	F	F
F	T	F
F	F	F

In English, other words, such as *also, but, furthermore, moreover,* and *while,* as well as semicolons, are used to form conjunctions. These terms, also called *conjunctions,* differ in connotation. For example, *but* and *while* suggest a con- *trast* between the two sentences that are conjoined ("Jane won the election, but John lost"). *And* sometimes connotes *temporal succession* in the sense of *and then* in addition to its conjunctive force ("Rosie finished the marathon and went to a dance that night"). As with the other logical connectives, however these rhetorical subtleties are ignored to concentrate on the logical force of conjunction as it affects the validity of arguments. The preceding table, called a **truth table,** assigns an unambiguous meaning to the dot symbol by stating conditions under which sentence forms connected by the dot are true or false. The following three truth tables completely define the other truth-functional connectives introduced thus far:

p	~*p*		*p*	*q*	*p* → *q*		*p*	*q*	*p* ∨ *q*
T	F		T	T	T		T	T	T
F	T		T	F	F		T	F	T
			F	T	T		F	T	T
			F	F	T		F	F	F

The tilde, or negation sign, is regarded as a **connective,** even though it does not connect two sentences. Negation is a "unary" connective; the other connectives are "binary." Because every negated sentence contains another sentence (the sentence that is negated), a negated sentence fits the definition of a "compound sentence."

One other truth-functional connective—the **material biconditional**—is used. In English, the expression closest in meaning to this connective is *if and only if.* The sentence "The roof leaks if and only if it is raining" means that if the roof leaks, then it is raining *and* if it is raining, the roof leaks. Thus, the material biconditional is equivalent to the conjunction of two material condi- tionals, in which the antecedent of one is the consequent of the other, and vice versa. Accordingly, we could use the arrow and the dot to express this relationship: "(*p* → *q*) • (*q* → *p*)." The left conjunct represents "*p* only if *q*," and the right conjunct represents "*p* if *q*." However, the relationship repre- sented by the material biconditional is common enough in argumentation to use a special symbol (double arrow) to denote it. The truth table for the mater- ial biconditional is:

p	*q*	*p* ↔ *q*
T	T	T
T	F	F
F	T	F
F	F	T

A material biconditional states that two sentences have the same truth value. It is true when both components are true and when both components are false; otherwise, a material biconditional is false.

III. SYMBOLIZING ENGLISH SENTENCES

To analyze English-language arguments in which validity apparently depends on truth-functional connections between sentences, lower-case italic letters ("*p*," "*q*," "*r*," "*s*," and so on) are used to denote simple sentences, and the symbols →, •, v, ~, and ↔ are used to denote truth-functional connectives. When arguments are symbolized, the resulting expressions are argument forms.

Sentence forms are symbolic expressions that consist of a single letter or letters (for sentences) connected in an appropriate way by logical symbols (for connectives). The relationship between sentence forms and English sentences is analogous to the relationship between argument forms and English-language arguments.

In addition to letters and symbols for connectives, some form of punctuation is necessary to avoid ambiguity in sentence forms. In English, various punctuation marks (for example, commas, dashes, semicolons) serve to eliminate ambiguity. Various special terms in English, such as *either, neither*, and *both*, also perform this function. The logical symbolism used here has just one form of punctuation—parentheses—which function as they do in arithmetic and algebra.

For example, the expression

$$7 + 5 \times 3$$

is ambiguous, because one value (36) is obtained when 7 is added to 5 and then multiplied by 3, and a different value (22) is obtained when 7 is added to the product of 5 and 3. When the expression is written

(1) $$7 + (5 \times 3)$$

the value is clearly 22. When the expression is written

(2) $$(7 + 5) \times 3$$

the value is 36. Parentheses indicate which expressions belong together and which arithmetic operations to perform first. To determine a numerical value for an expression, we perform the operation *within* parentheses first and the operation that is indicated by the *main connective* last. Parentheses indicate that the sign for addition in expression (1) and the sign for multiplication in expression (2) are the main connectives. In a similar way, parentheses indicate the main connective in sentence forms, indicating whether the sentence form in question is a conditional, a disjunction, a conjunction, a biconditional, or a negation.

The following examples illustrate how parentheses are used in translating English sentences into formal symbolism.

1. Either Andretti won the race and the prize money is large, or his backers will not be happy.

> p : Andretti won the race.
>
> q : The prize money is large.
>
> r : His backers will be happy.

(1) $\qquad\qquad\qquad\qquad (p \cdot q) \text{ v } {\sim}r$

In the English sentence, *either* serves to group together the components that precede *or*. Both *either* and the comma prevent us from understanding the sentence in the following way:

(2) $\qquad\qquad\qquad p \cdot (q \text{ v } {\sim}r)$ (incorrect translation)

As in the numerical example involving addition and multiplication, a difference in the placement of parentheses can make a difference to the truth value assigned to the compound sentence. Suppose that "p" is false, "q" is true, and "r" is false. Then "${\sim}r$" is true. Because (1) is a disjunction (a wedge "v" is the main connective) with a true disjunct, (1) is true. However, (2) is a conjunction (its main connective is •), and the first conjunct (p) is false. With the same assignment of truth values to the sentence letters, (1) is true and (2) is false.

2. Neither rain nor sleet can keep the postman away, but only Superman could deliver mail in this snowstorm.

> p: Rain can keep the postman away.
>
> q: Sleet can keep the postman away.
>
> r: Only Superman could deliver mail in this snowstorm.

$$ {\sim}(p \text{ v } q) \cdot r $$

In this sentence, *neither* and the comma indicate that the main connective is *but*, which is a conjunction. "*Neither* rain nor sleet can keep the postman away" has the same meaning as

(1) "It is not the case that either rain can keep the postman away or sleet can keep the postman away," or symbolically,

$$ {\sim}(p \text{ v } q) $$

Alternatively, the *neither . . . nor* could be rendered

(2) "Rain cannot keep the postman away and sleet cannot keep the postman away," or symbolically,

$$\sim p \cdot \sim q$$

We see that expressions (1) and (2) are equivalent by examining the following truth table:

			(1)			(2)
p	*q*	$(p \lor q)$	$\sim(p \lor q)$	$\sim p$	$\sim q$	$\sim p \cdot \sim q$
T	T	T	F	F	F	F
T	F	T	F	F	T	F
F	T	T	F	T	F	F
F	F	F	T	T	T	T

In this truth table, as in all standard truth tables, the initial columns display all possible truth values of the relevant sentence letters. The only sentence letters in this truth table are "*p*" and "*q*." The third column displays the truth value of "*p* ∨ *q*" for each combination of truth values of the sentence letters. The fourth column displays the values of "∼(*p* ∨ *q*)." The values in this column are opposite to the values in the preceding column because ∼ turns true sentences into false ones, and vice versa. The fifth and sixth columns display values of the negation of *p* (opposite to values in the first column) and the negation of *q* (opposite to values in the second column), respectively. The final column, which is identical to the ∼(*p* ∨ *q*)-column, gives the values of the conjunction of ∼*p* and ∼*q*. Thus, the table shows that whatever values are assigned to the sentence letters "*p*" and "*q*," expressions (1) and (2) always have the same truth value. When this relationship holds between two sentence forms, the forms are said to be **logically equivalent.**

The logical equivalence of the preceding expressions (1) and (2) is an example of **De Morgan's Laws.** The logician Augustus De Morgan (1806–1871) pointed out important similarities between some aspects of logic and ordinary algebra. The laws that bear his name can be stated in English:

1. The negation of a conjunction is logically equivalent to the disjunction of the negations of the conjuncts.

2. The negation of a disjunction is logically equivalent to the conjunction of the negations of the disjuncts.

3. The conjunction of two sentences is logically equivalent to the negation of the disjunction of their negations.

4. The disjunction of two sentences is logically equivalent to the negation of the conjunction of their negations.

In symbols, the laws can be expressed succinctly:

1. "~(p • q)" is logically equivalent to "~p v ~q"

2. "~(p v q)" is logically equivalent to "~p • ~q"

3. "p • q" is logically equivalent to "~(~p v ~q)"

4. "p v q" is logically equivalent to "~(~p • ~q)"

Exercise Set 9.2

Part One. Translate each of the following English sentences into a sentence form that most nearly captures the meaning of the English sentence, using the suggested sentence letters and their assigned interpretations. Be sure to use parentheses when necessary to prevent ambiguity.

p: Logic is easy.

q: Logic is fun.

r: Symbols can be used.

1. Logic is fun, but symbols cannot be used. Q & ~R
2. Logic is not easy unless symbols can be used. ~~~ If ~R ~?
3. Logic is fun only if symbols can be used. Q → R
4. Logic is easy, and logic is fun if symbols can be used. P • (r→q)
5. Logic is not fun if symbols can't be used. ~R → ~Q
6. Symbols can be used, or it is not the case that logic is easy.
7. Logic is fun if and only if it is easy.
8. Logic is neither easy nor fun.
9. It isn't true that symbols cannot be used.
10. Logic isn't easy if and only if symbols can't be used.
11. Logic is fun, but it isn't easy.
12. Logic is easy; moreover, it is fun.
13. Either symbols can be used, or logic is easy but not fun.
14. Logic is easy, and if symbols can be used, it is fun.
15. Symbols can be used, but logic is neither easy nor fun.

Part Two. Using the preceding interpretations for "p," "q," and "r," translate the following sentence forms into English sentences:

1. p • ~r
2. ~(p • r)

3. $\sim(q \vee r)$

4. $q \leftrightarrow \sim r$

5. $p \cdot (\sim r \rightarrow q)$

6. $(p \vee q) \cdot \sim(p \cdot q)$

7. $r \rightarrow (p \rightarrow q)$

8. $(r \cdot p) \rightarrow q$

9. $q \cdot (p \leftrightarrow q)$

10. $(q \rightarrow r) \cdot (r \rightarrow q)$

Part Three. Construct a truth table to show that the expressions "$p \leftrightarrow q$" and "$(p \rightarrow q) \cdot (q \rightarrow p)$" are logically equivalent. This will be a four-row truth table, similar to that showing the logical equivalence of "$\sim(p \vee q)$" and "$\sim p \cdot \sim q$." Be sure to include separate columns for "$p \rightarrow q$" and "$q \rightarrow p$."

Part Four. Construct a truth table to to compare each of the following pairs of sentences, and indicate whether the two members of each pair are logically equivalent to one another.

1. $p \rightarrow q, q \rightarrow p$

2. $p \rightarrow \sim q, \sim(p \rightarrow q)$

3. $p \rightarrow q, \sim(p \cdot \sim q)$

4. $p \rightarrow q, \sim p \vee q$

5. $(p \vee \sim p) \vee r, r$

6. $(p \rightarrow (q \rightarrow p)), (p \vee \sim p)$

IV. DETERMINING THE TRUTH VALUES OF COMPOUND SENTENCE FORMS

The truth values of compound sentence forms that are made up of simple sentences joined by truth-functional connectives can be determined on the basis of the truth values of the component simple sentences. Consider the following examples of sentence forms, when it is known that "p" is true, "q" is true, "r" is false, and "s" is false.

1. "$r \rightarrow (p \cdot q)$" is true.

This sentence form is a conditional with a simple (noncompound) sentence as the antecedent, and a conjunction as the consequent. Because its antecedent is false, it is a true conditional. We do not need to consider the truth value of the consequent, because any conditional with a false antecedent is true.

2. "$(p \vee r) \rightarrow (q \vee s)$" is true.

This sentence form is a conditional with a disjunction as its antecedent and another disjunction as its consequent. The antecedent has a true disjunct (p), so it is true. The consequent also has a true disjunct (q), so it is true. A conditional with a true antecedent and a true consequent is true.

3. "$p \cdot (r \vee q)$" is true.

This sentence form is a conjunction. Its first conjunct is a simple sentence (p), with a true value. Its other conjunct is a disjunction with one true disjunct (q), so this conjunct is also true. The conjunction of two true sentences is true.

4. "$(p \cdot r) \vee s$" is false.

This sentence form is a disjunction. Its second disjunct is a simple sentence with a false value. Its first disjunct is a conjunction with one false conjunct (r), so the conjunction is false. Thus, the disjunction has two false disjuncts and is false.

5. "$p \leftrightarrow \sim q$" is false.

This sentence form is a material biconditional. One of its components is a simple sentence (p) that is true. Its other component is the negation of a true sentence, so that component is false. Thus, the two components of the biconditional have different truth values, and the biconditional is false.

The general method for determining the truth values of compound sentence forms is to work from the innermost parentheses out, considering the sentences connected by the main connective last of all.

Exercise Set 9.3

Suppose that "p" is true, "q" is false, "r" is true, and "s" is false. What is the truth value (T or F) of each of the following compound sentence forms?

1. $p \vee q$
2. $q \vee s$
3. $p \cdot (q \vee \sim q)$
4. $(p \cdot q) \vee (r \cdot s)$
5. $(p \cdot r) \vee (q \cdot s)$
6. $p \rightarrow s$
7. $p \rightarrow (s \rightarrow r)$
8. $p \rightarrow (r \rightarrow s)$
9. $(p \cdot s) \rightarrow r$
10. $\sim(r \cdot s)$
11. $r \rightarrow (p \rightarrow (q \vee s))$
12. $r \cdot (q \rightarrow p)$
13. $\sim(r \vee s)$

14. $q \leftrightarrow s$

15. $(q \leftrightarrow r) \rightarrow p$

16. $p \rightarrow (q \rightarrow p)$

17. $(q \vee \sim q) \rightarrow p$

V. DETERMINING THE VALIDITY OR INVALIDITY OF ARGUMENT FORMS

Truth tables are used to prove the validity or invalidity of argument forms. Because every valid argument in which validity depends essentially on truth-functional connectives is an instance of a valid truth-functional *argument form*, the truth-table method provides an indirect test of validity for truth-functional *arguments* in English. Consider the following argument:

> If primitive peoples did not cross the Pacific Ocean, there would not be a strong resemblance between Polynesian artifacts and South American artifacts. But there is a strong resemblance, so primitive peoples did cross the Pacific.

Assume that sentence letters "p" and "q" are interpreted in the following way:
p: Primitive peoples crossed the Pacific Ocean.
q: There is a strong resemblance between Polynesian artifacts and South American artifacts.
Then the English-language argument is an instance of the following argument form:

$\sim p \rightarrow \sim q$
q
_____
p

To prove the validity of this form (and the argument that is an instance of the form), we construct a four-row truth table to display all possible combinations of the truth values of the component simple sentences (p, q):

(1)	(2)	(3)	(4)	(5)
p	q	$\sim p$	$\sim q$	$\sim p \rightarrow \sim q$
T	T	F	F	T
T	F	F	T	T
F	T	T	F	F
F	F	T	T	T

In addition to the two initial columns, others are provided for each premiss and the conclusion of the argument. Additional columns for compound sentence forms that are components of the premisses or the conclusion may also be included. (In this case, a column is provided for ~*p* and one for ~*q*. With these additional columns, the truth value of "~*p* → ~*q*" can be determined by looking at just those columns.)

To check the validity or invalidity of the argument form, look at the premiss columns (5) and (2) and the conclusion column (1). Notice any *rows* in which the premisses are true. (The first row is the only row in which both premisses are true.) Now check that row (or rows) to see whether the conclusion is true as well. If the conclusion is true in each row in which *all* the premisses are true, then the argument form is valid. If in some row the premisses are all true but the conclusion is false, then the argument form is invalid. The preceding argument form is valid. In the first row, the only row in which all the premisses are true, the conclusion is true as well.

Because a truth table displays all *possible* combinations of truth values of the premisses and conclusion, an examination of the truth table settles the question of whether it is *possible* for an argument in that form to have all true premisses and a false conclusion. By definition, an argument (also, an argument form) is valid if it is not possible for it to have all true premisses and a false conclusion.

Here is another example of an argument in English that can be tested by the truth-table method:

> If we drive nonstop to New York, we'll need at least two days to recover; for if we drive nonstop we'll be on the road for 24 hours, and if that happens we'll need at least two days to recover from the trip.

The conclusion is stated at the beginning of the argument, which is an instance of **hypothetical syllogism.** Assign sentence letters "*p*," "*q*," and "*r*" the following interpretations:

p: We drive nonstop to New York.
q: We'll be on the road for 24 hours.
r: We'll need at least two days to recover from the trip.

Then the argument is an instance of the following form:

$$p \to q$$
$$\underline{q \to r}$$
$$p \to r$$

This argument form contains three distinct sentence letters, so an eight-row truth table is required to display all possible combinations of their truth values. (In general, a table of 2^n rows is required when there are *n* distinct sentence letters.) In addition to the three initial columns for the sentence letters "*p*," "*q*," and "*r*," the truth table contains a column for each premiss and a column for the conclusion:

(1)	(2)	(3)	(4)	(5)	(6)
p	q	r	$p \rightarrow q$	$q \rightarrow r$	$p \rightarrow r$
T	T	T	T	T	T
T	T	F	T	F	F
T	F	T	F	T	T
T	F	F	F	T	F
F	T	T	T	T	T
F	T	F	T	F	T
F	F	T	T	T	T
F	F	F	T	T	T

In this truth table, columns (4) and (5) display truth values of the premisses, and column (6) displays the truth values of the conclusion. Both premisses are true in the first, fifth, seventh, and eighth rows. The conclusion is true as well in these rows. Thus, no row contains all true (T) premisses and a false (F) conclusion. This argument form is valid, and so is any English-language argument that is an instance of this form.

Truth tables can also be used to demonstrate the invalidity of argument forms. The invalidity of **affirming the consequent,** a fallacious argument form, is demonstrated in the following table:

(1)	(2)	(3)
p	q	$p \rightarrow q$
T	T	T
T	F	F
F	T	T
F	F	T

Here, the premisses are given in columns (2) and (3) and the conclusion is given in column (1). Notice that in this truth table, as in many others, the initial columns do "double duty." One of the sentence letters is a premiss, and the other is the conclusion. In Row 3, both premisses are true but the conclusion is false. The table thus shows that it is possible for an argument of this form to have all true premisses and a false conclusion.

Although the truth-table method can prove the invalidity of an argument *form,* we should remember that such a proof does *not* show that any English-language argument that is an instance of the form is invalid. Because not all valid arguments are valid truth-functional arguments, the English argument may be an instance of some other valid form. (Some valid forms, for example, depend on *intrasentence* connections rather than on *intersentence* connections.) To prove that an argument is invalid, it must be shown either that the argument could have all true premisses and a false conclusion or that the argument is not an instance of any valid argument form.

Indirect arguments, also called **proofs by contradiction,** which are discussed in Chapter 3, can be analyzed by using truth tables. Indirect arguments proceed by taking as a premiss the denial of the claim to be proved, and then showing that from this follows either the denial of the assumed premiss (which is the conclusion to be established), or some obviously false sentence, or even an outright contradiction. (In Latin, this type of argument is called *reductio ad absurdum.*) If a valid argument leads to an absurdity, then it must contain at least one false premiss.

As mentioned in Chapter 3, in ordinary language, the premiss that denies the conclusion in an indirect argument is frequently supported by an opponent but rejected by the person constructing the argument. Indirect argument is a powerful method of proof in mathematics. Students of higher mathematics encounter this method frequently and recognize that assuming the denial of what they are supposed to prove provides a convenient starting point for constructing many a proof.

Example

To prove that the square root of two is not a positive integer: Suppose that the square root of two is a positive integer. If the square root of two is a positive integer, then there must be a positive integer smaller than two, which when multiplied by itself is equal to two. But this cannot be so because the only positive integer smaller than two is one, and one times one is equal to one. Therefore, the square root of two is not a positive integer.

This argument can be understood as an instance of the following form

$$p$$
$$p \rightarrow q$$
$$\sim q$$
$$\overline{\sim p}$$

The first premiss is "The square root of two is a positive integer." This is the antecedent of the second (conditional premiss). The conditional premiss, with a consequent represented by q is true by definition. The third premiss, which is obviously true, denies the consequent of the conditional. But the conclusion of the argument is a sentence that contradicts the first premiss, and so that premiss is rejected as false. The following truth table shows that the argument form is valid:

(1)	(2)	(3)	(4)	(5)
p	q	$\sim p$	$\sim q$	$p \rightarrow q$
T	T	F	F	T
T	F	F	T	F
F	T	T	F	T
F	F	T	T	T

Columns (1), (4), and (5) are premiss columns, and column (3) is the conclusion. In this truth table—unlike the others we have considered so far—there are NO rows in which all the premisses are true. Although this may seem to invalidate the form, in fact it guarantees its validity. If there are no rows in which all of the premisses are true, then there can be no rows in which all the premisses are true and the conclusion is false! There are no rows in which all the premisses are true because the premisses contradict one another; at least one of the premisses must be false. Because the purpose of this argument is to show that the first premiss—which denies the conclusion—is false, this should not be surprising. Any argument in which it is *impossible* for all of the premisses to be true is valid, for in such arguments, it is automatically impossible for all of the premisses to be true and the conclusion to be false.

When proof by contradiction has more than one premiss, the argument might not indicate *which* of the premisses is false, only that at least one of them must be false. The preceding valid argument points to the first premiss as false because the other premisses are obviously true. In some proofs by contradiction, disputes arise concerning the source of trouble in the premisses. The method of proof by contradiction does not provide the answer to this problem.

Exercise Set 9.4

> Part One. Use truth tables to determine the validity or invalidity of each of the following argument forms. Be sure to say whether the form is valid or invalid.

1. $p \cdot q$
   p
   $\underline{{\sim}p \lor {\sim}q}$
   q

2. $(p \lor q) \rightarrow (p \cdot q)$
   $\underline{p \cdot q}$
   $p \lor q$

3. $(p \lor q) \rightarrow (p \cdot q)$
   $\underline{{\sim}(p \lor q)}$
   $p \cdot q$

4. $p \rightarrow q$
   $\underline{{\sim}(q \lor r)}$
   ${\sim}p$

5. $p \rightarrow q$
   $\underline{p \rightarrow {\sim}q}$
   ${\sim}p$

6. $p \rightarrow q$
   $\underline{\sim p \rightarrow q}$
   q

7. $\underline{p}$
   $p \vee q$

8. $p \rightarrow (q \rightarrow r)$
   $\underline{q \rightarrow (r \rightarrow s)}$
   $p \rightarrow s$

Part Two. Using sentence letters and connective symbols, symbolize the following arguments and construct truth tables to decide whether the resulting argument forms are valid or invalid.

1. Either the game has been sold out, or it has been canceled. If it's been sold out I won't be able to see it, and if it's been canceled I won't be able to see it. So I won't be able to see the game.

2. Either Jeremy won a scholarship, or he borrowed money for tuition. But he hasn't borrowed money. Therefore, Jeremy won a scholarship.

3. If it doesn't rain for two weeks in June, the garden will fail. If the garden fails, we won't have fresh tomatoes in July. So if it doesn't rain for two weeks in June, we won't have fresh tomatoes in July.

4. If the public is very interested in a sport like baseball, they'll pay plenty to see the games. The public does pay a lot to see baseball, so the public is very interested in baseball.

5. Professional baseball players can command big salaries, and they could do so only if the public supported them strongly. So the public strongly supports professional baseball players.

6. If I buy a new car, I'll be broke (because of the insurance payments). But if I buy an older car, I'll be broke (because of the cost of keeping it in shape). I must buy either a new car or an older car, so I'll be broke.

Part Three. Reconstruct the following arguments as truth functional arguments, using appropriate symbols, and following special instructions when indicated.

1. The following passage occurs in Sophocles's play *Antigone*. Antigone has admitted burying her brother, against the tyrant Creon's orders, and has been sentenced to death. Reconstruct her argument.

Antigone: This punishment will not be any pain.
Only if I had let my mother's son
Lie there unburied, then I could not have borne it.
This I can bear.

2. Reconstruct the following argument from *Les Liaisons Dangereuses* (C. de Laclos, translated by P. W. K. Stone):

> Either you have a rival or you don't. If you have one you must set out to please, so as to be preferred to him; if you don't have one you must still please so as to obviate the possibility of having one. In either case the same principle is to be followed: so why torment yourself?

3. Reconstruct the following argument of Bertrand Russell, using truth-functional connectives, and the suggested interpretations of sentences:

> In England under the blasphemy laws it is illegal to express disbelief in the Christian religion. It is also illegal to teach what Christ taught on the subject of non-resistance. [Therefore], whoever wishes to avoid being a criminal must profess to agree with Christ's teaching, but must avoid saying what that teaching was.

p: You express disbelief in the Christian religion.

q: You break the law.

r: You teach what Christ taught on the subject of nonresistance.

4. Consider the following passage from George Eliot's *Middlemarch*:

> Poor Mr. Casaubon was distrustful of everybody's feelings toward him, especially as a husband. To let anyone suppose that he was jealous would be to admit their (suspected) view of his disadvantages; to let them know that he did not find marriage particularly blissful would imply his conversion to their (probably) earlier disapproval. . . . All through his life Mr. Casaubon had been trying not to admit even to himself the inward sores of self-doubt and jealousy.
>
> Thus Mr. Casaubon remained proudly, bitterly silent.

Try to cast Mr. Casaubon's reasoning into argument form, stating the premises and the conclusion. Then select sentence letters, with appropriate interpretations, and construct the argument form that this argument fits. Use a truth table to test the validity of the form.

5. Consider the following argument from K. S. Shrader-Frechette's *Nuclear Power and Public Policy*:

> Now either nuclear power is safe and catastrophic accidents are impossible, in which case no limit on liability is needed to protect the nuclear industry from bankruptcy or on the other hand, nuclear power is not safe and catastrophic accidents are possible, in which case a limit on liability is needed to protect the nuclear industry from bankruptcy. If the limitation is needed, it can only be so because successful claims can be made against the industry. But successful claims can be made against the industry only when injury can be shown to be the result of a nuclear accident. And if

this can be shown, nuclear power is not safe. Hence one cannot argue consistently, both that there is a need for a limit on nuclear liability and that nuclear reactors are safe.

(1) Represent the form of this argument, using the following interpretations of sentences:

   p: Nuclear power is safe.

   q: Catastrophic accidents are possible.

   r: A limit on liability is needed to protect the nuclear industry from bankruptcy.

   s: Successful claims can be made against the industry.

   t: Injury can be shown to be the result of a nuclear accident.

(2) How many rows are there in the truth table for this argument form?

6. On the basis of the following passage from Beryl Markham's *West with the Night*, can you construct a truth-functional argument for the conclusion that elephants dispose of their dead in secret burial grounds? What is the form of the argument?

> There is a legend that elephants dispose of their dead in secret burial grounds and that none of these has ever been discovered. In support of this, there is only the fact that the body of an elephant, unless he had been trapped or shot in his tracks, has rarely been found. What happens to the old and diseased?

7. Regarding the use of compost, which would have to be applied at the rate of 100,000 pounds per acre instead of granular fertilizer, at a rate of 100 pounds per acre:

> If the compost were put down after planting, many seeds would be too deep for the plants to grow. If the compost were spread before planting, seeds would be planted in the compost alone and, because of the low water retention of most compost, many seeds would not generate.
>
> The only solution would be to work the compost into the soil. In order to qualify for federal subsidies, minimum tillage or no-till practice must be observed (that is, farmers are no longer allowed to plow their fields). Consequently, regulations must be revised before farmers will consider using compost.
>
> —Andrew C. Baumert (letter to *Science News* 9/18/93)

Reconstruct Baumert's argument contained in the preceding passage, using the following symbols:

   p : Compost is put on top of soil after planting.

   q : Plants can grow.

    r : Seeds can germinate.

    s : Compost can be tilled into the soil.

    t : Farmers will consider using compost.

    u : Government regulations are revised.

8. I reasoned, however, as follows

(1) either Kenneth is deeply and sincerely attached to Ned or he is not;

(2) if he is not so attached, then my pursuit of Ned will cause him no distress;

(3) if he is so attached, then either the attachment is reciprocal or it is not;

(4) if it is reciprocal, Ned will reject my advances and my pursuit of him will accordingly cause Kenneth no distress;

(5) if it is not reciprocal, Kenneth will suffer distress whether or not I pursue Ned;

(6) if Kenneth will suffer distress whether I pursue Ned or not, my pursuit of Ned cannot be the cause of Kenneth's distress;

(7) it is therefore logically impossible for my pursuit of Ned to cause Kenneth distress.

                                —Sarah Caudwell, *Thus Was Adonis Murdered*

VI. TAUTOLOGIES, SELF-CONTRADICTIONS, AND CONTINGENT SENTENCES

Some sentences have the interesting property of being true on the basis of their truth-functional structure alone. One example is "If it is snowing, then it is snowing." This sentence is an instance of the form "$p \rightarrow p$," and although it is apparently about the weather, its truth does not depend on what the weather is. Sentences that have this structural property are called **tautologies.** Truth tables can be used to determine whether sentence forms are tautologous. If the column under the sentence form contains only T's, that sentence form is tautologous. If a sentence is an instance of a tautologous sentence form, then that sentence is a tautology.

    Some truth tables of tautologous sentence forms follow:

1.

p	$p \rightarrow p$
T	T
F	T

This truth table shows that "$p \rightarrow p$" is a tautology. Any English conditional in which the antecedent and the consequent are identical is an instance of this tautologous form.

2.

p	$\sim p$	$p \vee \sim p$
T	F	T
F	T	T

Any English sentence that is a disjunction with two disjuncts, one of which is the denial of the other, is an instance of this tautologous form. Examples are:

(1) It is snowing or it is not snowing.

(2) John loves Mary or he does not.

3.

p	q	$q \rightarrow p$	$p \rightarrow (q \rightarrow p)$
T	T	T	T
T	F	T	T
F	T	F	T
F	F	T	T

An English instance of this tautologous sentence form is "If there's gold in the mine, then if the prospector finds gold then there's gold in the mine."

Tautologies belong to the class of sentences that are *logically true.* Their truth is solely a matter of their logical form. A sentence such as "If it is snowing, then it is snowing," tells us nothing at all about the weather, or anything else in the world. *Tautology* in the logician's vocabulary differs from the common usage of the term to refer to any trivial or uninteresting claim. Because of the empty or uninformative nature of logical tautologies, the two senses are related. Although logical tautologies do not provide information about what the world is like, these sentences have structural properties that interest logicians. For example, one widely held philosophical view of the nature of mathematical truths regards them as tautologies, and few people would deny the importance of mathematics.

In the same way that some sentences are true by virtue of logical structure rather than their connections with the way the world is, other sentences are false by virtue of their truth-functional logical structure. These sentences are called **self-contradictions.** In a truth table, the column under a self-contradiction contains only F's. An example of a self-contradictory sentence form is "$p \cdot \sim p$," as shown by the following truth table:

p	$\sim p$	$p \cdot \sim p$
T	F	F
F	T	F

The English sentence "It is snowing, and it is not snowing" is an instance of this self-contradictory form. Any conjunction that contains one conjunct that is the negation of another conjunct is self-contradictory. Less obvious forms of self-contradictory sentences also occur, such as

$$(p \rightarrow q) \cdot ((p \rightarrow r) \cdot (p \cdot \sim r)).$$

The truth tables for such self-contradictory sentence forms display all F's in the column under the main connective for the sentence.

Sentences that are neither tautologies nor contradictions are **contingent** sentences. The truth values of these sentences depend on (are contingent on) actual states of affairs. The truth-table column under a contingent sentence contains a mixture of T's and F's.

The following important relationship holds between the truth-functional validity of arguments and the tautologousness of sentences:

> An argument is valid truth-functionally if and only if its corresponding conditional is a tautology.

The **corresponding conditional** to an argument is a conditional sentence with the following structural properties:

1. The antecedent of the conditional is the conjunction of all of the premisses of the argument.

2. The consequent of the conditional is the conclusion of the argument.

The conditional corresponding to the form *affirming the antecedent (modus ponens)* is

$$((p \rightarrow q) \cdot p) \rightarrow q$$

Hypothetical syllogism has as its corresponding conditional

$$((p \rightarrow q) \cdot (q \rightarrow r)) \rightarrow (p \rightarrow r)$$

Exercise Set 9.5

1. Explain why any argument with a tautologous conclusion is valid.

2. Explain why any argument with a self-contradictory premiss is valid.

3. Explain why no valid argument can have all tautologous premisses and a contingent conclusion.

4. Is the following claim true? "If two sentence forms are logically equivalent, then the statement of their material biconditional is a tautology." Explain.

5. Explain why no simple sentence can be a tautology.

6. Write the corresponding conditionals for each of the following argument forms:

(1) $p \vee q$

   $\underline{p}$

   $\sim q$

(2) $p \rightarrow q$

   $p \vee r$

   $r \rightarrow \sim s$

   $\underline{s}$

   q

(3) $\underline{p \vee \sim p}$

   q

7. Construct truth tables to show whether the following sentence forms are tautologous, self-contradictory, or contingent. Be sure to say what the truth table shows.

   (1) $(p \rightarrow q) \rightarrow (q \rightarrow p)$

   (2) $p \rightarrow \sim p$

   (3) $\sim p \rightarrow p$

   (4) $q \rightarrow (p \vee \sim p)$

   (5) $(p \rightarrow q) \rightarrow (p \rightarrow (p \cdot q))$

8. Using sentence letters to represent simple sentences in English, translate each of the following into an appropriate sentence form that most closely captures the truth-functional structure of the sentence. Use a truth table to decide whether the sentence *as translated* is a truth-functional tautology, self-contradiction, or contingent sentence.

   (1) You can't win if you don't try.

   (2) The rain falls on both the rich and the poor.

   (3) It never rains but it pours.

   (4) You win some, and you lose some.

   (5) If you really love her, you'll tell her so.

   (6) You're either with me, or against me.

VII. LOGIC AND COMPUTERS: APPLICATION OF TRUTH-FUNCTIONAL LOGIC

The ability to perform calculations at incredible speeds is an important feature of modern computers. The speed of computers depends on their electronic components; the calculating ability of computers depends on their logical design. Although computers work at remarkable speeds, they can accomplish their tasks only when the problems they are to solve can be analyzed in terms of basic logical operations, such as negation, conjunction, and disjunction.

Following a few preliminary remarks, we briefly discuss the role of truth-functional logic in the logical design of computers, using a primitive adding machine as an example.

1. Representation of Numbers

Numerals are symbols that are used to name numbers. You are familiar with *Roman numeral symbols* (I, X, V, L, C, D, M) and with *Arabic numeral symbols* (0, 1, 2, and so on). In addition to the various types of symbols that name numbers, different *systems of numerals exist*. These numeral systems are distinguished by the number of distinct numeral symbols used to represent numbers.

i. Decimal System

The system familiar to all of us is the *decimal* system. It employs ten distinct symbols (0,1,2,3,4,5,6,7,8, and 9). The numbers zero through nine can each be represented by a single digit. Numbers greater than nine must be represented by more than one digit, using the *place system*, which employs powers of 10. (10^0 is equal to 1, 10^1 is equal to 10, 10^2 is equal to 100, and so on.)

In the decimal system, the rightmost digit stands for the number of units (10^0). The place left of that stands for the number of tens (10^1); the place left of that stands for the number of hundreds (10^2); and so on.

Examples

67 represents 6 tens and 7 units, or

$$(6 \times 10^1) + (7 \times 10^0)$$

342 represents 3 hundreds, 4 tens, and 2 units, or

$$(3 \times 10^2) + (4 \times 10^1) + (2 \times 10^0)$$

1001 represents 1 thousand, no hundreds, no tens, and 1 unit, or

$$(1 \times 10^3) + (0 \times 10^2) + (0 \times 10^1) + (1 \times 10^0)$$

The decimal system is sometimes called a **base-ten numeral system.**

ii. Binary System

In the binary system, sometimes called a **base-two numeral system,** there are only two digits (0 and 1). The numbers zero and one can each be represented by a single digit. Numbers greater than one must be represented by more than one digit, so a place system employing powers of two is used. In this system, the rightmost digit stands for the number of units (2^0, because any number raised to the 0 power is equal to one). The place left of that stands for the number of twos (2^1); the place left of that stands for the number of fours (2^2); and so on.

Examples :

1001 represents the number nine, because it signifies

$$(1 \times 2^3) + (0 \times 2^2) + (0 \times 2^1) + (1 \times 2^0).$$

111 represents the number seven, or

$$(1 \times 2^2) + (1 \times 2^1) + (1 \times 2^0).$$

The binary system is inconvenient for human calculators using paper and pencil, because it requires many more marks than are needed in the decimal system to represent numbers greater than one. Nevertheless, any number can be represented in either system; the fact that there are only two distinct symbols in the binary system is not a limitation in that sense. Furthermore, under some conditions, a binary system is more convenient than a decimal system. If information about numbers is transmitted as a series of electrical impulses on a wire, then it is simpler to distinguish only two types (using high current and low current) instead of ten types. Electrical impulses can be transmitted very quickly, so the disadvantage of having to write down long strings of symbols —as a human calculator who uses paper and pencil must—does not apply.

2. Binary Addition

Binary addition works exactly like addition in the decimal system. In the following addition table, the numbers above the lines (*rows p, q*) are the numbers to be added; below the lines, the left digit (c) is the carry digit and the right digit (s) is the sum digit:

p	1	1	0	0
q	1	0	1	0
cs	10	01	01	00

To summarize the table, the first column shows us that one plus one is equal to two (10 in binary notation); the second and third columns show us that zero and one added yield one (although it is written down here, the carry digit can be omitted when it is zero); and the final column gives the result of adding two zeros. The information about addition may be viewed in a form analogous to that of a truth table:

p	q	c	s
1	1	1	0
1	0	0	1
0	1	0	1
0	0	0	0

3. Constructing an Adder

To analyze addition as a *logical* operation, we consider which of our familiar truth-functional connectives can be used to capture the functions represented in the c and s columns.

In the c column, a high value (1) occurs when both p and q have the high value; otherwise the value is low (0). If we read 1 as T and 0 as F, the addition table for c is exactly analogous to the truth table for the dot that symbolizes logical conjunction ($\bullet$).

Turning now to the s column, we can see that when p and q have the same value, s takes the low value (0), whereas when p and q have different values, s takes the high value (1). This is exactly the opposite situation from the one represented by the material biconditional connective. So one way of representing this s function is

$$\sim(p \leftrightarrow q).$$

Another way of representing this s function is

$$(p \bullet \sim q) \vee (\sim p \bullet q).$$

Exercise Set 9.6

Construct a truth table to show that the above two sentence forms are logically equivalent to one another.

Now suppose that we have electrical switches that can physically realize the logical functions of conjunction, disjunction, and negation. For example:

Conjunction (See Figure 9-1): There are two input wires (p, q). When both wires carry high current (1), the single output wire from the switch carries high current. When either or both input wires carry low current (0), so does the output wire.

Disjunction (See Figure 9-2): This switch also has two input wires and one output wire. When either or both input wires carry high current, so does the output wire. When both input wires carry low current, so does the output wire.

Negation: (See Figure 9-3): This switch has one input wire and one output wire. It changes the current on the input wire from high to low and from low to high.

Using switches of this type, we can build our simple adding machine. We want to feed numbers, represented by impulses of high and low current, into the machine on the input wires p and q, and to have output wires that represent the carry digit c and the sum digit s.

Figure 9-4 is a "black box" representation of such a machine, so-called

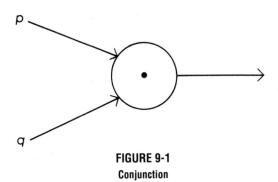

FIGURE 9-1
Conjunction

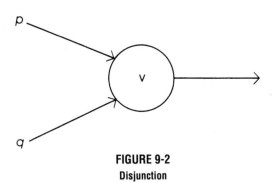

FIGURE 9-2
Disjunction

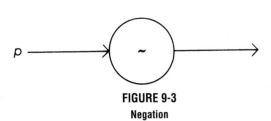

FIGURE 9-3
Negation

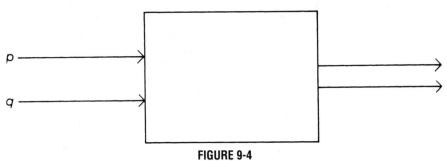

FIGURE 9-4
Adding Machine (external view)

because although we can observe the inputs and the outputs, we cannot see how the machine works.

The internal workings of the machine are represented in Figure 9-5.

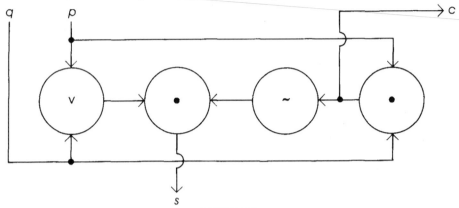

FIGURE 9-5
Adding Machine (internal view)

The simple adding machine, called a half adder, is primitive. Although it can add any two digits, it cannot add the carry digit from a previous addition. To construct a *full adder*, we need to consider binary addition for three digits (p, q, and a carry-in digit c_{in} from a previous addition). The following table provides the required information about binary addition:

p	q	c_{in}	c_{out}	s
1	1	1	1	1
1	1	0	1	0
1	0	1	1	0
1	0	0	0	1
0	1	1	1	0
0	1	0	0	1
0	0	1	0	1
0	0	0	0	0

Examination of this table reveals that c_{out} takes the high value in rows 1, 2, 3, and 5 (when all three inputs p, q, c_{in} are high, as they are in row 1, or when any two inputs are high and the third input is low). In row 2, p and q are high; in row 3, p and c_{in} are high; in row 5, q and c_{in} are high. Thus, we can express c_{out} as the following function of p, q, and c_{in}:

$$(p \cdot q \cdot c_{in}) \text{ v } (p \cdot q \cdot \sim c_{in}) \text{ v } (p \cdot \sim q \cdot c_{in}) \text{ v } (\sim p \cdot \sim q \cdot c_{in})$$

The same type of reasoning may be used to formulate s as a function of p, q, and c_{in}. The high value is assigned to s in rows 1, 4, 6, and 7. The high value is assigned whenever an odd number of components (either one or three) takes a high value; otherwise s is low. Thus, we can express s as the following function:

$$(p \cdot q \cdot c_{in}) \text{ v } (p \cdot \sim q \cdot \sim c_{in}) \text{ v } (\sim p \cdot q \cdot \sim c_{in}) \text{ v } (\sim p \cdot \sim q \cdot c_{in})$$

The full adder will have three input wires and two output wires. Using three types of switches to realize the functions of negation, conjunction, and disjunction, the adder might be constructed as shown in Figure 9-6.

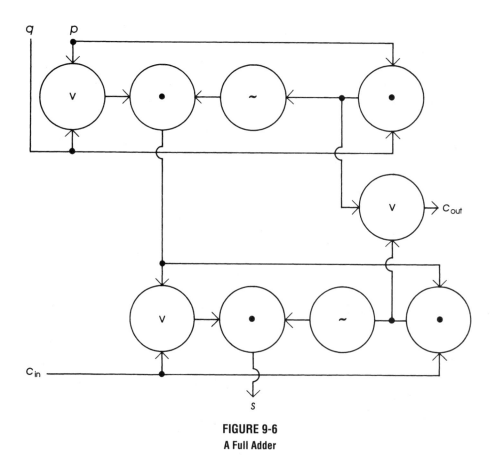

FIGURE 9-6
A Full Adder

Many logical problems of computer design resemble these rather simple problems just presented, although, of course, they can be considerably more complicated.

4. Disjunctive Normal Forms

A *disjunctive normal form* is a disjunction, each disjunct of which is a conjunction. Furthermore, each conjunction contains exactly one occurrence of every sentence letter in that sentence form; the one occurrence may be either negated or unnegated. (The preceding sentence forms for c_{out} and s are disjunctive normal forms.) It can be proved that for any truth-functional sentence form, there is a logically equivalent disjunctive normal form.

Sometimes it is desirable to design computers using only three kinds of switches (for negation, disjunction, and conjunction). In such cases, it is useful to have a method for translating sentence forms that contain other connectives into sentence forms that contain only tildes, dots, and wedges. One method for constructing the logically equivalent disjunctive normal form for any sentence form was first proposed by Lewis Carroll (*Symbolic Logic*):

1. Construct a truth table for the sentence form.

2. Note any rows in which the truth value of the sentence form is T.

3. For each row in which the sentence form is assigned T, form a conjunction in which each sentence letter occurs exactly once and is negated if and only if the sentence letter is assigned F in that row.

4. Form a disjunction using each of the conjunctions (constructed according to step 3) as disjuncts.

5. This disjunction is in disjunctive normal form and is logically equivalent to the original sentence form.

Exercise Set 9.7

1. Construct logically equivalent disjunctive normal forms for each of the following sentence forms:

    (1) $p \rightarrow q$

    (2) $p \leftrightarrow q$

    (3) $\sim(p \rightarrow q)$

    (4) $p \rightarrow \sim q$

2. Sometimes computers are designed with just one kind of switch, called a "nand" switch and symbolized by a stroke "|". This switch represents the negation of a conjunction:

$$\text{"}(p \mid q)\text{" is logically equivalent to "}\sim(p \cdot q).\text{"}$$

It is possible to use only the stroke connective to represent *any* truth-functional connection between sentences. Some examples are:

"$\sim p$" has the same truth table as "$p \mid p$."

"$p \rightarrow q$" has the same truth table as "$p \mid (q \mid q)$."

"$p \vee q$" has the same truth table as "$(p \mid p) \mid (q \mid q)$."

    Using only the stroke connective, construct a sentence form that is equivalent to:

    (1) $p \cdot q$

    (2) $p \leftrightarrow q$

3. Design a circuit with two input wires p and q and one output wire s, using only the connectives "$\sim$," "$\cdot$," and "$\vee$," that functions as an "exclusive or" switch.

4. Many lights are wired in such a way that they can be turned on or off at either end of a room. Use the logical connectives for conjunction, disjunction, and negation to work out a design for the circuit that controls these lights.

VIII. REVIEW

Chapter 9 was devoted to the study of various forms of truth-functional arguments, the translation of English arguments into argument forms, the use of symbols for sentence letters and connectives, and the use of truth-table tests to determine the validity and invalidity of argument forms. The *truth-functional connectives* represented in English by "if . . . then," "and," "or," "not," and "if and only if" were given truth-table definitions. Sentences that are true by virtue of their truth-functional structure (*tautologies*) and sentences that are false by virtue of their structure (*self-contradictions*) were also examined. The truth-table method for settling questions of validity and tautologousness can be cumbersome if many distinct sentence letters occur in the sentence forms and argument forms that are tested. An alternative method for proving validity or invalidity of argument forms and for determining whether sentence forms are tautologies, contingent sentence forms, or self-contradictions is presented in Appendix 1 to this text. This method is more convenient to use if more than four distinct sentence letters occur in an argument form or sentence form. In the last section of Chapter 9 an important application of truth-functional logic—the logical design of computers—was discussed, using the construction of a simple adder as an example.

A list of important definitions and argument forms covered in this chapter follows.

Truth-table definitions of logical connectives:

Conjunction:	p	q	$p \cdot q$
	T	T	T
	T	F	F
	F	T	F
	F	F	F

Disjunction:	p	q	$p \vee q$
	T	T	T
	T	F	T
	F	T	T
	F	F	F

Material Biconditional: p	q	$p \leftrightarrow q$
T	T	T
T	F	F
F	T	F
F	F	T

Material Conditional: p	q	$p \rightarrow q$
T	T	T
T	F	F
F	T	T
F	F	T

Negation:	p	$\sim p$
	T	F
	F	T

Some important valid argument forms:

Constructive Dilemma:

$$p \rightarrow q$$
$$r \rightarrow s$$
$$\underline{p \vee r}$$
$$q \vee s$$

Destructive Dilemma:

$$p \rightarrow q$$
$$r \rightarrow s$$
$$\underline{\sim q \vee \sim s}$$
$$\sim p \vee \sim r$$

Disjunctive Syllogism:

$$p \vee q$$
$$\underline{\sim p}$$
$$q$$

Hypothetical Syllogism:

$$p \rightarrow q$$
$$\underline{q \rightarrow r}$$
$$p \rightarrow r$$

Contingent Sentence: The truth or falsity of a contingent sentence depends on its content as well as on its logical structure. A sentence form is contingent if its column in a truth-table contains both T's and F's.

Corresponding Conditional: Every argument (and every argument form) has a corresponding conditional in which the antecedent is the conjunction of all of the premises and the consequent is the conclusion of the argument.

False Dilemma; Fallacy of Black-and-White Thinking: When we ignore a whole range of alternatives and think only in terms of extreme opposites (for example, "He is either my friend or my enemy"—when he could be neutral), we commit this fallacy. We are sometimes tempted to think this way when we construct arguments in the form of dilemmas and disjunctive syllogisms.

Logical Equivalence: Two sentences (or sentence forms) are logically equivalent if they always have the same truth value. If two sentences are logically equivalent, then the statement of their material biconditional is a tautology.

Self-Contradiction: A compound English sentence is a self-contradiction if it is false by virtue of its logical structure, regardless of its content. A sentence form is a truth-functional self-contradiction if its column in a truth-table contains only F's.

Tautology: A compound English sentence is a tautology if it is true by virtue of its truth-functional structure, regardless of its content. A sentence form is a tautology if its column in a truth-table contains only T's.

Truth-Table Test for Validity or Invalidity of Argument Forms: Construct a truth table with an initial column for each distinct sentence letter in the argument. (If there are n such letters, the truth table will have 2^n rows.) Construct a separate column for each premiss and the conclusion. (There may be additional columns for compound components of these sentence forms as well.)

If there is some row in which all of the premisses are assigned T and the conclusion is assigned F, the argument form is invalid. If there are no such rows, the argument form is valid.

Valid Truth-Functional English-Language Argument: An English-language argument is valid truth-functionally if it is an instance of some valid truth-functional argument form. (Note that a valid argument may also be an instance of some invalid argument form. An English-language argument is invalid only if there is no valid form of which it is an instance.)

Chapter Ten

CATEGORICAL SYLLOGISMS

I. INTRODUCTION

Discussions of deductive validity in earlier chapters include examples of obviously valid arguments, similar to the following:

(a) Every bat is a mammal.
No bird is a mammal.

No bird is a bat.

(b) All birds can fly.
Some mammals cannot fly.

Some mammals are not birds.

(c) Every president is a politician.
Some president is a statesman.

Some statesman is a politician.

Each is an example of a type of argument called *categorical syllogism*. In ordinary discourse we rarely encounter arguments that are expressed in the standard form of the preceding examples. When the arguments are spelled out that way they look so obvious, it seems pointless to state them completely, let alone to develop a set of rules to determine whether they are valid or invalid. In fact, a seventeenth-century author of a treatise on logic raised doubts about whether the formal rules of syllogistic reasoning, which he admitted to be "the only aspect of logic traditionally treated with any care," are "as useful as is generally believed." For, he says, "If any man is unable to detect by the light of reason alone the invalidity of an argument, then he is probably incapable of understanding the rules by which we judge whether an argument is valid—and still less able to apply those rules" (Arnauld 1964:175). Despite his doubts, however, Arnauld went on to write a long chapter about the subject.

Syllogistic reasoning is worth studying for a number of reasons. Although often incompletely stated, syllogisms pervade day-to-day reasoning. Children's "why" questions are often given answers that can be construed as syllogistic arguments, for example:

(d) Why do chickens have feathers?
Because they're birds and all birds have feathers.

(e) Do all birds fly?
No, ostriches are birds, but ostriches can't fly.

An understanding of the rules of the syllogism allows us to construct syllogistic arguments as well as to evaluate difficult syllogisms. Mastery of this common, well-understood type of reasoning also provides access to more difficult types.

In this chapter, the forms of categorical syllogisms are analyzed and two different methods for determining their validity are presented. **Categorical syllogisms,** like hypothetical syllogisms and disjunctive syllogisms (discussed in Chapter 9), are arguments with two premises. However, categorical syllogisms are *not* truth-functional arguments. Truth tables, which are used to investigate the intersentential structure of arguments, are not adequate to assess the formal validity of categorical syllogisms. Validity of these depends on intrasentence structure as well. All of the preceding categorical syllogisms are valid. If we represented the structure of these arguments by using sentence letters to denote simple sentences, each argument would be an instance of the obviously invalid form:

p

q

r

The connections between classes named by the subject terms and predicate terms of categorical sentences are essential to the forms by virtue of which these arguments are valid.

II. CATEGORICAL SENTENCES

In arguments (a), (b), and (c), each of the four types of categorical sentences occurs. If we let the upper-case italic letter *"S"* represent the subject terms and *"P"* represent the predicate terms, we can characterize the forms of the four types of categorical sentences in the following standard way:

1. Every S is P.

2. No S is P.

3. Some S is P.

4. Some S is not P.

The form of the first type of categorical sentence, "Every S is P," is the familiar **affirmative universal generalization,** which can also be stated "All S are P." This form is used to state that all the members of the *class* denoted by the term *"S"* are members of the *class* denoted by the term *"P."* Another way of saying the same thing is "the subject class is included in the predicate class." (The logic of categorical syllogisms is sometimes called "the logic of classes.") "Every junior at the University is an undergraduate" is an example of an affirmative universal sentence in which "junior at the University" refers to the subject class and "undergraduate" refers to the predicate class.

The second type of categorical sentence, "No S is P," is a **negative universal generalization.** This type of sentence states that no members of the class S are members of the class P. Alternatively, this sentence could be interpreted as "the subject and predicate classes do not overlap," or "the subject and predicate classes exclude one another." "No professional football player is a ballerina" is a negative universal sentence in which *professional football player* is the subject and *ballerina* is the predicate.

The third type of categorical sentence, "Some *S* is *P*," is an **affirmative particular generalization,** also called an **affirmative existential generalization.** This type of sentence says that at least one individual is a member of the class *S* and also of the class *P*. (This is a *general* sentence because no member is actually identified; the sentence simply says *some* such member does exist.) Another way of stating the same thing is "the subject and predicate classes overlap to the extent that they share at least one member." "Some dog is brown" is an example of an affirmative particular generalization.

The fourth type of categorical sentence, "Some *S* is not *P*," is a **negative existential** (or **particular**) **generalization**. Sentences of this form state that something (at least one thing) that is a member of the class *S* is not also a member of the class *P*. That is to say, at least one member of *S* is not identical with any member of *P*. This alternate formulation, although awkward in English, is useful in the discussion of an important feature of the negative existential generalization. "Some dog is not brown" or "At least one dog is not identical with any brown thing" is an example of a negative existential generalization.

1. Relationships among Categorical Sentences—the Traditional Square of Opposition

Syllogistic logic was developed by Aristotle more than 2,300 years ago. Aristotle was the first to formalize principles of valid arguments. He was so successful that much of what he developed has continued to be studied in logic classes from antiquity to the present day. Only the geometry developed by Euclid, at roughly the same time Aristotle achieved his results, has secured a similar position in Western intellectual history. In addition to his interest in the validity of syllogisms, Aristotle was concerned with various relationships among the four types of categorical sentences when each had the same subject and predicate. These relationships can be considered by displaying the four types of sentences in a square of opposition, shown in Figure 10-1.

(A) Every *S* is *P*.	(E) No *S* is *P*.
(I) Some *S* is *P*.	(O) Some *S* is not *P*.

FIGURE 10-1
Square of Opposition

The letters *A, E, I,* and *O* have been used since medieval times to denote the four types of categorical sentences. *A,* which represents the universal affirmative, is the first vowel of the Latin *Affirmo,* or "I affirm." *I,* which denotes the particular affirmative, is the second vowel of the same Latin word. *E,* which identifies the universal negative, is the first vowel of the Latin *Nego,* or "I deny," and *O*, which represents the particular negative, is the second vowel of the same Latin word.

According to Aristotle's system of logic, the following relationships hold between pairs of categorical sentences:

1. The *A* sentence and the *O* sentence are **contradictory** to one another, as are the *E* sentence and the *I* sentence.

To say that two sentences are *contradictories* means that when one sentence of the pair is true, the other sentence must be false. Clearly if "Every *S* is *P*" is true, then it must be false that "Some *S* is not *P*." And if it is true that "Some *S* is not *P*," then it cannot be the case that "Every *S* is *P*." With regard to the *E* and *I* sentences, if "No *S* is *P*," is true, "Some *S* is *P*" is false. Similarly, if it is true that "Some *S* is *P*," then it must be false that "No *S* is *P*." The sentence forms that are *diagonally* opposite one another on the square of opposition are "opposites" in the sense that they are logically contradictory to one another.

2. The *A* sentence and the *E* sentence are **contrary** to one another.

Two sentences are *contraries* when they could not both be true, although they could both be false. The sentences "Every dog is brown" and "No dog is brown" are contraries which are both false. The sentences "Every football player is an athlete" and "No football player is an athlete" are contraries, but only the second sentence is false. The sentence forms that are opposite one another at the *top* of the square of opposition are "opposites" in the sense that they are logically contrary to one another.

The terms *contradictory* and *contrary* also apply to pairs of sentences that are not categorical. For example, "My only brother weighs more than my only sister" and "My only sister weighs more than my only brother" are contraries, even though neither sentence is categorical. These sentences could not both be true, although they could both be false (if my siblings weigh exactly the same).

Referring to truth-functional sentence forms, any pair of the forms "*p*" and "*~p*" is a contradictory pair, regardless of whether "*p*" is a categorical sentence. (Remember that a sentence letter may represent any sentence whatsoever, although to capture structural relationships among sentences, sentence letters are used to represent *simple* sentences.) The sentences "It is raining" and "It is not raining" are contradictories.

For critical thinking, the distinction between contradictory and contrary pairs of sentences is important. It would be a mistake, for example, to conclude "Sally hates me" from the premiss "Sally doesn't love me." Although the sentences "Sally hates me" and "Sally loves me" are contrary to one another, they are not contradictory. Therefore, we cannot conclude that because one of them is false, the other must be true. They could both be false. The English term *incompatible* is ambiguous when it is applied to pairs of sentences that do not "agree" with one another. *Incompatible* sometimes refers to contraries, and sometimes refers to contradictories.

3. The *I* and the *O* sentences could not both be false, but they could both be true.

Sentences that are related to one another in this way are called **subcontraries** (because of their position beneath the contraries in the square of opposition). The English sentences "Some dog is brown" and "Some dog is not brown" are subcontraries; both are true. The pair "Some men are mortal" and "Some men are not mortal" are subcontraries, but only the first sentence is true. The sentences on opposite sides of the *bottom* of the square of opposition are "opposite" in the sense that they are subcontraries. Unlike contrary pairs of sentences, subcontraries are not usually mistaken for contradictories. When this mistake does arise, it can often be traced to confusion about the placement of *not* in English sentences. For example, the sentences

(i) Elizabeth II is the queen of England.

(ii) Elizabeth II is not the queen of England.

are contradictories. In sentence (i), inserting *not* after the verb has the same logical force as placing "It is not the case that" before sentence (i). Despite similarities in appearance, particular generalizations are logically different from (i) and (ii), and inserting a *not* after the verb has a different logical force from prefixing "It is not the case that." Consider the following pair of sentences:

(iii) Some women are queens.

(iv) Some women are not queens.

These sentences are not contradictories. They are both true, and they are subcontraries.

4. The *I* sentence is a logical consequence of (is implied by) the *A* sentence; and the *O* sentence is a logical consequence of (is implied by) the *E* sentence (see Figure 10-2).

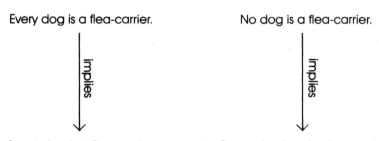

Every dog is a flea-carrier.

implies

Some dog is a flea-carrier.

No dog is a flea-carrier.

implies

Some dog is not a flea-carrier.

FIGURE 10-2

It seems reasonable to say that if it is true that every *S* is *P*, then some *S* is *P*. Similarly, if "No *S* is *P*," is true, then it must be the case that "Some *S* is not *P*." This relationship between the *A* and *I* sentences, and between the *E* and *O* sentences is called **subimplication,** because the sentences at the top of the square of opposition *imply* the sentences below them. If the *A* sentence is true, then the *I* sentence must be true as well; if the *E* sentence is true, then the *O* sentence must be true also.

The relationships among categorical sentences in the Aristotelian square of opposition can be represented by arrows, as shown in Figure 10-3.

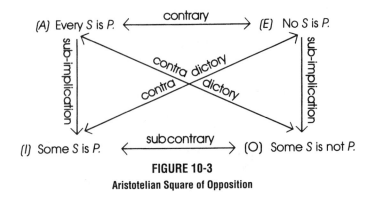

FIGURE 10-3
Aristotelian Square of Opposition

Despite a superficial grammatical similarity between universal sentences and particular sentences, their logical structures are distinct. Universal sentences are interpreted by contemporary logicians as conditional sentences in which the pronoun in the consequent refers back to the subject of the antecedent clause: "If anything is *S*, then it is *P*"; "If anything is *S*, then it is not *P*." Particular sentences, in contrast, assert that there is some individual that has some property (or, in the negative case, that lacks the property): "Something that is *S* is also *P*"; "Something that is *S* is not *P*." Particular sentences are interpreted as conjunctions rather than as conditionals.

One logically important feature of the *A* and *E* forms of categorical sentences in English is that they can be true even when no members of the subject class exist ("All ghosts are invisible"). Universal generalizations sometimes are used when we *hope* there will be no members of the subject class ("Every student who does not meet the deadline for term papers will receive a failing grade"). Thus, it seems reasonable to say that these universal categorical sentences lack **existential import.** Particular sentences, in contrast, are understood always as either asserting or denying that some (existing) individual has a property. Particular sentences, unlike some universal sentences, have existential import.

2. Existential Import and the Modern Square of Opposition

For the purpose of systematizing logic, modern logicians view universal categorical statements as conditional sentences, and deny existential import to

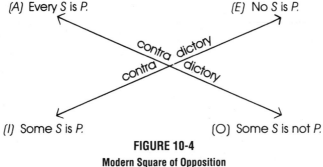

FIGURE 10-4
Modern Square of Opposition

them. Thus, they adopt a restricted form of the Square of Opposition. In the modern systems of logic, universal generalizations are regarded as material conditionals, which are false only when they have a true antecedent and a false consequent. In other words, any conditional that has a false antecedent is true. Consider the sentence: "Every ghost is invisible." Rephrased in conditional form, it becomes "If anything is a ghost, then it is invisible." But ghosts do not exist, so the antecedent is false. Then, interpreting the conditional as a material conditional, "Every ghost is invisible" is true. The same sort of reasoning, however, applies to the negative universal generalization "No ghost is invisible," which is also true because it has a false antecedent. Understood in this way, the *A* sentence and the *E* sentence can both be true, and so they are no longer contraries. If universal generalizations are understood as material conditionals, the square of opposition is drastically simplified. Most of the relationships that were recognized by Aristotle between forms of categorical sentences with the same subject and predicate terms no longer hold. Only the contradictory relationships between the pairs of categorical sentences diagonally opposite one another remain intact (see Figure 10-4).

The modern interpretation of universal generalizations as conditionals is no closer to their "true meaning" than the Aristotelian interpretation. Clearly, in some contexts of ordinary language, universal generalizations are understood as having existential import. Nevertheless, the decision to interpret universal sentences as material conditionals and existential sentences as conjunctions is justified in logical terms because it facilitates a comprehensive logical system that is able to account for more complex sorts of arguments than the Aristotelian system.*

If universal generalizations are interpreted as material conditionals:

> (*A*) If anything is an *S*, then it is a *P*.
> (*E*) If anything is an *S*, then it is not a *P*.

then it is possible for the *A* sentence to be true (when there are no *S*'s) while the corresponding *I* sentence is false, for the *I* sentence asserts that some *S* is

---

*See "Truth-Functional Conditionals and Modern vs. Traditional Syllogistic," R. B. Angell, 1986.

P. The *I* sentence has existential import. Similarly, it is possible for the *E* sentence to be true while the corresponding *O* sentence is false. Thus, the relationships of subimplication do not hold in the modern interpretation. Furthermore, the *I* and *O* sentences can both be false, when there are no *S*'s, so the relationship of subcontraries also fails to hold.

Consider the following four categorical sentences in which *unicorn* is the subject term and *white things* is the predicate term:

> *A*: Every unicorn is a white thing.
> *E*: No unicorn is a white thing.
> *I*: Some unicorn is a white thing.
> *O*: Some unicorn is not a white thing.

Because unicorns do not exist, the *A* and *E* sentences are both true, and the *I* and *O* sentences are both false. The *A* sentence does not imply the *I* sentence; the *E* sentence does not imply the *O* sentence. *A* and *E* are not contraries; *I* and *O* are not subcontraries. However, *A* and *O* are contradictories, as are *E* and *I*; if one member of these pairs is true, the other is false.

Using sentence forms to represent sentences suppresses the content of those sentences to focus on structural considerations. The logically interesting feature of categorical sentences is the nature of the relationship between the subject class and the predicate class. Does one class include or exclude the other? Do the two classes share a common member? Does some member of one class fail to belong to the other class? Some advantages of employing sentence forms rather than sentences to analyze the validity or the invalidity of arguments are already familiar. In Chapter 11, some previously introduced symbolic techniques are developed to show how modern treatments of the logic of classes can be extended to more complex systems.

Even though the simpler modern square of opposition is normally used in contemporary formal treatments of syllogisms, the relationships among categorical sentences in the traditional Aristotelian square of opposition are important in everyday reasoning in ordinary language. For that reason, they repay our careful attention. Arguments in ordinary reasoning often depend on one sentence being contrary to another, or subcontrary to another, or a subimplication of another. We should be able to recognize and assess such arguments in ordinary contexts.

Exercise Set 10-1

> Part One. Using Aristotle's account of the relationships between categorical sentences as presented in the traditional square of opposition, answer each question with a *categorical sentence* in English.

1. What is the contradictory of "All fiddlers are bass fiddlers"?
2. What is the contrary of "No politicians are statesmen"?

3. What is the contradictory of "Some politicians are statesmen"?

4. What is the subcontrary of "Some cats are Persians"?

5. What sentence must be true if "All cats are Persians" is true?

6. What sentence must be true if "No cats are Persians" is true?

7. What is the contradictory of "Some cats are not domestic"?

8. What is the contradictory of "No football players are pre-med students"?

9. What sentence is contrary to "All doctors are rich"?

10. What is the subimplication of "No rich persons are doctors"?

Part Two. Give an English sentence (it need not be categorical) that is contrary to each of the following:

1. It never rains in southern California.

2. Mary Ann has two blue eyes.

3. His only pet is a dog.

4. Johnny is rich.

5. Chocolate desserts are delicious.

6. Chocolate is my favorite flavor.

7. You always complain about the homework.

8. When it rains, it pours.

9. Many a hero has gone unsung.

10. Parakeets are the easiest pets to keep.

Part Three. Give an English sentence (it need not be categorical) that is contradictory to each of the following:

1. Peas are not usually eaten with a knife.

2. Carrots are orange.

3. Baseball is less interesting than football.

4. Every rose has its thorn.

5. The grass is always greener on the other side of the fence.

6. This movie glorifies criminals.

7. Mary Stuart was the only reigning queen of Scotland.

8. It never rains but it pours.

9. Old soldiers never die.

10. The ozone hole over Antarctica is expanding.

III. TRANSLATING ENGLISH SENTENCES INTO STANDARD CATEGORICAL FORMS

With sufficiently clever linguistic manipulation, many sentences that do not appear to be categorical can be adjusted to fit one of the four standard categorical forms. For example, the sentence "It never rains but it pours," can be "translated" into "Every time of raining is a time of pouring," which is a standard *A* sentence.

1. *A* Sentences

Consider the following English sentences:

1. All trespassers are persons who will be prosecuted.
2. Trespassers will be prosecuted.
3. Anyone who trespasses will be prosecuted.
4. If anyone trespasses, that person will be prosecuted.
5. No trespasser will fail to be prosecuted.
6. It is false that some trespassers will not be prosecuted.
7. All persons who will not be prosecuted are nontrespassers.

All of these sentences are equivalent to one another in the logically important sense that each states that the class of trespassers is included in the class of persons who will be prosecuted. The following remarks about each of these sentences are designed to make this equivalence apparent:

1. This sentence is clearly equivalent to "Every trespasser is a person who will be prosecuted." *Trespassers* denotes the subject class, and *persons who will be prosecuted* denotes the predicate class. We can regard "All *S* are *P*" as another standard rendering of the *A* sentence.

2. In English, the *quantifier* (*every, all,* or *some*) may be omitted when the context shows which quantifier is intended. For example, the sentence "Whales are mammals" is interpreted as "Every whale is a mammal." But the second sentence in "Watch your language. Children are present," is understood to mean "Some child is present." Noun phrases such as "persons who," "things which," and similar expressions can also be omitted from predicate terms.

3. In this sentence, "Anyone who trespasses" means the same as "all trespassers."

4. This translates the *A* sentence into a conditional form: "If anything is an *S*, then it is a *P*."

5. This sentence is obviously equivalent to the *E* form: "No trespassers are persons who will not be prosecuted." In addition to changing the *all* in the

original sentence (1) to *no*, the predicate, "persons who will be prosecuted" has been replaced by "persons who will not be prosecuted." In general, an *A* sentence may be transformed to an equivalent *E* sentence in the following two steps:

(1) Replace "every" (or "all") with "no." The change from an affirmative to a negative sentence, or a negative sentence to an affirmative sentence, is called a change in **quality**.

(2) Replace the predicate term of the sentence with its **complement**. The complement of a class is the class of all things that are not in the original class. For example, the complement of the class of cats is the class of noncats; the complement of the class of nonmen is the class of men. The term that refers to the complement class is called the **complement** of the original term.

The process of changing the quality of a categorical sentence and replacing the predicate term with its complement is called **obversion**. When any categorical sentence (*A*, *E*, *I*, or *O*) is **obverted**, a sentence that is equivalent in meaning to the original sentence results.

6. This sentence is equivalent to the *denial* of an *O* sentence: "*It is not the case that* some trespassers are persons who will not be prosecuted." The *O* sentence that is contradictory to "All trespassers are persons who will be prosecuted" is "Some trespassers are persons who will not be prosecuted." The denial of the contradictory of a sentence is logically equivalent to the original sentence.

7. In this sentence, the subject term is the complement of the predicate term in (1) and the predicate is the complement of the subject term in (1). This transformation is called **contraposition.** The contraposition of *A* sentences yields *A* sentences that are equivalent in meaning to the original sentence.

The relationship between subject and predicate in the *A* sentence can be represented graphically in the *Venn diagram* * of the *A* sentence shown in Figure 10-5.

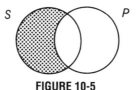

FIGURE 10-5

* After John Venn (1834-1923), an English clergyman who made important contributions to mathematics and logic.

Against a background of all of the types of things in the universe, the overlapping circles represent two classes, or types of things in that universe: S's and P's. These classes may or may not have members. Shading is used to indicate the emptiness of a region. Thus, for the A sentence, the region in the S circle that lies outside the P circle is shaded, for any S's (if there are any) must lie within the part of the S circle that is included in the P circle.

2. *E* Sentences

Consider the following English sentences:

1. No whales are fish.

2. Whales aren't fish.

3. Nothing that's a whale is a fish.

4. None but nonfishes are whales.

5. If anything is a whale, then it is not a fish.

6. All whales are nonfish.

7. It is false that some whales are fish

Each of these sentences says that the class of whales and the class of fish is nonoverlapping, or, in other words, that no members are common to both classes. Comments on each of these sentences follow:

1. This sentence is in standard E form.

2. This sentence is equivalent to the categorical A sentence "All whales are nonfish." In ordinary English, it is tempting to say "All whales are not fish," but this sentence is ambiguous; it leaves open the possibility that some whales are fish. The original sentence (2), however, denies that any whales are fish. The sentence form "All S are not P" is not a categorical form, and, because it is ambiguous, is not equivalent to the categorical "All S are non$P$," which is a variant of the A form.

3. "Nothing that's a whale" in this context has the same meaning as "no whales," and "is a fish" agrees better grammatically with this version than "are fish."

4. "None but nonfishes are whales" means the same as "Only nonfishes are whales" or "If anything is not a nonfish, then it is not a whale." This in turn is equivalent to "If anything is a fish, then it is not a whale." This sentence states that that the classes of fish and whales do not overlap (they contain no members in common), which is what the original E sentence (1) says.

5. This is the standard translation of the E sentence into an equivalent conditional. "No S is P" becomes "If anything is an S, then it is not a P."

6. This sentence represents the standard transformation of an *E* sentence into an equivalent *A* sentence by obversion. The quality of the sentence is changed from negative to affirmative, and the predicate term is replaced by its complement.

7. This sentence is the denial of the contradictory of the original *E* sentence (1). In general, the categorical sentence "No *S* are *P*" is equivalent to the noncategorical sentence "It is false that some *S* are *P*."

E sentences (including all the English variants of the standard form of *E* sentence) can be represented by the Venn diagram shown in Figure 10-6.

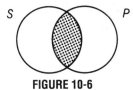

FIGURE 10-6

As in the Venn diagram of the *A* sentence, the two circles represent the classes *S* and *P*. Shading in the overlapping area indicates that this region is empty. In other words, no things are members of both classes.

Inspection of the Venn diagram shows that the sentence forms "No *S* is *P*" and "No *P* is *S*" are equivalent. Thus, the subject term and the predicate term can be interchanged in an *E* sentence without changing the meaning of the sentence. This transformation is called **conversion.** Conversion does not preserve meaning in *A* sentences. For example, "All elephants are mammals," does not mean "All mammals are elephants." Examination of the Venn diagram of the *A* sentence makes its lack of symmetry with respect to subject and predicate terms apparent.

3. *I* Sentences

The following are all English variations of the same *I* sentence:

1. Some logical principles are things difficult to grasp.

2. Some logical principles are difficult to grasp.

3. Some things are both logical principles and difficult to grasp.

4. There are logical principles that are difficult to grasp.

5. Some logical principles are not things that are not difficult to grasp.

6. Some logical principles are not easy to grasp.

7. It is not the case that no logical principles are difficult to grasp.

8. It is not the case that all logical principles are easy to grasp.

9. Some things that are difficult to grasp are logical principles.

Some of these equivalencies are discussed below. The rest are left as exercises for the reader. (Treat "easy to grasp" and "difficult to grasp" as complementary.)

1. This sentence is in the standard *I* form.

3. This form displays the conjunctive nature of *I* sentences.

5. An *O* form that is equivalent to the *I* form can be constructed by changing the quality from affirmative to negative and replacing the predicate term with its complement (obversion).

7. The *E* sentence that is the contradictory of the *I* sentence is negated. The resulting sentence is equivalent to the original *I* sentence.

9. Because the *I* sentence has the logical form of a conjunction and because the order of the conjuncts is irrelevant to the truth of the conjunction, "Some *S* are *P*" is equivalent to "Some *P* are *S*." As in the *E* sentence, the subject and predicate terms in the *I* sentence may be interchanged without changing the meaning of the sentence. Conversion preserves meaning in *I* sentences.

In constructing the Venn diagram for the *I* sentence, two overlapping circles are again used to represent the classes *S* and *P*. An **x** represents a member (or members) of a class. Because the *I* sentence says that the classes *S* and *P* share at least one member, an **x** is placed in the overlapping region, as shown in Figure 10-7.

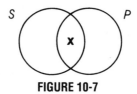

FIGURE 10-7

4. *O* Sentences

The following are all English variations of the same *O* sentence:

1. Some runners are not vegetarians.

2. Some runners are nonvegetarians.

3. Some nonvegetarians are runners.

4. Not all runners are vegetarians.

5. There are nonvegetarian runners.

6. Some nonvegetarians are not nonrunners.

The principles by virtue of which these sentences are equivalent to one another have been introduced already. The first sentence (1) is in standard *O* form. The second sentence (2) is the obverse of (1). The quality of sentence (1) is changed from negative to affirmative (that is, from an *O* sentence to an *I* sentence), and the predicate term is replaced by its complement. Sentence (3) is the converse of (2), in which the subject and predicate terms of that *I* sentence are interchanged. Sentence (4) is the denial of the *A* sentence that is contradictory to the original *O* sentence. Sentence (5) exhibits the conjunctive nature of the *O* sentence. Finally, sentence (6) is the **contrapositive** of sentence (1). Contraposition preserves meaning in *O* sentences as well as in *A* sentences.

Again, using overlapping circles and an **x** to show that a class has some member, the Venn diagram in Figure 10-8 represents all variants of the *O* sentence. In this case, the **x** is drawn outside the *P* circle but within the *S* circle.

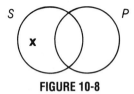

FIGURE 10-8

Exercise Set 10.2

For each of the following English sentences, construct an English sentence in one of the four standard categorical forms that captures the meaning of the original sentence. Draw a Venn diagram for each sentence and clearly label the subject-class circle and the predicate-class circle.

1. Only a mother could love him.
2. If students don't keep up with the assignments, they're lost.
3. The longest mile is the last mile home.
4. Happy is the bride the sun shines on.
5. No one may be admitted except juniors and seniors.
6. Not all apples are red.
7. If it isn't genuine, it isn't worth owning.
8. The home team always wins at football.
9. Valuable lessons are never easily learned.
10. Not every good dancer is a good person.
11. American warships are in the Indian Ocean.
12. The easiest course is not always the most satisfying.

13. It never rains in southern California.

14. She brings sunshine everywhere she goes.

15. Cosmic radiation is all around us.

16. Times like these try persons' souls.

17. It's an antique only if it's more than 100 years old.

18. The last exercise is always the best.

IV. TESTING FOR VALIDITY WITH VENN DIAGRAMS

Categorical syllogisms in standard form are arguments with two premises and a conclusion that also have the following properties:

1. Both the premises and the conclusion are standard-form categorical sentences.

2. Only three terms occur in the argument. One term, called the *middle term*, occurs once in each premiss; each of the other two terms, called *end terms*, occurs once in a premiss and once in the conclusion.

In representing the forms of these arguments, *S* refers to the subject term of the conclusion, *P* refers to the predicate term of the conclusion, and *M* refers to the term that occurs in both premises.

Recall the definition of deductive validity: In all circumstances in which the premises are true, the conclusion is true as well. In deductive arguments, we say that the information contained in the conclusion is already at least implic-

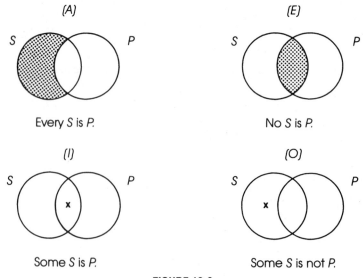

FIGURE 10-9

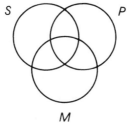

FIGURE 10-10

itly contained in the premisses. The information contained in categorical sentences can be represented in Venn diagrams. A Venn diagram can show whether one class is included in another, one class excludes the other, classes share a common member, or one class has a member that lies outside the other class (see Figure 10-9).

To apply the Venn diagram technique to categorical syllogisms, use three overlapping circles—one for each of the three terms in the argument. The circles are arranged in the standard way shown in Figure 10-10.

To test a syllogism for validity, use shading or **x**s to mark all information contained in the premisses on this standard blank diagram. Then inspect the diagram to see whether the information in the conclusion sentence can be read off the diagram. If the conclusion can be read off, then the argument is a valid syllogism. If the conclusion cannot be read off the diagram, then the argument is not a valid syllogism.

Examples

(a)   All sensitive persons are dreamers.   All *S* are *M*.
         All dreamers are poets.   All *M* are *P*.
         ———————————————————   ——————————
         All sensitive persons are poets.   All *S* are *P*.

In this argument, *S* is the class of sensitive persons, *P* is the class of poets, and *M* is the class of dreamers.

To diagram the first premiss, consider only the two circles labeled *S* and *M*. The first premiss is an *A* sentence, with *S* as the subject term. Thus, all of the *S* circle that lies outside the *M* circle is shaded, as shown in Figure 10-11.

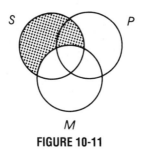

FIGURE 10-11

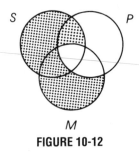

FIGURE 10-12

To diagram the second premiss, consider the two circles labeled P and M. The second premiss is also an A sentence with M as the subject term, so all of the M circle that does not lie within the P circle is shaded, as shown in Figure 10-12.

After diagramming these two premisses, inspect the Venn diagram to see whether the conclusion can be read off. The conclusion is an A sentence with S as the subject term and P as the predicate term. On the diagram, all of the S circle that lies outside the P circle has been shaded. (A part that lies inside the P circle has been shaded as well, but this does not conflict with the claim that if anything is an S then it is a P; it simply provides the additional information that any of the S's that are P's are M's as well.) Thus we can read off the sentence "All S are P" from the Venn diagram, and the argument is shown to be valid.

(b)   All statesmen are honorable persons.   All S are M.
         Some honorable persons are politicians.   Some M are P.
         ─────────────────────────────────   ──────────────
         Some statesmen are politicians.   Some S are P.

In Figure 10-13, the first premiss, "All S are M," is diagrammed by shading the part of the S circle that lies outside the M circle.

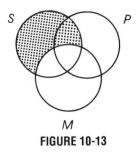

FIGURE 10-13

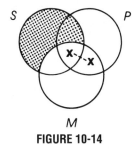

FIGURE 10-14

In Figure 10-14, the information contained in the second premiss, "Some *M* are *P*" is added to the diagram of the first premiss. The overlapping region between the *P* circle and the *M* circle is itself divided into two parts. One part lies within the *S* circle; the other part lies outside. Because the information in the premiss tells us only that a member exists somewhere in this overlap, we cannot locate an **x** definitely in one region or the other. Instead, we use the "floating **x**" (two **x**s connected by a dashed line) to indicate that a member lies somewhere in that region.

However, when we try to read off the conclusion "Some *S* are *P*," we see that the diagram tells us only that an **x** might lie in the region overlapping *S* and *P* or that it might lie in the region overlapping *P* and *M* but outside of *S*. Thus, we cannot read off the conclusion from the diagrammed premisses, and the syllogism is invalid. It is possible for both premisses to be true and the conclusion to be false.

(c)	No unicorns are black things.	No *S* are *M*.
	Some black things are dogs.	Some *M* are *P*.
	No unicorns are dogs.	No *S* are *P*.

In the Venn diagram in Figure 10-15, the first premiss requires shading the overlapping area between the *S* and the *M* circles. An **x** is then drawn in the overlapping area between the *M* and the *P* circles to represent the second pre-

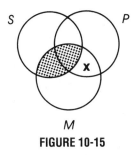

FIGURE 10-15

miss. In this case, as a result of diagramming the first premiss, we can see that the area of overlap between M and P that also lies within the S circle is empty, so a "floating **x**" is not needed. The **x** can only be drawn in the area between M and P that is unshaded. (Shading indicates emptiness; therefore no members can be found in a shaded area. The use of floating **x**s in Venn diagrams can be minimized by always first diagramming any universal premiss.) To read off the conclusion from this diagram, the area of overlap between the S and the P circles would have to be shaded. Because this is not the case, the syllogism is invalid.

(d)	No intelligent persons are gluttons.	No P are M.
	Some famous persons are gluttons.	Some S are M.
	Some famous persons are not intelligent.	Some S are not P.

The first premiss is diagrammed in Figure 10-16 by shading the overlapping region between the P and the M circles. The second premiss requires placing an **x** in the overlap between the S and the M circles. The **x** is placed in the unshaded portion of this overlap. In order to read off the conclusion, an **x** must be in the portion of the S circle that lies outside the P circle. This is the case, and so the diagram shows the validity of this syllogism.

(e)	Some animals are furry.	Some S are M.
	Some furry things are cats.	Some M are P.
	Some animals are cats.	Some S are P.

To diagram the first premiss, place an **x** in the overlap between S and M. This overlap contains two parts—one within and one outside the P circle (see Figure 10-17). The premiss does say where to place the **x**, so a floating **x** must be used. The second premiss says that a member of both P and M does exist but does not say whether this member belongs to S. Therefore, another floating **x** is used. The conclusion requires that an **x** be in the overlapping region between S and P. But because both **x**s are floating, we cannot tell whether either **x** lies in that region. Thus, the conclusion cannot be read off the diagram, and the syllogism is invalid.

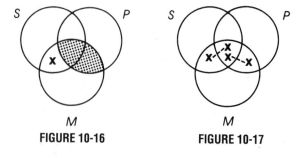

FIGURE 10-16 FIGURE 10-17

Exercise Set 10.3

Part One. For each of the following syllogisms:

(i)   Identify the *S*, *M*, and *P* terms.

(ii)   Draw a Venn diagram.

(iii) Tell whether the syllogism is valid or invalid.

Remember that diagramming will be simplified if universal premisses are diagrammed first. This will minimize the use of floating **xs**.

1. All animals feel pain. All things that feel pain are able to think. Therefore, all animals are able to think.

2. All patriots are chauvinists. Some chauvinists are fanatics. Therefore, some patriots are fanatics.

3. No good persons are cruel to animals. Some children are cruel to animals. Therefore, some children are not good persons.

4. No elephants are easy to train. Some dogs are not easy to train. Some dogs are not elephants.

5. All messengers who bring bad news are unwelcome. All messengers who bring bad news are punished. Therefore, some unwelcome persons are punished.

6. Some awards are worthless. Some worthless things are fun to have. Therefore, some awards are fun to have.

7. All diets require will power. No things that require will power are simple. Therefore, no diets are simple.

8. Some syllogisms are not valid arguments. All syllogisms have two premisses. Therefore, some arguments with two premisses are not valid.

9. No syllogisms are arguments with four terms. Some arguments with four terms are invalid. Therefore, no syllogisms are invalid.

10. Some arguments are invalid. Some invalid arguments are not syllogisms. Therefore, some arguments are not syllogisms.

Part Two. Regard each of the following pairs of sentences as premisses. Using an appropriately labeled three-circle Venn diagram, tell what syllogistic conclusion, if any, can be drawn from these premisses.

1. No football players are weaklings.

   No ballerinas are weaklings.

2. Some dogs have fleas.

   Some things with fleas are good pets.

3. No students are boring.

   Some professors are boring.

4. All mariners are sailors.

   All mariners love the sea.

5. Some valuable things are inexpensive.

   Some inexpensive things are not bargains.

6. No valuable thing is free of charge.

   All immunizations at the Health Center are free of charge.

7. All champions are hard workers.

   Some hard workers are unsuccessful.

8. All birds are egg-layers.

   Some mammals are egg-layers.

9. No birds are cold-blooded.

   All reptiles are cold-blooded.

10. All reptiles are cold-blooded.

   Some dinosaurs are not cold-blooded.

   Part Three. Suppose we follow the strategic rule of always diagramming universal premises before particular premises. This reduces the need for floating **x**s. Question: If, after diagramming universal premises, a floating **x** remains, is the form invalid? Explain why or why not.

V. DISTRIBUTION OF TERMS

A term is said to be **distributed** in a categorical sentence just in case that sentence says something about every member of the class to which the term refers. In the *A* sentence, for example, the subject term is distributed. The sentence "All logic students are hard working," says that *every* logic student is a hard-working person. However, the predicate term in the *A* sentence is not distributed, because that sentence does not say something about every hard-working person.

In the *E* sentence, both the subject and predicate terms are distributed. The sentence "No NFL football player is a ballerina" says of every NFL football player that he is not a ballerina and also says of every ballerina that she is not an NFL football player.

In the *I* sentence, neither the subject term nor the predicate term is distributed. This sentence says only that the two classes share at least one member. The *I* sentence says nothing about every member of either the subject class or the predicate class.

In the *O* sentence, the subject term is not distributed. In *O* sentences, as in *I* sentences, the subject term refers to only some member or members ("some" may mean more than one) of the class, not to every member. The predicate term, however, is understood as distributed in the *O* sentence. The awkward alternate formulation of the *O* sentence presented earlier ("At least one member of *S* is not identical with any member of *P*") illustrates that, in a roundabout way, the *O* sentence says something about each and every member of the *P* class—namely, that at least one member of *S* is not identical with it. Thus, the claim that "Some dogs are not brown" means "At least one dog is not identical with any brown thing," and the latter sentence is regarded as referring to all brown things.

These principles concerning the distribution of terms, which play an important role in the second method for assessing the validity of categorical syllogisms, can be summarized as follows:

Universal sentences: Subject term is distributed.

Negative sentences: Predicate term is distributed.

Fallacies of distribution can occur if the distinction between using a term distributively (to refer to every member of a class) and using a term collectively (to refer to the class as a whole) is not recognized. Consider the following arguments, neither of which is a categorical syllogism:

1. I infer that this stew will be delicious because each ingredient that went into it is delicious.
2. Mary's room at college must be large, for she lives in a very large dormitory.

In the first of these arguments, the conclusion that a *collective whole* (a stew) has a certain property is based on the information that its *parts* (distributively or individually) have that property. But this type of inference is not reliable. You can put together a collection of individually fine football players and end up with a poor team, and you can gather fine singers into a choir that sings badly. What is true of the parts is not *necessarily—or even probably*—true of the whole. The mistake of reasoning that what is true of the parts of a whole is also true of the whole, or that what is true of the individual members is true of the class, is called the **fallacy of composition**.

The second argument depends on the principle that what is true of the whole must be true of its parts. But this is also mistaken. Very large machines can be constructed from parts that are individually very small. A herd of cattle can be small even though none of its members is small. The fallacy involved in argument (2) above is called the **fallacy of division.** Like the fallacy of composition, the fallacy of division involves confusing the distributive use of a term with its collective use.

Exercise Set 10.4

1. The following argument occurs in Book V of Lucretius's (c. 100-55 B.C.) great philosophical poem *On the Nature of the Universe*. What fallacy does Lucretius apparently commit here?

> In the first place, since the elements of which we see the world composed—solid earth and moisture, the light breaths of air and torrid fire—all consist of bodies that are neither birthless nor deathless, we must believe the same of the world as a whole.

2. Does the following argument commit a fallacy of distribution?

> Science tells us that physical objects are made up entirely of tiny particles—electrons, positrons, neutrons, and so on—that are invisible, although their motions can be detected by sophisticated instruments. Science also tells us that these particles are in constant motion and that there are spaces between them. Yet we can see physical objects, feel their solidity, and see that they are not always in motion. So science must be wrong; physical objects cannot be composed of atomic and subatomic particles.

3. What fallacy occurs in the following passage?

> What is prudence in the conduct of every private family can hardly be folly in that of a great kingdom.
>
> —Adam Smith, *Wealth of Nations*

VI. RULES FOR TESTING THE VALIDITY OF SYLLOGISMS

Venn diagrams provide a general method of determining which conclusions follow validly from premises in categorical syllogisms. This technique is simple to apply. Various other techniques can be used also to determine whether syllogisms are valid or invalid. Deductive logicians are less concerned with assessing the validity of *particular arguments* than with formulating and testing *general principles* related to valid forms of argument. The truth tables introduced in the preceding chapter and the proof method discussed in Appendix 1 embody such general principles for truth-functional arguments. A number of different systems of principles governing "what-follows-from-what" in categorical syllogisms have been investigated by many logicians, beginning with Aristotle himself.

Aristotle's treatment of syllogisms differed from the Venn-diagram method. His approach to the problem employs the concept of a **figure of a syllogism.** In categorical syllogisms, the *S* term (the subject term of the conclusion) can be either the subject or the predicate of the premise in which it occurs; similarly, the *P* term (the predicate term of the conclusion) can be either the subject or the predicate of the premiss in which it occurs. Thus, four possible arrangements, or figures of the syllogism can be distinguished:

$$
\begin{array}{cccc}
MP & PM & MP & PM \\
SM & SM & MS & MS \\
\hline
SP & SP & SP & SP
\end{array}
$$

Because the order in which the premisses of an argument are stated has no bearing on the validity of the argument, variations in form that depend on this feature do not need to be considered. All premisses and conclusions of these arguments are sentences in *A*, *E*, *I*, or *O* form. These four types of sentences, taken three at a time (two sentences as the premisses and one sentence as the conclusion), can be combined in 64 ways, and each of the 64 combinations (called moods of the syllogism) can occur in each of the four figures. Therefore, 256 forms of categorical syllogisms are possible, only a few of which are valid. Venn diagrams can be used to test each form.

Aristotle's own system of principles for testing validity was less tedious than drawing 256 Venn diagrams. He took as axioms those syllogisms in the first figure that were obviously valid and showed that all valid forms in the other figures could be reduced (by obverting sentences, exchanging subject and predicate terms in *E* and *I* sentences, and other transformations discussed in Section III) directly or indirectly to these obviously valid forms. To show the invalidity of forms, Aristotle used the method of counterexample, providing arguments in those forms with obviously true premisses and obviously false conclusions. Aristotle's treatment of syllogistic logic was in many ways similar to Euclid's treatment of geometry as a deductive system. (For a discussion of Aristotle's treatment, see B. Mates, *Elementary Logic*.)

1. Three Rules for Valid Syllogisms

In this section, we consider a system of three rules for testing the validity of categorical syllogisms. This system of rules is another alternative to the Venn-diagram method. Some people find it easier to use than the diagrams.

Assuming the modern interpretation of universal generalizations, all of the properties required for a syllogism to be valid can be stated compactly in the three following rules.*

1. *The middle term must be distributed exactly once.* (This means that the middle term must be distributed in one of the premisses and undistributed in the other premiss. The middle term does not occur in the conclusion.)

---

* These rules are presented by W. Salmon in *Logic*, 3rd ed. He adapted them from a set given by J. T. Culbertson, *Mathematics and Logic for Digital Devices*.

2. *No end term can be distributed exactly once.* (This means that the *S* term can be distributed in the conclusion *if and only if* it is distributed in a premiss; the same is true for the *P* term.)

3. *The number of negative conclusions must equal the number of negative premisses.* (That is to say, there can be a negative conclusion if and only if there is exactly one negative premiss.)

Although these requirements are not immediately obvious, they are easy to memorize and provide a simple way of testing the validity of categorical syllogisms.

If a categorical syllogism violates *none* of these three rules, then it is valid. If *any* one of these rules is violated, then the syllogism is invalid.

Understanding what it means for a term to be distributed is crucial to seeing why these rules work. However, *applying* these rules to syllogisms requires only knowing *which* terms are distributed—not what *distribution* means.

If a term is distributed in the conclusion, then the conclusion says something about every member of the class to which the term refers. In any valid syllogism, the occurrence of that term in the premiss must be distributed as well; otherwise, the conclusion would "go beyond" the premiss in the sense that the conclusion—but not the premiss—would say something about every member of that class.

For similar reasons, one of the occurrences of the *middle term* (the *M* term, which occurs in each premiss but not in the conclusion) must be distributed, because it is through the middle term that the *S* and *P* terms (*end terms*) are connected. This connecting function of the middle term shows up clearly in Venn diagrams. If one of the premisses did not say something about every member of a class, then there might be no connection between the subject term and the predicate term of the conclusion, for the subject class might be connected with one part of the class denoted by the middle term while the predicate class might be connected with a separate part of the class denoted by the middle term. When the middle term is not distributed in a categorical syllogism, the **fallacy of the undistributed middle** is committed.

The preceding remarks offer *partial* justification for the rules. A justification has been given for why the middle term must be distributed at *least* once, but nothing has been said about why it must be distributed at *most* once. (If the Aristotelian interpretation of universal generalizations is adopted, the rule is revised to read "The middle term must be distributed at least once." A revised system of rules also permits deducing a particular conclusion from two universal premisses. This is to be expected, given the Aristotelian principle of subimplication.) It has been shown why an end term that is distributed in the conclusion must be distributed in the premiss, but it has not been shown why an end term that is distributed in the premiss must also be distributed in the conclusion. All of the other less obvious features of the rules can be justified, but the proofs are often tedious "proofs by cases," in which one must go through all the possible figures of the syllogism in which the rule is applicable to show why it works.

For example, to show that no valid categorical syllogism can have two negative premisses, we note that each negative premiss either states that the middle term and the end terms completely exclude one another or that some member of one of these classes does not belong to the other class. From this, however, it may not be apparent that nothing at all can be said with certainty in the conclusion about the relationship between the two end terms. In a "proof by cases," we can use Venn diagrams to consider the following possibilities.

     (i) Both premisses are *E* sentences.

Because the subject and the predicate terms are interchangeable in *E* sentences, we do not need to consider each figure separately. The Venn diagram for any syllogism with two *E* premisses looks like the one shown in Figure 10-18.

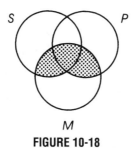

M

FIGURE 10-18

An inspection of the Venn diagram shows that no conclusion relating the end terms can be drawn from such premisses.

     (ii) Both premisses are *O* sentences.

If the middle term is not the predicate term in at least one of the *O* sentences, then the middle term is undistributed. Thus, the third figure is invalid:

$$MP \quad (O)$$
$$\underline{MS} \quad (O)$$
$$SP$$

For the other three figures, Venn diagrams will show that no syllogistic conclusion can be drawn from two *O* premisses.

(iii) One premiss is an *E* sentence, and the other premiss is an *O* sentence.

There are two possibilities:

(1) The premiss containing the *P* term is the *E* sentence. Two Venn diagrams are relevant here (see Figure 10-19). The left one diagrams "Some *S* are not *M*"; the right one diagrams "Some *M* are not *S*. " Neither shows a syllogistic conclusion.

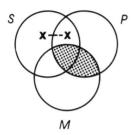 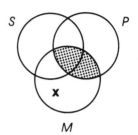

FIGURE 10-19

(2) The premiss containing the *S* term is the *E* sentence. Two Venn diagrams are relevant here (see Figure 10-20). The left one diagrams as "Some *P* are not *M*"; the right one diagrams "Some *M* are not *P*." Neither yields a syllogistic conclusion.

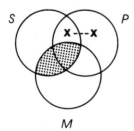 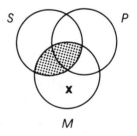

FIGURE 10-20

A *part* of the third rule has thus been justified in this "proof by cases," for we have shown that any syllogism with two negative premises is invalid, whether the conclusion is affirmative or negative. (Obviously, any syllogism can have only one conclusion.)

Exercise 10.5

1. Show, by a demonstration similar to the preceding "proof by cases" that any syllogism in which the number of negative conclusions is greater than the number of negative premises is invalid. Be sure to consider all possibilities.

2. According to the three rules given above, some *forms* of syllogisms are invalid, although English-language arguments that are instances of those forms are valid. Consider the following:

No graduate school to which I applied accepted me.
Every graduate school to which I applied is a high-ranked school.

Some high-ranked schools did not accept me.

(1) Represent the form of this syllogism as it is stated.

(2) Which of our three rules does this *form* violate?

The rules given in this chapter are designed to distinguish valid and invalid forms according to the modern interpretation of universal generalizations. According to the modern interpretation, no particular conclusion can be drawn validly from two universal premisses. The rules concerning distribution of end terms and middle term guarantee that this is so. If generalizations are interpreted in Aristotle's manner, however, which is to say if generalizations are understood as having existential import, then a different set of rules will be appropriate, and some forms that are invalid under the modern interpretation will be valid under the new set of rules. While the question of which *forms* are valid is tied to the system of logical rules, we must remember that an English-language argument can be an instance of several different forms. The English-language argument in Exercise Set 10.5 #2, for example, is valid. Using the modern system of logic to show its validity, however, requires explicitly stating the implicit premiss regarding the existence of high-ranked schools. With the addition of this third premiss, the argument no longer has the form of a syllogism, but the argument can be shown to be valid by the formal criteria of the logic of quantifiers that is discussed in Chapter 11.

2. Examples of Using the Rules to Test Validity

Remember that the subject terms are distributed in universal sentences and that the predicate terms are distributed in negative sentences. All distributed terms will be denoted by the subscript $_d$ in the argument forms.

(a)   All soldiers are brave persons.   All M_d are S.
        Some soldiers are not daredevils.   Some M are not P_d.

        Some brave persons are not daredevils.   Some S are not P_d.

1. The middle term is distributed in the first premiss but not in the second premiss. Thus, the middle term is distributed exactly once.

2. S is not distributed in the first premiss or in the conclusion. P is distributed in both the second premiss and in the conclusion. Thus, no end term is distributed exactly once.

3. The second premiss is the only negative premiss. The conclusion is negative. Thus, the number of negative premisses is equal to the number of negative conclusions.

The syllogism is valid.

(b) All football fans are fanatics.   All P_d are M.
     Some fanatics are silly people.   Some M are S.

     Some silly people are football fans.   Some S are P.

1. The middle term is not distributed in either of the premisses.

The syllogism is invalid. (Violation of one rule is sufficient to show invalidity. However, notice that the second rule is also violated, because P is distributed exactly once.)

(c) No difficult subjects are worthless.   No M_d are P_d.
     Some logic classes are not difficult.   Some S are not M_d.

     Some logic classes are not worthless.   Some S are not P_d.

1. The middle term is distributed in both premisses.

The syllogism is invalid. (Also note that the third rule is violated because of the two negative premisses and one negative conclusion.)

Exercise Set 10.6

> Part One. Identify the premisses and the conclusions of the following categorical syllogisms. Put the premisses and the conclusions into standard categorical form. Use the rules you have learned in this section to determine the validity or invalidity of the arguments. If a syllogism is invalid, specify which rule or rules it violates.

1. Some birds are nonflyers, for ostriches are birds and all ostriches are nonflyers.

2. No persons who aren't in great shape are runners, so no smokers are runners, for all smokers are persons who aren't in great shape.

3. Not all generals are warmongers, but some admirals are warmongers; so no admirals are generals.

4. Some bridge games are interesting to observe, but no canasta games are interesting to observe. Hence, some bridge games are not canasta games.

5. Whales have lungs, but no fish do; so whales aren't fish.

6. All gem stones are expensive, but some cubic zirconias are not expensive; so cubic zirconias are not gem stones.

7. All feminists supported the ERA, but some women did not support the ERA. Hence, some feminists are not women.

8. All porpoises are mammals, but no fish are mammals; so no porpoises are fish.

9. Ostriches never fly, but birds always do; so ostriches aren't birds.

10. Not all sofas are beds, but some beds are uncomfortable; so some sofas are uncomfortable.

> Part Two. Some systems of rules for valid syllogisms include the following rule:

No syllogistic conclusion can be drawn from two particular premisses.

Provide a justification for this rule. (*Hint*: You may provide a "proof by cases," using Venn diagrams to support each case. Or you may appeal to the set of three rules for a valid syllogism and show that this rule follows from that set.)

VII. REDUCING THE NUMBER OF TERMS IN SYLLOGISMS

By definition, a categorical syllogism cannot contain more than three terms. However, many arguments that do contain more than three terms can be transformed to equivalent categorical syllogisms. Some categorical syllogisms contain more than three terms because **synonyms** are used in the argument. Synonyms, like other rhetorical devices, make the language of arguments more interesting and can increase an argument's persuasive force. When reconstructing these arguments to assess their validity, the number of terms can be reduced by treating synonyms as multiple occurrences of the same term.

In other cases, arguments contain both pairs of a complementary set of terms. It may be possible to reduce the number of terms by obversion (changing the quality and replacing a predicate term with its complement). Because obversion can reduce the number of terms only when the extra term occurs in the predicate position, it may be necessary to exchange the subject and predicate terms before obverting. (Remember, this exchange is legitimate only in *I* and *E* sentences.) Consider the following argument, in which both premisses are categorical sentences and the conclusion is a categorical sentence, but which contains four terms:

All puzzles are interesting.
All logic exercises are puzzles.
———————————————————
No logic exercises are noninteresting.

The terms *interesting and noninteresting* are complementary. If the first premiss is obverted, it becomes "No puzzles are noninteresting." This categorical sentence is equivalent to "All puzzles are interesting." The number of terms in the new equivalent syllogism is now only three, and the syllogism can be tested by the rules for a valid syllogism or by the Venn-diagram method:

No *M* are *P*
All *S* are *M*

No *S* are *P*

A different way to reduce the number of terms in this English argument is to obvert the conclusion instead of the first premiss. Then, the conclusion becomes "All logic exercises are interesting." Again, a categorical syllogism results, but of the following form:

All *M* are *P*
All *S* are *M*

All *S* are *P*

In this form, the *P* term is *interesting,* whereas in the preceding form, the *P* term is *noninteresting.* Is this a valid form of syllogism?

The following argument contains five terms:

Some nonbelievers are freethinkers, because no believers are atheists and some atheists are nonfreethinkers.

Letting *P* represent freethinkers, *S* represent believers, and *M* represent atheists, this argument has the following form:

No *S* are *M*
Some *M* are non-*P*

Some non-*S* are *P*

The second premiss can be obverted: Change the *I* sentence to an *O* sentence, and change non-*P* to *P* (Some *M* are not *P*).

Next, reduce the pair of terms *S* and non-*S.* Begin by exchanging the subject and the predicate terms in the conclusion. This is legitimate, because the conclusion is an *I* sentence (Some *P* are non-*S*).

Then, this sentence can be obverted to yield

Some *P* are not *S.*

The reconstructed argument, which contains only three terms, has this form:

No *S* are *M*
Some *M* are not *P*

Some *P* are not *S*

Is this a valid form of syllogism?

Exercise Set 10.7

> Reconstruct each of the following arguments as a categorical syllogism in standard form. Test each syllogism for validity, using either the rules for a valid syllogism or Venn diagrams.

1. Some men are nonsexists, since all sexists oppose equal rights for women and some men do not oppose equal rights for women.

2. Some strong persons are sensitive, but no poets fail to be sensitive. Hence, some poets are strong persons.

3. All modern-style architecture is without ornamentation, but some recently constructed buildings are ornate; so not all new buildings are in the modern style.

4. Some edible things are nonpoisonous, for all insects are edible and some insects are poisonous.

5. No man is willing to die; but women aren't men, so some women are not unwilling to die.

6. No one who speaks Latin lives in Latin America; but not all Latin Americans live there, so some Latin Americans are Latin speakers.

7. Carrot eaters are health-food freaks, and no one who is crazy about health food eats chocolate; so chocolate-freaks aren't carrot eaters.

8. All rooms look their best if they are used by the people they belong to. Unless a room is arranged in a way that allows it to function comfortably, it will never be used. Therefore no room will look its best until it is comfortably arranged.

   —M. Hampton, *House and Garden*, March 1987

(Exercises 9-11 are from *The Art of Thinking*, also called *Port-Royal Logic*. This seventeenth-century logic text was designed by Antoine Arnauld to teach a young nobleman everything there was to know about logic in ten days.)

9. That which has no parts cannot perish by dissolution of its parts.
   The soul has no parts.
   _____

   The soul cannot perish by dissolution of its parts.

10. No virtue is offensive.
    Some zeal is not inoffensive.
    _____

    Some zeal is nonvirtuous.

11. All liars are unbelievable.
    Every upright person is believable.
    _____

    All liars are persons who are not upright.

VIII. RECONSTRUCTING ORDINARY-LANGUAGE ARGUMENTS AS SYLLOGISMS

Many arguments that are incompletely stated in English or that contain sentences not in categorical form can be construed as categorical syllogisms.

Examples

(a) Consider the following passage from Simone de Beauvoir's *The Ethics of Ambiguity*:

> In *Plutarch Lied*, Pierrefeu rightly says that in war there is no victory which can not be regarded as unsuccessful, for the objective which one aims at is the total annihilation of the enemy and this result is never attained.

This argument can be stated in syllogistic form:

All successful victories in war achieve total annihilation of the enemy.
No actual victories in war achieve total annihilation of the enemy.
_____

No actual victories in war are successful victories in war.

(b) The following argument, from Chapter 12 of Leo Tolstoy's *What is Art?*, can also be recast as a syllogism:

> Accustoming people to something resembling art disaccustoms them to the comprehension of real art. And that is how it comes about that none are more dull to art than those who have passed through the professional schools and have been most successful in them. Professional schools produce an hypocrisy of art.

Syllogistically, this argument can be expressed

All who have successfully passed through professional schools of art have been accustomed to something resembling art.
All who have been accustomed to something resembling art are persons most dull to real art.
_____

All who have successfully passed through professional schools are persons most dull to real art.

(c) The next argument is from St. Augustine's *Confessions*, Book X. When an unstated (but obviously intended) premiss is supplied, it can be viewed as a categorical syllogism:

> [A] happy life is not seen with the eye, because it is not a body.

In syllogistic form, this argument becomes

No happy lives are bodies.
(All things that can be seen with the eye are bodies.)   *Implicit premiss*

No happy lives are things that can be seen with the eye.

(d) The final example is taken from *The Mismeasure of Man* by Stephen Jay Gould:

> If I had any desire to lead a life of indolent ease, I would wish to be an identical twin, separated from my brother and raised in a different social class. We could hire ourselves out to a host of social scientists and practically name our fee. For we would be exceedingly rare representatives of the only really adequate natural experiment for separating genetic from environmental effects in humans—genetically identical individuals raised in disparate environments.

A syllogistic reconstruction of this argument is

All who are genetically identical individuals raised in disparate environments are representatives of the only adequate natural experiment for separating genetic from environmental effects in humans.
All representatives of the only adequate natural experiment for separating genetic from environmental effects in humans are persons who can command a sufficient fee from social scientists to lead a life of indolent ease.

All genetically identical individuals raised in disparate environments are persons who can command a sufficient fee from social scientists to lead a life of indolent ease.

IX. QUASI-SYLLOGISM AND SORITES

1. Quasi-Syllogisms

A syllogism with one universal premiss, another premiss stating that a given individual is a member of the subject class, and a conclusion stating that the individual is a member of the predicate class, such as

All men are mortal.
Socrates is a man.

Socrates is mortal.

is called a **quasi-syllogism.** This is obviously an instance of a valid form of reasoning. Strictly speaking, however, it is not a *categorical* syllogism because sentences such as "Socrates is a man" (called **singular** sentences) are not categorical. Some treatments of syllogistic logic handle this fundamental form of argument by interpreting singular sentences as disguised universal generalizations:

All members of the class in which the only member is Socrates are men.

If the singular sentences are interpreted in this way, the preceding quasi-syllogism above becomes an instance of the valid form:

All *M* are *P*
All *S* are *M*
———————
All *S* are *P*

Quasi-syllogisms can also occur with negative universal premisses:

No whales are fishes.
Shamu is a whale.
———————
Shamu is not a fish.

The conclusion in this syllogism is interpreted as

No members of the class whose only member is Shamu are fishes.

Interpreting the singular premiss as in the other quasi-syllogism, this quasi-syllogism becomes an instance of the valid categorical form:

No *M* are *P*
All *S* are *M*
———————
No *S* are *P*

An alternative way of interpreting the quasi-syllogism is discussed in Chapter 11.

2. Sorites

A **sorites** is an argument with more than two categorical sentences as premisses from which a final categorical conclusion may be drawn by performing a series of syllogistic inferences. In a sorites with three premisses, the intermediate syllogistic conclusion drawn from a pair of the stated premisses is used as an additional premiss and combined with the third premiss to yield the final conclusion of the argument.

In a sorites with more than three premisses, the process of drawing intermediate conclusions and using them as additional premisses is performed as often as required to reach the final conclusion. Lewis Carroll, the brilliant logician who is best known as the author of *Alice in Wonderland*, discusses this type of argument in his *Symbolic Logic*. All of the following examples are taken from this work. Solutions to the first two examples are given. The remaining sets of premisses are intended as exercises.

Examples of Premisses for Soriteses

(a) (i) No ducks waltz.
   (ii) No officers ever decline to waltz.
   (iii) All of my poultry are ducks.

Taking *ducks* as a middle term, the first and third premisses can be combined to yield the intermediate conclusion:

   (iv) No poultry of mine waltz.

"No officers ever decline to waltz" can be obverted to obtain "All officers waltz." This can then be combined with the intermediate conclusion (iv) to yield the final conclusion:

   (v) No officers are poultry of mine.

The conclusion "No poultry of mine are officers," which is equivalent to (v), could also be drawn from the same premisses.

(b) (i) No potatoes of mine that are new have been boiled.
   (ii) All my potatoes in this dish are fit to eat.
   (iii) No unboiled potatoes of mine are fit to eat.

Taking *things that are fit to eat* as a middle term, premisses (ii) and (iii) can be combined to provide an intermediate conclusion:

   (iv) No unboiled potatoes of mine are my potatoes in this dish.

Before this intermediate conclusion can be combined with (i), the number of terms must be reduced. "Potatoes of mine" is equivalent to "my potatoes." Because "boiled" and "unboiled" are complementary, we obvert (i), in which "boiled" occurs in the predicate position. Obverting (i) yields

   (v) All potatoes of mine that are new are unboiled (potatoes of mine).

Combining (iv) and (v), yields the conclusion:
   No potatoes of mine that are new are potatoes of mine in this dish.
Or, less awkwardly, "None of my new potatoes are in this dish."

Exercise Set 10. 8

1. Show that the conclusion "All of my new potatoes are unfit to eat" also follows from the first three premisses in (b).

2. Draw an appropriate syllogistic conclusion from the following three premisses:

    (i) No one takes the *Times* unless he is well educated.

    (ii) No hedgehogs can read.

    (iii) Those who cannot read are not well educated.

3. Draw an appropriate syllogistic conclusion from the following three premisses:

    (i) Every one who is sane can do logic.

    (ii) No lunatics are fit to serve on a jury.

    (iii) None of your sons can do logic.

4. Draw an appropriate syllogistic conclusion from the following three premisses:

    (i) All hummingbirds are richly colored.

    (ii) No large birds live on honey.

    (iii) Birds that do not live on honey are dull in color.

5. Draw an appropriate syllogistic conclusion from the following four premisses:

    (i) No birds, except ostriches, are nine feet high.

    (ii) There are no birds in this aviary that belong to anyone but me.

    (iii) No ostrich lives on mince pies.

    (iv) I have no birds less than nine feet high.

6. Reconstruct Woodward's argument in the following passage as a quasi-syllogism. Is it valid?

> Robert S. Woodward, then president of the Carnegie Institution, reacted with silence to a new archaeology department. He did remark to his colleagues at the institution that archaeology exists to aid museums in the acquisition of collections, and since the Carnegie had no museums, archaeology was therefore not part of the Carnegie's mission.
>
> —Brunhouse 1971, p. 67, quoted by D. R. Givens

X. REVIEW

Not surprisingly, an extensive specialized terminology has developed in connection with a subject that has been studied in classrooms for more than 2,000 years. Although some of this terminology is used predominantly in logic classes, much of it has found its way into the everyday vocabulary of educated people. A list of the important new terms used in this chapter, with brief definitions, follows.

Categorical Sentence: Letting "*S*" represent the subject term and "*P*" represent the predicate term, the four standard categorical sentence forms are:

1. Every *S* is *P*. (Universal affirmative, or *A* sentence)

2. No *S* is *P*. (Universal negative, or *E* sentence)

3. Some *S* is *P*. (Particular affirmative, or *I* sentence)

4. Some *S* is not *P*. (Particular negative, or *O* sentence)

Categorical Syllogism: The following features characterize this type of argument:

1. Two premisses, and a conclusion, each of which is a categorical sentence.

2. Only three terms occur in the argument. The middle term occurs once in each premiss; the two end terms occur once in one of the premisses and once in the conclusion.

Complementary Terms: A pair of terms is complementary when one term of the pair refers to a class and the other term of the pair refers to its *complement* (the class consisting of all things that are not members of the original class).

Contradictory Sentences: When one sentence in a pair is the negation of the other sentence, the pair of sentences is contradictory. In a pair of contradictory sentences, one is true and the other is false. For categorical sentences with the same subjects and predicates, the *A* and *O* sentences are contradictory, as are the *E* and *I* sentences.

Contraposition: The *contrapositive* of an *A* or an *O* sentence is formed by exchanging the positions of the subject and predicate terms and replacing each with its complement. Contraposition preserves meaning for *A* and *O* sentences, but not for *I* and *E* sentences.

Contrary Sentences: When a pair of sentences is related in such a way that they could both be false but could not both be true, the sentences are contrary to one another. In the Aristotelian interpretation of categorical sentences, the *A* and *E* sentences which share the same subject and predicate terms are contraries.

Conversion: A categorical sentence is *converted* when the subject and predicate terms are interchanged. Converting *I* and *E* sentences yields sentences with the same meaning as the original sentences; converting *A* and *O* sentences does not.

Distribution of Terms: When a sentence says something about every member of a class, the term referring to that class is said to be *distributed*. In universal categorical sentences, the subject terms are distributed; in negative categorical sentences, the predicate terms are distributed.

Existential Import: When a sentence asserts the existence of some object, the sentence has existential import. Universal categorical sentences, when understood as material conditionals, lack existential import. Particular categorical sentences have existential import.

Fallacies of Distribution: Mistakes in reasoning that occur when a term that is used collectively in the premisses is interpreted distributively in the conclusion (**fallacy of division**) or when a term that is used distributively in the premisses is interpreted collectively in the conclusion (**fallacy of composition**).

Fallacy of the Undistributed Middle: This fallacy occurs in syllogistic arguments in which the middle term is undistributed in either premiss.

Figure of a Syllogism: The "figure" refers to the arrangement of the end terms ("*S*" and "*P*") and the middle term ("*M*") in the premisses. The four figures are:

MP	*PM*	*MP*	*PM*
SM	*SM*	*MS*	*MS*
SP	*SP*	*SP*	*SP*

Obversion: A categorical sentence is *obverted* when the quality of the sentence is changed and the predicate term is replaced with its complement. The resulting sentence is a categorical sentence that is logically equivalent to the original sentence.

Quality of a Categorical Sentence: The quality of a categorical sentence refers to whether the sentence is negative or affirmative. The quality of *A* and *I* sentences is affirmative; the quality of *E* and *O* sentences is negative.

Quasi-Syllogism: A three-term syllogism with a universal premiss, a singular premiss, and a singular conclusion.

Sorites: An argument with more than two categorical sentences as premisses and with a categorical conclusion that is reached by drawing an *intermediate* syllogistic conclusion from two of the premisses and then using this conclusion in combination with another premiss to draw a further syllogistic conclusion. This pattern is repeated, using the remaining premisses, until the final conclusion is reached.

Subcontrary Sentences: When a pair of sentences is related in such a way that they could both be true but could not both be false, the sentences are subcontraries. Under the Aristotelian interpretation of categorical sentences, *I* and *O* sentences with the same subject and the same predicate terms are subcontraries.

Venn Diagrams: Sets of overlapping circles, which can be marked to indicate class membership, class exclusion, and class inclusion. These diagrams are used to exhibit the relations between classes in categorical sentences and to test for the validity of syllogisms.

Exercise Set 10.9

Part One. For each of the following incomplete arguments, supply a premiss that will make the argument a valid categorical syllogism or quasi-syllogism. (Use the rules for valid syllogisms or Venn diagrams, if helpful.)

1. Marijuana should not be legalized because it is potentially dangerous.

2. Marijuana should be legalized because it is no more dangerous than alcohol, which is legal.

3. Abernathy must be rich, since he never wears an overcoat.

4. Female office workers work just as hard as male office workers and are just as productive. Therefore, female office workers should receive the same pay as male office workers in comparable positions.

5. Since John gets sick only when he is nervous, he must have psychogenic illness.

6. Not all socialists deserve to be persecuted, for some socialists are champions of human rights.

7. Those who do not sin need not fear God, so you don't need to be afraid of God.

8. Terry is a mathematician, so she must be musically talented.

9. You had no right to take away his gun, because that gun was private property.

10. If you failed, it's because you didn't try hard enough.

Part Two. What syllogistic conclusion, if any, can be validly drawn from the following pairs of premisses? (The rules for valid syllogisms or Venn diagrams will prove helpful.)

1. All beautiful things are expensive. Some beautiful things are made of inexpensive materials.

2. Some sailors are adventurous. Some adventurous persons like long sea voyages.

3. Whoever lives by the sword will perish by the sword. Some soldiers perish by the sword.

4. Whatever goes up must come down. Stock prices are going up.

5. Anything I say can be misinterpreted. Some misinterpretations are harmless.

6. All grains are cereals. Some fruits are grains.

7. No salt is an element. Some salts are soluble.

8. All metals are fusible. Some conductors are nonmetals.

9. All gondolas are boats. All gondolas have gondoliers.

10. All children like candy. Some adults like candy.

11. All first basemen are athletes. No catchers are first basemen.

Part Three. Reconstruct each of the following arguments as a categorical syllogism, supplying plausible premisses when necessary. Test each syllogism for validity, using the rules for valid syllogisms or Venn diagrams.

1. Some valid arguments have false conclusions, but not all syllogisms are valid; so some syllogisms have true conclusions.

2. None but the rich can afford to be idle. Anyone who can afford to be idle is a threat to the Puritan work ethic, so some rich persons threaten the Puritan work ethic.

3. Skillfully handcrafted items that are beautiful, enduring, and useful are never inexpensive, so Navajo rugs command a high price.

4. A clever cook avoids making souffles for dinner parties. No home economics major is not a clever cook. Therefore, no home economics major fails to avoid making souffles for dinner parties.

5. Some custards are soft, but no ices are soft; so some ices are not custards.

6. Fallacious arguments are unconvincing. None of your arguments is fallacious. Therefore, all of your arguments are convincing.

7. Some professors are ignorant. None who is ignorant is fit to teach college students. So some who are unfit to teach college students are professors.

8. He who hesitates is lost, but the lost shall be found; so hesitators won't stay lost.

9. All reporters are aggressive. None but reporters have daily deadlines. So no nonaggressive persons have daily deadlines.

10. Syllogisms all have two premisses. Not all syllogisms are categorical. So some noncategorical syllogisms have two premisses.

11. Decent newspapers cannot attain a wide circulation, for they do not emphasize sensational material. We all know that papers that emphasize sensational material attain a wide circulation.

Chapter Eleven

ARGUMENTS IN WHICH VALIDITY DEPENDS ON RELATIONSHIPS

I. INTRODUCTION

Two important types of arguments, truth-functional arguments and categorical syllogisms, are analyzed in preceding chapters to show that validity depends on the *form* of the arguments. The validity of truth-functional arguments depends on logical connections among the sentences that make up the argument, whereas the validity of categorical syllogisms depends on logical connections between the subject terms and the predicate terms within sentences. In the analysis of both truth-functional and syllogistic arguments, the *content* of the arguments is ignored to focus on logically important structural features of the arguments. To express the forms of these arguments in a general way, simple sentences in truth-functional arguments and class terms in categorical syllogisms are represented by letters of the alphabet. In the case of truth-functional arguments, logical symbols are used to represent the truth-functional connectives *and, not, or, if . . . then,* and *if and only if.*

Logicians operate on the assumption that *any* deductively valid argument is an instance of *some* valid argument form. Accordingly, the history of logic has been the history of an increasing awareness of the formal properties of arguments that are recognized intuitively as valid. Aristotle's theory of syllogisms was the first formal account of arguments. Shortly after Aristotle, the Stoic logicians developed a comprehensive theory of the forms of truth-functional arguments. Only much later did another important class of arguments receive formal treatment. The validity of these arguments depends on certain formal properties of *relationships* mentioned in them. These **relational arguments** are the subject of this chapter. The formal symbolism developed to handle relational arguments draws on both the logic of classes and truth-functional logic. By studying relational logic, even briefly, we can glimpse some of the power of modern symbolic techniques for unifying the study of deductive reasoning.

II. EXAMPLES OF RELATIONAL ARGUMENTS

The following arguments are obviously valid:

1. New Maseratis are more expensive than new Cadillacs.
   New Cadillacs are more expensive than new Fords.
   _____
   New Maseratis are more expensive than new Fords.

2. Jill is older than Jack.
   _____
   Jack is not older than Jill.

3. One British pint is equal to 570 milliliters.
   _____
   570 milliliters is equal to one British pint.

Using only the techniques of truth-functional logic and syllogistic logic, we cannot represent the forms by virtue of which any of these arguments are valid. In each case, the validity of the argument depends essentially on some property of the relationships ("more expensive than," "older than," "equal to") referred to in the arguments, rather than merely on connections among the sentences in the argument or on how the subjects and predicates of the sentences are connected.

III. IMPORTANT PROPERTIES OF RELATIONSHIPS

Argument (1) is valid because if one thing is more expensive than a second, and the second is more expensive than a third, then the first is more expensive than the third. When a relationship, such as "more expensive than" exhibits this feature, the relationship is said to be **transitive.** Many ordinary relationships are transitive. Some examples of transitive relationships are: "older than," "younger than," "prettier than," "equal to," "greater than," "ancestor of," "descended from."

Not all relationships are transitive. Some are **intransitive.** If the fact that one member is related to a second and the second has the same relationship to a third *rules out* the first member standing in that relation to the third, the relationship is intransitive. The following argument is valid because the relationship "mother of" is intransitive:

Ruth is the mother of Betty.
Betty is the mother of Claudia.

Ruth is *not* the mother of Claudia.

Other examples of intransitive relationships are "father of" and "twice as large as."

Nontransitive relationships are neither transitive nor intransitive. ("Transitive" and "intransitive" are contrary terms, not contradictories.) If the first member has a nontransitive relationship to a second, and the second has that same relationship to a third, then the first member might or might not be related to the third in that way.

"Cousin of" is a nontransitive relationship. If James is a cousin of Alice and Alice is a cousin of Richard, James could be Richard's cousin—but maybe not. No conclusion can be drawn regarding the relationship between the first and third members on the basis of a nontransitive relationship between the first and second and the second and third. Some other nontransitive relationships are "takes a class with," "likes some of the same foods as," "is a friend of," "loves," and "is in a carpool with."

All of the relationships mentioned thus far relate pairs of things or individuals. These are called **binary** or two-termed relationships. The two things that are related by a binary relationship are called the **terms** of the relation. Not all relationships are binary. In the sentence "Clarissa bought her books from

Edward," a relationship connects three terms: Clarissa, her books, and Edward. The following sentence involves a four-term relationship: "Tony gave money to Sally for the hospital fund-raiser." Although constructing English sentences involving relationships with more than four or five terms is awkward, in theory, any number of terms can be related. To avoid complexities, and to focus on some important properties of relationships that relate only two terms, the discussion in this chapter is confined to binary relationships.

Any binary relationship belongs to *exactly one* of the following categories: transitive, intransitive, or nontransitive.

The relationship ("older than") mentioned in argument (2) in Section II is transitive. However, the validity of this argument does not depend on the transitivity of that relationship but on another of its properties. "Older than" is an **asymmetric relationship.** If the first member is related by an asymmetric relationship to the second, then the second is *not* related to the first in that way. "Greater than," "less than," "weighs more than," and "mother of" are examples of asymmetric relationships.

If the fact that the first member has a relationship to the second *implies* that the second has that same relationship to the first, then the relationship is said to be **symmetric.** "Equal to," "weighs the same as," "not identical with," and "sibling of" are all symmetric relationships. The validity of argument (3) in Section II depends on the symmetry of "equal to."

In **nonsymmetric** relationships, the fact that the first member is related to the second *neither* implies *nor* rules out the second member standing in that relationship to the first. "Brother of" is a nonsymmetric relationship. Two individuals can be related in such a way that one is the brother of the other but the second is not brother of the first (when the second is female). In the case of two males, if the first is brother to the second, then the second is brother to the first. Because either situation is possible for two arbitrarily selected individuals who can stand in that relationship to one another, "brother of" is a nonsymmetric relationship.

Every binary relationship falls into *exactly one* of these three categories: symmetric, asymmetric, or nonsymmetric.

Relationships that relate an individual or a thing to itself are called **reflexive** relationships. "Identical with" is a reflexive relationship; everything is identical with itself. Other examples of reflexive relationships are "equal to" and "is the same color as."

Irreflexive relationships are those that no individual or thing can have to itself. Examples of irreflexive relationships are "unequal to," "different from," "not the same as," and "greater than."

Some relationships are **nonreflexive.** Individuals or things *might* or *might not* bear such relationships to themselves. "Loves," for example, is nonreflexive; some persons love themselves, but others do not.

Some find it odd to regard a relationship as two-termed when the "two" things being related are one and the same. Nevertheless, it makes perfectly good sense to speak of a thing's either having or failing to have some relationship to itself. In general, the two terms in any binary relationship need not refer to distinct individuals.

Exercise Set 11.1

Part One. State whether each of the following relationships is

(1) Transitive, intransitive or nontransitive.

(2) Symmetric, asymmetric, or nonsymmetric.

(3) Reflexive, irreflexive, or nonreflexive.

1. Loves

2. Cousin of

3. Belongs to

4. Looks like

5. Less than

6. Is preferred to

7. Is taller than

8. Is identical with

9. Is the same age as

10. Plays better than

Part Two. Name ten additional binary relationships, and categorize each
as transitive, symmetric, reflexive, and so on.

IV. USING QUANTIFIERS TO EXPRESS RELATIONSHIPS

Aristotle used *variables* (letters of the alphabet) to represent class terms when
he formulated principles of reasoning. Using variables in this way simplifies
the expression of principles and makes it easier to recognize the formal properties of arguments. The use of letters to represent sentences in truth-functional logic is a twentieth-century innovation. Some grasp of the simplicity
gained by applying this technique is evident when the modern formulation of
affirming the antecedent:

$$p \rightarrow q$$
$$\underline{p}$$
$$q$$

is compared with the formulation of the ancient Stoic logicians:

If the first, then the second.
The first.
Therefore, the second.*

---

* Benson Mates, *Elementary Logic,* p. 214.

When truth-functional argument forms involve numerous simple sentences, the use of sentence letters is even more attractive. (For instance, try to express one of the dilemma forms of argument using expressions such as "the first," "the second," "the third," and so on.)

Twentieth-century developments in the symbolization of logic facilitate the expression of relationships. The symbolic languages used by modern logicians provide an adequate formulation of categorical syllogisms as well, and, by employing symbols common to various types of arguments, serve to make apparent the structural similarities among truth-functional arguments, syllogistic arguments, and relational arguments.

In the following sections we will speak of *translating* English expressions into artificial symbolic language. These translations are not intended to capture all of the nuances that could be expressed in the English language. Their purpose is to identify the features of arguments that are important for determining their validity. The symbols introduced here are designed to capture only those features.

For any translation to be possible, the symbols of the artificial language must be *interpreted*. **Interpretations** specify the meanings of the symbols to the extent that truth conditions (the conditions under which sentences in the artificial language are true or false) are clearly specified. Truth tables have already been used for this purpose with the symbols of truth-functional logic. Because the same connectives are used here, the following summary is provided ("*p*" and "*q*" are sentence letters, which can be used to represent complex as well as simple sentences):

1. "$\sim p$" is true if and only if "*p*" is false.

2. "$(p \vee q)$" is false only in cases when both "*p*" and "*q*" are false; otherwise, it is true.

3. "$(p \cdot q)$" is true only in cases when both "*p*" and "*q*" are true; otherwise, it is false.

4. "$(p \to q)$" is false whenever "*p*" is true and "*q*" is false; otherwise, it is true.

5. "$(p \leftrightarrow q)$" is true whenever "*p*" and "*q*" have the same truth value; otherwise, it is false.

Other features of interpretations are discussed in context as they arise.

1.   Symbolizing the Universal Quantifier

In the universal affirmative sentence form "All *S* are *P*," *all* is a **universal quantifier.** Chapter 10 discusses the logical structure and different ways of expressing universal affirmative sentences. In accord with the modern interpretation of universal affirmatives, they can be expressed as conditionals:

If anything is an *S* then it is a *P*.

An equivalent conditional formulation is:

For any individual (person, place, or thing), if it is an *S*, then it is a *P*.

The universal quantifier is commonly symbolized by a lowercase italic letter from the end of the alphabet enclosed in parentheses. Examples are

(*x*) Read: "For any *x*"

(*y*) Read: "For any *y*"

(*z*) Read: "For any *z*"

In symbolizing the universal affirmative sentence, the same letter that is in the quantifier is used in place of pronouns such as *it* to refer to the same individual. Thus, to symbolize "For any individual, if it is an *S* then it is a *P*," write

$(x)(Sx \rightarrow Px)$

Parentheses enclose the expression following the quantifier to indicate that the *x*'s in this expression are those referred to by the quantifier that precedes the expression. Lowercase letters from the end of the alphabet that are used in this way are called **individual variables;** the uppercase italic letters used to represent *classes* of individuals are called **predicate letters.**

Now, suppose that we want to translate the English categorical sentence "All suffragettes are feminists" into a symbolic sentence that represents the meaning of the English sentence as closely as possible. The first step is to specify a **domain of interpretation,** or the *set of all individuals* referred to in the artificial language. This domain may vary from interpretation to interpretation. When numbers are the only individuals referred to, the *set of all numbers* can be chosen as the domain of interpretation. In another situation, persons might be the only individuals referred to, so the *set of all persons* can be taken as the domain. In general, the domain of interpretation can be any nonempty set of individuals. To simplify matters for all interpretations in this chapter, unless otherwise noted, the domain of interpretation consists of the set of all individuals. (The members of this domain are all persons, things, numbers, and so on.)

Predicate letters are interpreted as referring to *classes* (sets) of individuals in the domain. To translate "All suffragettes are feminists," let one predicate letter (*S*) denote the class of suffragettes, and a second predicate letter (*F*) denote the class of feminists. Then "All suffragettes are feminists" is translated "$(x)(Sx \rightarrow Fx)$."

The universal negative sentence ("No *S* are *P*") has a structure similar to the universal affirmative and is written

$(x)(Sx \rightarrow \sim Px)$

(For any individual, if it is an *S*, then it is not a *P*).

To translate the sentence "No Chihuahuas are guide dogs," let the predicate letter "G" denote the class of guide dogs and "C" denote the class of Chihuahuas:

$(x)(Cx \rightarrow \sim Gx)$,

(If anything is a Chihuahua then it is not a guide dog.)

2. Symbolizing the Existential Quantifier

The quantifier *some* is called the **existential quantifier.** Particular affirmative sentences and particular negative sentences assert both that some individual *exists* and that the individual either *has* or *lacks* some property. These sentences are therefore said to have **existential import.** On the modern interpretation, universal sentences are said to lack existential import because they do not assert the existence of anything.

As noted in Chapter 10, the structure of *I* and *O* sentences differs from that of universal sentences. Particular generalizations resemble conjunctions rather than conditionals. The *I* sentence:

Some *S* are *P*

is understood to mean

Some individual exists that is an *S* and also a *P*.

The *O* sentence:

Some *S* are not *P*

is understood to mean

Some individual exists that is an *S and* not a *P*.

The existential quantifier is symbolized by a backward "E" followed by an individual variable, both enclosed in parentheses: $(\exists x)$.

To symbolize the existential, or particular, affirmative categorical sentence, write

$(\exists x)(Sx \cdot Px)$

which can be read: "There is some *x* such that it is *S* and it is *P*."

To symbolize the existential (particular) negative categorical sentence, write

$(\exists x)(Sx \cdot \sim Px)$

which can be read: "There is some *x* such that it is *S* and it is not *P*."

Exercise Set 11.2

Assign predicate letters to classes, and translate the following sentences into the symbolic language:

1. Some dogs have fleas.
2. Some cats are not independent.
3. No dogs are vegetarians.
4. All cats are independent.
5. There are wild cats.
6. Cats are quadrupeds.
7. Not all dogs bark.
8. All dogs bark and all cats meow.
9. Some dogs bark, but some do not.
10. Dogs and cats are fine pets.
11. If some cats are wild, then some are tame.
12. If no dogs are cats, then no cats are dogs.

3. Symbolizing Relational Sentences

The symbols used to represent categorical sentences can be adapted to express relationships. The class terms that occur in categorical sentences can be thought of as **one-place** or **monadic** predicates. In the symbolic language, we indicate that an individual x is a member of a class S by writing a predicate letter followed by a single individual variable: Sx. In a similar manner, binary relationships can be represented by **two-place predicates**. Predicate letters can be used to indicate that an individual x stands in a relationship R to an individual y by writing that predicate letter followed by the pair of variables, taken in the proper order: Rxy.

Two-place predicate letters are thus interpreted as referring to sets of **ordered pairs** of individuals in a particular relationship. For example, let the predicate letter "L" denote the set of all pairs of individuals such that the first member of the pair loves the second member of the pair. In specifying such interpretations, we can use the following notation:

L: __ loves . . .

Generalizations that involve relationships can be expressed symbolically by using quantifiers, predicate letters, and individual variables. For example, if we interpret "L" as before, we can translate "Everything loves everything" into symbols:

$(x)(y)Lxy$

To translate the sentence "Everybody loves everybody," a predicate letter (P) is used to represent the class of persons:

$$(x)(y)((Px \cdot Py) \rightarrow Lxy)$$

which can be read: "Given any x and any y, if x is a person and y is a person then x loves y." Notice that if the domain of interpretation is limited to the set of all persons, then "Everybody loves everybody" can be translated

$$(x)(y)Lxy$$

When the domain of interpretation is not limited to persons, the expression

$$(\exists x)(\exists y)Lxy$$

can be read "Something loves something."

Again, letting P refer to the class of persons, and L to the set of ordered pairs such that the first member loves the second member, "Somebody loves somebody" is translated:

$$(\exists x)(\exists y)(Px \cdot Py \cdot Lxy)$$

In contrast to *generalizations* about relationships, sentences such as "Ruth is the mother of Betty" state that some specific individual is related to another specific individual. In the standard symbolic language, lowercase letters from the earlier part of the alphabet (a-t) are assigned to individuals in the domain of interpretation. These letters, called **individual constants,** perform the same function in the symbolic language as proper names in ordinary language. For example, the sentence "Socrates is mortal" can be symbolized by interpreting s to refer to Socrates and M to refer to the class of mortals and writing

$$Ms$$

Socrates, one of the most important philosophers of all time, was married to Xanthippe. Interpreting "H" to refer to "___ is husband of . . . ," "s" to refer to Socrates, and "a" to refer to Xanthippe, then

$$Hsa$$

is true, for it says that Socrates is the husband of Xanthippe. Given the same interpretation,

$$Has$$

is false, for it says that Xanthippe is the husband of Socrates. Because "husband of" is an asymmetric relationship, the order of the individual constants makes a difference to the truth of the sentence.

Using quantifiers, individual variables, and two-place predicate letters, important properties of binary relationships can be conveniently and precisely characterized. Let R be some two-place relationship. Then any of the following properties of R can be expressed symbolically:

1. R is reflexive: $(x)\,Rxx$

The symbolic formula is read: "Given anything, it stands in relationship R to itself."

2. R is irreflexive: $(x)\sim Rxx$

"Given anything, it is not related by R to itself."

3. R is nonreflexive: $\sim(x)Rxx \bullet \sim(x)\sim Rxx$

"It is not the case that R is reflexive, and it is not the case that R is irreflexive. (Or, "R is not reflexive, and R is not irreflexive.")

4. R is symmetric: $(x)(y)(Rxy \rightarrow Ryx)$

"Given any x and any y (not necessarily distinct), if x bears relationship R to y, then y bears relationship R to x."

5. R is asymmetric: $(x)(y)(Rxy \rightarrow \sim Ryx)$

"Given any x and any y (not necessarily distinct), if x bears relationship R to y, then y does not bear relationship R to x."

6. R is nonsymmetric: $\sim(x)(y)(Rxy \rightarrow Ryx) \bullet \sim(x)(y)(Rxy \rightarrow \sim Ryx)$

"R is not symmetric, and R is not asymmetric."

7. R is transitive: $(x)(y)(z)((Rxy \bullet Ryz) \rightarrow Rxz)$

"For any three individuals x, y, z (not necessarily distinct), if the first bears relationship R to the second and the second bears relationship R to the third, then the first bears relationship R to the third."

8. R is intransitive: $(x)(y)(z)((Rxy \bullet Ryz) \rightarrow \sim Rxz)$

"For any three individuals x, y, z (not necessarily distinct), if x bears relationship R to y and y bears relationship R to z, then x does not bear relationship R to z."

Exercise Set 11.3

Express each of the following in symbols, providing interpretations for symbols when necessary. To simplify translations, let the domain of interpretation be the set of all persons.

1. R is nontransitive.
2. Mary loves someone.
3. John loves himself.
4. John loves himself and Mary.

5. Mary does not love John.

6. Someone loves Mary.

7. Everyone loves John.

8. No one loves John.

9. Mary loves no one.

10. Everyone loves John, or everyone loves Mary.

11. Not everyone loves himself.

12. Someone does not love himself.

4. Multiple Quantifiers

To symbolize most generalizations involving relational properties, more than one quantifier is needed. For example, two universal quantifiers are needed to state that a relationship is symmetric, and three universal quantifiers are required to state the transitivity of a relationship. When multiple quantifiers are all of the same type (all universal or all existential), the order in which they are placed at the beginning of the symbolized expression is irrelevant. Assuming that R is interpreted the same way in each case, there is no difference in meaning among the following:

(1) $(x)(y)(z)((Rxy \cdot Ryz) \to Rxz)$;

(2) $(y)(x)(z)((Rxy \cdot Ryz) \to Rxz)$;

(3) $(z)(y)(x)((Rxy \cdot Ryz) \to Rxz)$.

Likewise, there is no difference in meaning between

(1) $(\exists x)(\exists y)(Rxy \cdot Ryx)$ and

(2) $(\exists y)(\exists x)(Rxy \cdot Ryx)$

However, when both existential and universal quantifiers are used in a single expression, reordering the quantifiers might change the meaning of the expression. Consider the sentence "Everybody has a mother."

Limit the domain of interpretation to the set of persons, and assign the predicate letter M to the set of ordered pairs such that the first is the mother of the second:

$M:$ ___ is the mother of . . .

Then the translation of the English sentence is

$(x)(\exists y)(Myx)$.

The symbolic sentence can be read: Given any x, there is some y such that y is the mother of x. In other words, the sentence says that for any person, that person has a mother.

If the order of the quantifiers is reversed, the symbolic sentence becomes

$(\exists y)(x)(Myx)$

Based on the same interpretation, this sentence is read

There is some y such that given any x, y is the mother of x.

In other words, this sentence says that someone is the mother of everyone! When *someone* occurs at the beginning of the expression, it means "some one person," but no one person is the mother of everyone. When *someone* occurs in the position shown in the first translation, it means "someone or other," and it is true that every person has someone or other as a mother. Thus, although these two symbolic expressions differ only in the order in which the quantifiers are placed at the beginning of the expression, they do not mean the same thing.

Exercise Set 11.4

Using the set of persons as the domain of interpretation and interpreting L as " ____ loves . . . ," express each of the following in symbolic language.

1. Everyone loves someone (or other).
2. No one loves everyone.
3. No one loves anyone.
4. Someone loves everyone.
5. There is someone whom no one loves.
6. If everyone loves someone then no one is unloved.

5. The Fallacy of Every and All

It was—and is—widely believed that nothing happens without a cause. In antiquity, the claim "Everything that happens has a cause" was used as a premiss to infer that some "first cause" exists for everything. If this argument is valid, however, it must be an instance of some form other than the following:

$$\frac{(x)(\exists y)Cyx}{(\exists y)(x)Cyx}$$

because this form is invalid. Based on the intended interpretation (C: ____ causes . . .), the symbolization provides a reasonable translation of the argument, as stated.

This argument form, however, is shown to be invalid by a counterexample, which is an argument in that form with all true premises and a false conclusion. Using the set of all persons as the domain of interpretation, assign C to the set of all ordered pairs such that the first is the mother of the second:

C: ___ is mother of . . .

Under this interpretation, the single premiss of the argument is obviously true, but the conclusion is obviously false:

Everyone has a mother.

Someone is everyone's mother.

For an argument form to be valid, it must be valid under any interpretation of the predicate letters.

This fallacious form of argument is called the **fallacy of every and all.** We must remember, however, that an argument which is an instance of some fallacious *argument form* might not be an *invalid argument*. An argument is invalid only if it is not an instance of *any* valid argument form. Nevertheless, as with truth-functional arguments that were instances of invalid truth-functional forms, we should at least suspect invalidity when an argument is an instance of an invalid form *and* when no analysis of the argument is provided to show that it is an instance of some valid form.

Aristotle's argument for the existence of a first cause, or "prime mover," actually involved at least one further premiss, which stated that an infinite series of causes and effects is impossible. We might symbolize Aristotle's rejection of an infinite regress of causes—the claim that some cause must exist that is not the effect of any other cause—as shown

$(\exists y)((\exists x)(Cyx) \cdot \sim(\exists z)(Czy))$

Or, "There is a y such that y causes some x and no z causes y."

The addition of this premiss does not allow us to conclude the existence of only one "first cause," however, for there could be more than one "uncaused cause." (*Some* means "at least one"; it does not mean "exactly one.")

It is difficult to analyze some of Aristotle's arguments because of problems with translating the ancient Greek language and because the texts, which were essentially his students' lecture notes, suffer from incompleteness and alterations. Many scholars, however, impute the *fallacy of every and all* to Aristotle in more than one context. In commenting on Aristotle's apparent use of the premiss that every action has a final end to support the conclusion that there is one and the same end to all actions, called the "Supreme Good," a contemporary philosopher has said in defense of the founder of logic:

> This is a type of reasoning [relational logic] that lies beyond the reach of his own formal logic. He may, for this reason, have been more easily deceived by this fallacy.*

One benefit of modern techniques of symbolization is their ability to expose such fallacious reasoning, thus making it easier for us to understand and to avoid the fallacies.

V. SYMBOLIZING ARGUMENTS

Another advantage of modern symbolic languages lies in their capacity to reveal important structural similarities that are shared by various types of arguments. Consider, for example, the following quasi-syllogism:

All princesses are beautiful.
Diana is a princess.
_____

Diana is beautiful.

Assign predicate letters and the individual constant d in the following way:

P: the class of princesses
B: the class of beautiful persons
d: Diana.

Then, the argument can be translated

$(x)(Px \rightarrow Bx)$
Pd
_____

Bd

This form resembles the form of *affirming the antecedent*:

$p \rightarrow q$
p
_____

q

Consider, moreover, that a universal generalization is a sentence that says something about every individual in the domain of interpretation. If what the universal generalization says is true of every individual in the domain, then it

---

* D. J. O'Connor, "Aristotle," in *A Critical History of Western Philosophy,* edited by D. J. O'Connor.

must be true of any *particular* individual in the domain. For example, based on the given interpretation, if

$(x)(Px \rightarrow Bx)$

is true, then so is the conditional sentence

$Pd \rightarrow Bd$
(If Diana is a princess, then Diana is beautiful).

If the first premiss of the original argument is replaced with a particular instance of the generalization ($Pd \rightarrow Bd$), then the argument becomes

$Pd \rightarrow Bd$
Pd
───────
Bd

This argument is an instance of the form of affirming the antecedent and is therefore a valid argument form. The original quasi-syllogism is thus shown to be valid because it cannot have all true premisses and a false conclusion. This treatment of the singular premisses of quasi-syllogisms seems less arbitrary than the treatment suggested in Chapter 10. There, sentences such as "Diana is a princess" were treated as a type of universal generalization: "All members of the class of which Diana is the only member are princesses," which seemed artificial because universal generalizations lack existential import. The singular sentence "Diana is a princess," however, would be regarded as false if she did not exist.

A detailed discussion of the systems of logic that employ quantifiers is beyond the scope of this text. It is worth noting, however, that all these systems have a rule of inference that permits inferring particular instances from universally quantified sentences. Additional rules, subject to various restrictions, allow removing existential quantifiers and replacing both types of quantifiers after they have been removed. With this in mind, consider the similarity between the following syllogistic form of argument and the truth-functional form of hypothetical syllogism:

$(x)(Sx \rightarrow Mx)$	$p \rightarrow q$
$(x)(Mx \rightarrow Px)$	$q \rightarrow r$
$(x)(Sx \rightarrow Px)$	$p \rightarrow r$

Similarities between syllogistic arguments, truth-functional arguments, and relational arguments also become apparent when this symbolic language is used. For example, the validity of the argument "Marcy ran faster than Sam, and Sam ran faster than Carrie; therefore, Marcy ran faster than Carrie," depends on the true, but unstated, premiss that "ran faster than" is a transitive relationship. The argument can be symbolized, using the following interpretation:

R: ___ ran faster than . . .
m: Marcy
s: Sam
c: Carrie

$$(x)(y)(z)((Rxy \cdot Ryz) \to Rxz)$$
$$\underline{Rms \cdot Rsc}$$
$$Rmc$$

Again, the symbolism shows the similarity between this form and *affirming the antecedent.*

The value of symbolic techniques in modern logic should not be underestimated. The development of appropriate symbols has allowed advances in this field similar to the advances in mathematics that resulted from replacing the system of Roman numerals with the system of Arabic numerals.

VI. REVIEW

In Chapter 11, some relational arguments have been introduced. In these, validity depends on the properties of binary relationships referred to in the arguments. Representing these arguments with the symbolic techniques of modern logic facilitates expression of the forms of these arguments, and exposes similarities between these forms and familiar truth-functional forms.

Every binary relationship falls into exactly one of each of the following categories:

1. Transitive, intransitive, nontransitive.

2. Symmetric, asymmetric, nonsymmetric.

3. Reflexive, irreflexive, nonreflexive.

You should review the definitions presented in this chapter of these properties of relationships and be able to categorize examples of binary relationships according to these properties.

In many arguments in which validity depends on some property of a relationship referred to in the argument, the premises do not include a statement of that property. You should be able to recognize such unstated premises and to supply them when you reconstruct these arguments.

You should be able to translate categorical sentences and sentences involving relationships from English into the logical symbolism that reveals their logical structure. To do this, you need to remember that universal sentences are to be treated as quantified conditional sentences and that existential (particular) sentences are to be treated as quantified conjunctions.

Finally, you should be able to recognize apparent instances in English of the **fallacy of every and all.** This fallacy occurs when sentences containing both universal and existential quantifiers are treated as if truth is always preserved when the order in which their quantifiers occur is exchanged. The ability to symbolize such English sentences helps us to avoid this fallacy.

Exercise Set 11.5

Part One. For each of the following arguments, name the property of the relationship that makes the argument valid.

1. Horses can outrun greyhounds, and greyhounds exist. But greyhounds can outrun rabbits, so horses can outrun rabbits.

2. Seven is greater than the square root of 48, so the square root of 48 is not greater than 7.

3. John is married to Sarah, so Sarah is married to John.

4. Marianne's hair is the same color as Caroline's, and Caroline is a blond, so Marianne is a blond.

Part Two. Relationships that are transitive, symmetric, and reflexive are called **equivalence relationships.** Give three examples of equivalence relationships.

Part Three. Relationships that are transitive, asymmetric, and irreflexive are called **ordering relationships.** Give an example of an ordering relationship.

Part Four. When an individual *a* is related by a relationship *R* to individual *b*, then *b* is said to be related to *a* by a relationship called the *converse of R.* What is the converse of each of the following relationships?

1. Husband of

2. Parent of

3. Greater than

4. Greater than or equal to

5. Owned by

Part Five. When a relationship is symmetric, what can we say about its converse?

Part Six. Provide a suitable interpretation and translate the following into the symbolic language developed in this chapter, using relational predicates when appropriate:

1. Cats make better pets than dogs.

2. Some cats are smarter than any dog.

3. Every dog fears some cat.

4. Some cat is feared by every dog.

5. Christopher is Virginia's brother.

6. Not everyone has a cousin.

7. Cats and dogs are smarter than goldfish.

8. Snakes eat mice.

9. Every rich woman owns a piano.

10. Some people who are not rich own pianos.

11. Christopher plays pianos.

12. "Cousin of" is not a transitive relationship.

Part Seven. Provide a suitable interpretation and symbolize all four of the arguments in Exercise I of this set. Be sure to symbolize the unstated premisses concerning the properties of the relationships involved as well as the stated premisses.

Part Eight. G. E. M. Anscombe, in *An Introduction to Wittgenstein's Tractatus,* draws attention to the following argument. What is wrong with it?

At all times there is a possibility of my abstaining from smoking. Therefore, there is a possibility of my abstaining from smoking at all times.

Part Nine. Construct (or find) an example of an argument in English that apparently commits the *fallacy of every and all*.

Part Ten. Give an example of a relationship that is reflexive but not symmetric.

Appendix 1

PROOF METHOD FOR TRUTH-FUNCTIONAL LOGIC

I. INTRODUCTION

Truth tables can be used to demonstrate the validity or the invalidity of any truth-functional argument form. However, these tables become unwieldy when an argument form contains more than four distinct sentence letters. An argument form with five distinct letters requires a truth table with 32 rows to show all of the possible combinations of truth values. Six sentence letters require a 64-row truth table, and adding just one more sentence letter requires an additional 64 rows. The chief advantage of applying other **proof methods** to truth-functional logic is their brevity compared to truth tables. The proof method presented here is a **tree method,** modeled on a simplified version of proof methods developed by Gerhard Gentzen.* The method is also called a **natural deduction** method, because it uses an intuitively plausible set of rules to show whether a conclusion follows from a set of premises. This method is simple to use, and it always works—that is to say, for the class of argument forms that it is designed to handle (i.e., truth-functional argument forms), it always provides an answer to the question of whether a given sentence form (the conclusion) follows truth-functionally from a specific set of sentence forms (the premisses).

We use the logical symbols already introduced for negation ($\sim$), conjunction ($\bullet$), disjunction (v), material conditional ($\rightarrow$), and material biconditional ($\leftrightarrow$). We also use the gate symbol ($\vdash$) to indicate the relationship of *logical consequence,* or *following from.* The conclusion in a deductively valid argument is a logical consequence of, or follows from, the premisses of that argument. Instead of writing an argument form, such as *modus ponens,* in the standard form

$$p \rightarrow q$$
$$\underline{p}$$
$$q$$

we have used thus far, we now write the same argument forms in the following way:

$$p \rightarrow q, p \vdash q$$

Premisses, separated from one another by commas, are written to the left of the gate; the conclusion is written to the right of the gate. The preceding expression, which is called a **sequent,** may be read "q follows from the premisses $p \rightarrow q$ and p."

The strings of the sentence forms on the left and the right sides of the gate in a sequent are called **sequences**. In our example, the sequence on the left

---

*See Stig Kanger, "A Simplified Proof Method for Elementary Logic," in *Computer Programming and Formal Systems*, edited by P. Braffort & D. Hirschberg.

has two members ($p \rightarrow q$ and p); it is a sequence of "length two." The sequence on the right has one member (q); it is a sequence of "length one." Sequences may be of "length zero," in which case they are called **empty sequences**, or their length may be equal to any positive integer. All sequences are finite in length.

We have seen that when the length of a sequence on the left side of the gate is greater than one, the members of the sequence are separated by commas and each comma on the left is read as "and." When more than one member of the sequence appears on the right side of the gate, these members are also separated by commas, but each comma on the right is read as "or." For example, we may read the sequent

$$p \vee q, p \rightarrow r, p \rightarrow s, \sim q \vdash r \cdot s, t \rightarrow p$$

as "Either $r \cdot s$ or $t \rightarrow p$ follows from the premisses $p \vee q$, and $p \rightarrow$ r, and $p \rightarrow s$, and $\sim q$."

An empty sequence to the left of the gate indicates a true (although unspecified) premiss. An empty sequence to the right of the gate indicates a true conclusion.

Examples

(a)   Read the sequent

$$\vdash p \rightarrow (q \vee \sim q)$$

as "$p \rightarrow (q \vee \sim q)$ follows from any true premiss."

(b)   Read the sequent

$$p, p \rightarrow q, \sim p \vdash$$

as "Any true conclusion follows from p, and $p \rightarrow q$, and $\sim p$."

If a sentence form follows from any true premiss, then that sentence form must itself always be true. A sentence form that follows from any true premiss whatsoever is a **tautology.** Similarly, if a set of premisses deductively yields any true conclusion whatsoever, that set of premisses must be **contradictory.**

II. THE PROOF METHOD

In the following discussion, we use the roman capital letters "A" and "B" to refer to sentence forms. The sentence forms thus denoted may be either simple or complex. We will use the script capital letters "$\mathcal{D}$," "$\mathcal{E}$," "$\mathcal{F}$," and "$\mathcal{G}$" to denote finite and possibly empty sequences of sentence forms.

The proof method employs eleven rules or postulates, which include one axiom and ten rules of inference. Postulates P.1–P.11 are presented schematically here, with brief comments.

P.1 $\mathcal{D}$, A, $\mathcal{E}$ ⊢ $\mathcal{F}$, A, $\mathcal{G}$ (axiom)

In this sequent, the same *sentence form* (A) occurs both to the left and to the right of the gate; on both sides, it is separated from the other *sequences of sentence forms* ($\mathcal{D}$, $\mathcal{E}$, $\mathcal{F}$, $\mathcal{G}$) by commas. This means that a *disjunction* that contains A is said to follow from a set of premisses that includes A. Such a disjunction could not fail to follow, for if A is a true premiss, then the disjunction contains a true disjunct and the disjunction is true also. Thus, all the premisses cannot be true while the conclusion is false. In our proof method, this instance of the *consequence relationship* is considered to be a fundamentally valid argument form (an *axiom scheme*).

The rules of inference in this proof method are used to eliminate connectives, with the goal of "reducing" the original argument form to a series of simpler forms that are instances of the axiom. Each of the rules of inference (P.2–P.11) allows us to eliminate a main connective in a sentence form on either the left or the right of the gate.

P.2
$$\frac{\mathcal{D} \vdash \mathcal{F}, {\sim}A, \mathcal{G}}{A, \mathcal{D} \vdash \mathcal{F}, \mathcal{G}}$$
(eliminates $\sim$ on right)

P.3
$$\frac{\mathcal{D}, {\sim}A, \mathcal{E} \vdash \mathcal{F}}{\mathcal{D}, \mathcal{E} \vdash A, \mathcal{F}}$$
(eliminates $\sim$ on left)

P.4
$$\frac{\mathcal{D} \vdash \mathcal{F}, A \cdot B, \mathcal{G}}{\mathcal{D} \vdash \mathcal{F}, A, \mathcal{G} \qquad \mathcal{D} \vdash \mathcal{F}, B, \mathcal{G}}$$
(eliminates • on right)

P.5
$$\frac{\mathcal{D}, A \cdot B, \mathcal{E} \vdash \mathcal{F}}{\mathcal{D}, A, B, \mathcal{E} \vdash \mathcal{F}}$$
(eliminates • on left)

P.6
$$\frac{\mathcal{D} \vdash \mathcal{F}, A \vee B, \mathcal{G}}{\mathcal{D} \vdash \mathcal{F}, A, B, \mathcal{G}}$$
(eliminates v on right)

P.7
$$\frac{\mathcal{D}, A \vee B, \mathcal{E} \vdash \mathcal{F}}{\mathcal{D}, A, \mathcal{E} \vdash \mathcal{F} \qquad \mathcal{D}, B, \mathcal{E} \vdash \mathcal{F}}$$
(eliminates v on left)

P.8
$$\frac{\mathcal{D} \vdash \mathcal{F}, A \rightarrow B, \mathcal{G}}{A, \mathcal{D} \vdash \mathcal{F}, B, \mathcal{G}}$$
(eliminates $\rightarrow$ on right)

P.9
$$\frac{\mathcal{D}, A \rightarrow B, \mathcal{E} \vdash \mathcal{F}}{\mathcal{D}, \mathcal{E} \vdash A, \mathcal{F} \qquad \mathcal{D}, B, \mathcal{E} \vdash \mathcal{F}}$$
(eliminates $\rightarrow$ on left)

P.10
$$\frac{\mathcal{D} \vdash \mathcal{F}, A \leftrightarrow B, \mathcal{G}}{A, \mathcal{D} \vdash \mathcal{F}, B, \mathcal{G} \qquad B, \mathcal{D} \vdash \mathcal{F}, A, \mathcal{G}}$$
(eliminates $\leftrightarrow$ on right)

P.11
$$\frac{\mathcal{D}, A \leftrightarrow B, \mathcal{E} \vdash \mathcal{F}}{\mathcal{D}, \mathcal{E} \vdash A, B, \mathcal{F} \qquad A, B, \mathcal{D}, \mathcal{E} \vdash \mathcal{F}}$$
(eliminates $\leftrightarrow$ on left)

When we want to show that one sequence follows from another, we write the premiss sequence, followed by a gate, followed by the conclusion. Then we draw a line below that sequent and construct a "tree" of sequents below it, using the rules of inference (P.2–P.11). If we are able to construct a tree with an instance of P.1 (the axiom) at the bottom of every branch, the proof has succeeded. If the sequence on the right is a logical consequence of the sequence on the left, we will always be able to construct such a tree.

In addition to the axiom and rules of inference of the proof method, one strategic rule for constructing proofs should be noted. Frequently, we may be able to continue a branch of the tree in more than one way, since we have more than one main connective to eliminate. When this happens, we always prefer applications of P.2, P.3, P.5, P.6, and P.8 to applications of the other rules. Our preference for these rules will minimize tree branching, because these rules themselves do not branch. Before we focus on considering the justification of inference rules, we will consider some examples of proofs.

Examples

(a) To show that $p \vee q$ follows from p we construct the following tree:

$$\frac{p \vdash p, \vee q \quad \text{(apply P.6)}}{p \vdash p, q \quad \text{(axiom)}}$$

Here, only one main connective (the $\vee$ on the right) can be eliminated. Thus, P.6 is the appropriate rule. In applying P.6 to the sequent on the top line, A represents p, the sentence form to the left of the connective, and B represents q, the sentence form to the right of the connective. $\mathcal{D}$ represents the sequence that is left of the gate (p). $\mathcal{F}$ and $\mathcal{G}$ are the sequences to the right and the left of the sentence form A $\vee$ B, respectively; in this example, $\mathcal{F}$ and $\mathcal{G}$ are empty sequences. In the sequent below the line, the same sequence $\mathcal{D}$ (p) is to the left of the gate. On the right of the gate, the $\vee$ has been eliminated and replaced by a comma. The sequent below the line is an instance of the axiom, for the same sentence form (namely, p) occurs, separated from other sentence forms by commas, on the right of the gate, and also on the left. Thus, we have shown that $p \vee q$ follows deductively from p.

(b) To show that q follows from $p \rightarrow q$, $\sim p \rightarrow r$, and $\sim q \rightarrow \sim r$, we construct the following tree:

(1) $\qquad\qquad\quad \dfrac{p \rightarrow q,\ \sim p \rightarrow r,\ \sim q \rightarrow \sim r \vdash q}{}$

(2) $\dfrac{\sim p \rightarrow r,\ \sim q \rightarrow \sim r \vdash p, q}{} \qquad \dfrac{q,\ \sim p \rightarrow r,\ \sim q \rightarrow \sim r \vdash q^*}{}$

(3) $\dfrac{\sim q \rightarrow \sim r \vdash \sim p, p, q}{} \qquad\qquad r,\ \sim q \rightarrow \sim r \vdash p, q$

(4) $\quad p,\ \sim q \rightarrow \sim r \vdash p, q^* \qquad\qquad \dfrac{r \vdash \sim q, p, q}{} \qquad \dfrac{r,\ \sim r \vdash p, q}{}$

(5) $\qquad\qquad\qquad\qquad\qquad\qquad\quad q, r \vdash p, q^* \qquad\qquad r \vdash r, p, q^*$

Line (1) contains the sequent, with the premisses on the left and the conclusion on the right of the gate. The only main connectives are $\rightarrow$s to the left of the gate, so the only applicable rule is a branching one, P.9, which could be applied to any of the three sentence forms that make up the sequence on the left.

In this proof, P.9 is applied to the first conditional, $p \rightarrow q$. Thus, A is p, and B is q. $\mathcal{D}$, which refers to any sequence to the left of A $\rightarrow$ B, is empty, and $\mathcal{E}$ denotes the sequence $\sim p \rightarrow r$, $\sim q \rightarrow \sim r$. $\mathcal{F}$ refers to everything to the right of the gate (in this case, q).

Line (2) is the result of applying P.9 to $p \rightarrow q$ in line (1). The right-hand branch ends in an axiom (indicated by the *), with an occurrence of the sentence form q on both the right and the left sides of the gate. That branch is now complete. The left branch is not an instance of the axiom but contains further connectives that may be removed. Again, the only main connectives are the $\rightarrow$s on the left, so P.9 is applicable.

Line (3) is the result of applying P.9 to $\sim p \rightarrow r$ in line (2). Here, A is $\sim p$ and B is r. $\mathcal{D}$ is empty, $\mathcal{E}$ is $\sim q \rightarrow \sim r$, and $\mathcal{F}$ is the sequence p, q. Neither of these branches is an instance of the axiom, but connectives remain, so each branch is continued.

In the left branch of the tree, a main connective on the right is a negation sign. Our strategy rule tells us to prefer the application of P.2 over any of the branching rules. Applying P.2 gives us p as A and $\sim q \rightarrow \sim r$ as $\mathcal{D}$. $\mathcal{F}$ is empty, and $\mathcal{G}$ is the sequence p, q to the right of $\sim$A. After applying P.2, this branch ends in an instance of the axiom on the left branch of line (4).

In the right branch of the tree, the only main connective is once more a $\rightarrow$ on the left side of the gate, so that P.9 is applicable. Line (4), on the right gives the result of applying this branching rule. Neither branch ends in an axiom at this stage, so both branches continue.

In the left branch, a negation on the right is eliminated by applying P.2, which results in the branch ending in an axiom on line (5). In the right branch, there is a negation on the left, which is eliminated by applying P.3; that branch also ends in an axiom on line (5).

Thus, each branch of the tree ends in an axiom, and we have succeeded in proving that q is a consequence of $p \rightarrow q$, $\sim p \rightarrow r$, and $\sim q \rightarrow \sim r$.

(c) To show that $\sim q$ is not a consequence of $p \rightarrow q$ and $\sim p$, we construct the following tree:

(1) $\underline{\quad p \rightarrow q, \; \sim p \vdash \sim q \quad}$

(2) $\underline{\quad p \rightarrow q \vdash p, \; \sim q \quad}$ (P.3 applied to $\sim p$)

(3) $\underline{\quad q, p \rightarrow q \vdash p \quad}$ (P.2 applied to $\sim q$)

(4) $q \vdash p, p \qquad q, q \vdash p$ (P.9 applied to $p \rightarrow q$)

In this case, we see two branches on line (4) that do not end in axioms. Whenever at least one branch does not end in an axiom and cannot be extended because no more connectives can be removed, we have a proof that the alleged conclusion does not follow from these premises—that the argument form is invalid.

(d) To show that $\sim(p \cdot q) \leftrightarrow (\sim p \vee \sim q)$ is a tautology, we construct the following tree:

(1) $\qquad \vdash \sim(p \cdot q) \leftrightarrow (\sim p \vee \sim q) \qquad$ (P.10)

(2) $\underline{\sim(p \cdot q) \vdash \sim p \vee \sim q}$ (P.3) $\underline{\sim p \vee \sim q \vdash \sim(p \cdot q)}$ (P.2)

(3) $\underline{\vdash p \cdot q, \sim p \vee \sim q}$ (P.6) $\underline{p \cdot q, \sim p \vee \sim q \vdash}$ (P.5)

(4) $\underline{\vdash p \cdot q, \sim p, \sim q}$ (P.2) $\underline{p, q, \sim p \vee \sim q \vdash}$ (P.7)

(5) $\underline{p \vdash p \cdot q, \sim q}$ (P.2) $\underline{p, q, \sim p \vdash}$ (P.3) $\underline{p, q, \sim q \vdash}$ (P.3)

(6) $\underline{q, p \vdash p \cdot q}$ (P.7) $p, q \vdash p^*$ $p, q \vdash Q^*$

(7) $p, q \vdash q^*$ $p, q \vdash q^*$

Note that each branch of this tree ends in an axiom. To prove that a sentence form is a tautology, it is sufficient to show that the sentence form follows from any true premiss. Thus, we set up the proof by placing an empty sequence to the left of the gate and the supposed tautology to the right of the gate. If every branch does end in an axiom, we have shown that the sentence follows from any true premiss and that it must itself be true. If some branch fails to end in an axiom and cannot be continued, then the sentence form is not a tautology.

Exercise Set A-1

I. Use the proof method to determine the validity or the invalidity of each of the following argument forms:

1. $\dfrac{p \to q}{p \to (p \cdot q)}$

2. $\dfrac{p \vee q}{\sim p \vee \sim q}$

3. $\dfrac{p \to (q \to r)}{(p \to q) \to r}$

4. $\dfrac{p \to (q \to r)}{(p \cdot q) \to r}$

5. $p \to (q \to r)$
$\dfrac{(q \to r) \to s}{p \to s}$

6. $p \to (q \to r)$
$\dfrac{q \to (r \to s)}{p \to s}$

7. $(p \vee q) \to (p \cdot q)$
$\dfrac{p \cdot q}{p \vee q}$

II. Use the proof method to determine whether or not the following sentence form is *tautologous:*

$$(p \to (q \to r)) \to ((p \to q) \to (p \to r))$$

How many rows would a truth table require to show this? How many lines would it take you to construct a truth table for this sentence form?

III. Use the proof method to show whether or not the following sentence form is a *self-contradiction:*

$$(p \rightarrow q) \cdot (q \rightarrow r) \cdot p \cdot \sim r$$

III. JUSTIFYING THE RULES OF INFERENCE

A deductive rule of inference is *justified* when it can be shown that the use of the rule will never lead from true premises to a false conclusion—or, in other words, when it can be shown that the rule is *truth-preserving.*

When we remove connectives by using the rules of inference in this proof method, we reduce a complicated sequent (argument form) to a series of *less complicated* sequents, in the sense that each of the sequents below the lines has fewer truth-functional connectives than the sequents above the lines. What we want to show is that the use of any of the rules P.2–P.11 for eliminating connectives will result in sequents below the line with right-hand sequences that are the logical consequences of their left-hand sequences if and only if the right-hand sequence above the line is a logical consequence of its left-hand sequence.

The rules of inference used in this proof method depend for their justification on:

1. The definition of *logical consequence,* which states that a sentence (or sentence form) A is a logical consequence of a set of sentences (or sentence forms) $\mathcal{D}$ if it is impossible for all of the sentences (sentence forms) in the set $\mathcal{D}$ to be true while the sentence (sentence form) A is false.

2. The definitions of the *truth-functional connectives* ($\sim$, v, $\cdot$, $\rightarrow$, $\leftrightarrow$).

3. The understanding that commas to the left of the gate represent "and" and that commas to the right of the gate represent "or."

In each rule, we note that the sequences $\mathcal{D}$, $\mathcal{E}$, $\mathcal{F}$, and $\mathcal{G}$ simply reappear unchanged in sequents below the line. They are never dropped or modified in any way. For this reason, we can ignore their content in justifying rules P.2–P.11. In other words, we can simply regard these sequences as *empty sequences* and focus on how the removal of the connectives that relate A and B affects the consequence relationship.

Justification of P.2

P.2 $$\frac{\mathcal{D} \vdash \mathcal{F}, \sim A, \mathcal{G}}{A, \mathcal{D} \vdash \mathcal{F}, \mathcal{G}}$$ (eliminates $\sim$ on right)

If we regard the sequences $\mathcal{D}$, $\mathcal{F}$, and $\mathcal{G}$ as empty, then the sequent above the line says that $\sim A$ is a consequence of an empty sequence. This means that $\sim A$ must be a tautology. Then A itself must be a self-contradiction, since A is equivalent to the denial of $\sim A$, and the denial of a sentence form that must be true is a sentence form that must be false. But if A is a self-contradiction, then any conclusion, including an empty sequence, follows from it. The sequent below the line says that an empty sequence follows from A, and this is so if and only if ~A follows from an empty sequence.

Justification of P.3

P.3
$$\frac{\mathcal{D},\ \sim\!A,\ \mathcal{E} \vdash \mathcal{F}}{\mathcal{D},\ \mathcal{E} \vdash A,\ \mathcal{F}}$$ (eliminates ~ on left)

Again, we assume that $\mathcal{D}$, $\mathcal{E}$, and $\mathcal{F}$ are empty. Then the sequent above the line in P.3 says that an empty sequence follows from ~A. Thus, ~A is a self-contradiction. But this means that A is a tautology, and a tautology follows from an empty sequence. So the consequence relationship holds in the sequent below the line in P.3 if and only if it holds in the sequent above the line.

Justification of P.4

P.4
$$\frac{\mathcal{D} \vdash \mathcal{F},\ A \cdot B,\ \mathcal{G}}{\mathcal{D} \vdash \mathcal{F},\ A,\ \mathcal{G} \qquad \mathcal{D} \vdash \mathcal{F},\ B,\ \mathcal{G}}$$ (eliminates • on right)

P.4 allows us to eliminate a conjunction (•) on the right side of the gate. If a conjunction follows from any premisses—including the *empty set* of premisses—then each of the conjuncts separately follows from those same premisses. Thus, there are two sequents below the line, and each of these sequents contains one conjunct on the right side of the gate. Conversely, if each of two sentence forms follows from identical sets of premisses, then their conjunction follows from that set of premisses.

Justification of P.5

P.5
$$\frac{\mathcal{D},\ A \cdot B,\ \mathcal{E} \vdash \mathcal{F}}{\mathcal{D},\ A,\ B,\ \mathcal{E} \vdash \mathcal{F}}$$ (eliminates • on left)

P.5 allows us to eliminate a conjunction (•) on the left side of the gate. Consider an argument form with a conjunction with two members (A and B) as its only premiss. A conjunction is true if and only if both of its conjuncts are true. If the conclusion follows from this premiss, then the conclusion clearly follows from the two premisses A and B. If the conclusion does not follow from A • B, then it will not follow from the two separate premisses A and B. In P.5, a conjunctive premiss above the line is simply split into two separate premisses below the line. (Remember that the comma on the left side of the gate is read as "and.") All other sequences ($\mathcal{D}$, $\mathcal{E}$, and $\mathcal{F}$) are simply carried along without alteration.

Justification of P.6

P.6
$$\frac{\mathcal{D} \vdash \mathcal{F},\ A \lor B,\ \mathcal{G}}{\mathcal{D} \vdash \mathcal{F},\ A,\ B,\ \mathcal{G}}$$ (eliminates v on right)

The justification of P.6 is quite obvious if we consider that commas on the right side of the gate are read as "or." To apply P.6, a wedge (v) on the right side of the gate is replaced by a comma. If the disjunction A v B follows from the premisses on the left, then either A follows from those premisses or B does. If the disjunction does not follow, then it is not true that either A or B follows from the premisses.

Justification of P.7

P.7
$$\frac{\mathcal{D}, \text{A v B}, \mathcal{E} \vdash \mathcal{F}}{\mathcal{D}, \text{A}, \mathcal{E} \vdash \mathcal{F} \quad \mathcal{D}, \text{B}, \mathcal{E} \vdash \mathcal{F}} \quad \text{(eliminates v on left)}$$

If a conclusion follows from a disjunction (A v B), the conclusion must be true if either A is true or B is true. However, this is equivalent to saying that the conclusion follows from A and also from B. Thus, there are two sequents below the line, and each sequent contains one disjunct as a premiss. Also, if a conclusion follows from either of two premisses considered separately, then it clearly follows from the disjunction of those same premisses.

Justification of P.8

P.8
$$\frac{\mathcal{D} \vdash \mathcal{F}, \text{A} \rightarrow \text{B}, \mathcal{G}}{\text{A}, \mathcal{D} \vdash \mathcal{F}, \text{B}, \mathcal{G}} \quad \text{(eliminates} \rightarrow \text{on right)}$$

If a material conditional follows from some premisses, this means that if all of the premisses are true, then the conditional is also true. But if the conditional is true, then it cannot be the case that its antecedent is true and its consequent is false. Thus, if the antecedent of the conditional is added to the premisses, then the consequent must follow from those premisses supplemented by its antecedent. Similarly, if B follows from premisses that include A, then the sentence form A → B will be true if those premisses (excluding A) are all true. This justifies the application of P.8.

Justification of P.9

P.9
$$\frac{\mathcal{D}, \text{A} \rightarrow \text{B}, \mathcal{E} \vdash \mathcal{F}}{\mathcal{D}, \mathcal{E} \vdash \text{A}, \mathcal{F} \quad \mathcal{D}, \text{B}, \mathcal{E} \vdash \mathcal{F}} \quad \text{(eliminates} \rightarrow \text{on left)}$$

Consider that A → B is logically equivalent to ~A v B. If we apply P.7 to the sequent $\mathcal{D}$, ~A v B, $\mathcal{E} \vdash \mathcal{F}$, we obtain sequents $\mathcal{D}$, ~A, $\mathcal{E} \vdash \mathcal{F}$ and $\mathcal{D}$, B, E ⊢ $\mathcal{F}$ below the line. If we then apply P.3 to $\mathcal{D}$, ~A, $\mathcal{E} \vdash \mathcal{F}$, we obtain $\mathcal{D}$, $\mathcal{E} \vdash$ A, $\mathcal{F}$. This sequent and the sequent $\mathcal{D}$, B, $\mathcal{E} \vdash \mathcal{F}$ occur below the line in the application of P.9.

Justifications of P.10 and P.11

P.10
$$\frac{\mathcal{D} \vdash \mathcal{F}, \text{A}, \leftrightarrow \text{B}, \mathcal{G}}{\text{A}, \mathcal{D} \vdash \mathcal{F}, \text{B}, \mathcal{G} \quad \text{B}, \mathcal{D} \vdash \mathcal{F}, \text{A}, \mathcal{G}} \quad \text{(eliminates} \leftrightarrow \text{on right)}$$

P.11
$$\frac{\mathcal{D}, \text{A} \leftrightarrow \text{B}, \mathcal{E} \vdash \mathcal{F}}{\mathcal{D}, \mathcal{E} \vdash \text{A}, \text{B}, \mathcal{F} \quad \text{A}, \text{B}, \mathcal{D}, \mathcal{E} \vdash \mathcal{F}} \quad \text{(eliminates} \leftrightarrow \text{on left)}$$

These justifications are left as exercises. In each case, consider that A ↔ B is logically equivalent to (A → B) • (B → A).

It is interesting to note that this proof method may be used effectively even when the user does not understand the justifications of the rules of inference or why they work. The rules work in such a way that machines may be designed to test the validity of argument forms as well as to test whether sentence forms are tautologous or self-contradictory. If you have some computer experience, you might try to write a program for generating proofs using this proof method.

Exercise Set A-2

I. Use the proof method to decide whether the last sentence form is a logical consequence of the remaining sentence forms:

1. $p \rightarrow q$
   $\sim p \rightarrow r$
   $\sim q \rightarrow r$
   $\sim q$

2. $p \rightarrow q$
   $r \rightarrow \sim s$
   $q \rightarrow r$
   $p \rightarrow \sim s$

3. $(p \cdot q) \rightarrow (r \cdot s)$
   $\sim(q \vee s)$
   $t \rightarrow (\sim q \rightarrow (p \cdot r))$
   $\sim t$

4. $p \rightarrow q$
   $r \rightarrow s$
   $\sim s \rightarrow p$
   $q \rightarrow r$
   $\sim s \rightarrow t$

5. $(p \rightarrow q) \vee (r \rightarrow s)$
   $(p \rightarrow s) \vee (r \rightarrow q)$

6. $(p \leftrightarrow q) \rightarrow r$
   $\sim r$
   $\sim p \cdot q$
   s

II. Use the proof method to determine which of the following are tautologies. Take care to identify the main connectives correctly.

1. $(p \rightarrow q) \vee (\sim p \rightarrow q)$
2. $(p \rightarrow q) \rightarrow ((r \rightarrow (q \rightarrow s)) \rightarrow (r \rightarrow (p \rightarrow s)))$
3. $((p \rightarrow q) \rightarrow (q \rightarrow r)) \leftrightarrow (q \rightarrow r)$
4. $((p \rightarrow q) \rightarrow r) \rightarrow ((p \rightarrow r) \rightarrow r)$
5. $(\sim p \rightarrow r) \rightarrow ((q \rightarrow r) \rightarrow ((p \rightarrow q) \rightarrow r))$
6. $\sim(p \rightarrow q) \leftrightarrow (p \rightarrow \sim q)$

III. Using sentence letters to represent simple sentences, translate each of the following English arguments into argument forms. Then use the proof method to determine the validity or the invalidity of each argument form.

1. Either the economy will improve or the stock market will crash. If the stock market crashes, banks will fail. But banks will not fail. So it is not the case that if the economy improves, the banks will fail.

2. The president is happy if and only if his favorite bills are passed by Congress. If the president is happy, his staff feels good. But if the staff members feel good, they are in no condition to work for the bills, and if that is the case, the President's favorite bills will not be passed by Congress. Therefore, the President is unhappy.

3. If the Republicans choose a good candidate, they will win the election unless there is a split in the party. It is not true that if the Republicans meet in Chicago, there will be a split in the party. But if they meet in Chicago, they will choose a good candidate. So they will choose a good candidate, and they will win the election.

4. If some archaeologists are correct, then the first humans entered North America across the Bering Strait 30,000 years ago. If they crossed the Bering Strait 30,000 years ago, they must have spent time in what is now Alaska. If they spent time in what is now Alaska, they must have left artifacts with radio-carbon dates about 30,000 years old. If such artifacts are there, they will be uncovered if the archaeologists excavate. So if the archaeologists excavate and if some archaeologists are correct, then they will uncover 30,000 year-old-artifacts in Alaska.

Appendix 2

INDEX OF FALLACIES

From the time of Aristotle, fallacies have been studied in both informal and formal accounts of reasoning, In this text, the fallacies have been treated for the most part as departures from correct standards of reasoning. Accordingly, they were introduced in connection with the correct patterns of reasoning that they superficially resemble. A more traditional way of handling fallacies is to treat them in a separate chapter, classifying them into three groups: material (for example, *the appeal to pity*), verbal (*equivocation*), and formal (*affirming the antecedent*). This Appendix lists the fallacies treated in the text, with a brief explanation of each type. For a more traditional discussion, you may want to read the brief article "Fallacy" in the *Encyclopedia Brittanica,* which also contains useful references to some of the classical treatments of the subject.

Ad Baculum: (*See* **Appeal to Force**)

Ad Hoc Reasoning: (Chap. 8, p. 268) This fallacious form of reasoning occurs when auxiliary hypotheses are rejected (or brought forth) arbitrarily, merely to save a favored hypothesis. Hypotheses are tested by deriving predictions from them and observing whether the predictions are true. Usually, however, predictions cannot be derived from the hypothesis to be tested without the aid of additional assumptions (auxiliary hypotheses). These provide the links between the predictions with the hypothesis that is tested. When the auxiliary hypotheses have no independent justification, they are called *ad hoc* assumptions. To invoke such assumptions is to be guilty of *ad hoc* reasoning. For example, auxiliary hypotheses concerning the reliability of observers and instruments of observation are often required to show that some observation supports an hypothesis. If an observation fails to support an hypothesis, and the blame is laid on a faulty instrument—*without any independent evidence that the instrument is at fault*—one should suspect the fallacy of *ad hoc* reasoning.

Ad Hominem: (*See* **Fallacious Argument Against the Person**)

Ad Misericordium: (*See* **Appeal to Pity**)

Affirming the Consequent: (Chap. 7, p. 243) This fallacious form of argument resembles the valid form of denying the consequent. Its structure involves a conditional premiss (If p then q), an additional premiss that affirms the consequent (q), and a conclusion that affirms the antecedent (p). The form is fallacious because instances of it can have all true premisses and a false conclusion. A truth table can be used to show that the form is fallacious, or a counter-example with obviously true premisses and an obviously false conclusion will also show that the form is fallacious.

Appeal to Force: (Chap. 3, p. 87) This fallacy occurs when a threat of force is somehow put forth as evidence, or taken as evidence, for a conclusion.

Appeal to Pity: (Chap. 3, p. 88) This fallacy occurs when sympathy or pity for the circumstances of some person or persons is somehow put forth as evidence, or taken as evidence, for a conclusion.

Biased Statistics: (Chap. 4, p. 134) Fallacious arguments that depend on biased statistics might have the same structure as correct inductive arguments, but they are based on samples that have not been designed to capture the relevant variety in the population. We have reason to believe that the samples in such fallacious arguments are not representative of the populations from which they are selected.

Black-and-White Thinking: (Chap. 1, p. 28; Chap. 9, p. 290) When we ignore a whole range of alternative possibilities and focus only on the extremes (for example, best-worst, priceless-worthless, friend-foe), and we frame an argument, such as a disjunctive syllogism or dilemma, in terms of the extremes, we commit the fallacy of **Black-and-White Thinking.** Other names for the fallacy are **False Dilemma,** and **False Choice.**

Circular Reasoning: (Chap. 4, p. 141) This fallacy occurs when the truth of the conclusion is already assumed in premises that are no more plausible than the conclusion they are supposed to support. If the conclusion of an argument is in doubt, then premises that are equally dubious provide little reason to believe the conclusion. (Circular arguments are deductively valid because their conclusions cannot be false if all their premises are true, but the accusation of circularity concerns the persuasiveness of an argument in a given context rather than its formal validity.)

Composition: (Chap. 10, p. 347) This fallacy occurs when a term that is used distributively (referring to each member of a class or each part of a whole) in the premises is interpreted collectively (referring to the class or the whole) in the conclusion. In such cases, the term is used in different senses in the premises and in the conclusion.

Confusing Cause and Effect: (Chap. 5, p. 184) This fallacy occurs when insufficient attention is given to causal ordering, leading to misidentification of which is cause and which is effect in a causal relationship. Since it is understood that effects cannot precede their causes, most instances of this fallacy result from carelessness in sorting out which event is temporally prior to the other.

Confusing Coincidental Relationships with Causal Relationships (Post Hoc): (Chap. 5, p. 182) Temporal succession of events is not adequate evidence of a causal relationship between them; one needs some evidence that the connection is regular. But if an event is unusually interesting or important, we look for its cause, and sometimes (fallaciously) identify some pertinent preceding event as "the cause" on grounds of precedence alone.

Confusing the Harm or Benefits That Result from Holding a Belief with Evidence for It (Consequential Fallacy): (Chap. 5, p. 187) The name of the fallacy describes it. We are in danger of committing this fallacy when our ability to assess evidence for a claim is clouded by a desire to achieve the perceived benefits that would result if a claim were true or to avoid the perceived harms if a claim were false.

Denying the Antecedent: (Chap. 7, p. 243) This fallacy occurs when we offer or accept as valid the following form of argument:

If *p* then *q*, but not *p*, therefore not *q*.

This invalid form resembles the valid form of denying the consequent.

Division: (Chap. 10, p. 347) This fallacy occurs when a term that is used collectively in the premises is interpreted distributively in the conclusion. As in the fallacy of composition, the term is used in one sense in the premises and a different sense in the conclusion.

Equivocation: (Chap. 2, p. 47) If the conclusion of an argument depends on a shift in meaning of an ambiguous term, phrase, or grammatical construction in the context of that argument, the fallacy of equivocation is committed. When the middle term in a categorical syllogism is used equivocally, the result is a **fallacy of four terms** (as opposed to the three terms required for a valid syllogism).

Every and All: (Chap. 11, p. 379) Sentences that contain both universal and existential quantifiers (every, all, none, some) can change meaning when the order of the quantifiers is reversed. For example, *someone* in "Everyone loves someone" means "someone or other" whereas *someone* in "Someone is loved by everyone" means "some one person." The first sentence follows from the second, but the second does not follow from the first. If the conclusion of an argument depends on failure to recognize such a shift in meaning, the fallacy of every and all is committed.

Fallacies of Distribution: (*See* **Composition,** and **Division**)

Fallacious Appeal to Consensus: (Chap. 4, p. 112) Arguments that offer majority opinion as a reason to believe some claim are fallacious *unless* there is a good reason to believe that the majority opinion on the subject matter of the claim is correct. In general, the mere fact that many people or even most people believe a claim is not good evidence for it.

Fallacious Argument Against the Person: (Chap. 4, pp. 109–110) An argument that concludes a claim is false because it was made by a particular person is fallacious *unless* good reasons support the belief that most of what that person says about the subject matter of the conclusion is false. Sometimes the character of the person is attacked (**Abusive ad Hominem**), sometimes the person's circumstances are attacked (**Circumstantial ad Hominem**), and sometimes the person is attacked for somehow being associated with the position criticized in the argument (**Tu Quoque**).

Fallacious Argument from Authority: (Chap. 4, p. 106) An argument that concludes that some claim is true because some authority figure says so is fallacious *unless* (1) the so-called authority is a genuine expert who is speaking in his or her area of expertise, and (2) no substantial disagreement exists among authorities in that subject area.

Fallacy of Confusing an Originating Cause with a Sustaining Cause: (Chap. 5, p. 188) Assumes that because a particular cause was required to bring something into existence it is also necessary to maintain that thing's existence.

Fallacy of the Undistributed Middle: (Chap. 10, p. 350) In a correct categorical syllogism, the term that occurs in both premises must be distributed in one of its occurrences. If it is not, the fallacy of the undistributed middle is committed.

False Analogy: (Chap. 4, p. 120) This fallacy occurs when the relevant dissimilarities between the types of objects mentioned in the premises of an analogical argument are ignored. For example, to argue that the current president of the United States could use the same methods as Franklin Roosevelt to overcome unemployment, merely because the current president has similar powers to create agencies, enact emergency legislation, and so forth, ignores many relevant differences in the economic background of the two eras.

False Dilemma: (*See* **Black-and-White Thinking**)

Gamblers Fallacy: (Chap. 6, p. 221) This fallacy occurs if we interpret what happens "on average" or "in the long run" in such a way as to suppose that departures from what is average will be corrected in the short run. The fallacy is named for the gambler who hopes to overcome losses by betting, for example, that a tail is bound to come up after a run of heads.

Genetic Fallacy: (Chap. 5, p. 186) This fallacy occurs whenever some nonevidential feature connected with the origin of a claim (such as who said it, how it first came to be believed, how old it is) is taken as evidence for or against it. This fallacy is closely related to fallacious appeals to authority, fallacious ad hominems, and fallacious appeals to consensus, which can all be considered variants of the genetic fallacy.

Hasty Generalization: (Chap. 4, p. 134) This fallacy, also called "leaping to a conclusion," occurs in inductive reasoning when a conclusion is drawn from a sample that is too small.

Ignoring a Common Cause: (Chap. 5, p. 183) When we carelessly or without sufficient evidence attribute a direct causal relationship between two events that are only indirectly related to one another through a common underlying cause of both, we commit this fallacy. The fallacy would occur, for example, if we were to argue that red spots cause a child to have a fever, without considering that both features could be symptoms of some underlying cause, such as a measles virus.

Incomplete Evidence: (Chap. 4, p. 103) When we construct or evaluate an inductive argument, we must take account of all available relevant evidence that would affect the truth of the conclusion. If we deliberately ignore or carelessly fail to obtain such evidence, we commit this fallacy.

Misleading Vividness: (Chap. 4, p. 136) This fallacy occurs when some particularly vivid information is weighted disproportionately so that a substantial amount of statistical support for a conclusion is deemed less important than it really is.

Post Hoc: (*See* **Confusing Coincidental Relationships with Causal Relationships**)

Slippery Slope: (Chap. 4, p. 128) This fallacy incorrectly reasons that the arbitrariness of marking a distinction along some continuum shows that no distinction is possible. It ignores the fact that numerous small differences can make a big difference and fails to discriminate where discrimination is possible and appropriate. For example, to argue that anyone who takes a sip of wine is bound to become an alcoholic is to commit the fallacy of the slippery slope.

Tu Quoque: (*See* **Fallacious Argument Against the Person**)

BIBLIOGRAPHY

Allen, Gary. *None Dare Call It Conspiracy,* 1972, Council Press, Rossmoor, California.

Angell, R. B. "Truth-Functional Conditionals and Modern vs. Traditional Syllogisms," 1986, *Mind* 95, 210–233.

Anscombe, G. E. M. *An Introduction to Wittgenstein's Tractatus,* 2nd ed., 1959, Harper and Row, New York.

Aristotle. *The Works of Aristotle,* ed. W. D. Ross, 1921, Oxford University Press, Oxford.

Arnauld, Antoine. *The Art of Thinking,* trans. J. Dickoff and P. James, 1964, Bobbs-Merrill Co., Indianapolis.

Asimov, Isaac. *The Intelligent Man's Guide to the Biological Sciences,* 1960, Basic Books, New York.

Asimov, Isaac. *The Intelligent Man's Guide to the Physical Sciences,* 1960, Basic Books, New York.

Augustine, Saint. *The Confessions of St. Augustine,* trans. E. B. Pusey, 1951, Pocket Books, New York.

Binford, Lewis. *Bones,* 1981, Academic Press, New York.

Bloom, Alan. *The Closing of the American Mind,* 1987, Simon and Schuster, New York.

Bok, Sissela. *Secrets,* 1984, Oxford University Press, Oxford.

Boorstin, Daniel J. *The Discoverers,* 1983, Random House, New York.

Boswell, James. *Boswell for the Defense,* ed. W. K. Wimsatt, Jr. and F. A. Pottle. 1959, McGraw-Hill, New York.

Boswell, James. *Boswell on the Grand Tour,* ed. F. Brady and F. A. Pottle, 1955, McGraw-Hill, New York.

Boswell, James. *In Search of a Wife,* ed. F. Brady and F. A. Pottle, McGraw-Hill, New York, 1956.

Boswell, James. *Life of Johnson,* ed. C. G. Osgood, 1917, Charles Scribner's Sons, New York.

Boswell, James. *The Ominous Years,* ed. C. Ryekamp and F. A. Pottle, 1963, McGraw-Hill, New York.

Braffort, P. and D. Herschberg. *Computer Programming and Formal Systems,* 1967, North Holland, Amsterdam.

Bridgman, P. W. *The Logic of Modern Physics,* 1927, Macmillan, New York.

Campbell, Keith. *Body and Mind,* 1970, Doubleday, Garden City, New York.

Carroll, Lewis. *Alice's Adventures in Wonderland,* 1962, Macmillan Co., New York.

Carroll, Lewis. *Symbolic Logic,* 1958, Dover Publications, New York.

Caudwell, Sarah. *Thus Was Adonis Murdered,* 1981, Scribner, New York.

Chesterfield, Lord (Philip Dormer Stanhope). *Lord Chesterfield's Letters,* 1929, A. L. Burt Co., New York.

Chesterton, G. K. *The Father Brown Omnibus,* 1951, Dodd, Mead and Co., New York.

Childs, J. R. *Casanova: A Biography Based on New Documents,* 1961, Allen and Unwin, London.

Cornelisen, Ann. *Any Four Women Could Rob the Bank of Italy,* 1983, Penguin Books, New York.

Culbertson, James T. *Mathematics and Logic for Digital Devices,* 1958, D. Van Nostrand Co., New York.

Darwin, Charles. *The Origin of Species,* 1903, Hurst And Co., New York.

De Beauvoir, Simone. *The Ethics of Ambiguity,* trans. B. Frechtman, 1964, Citadel Press, New York.

Deetz, James. *Invitation to Archaeology,* 1967, Natural History Press, Garden City, New York.

Descartes, René. *Discourse on Method and Meditations on First Philosophy,* trans. Donald A. Cress, 1980, Hackett Publishing Co., Indianapolis.

Devlin, Patrick Lord. *The Enforcement of Morals,* 1965, Oxford University Press, London, Oxford, New York.

Dickens, Charles. *Our Mutual Friend,* 1894, Houghton Mifflin, Boston.

Doyle, Sir Arthur Conan. *The Annotated Sherlock Holmes,* ed. W. S. Baring-Gould, 1967, Clarkson N. Potter, New York.

Dunn, L. C. and T. H. Dobshansky. *Heredity, Race, and Society,* 1946, Penguin Books, New York.

Durrell, Lawrence. *Prospero's Cell and Reflections on a Marine Venus,* 1960, Dutton, New York.

Eliot, George. *Felix Holt,* n.d., John W. Lovell Co., New York.

Eliot, George. *Middlemarch,* n.d., John W. Lovell Co., New York.

Ehrlich, Paul. *The Population Bomb,* 1968, Ballantine Books, New York.

Firestone, Shulamith. *The Dialectic of Sex,* 1971, Jonathan Cape, New York.

Fowles, John. *Daniel Martin,* 1977, Little, Brown Co., Boston.

Frankfurt, Harry. *Demons, Dreamers, and Madmen,* 1970, Bobbs-Merrill Co., Indianapolis.

Freud, Sigmund. *The Basic Writings of Sigmund Freud,* trans. and ed. A. A. Brill, 1956, Modern Library, New York.

Fussell, Paul. *Class,* 1983, Summit Books, New York.

Galbraith, J. K. *The Affluent Society,* 1976, Houghton Mifflin, Boston.

Gish, Duane. *Evolution? The Fossils Say No!* 1979, Creation-Life Publishers, New York.

Gissing, George. *The Odd Woman,* 1971, W. W. Norton, New York.

Givens, D. R. "Sylvanus G. Morley and the Carnegie Institution's program of Mayan research." In *Rediscovering Our Past: Essays on the History of American Archaeology,* 1992, ed. by J. E. Reyman, Avebury, Aldershot UK, pp. 137-144.

Glob, P. V. *The Bog People,* 1971, Ballantine Books, New York.

Goodin, R. E. *No Smoking,* 1989, University of Chicago Press, Chicago.

Goodman, Nelson. *Ways of Worldmaking,* 1987, Hackett Publishing Co., Indianapolis.

Gould, R. A. *Living Archaeology,* 1980, Cambridge University Press, Cambridge.

Gould, Stephen J. *The Flamingo's Smile,* 1985, W. W. Norton, New York.

Gould, Stephen J. *The Mismeasure of Man,* 1981, W. W. Norton, New York.

Greene, T. M. *The Arts and the Art of Criticism,* 1973, Gordian Press, New York.

Guthrie, W. K. C. *The Greeks and their Gods,* 1955, Beacon Press, Boston.

Hacking, Ian. *The Emergence of Probability,* 1975, Cambridge University Press, Cambridge.

Hamilton, Edith. *The Greek Way,* 1971, W.W. Norton, New York.

Harris, Marvin. *The Rise of Anthropological Theory,* 1968, Thomas Y. Crowell Co., New York.

Hume, David. *Dialogues Concerning Natural Religion,* ed. N. Pike, 1970, Bobbs-Merrill Co., Indianapolis.

Hume, David. *A Treatise of Human Nature,* ed. L. A. Selby-Bigge, 1888, Oxford University Press, London.

Huxley, Julian. *New Bottles for Old Wine,* 1957, Harper and Brothers, New York.

Irving, Washington. *Bracebridge Hall,* 1871, H. M. Caldwell Co., New York.

Jochim, M. A. *Strategies for Survival,* 1981, Academic Press, New York.

Jolly, C. and F. Plog. *Physical Anthropology and Archaeology,* 2nd ed., 1979, Alfred A. Knopf, New York.

Kitcher, Philip. *Abusing Science,* 1982, MIT Press, Cambridge, Massachusetts.

Koestler, Arthur. *The Invisible Writing,* 1954, Macmillan Co., New York.

Laclos, C. de. *Les Liaisons Dangereuses,* trans. P. W. K. Stone, 1961, Penguin Books, Baltimore.

Lenin, V. I. *Collected Works* Vol. 14, 1927, V. I. Lenin Institute, Moscow.

Levi, E. H. *An Introduction to Legal Reasoning,* 1970, University of Chicago Press, Chicago.

Livingstone, David. *The Geographical Tradition,* 1992, Blackwell, Oxford.

Lucretius. *On the Nature of the Universe,* trans. E. E. Latham, 1951, Penguin Books, Baltimore.

Maalfjit, A. de W. *Images of Man,* 1974, Alfred A. Knopf, New York.

Maclean, Norman. *Young Men and Fire,* 1992, University of Chicago Press, Chicago.

MacMahon, B. and T. F. Pugh. *Epidemiology,* 1978, Little Brown Co., Boston.

MacMahon, B., T. F. Pugh, and J. Ipsen. *Epidemiologic Methods,* 1960, Little, Brown Co., Boston.

Malone, Michael. *Handling Sin,* 1986, Little, Brown Co., Boston.

Mates, Benson. *Elementary Logic,* 2nd ed., 1972, Oxford University Press, New York.

Mill, John Stuart. *A System of Logic,* 8th ed., 1874, Harper and Bros., New York.

Millett, Kate. *Sexual Politics,* 1970, Doubleday Co., Garden City, New York.

Morris, H. M. *Introducing Creationism in the Public Schools,* 1975, Creation Life Publishers, San Diego.

Morris, Herbert. *On Guilt and Innocence,* 1976, University of California Press, Berkeley.

Mumford, Lewis. *Technics and Human Development,* 1966, Harcourt Brace, New York.

Murphy, J. G. *Civil Disobedience and Violence,* 1971, Wadsworth Publishing Co., Belmont, California.

Murray, Gilbert. *The Literature of Ancient Greece,* 1956, University of Chicago Press, Chicago.

Newman, J. R. *The World of Mathematics,* 1956, Simon and Schuster, New York.

Nisbet, R. and L. Ross. *Human Inference: Strategies and Shortcomings of Social Judgment,* 1980, Prentice-Hall, Englewood Cliffs, New Jersey.

Nietzsche, Friedrich. *The Philosophy of Nietzsche,* 1927, Modern Library, New York.

O'Connor, D. J., ed. *A Critical History of Western Philosophy,* 1964, Free Press, New York.

Phillips, G. D. *Evelyn Waugh's Officers, Gentlemen, and Rogues,* 1975, Nelson-Hall, Chicago.

Pliny the Elder. *The Natural History of Pliny,* trans. John Bostock, 1855, H. G. Bohn, London.

Reid, Thomas. *Works,* 6th ed., ed. W. Hamilton, 1863, Edinburgh.

Renfrew, C. and P. Bahn. *Archaeology: Theories, Methods, and Practice,* 1991, Thames and Hudson, Ltd., New York.

Rousseau, Jean-Jacques. *The Social Contract,* ed. C. M. Sherover, 1974, New American Library, New York.

Routley, R. and V. "Nuclear power," In *And Justice for All,* edited by T. Regan and D. Van De Veer, 1982, Rowman and Allanheld, Totowa, New Jersey.

Russell, Bertrand. *My Philosophical Development,* 1959, Simon and Schuster, New York.

Russell, Bertrand. *Religion and Science,* 1961, Oxford University Press, New York.

Russell, Bertrand. *Skeptical Essays,* 1928, W. W. Norton, New York.

Sabloff, Jeremy. *The Cities of Ancient Mexico: Reconstructing a Lost World,* 1989, Thames and Hudson, Ltd., New York.

Salmon, Wesley. *Logic,* 3rd ed., 1983, Prentice-Hall, Englewood Cliffs, New Jersey.

Salmon, Wesley. *The Foundations of Scientific Inference,* 1967, University of Pittsburgh Press, Pittsburgh.

Shakespeare, William. *Merchant of Venice,* 1965, Airmont Publishing Co., New York.

Shakespeare, William. *King Lear,* 1966, Airmont Publishing Co., New York.

Shrader-Frechette, Kristin. *Nuclear Power and Public Policy,* 1980, D. Reidel, Dordrecht, Holland.

Singer, Peter, *et al. Embryo Experimentation,* 1990, Cambridge University Press, Cambridge.

Skyrms, Brian. *The Dynamics of Rational Deliberation,* 1990, Harvard University Press, Cambridge, Massachusetts.

Smith, Adam. *The Wealth of Nations,* 1863, Adam and Charles Black, Edinburgh.

Smith, A. H. *The Mushroom Hunter's Field Guide,* 1958, University of Michigan Press, Ann Arbor.

Storr, Anthony. *The Psychodynamics of Creativity,* 1977, Geigy Pharmaceuticals, Ardsley, New York.

Suppes, Patrick. *A Probabilistic Theory of Causality,* 1970, North-Holland, Amsterdam.

Swartz, Robert J. *Perceiving, Sensing and Knowing,* 1965, Anchor Books, Garden City, New York.

Tannen, Deborah. *You Just Don't Understand: Men and Women in Conversation,* 1991, Ballantine, New York.

Thompson, J. Eric S. *Maya Archaeologist,* 1963, University of Oklahoma Press, Norman.

Tolstoy, Leo. *The Death of Ivan Ilych and Other Stories,* 1960, New American Library, New York.

Tolstoy, Leo. *What Is Art?,* 1960, Liberal Arts Press, Indianapolis.

Trevelyan, G. M. *English Social History,* 1942, Longmans, Green, London.

Tuttle, M. *America's Neighborhood Bats,* 1992. University of Texas Press, Austin.

Twain, Mark. *The Writings of Mark Twain,* 1899-1922, F. Collier and Sons Co., New York.

Van Fraassen, Bas. *The Scientific Image,* 1980, Oxford University Press, Oxford.

Wesley, John. *The Journal of John Wesley,* ed. P. L. Parker, 1974, Moody, Northbrook, Illinois.

Westfall, Richard S. *The Construction of Modern Science: Mechanisms and Mechanics,* 1971, Cambridge University Press, Cambridge, United Kingdom.

Wharton, Edith. *The Custom of the Country,* 1913, Charles Scribner's Sons, New York.

White, Antonia. *Frost in May,* 1981, Penguin Books, London.

White, Tim. *Prehistoric Cannibalism at Mancos 5MTUMR-2346,* 1992, Princeton University Press, Princeton, New Jersey.

Wilde, Oscar. *The Plays of Oscar Wilde,* Modern Library, New York.

Wootton, Barbara. *Crime and the Criminal Law,* 1963, Stevens, London.

Young, Agatha. *The Men Who Made Surgery,* 1961, Hillman Books, New York.

Zinsser, William. *On Writing Well,* 2nd ed. 1980, Harper and Row, New York.

ANSWERS TO ODD-NUMBERED EXERCISES

CHAPTER ONE

Exercise Set 1.1 (pp. 5–11)

1. Gathering evidence beyond your friend's word seems unimportant here since little will be lost if the information given is incorrect.

3. She may request a written excuse from Student Health Service if she will not accept your word for the illness.

5. (1) No evidence is offered.

(2) It is reasonable to regard the description as accurate, barring an earthquake or other disaster in the time since the account was written.

(3) Evidence should be sought because military invasions have important effects on human lives and property.

7. (1) a. Shallow cultivation controls weeds effectively.

b. Experiments have shown that hoeing or tilling the top 2 to 4 inches of soil before seed sprouts can set eventually exhausts most of the vast supply of weed seeds that lie dormant in the soil.

(2) The preceding assertion (b), which reports physical evidence is offered as verbal evidence in support of (a).

(3) No, because the probable benefits of the alternative to poisoning the earth outweigh a possible reduction in home garden yields.

(4) Yes, it would be worthwhile to try a shallow-cultivation test plot because of the economic consequences of crop loss.

9. Evidence: In telephone interviews with the reporter, four insurance agents from different companies quoted costs that varied by as much as $200 for identical automobile insurance policies for a 20-year-old male college student with no history of automobile accidents, when the make and model of the automobile were specified.

11. (1) The title is misleading because the article offers a better way to teach reading instead of an argument for not teaching reading.

(2) A report, based on decades of research, issued by the Commission on Reading, is cited as evidence.

13. (1) An emotional appeal to fear.

(2) No.

15. Lear asks for physical evidence in the form of his daughter's breath.

17. (1) Because no information about other possible sources of exposure to lead are mentioned, the evidence is not persuasive that lower classes absorbed less lead than upper classes.

(2) Because the lower classes are likely to be closely involved with making, installing, and maintaining products that contain lead, they might be more susceptible to lead poisoning.

19. (1) The football player must spend five or six hours a day working at the "job" of football.

(2) "Real jobs" are jobs for which pay is normally received. By definition, amateur sports are not professional (for pay), and those who participate in scholastic sports are counted as amateurs. Participation in college sports, for example, does not disqualify a player's amateur status, even if the player is "paid" in the form of tuition, room, and board.

(3) No. Practice time for amateur performance in the arts is not considered work for pay. Many students study (work) five or six hours a day without expecting to be paid for this work.

Exercise Set 1.2 (pp. 18–23)

Part One

1. Identical twins, who have the same genes, are more likely to have the same blood pressure than fraternal twins, who share half the same genes.

   High blood pressure is inherited.

3. In England under the blasphemy laws it is illegal to express disbelief in the Christian religion.
   It is also illegal to teach what Christ taught on the subject of nonresistance.

   Whoever wishes to avoid being a criminal must profess to agree with Christ's teachings but must avoid saying what that teaching was.

5. A coin has been tossed twelve times and has shown a "head" each time.

   The coin is unfair.

7. The exercise, training, and development of our powers of discriminating among works of art are plainly aesthetic activities.

   The aesthetic properties of a picture plainly include not only those found by looking at it but also those that determine how it is to be looked at.

9. Over a period of two years now, I have tested my instrument (or rather dozens of my instruments) by hundreds and thousands of experiments involving thousand and thousands of objects, near and far, large and small, bright and dark.

I do not see how it can enter the mind of anyone that I have simplemindedly remained deceived in my observation.

11. [Evolutionary theory] offers a unified set of problem-solving strategies that can be applied, by means of independently testable assumptions, to answer a myriad of questions about the characteristics of organisms, their interrelationships, and their distributions.

Evolutionary theory merits a place among the sciences.

13. [T]he seat and origin of the plague had always been in the 'Liberties' outside the city where the poorest dwelt.
[A]s these districts were not burnt down they were not rebuilt.
[I]n 1722 'they were still in the same condition as they were before.'

[T]he 'rebuilding of London' due to the Fire was not the main reason why the plague disappeared from London after its last great effort.

Note: The first sentence of the exercise ("The [Great Fire of London (1666)] and rebuilding made little improvement in the sanitary and moral conditions of the slum populations" is an alternative statement of the conclusion. The conclusion is stated twice for emphasis.

Part Two

Indicator words are italicized.

1. *Since* women tend to do better on essay tests than on timed, multiple-choice tests, and *since* men tend to do better on timed, multiple-choice tests, *therefore* SAT tests are biased in favor of men.

3. The year 1859 is perhaps the most important one in the history of biology to date, *for* in that year Charles Darwin published his theory of evolution by natural selection, which has deeply affected not only biology, but other branches of human thought as well.

5. *Since* with no legal, regulated disposal facilities available, illegal dumping becomes more attractive, and *since* far more damage will be done to the environment from illegal dumping than from regulated, legal disposal, *it follows that* hazardous-waste disposal facilities are essential to the protection of Pennsylvania's environment.

Part Three

1. This sentence, which is not an argument, explains why the parents object to *Romeo and Juliet.* The word *Because* signals that a causal explanation is offered. The parents in question, however, might construct the following argument:

Romeo and Juliet portrays teen lust, drug use, and suicide.
Such subjects are not appropriate for high school literature classes.

Romeo and Juliet should not be required reading in high school.

3. Not an argument: *Since* as used here indicates the passage of time (since the 1967 war).

5. Not an argument: *Thus* in this passage merely introduces examples.

7. Not an argument: *For* is used to introduce the causal explanation of why the eerie scene of town with only one main street with a few stores and houses occurs over and over again in Ireland.

9. This passage could be interpreted either as a causal explanation of why describing how a process works is valuable, or—from another point of view—it could be offered as an argument to persuade someone that describing how a process works *is* valuable.

Exercise Set 1.3 (pp. 24–25)

1. (1) Its [nuclear fuel's] normal waste products do not cause significant atmospheric or water pollution.

   Nuclear fuel is cleaner than fossil fuels with respect to normal waste.

   (2) The waste nuclear fuels does produce is very dangerous and lasts for centuries.
   Nuclear fuels also have the possibility of dramatic pollution from escaped radiation, such as occurred at Chernobyl.

   Overall, fossil fuels are cleaner than nuclear fuel.

3. (1) Cycads are rare and have an uncertain future.

   Cycads should claim our interest.

   (2) Cycads appear but little changed from ancestors that flourished along with dinosaurs and our own insectivorous antecedents.
   They are, in a true sense, living fossils.

   Cycads are valuable to students of plant evolution.

   (3) Cycads are valuable to students of plant evolution.

   Cycads should claim our interest.

5. (1) These drugs (LSD, DOM, and other LSD-like drugs) elicit a common set of effects: sensory perceptual (examples given); psychic (examples given); and somatic (examples given).
   These drugs display cross-tolerance (the term is defined and an example is given).

   The grouping of these drugs is not arbitrary or simply for convenience.

   (2) It may be argued, and perhaps correctly so, that drugs such as marijuana and PCP should also be classified as hallucinogenic.
   But marijuana and PCP show no evidence of cross-tolerance with LSD-like drugs.

   Marijuana and PCP do not belong to the class of LSD-like drugs.

Exercise Set 1.4 (pp. 30–31)

Part One

1. Statistical

3. Statistical

5. Ideally, this is a universal generalization. In real life, it is statistical.

7. Universal

9. Universal

Part Two

1. Women office workers work equally as hard as men office worker and are equally productive.
   Equal work deserves equal pay.

   Women office workers should receive the same pay as men in comparable positions.

3. Nuclear power is less damaging to the environment than fossil fuels.
   In general, fuels that are less damaging to the environment should be preferred to those that harm the environment more.

   Nuclear power should be used.

5. Marijuana is no more dangerous than alcohol, which is already legal.
   Substances should not be declared illegal if they are no more dangerous than substances that are already legal.

   Marijuana should not be illegal.

7. Marijuana leads to the use of harder drugs, such as heroin.
   No drug that leads to use of hard drugs should be legal.

   Marijuana should not be legal.

   In this argument the first premises is probably less plausible than the generalization.

9. Prices have been rising for a long time now.
   *Whenever prices have been rising for a long time, they go down.***

   Prices are bound to drop soon.

11. The past six tosses of the coin have been heads.

    A head will show on the next toss of the coin.

---

*This generalization is questionable. Good reasons exist for not adding to the supply of available harmful substances. Difficulties in prohibiting the use of substances that are firmly entrenched in the culture may argue against their prohibition, but the same arguments do not apply to admitting new harmful substances.

**The generalization is too vague to serve as a suitable premiss. In general, it is true that prices fluctuate, but that premiss does not lead to the conclusion that prices are bound to drop soon.

It is difficult to find a plausible generalization to support the conclusion. If the coin is fair, the chance for a head on the next toss is 0.50, as for any other toss. If the coin is weighted for heads, the next toss is more likely to be a head, but the past six tosses that landed heads are not strong evidence that the coin is weighted.

Exercise Set 1.5 (pp. 34–37)

1. (1) 1.4 million abortions per year are now being performed.
    If abortion is made illegal, half those women will have babies.

    If the bill is passed and abortions are made illegal, at least another 700,000 babies will be born next year.

   (2) About two-thirds of the 700,000 mothers (400,000) will collect welfare. Instead of a single cost of $125 for an abortion, we will pay $1,000 to $1,500 for a delivery, and at least $100,000 to support these welfare children until they reach maturity.

    The human-life bill would cost taxpayers $40 billion each year.

   Additional material: The proponent of the argument claims that the bill will leave government on our backs and put government in our bedrooms. He also claims that half of the women who want abortions will get them illegally or go out of the country for abortions. This material encourages a negative attitude towards the bill.

3. (1) Last year the national organization of Jaycees voted to kick out the women members that they had previously recruited.
    They also voted to kick out the chapters who would not kick out the women they had previously invited.

    Who says that chauvinists are chivalrous?*

   (2) (The Minnesota court's argument)
    The Jaycees were soliciting memberships, which makes them a public business.
    Public businesses are forbidden to discriminate.

    The Jaycees are forbidden to discriminate.

5. A good dark suit, white shirt and conservative tie are authority symbols.

    A good dark suit, etc. are a young man's best wardrobe friends, if he's applying for a white-collar job in a big range of business and professional categories.

   Additional material: The author's remarks about wearing signs is intended to prepare the reader or listener for his argument that clothes carry a message that help find a young man a job.

---

*The conclusion, stated as a rhetorical question, is that these chauvinists are not chivalrous, but are instead very impolite.

7. If people differ in the aims (inner contexts) of their lives, they will differ in the externals as well.

Ladies in highest society and prostitutes share the same fashions, the same tastes, the same amusements, the same employment of all means to allure.

Life in our upper class is simply a brothel. (That is to say, women in our society have the same interests in life as prostitutes.)

Additional material: The opening paragraph prepares us for the argument by remarking on the shamelessness of society and saying that our familiarity with this situation blinds us to its true nature.

9. The last of the great pyramids at Giza on the Nile were built nearly 3000 years before the great pyramids of the Sun and the Moon in Teotihuacan, or the well-known pyramids in the Maya lowlands.

It is difficult to imagine a boatload of ancient Egyptians arriving in Mexico, then introducing a monumental activity that had not been practiced in their homeland for millennia.

It is more likely that a boatload of foreigners—with no nearby support and no clear military or technological advantage—would be killed before they got far from the beach than be able to introduce a new architectural style.

The pyramids are shaped differently and serve different purposes.

Theories that link the pyramids of Egypt and Mexico are not well supported.

Exercise Set 1.6 (pp. 39–44)

1. You are through [smoke]jumping at forty.

There are few administrative or maintenance openings [in smokejumping].

There is very little chance of a longtime future in smokejumping.

Additional material—"for those who think of lasting that long" warns the reader of the danger of parachuting into a forest fire to fight the fire.

3. The transit of Venus was accurately observed and recorded.

Kangaroos were discovered.

Ethnographic studies of indigenous peoples were carried out.

The New Zealand coastline was charted.

A vast amount of material was collected and shipped back to the Royal Society—thousands of plants, for example.

Scientifically, Cook's first voyage to the South Pacific was hugely successful.

A possible obvious implicit generalization: Any expedition that succeeds in discovering and collecting new plants and animals, and in improving astronomical, geographic, and ethnographic knowledge is a scientific success.

5. Poetry cannot be translated. (Or—We cannot have the beauties of poetry but in its original language.)
   We would not be at the trouble to learn a language when we can have all that is written in it just as well in translation.

   It is the poets who preserve language. (Or—We learn new languages primarily for the poetry in that language.)

7. Firestone is offering a causal explanation of why so few women have been great artists, philosophers, and writers; she is not presenting an argument.

9. Wassersug's argument:

   The Clean Air Act is the rule of the land.
   Implicit premiss: *Whatever is the rule of the land must be enforced.*

   The Clean Air Act as now written must be enforced.

   Background information: Pennsylvania may not lose the money because the Act may be revised.

11. The very strength of these alcoholic full-fruited wines with considerable residual sugar cuts through the heaviness of chocolate.
    Implicit generalization: *Heavy desserts require a wine that can cut through the heaviness.*

    The proper use for late-harvest Zinfandels is with chocolate desserts.

    Additional material: The author states his preference and tells what led him to change his mind about the proper dessert wine for chocolate desserts.

13. We are inclined to give the *thought* the benefit of what has pleased us in the form of the joke. (Or—we are apt to believe what has pleased us.) It would spoil the source of the pleasure if we found anything wrong (incorrect) that had given us enjoyment.
    The thought tends to wrap itself in a joke because in this way it recommends itself to our attention, seems to be more significant, and so forth.

    (This passage could also be interpreted as a causal explanation of why people present messages that they want to be accepted "wrapped in a joke.")

15. An argument:

    If a person is known to lie occasionally, it is not reasonable to accept something simply on the ground that he testifies to it.
    The senses have been discovered to be capable of deception,

    It is not reasonable to regard a belief as solid or permanent merely because it is based on sensory evidence.

    In addition, the following two conditional sentences are put forth:

    (1) It may turn out that the occasion on which the senses provided the evidence for the belief was one on which the senses were deceptive; then the belief would have to be abandoned.

(2) If occasions on which the senses are absolutely reliable can be distinguished from those on which they are likely to deceive, then it might still be reasonable to regard some sensory beliefs as permanent and indubitable.

17. To the trivial all things are trivial.

A critic with limited powers of observation, a weak imagination, and a restricted scale of values must remain blind to artistic greatness and incapable of distinguishing artistic profundity from artistic triviality.

If great art is a product of a great soul, only a critic of spiritual stature can hope to recognize and appreciate artistic greatness when he sees it.

19. The key features of dietary cannibalism involve close, detailed similarities in the treatment of animal and human remains.

If it is accepted that the animal remains in question were processed as food items, then it can be suggested by analogy that the human remains, subjected to identical processing were also eaten.

Evidence for dietary cannibalism is found in patterns of bone modification and discard.

21. According to the King, Rule forty-two ("All persons over . . .") is the oldest rule in the book.

The oldest rule in the book ought to be rule number one.

"All persons over one mile high to leave the courtroom" ought to be rule number one.

Additional material: the context of Alice's dispute with the King.

23. Here Koestler sets up an elaborate threat, thinly disguised as an argument, to force agreement with his point about the absence of free will in humans.

25. (1) God's existence is taught in the Holy Scriptures.

God's existence is to be believed in.

(2) The Holy Scriptures have God as their source.

The Holy Scriptures are to be believed.

(3) Faith is a gift from God.

God who gives the grace that is necessary for believing the Scriptures can also give us the grace to believe he exists.

Those with the faith can accept arguments (1) and (2).

(4) Unbelievers (who lack the gift of faith) would judge arguments (1) and (2) as circular. (An argument is circular when it assumes in the premisses that which is to be proven in the conclusion.)

Arguments (1) and (2) cannot convince unbelievers.

CHAPTER TWO

Exercise Set 2.1 (p. 49)

1. "Good," when applied to a skill such as dancing, means a high level of technical expertise. When applied to a person, "good" refers to moral goodness.

3. "All women are not feminists" could mean either "No women are feminists" or "Some women are not feminists." If the first interpretation is adopted, the premises support the conclusion, but the first premiss is false. If the second interpretation is adopted, the first premiss is true, but the premises do not provide evidence for the conclusion.

5. In this case, the ambiguity arises not because of a double meaning of any words or phrases used by the oracle, but instead because of lack of specification of whose empire would be destroyed. Of the two possibilities, Croesus, who had framed his question in terms of his own success in a war against Persia, considered only the destruction of the Persian empire.

7. Jack uses *business* in the sense of personal matters; Algernon uses *business* in the sense of financial affairs.

Exercise Set 2.2 (pp. 51–52)

1. Usually, when we contrast *vegetable* and *fruit,* we are talking about different ways of serving foods and and the different functions that they serve as snacks or parts of meals. In this sense, typical fruits are apples, peaches, pears, and oranges. They are naturally sweet, and can be served as desserts with or without added sweetening, in pastry, and so forth. In the same context, vegetables are less sweet, and are typically served unsweetened as part of an entree, main course, or salad. Tomatoes are usually eaten as vegetables although they also are made into sweetened preserves. In the botanical sense, the fruit of a plant is the part that contains the seed—as the edible portion of the tomato does—and *vegetable* is a general term referring to both edible and inedible plants—as in the guessing game called "Animal, vegetable, or mineral?".

   If edible fruits and vegetables were subjected to different import duties or taxes, it would be important to specify the category of such items as tomatoes, pumpkins, and other plants that might be classified in either group.

3. Most common nouns have some element of vagueness, in the sense that sometimes it's not clear whether the term applies. This is not to say that common nouns are vague in most of their occurrences. The context normally clarifies any problematic vagueness.

Exercise Set 2.3 (p. 53)

1. The definition is circular.

3. The definition is too broad, because forks are not the only utensils for eating foods. The definition is also too narrow, for some forks (forks in roads and forks in forklifts) are not utensils for eating foods.

5. The definition is too narrow, for *overture* applies to other sorts of opening moves.

Exercise Set 2.4 (p. 57)

1. *Adult* refers to a level of maturity. Being an adult has physical, mental, and emotional components, but these are not easily correlated with calendar age. The components might be differently developed in any given individual, so we can say, for example, that a person is mentally an adult but emotionally a child. Moreover, not everyone agrees about the levels required in each of the three categories. In addition, *adult* can refer to sexually explicit materials, as in "adult video."

Exercise Set 2.5 (p. 60)

1. *Fragile* carries the positive emotive sense of something worth preserving though easily broken. *Weak* has a more negative emotive tone. Ignoring emotive force, the intensional meaning is somewhat different, because *fragile* is used primarily to refer to brittle objects, such as glass, whereas *weak* refers more generally to a lack of strength and also can be used to refer to very pliable (definitely nonbrittle) objects.

3. *Mexican-American* refers to Americans with Mexican ancestors and is emotively more neutral than *Chicano,* which signifies a certain pride in Latin-American ancestry. The intensional meaning of the two terms differs also because *Chicano* can be applied to those with Puerto Rican, Cuban, and other Latin heritages.

5. *Chairperson* is employed as a gender-neutral term as opposed to the masculine *chairman*. Given the long-accepted usage in which *chairman* has been applied to both males and females, the newer term *chairperson* probably has greater emotive force because it makes an antisexist statement in implementing a change towards gender-neutrality in the language.

7. *Usherette* involves a diminutive suffix, and means "little usher." The term suggests diminished capacity or responsibility and when used to denote a female usher suggests that female ushers are less able or less responsible than male ushers. Because *usher* is a gender-neutral term, it can be used for male or female.

9. The saying "A house is not a home" draws on the emotive difference between these two terms, suggesting that the home is made from the human relationships of those who live together whereas a house merely provides shelter from the elements. Architecturally, houses are normally freestanding or semi-detached, relatively permanent structures, whereas homes may be in apartments, tents, hotels, castles, trees, boats, or a variety of other places.

11. *College,* which suggests a group of colleagues working together for some common goal, has a more personal emotive tone than *university,* which suggests a widespread range of interests, goals, pursuits, and so forth. To many, *university,* which signifies a number of different colleges (College of Business, College of Nursing, College of Liberal Arts) gathered under a single unit and granting advanced degrees, suggests a more significant educational institution than *college*. Both terms have various nonoverlapping intensional meanings.

13. *Man* can be used as an emotively neutral term to denote an adult male, or it can be used to suggest strength, power, bravery (He's a real man). *Gentleman* is colloquially used as a polite term to refer to any man. It is also used to refer to a man with a certain level of breeding, manners, or some other distinction.

Exercise Set 2.6 (p. 61)

1. *And* is a conjunction used to connect components in such a way that the compound formed is true when both components are true but false otherwise, as in "Washington and Lincoln were both great presidents."

3. "Neither rain nor snow will keep the fans away from Sunday's game" means the same as "Rain will not keep the fans away from Sunday's game and snow won't either."

Exercise Set 2.7 (p. 64)

1. (1) When I bite into this lemon it makes my mouth pucker.

(3) Frank is making plans to go to State University next year even though without a scholarship he cannot possibly manage to do so. He says that this time he knows he'll win the scholarship.

Exercise Set 2.8 (pp. 65–67)

1. Intensional, lexical definition.

3. Theoretical definition.

5. Verbal extensional definition. (Platypuses and echidnas are the only two types of monotremes.)

7. Persuasive definition, conveying a negative attitude towards a particular style in art and literature.

9. Stipulative definition.

11. Implicit definition.

13. Lexical definition.

15. Persuasive definition.

17. Persuasive definition.

19. Lexical definition.

CHAPTER THREE

Exercise Set 3.1 (p. 78–80)

Part One

1. True   3. True   5. False

Part Two

1. Because there is a specific person (John) who is the brother of Mary, there is someone who is the brother of Mary, which means that Mary has a brother.

3. Because black swans are an instance of nonwhite swans, the general claim that not all swans are white is true.

5. The conclusion follows from the premiss and the mathematical calculation involved in counting the hours from 11 A.M. to 2 P.M.

7. The conclusion follows from the premisses and multiplication of 150 by 4.

9. Again, mathematical calculations, on the figures given in the premisses, yield the conclusion.

Part Three

1. Voters could change their minds between the time of the survey and the time of the voting; or, the survey might be unreliable.

3. Greer's problem might have been dietary instead of heat exhaustion, and thus it might have been repaired by some "quick fix," such as a dose of sugar.

5. The costs of monitoring patients in single rooms or the conversion costs might not be compensated by the features the author mentions.

Exercise Set 3.2 (pp. 85–87)

Part Two

1. Premiss: The introduction of cooperative marketing into Europe greatly increased the prosperity of the farmers.
   Conclusion: A similar system in the United States will greatly increase the prosperity of our farmers.
   —Argument that concludes that a particular kind of similarity holds on the basis of other known similarities. (The similarities on which the argument depends are not explicitly stated—presumably, they are the similar situation of American and European farmers.)

3. Premiss: In a group of 6,634 men and women, those who consumed at least one gram of calcium per day lowered their risk of high blood pressure by about 12 percent.
   Conclusion: Calcium guards against hypertension.
   —Generalizing on the basis of a sample.

5. This passage gives an argument by Ptolemy, an important ancient astronomer, for the value of astrology.

Premisses: Study of the stars and moon allows predictions of tempests, gales and so forth.
   Conclusion: Similar knowledge of the constitution of the heavens will allow prediction of destiny and disposition of human beings.
   —Argument that concludes that a particular kind of similarity holds on the basis of other known similarities. (Again, the precise similarities are not mentioned, but presumably they involve the claim that human temperaments, and so forth are natural events, like gales and tempests.)

7. Premisses: These ostensibly primitive poems show a length and complexity of composition that can be only the result of many generations of artistic effort.
   They speak a language out of all relation to common speech, full of forgotten meanings and echoes of past states of society; a poet's language, demonstrably built up and conditioned at every turn by the needs of the hexameter metre.
   Conclusion: The *Iliad, Odyssey, Erga,* and *Theogony* are not the first hexameter poems.

—Murray's conclusion is based on causal reasoning concerning what accounts for the sophistication of ancient epic poetry. It is possible to interpret this passage as an extended argument with an inductive and a deductive part. If we interpret the first premiss to say that the complexity of the poems can be accounted for *only* by recognizing them as late members in a developing series of earlier, but similar (and lost-to-us) epic poems, the conclusion here follows deductively from that claim. The premiss of the deductive argument then could be considered as a conclusion drawn inductively from the evidence presented in the second premiss.

9. Premisses: Construction spending rose 1.4 per cent in December, the second straight monthly gain.

Orders to U.S. factories for new manufactured goods rose a strong 4.8 per cent.

Conclusion: The economy soon will be in good shape.

—In this argument, we conclude something about the future on the basis of what has already happened.

Exercise Set 3.3 (pp. 89–90)

1. Borden's status as an orphan does not have a bearing on the evaluation of evidence that she killed her parents. The fallacy is an appeal to pity.

3. His concern for crime is not evidence that the Senator is able to do anything about it, though fear of crime might cloud judgment. If the other candidates refuse even to acknowledge the crime problem, however, Ess's concern may be relevant to the voter's decision.

5. One instance of eating fish followed by a headache the next day is not sufficient to support the generalization.

Exercise Set 3.4 (pp. 91–92)

1. A group of houseplants that was exposed to four hours of fluorescent light in addition to normal daylight grew much more quickly and were generally greener and healthier looking than others that were not exposed to the additional lighting.

Fluorescent light is good for houseplants.

—Inductive. Conclusion is a generalization based on what happens in a sample.

3. Any individual dependence [i.e., loss of liberty] is so much force denied to the body of the State.
Liberty cannot subsist without equality.

The greatest good aimed at in every system of legislation is liberty and equality.

—This argument is probably intended to be deductive. The first premiss attempts to link in a deductive manner individual liberty with the strength of the State.

5. This is an inductive argument, a generalization about the effectiveness of carbolic acid, based on the sample results tabulated in the passage.

7. <u>Two or more elements are associated within a geological deposit.</u>

   A roughly coincidental contextual relationship holds between the events from which the elements were derived.

—Intended to be deductive, as signaled by the use of "implied." The conclusion is weak and guarded, in contrast to the stronger conclusion that others have drawn and that Binford rejects.

9. (1) <u>Today the main salmon run up the Bann occurs in midsummer.</u>
   <u>In Mesolithic times, there may have been a late spring run.</u>
   <u>Lower water temperatures make it unlikely that the salmon run would continue beyond the fall.</u>

   Salmon bones indicate summer occupation.

   (2) <u>Eels run downstream in the fall.</u>

   Eel bones indicate fall residence.

   (3) <u>Hazelnuts are ready for picking by midfall.</u>
   <u>Water-lily seeds are best collected in September.</u>

   Hazelnuts and water-lily seeds indicate fall residence.

—These three arguments are inductive, based on what usually happens. They jointly support the overall conclusion that the site was occupied in the seasons indicated by the remains of salmon bones, eel bonds, hazelnuts, and water-lily seeds.

11. <u>He took leave of us a quarter of an hour before he died, and asked us to take Voloyda away.</u>

   He was conscious to the last moment.

—Intended to be deductive. An obvious implicit premiss: When a person makes farewells and sensible requests, that person is conscious.

   A second, incomplete argument based on similarities also occurs:

<u>Three days of frightful suffering and then death!</u>

That might suddenly, at any time, happen to me.

—Implicit premiss: The dead man was similar to me in many respects.

13. <u>Per capita consumption of beer in the United States last year reached an all-time high.</u>
   <u>Beer sales for the past several years have been going up 4 percent to 5 percent annually.</u>
   <u>This year—a recession year—the rise is around 2 percent.</u>

   Everything is heading up for the beer business.

   —Inductive, based on what has already happened.

15. Climate has a great influence on bodily functions.
    All of the places in which men of great intellect have been found . . .
    have an unusually dry atmosphere.

    Genius is dependent on dry air, and so on.

—Probably intended to be deductive, but the connection between dry air, rapid body functions, and genius has not been established, and no plausible generalization seems to connect them.

17. The means of command and control are inevitably vulnerable to nuclear destruction.

    A nuclear war could not be limited and prevented from escalating into an all-out civilization-shattering exchange.

—Inductive, signaled by "it is extremely doubtful."

19. Early man could not have known the social advantages of incest taboos.

    Social functions of incest taboos cannot account for their origins.

    —Intended to be deductive. Missing premiss: Customs cannot be accounted for by their social advantages unless those who originate the customs are aware of those advantages. (Sociobiologists, among others, would deny such a premiss.)

21. To be able to read the classics you have to know "from where" you are reading them.
    If not, both the book and the reader will be lost in a timeless cloud.

    The greatest "yield" from reading the classics will be obtained by someone who knows how to alternate them with the proper dose of current affairs.

    —Intended to be deductive.

23. The past four presidents of the United States have supported equality of races and civil liberties.
    We do not have equality of races, and erosion of our civil liberties continues.

    Congress or some other force must be preventing our presidents from bringing about the reforms they want.

    —Intended to be deductive, though the vague "some other force" in the conclusion trivializes the argument. The suggestion that Congress is at fault is ungrounded.

25. Blacks can "pass" as whites.
    "Looking black" is different from being black.

    Skin hue is neither a necessary nor a sufficient condition for being classified as black in our culture.

    —Deductive.

CHAPTER FOUR

Exercise Set 4.1 (pp. 102–103)

Part One

1. R: Professional hair dyes   A: Peroxide dyes

Strong (percentage close to 100 percent)

3. R: Students who registered this term   A: Students favoring the fee

Not strong (only 75 percent)

5. R: German shepherds   A: dogs easy to train

Reasonably strong ("most")

7. R: Cigarette smokers   A: those who die from lung cancer

Strong (97 percent)—but consider the consequences if you are in the 3-percent group!

Part Two

1. Most wild mushrooms are poisonous.
   The mushrooms the collector gathers are wild.
   _____

   The mushrooms the collector gathers are poisonous.

3. Hardly any Independents are election winners.
   The incumbent will run as an Independent.
   _____

   The incumbent will not win the election.

5. More than two-thirds of students who enter the college earn degrees.
   You are a student who entered the college.
   _____

   You will earn a degree.

Exercise Set 4.2 (pp. 104–105)

1. Ambassadors to important posts, such as the UN, are very likely to be fluent in several languages, including English.

3. Being president of GM is a high-paid job.

5. People who are so committed to the benefits of exercise that they write books and make videos about it are not likely to stop merely because they turn 50.

Exercise Set 4.3 (pp. 107–108)

1. The creationist critics of evolutionary biology are not experts in that field; therefore they are speaking outside of their area of expertise.

Exercise Set 4.4 (pp. 115–116)

Part One

1. This is an argument against the person, based on Colson's record as a perjurer in the Watergate affair. It is a relatively strong *ad hominem.*

Most of what Colson says about Watergate is false.
Colson says that the CIA knew about Watergate in advance.

The CIA did not know about Watergate in advance.

3. This is a fallacious *ad hominem.* Their status as prisoners does not render most of what they say about prison conditions false.

5. This is a fallacious argument from consensus. "Most people" does not constitute an authority on the dangers of marijuana.

7. This is a fallacious circumstantial *ad hominem.*

9. This is a fallacious appeal to authority. Wesley, though a holy man, was no legitimate medical authority.

Part Three

The argument is :

Most English-speaking people pronounce *otiose* as o´-shi-os.

The correct pronunciation of *otiose* is o´-shi-os.

This argument is not an appeal to consensus, but is deductively correct, because, by definition, the pronunciation accepted by the majority of language speakers is the correct pronunciation.

Part Five

This is an attack on the fallacious appeal to authority. All of Huxley's examples refer to persons of some distinction in one field making pronouncements on another area outside their special area of expertise.

Exercise Set 4.5 (pp. 123–127)

1. Tar (extracted from cigarette smoke) when smeared on the skin of mice in laboratories causes skin cancers.
   Implicit points of analogy: Mice skin is similar to human lung tissue.
   Additional implicit premiss: Tar from cigarette smoke clings to smokers' lungs.

Cigarette smoking causes lung cancer in humans.

—Although the conclusion is believable on other grounds, the preceding argument is weak in the absence of information required to establish relevant similarities between mice skin and lung tissue, as well as information about the amounts of accumulated tar required to produce cancers.

3. This argument depends on an implicit claim that an analogy or similarity must exist between cause and effect. It is not a good argument from analogy.

5. Chimps have a limited capacity to use tools.
   Other great apes are similar to chimps in intelligence.

   Other great apes will have a capacity for tool use similar to chimps.

   —The argument is good and is strengthened by the implicit premiss that other apes resemble chimps not only in intelligence but also in body structure and manual dexterity.

7. The planets are attracted to the sun in inverse proportion to the square of the distance between the planet and the sun.
   The electrons are attracted to the nucleus of an atom in inverse proportion to the square of the distance between the electron and the nucleus.
   Planets revolve around the sun in orbits.

   Electrons revolve around the nucleus in orbits.

   —The argument is strong.

9. A chemist was held liable for injuries caused by a hair-wash he compounded, judging him guilty of fraud.
   A gun seller sold a defective gun that blew up in the plaintiff's hand.
   The gun seller's negligent behavior was similar in relevant respects to the chemist's fraudulent behavior.

   The gun seller was held liable.

   —Relatively strong, though the implicit similarities between failing to protect consumers against a fraudulent product (a worthless, but dangerous hairwash) and an inherently dangerous product (a defective gun) should be further spelled out.

11. The servant's argument:

   My master encourages me to lie for his benefit.

   My master allows me to lie for my own benefit.

   The strength of the argument depends on the degree of relevant similarity between the servant's own lies and the lies told for the master. Johnson doubts that the servant will distinguish "little white lies" told for social purposes from other sorts of lies.

13. The bending of the twig shapes the tree.

   The education a person has shapes the person's mind.

   The conclusion is plausible on other grounds, but the degree of relevant analogy between young trees and uneducated minds is not great.

15. Some highly civilized persons today feel about abortion the way some highly civilized persons in earlier times felt about slavery—that it is a normal human institution.
   It would not have been appropriate in earlier times to scorn Jefferson for owning slaves.

   It is not appropriate now for pro-life folk to scorn a woman who terminates a pregnancy by abortion.

   —Similarities *do* exist in the passions felt by abolitionists for their cause and pro-lifers for theirs; many relevant differences also exist between slavery and abortion. Buckley's argument ostensibly promotes tolerance for abortion, but in reality it condemns abortion by placing it in the same moral category as slavery.

17. A continuous gradation of color patches from yellow through orange into
    red can be divided into two classes [reddish and yellowish] by choos-
    ing some criterion of demarcation in the center of the orange range.
    The fossil record of a sequence of organisms showing gradual changes
    from reptile to mammal has been divided by taxonomists for conve-
    nience into two classes, reptile and mammal.
    It would be absurd to say on the basis of a decision to divide the contin-
    uum of color patches that no continuum exists.

    It is absurd to say on the basis of taxonomist's decision to divide the
    sequence of organisms into two classes that no continuum exists.

—The point that drawing divisions in a continuum does not destroy a continuum
is correct, but creationists might not be moved by Kitcher's analogy because they
would question the similarity between the continuum found in the color spectrum and
the "gappy" continuum of the fossil record.

19. (1) The ancients were similar to us in preferring to use precious materials for symbolic artifacts.

(2) The ancients were similar to us in regarding certain parts of the body as particularly significant.

(3) The ancients were similar to us in their desire to cover less valuable materials with
more valuable materials.

Exercise Set 4.7 (pp. 138–140)

1. Premiss: Two pure samples of copper have boiling points of 2,567° C.
   Conclusion: 2.567° C. is the boiling point of copper.
   —Small sample is adequate because of uniformity of samples of pure copper.

3. Premiss: 70 percent of heroin users in the sample had tried marijuana first.
   Conclusion: 70 percent of marijuana users will go on to heroin.

—Fallacy, because the sample, though large, is biased since it encompasses only heroin
users.

5. Premiss: The number of rooms in six excavated sites in the Upper Little Colorado
region was equal to . . .
   Conclusion: The number of rooms in pueblo sites in AZ, NM, and CO is . . .
   —Weak, perhaps fallacious. More information about the uniformity of pueblo populations is needed. The sample is small, and is taken from a small region of the states
mentioned in the conclusion.

7. Premiss: In a questionnaire, 48 percent of pet owners responded that the animal
was a human family member.
   Conclusion: Overestimating the importance of pets to people is impossible.
   —The conclusion is too strong for the small amount of evidence presented.

9. Premiss: Once when Conny van Rietschoten tossed coins into the sea to bring wind,
wind occurred.
   Conclusion: Tossing coins into the sea brings wind.
   —Fallacy of biased statistics and insufficient statistics.

11. Premiss: Data on male-female speech patterns at seven university faculty meetings, in
which with one exception men spoke more often, and with no exceptions spoke longer.

Premiss: When a public lecture is followed by questions or a talk show host opens the phone lines, the first voice is almost always a man's.

Premiss: When men ask questions or offer comments they tend to talk longer (52.7 seconds for men; 23.1 seconds for women).

Conclusion: Men talk more.

—Acceptable.

Exercise Set 4.8 (pp. 144–149)

1. Statistical syllogism:

80 percent to 90 percent of those who follow the special diet produce the boy or girl babies they want.

The woman who wants a boy (girl) will follow the special diet for a boy (girl).

The woman who wants a boy (girl) will produce a boy (girl).

Inductive generalization:

In a study of 47 French couples from 1970 to 1980, 39 (83 percent) produced a child of the sex they wanted.

In Canada, a study of 224 couples on special diets revealed an 80 percent success rate.

In five health centers in Paris and five outside the city, the success rate is approximately 90 percent.

From 80 percent to 90 percent of all couples who follow the special diet will produce a child of the sex they want.

3. Johnson uses an analogy between military service—where beatings by superior officers are permitted—and schools. The argument is weak because of the strong dissimilarities between the two cases. For example, the purpose of the military is to provide defense for the country; therefore instant and unquestioning obedience has value. But the purpose of schools is to train young minds, to develop responsible citizens who can think for themselves. Pufendorf is a legal scholar. What he says about the legality of the beatings does not necessarily extend to the moral justification of the practice, which is what seems to be in question here.

5. The argument is based on (unstated) analogies between humans and experimental animals. Premises state the effects of the drug on those animals.

7. Inductive generalization. Reasonably strong, assuming that the tests were fair.

9. Statistical syllogism. Probably violates the requirement of total evidence because most young women who are divorced do not receive such large alimony payments.

11. Analogical argument. Depends on relevant similarities, stated in the premises, between macaque monkeys and humans.

13. Inductive generalization. Based on relatively small sample, but from widely scattered areas. Reasonably strong argument, assuming reports about the use of dingoes were accurate.

15. Statistical syllogism:

Most heads of household earning more than $40,000 per year own some
    stocks or bonds.
The person to whom the letter is addressed is a head of household who earns
    more than $40,000 per year.

The person to whom the letter is addressed owns some stocks or bonds.

17. (1) *Ad hominem*

    (2) Analogy

CHAPTER FIVE

Exercise Set 5.1 (pp. 154–155)

1. Some area of the main road leading to the place of work had nails, glass,
or other sharp objects on it.

3. A drought may be affecting trees, or an insect infestation, such as a gypsy
moth attack.

5. Fire hydrants on your street were flushed that day.

7. An outstanding teacher works with student and coaches them to compete in scholarship competitions.

Exercise Set 5.2 (p. 156)

1. One of the plants could have been a weakling; one could be planted in a sunnier
place; or one might have been attacked by insects or disease.

3. Your oven thermostat might have broken, or you might have been careless in following the recipe the second time.

5. The shirt has been washed and has shrunk.

7. The IRS has hired additional auditors and is checking more returns.

Exercise Set 5.3 (pp. 163–167)

1. (1) The decreased rate of mortality in one group of encephalitis patients.

(2) Members of one group were given ara-A. Members of the other group were given
an inert substance.

(3) Joint Method.

(4) The drug ara-A causes a decrease in the rate of mortality among patients with
encephalitis.

3. (1) Lower rate among junior high students of taking up smoking.

(2) Two groups of students were questioned about smoking habits. One group was
given antismoking propaganda, and the other group was not. Ten weeks later, both
groups were questioned a second time.

(3) Joint Method.

(4) Antismoking propaganda caused a lower rate of taking up smoking.

5. (1) Rate of dental caries.

(2) Records of the past 100 years show a steady increase in the per capita consumption of sucrose, from about 20 pounds per year in 1820 to more than 100 pounds per year today, with an almost parallel rise in dental caries. In Europe and Japan, the consumption of sucrose was restricted during wartime, and there was a dramatic decrease in caries.

(3) Concomitant Variation.

(4) Increase (decrease) in rate of consumption of sucrose causes increase (decrease) in rate of dental caries.

7. (1) Higher than normal rate of malignant skin cancer among members of the D. C. police department.

(2) All twelve policemen afflicted with skin cancer had used tear gas to quell riots and demonstrations between 1968 and 1971.

(3) Method of Agreement.

(4) One chemical component of tear gas apparently causes skin cancer.

9. (1) Death rates during three years in forty-six American cities.

(2) In twenty-four of the cities, the water was fluoridated. In twenty-two of the cities, the water was not fluoridated. No difference in death rates between the two groups was observed.

(3) Joint Method.

(4) Fluoridation of water does not cause increased death rates.

11. (1) Higher incidence of lung cancer in women of Xuan Wei County.

(2) Use of smoky coal for cooking and heating; variation in time spent indoors by men and women.

(3) Concomitant Variation.

(4) Greater exposure to smoky coal is the cause of higher incidence of lung cancer in women.

13. (1) Rate of heart disease.

(2) Diagonal crease in earlobe.

(3) Joint Method.

(4) A diagonal crease in an ear lobe may foretell heart disease.

15. (1) Increased rate of suicide among women.

(2) Smoking one to twenty-four cigarettes daily; smoking twenty-five or more cigarettes daily.

(3) Joint Method (also Concomitant Variation).

(4) Smoking is linked to increased rate of suicide in women.

Exercise Set 5.4 (pp. 171–173)

1. In Exercise 1 of set 5.3, a control group of patients with the disease receive an inert substance, and an experimental group of patients receive ara-A. Randomized experimental design.

In Exercise 2, an experimental group of brains of former Alzheimer's patients shows loss of neurons, and a control group of brains of those without the disease does not show loss. Retrospective.

In Exercise 3, an experimental group of junior-high students is given antismoking propaganda, and no propaganda is given to a control group. Randomized experimental design.

In Exercise 4, one group of patients is fed polished rice; the other group unpolished rice. Randomized experimental design.

In Exercise 5, a "self-selected" group on war rations received less sucrose; otherwise, the amount of sucrose increased each year. Retrospective.

(The other exercises also exemplify features of controlled experiments.)

3. The study would have been more convincing by withholding the toothpaste from a control group of those with colds and then comparing the two groups for how quickly the colds improved.

5. Use of volunteers constitutes a self-selected group, not necessarily representative of the population. The graduate school population from which the volunteers came is also likely to differ from the general population in relevant ways with respect to alcoholic behavior.

Exercise Set 5.5 (pp. 177–178)

1. Having enough time can be considered a necessary condition for passing an exam.

3. The invitation from Jean might have been both necessary and sufficient, or sufficient, or probabilistic. More contextual information is needed to decide.

5. Oily rags stored in a closet are are highly susceptible to spontaneous combustion, thus making fire highly probable, given a background of standard conditions, such as normal temperatures and oxygen supplies.

7. Although infection with the virus is necessary and sufficient for the disease, contact with someone who has the disease is a probabilistic cause for a nonimmunized person's contracting the disease.

9. Reduced atmospheric pressure (such as that found at high altitudes) is a sufficient cause for lowering boiling points of substances. Lower boiling points are sufficient causes for longer cooking times of foods that are prepared in boiling liquid.

11. Lethal injections are a sufficient cause of death.

13. The assassination of the Archduke is often cited as the proximate cause of World War I. Any major war is the result of a complicated set of causes, not merely a single event—though a single event may provide the spark that ignites the explosive situation that has developed over time.

15. Worry about the deficit may have been a contributing necessary cause, or a partial probabilistic cause.

17. Pollination is necessary for fruit production. Bees are the normal agents of pollination, but it can be accomplished in other ways.

19. Lower levels of T-cells are probabilistically related to severe heart disease.

Exercise Set 5.6 (pp. 191–194)

Part One

1. Ignoring a common cause.

Part Two

1. Post hoc.

3. Post hoc.

5. Ignoring a common cause. The crankiness and later cold symptoms are probably both results of the onset of the cold. (The regularity of the connection argues against this example being an instance of post hoc.)

7. Genetic fallacy.

9. Genetic fallacy. This is also an example of circumstantial ad hominem.

11. Confusing an orginating cause with a sustaining cause.

Part Three

1. Confusing cause and effect.

3. Ignoring a common cause.

Part Four

1. The warning is against assuming a general cause (sodium) when the cause is more specific—sodium chloride.

3. The warning is against failing to see that the same cause (depression) could be operative at different ages in different socioeconomic groups.

CHAPTER SIX

Exercise Set 6.1 (pp. 207–208)

Remember that the point of the exercise is to provide the right setup for calculating the probabilities rather than demonstrating skill in arithmetic. You may use a calculator to add, subtract, multiply, or divide. Or you may show how to set up the problem without doing the calculations.

1. Pr (Ace will be drawn) = 4/52; Pr (King will be drawn) = 4/52.

Pr (Ace or King will be drawn) = 4/52 + 4/52 = 8/52 (or 2/13).

(Rule 3, disjuncts are mutually exclusive.)

3. $(1/2 \times 1/2 \times 1/2) = 1/8$.

(Rule 4, conjuncts are independent.)

5. $(1/2 + 1/2) = 1$.

(Rule 3, disjuncts are mutually exclusive.)

7. Pr (First card is ace and second card is ace and third card is ace and fourth card is ace) = $(4/52 \times 3/51 \times 2/50 \times 1/49) = 24/6497400$ (or 1/270725).

(Rule 4, the conjuncts are not independent.)

The probability of obtaining the sequence in the second part of the problem is $(1/52 \times 1/51 \times 1/50 \times 1/49) = 1/6497400$.

(Rule 4, conjuncts are not independent.) The same four cards can occur in 24 different (mutually exclusive) orders, each with a probability of $1/6497400$. Therefore, the probability of getting those four cards, in any order, is $24/6497400$.

9. (1) Pr (Male will be alive and Female will be alive) = $(.840 \times .910) = 0.764$.

(Rule 4 is used; the conjuncts are independent.)

(2) Yes, their life expectancies are no longer independent because in their life together they will share many of the same risks and benefits.

11. Pr (Hand will be improved) = Pr (Draw Ax or draw xA or draw any pair).

These possibilities are mutually exclusive. The probability of drawing an ace and any other card can be calculated thus:
Pr (Ax or xA) = $(1/47 \times 46/46) + (46/47 \times 1/46) = 92/2162$.

(Rule 4 is used to calculate the probability of Ax and also the probability of xA. Rule 3 is used to calculate the probability of Ax or xA.)

Because you hold three aces and have discarded two non-aces, the 47 cards remaining in the deck include one ace, two sets of three matching cards, and ten sets of four matching cards. You can draw a pair by drawing a pair from the sets of three or from the sets of four. Your chance of drawing a pair from the sets of three is equal to the probability that the first card drawn will be one of those six $(6/47)$ times the probability that the second card drawn will be its mate $(2/46)$, according to Rule 4; $6/47 \times 1/46 = 12/2162$. Your chance of drawing a pair from the set of four is equal to the probability that the first card drawn will be from one of those sets of four $(40/47)$ times the probability that the second card will be its mate $(3/46)$, again using Rule 4; $40/47 \times 3/46 = 120/2162$. These two ways of drawing pairs are mutually exclusive, so the probability of drawing a pair is $12/2162 + 120/2162 = 132/2162$, by Rule 3. So, the probability of improving your hand by drawing an ace and some other card, or by drawing a pair is equal to $92/2162 + 132/2162$, which is $224/2162$. Thus, your chance of improving your hand is 0.1036, or slightly better than 10 percent.

13. The probability of getting at least one right answer out of five is equal to 1 minus the probability of getting all five wrong (by the theorem "If Pr $(b|e) = n$, then Pr (not $b|e) = 1 - n$"). Using the method of coin tossing to answer a given True-False question, the probability that you will have the wrong answer is $1/2$. Because coin tosses are independent, the probability of getting five wrong answers in five tosses of a coin, is $1/2 \times 1/2 \times 1/2 \times 1/2 \times 1/2 = 1/32$. So the probability of getting at least one right answer using this method is $31/32$, or about 97 percent.

Exercise Set 6.2 (pp. 224–227)

1. (1) .001

(2) $.001 \times \$500 = \$0.50 - \$1.00 = -\$0.50$

(3) $.001 \times (\$500 \times 3) = \$1.50 - \$3.00 = -\$1.50$

(4) $(.001 \times \$500) + (.001 \times \$500) + (.001 \times \$500) = \$1.50 - \$3.00 = -\$1.50$

3. (1) Decision under uncertainty

(2) Yes, because the sole purpose of the charity dinner is to raise money.

(4)

	Rain	**No Rain**
Indoors	$440	$170
Outdoors	$80	$500

No action dominates. If there is a satisfactory action, it is to have an indoor buffet. If there is no satisfactory action, the gambler would choose the outdoor picnic; the cautious player would choose the indoor supper. The calculator would see that the average utility of the indoor supper is $305, the average utility for the outdoor picnic is $290, and would choose the indoor supper.

5. (1) Maximize expected utility (because this is a decision under risk).

(2) It is reasonable to equate units of utility with profits and losses.
Expected utility for new special: $(1/2 \times \$250) + (1/2 \times -\$50) = \$100$.
Expected utility for usual special : $100
Because the expected utilities are the same, it is reasonable to choose either action.

7.

	States of the World		
	Attend 3	**Attend 4**	**Attend 5**
Buy a season ticket	1/3 (−$100)	1/3 (−$100)	1/3 (−$100)
Pay as you go	1/3 (−$75)	1/3 (−$100)	1/3 (−$125)

The utilities are based on cost of tickets only, and the point is to maximize the expected utility. The expected utility of buying a season ticket is −$100, which is what it costs no matter how many operas you attend. The expected utility of paying as you go is $(-\$25) + (-\$33.33) + (-\$41.69) = -\$100.02$. With these probabilities, season tickets provide only a minimal advantage ($.02). Notice that if other values, such as convenience of having a season ticket and the ability to give—or perhaps sell—unused tickets, were considered, the decision would probably be to buy a season ticket.

9. (1) Pr (Epidemic) × Pr (Flu, given epidemic and no vaccination) = $0.6 \times 0.4 =$ 0.24.

(2) The utility of having the flu is figured in days lost to illness: −9, and so the expected utility of having the flu is 0.24×-9 days $= -2.16$ days.

(3) The expected utility of having the shot is 0.10×-2 days $= -0.20$ days.

(4) Get the shot.

11. One way to set up the problem assigns utilities solely on the basis of dollar cost:

	States of the World		
	Get the jacket	**Miss out**	**Expected Utility**
Actions			
Buy now	1 (−100)	0 (−110)	−100
Wait three days	1/2 (−50)	1/2 (−110)	−80

On this basis, it would be better to wait three days and try to buy the jacket you like. If, however, as the statement of the problem indicates, price is not the only consideration, you would want to place some added value on the preferred jacket. For example, this might be done by adding a $50 premium to obtaining that jacket. Consider the following matrix:

States of the World

	Get the jacket	Miss out	Expected Utility
Actions			
Buy now	1 (−100 +50)	0 (−110)	−50
Wait three days	1/2 (−50 +50)	1/2 (−110)	−55

On the basis of this decision matrix, it would be better to buy now and not miss out.

CHAPTER SEVEN

Exercise Set 7.1 (p. 235)

1. If you do well in math and logic classes, then you keep up with the assignments.

3. If you want something very much, then you work hard for it.

5. If life has no complications, then life is uninteresting.

(Or, if life is interesting, then life has complications.)

7. If you really want to pass it, then you can pass this class.

9. If a student passes one course in logic, then the student fulfills the logic requirement.

Exercise Set 7.2 (pp. 238–239)

Part One

1. If q, then p (True).

3. If q, then q (True).

5. If q, then p (True).

7. If q, then p (True).

9. If not q then p (True).

Part Two

1. (1) Sally won the marathon.

(3) Rita phoned Larry. She went to his apartment.

Exercise Set 7.3 (p. 240)

1. If Charlie will go to the dance, then Sally will go to the dance.
   Charlie will go to the dance.

   Sally will go to the dance.

3. If you are persistent, then you will be elected.
   You are persistent.

   You will be elected.

Exercise Set 7.5 (pp. 246–248)

1. If our school's team wins all its football games this season, then the team
      will be invited to play in a postseason bowl game.
   The team will be invited to play in a postseason bowl game.

   The team will win every game this season.

   (Affirming the consequent)

3. If the Steelers beat the Oilers, then the Steelers will go to the playoffs.
   The Steelers beat the Oilers.

   The Steelers will go to the playoffs.

   (Affirming the antecedent)

5. If it does not rain on Thursday, then the picnic will be held on Thursday.
   It will not rain on Thursday.

   We'll have the picnic on Thursday.

   (Affirming the antecedent)

7. If primitive people did not cross the Pacific Ocean, then there would not
      be a strong resemblance between Polynesian artifacts and South Ameri-
      can artifacts.
   But there is a strong resemblance (i.e., it is not the case that there is no
      strong resemblance) between those artifacts.

   Primitive people did cross the Pacific Ocean (i.e., it is not the case that
      primitive people did not cross the Pacific Ocean).

   (Denying the consequent)
   Note: Although this argument is valid, the link between antecedent and consequent
   in its conditional premiss is dubious.

9. If coyotes howl, then there's a moon.
   There will be a moon tonight.

   Coyotes will howl tonight.

   (Affirming the consequent)

11. If 2 is not a prime number, then there is a positive integer smaller than 2 and greater than 1 which evenly divides 2.
But there are no positive integers smaller than 2 and greater than 1.

2 is a prime number.

(Denying the consequent)

13. If we can have all that is written in a language in translation, then we will not take the trouble to learn it.
We cannot have all that is written in the language in translation (i.e., poetry cannot be translated).

We take the trouble to learn it.

(Denying the antecedent)

15. If a judgment of acquittal by reason of insanity is inappropriate in the Washington case, then a jury verdict of guilty would violate the law or the facts.
The jury verdict of guilty does not violate the law or the facts.

A judgment of acquittal by reason of insanity is inappropriate in the Washington case.

(Denying the consequent)

17. If the simple utilitarian model is correct, then there will be a wide but more-or-less even pattern of dispersal of axes in all directions from the quarry source.
There is not a more-or-less even pattern of dispersal of axes from the quarry source.

Implicit conclusion: The simple utilitarian model is not correct.

(Denying the consequent)

19. If it wasn't the Major, then it was the Bruce chap.
It wasn't the Major.

It is the Bruce chap.

(Affirming the antecedent)

CHAPTER EIGHT

Exercise Set 8.1 (pp. 261–264)

Note: When no auxiliary hypotheses are mentioned, assume the usual constraints on capability of observers, accuracy of reported data, and so forth.

1. (1) Hypothesis: The high-cholesterol diet is the cause of the high incidence of heart attacks.

(2) Observable prediction: Reducing cholesterol in the diets of people in this area will be followed by a reduction in the incidence of heart attacks.

(3) Alternative: The hard work that the men do is the cause of the high incidence of heart attacks.

(4) Current medical theory gives the original hypothesis somewhat higher probability than the hard work hypothesis.

3. (1) Hypothesis: Intellectual achievements of Jews are (partly) caused by inherited myopia.

(2) Observable prediction: A random sample of myopic non-Jews will contain a higher proportion of intellectuals than a comparable sample of non-Jews who are not near-sighted.

Auxiliary: Those who are unfit for sports turn to intellectual pursuits.

(3) Alternative: Intellectual achievements are the result of greater-than-average intellectual abilities, a high cultural valuation of intellectual achievement, or both.

(4) The original hypothesis has a low prior probability. Burt's theories on this topic border on "crank," and no other evidence supports his views.

5. (1) Counseling and home placement programs can substantially reduce the number of juveniles incarcerated for minor offenses.

(2) Observable prediction: Implementation of a program of counseling is followed by a reduction of 43 percent from preprogram levels in the total number of offenders placed in detention. Auxiliary hypotheses: Statistics are accurate. The reduction cannot be accounted for entirely by the national trend towards reduction.

(3) Alternative hypothesis: Judges and prosecutors might have been unwilling to commit juveniles to detention while testing the program.

(4) The original hypothesis has a reasonably high probability because social theory indicates that adolescents need guidance and support. If this program provides support and nothing else does, the program has a reasonably high probability of success.

7. (1) A contributing cause of the manatee's death was a sharp drop in water temperature.

(2) Water temperature measures significantly below normal (64 degrees instead of 75 to 78 degrees).

(3) One alternative cause of death was considered: old age—another is some unknown disease.

(4) Hypothesis is not implausible, but needs further support by seeking information about (captive) manatee's requirements for warm water or a steady water temperature.

9. (1) Catfish slime has healing properties.

(2) A cut that normally takes ten days to heal, heals in three days when catfish slime is applied to it.

(3) No alternative for the quick-healing cut is suggested, and little information about it is given to propose an alternative, though the healing could come from some other feature of the catfish-catching situation.

(4) Not totally implausible: Many natural substances, such as sheep fat, have healing properties when spread on cuts.

11. (1) Ultrasound exposure in the womb may be a contributing cause to left-handedness.

(2) Weak association found between left-handedness in eight- and nine-year-olds and ultrasound exposure when they were in the womb.

(3) Because the association is weak, it may be a chance phenomenon.

(4) Not totally implausible: A possible mechanism is suggested, but many other causes could be invoked for left-handedness. The report of the study, for example, does not mention any hereditary factors.

Exercise Set 8.2 (p. 266)

1. Hypothesis: The infrared light treatment cures colds.
   Because colds usually heal within a week in any case, the treatment has not been shown to be effective.
   (Biased statistics)

Exercise Set 8.3 (pp. 271–274)

Note: "Alternative" here refers to a hypothesis that could account for the observation.
1. Hypothesis: Student missed exam because of family crisis.
   Plausible, in view of student's advance notice to this effect.
   Disconfirming observation: Student is seen on campus immediately after exam.
   Alternative hypothesis: Student was not prepared to take the exam.

3. Hypothesis: Oxygen in the air was the cause of the failure of cauterization to cure gangrene.
   Disconfirming observation: Oxygen was always present, but sometimes gangrene was cured and sometimes not.
   Alternative: Something other than oxygen caused gangrene to reappear.

5. Hypothesis: Protein is a major attribute of food desirability. (Plausible because high-quality protein is a requirement for survival.
   Disconfirming observation: Proteins are not recognized as such by most people in the world and thus do not figure in their evaluations of food.
   Alternative: The Fat Hypothesis.

7. Hypothesis: Light consists of tiny waves. Plausible on the basis of some similarity between the behavior of water and light.
   Disconfirming observations: Light rays travel in straight lines and cast sharp shadows. Light rays cannot go around obstacles. Light rays can travel through a vacuum (assuming the auxiliary hypothesis that space is a vacuum).
   Alternative: Light consists of tiny particles.

9. Applying external heat to people suffering from effects of extreme cold is helpful. (Initially plausible because external heat helps those suffering from effects of moderate cold.)
   Disconfirming observation: Sitting in front of heaters after exposure to extreme cold made no difference in body temperature.
   Alternative: Shivering and exercise help more.

Exercise Set 8.4 (pp. 276–278)

1. a.

(1) $100/300 \times 50/100 = 1/6$

(2) $200/300 \times 150/200 = 1/2$

(3) $(100/300 \times 50/100) + (200/300 \times 50/200) = 1/6 + 1/6 = 1/3$

b.

(1) $(1/3 \times 1/2)/[(1/3 \times 1/2) + (2/3) \times 1/4)] = 1/2$

(2) $(2/3 \times 1/4)/[(2/3 \times 1/4) + (1/3) \times 1/2)] = 1/2$

3. (1) 1/6

(3) 3/4

(5) $[(1/6) \times (3/4)] + [(5/6) \times (1/4)] = 8/24 = 1/3$

Exercise Set 8.5 (pp. 280–281)

1. (1) 0.05 (1/20)

(3) $(0.05 \times 0.80)/(0.05 \times 0.80) + (0.95 \times 0.20) = 0.04/(0.04 + 0.19) = 0.04/0.23 = 0.17$

3. (1) $(0.2 \times 0.00085) + (0.8 \times 0.00015) = 0.00017 + 0.00012 = 0.00029$

(2) $(0.1 \times 0.00065) + (0.9 \times 0.00001) = 0.000074$

(3) $(0.7 \times 0.00029)/[(0.7 \times 0.00029) + (0.3 \times .000074)] =$

$[0.000203/(0.000203 + 0.0000222)] = (0.000203/0.0002252) = 0.901$

(4) $0.2 \times 0.00085/[(0.2 \times 0.00085) + (0.8 \times 0.00015] =$

$0.00017/(0.00017 + 0.00012) = 0.00017/0.00029 = 0.586$

5. The advisory group judged that the prior probability of the dietary fat hypothesis was too low to justify the cost of testing it.

Exercise Set 8.6 (pp. 283–284)

1. This enhances the prior probability of H, and makes it more worthwhile to test *H* than it would be if *H* did not have this relationship to other well-supported hypotheses.

3. Hypothesis: Visitors from some advanced civilization, possibly from another planet, are responsible for some fabulous earthworks found in pre-Columbian American sites.

Prediction: The intricate patterns of earthworks can only be appreciated from an aerial perspective. (Many other examples of false hypotheses with true predictions exist.)

5. In one sense, the answer is an easy "no," because no scientific hypothesis is ever *conclusively* established. Undiscovered or unappreciated evidence may threaten even our most cherished hypotheses. If "conclusively" means "absolutely confirmed," in our guarded use of that term, the answer is still "no" because true prediction is only part of what is required for strong or "absolute" confirmation. Hypotheses that make all true predictions, but that themselves cannot be falsified, are not scientifically valuable. Hypotheses that make true predictions, but that would require throwing out most of the best scientific knowledge that is currently available, will not be easily accepted.

7. No. When hypotheses are treated as premises from which to deduce predictions, they normally require additional premises to support a prediction. Any interesting scientific hypothesis is embedded in a complex of other hypotheses and cannot be tested without assuming the truth of some of these others. In addition, if a specific observa-

tion is to follow from a hypothesis, some assumptions must be made about the instruments used, the competence of observers, and so forth.

9. In almost any case more than one hypothesis is compatible with the scientific evidence. Whether all of these hypotheses are equally plausible in the light of what is already known is another question. Sometimes scientists count themselves fortunate to come up with even one hypothesis that can accommodate the evidence and not fly in the face of what is already known. In other cases, such as the example about the worked mammoth bones, several hypotheses could account for what has been observed. Rarely is a scientist in a position of contemplating a large array of hypotheses, all equally able to account for the data.

11. No, crucial tests are interesting and yield valuable results, but being able to perform them is not an everyday matter in scientific investigations.

13. We do assume that the auxiliary hypotheses are true in the context of testing a hypothesis that depends on those auxiliaries to yield observable predictions. Nevertheless, the auxiliary hypotheses can be tested in other circumstances. Ideally, auxiliary hypotheses have already been tested and confirmed in other contexts. One can always go back and re-examine them if necessary, but it is better to work with well-confirmed auxiliary hypotheses.

15. If one is using Bayes's theorem as a model of hypothesis testing, and the prior probability is zero, then the posterior probability will be zero also. Therefore, no test would make a difference. Intuitively, using an informal Bayesian model, if the prior probability is zero, the hypothesis is hardly worth testing for it is difficult to see what evidence would increase its probability. The situation is dramatically different if the hypothesis has even a very low prior probability, for in that case, some unexpected result that could be accounted for by no other known hypothesis could raise the posterior probability significantly.

17. If the hypothesis already has a probability close to one, further testing cannot raise it much. Or, if an alternative hypothesis has the same observational predictions, the probability of the tested hypothesis will not be raised by much relative to the probability of the alternative.

19. The skull might have been displayed on a pole or stick (this would account for the pierced base). The "ring" of stones might have been a result of natural forces, such as water movement through the cave.

CHAPTER NINE

Exercise Set 9.1 (pp. 293–294)

1. Hypothetical syllogism

3. Disjunctive syllogism

5. Constructive dilemma

7. Constructive dilemma (with a tautological disjunctive premiss)

9. Hypothetical syllogism

11. Hypothetical syllogism

Exercise Set 9.2 (pp. 299–300)

1. $q \cdot \sim r$

3. $q \rightarrow r$

5. $\sim r \rightarrow \sim q$

7. $q \leftrightarrow p$

9. $\sim\sim r$

11. $q \cdot \sim p$

13. $r \vee (p \cdot \sim q)$

15. $r \cdot \sim(p \vee q)$

Part Two

1. Logic is easy, and symbols cannot be used.

3. Logic is not fun, and symbols cannot be used.

5. Logic is easy, and if symbols cannot be used, then logic is fun.

7. If symbols can be used, then if logic is easy, then logic is fun.

9. Logic is fun, and logic is easy if and only if it is fun.

Part Four

1.

p	q	$p \rightarrow q$	$q \rightarrow p$	
T	T	T	T	
T	F	F	T	Not equivalent, shown by
F	T	T	F	rows 2 and 3
F	F	T	T	

3.

p	q	$p \rightarrow q$	$\sim q$	$p \cdot \sim q$	$\sim(p \cdot \sim q)$	
T	T	T	F	F	T	
T	F	F	T	T	F	Equivalent
F	T	T	F	F	T	
F	F	T	T	F	T	

5.

p	r	$p \vee \sim p$	$(p \vee \sim p) \vee r$	
T	T	T	T	
T	F	T	T	Not Equivalent
F	T	T	T	
F	F	T	T	

Exercise Set 9.3 (pp. 301–302)

1. T

3. T

5. T

7. T

9. T

11. F

13. F

15. T

17. T

Exercise Set 9.4 (pp. 306–310)

1.

p	q	$\sim p$	$\sim q$	$\sim p \vee \sim q$	$p \cdot q$	
T	T	F	F	F	T	
T	F	F	T	T	F	Valid
F	T	T	F	T	F	
F	F	T	T	T	F	

3.

p	q	$p \vee q$	$\sim(p \vee q)$	$p \cdot q$	$(p \vee q) \to (p \cdot q)$	
T	T	T	F	T	T	
T	F	T	F	F	F	Invalid
F	T	T	F	F	F	
F	F	F	T	F	T	

5.

p	q	$\sim p$	$\sim q$	$p \to q$	$p \to \sim q$	
T	T	F	F	T	F	
T	F	F	T	F	T	Valid
F	T	T	F	T	T	
F	F	T	T	T	T	

7.

p	q	$p \vee q$	
T	T	T	
T	F	T	
F	T	T	Valid
F	F	F	

Part Two

Note : Truth tables are not shown here.

1. p The game has been sold out.
   q The game has been canceled.
   r I won't be able to see the game.

$p \vee q$
$p \rightarrow r$
$\underline{q \rightarrow r}$ Valid
r

3. p It doesn't rain for two weeks in June.
   q The garden will fail.
   r We won't have fresh tomatoes in July

   $p \rightarrow q$
   $\underline{q \rightarrow r}$ Valid
   $p \rightarrow r$

5. p Professional baseball players can command big salaries.
   q The public strongly supports them.

   p
   $\underline{p \rightarrow q}$ Valid
   q

Part Three

1. p I let my mother's son lie there unburied.
   q I can bear this pain.
   $\sim q \rightarrow p$
   $\underline{\sim p}$
   q

3. $p \rightarrow q$
   $\underline{r \rightarrow q}$
   $\sim q \rightarrow (\sim p \bullet \sim r)$

5. $((p \bullet \sim q) \rightarrow r)$
   $r \rightarrow s$
   $s \rightarrow t$
   $\underline{t \rightarrow \sim s}$
   $\sim (r \bullet p)$ This requires a 32-row truth table.

7. $p \rightarrow \sim q$
   $\sim p \rightarrow \sim r$
   $t \rightarrow s$
   $\underline{\sim u \rightarrow \sim s}$
   $t \rightarrow u$

Exercise Set 9.5 (pp. 312–313)

1. If an argument has a tautologous conclusion, then the conclusion cannot be false. So, no matter what truth value the premisses have, the argument cannot have all true premisses and a false conclusion.

3. If the premisses are all tautologies, then they will always be true. If the conclusion is a contingent sentence then it could be false. So it would be possible for such an argument to have all true premisses and a false conclusion.

5. No simple (noncompound) sentence can be a tautology, because such a sentence could be assigned a value of either T or F. Such a sentence lacks the structure that could make it tautologous.

7. (1)

p	*q*	($p \rightarrow q) \rightarrow (q \rightarrow p$)			
T	T	T	T	T	
T	F	F	T	T	Contingent
F	T	T	F	F	
F	F	T	T	T	

(3)

p	~*p*	~*p* $\rightarrow$ *p*	
T	F	T	Contingent
F	T	F	

(5)

p	*q*	($p \rightarrow q) \rightarrow (p \rightarrow (p \bullet q$))				
T	T	T	T	T	T	
T	F	F	T	F	F	Tautology
F	T	T	T	T	F	
F	F	T	T	T	F	

Exercise Set 9.7 (pp. 320–321)

1.(1)

p	*q*	($p \rightarrow q$)
T	T	T
T	F	F
F	T	T
F	F	T

Following Carroll's method, the sentence form is true in rows 1, 3, and 4. So the required disjunctive normal form is:

($p \bullet q$) v (~$p \bullet q$) v (~$p \bullet$ ~q)

(2)

p	*q*	($p \leftrightarrow q$)	
T	T	T	
T	F	F	($p \bullet q$) v (~$p \bullet$ ~q)
F	T	F	
F	F	T	

(3)

p	q	$\sim(p \to q)$
T	T	F
T	F	T
F	T	F
F	F	F

$p \cdot \sim q$

(4)

p	q	$(p \to \sim q)$
T	T	F
T	F	T
F	T	T
F	F	T

$(p \cdot \sim q) \vee (\sim p \cdot q) \vee (\sim p \cdot \sim q)$

3. The exclusive *or* connects two sentences in such a way that if one is true, the other is false, or in other words, it has the value "true" when its components have different values, and it has the value "false" when the components have the same value.

p	q	p **exclusive or** q
T	T	F
T	F	T
F	T	T
F	F	F

Thus, the exclusive *or* is the denial of material equivalence:

p	q	$(p \leftrightarrow q)$	$\sim(p \leftrightarrow q)$
T	T	T	F
T	F	F	T
F	T	F	T
F	F	T	F

To design the connective using only $\sim$, $\cdot$, and v, use the truth table to construct the disjunctive normal form for the denial of material equivalence:

$(p \cdot \sim q) \vee (\sim p \cdot q)$

For a switch diagram of *s*-function, see Figure 9-5 in text.

CHAPTER TEN

Exercise Set 10.1 (pp. 332–333)

Part One

1. Some fiddlers are not bass fiddlers.

3. No politicians are statesmen.

5. Some cats are Persians.

7. All cats are domestic.

9. No doctors are rich.

Part Two

1. It always rains in southern California.

3. His only pet is a cat.

5. Chocolate desserts are yucky.

7. You never complain about the homework.

9. Few heroes have gone unsung.

Part Three

1. Peas are usually eaten with a knife.

3. Baseball is not less interesting than football.

5. The grass is not always greener on the other side of the fence.

7. Mary Stuart was not the only reigning queen of Scotland.

9. Old soldiers sometimes die.

Exercise Set 10.2 (pp. 339–340)

1. Every person who could love him is a mother.

L: Persons who could love him

M: Mothers

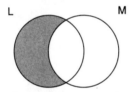

3. Every mile that is longest is a mile that is the last mile home.

M: Mile that is longest

H: Last mile home

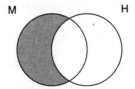

5. Every person who is admitted is a junior or a senior.

A: Person who is admitted

J: Junior or senior

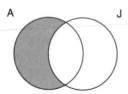

7. Every thing worth owning is a genuine thing.

T: Things worth owning

G: Genuine things

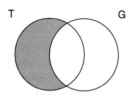

9. No valuable lessons are easily learned lessons.

V: Valuable lessons

E: Easily learned lessons

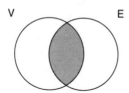

11. Some American warships are ships in the Indian Ocean.

A: American warships

I: Ships in the Indian Ocean

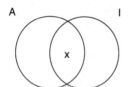

13. No times of raining are times in southern California.

R: Times of raining

S: Times in southern California

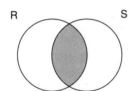

15. All places around us are places with cosmic radiation.

P: Places around us

C: Places with cosmic radiation

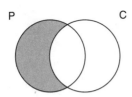

17. All antiques are objects more than 100 years old.

A: Antiques

O: Objects more than 100 years old

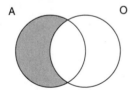

Exercise Set 10.3 (pp. 345–347)

Part One

1. S: Animals

P: Things able to think

M: Things that feel pain

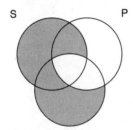

3. S: Children

P: Good persons

M: Persons who are cruel to animals

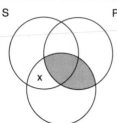

Valid

5. S: Unwelcome persons

P: Persons who are punished

M: Messengers who bring bad news

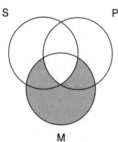

Invalid

7. S: Diets

P: Things that are simple

M: Things that require will power

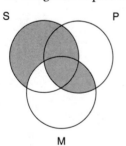

Valid

9. S: Syllogisms

P: Invalid arguments

M: Arguments with four terms

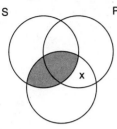

Invalid

Part Two

1. No syllogistic conclusion.

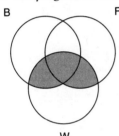

3. Some professors are not students.

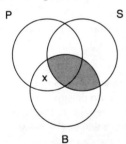

5. No syllogistic conclusion.

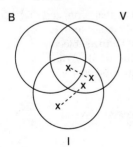

7. No syllogistic conclusion.

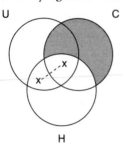

9. No birds are reptiles.

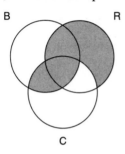

Exercise Set 10.4 (pp. 348–349)

1. Fallacy of composition.

3. Fallacy of composition.

Exercise Set 10.5 (pp. 353–354)

Because by definition an argument has only one conclusion, we consider only the cases that have a negative conclusion but no negative premisses.

1. The conclusion is an *E* sentence:

Because both end terms are distributed in the *E* sentence, each must be distributed in its occurrence in the premisses. Because, by supposition, there are no negative premisses, and because no terms are distributed in *I* sentences, both premisses must be *A* sentences with the end terms as subjects. But then the middle term will be the predicate of an *A* sentence in both cases and will not be distributed.

2. The conclusion is an O sentence:

Because only the predicate term is distributed in the *O* sentence, that term, and that term only, must be distributed in exactly one premiss. Because neither term is distributed in *I* sentences, the predicate term of the *O* sentence must be the subject term of a premiss that is an *A* sentence. If the middle term is to be distributed, then the other premiss must also be an *A* sentence, with the middle term as its subject. Therefore we need consider only the following form:

Every *P* is an *M*

Every *M* is an *S*

Some *S* are not *P*

This syllogism is shown to be invalid in the following Venn diagram.

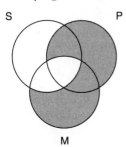

Exercise Set 10.6 (p. 355)

Part One

1. Every ostrich is a bird.
   Every ostrich is a nonflyer.

   Some birds are nonflyers.

   Invalid—middle term is distributed twice.

3. Some generals are not warmongers.
   Some admirals are warmongers.

   No admirals are generals.

   Invalid—both end terms are distributed in the conclusion but not in the premisses.

5. No fish have lungs.
   All whales have lungs.

   No whales are fish.

   Valid.

7. Some women did not support the Equal Rights Amendment.
   All feminists supported the Equal Rights Amendment.

   Some feminists are not women.

   Invalid—*women* is distributed in the conclusion, but not in the first premiss; *feminist* is distributed in the second premiss, but not in the conclusion.

9. All birds fly.
   No ostriches fly.

   No ostriches are birds.

   Valid.

Exercise Set 10.7 (p. 357)

1. All sexists oppose equal rights for women.
   Some men do not oppose equal rights for women.

   Some men are not sexists.

   Valid.

3. Some new buildings are ornate.
   No modern-style architecture is ornate.
   _____
   Some new buildings are not modern-style architecture.

   Valid

5. No man is willing to die.
   No woman is a man.
   _____
   Some women are willing to die.

   Invalid—violates all three rules for the syllogism.

7. All carrot eaters are health-food freaks.
   No health-food freak is a chocolate eater.
   _____
   No chocolate eater is a carrot eater.

   Valid

9. Every thing which has no parts is a thing that cannot perish by dissolution of its parts.
   Every thing that is a soul is a thing that has no parts.
   _____
   Every thing that is a soul is a thing that cannot perish by dissolution of its parts.

   Valid.

11. Every liar is unbelievable.
    No upright person is unbelievable.
    _____
    No liar is an upright person.

    Valid.

Exercise Set 10.8 (p. 362)

1. All potatoes of mine that are new are unboiled. (Obversion of i)
   No unboiled potatoes of mine are fit to eat. (iii)
   _____
   No potatoes of mine that are new are fit to eat (*)

   All of my new potatoes are unfit to eat. (Obversion of *)

3. Every one who is sane can do logic. (i)
   No sons of yours can do logic. (iii)
   _____
   No sons of yours are sane. (iv)

   All sons of yours are lunatics. (Obversion of iv)
   No lunatics are fit to serve on a jury. (ii)
   _____
   No sons of yours are fit to serve on a jury.

5. All of my birds are (at least) nine feet high. (iv)
   All birds that are nine feet high are ostriches. (i)

   All of my birds are ostriches. (v, from iv and i)
   All of the birds in this aviary are mine. (ii)

   All of the birds in this aviary are ostriches. (vi, from v and ii)
   No ostrich lives on mince pies. (iii)

   No bird in this aviary lives on mince pies. (vii, from vi and iii)

Exercise Set 10.9 (pp. 365–366)

Part One

1. No potentially dangerous substance should be legalized.

3. No rich men wear overcoats.

5. All persons who get sick only when nervous have psychogenic illness.

7. You do not sin.

9. None have the right to take away private property.

Part Two

1. Some expensive things are made of inexpensive materials.

3. No conclusion (undistributed middle term).

5. No conclusion (undistributed middle; end term distributed in premiss but not conclusion).

7. Some soluble things are not elements.

9. No conclusion (middle term distributed twice).

11. No conclusion (middle term distributed twice).

Part Three

1. Some valid arguments have false conclusions.
   Some syllogisms are not valid.

   Some syllogisms do not have false conclusions.

   Invalid—end term distributed in conclusion but not in premiss.

3. All skillfully handcrafted items that are beautiful . . . are expensive.
   All Navaho rugs are skillfully handcrafted items. . . .

   All Navaho rugs are expensive.

   Valid.

5. No ices are soft.
   Some custards are soft.

   Some ices are not custards.

   Valid.

7. No persons who are ignorant are fit to teach college students.
Some professors are ignorant.

Some professors are not fit to teach college students.

Valid.

9. All who have daily deadlines are reporters.
All reporters are aggressive.

All persons who have daily deadlines are aggressive. (By conversion and obversion)

Valid.

11. All newspapers that emphasize sensational material attain a wide circulation.
No decent newspapers emphasize sensational material.

No decent newspapers attain a wide circulation.

Invalid—middle term distributed twice; end term is distributed in the conclusion but not in the first premiss.

CHAPTER ELEVEN

Exercise Set 11.1 (p. 371)

1. Nontransitive, nonsymmetric, nonreflexive.

3. Nontransitive, nonsymmetric, nonreflexive.

5. Transitive, asymmetric, irreflexive.

7. Transitive, asymmetric, irreflexive.

9. Transitive, symmetric, reflexive.

Exercise Set 11.2 (p. 375)

Domain of interpretation: The set of all things.

D: Dogs

F: Things that have fleas

I: Independent things

C: Cats

V: Vegetarians

W: Wild things

Q: Quadrupeds

B: Things that bark

M: Things that meow

P: Fine pets

1. $(\exists x)(Dx \cdot Fx)$

3. $(x)(Dx \rightarrow \sim Vx)$

5. $(\exists x)(Wx \cdot Cx)$

7. $(\exists x)(Dx \cdot \sim Bx)$

9. $(\exists x)(Dx \cdot Bx) \cdot (\exists x)(Dx \cdot \sim Bx)$

11. $(\exists x)(Cx \cdot Wx) \rightarrow (\exists x)(Cx \cdot \sim Wx)$

Exercise Set 11.3 (pp. 377–378)

Domain: Persons

m: Mary   *j*: John   *L*:____ loves . . .

1. $\sim(x)(y)(z)((Rxy \cdot Ryz) \rightarrow Rxz)$

3. *Ljj*

5. $\sim Lmj$

7. $(x)Lxj$

9. $(x) \sim Lmx$

11. $(\exists x)\sim Lxx$

Exercise Set 11.4 (p. 379)

Domain: Persons

L:____ loves . . .

1. $(x)(\exists y)\, Lxy$

3. $(x)(y)\sim Lxy$

5. $(\exists x)(y)\sim Lyx$

Exercise Set 11.5 (pp. 384–385)

1. Transitivity of *can outrun*.

3. Symmetry of *is married to*.

Part Three.

Less than.

Part Five.

It is also symmetric.

Part Six

Domain of interpretation: The set of all things.

C: cats   *B*: ___ makes a better pet than . . .   *F*: ___ fears . . .

D: dogs   *T*: ____ is smarter than . . .   *S*: ___ is the brother of . . .

G: goldfish	*R:* ____ is cousin of . . .
S: snakes	*E:* ____ eats . . .
M: mice	*O:* ____ owns . . .
P: pianos	*W:* ____ plays . . .
F: women	*c:* Christopher
R: rich persons	*v:* Virginia

1. $(x)(y)((Cx \cdot Dy) \rightarrow Bxy)$

3. $(x)(\exists y)(Dx \rightarrow (Cy \cdot Fxy))$

5. Scv

7. $(x)(y)(((Cx \vee Dx) \cdot Gy) \rightarrow Txy)$

9. $(x)(\exists y)((Fx \cdot Rx) \rightarrow (Py \cdot Oxy))$

11. $(\exists x)(Px \cdot Wcx)$

Part Seven

1. Domain of interpretation: The set of all things.

H: horses   *G:* greyhounds   *C:* rabbits

O: ____ can outrun . . .

$(x)(y)((Hx \cdot Gy) \rightarrow Oxy)$

$(\exists y)(Gy)$

$(x)(y)((Gx \cdot Cy) \rightarrow Oxy)$

$\underline{(x)(y)(z)((Oxy \cdot Oyz) \rightarrow Oxz)}$

$(x)(y)((Hx \cdot Cy) \rightarrow Oxy)$

3. Domain of interpretation: Persons.

j: John   *s:* Sarah   *M:* ____ is married to . . .

Mjs

$\underline{(x)(y)(Mxy \rightarrow Myx)}$

Msj

APPENDIX 1

Exercise Set A.1 (pp. 392–393)

Part One

1.

$$\frac{\frac{p \rightarrow q \vdash p \rightarrow (p \cdot q)}{\frac{p, p \rightarrow q \quad \vdash p \cdot q}{p, p \rightarrow q \vdash q}}}{^*p, p \rightarrow q \vdash p \qquad \frac{p, p \rightarrow q \vdash q}{^*p \vdash p, q \qquad ^*p, q \vdash q}}$$

Valid

3.
$$\frac{p \rightarrow (q \rightarrow r) \vdash (p \rightarrow q) \rightarrow r}{}$$

$$p \rightarrow q, p \rightarrow (q \rightarrow r) \vdash r$$

$$\frac{p \rightarrow (q \rightarrow r) \vdash p, r \qquad\qquad q, p \rightarrow (q \rightarrow r) \vdash r}{}$$

$$\vdash p, p, r \qquad q \rightarrow r \vdash p, r$$

There is need to continue the tree, since there is a branch that does not terminate in an axiom. Invalid.

5.
$$\frac{p \rightarrow (q \rightarrow r), (q \rightarrow r) \rightarrow s \vdash p \rightarrow s}{}$$

$$p, p \rightarrow (q \rightarrow r), (q \rightarrow r) \rightarrow s \vdash s$$

$$*p, (q \rightarrow r) \rightarrow s \vdash p, s \qquad\qquad p, q \rightarrow r, (q \rightarrow r) \rightarrow s \vdash s$$

$$*p, q \rightarrow r \vdash q \rightarrow r, s \quad *p, q \rightarrow r, s \vdash s$$

Valid.

7.
$$\frac{(p \vee q) \rightarrow (p \cdot q), p \cdot q \vdash p \vee q}{}$$

$$(p \vee q) \rightarrow (p \cdot q), p, q \vdash p \vee q$$

$$*(p \vee q) \rightarrow (p \cdot q), p, q \vdash p \quad *(p \vee q) \rightarrow (p \cdot q), p, q \vdash q$$

Valid.

Part Three

$$\frac{(p \rightarrow q) \cdot (q \rightarrow r) \cdot p \cdot \sim r \vdash}{}$$

$$p \rightarrow q, q \rightarrow r, p, \sim r \vdash$$

$$\frac{p \rightarrow q, q \rightarrow r, p \vdash r}{}$$

$$*q \rightarrow r, p \vdash p, r \qquad\qquad q, q \rightarrow r, p \vdash r$$

$$*q, p \vdash q, r \quad *q, r, p \vdash r$$

Self-contradiction.

Exercise Set A.2 (pp. 396–397)

Part One

1.
$$\frac{p \rightarrow q, \sim p \rightarrow r, \sim q \rightarrow r \vdash \sim q}{}$$

$$q, p \rightarrow q, \sim p \rightarrow r, \sim q \rightarrow r \vdash$$

$$\frac{q, \sim p \rightarrow r, \sim q \rightarrow r \vdash p \qquad\qquad q, q, \sim p \rightarrow r, \sim q \rightarrow r \vdash}{}$$

$$\frac{q, \sim q \rightarrow r \vdash \sim p \qquad\qquad q, r, \sim q \rightarrow r \vdash p}{}$$

$$q \vdash \sim q, \sim p \qquad q, r \vdash \sim p$$

$$\frac{q, q \vdash \sim p}{}$$

$$p, q, q \vdash$$

This branch does not terminate in an axiom. The last sentence form ($\sim q$) is not a consequence of the others.

3.

$$\underline{(p \bullet q) \to (r \bullet s),\ \sim(q \lor s),\ t \to (\sim q \to (p \bullet r)) \vdash \sim t}$$

$$\underline{t,\ (p \bullet q) \to (r \bullet s),\ \sim(q \lor s),\ t \to (\sim q \to (p \bullet r)) \vdash}$$

$$\underline{t,\ (p \bullet q) \to (r \bullet s),\ t \to (\sim q \to (p \bullet r)) \vdash q \lor s}$$

$$\underline{t,\ (p \bullet q) \to (r \bullet s),\ t \to (\sim q \to (p \bullet r)) \vdash q,\ s}$$

$$\underline{t,\ t \to (\sim q \to (p \bullet r)) \vdash p \bullet q,\ q,\ s} \quad \text{(other branch to be continued)}$$

$$\text{*}t \vdash t,\ p \bullet q,\ q,\ s \qquad \qquad \underline{t,\ \sim q \to (p \bullet r) \vdash p \bullet q,\ q,\ s}$$

$$\underline{t \vdash \sim q,\ p \bullet q,\ q,\ s} \qquad \underline{t,\ p \bullet r,\ \vdash p \bullet q,\ q,\ s}$$

$$\text{*}q,\ t \vdash p \bullet q,\ q,\ s \qquad \underline{t,\ p,\ r \vdash p \bullet q,\ q,\ s}$$

$$\text{*}t,\ p,\ r \vdash p,\ q,\ s \qquad t,\ p,\ r \vdash q,\ q,\ s$$

One branch does not terminate in an axiom. The unfinished branch of the tree does not need to be completed. The last sentence form ($\sim t$) is not a consequence of the other.

5.

$$\underline{(p \to q) \lor (r \to s) \vdash (p \to s) \lor (r \to q)}$$

$$\underline{(p \to q) \lor (r \to s) \vdash p \to s,\ r \to q}$$

$$\underline{p,\ (p \to q) \lor (r \to s) \vdash s,\ r \to q}$$

$$\underline{p,\ r\ (p \to q) \lor (r \to s) \vdash s,\ q}$$

$$\underline{p,\ r,\ p \to q \vdash s,\ q} \qquad \underline{p,\ r,\ r \to s \vdash s,\ q}$$

$$\text{*}p,\ r \vdash p,\ s,\ q \quad \text{*}p,\ r,\ q \vdash s,\ q \quad \text{*}p,\ r \vdash r,\ s,\ q \quad \text{*}p,\ r,\ s \vdash s,\ q$$

Consequence.

Part Two

1.

$$\underline{\vdash (p \to q) \lor (\sim p \to q)}$$

$$\underline{\vdash p \to q,\ \sim p \to q}$$

$$\underline{p \vdash q,\ \sim p \to q}$$

$$\underline{\sim p,\ p \vdash q,\ q}$$

$$p \vdash p,\ q,\ q$$

Tautology.

3.

$$\vdash ((p \to q) \to (q \to r)) \leftrightarrow (q \to r)$$

$$\underline{(p \to q) \to (q \to r) \vdash q \to r} \quad \underline{q \to r \vdash (p \to r) \to (q \to r)}$$

$$\underline{q,\ (p \to q) \to (q \to r) \vdash r} \qquad \text{*}p \to r,\ q \to r \vdash q \to r$$

$$\underline{q \vdash p \to q,\ r} \quad \underline{q,\ q \to r \vdash r}$$

$$\text{*}q,\ p \vdash q,\ r \qquad \text{*}q \vdash q,\ r \quad \text{*}q,\ r \vdash r$$

Tautology.

5.

$$\vdash (\sim p \to r) \to ((q \to r) ((p \to q) \to r))$$

$$\sim p \to r \vdash (q \to r) \to ((p \to q) \to r)$$

$$q \to r, \sim p \to r \vdash (p \to q) \to r$$

$$p \to q, q \to r, \sim p \to r \vdash r$$

$$q \to r, \sim p \to r \vdash p, r \qquad q, q \to r, \sim p \to r \vdash r$$

$$\sim p \to r \vdash q, p, r \qquad {}^*r, \sim p \to r \vdash p, r \qquad {}^*q, \sim p \to r \vdash q, r \quad {}^*q, r \sim q, r \sim p \to r \vdash r$$

$$\vdash \sim p, q, p, r \qquad {}^*r, \vdash q, p, r$$

$${}^*p \vdash q, p, r$$

Tautology.

Part Three

1. p: The economy will improve. q: The stock market will crash. r: Banks will fail.

$$(p \vee q), (q \to r), \sim r \vdash \sim (p \to r)$$

$$p \vee q, q \to r, \sim r \vdash \sim (p \to r)$$

$$p \to r, p \vee q, q \to r, \sim r \vdash$$

$$p \to r, p \vee q, q \to r \vdash r$$

$$p \vee q, q \to r \vdash p, r \qquad {}^*r, p \vee q, q \to r \vdash r$$

$${}^*p, q \to r \vdash p, r \qquad q, q \to r \vdash p, r$$

$${}^*q \vdash q, p, r \qquad {}^*q, r \vdash p, r$$

Valid.

3. p: The Republicans choose a good candidate.

   q: They will win the elcetion.

   r: There is a split in the party.

   s: They meet in Chicago.

   $p \to (q \vee r)$

   $\sim (s \to r)$

   $s \to p$

   ────────

   $p \cdot q$

Valid.

$p \rightarrow (q \vee r), \sim(s \rightarrow r), s \rightarrow p \vdash p \cdot q$

$\overline{\qquad\qquad p \rightarrow (q \vee r), s \rightarrow p \vdash s \rightarrow r, p \cdot q \qquad\qquad}$

$\overline{\qquad\qquad s, p \rightarrow (q \vee r), s \rightarrow p \vdash r, p \cdot q \qquad\qquad}$

$\overline{*s, p \rightarrow (q \vee r) \vdash s, r, p \cdot q \quad s, p \rightarrow (q \vee r), p \vdash r, p \cdot q}$

$\overline{\qquad *s, p \rightarrow (q \vee r), p \vdash r, p \quad s, p \rightarrow (q \vee r), p \vdash r, q \qquad}$

$\qquad\qquad *s, p \vdash p, r, q \quad \underline{s, q \vee r, p \vdash r, q}$

$\qquad\qquad\qquad *s, q, p \vdash r, q \quad *s, r, p \vdash r, q$

Valid.

Index